Point/Counterpoint focuses on areas of controversy or disagreement within HRM, offering the arguments for and against a position, along with some conclusions that leave room for interpretation by the student.

Outsourcing *(Ch. 1)*
Best Practices or Contingency Approach? *(Ch. 2)*
Too Much Human Resources Regulation? *(Ch. 3)*
Wages and Conditions in Foreign Plants *(Ch. 4)*
Should Work Be Designed for Teams? *(Ch. 5)*
Using Realistic Job Previews *(Ch. 6)*
Selecting for Fit Versus Skill *(Ch. 7)*
Employee Retention *(Ch. 8)*
360-Degree Feedback *(Ch. 9)*
Training for Future Jobs *(Ch. 10)*
What Should Be the Basis for Compensation? *(Ch. 11)*
Team Versus Individual Incentives *(Ch. 12)*
Should Organizations Adopt Cafeteria Plans for Benefits? *(Ch. 13)*
Are Labor Unions Still Necessary? *(Ch. 14)*
Not Enough Stress? *(Ch. 15)*
Should Organizations Strive to Increase Diversity? *(Ch. 16)*
Should You Work at Home? *(Ch. 17)*

HR Legal Brief describes specific legal issues that are especially important and related to the chapter topic. Relevant laws and regulations are discussed throughout the text, but this section calls attention to issues that either are the focus of significant public interest, or are so important that they are likely to dominate HR practice in the future.

Paying the Price *(Ch. 1)*
Sexual Harrassment in the Army *(Ch. 3)*
Child Labor and International Business *(Ch. 4)*
Goodyear Stops Labeling 10 Percent of Its Workers as the "Worst" *(Ch. 9)*
Stock Options as Incentives *(Ch. 12)*
Legislating Domestic Partner Benefits? *(Ch. 13)*
The Merits of Diversity Training? *(Ch. 16)*
When Is Temporary Permanent? *(Ch. 17)*

HR Around the Globe discusses HR practices from outside the U.S., offering a useful background for students who will be working in a global economy.

Blending the Multinational Mix *(Ch. 2)*
Toyota Wants Only the Best *(Ch. 4)*
Exporting Jobs? *(Ch. 8)*
Teaching Language Skills for a Global Workforce *(Ch. 10)*
Global Benefits: Similarities and Differences *(Ch. 13)*
International Assignments and Career Development *(Ch. 15)*
Too Little Diversity? *(Ch. 16)*

HR Tech Talk discusses how technology has affected HR practices.

Internships Go Virtual as Firms Seek Ways to Save *(Ch. 6)*
Using Computers to Hire People *(Ch. 7)*
Negotiating Salaries on the Web *(Ch. 11)*
Too Much Technology? *(Ch. 15)*

HR in the 21st Century identifies a trend or practice that the authors see as growing, then discusses why it is expected to become more common in the future.

A Shortage of Workers? *(Ch. 1)*
Easy Come, Easy Go *(Ch. 2)*
What's in a Job Title? *(Ch. 5)*
Job Seekers Take Creativity to a New Level *(Ch. 6)*
The Fine Print: Hiring Through Handwriting Analysis *(Ch. 7)*
The Hidden Cost of Layoffs *(Ch. 8)*
Absenteeism as an Entitlement *(Ch. 8)*
Training for the MTV Generation *(Ch. 10)*
Minimum Wage…or Minimum Wages? *(Ch. 11)*
Pay for Morale? *(Ch. 12)*
Taking It with You *(Ch. 13)*
Emerging Trends in Unionization *(Ch. 14)*
Building the Perfect Work Environment *(Ch. 15)*
On the Horizon, a Labor Shortage Looms *(Ch. 16)*
An Eye for an Eye *(Ch. 17)*

Human Resource Management

SECOND EDITION

Human Resource Management

Angelo S. DeNisi

Texas A&M University

Ricky W. Griffin

Texas A&M University

Houghton Mifflin Company

Boston   New York

For Adrienne, Jessica, and Rebecca—
the women who mean the most to me (AD)

For Matt, who makes my daughter smile (RWG)

VP, Editor-in-Chief: George Hoffman
Associate Sponsoring Editor: Susan M. Kahn
Editorial Assistant: Kira Robinson-Kates
Associate Project Editor: Kristin Penta
Senior Composition Buyer: Sarah Ambrose
Senior Photo Editor: Jennifer Meyer Dare
Senior Art and Design Coordinator: Jill Haber
Senior Manufacturing Coordinator: Marie Barnes
Senior Marketing Manager: Steven W. Mikels
Marketing Associate: Lisa E. Boden

Cover images:
© Steve Edson/Photonica (top left)
© Ryoichi Utsumi/Photonica (top right)
© Paul Winter/Photonica (bottom)

Photo and cartoon credits appear on page 611.

Printed in the U.S.A.

Library of Congress Control Number: 2002109430

ISBN: 0-618-31277-3

1 2 3 4 5 6 7 8 9 – DOW – 08 07 06 05 04

Brief Contents

Contents

Chapter 12 Incentives and Performance-Based Rewards 381

Angelo S. DeNisi

Angelo S. DeNisi is the B. Paul N. and Rosalie Robertson Chair in Business Administration and the Head of the Department of Management at Texas A&M University. After receiving his Ph.D. in Industrial/Organizational Psychology from Purdue University, Angelo taught at Kent State University, the University of South Carolina, and Rutgers University before moving to Texas A&M. He has taught HR courses for undergraduates, MBAs, Executive MBAs, MS in HR students, and Ph.D. students. He has also taught classes and conducted seminars on various HR topics in Singapore, Madrid, Jerusalem, Beijing, Kuala Lumpur, Hong Kong, Santo Domingo, and Jakarta. He is a Fellow of the Academy of Management, and has served as Editor of the *Academy of Management Journal*, a member of the Board of Governors, and the Chair of both the Human Resources Division and the Organizational Behavior Division. He is a Fellow of The Society for Industrial and Organizational Psychology (SIOP) and the American Psychological Association, and a past SIOP President. In addition, he is a Fellow of the Southern Management Association, and he served on the Board of Governors of the Southern Management Association. Most of his research has focused on issues of performance appraisal and feedback, but he has also written on job analysis, managing persons with disabilities at work, and problems associated with expatriate management. His research has been funded by such organizations as the National Science Foundation and the Army Research Institute, and has appeared in such journals as the *Academy of Management Journal, Academy of Management Review, Journal of Applied Psychology, Psychological Bulletin, Journal of Personality and Social Psychology,* and *Industrial and Labor Relations Review.* He has also published a book about his research entitled *Cognitive Approach to Performance Appraisal: A Program of Research,* and is co-editor of *Managing Knowledge for Sustained Competitive Advantage.*

Angelo has received a number of honors over the years, including being named Honorary Professor, Department of Management, City University of Hong Kong; and External Examiner, Human Resource Consulting/Management, Nanyang Business School, Nanyang Polytechnic University, Singapore. His research has also been honored, including winning awards such as The William Owens Award for the Outstanding Publication in Industrial and Organizational Psychology, 1998; Outstanding Publication in Organizational Behavior, Organizational Behavior Division of the Academy of Management, 1997; and Best Paper in Organizational Communications, Organizational Communications Division of the Academy of Management, 1992.

Ricky W. Griffin

Ricky W. Griffin is Distinguished Professor of Management, holds the Blocker Chair in Business, and currently serves as the Executive Associate Dean at the Mays Business School at Texas A&M University. He formerly served as Director of the Center for Human Resource Management and as the Head of the Department of Management at Texas A&M. His research interests include workplace aggression and violence, executive skills and decision making, and workplace culture. Ricky's research has been funded by the Office of Naval Research and the Global Research Consortium and has been published in such journals as *Academy of Management Review*, *Academy of Management Journal*, *Administrative Science Quarterly*, and *Journal of Management*. He has also served as Editor of *Journal of Management*. Ricky has served the Academy of Management as Chair of the Organizational Behavior Division. He has also served as President of the Southwest Division of the Academy of Management and on the Board of Directors of the Southern Management Association. Ricky is a Fellow of both the Academy of Management and the Southern Management Association. He has also co-edited several scholarly books, including *Dysfunctional Behavior in Organizations* and the *Dark Side of Organizational Behavior*.

Ricky has been a visiting scholar at the Warsaw School of Management in Poland and at the University of South Africa in Pretoria, South Africa. He has won numerous awards for his research, including the Outstanding Publication in Organizational Behavior award and the Best Paper award, each presented by the Organizational Behavior Division of the Academy of Management. He is also the author of several market-leading textbooks, including *Management* (8th Edition), *Organizational Behavior* (7th Edition), *Business* (7th Edition) and *International Business* (4th Edition). In addition, his texts are widely used in dozens of countries, adapted for use in countries such as Australia and Canada, and have been translated into numerous foreign languages, including Russian, Chinese, Spanish, and Polish.

...And the Changes Continue

When we wrote the preface for the first edition of this book, we focused on how much the world was changing and how this would impact the business environment our students would enter. But that was early in 2001—and the changes we have seen since then have been staggering. Of course, September 11, 2001 is a day Americans will never forget. We went from feeling safe and secure to realizing that we were neither. Issues concerning security have become paramount in the business world as well as in our everyday lives. Those tragic events also made it abundantly clear that the U.S. was part of a changing world and that events thousands of miles away could affect our lives in dramatic ways.

We've also seen amazing things happen in the area of corporate corruption. There have always been scandals and bankruptcies, but the rash of such disclosures—at Enron, WorldCom, and others—has been unique. We've been able to observe exactly what can happen when corporate greed is allowed to grow unchecked and is even rewarded. People with pension plans from every sector of the country and the economy were also awakened to the fact that what happened in Houston at Enron could affect them as well.

We've seen more wars and, as we write this, the United States has major troop commitments in Iraq and Afghanistan, and North Korea is ready to test nuclear weapons. Yes, things have continued to change in many ways. But these changes have also made it clear that people are an important component of everything that happens. More organizations are coming to appreciate the importance of human resources as a source of competitive advantage, and many of the events of recent years have made it clear that how people are managed anywhere in the world will affect us and everyone else. Therefore, it may be even more important today that students are prepared to manage human resources at work. Whether they enter careers in human resource management, engineering, accounting, or construction, they will need to manage people, and we wrote this book to help those students do that better.

What's Different About Our Text?

We view our book as different from others in the field in a number of fundamental ways. We cover important topics that are covered only briefly, if at all, in other texts. We have also expanded the number of special features throughout the book. We believe these features help bring to life the concepts we are discussing. We have also tried to continue to deal with the real HR issues that will have an impact on students throughout their careers in business. *It remains our point of view that all future managers need to understand HR issues, and this assumption has guided everything we have done in this book.*

What's Changed in the Second Edition?

Over the past few years, we have received comments and feedback from colleagues and students who have used our book. We have taken their suggestions and criticisms seriously to make our book as useful as we can. The publisher has also solicited feedback from colleagues who chose to use some of the competing HR texts that are available in the market. We took their feedback very seriously as they told us some reasons why they didn't use our book. But let us be more specific about the changes that resulted from these comments.

We have incorporated many more court cases and legal decisions that are relevant to HR. We believe that this will help students get a more complete picture of the legal environment in which organizations operate. We have also added a lot more material on the impact of technology on the way in which human resources are managed.

We have added a completely new chapter on "sizing" the organization (Chapter 8). In this chapter, we deal with downsizing, termination, absenteeism, and turnover issues, all of which are critical for the HR manager. We touched on most of these issues in the earlier edition, but there is much more discussion of these topics, and they are all discussed as part of the process through which organizations grow and shrink. We have reduced some of our coverage of more traditional forms of job analysis and replaced this with discussion of some more recent issues. We also changed this chapter (Chapter 5) by incorporating material on job design and job enrichment. We've also combined our discussion of career issues with our coverage of the physical work environment, and have greatly expanded the discussion of knowledge management and managing knowledge workers throughout the text. We've also tried to do an even better job of cross-referencing topics and issues across chapters.

Another major change in this edition is the addition of two sets of learning points at the end of every chapter. As already noted, we believe that the topics we cover in this book are of relevance to students who are entering the HR field as well as for those students who go into other careers. But we realize that what they might need to take away from a discussion of selection, for example, might be quite different. So we have added two sets of key points. One set is designed with the future HR manager in mind. Some of these points are more technical in nature and are truly relevant only to the future HR manager. The other set is designed for non-HR managers. These tend to be more strategic in nature and take more of a "big picture" perspective. These are the kinds of things one should know to manage any organization.

Finally, we've included the latest research findings throughout the book, and we've updated examples, cases, and even the cartoons and pictures. We hope that all of these changes will help students understand the importance of the issues being discussed, and also understand how each relates to every other issue discussed. Above all, we hope we have written a "user friendly" text.

On the other hand, there are a number of things that have *not* changed in this second edition. These are things we believe we got right the first time around. Therefore, although we've updated the entire book, there are things we hope you liked in the first edition that have been retained and enhanced. Therefore, you will find that every chapter includes:

- An opening real-world case highlighting a recent event, issue, or trend that illustrates a major point or theme in the chapter

- A more detailed closing case with questions to guide discussion

- A Point/Counterpoint feature that focuses on an area of controversy or disagreement within HRM, offering the arguments for and against a position, along with some conclusions that leave room for interpretation by the student

- A Chapter Summary and Review and Discussion questions to help students review, test, and apply what they have learned

- An Ethical Dilemmas in HR Management scenario that presents a situation related to the chapter material and asks students to discuss what they believe would be the response of most managers

- An HR Internet Exercise encouraging website investigation to see how organizations are really approaching issues discussed in the chapter

- A Building HR Management Skills exercise that requires students to apply the information from the chapter to a specific problem

We have included other features throughout the book where relevant.

- HR in the 21st Century sections identify a trend we see as growing, then discuss why the trend or practice is expected to become more common in the future, when students are ready to move into management.

- HR Legal Brief sections describe specific legal issues that are especially important and related to the chapter topic. Relevant laws and regulations are discussed throughout, but this section calls attention to legal issues that either are the focus of significant public interest or are so important that they are likely to dominate HR practice in the future.

- HR Around the Globe sections discuss noteworthy HRM practices from outside the U.S., offering a useful background for students who will be working in an increasingly global economy.

- HR Tech Talk sections discuss how technology has affected HR practices.

- The Lighter Side of HR feature reinforces important points made in the chapter with amusing cartoons accompanied by serious captions.

An Effective Teaching and Learning Package

We are pleased to provide a comprehensive set of supplements to help both instructors and students.

- *Student and Instructor Websites.* Student and instructor websites provide additional information, guidance, and activities that will help enhance the concepts presented in the text. The student site, accessible through unique passkeys packaged with new textbooks, includes the Internet exercises from the text (with updates as necessary), hyperlinks to the companies highlighted in each chapter, complete and chapter-by-chapter glossaries, flashcards for reviewing key terms, and ACE self-tests. The instructor site provides downloadable versions of the lecture outlines from the Instructor's Resource Manual that can be edited or used as is, PowerPoint slides, and the Video Guide.

- *Instructor's Resource Manual with Test Bank.* This resource includes for each chapter the list of learning objectives, a detailed lecture outline, suggested answers to all text questions and end-of-chapter activities, and the test bank. The Test Bank includes both recall and application oriented multiple-choice, essay, short answer, and scenario-based questions.

- *HM ClassPrep with HM Testing CD.* This new CD-ROM is designed to assist the instructor with in-class lectures and test preparation. *HM ClassPrep* includes the complete *Instructor's Resource Manual* in electronic format to allow for easy customization. It also includes the Power-Point slides. *HM Testing* includes all of the content found in the printed *Test Bank* and allows instructors to select specific questions, select random questions, edit questions, and add questions to produce tests for easy administration. Tests can be printed as is or in multiple versions for duplication or administered via a network system, modem, or personal computer. The program includes a grading function that lets instructors set up a class, record grades from tests or assignments, and analyze grades and produce class and individual statistics.

- *PowerPoint Slides.* PowerPoint slides on the instructor website and HM ClassPrep CD provide an effective presentation tool for lectures and include an outline of the text chapters and selected key figures.

- *Color Transparencies.* Full color transparencies illustrate major topics in the text. Two types of transparencies are included: highlights of key figures from the text and additional images that can be used to enhance lecture presentation.

- *Video Package.* To illustrate important concepts from the text, real-world video examples from leading organizations are provided. The video segments run from 10 to 20 minutes to allow time for classroom discussion. The Video Guide provides suggested uses, teaching objectives, an overview, and issues for discussion for each video segment.

A Final Word

As we noted in the preface to our first edition, what sets our book apart from many others you may have seen is not the content, but the approach. It is always our goal to present the most current information, based on the best research we can find, and to present that information in a way that is easy to understand and engaging. We make extensive use of cases and special features to try to bring the topics we cover to life for students. These were our goals in the first edition, and they remain our goals for this edition. What we have done is to take these ideas and update and expand how we apply them to the topic of Human Resource Management. As a result, the new edition has a new look, covers some new topics and includes some new features, but we hope that it remains a well-informed, user-friendly text. We also hope that both students and instructors will benefit from this approach.

Acknowledgments

A project such as this is never the result of just one or two people's efforts. There are many people who have contributed to this book, in different ways, over the years. First, we must thank the many (indeed, more than we would like to admit) students who have taken our classes over the years. They endured the process of climbing a learning curve as we learned how and what to teach, and they were the "guinea pigs" whenever we decided to try new ideas or approaches. But, more than that, authors form ideas about how a text should be written only by spending a lot of time observing students using other texts. So, to all the students who complained about the texts we assigned them, we apologize, and hope that this book will better meet students' needs, challenge their minds, and engage their interest.

Our colleagues have also helped us form ideas through discussions, as well as through the feedback they provided over the years. These discussions and conversations were critical for crystallizing the concepts that appear in this book. Other feedback from colleagues helped develop better writing skills, and allowed each of us to be able to communicate our ideas more clearly. Therefore we thank all those colleagues from the University of Houston, Purdue University, the University of Missouri, Kent State University, the University of South Carolina, Rutgers University, and of course from Texas A&M University. Somewhere along the line, though, some people played an even greater role in guiding and developing our ideas. We must therefore specifically thank and acknowledge the efforts and help of our mentors John Ivancevich and Ernest McCormick.

As we actually started writing this book, a number of other people played a role that should be acknowledged. We want to thank the reviewers of this text for spending time reading drafts of chapters and providing useful feedback for us on how to make them better. In particular, we want to thank:

Paula Becker Alexander
Seton Hall University

Debra A. Arvanites
Villanova University

Sheila R. Baiers
Kalamazoo Valley Community College

Janet C. Barnard
Rochester Institute of Technology

Kevin Carlson
Virginia Tech

Jennifer Carney
(MBA candidate)
Georgia State University

Suzanne Clinton
Cameron University

Gwendolyn M. Combs
University of Nebraska–Lincoln

Mary L. Connerley
Virginia Tech

Robert R. Cordell
West Virginia University at Parkersburg

Barbara J. Durkin
SUNY, College at Oneonta

Dyanne J. Ferk
University of Illinois–Springfield

Maureen J. Fleming
The University of Montana

Donald G. Gardner
University of Colorado

Carol B. Gilmore
University of Maine

Audrey Guskey
Duquesne University

Barbara L. Hassell
University of North Texas

Micki Kacmar
Florida State University

Gundars Kaupins
Boise State University

Alice E. Nuttall
Kent State University, Tuscarawas Campus

Stephen Owens
Western Carolina University

Robert Paul
Kansas State University

Alex Pomnichowski
Ferris State University

Paul R. Reed
Sam Houston State University

Shelton Rhodes
Bowie State University

Joan B. Rivera
West Texas A&M University

Rebecca A. Thacker
Ohio University

Charles N. Toftoy
George Washington University

J. Bruce Tracey
Cornell University

Carolyn Wiley
The University of Tennessee at Chattanooga

We also want to thank the professionals at Houghton Mifflin, especially Susan Kahn, George Hoffman, and Kristin Penta, who at various times encouraged, threatened, supported, and browbeat us to get the book finished, and to make it the best we could. We are especially indebted to Ms. Penta, who labors under the handicap of being a Red Sox fan. We hope you are pleased with the final product.

Finally, we must thank family and friends for their support through the entire process. These are the folks who had to listen to brilliant ideas (even when they weren't so brilliant), and our complaints about unreasonable reviewers (who truly weren't) and those editors who kept pressuring us to get the book finished (who really did). Without their help, this book would never have been completed. We are especially indebted to Glenda Griffin and Adrienne Colella, who play the multiple roles of wives, partners, collaborators, colleagues, and best friends. It is with all our love, respect, and appreciation that we dedicate this book to them.

Angelo S. DeNisi
Ricky W. Griffin

PART ONE

An Overview of Human Resource Management

1

CHAPTER OBJECTIVES

After studying this chapter you should be able to:

■ Characterize contemporary human resource management perspectives.

■ Summarize the evolution of the human resource function in organizations.

■ Describe human resource management today in terms of the impact of the electronic age and its basic tasks, functions, and systems.

■ Identify and discuss the fundamental goals of human resource management in organizations.

■ Discuss the responsibilities for human resource management in terms of staff and management functions and describe the human resource management department.

■ Discuss human resource managers in terms of their professionalism and careers.

The Nature of Human Resource Management

Southwest Airlines is one of the most successful firms in the world today. Unlike other major airlines, however, Southwest does not fly international routes, serve meals on any of its flights, subscribe to any computerized reservation system, or have pre-assigned seating or business- or first-class compartments, and it refuses to transfer bags to other airlines. It boasts the lowest costs and highest profits and regularly has the highest levels of efficiency, productivity, and customer satisfaction in the airline industry today. It is also recognized as one of the most-admired companies in the United States.

One key to Southwest's success is the culture created by the firm's legendary cofounder and long-time chief executive officer (CEO) Herb Kelleher, affectionately known as "Uncle Herbie" to Southwest employees. From the company's earliest days, Kelleher decided to make all his employees feel like part of one big team. For instance, Kelleher established a policy that no employee would be laid off, and he sometimes pitched in when a ticket counter or luggage conveyor became too crowded. And for years Southwest has offered innovative compensation and advancement opportunities and stressed employee involvement in every phase of the firm's operations. As a result of this unique culture, Southwest routinely makes *Fortune* magazine's annual list of the best places to work.

What does it take to work for Southwest Airlines? Obviously, candidates need to have the requisite skills

> *"My challenge is just don't screw it up."*
>
> (James Parker, Southwest Airlines CEO)*

necessary to perform the job for which they are being considered. But beyond technical skills, successful applicants must also demonstrate the capacity to get along with others, to be a team player, and to be willing to pitch in wherever needed. In return for these qualities, Southwest provides a flexible, stimulating, and enjoyable work environment; reasonable pay; good benefits; opportunities to advance; and job security.

Southwest's approach to dealing with its employees has paid big dividends. For instance, they do indeed view themselves as part of one big team and strive to work together in the best interests of the company. The firm has the lowest turnover in the industry and a workforce committed to flexibility and innovation. During the Persian Gulf Crisis in 1990–1991, more than one-third of the airline's employees took a voluntary pay cut to help offset higher jet-fuel prices so the firm could remain profitable. And Southwest reciprocated in 2001 when it became the only major U.S. airline not to eliminate jobs in the wake of the September 11, 2001, terrorist attacks.

When Kelleher recently retired, some observers worried that the firm's culture might falter. But so far, at least, that has not been the case. Under the leadership of Colleen Barrett, president, and James Parker, CEO, Southwest hasn't missed a beat. In Parker's own words, "One thing I'll always think about is 'What would Herb do?' …This is a superb company that has been successful. My challenge is just don't screw it up."[1] ■

Southwest Airlines clearly recognizes the value of people in the success of its business. If Southwest needs a new airplane or a new information system for managing its flight operations, it can just buy them. Neither of these assets can give the firm a sustained competitive advantage, however, because Jet Blue, United, or American can easily buy the exact assets. But the people who work for Southwest have an unusual relationship with their employer and provide the firm with a rare and valuable set of resources that its competitors cannot easily duplicate or sustain. Indeed, it is the quality and character of these human resources that sets Southwest apart from other airlines.

Regardless of their size, mission, market, or environment, all organizations strive to achieve their goals by combining various resources into goods and services that will be of value to their customers. But many different resources are available. Economists traditionally thought in terms of concrete physical resources. In this view organizations draw on financial resources such as ownership investment, sales revenues, and bank loans to provide capital and to cover expenses necessary to conduct business. Material resources such as factories, equipment, raw materials, computers, and offices also play an important role in the actual creation of goods and services and are easy to think about when we discuss a firm's resources. But increasingly managers are beginning to view less tangible resources as the most critical for gaining a competitive advantage.

For example, successful organizations need information about consumers and the firm's competitive environment to help managers make decisions, solve problems, and develop competitive strategies. Many people refer to such resources as knowledge-based resources.[2] That is, organizations need to know how to get information and how to use that information. We will discuss knowledge-based resources and knowledge workers later in this chapter, and throughout the book, but for now it is sufficient to note that most (but not all) of this critical knowledge tends to reside in the people in the organization. Therefore, many experts in the field have come to recognize that no set of resources is more vital to an organization's success than its human resources.[3]

An organization's **human resources** are the people it employs to carry out various jobs, tasks, and functions in exchange for wages, salaries, and other rewards. The chief executive officer responsible for the overall effectiveness of the organization, the advertising manager responsible for creating newspaper ads, the operations manager sent to open a new manufacturing facility in Taiwan, the financial analyst who manages the organization's cash reserves, and the

CEO Jim Parker has continued to lead Southwest Airlines to dominance in the U.S. airline industry. Among U.S. carriers, for instance, Southwest spends less per seat mile than any competitor and its planes spend more time in the air (versus at the gate) than any other airline. Yet, Southwest also has a higher proportion of unionized employees than any other airline in the country. The secret? Southwest recruits employees who fit its climate of high morale and high customer satisfaction, and then rewards these people for working harder and smarter by providing job security and profit sharing.

■ **Human resources** are the people an organization employs to carry out various jobs, tasks, and functions in exchange for wages, salaries, and other rewards.

custodian who cleans the offices after everyone else goes home are all human resources. And in his or her own way, each is a vital ingredient that helps determine the overall effectiveness—or lack of effectiveness—of the organization as it strives to accomplish its goals and objectives. At Southwest Airlines, Colleen Barrett and James Parker, working in concert with the firm's pilots, flight attendants, ground staff, maintenance workers, and myriad other employees comprise the firm's human resources.

■ **Human resource management** is the comprehensive set of managerial activities and tasks concerned with developing and maintaining a qualified workforce—human resources— in ways that contribute to organizational effectiveness.

Human resource management refers to the comprehensive set of managerial activities and tasks concerned with developing and maintaining a qualified workforce—human resources—in ways that contribute to organizational effectiveness. As we will see, organizations that once paid only lip service to human resource issues are increasingly recognizing the dramatic impact that effective human resource management can have in all areas of an organization. Indeed, effective human resource management is becoming a vital strategic concern for most organizations today.[4]

In this chapter we will explore the nature of human resource management in a way that provides a useful framework for the more detailed discussions in subsequent chapters. We begin by looking at a contemporary view of human resource management and the important role this process plays in organizational effectiveness. But the human resource function was not always held in such high esteem, and so we briefly trace how human resource management has evolved to its present role in modern organizations. We then look at contemporary human resource management more closely. The goals of the human resource management function are then identified and discussed. Next, we examine how the responsibilities for human resource management are shared as staff and management functions. The human resource department in different kinds of organizations is then discussed. Finally, we focus on the professionalism and career development of human resource managers themselves.

CONTEMPORARY HUMAN RESOURCE MANAGEMENT PERSPECTIVES

In most of today's organizations the role of human resource management has become quite important.[5] As noted below, the real emergence of human resource management as a critical management function probably came with the passage in 1964 of the Civil Rights Act. This law and the court cases that followed from it made it clear that organizations had to find ways to hire, reward, and manage people effectively while ensuring that they worked within the limits of the law. In this context, the human resource management function came to require dedicated professionals who could balance legal and ethical concerns with the need that organizations have to survive and be profitable.

But the human resource management function has become more than the legal enforcement arm of the organization. Top management has come to understand that, if properly managed, human resources can be an important source of competitive advantage in an increasingly competitive world. In fact, as noted earlier, human resources are the organization's most important resources. Hiring the right people and then equipping them with the right skills and abilities can substantially affect the quality and quantity of whatever goods or services the organization produces. And properly motivated and committed employees can add immeasurable value to an organization's bottom line. Given the shift in competitiveness, top executives in most firms now see that human resource management practices and policies significantly affect their ability to formulate and implement strategy in any area, and that other strategic decisions significantly affect the firm's human resources as well.

It was only natural, therefore, that human resource management would eventually be elevated to the same level of importance and status as other major functional areas of the firm.[6] The top human resource executive at most companies today has vice presidential or executive vice presidential status and is a fully contributing member of the firm's executive committee, the executive body comprised of key top managers that makes major policy decisions and sets corporate strategy. Although a few managers and organizations still use terms like *personnel management* or *employee relations,* most firms now use the term *human resource management* to reflect more accurately the sophistication and maturity of the function. In keeping with this trend, we will also use the human resource management terminology throughout this book. Some organizations have already gone beyond the human resource management terminology and use specialized terminology that fits their corporate culture more closely. The top human resource executive at Southwest Airlines, for example, has the title of Vice President for People. This trend is on the rise, and other firms are also recognizing the importance of human resources as knowledge resources and have started using titles such as Chief Knowledge Officer.

Many aspects of the modern human resource management function actually date back to the 1980s and 1990s. During this period, it became apparent to many firms that they were not able to compete effectively in the global marketplace. Some of these firms went out of business and the employees lost their jobs. Others were acquired by other, more successful firms, and in the aftermath many employees of the acquired firm were seen as redundant and so were let go. Still other firms sought mergers with former or potential competitors in the hope of forming a new joint enterprise that could compete successfully. But again, in most cases, following such mergers companies often did not find the same need for as many employees, and many workers lost their jobs. Finally, those firms struggling to be competitive often concluded that they could be more efficient with fewer employees, and we saw the beginning of an era of downsizing, rightsizing, or reengineering. Whatever it was called, though, fewer and fewer jobs were available. Note, however, that a "no layoff" policy is one of the major features of management at Southwest Airlines.

Each of these responses resulted in a profound impact on the human resource management function. It was often the job of the human resource management department to determine how and when layoffs would take place. This is not a pleasant part of anyone's job, and a lot of hard feelings were associated with these decisions (we will discuss these issues in more detail in Chapter 8). When firms went out of business, the human resource management department was usually charged with making sure that applications for unemployment were filed and that employees received due notice of closings. When a merger or acquisition took place, it was often the role of the human resource manager to help integrate the two workforces and workplace cultures. And as our feature HR in the 21st Century illustrates, it will be human resource managers who, ironically, will take the lead in addressing a projected future shortage of workers.

HR in the 21st Century

A Shortage of Workers?

Layoffs have become common in the U.S. economy as businesses face slowing demand and a slackening high-tech sector. In October 2002, for instance, 4.1 million persons, out of a workforce of 130 million, in the United States were unemployed.

However, James E. Oesterreicher, labor expert, says, "The U.S. faces a worker gap and a skills gap—and both are right around the corner." Even as the economy remains stalled, unemployment has held steady, at a modest 5.6 percent. Labor shortages are beginning in health care and construction. Harvard economist Dale W. Jorgenson claims, "If employers thought the '90s were the decade of the worker, the next decade will be even more that way."

Retirement of aging baby boomers is just one reason for the shortage. Another factor is the lower numbers of twenty-somethings entering the workforce. There are no untapped pockets of labor supply, such as women or immigrants, that contributed workers during the 1990s. In addition, work attitudes have shifted, and workers are more willing to leave jobs to gain time for leisure or family. The productivity gains that occurred over the last decade may be at a limit. "It would be almost impossible to match the increases of the past 20 years," says David T. Ellwood, Harvard economist. Finally, the pool of new labor

> *"The U.S. faces a worker gap and a skills gap...."*
>
> (James E. Oesterreicher, labor expert)*

entrants, such as welfare-to-work recipients, is almost depleted.

Employers may choose to offer incentives to attract applicants, or they may concentrate on better retention of current employees. Workers can best prepare themselves for the change by seeking higher education, especially in technical or professional fields. Ellwood states, "If you believe that technological change isn't going to slow down, we're not going to have enough college-educated workers to meet the demand." While layoffs grew in 2002, they grew much more rapidly for low-skilled workers than for professionals. John Challenger, CEO of an outplacement firm, claims, "Even when the economy is fully recovered and companies are back in expansion mode, we may not see a revival in hiring of the rank-and-file worker." The proverb "A rising tide raises all boats," may be true, but it may not raise all boats equally.

Sources: Aaron Bernstein, "Too Many Workers? Not for Long," *BusinessWeek*, May 20, 2002 (*quote on p. 78); "Lower Paid Workers Face Job Cuts," *CNN Money*, September 10, 2002; "Statement of U.S. Secretary of Labor Elaine L. Chao on Unemployment Numbers for October 2002," U.S. Department of Labor, November 23, 2002, www.dol.gov, accessed on November 23, 2002; "Table A-7. Reason for Unemployment," U.S. Bureau of Labor Statistics, November 1, 2002, www.bls.gov, accessed on November 23, 2002.

■ **Outsourcing** is the process of hiring outside firms to handle basic human resource management functions, presumably more efficiently than the organization.

As other organizations looked for new ways to be competitive and reduce costs, they often looked for activities within the company that could be done more efficiently by outsiders. For example, it became common for companies to fire their cleaning and maintenance employees and hire an outside cleaning firm to save money. But it also became somewhat common for companies to reduce the size of their human resource management staffs and turn to outside help for specific projects. This practice, commonly known as **outsourcing,** has resulted in smaller human resource staffs within companies and more reliance on outside consultants to provide the services that were once provided by those staffs. Thus, while the importance of human resource management activities is growing, the importance of human resource departments may be shrinking, and the size of most human resource management functions is certainly shrinking. Regardless of whether internal employees do the work or it is outsourced to consultants, the activities carried out by human resource managers are indeed growing in importance. Is outsourcing the most effective way to deal with human resource management issues? Our Point/Counterpoint feature presents some arguments on both sides of this question.

POINT | **COUNTERPOINT**

Outsourcing

Outsourcing refers to an organization contracting with an outside provider for services formerly provided inside the organization. Typically, the organization determines its core functions and then outsources all other activities. In some cases all human resource activities are outsourced, but more typically, only activities that are fairly routine, such as enrolling employees in benefits programs, or even administering those programs, are outsourced.

POINT... Outsourcing makes sense for organizations because...	COUNTERPOINT... On the other hand, outsourcing could be a problem because...
The need for full-time, permanent employees is reduced.	Higher-paid jobs within large corporations will be replaced by low-paying jobs with vendors.
Jobs that deal with routine and dull tasks are eliminated from the organization.	Organizations will have fewer entry-level jobs, making it more difficult for some people to start careers.
Fewer employees are working in marginal jobs, where satisfaction might be low.	Employees providing outsourced services will have fewer benefits and less security.
When budgets get tighter, costs can be reduced by dropping programs, but no permanent employees will lose their jobs.	No new human resource managers will be gaining important experience to replace those managers dealing with strategic issues when necessary.
Managers in human resources can spend their time dealing with larger strategic issues that are better suited to their abilities.	An activity that is outsourced can no longer be a source of competitive advantage because many other organizations that use the same vendor will have the same programs.
Vendors who provide services for several organizations can provide those services at a lower cost than if the organization provides the services itself.	Fewer employees will feel committed to their organizations.

So... It probably makes sense for an organization to outsource certain activities, especially those that are totally routine, can be performed more efficiently by outside vendors, and are not seen as a potential source of competitive advantage. However, an organization must also recognize the downsides to outsourcing so that it is not the solution to all human resource problems. It is especially critical to ensure that some new managers are always gaining experience and are ready to move up to the level of strategic decision making when they are needed.

These trends continue today. Although the merger and acquisition mania of a few years ago has subsided, a large number of mergers and acquisitions still take place every year. Furthermore, many of these transactions now involve firms from different countries. Even without a formal merger between parties, the number of joint ventures, especially with firms from China and other emerging economies, is growing at a rapid pace. Thus, the challenges of how to manage a proper-size workforce as well as the challenges involved in integrating workforces from different cultures (national as well as corporate) will continue to be important for human resource management in the future.

In addition, the legal imperatives that in large part helped elevate the importance of the human resource management function are changing and becoming more complex. In what has been termed a post–affirmative action world, issues regarding differential test performance of members of different ethnic and racial groups, especially in high-stakes situations (where jobs or entrance into academic institutions are involved) are becoming more rather than less complex. How do we address differences in test scores in a society where credentialing and accountability are becoming more important, and when we still haven't figured out how to deal with the diversity our society presents us?[7]

Furthermore, following the events of September 11, 2001, and their aftermath, employers and employees need to deal with entirely new challenges.[8] Questions of security (in every sense of the word) have become more important. For example, issues related to how to select, train, and motivate airport security personnel, who are the first line of defense against terrorism, fall squarely under the purview of human resource management. By extension, the same complexities confront many other kinds of organizations as well, including—but not limited to—any that could conceivably be a target for other terrorist attacks. At the same time, organizations must find a balance between these security needs and the need (both ethical and legal) to recognize the rights and privileges of all employees and not to engage in stereotyping or illegal profiling. The importance of the human resource management function will clearly grow over the years in all these areas.

But before moving on to a more detailed discussion of the tasks and functions of modern human resource management, it is useful to consider how we arrived where we are today. The struggle of human resource management for legitimacy within the organization, and how that legitimacy came about, is due in large part to the history of how human resource management developed.

EVOLUTION OF THE HUMAN RESOURCE FUNCTION

■ **Scientific management,** one of the earliest approaches to management, was concerned with how to structure individual jobs to maximize efficiency and productivity.

Even though businesses have existed for literally thousands of years, the practice of management itself has only been of special interest and concern for about 100 years or so.[9] Many early businesses were small enterprises and farms run by families interested only in supporting themselves and in providing security for family members. The industrial revolution of the eighteenth century, however, sparked a greater interest in business growth and expansion, and large-scale business operations began to emerge throughout Europe and the United States. As these businesses grew and became increasingly complex, owners began to step aside and turn the operation of their firms over to full-time professional managers. Owners who remained in control of their businesses still found it necessary to rely on managers to oversee a portion of their operations. This transition, in turn, resulted in greater awareness of the various functions of management that were necessary for long-term organizational success.[10]

While a few early management pioneers and writers like Robert Owen, Mary Parker Follette, and Hugo Munsterberg recognized the importance of people in organizations, the first serious study of management practice—set during the early years of the twentieth century—was based on scientific management.[11] **Scientific management,** in turn, was concerned with how to structure individual jobs to maximize efficiency and productivity. The major proponents of scientific management, such as Frederick Taylor, and Frank and Lillian Gilbreth, had backgrounds in engineering and often used time-and-motion studies in which managers used stopwatches to teach workers precisely how to perform each task that comprised their jobs. In fact, scientific management was concerned with every motion a worker made, and there were many examples of how changes in movements or in the placement of some piece of equipment led to increased productivity.

The Lighter Side of HR, however, illustrates an argument made by critics of scientific management—that labor would use the production standards established by management as a way to work even more slowly. Other critics argued that individual workers were generally valued only in terms of their capacity to perform assigned tasks as efficiently and as productively as possible. Still, scientific management helped augment the concepts of assembly-line production, division of labor, and economies of scale that gave birth to the large businesses that transformed domestic and international economies throughout the twentieth century.[12]

The Lighter Side of HR

Some people might think that the popularity of workplace comic strips such as *Dilbert* and *Cathy* is a recent phenomenon. But in reality, the workplace has been a source of comic humor for over a century, dating back to political and editorial cartoon features often centered on labor and labor-management conflicts. The cartoon below, for example, is from around the turn of the last century. It depicts how some critics of scientific management thought that labor might use Taylor's time-and-motion study ideas against management. The bricklayers in the cartoon, for example, have apparently been successful in getting work rules approved that allow them five minutes between motions. They are now waiting for the timer to hit the five-minute mark again, so that they can perform their next task.

(© Bettmann/Corbis)

MODERN BRICK-LAYING IN CHICAGO.

Origins of the Human Resource Function

As businesses such as General Motors (started in 1908), Bethlehem Steel (1899), Ford Motor Company (1903), Boeing (1916), and the other industrial giants launched during this era expanded rapidly and grew into big companies, they obviously needed to hire more and more workers. Ford, for example, increased its manufacturing capacity from 800 cars per day in 1910 to 9,109 cars per day by 1925.[13] At the same time, its workforce increased from less than 200 workers to several thousand workers. This same pattern of growth and hiring was being repeated in literally hundreds of other businesses across dozens of industries. These workers were needed to perform operating jobs created to produce ever-greater quantities of the products sold by the businesses. In the early days of this business explosion, the foreman, or first-line supervisor, usually hired new workers. Office workers were also needed, so people with titles such as office manager hired clerks and secretaries.

As these businesses became more complex and as their hiring needs became more complicated, however, the task of hiring new employees became too time-consuming for a first-line supervisor or office manager to perform. In addition, extra administrative duties were being added. For example, in 1913 Ford was paying its unskilled employees $2.34 per nine-hour day. Because the pay was so low and the work was both monotonous and tiring, the firm was also experiencing a turnover rate of almost 400 percent per year. Thus, the firm had to replace its average worker four times each year. It was hiring workers to fill new jobs while also

As noted in the text, in 1913 Ford way paying workers like these $2.34 per nine-hour day. Because this wage was so low and the work so boring, the average worker only stayed on the job for a few months before seeking better opportunities. But very shortly after this photograph was taken, Ford revolutionized by boosting pay to a minimum of $5 a day and shortening the workday itself to 8 hours. As a result, turnover dropped sharply, and Ford could have its pick of the droves of workers who showed up looking for jobs. This trend, in turn, led directly to the creation of what would eventually evolve into one of the first "personnel" departments anywhere.

■ The **human relations era** supplanted scientific management as the dominant approach to management during the 1930s. It was marked by an emphasis on finding ways to keep workers happy, since it was assumed that "happy workers were productive workers".

■ The human relations era was instigated by the **Hawthorne studies,** a series of studies conducted to test some principles of scientific management. The pattern of results seemed to contradict some of the ideas of scientific management, and the human relations era emerged as a result of efforts to explain the results of these studies.

hiring workers to replace those who quit. In 1914 Henry Ford made a dramatic effort to attract and retain higher-quality workers by boosting the firm's pay to a minimum of $5 for an eight-hour day.[14] This action attracted a groundswell of new job applicants and almost overwhelmed first-line supervisors, who were then hiring new employees while overseeing the work of existing workers.

As a result of growth and complexity, most large businesses, including Ford, started to hire their new employees through newly created specialized units. Ford, for example, called this unit the employment department. While these units were initially created to hire those new employees, they also began to help manage the existing workforce. For example, the emergence and growth of large labor unions like the United Auto Workers and the passage of the Fair Labor Standards Act in 1938 (which established a minimum wage) and the National Labor Relations Act in 1935 (which dealt with unionization procedures) made it necessary for businesses to have one or more managers represent the interests of the business to organized labor and to administer the emerging set of laws and regulations that governed labor practices.

Meanwhile, other developments, many taking place in other parts of the world, provided organizations with some of the tools they would need to manage these employment processes more effectively. For example, in England, the work of Charles Darwin popularized the idea that individuals differed from each other in important ways. In France, the work of Alfred Binet and Theophile Simon led to the development of the first intelligence tests and, during the course of World War I, several major armies tried using these tests to assign soldiers to jobs. These attempts at staffing continued in the private sector after the end of World War I, and by 1923 *Personnel Management* by Scott and Clothier was already spelling out how to match a person's skills and aptitudes with the requirements of the job.

Another important ingredient in the origins of the human resource function during this period was the so-called **human relations era,** which emerged following the **Hawthorne studies.** Between 1927 and 1932, the Western Electric Company sponsored a major research program at its Hawthorne plant near Chicago. This research, conducted by Roethlisberger and Mayo, revealed for perhaps the first time that individual and group behavior played an important role in organizations and that human behavior at work was something managers really needed to understand more fully. One of the Hawthorne studies suggested, for example, that individual attitudes may have been related to performance, while another suggested that a work group may have established norms to restrict the output of its individual group members.[15] Prior to this work, many managers paid almost no attention to their employees as people but instead viewed them in the same way they viewed a machine or a piece of equipment— as an economic entity to be managed dispassionately and with concern only for resource output.

Stimulated by the findings of the Hawthorne studies, managers began to focus more and more attention on better understanding the human character of their employees. During this era, for example, Abraham Maslow popularized his **hierarchy of human needs.**[16] And Douglas McGregor's well-known **Theory X** and **Theory Y** framework also grew from the human relations movement.[17] The basic premise of the human relations era was that if managers could make their employees more satisfied and happier, they would work harder and be more productive. Today, researchers and managers alike recognize that this viewpoint was overly simplistic and that both satisfaction and productivity are complex phenomena that affect and are affected by many different factors. Nonetheless, the increased awareness of the importance of human behavior stimulated during this period helped organizations to become even more focused on better managing their human resources. These organizations saw effective management of human resources as a means of potentially increasing productivity and, incidentally, as a way of slowing the growth of unionism, which was beginning to gain popularity.

■ Abraham Maslow's **hierarchy of human needs** was developed during the human relations era. This view of human needs suggests that people are motivated to satisfy one level of needs at a time, and that we progress from trying to satisfy physiological needs and safety needs to trying to satisfy social needs and esteem needs, and finally work to satisfy self-actualization needs.

■ Douglas McGregor's **Theory X** and **Theory Y** framework grew from the human relations movement. This framework characterized two different views of workers and what we should expect from them. Theory X suggested that workers were basically lazy and needed to be coerced into working harder. Theory Y suggested that workers were motivated to do their best and so required a much different type of management style.

Personnel Management

We noted earlier that as organizations grew, they began to create specialized units to cope with their increasing hiring needs, to deal with government regulations, and to provide a mechanism for better dealing with behavioral issues. During the 1930s and 1940s these units gradually began to be called **Personnel Departments** (the word *personnel* was derived from an Old French word that meant "persons"). They were usually set up as special, self-contained departments charged with the responsibility of hiring new workers and administering basic human resource activities like pay and benefits. The recognition that human resources needed to be managed and the creation of personnel departments also gave rise to a new type of management function—**personnel management.**[18]

During this period, personnel management was concerned almost exclusively with hiring first-line employees such as production workers, salesclerks, custodians, secretaries, blue-collar workers, unskilled labor, and other operating employees. Issues associated with hiring, developing, and promoting managers and executives did not surface until later. The manager who ran the personnel department was soon called the **personnel manager.**

■ **Personnel Departments,** specialized organizational units for hiring and administering human resources, became popular during the 1930s and 1940s.

■ **Personnel management,** a new type of management function, grew from the recognition that human resources needed to be managed.

■ The manager who ran the personnel department was called the **personnel manager.**

Personnel management took another step forward in its evolution during World War II. Both the military and its major suppliers developed an interest in better matching people with jobs. That is, they wanted to optimize the fit between the demands and requirements of the jobs that needed to be performed and the skills and interests of people available to perform them. Psychologists were consulted to help develop selection tests, for example, to assess individual skills, interests, and abilities more accurately. During the 1950s the lessons learned during the war were adapted for use in private industry. New and more sophisticated techniques were developed, especially in the area of testing, and companies also began to experiment with more sophisticated reward and incentive systems. Labor unions became more powerful and demanded a broader array of benefits for their members. In addition, government legislation expanded and continued to add complexity to the job of the personnel manager.

Still, from the first days of its inception until the 1970s, personnel management was not seen as a particularly important or critical function in most business organizations. While other managers accepted personnel as a necessary vehicle for hiring new operating employees, personnel management was also seen primarily as a routine clerical and bookkeeping function. For example, personnel was responsible for placing newspaper ads to recruit new employees, filling out paperwork for those employees after they were hired, and seeing that everyone was paid on time.

While other organizational units like marketing, finance, and operations grew in status and importance, the personnel department of most organizations was generally relegated to the status of necessary evil that had to be tolerated but that presumably contributed little to the success of the organization. Its offices were often drab and poorly equipped and were often located away from the central activity areas of the organization. And personnel managers themselves were often stereotyped as individuals who could not succeed in other functional areas and who were assigned to personnel either because the organization had nothing else for them to do or as a signal that the individual was not deemed to be a candidate for promotion to a higher-ranking position.

HUMAN RESOURCE MANAGEMENT TODAY

As noted earlier, the first real impetus for the increased importance for the role of human resource management came with the passage in 1964 of the Civil Rights Act. This law made it illegal for employers to consider factors such as gender, religion, race, skin color, or national origin when making employment-related decisions. The 1964 Civil Rights Act, combined with several subsequent amendments, executive orders, and legal decisions, made the processes of hiring and promoting employees within the organization far more complex. Thus, it quickly became critically important to organizations that those responsible for hiring and promoting employees fully understand the legal context within which they functioned. For example, ethical and moral issues aside, improper or inappropriate hiring practices left the organization open to lawsuits and other legal sanctions, accompanied by large fines, judgments, and new expenses. (We discuss the 1964 Civil Rights Act and related regulation more fully in Chapter 3.)

Human Resource Management in the Electronic Age

Through the years, as social and market dynamics changed, dramatic changes in technology also affected how we manage human resources. Some of these changes were related to the technologies available for measurement, although new technologies such as television, videotaping, and facsimile machines were also important for the development of the human resource management function. In recent years, however, the popularity of the Internet has had a profound impact on the human resource management function, and that impact is still developing and growing.

The widespread use of electronic technology and the Internet has not drastically affected the basic approach to how we manage human resources, but it has certainly had a major effect on how many human resource management systems are delivered. For example, in Chapter 5 we discuss methods for conducting job analysis, but we also note that the new O*NET system may allow many organizations to obtain the job analysis information they need online from a database. Chapter 6 discusses issues of recruiting, but one of the more popular ways for job seekers to search for jobs is by accessing one of the many websites for job searches. As a result, most organizations have come to realize that they must post job openings online with these services, in addition to using more traditional methods. Our discussion of selection techniques in Chapter 7 also includes discussion of online testing and other ways in which the Internet has changed the way organizations select employees. Training programs can now be purchased from vendors and provided to employees online, allowing them to take classes and training programs on their own schedule. Information systems, including information on benefits, make it easier for employees to check their benefit coverage and change it if desired.

Have these new applications of technology made human resource management easier? Clearly, it is easier now for management to deliver information and communicate with employees. But the openness of communications also means that employees can communicate with management, and this presents new challenges to managers. Electronic systems for communication and monitoring also bring up new challenges for the legal system (discussed in Chapter 3), and have led to new discussions about ethics and privacy. Thus, the new technology has made human resource management easier in some ways but more complicated in others. Have these new applications of technology made the management of human resources more effective? This question is important, but there is little data addressing it. Nonetheless, we will discuss the opportunities and challenges presented by new technology and the Internet throughout the book.

One other way in which technology has affected the human resource management function needs to be discussed. As organizations introduced new technologies for manufacturing, communication, and human resource management, they also increased their need for more specialized employees. **Knowledge workers** include any employees whose jobs are to acquire and apply knowledge, and they contribute to the organization by the nature of what they know and how well they can apply what they know. Although knowledge workers include more than workers who deal with computer technology (scientists and lawyers, for example, are usually considered knowledge workers), the explosion of technology at work has led to a huge increase in the need for workers who can learn and apply the management of this technology. These employees present special problems for recruitment, retention, and compensation, as well as for motivation; we will discuss these challenges throughout the book, but provide detailed coverage in Chapter 17.

■ **Knowledge workers** are employees whose jobs are primarily concerned with the acquisition and application of knowledge, and they contribute to an organization through what they know and how they can apply what they know.

Human Resource Management Tasks and Functions

It is clear that the human resource management function has changed over the years and continues to change. As human resource management was becoming more important because of the increasingly complex legal environment, other changes in the world of work led to other pressures to manage human resources more effectively. Changes in the competitive landscape, combined with rapid advances in technology and communication, made it more important than ever for organizations to use their resources wisely and to capitalize on the full value of those resources. At the same time, however, there was increasing concern over what was called quality-of-work-life issues. While managers were becoming increasingly concerned with ways to improve productivity and competitiveness, they also began to realize that it was important for workers to feel that their jobs were a source of personal satisfaction and growth. Successful organizations were those that could maximize effectiveness while at the same time make work more meaningful and fulfilling.

As noted earlier, human resources are an organization's most important resources. Hiring the right people and then equipping them with the right skills and abilities can substantially affect the quality and quantity of whatever goods or services the organization produces. Properly motivated and committed employees can add immeasurable value to an organization's bottom line. Given the shift in competitiveness, top executives in most firms began to see that human resource management practices and policies significantly affected their ability to formulate and implement strategy in any area and that other strategic decisions significantly affected the firm's human resources as well.

Thus, a combination of historical forces and legal pressures and the increased need to gain competitive advantage has led to our contemporary view of human resource management. Figure 1.1 shows the major tasks and functions that comprise human resource management today. This figure also represents the framework around which this book is organized. As you can see, one set of tasks and functions, covered in Part Two of the book, involves the environment within which human resource management occurs. To function effectively within the environment, most experts today agree that it is necessary to adopt a strategic perspective on human resource management.[19] That is, all aspects of the human resource management system should be coordinated, and together they should support the strategic goals of the organization. We will discuss strategic human resource management in more detail in Chapter 2.

The legal environment of human resource management, as already noted, is also of importance to organizations. Organizations that do not understand their legal environment are almost certain to encounter difficulties in almost every aspect of human resource management and may face financial and legal penalties as a result. Understanding the legal environment begins with equal employment opportunity and requires a complete understanding of protected classes in the workforce and what organizations must do to ensure that members of those classes have the same chances for success in the organization as do any other employees. Numerous special legal issues regarding compensation, benefits, labor relations, working conditions, training practices, and other related areas of human resource management must also be understood and considered by all managers. Chapter 3 provides in-depth coverage of these and other legal issues confronting human resource managers today.

FIGURE 1.1   The Human Resource Management Process

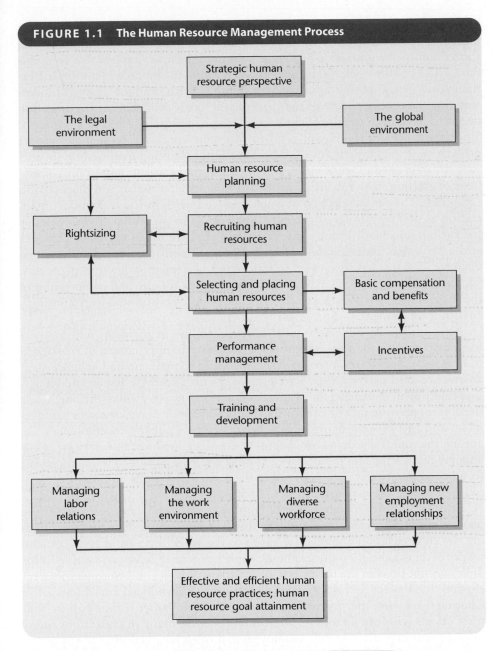

Another vital dimension of the environment of human resources is the international context in which the organization functions. Large multinationals like Ford, Sony, and Unilever clearly have numerous international human resource issues to manage. But many smaller firms are also venturing into foreign markets. Even purely domestic firms may find themselves buying from, selling to, and/or competing with businesses in other countries. Thus, all managers today must have an appreciation of the international business environment. Chapter 4 explores the various issues associated with managing human resources in an international company and with taking a global approach to human resource management itself.

Staffing the organization (acquiring and maintaining the appropriate mix of human resources needed by the organization) is another fundamental human resource management function and is the subject of the four chapters that comprise Part Three of this book. Staffing begins with human resource planning (determining the organization's future human resource needs) and job analysis (understanding the precise nature of the current and future jobs that the organization needs to have performed). These and related issues are covered in Chapter 5. Since most organizations will need to hire new employees either to support growth or to replace employees who have left, recruiting qualified applicants who are interested in working for the organization is also an important component of staffing. The recruiting process and associated issues are discussed in Chapter 6. The actual selection of employees—either outsiders to join the organization as new employees or current employees to be promoted or reassigned—for various jobs involves the appropriate and effective use of various techniques and a thorough understanding of both legal and performance-related factors. Chapter 7 is devoted to various selection and placement issues and processes. Chapter 8 addresses issues associated with adjusting the size and composition of the organization's workforce to fit its business needs best as the firm's business environment changes.

After employees have been given their initial job assignments and are performing their jobs (or after current employees have been promoted or reassigned to new jobs), human resource managers also help to maintain and enhance their motivation and performance. Part Four is devoted to these issues and topics. The first step in enhancing motivation and performance is to measure and assess the current performance of employees. Various methods of performance management and the process of providing performance feedback to employees are among the topics discussed in Chapter 9. Another fundamental element in enhancing motivation and performance in most organizations is to train employees to work more effectively by providing them with new skills and abilities. Employee training and management development are covered in Chapter 10.

Another important component of employee motivation and retention is the management of compensation and benefits. Part Five covers the issues surrounding the compensation and rewards given to the workforce. All employees who work for an organization, for example, expect to receive basic compensation for their contributions to the organization. A variety of issues and considerations regarding basic wage and salary administration are introduced and discussed in Chapter 11. Given that many employees will work harder if they believe that their efforts will lead directly to additional rewards, many organizations today offer various incentives to their employees and often base certain rewards on actual performance. Chapter 12 covers both traditional and innovative incentives and performance-based rewards. Beyond wages, salaries, and incentives, most organizations also provide various benefits to their employees; Chapter 13 is therefore devoted to employee benefits and services.

The ongoing management of the existing workforce, covered in the four chapters of Part Six, is also at least the partial responsibility of human resource managers. Organized labor—unions and other labor groups—is a critical element in this set of tasks and functions. As we will see in Chapter 14, understanding the unionization process, the process of collective bargaining, and the processes of negotiating and administering labor agreements are vital parts of labor relations. Chapter 15 focuses on various issues associated with the work environment, including discipline, grievances, and conflict in organizations. An array of other ongoing issues associated with the work environment, including employee rights, employee safety and health, quality-of-life programs, and health and stress management programs, are also covered in this chapter.

Many organizations today are also confronting the need to understand and manage diversity in their workforce, which is becoming more and more diverse in terms of gender, ethnicity, age distributions, and so forth. While it is important that people are treated fairly and that organizations avoid any form of discrimination, it is also important that differences among people be recognized and appreciated. Workforce diversity is thus the topic of Chapter 16. Because of the dynamic nature of human resource management, its practitioners must also remain alert to new issues, challenges, and opportunities. Chapter 17 introduces and discusses some of the other more important contemporary human resource challenges. Key topics include workplace and workforce transitions, organizational change, technology, participation and empowerment, changes in job assignments and/or job responsibilities, termination, and retirement, as well as the use of contingent workers (part-time employees, temporary workers, contract workers, and so forth).

In addition to following this framework throughout the book, another perspective also shapes the material covered here. Many human resource functions are the responsibility of managers who may not have had formal training in the fundamentals of human resource management. In fact, many students who elect or who are required to take a survey course in human resource management do not plan to become human resource management professionals. On the other hand, many other students may plan to work in the human resource field. Regardless of your specific intentions, both future and current managers need to know the basic concepts about the management of human resources.

The level of detail and the importance of specific elements of an area will vary, however, depending on whether you plan to be a professional human resource manager or not. Therefore, we will end each chapter with two different chapter summaries. One will present the major learning points for the human resource management professional. You will need to understand these points if you plan to do this kind of work for a living. The second summary will present learning points for the reader who is not planning to become a human resource manager. We assume that these readers plan to move into some type of management position, however, and so we will outline the points that any manager should take away to be effective in his or her job.

The Human Resource Management System

The preceding section discussed the various tasks and functions of human resource management from the perspective of discrete, self-contained activities. In reality, however, these tasks and functions are highly interrelated and do not unfold in a neat and systematic manner. Each of the various tasks and functions can affect and/or be affected by any of the other tasks and functions. And most basic human resource functions are practiced on an ongoing and continuous basis. For example, on any given day a human resource manager may need to help develop a recruiting strategy for hiring new sales representatives, set the base starting salary for a newly hired engineer, approve a pay raise for another engineer, negotiate with a vendor for a particular new employee benefit, oversee a training program for employees transferring to a new plant, resolve a union grievance about working hours, and terminate a problem employee.

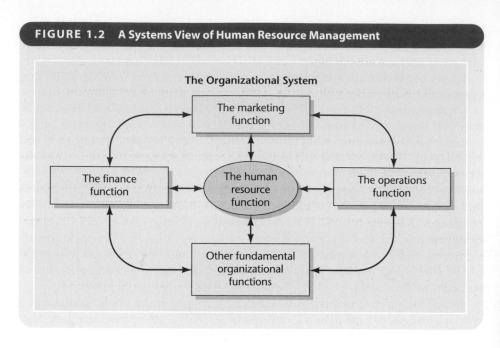

FIGURE 1.2   A Systems View of Human Resource Management

The Organizational System

The marketing function

The finance function

The human resource function

The operations function

Other fundamental organizational functions

■ A **human resource management system** is an integrated and interrelated approach to managing human resources that fully recognizes the interdependence among the various tasks and functions that must be performed.

Indeed, it is truly appropriate to think of human resource management as a system. A system is an interrelated set of elements functioning as a whole. A **human resource management system** is an integrated and interrelated approach to managing human resources that fully recognizes the interdependence among the various tasks and functions that must be performed. This viewpoint is illustrated in Figure 1.2. The basic premise of this perspective is that every element of the human resource management system must be designed and implemented with full knowledge and understanding of, and integration with, the various other elements. For example, poor recruiting practices will result in a weak pool of applicants. Even if the organization has sophisticated selection techniques available, it will not make much difference without a pool of truly qualified applicants from which to choose. As a result, there will be a greater need for training before a new employee starts work to provide him or her with the necessary skills. Subsequent performance appraisals will also be more difficult because it may take longer before these employees are truly proficient in their jobs, and this situation will affect how much they are paid.

Figure 1.2 also illustrates another useful systems-based perspective on human resource management. Many systems are themselves comprised of subsystems—systems within a broader and more general system. By viewing the overall organization as a system, human resource management then can be conceptualized as a subsystem within that more general organizational system. As the figure shows, the human resource management subsystem both affects and is affected by the other functional subsystems throughout the organization. This perspective can help reinforce the idea that human resource management must be approached from the same strategic vantage point afforded the other areas within the organization. Failure to do so can result in unanticipated consequences, poor coordination, and less effective performance.

For example, if the organization makes a strategic decision to compete on the basis of high-quality service, it will almost certainly need to use several mechanisms to do so. For example, the organization will need to recruit and subsequently hire more qualified new workers and to provide more training to both new and current workers. Similarly, if the financial function of an organization dictates that major cost cutting be undertaken, some portion of those costs may come from the human resource area. Thus, human resource managers may need to reduce the size of the workforce, attempt to renegotiate labor contracts for a lower pay rate, defer payment of some benefits, and so forth.

The increasing globalization of business also reinforces the need to view the human resource management function from a systems perspective. That is, human resource managers must take a global perspective in managing people. Within the borders of their own country, human resource managers must consider the social norms, individual expectations, and so forth, that shape worker behaviors. Cross-national assignments for managers are also an important consideration for many businesses today. Thus, the global perspective on human resource management includes the need to understand domestic similarities and differences in managing human resources in different countries and the role of international assignments and experiences in the development of human resource skills and abilities.

GOALS OF HUMAN RESOURCE MANAGEMENT

We have already defined human resource management, but it is both important and useful at this juncture to identify and discuss more specifically the basic goals of human resource management in modern organizations.[20] Figure 1.3 illustrates the four basic goals of the human resource management function in most organizations today.

Facilitating Organizational Competitiveness

All organizations have a general set of goals and objectives that they try to accomplish. Regardless of the time horizon or the level of specificity involved in these goals, they are generally intended to promote the organization's ability to be competitive in its efforts to fulfill its purpose or mission. For example, busi-

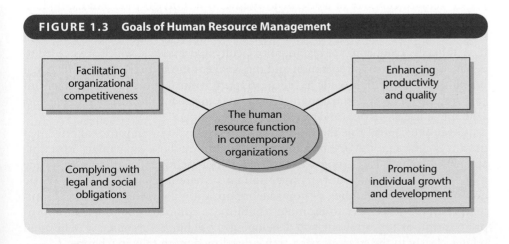

FIGURE 1.3   Goals of Human Resource Management

Although different types of organizations have different goals, this does not mean that they cannot work together towards a common goal. Recently, for example, New York Mayor Michael Bloomberg chose Joel Klein (CEO of Bertelsmann Inc.) to run the New York City Department of Education. Klein, in turn, put together a team of other business leaders who are concerned about our country's schools, including Jack Welch, former CEO of GE. In doing so, Bloomberg and Klein ignored educational insiders in favor of a new, more business-oriented approach. Their strategies for improving education include centralizing control, increasing accountability, revamping the culture to be more open to sharing ideas, and controlling budgets. The coming years will show whether this experiment is successful, but it is a rare case of a government organization turning to a business organization for help in dealing with a challenge.

ness organizations like Microsoft, Wal-Mart, Nestlé, and Toyota exist primarily to make a profit for their owners. Thus, their goals and objectives usually deal with sales or revenue growth, market share, profitability, return on investment, and so forth. Other organizations exist for different purposes and so they have goals other than increased profitability. Educational organizations like Ohio State University, Houston Community College, and the St. Louis Independent School District have their unique purposes, for example. The same can be said for health-care organizations like the Mayo Clinic, governmental organizations such as the U.S. Federal Bureau of Investigation (FBI), State of Missouri's Revenue Department, and charitable organizations like the United Way.

Even though people often associate competitiveness only with businesses, each of these other types of organizations must also be managed effectively and compete for the right to continue to work toward fulfillment of its purpose. For example, a state university that misuses its resources and does not provide an adequate education for its students will not be held in high regard. As a result, the university will have difficulty competing for high-quality faculty and students, which are needed to enhance the university's reputation and thus make it more competitive. Similarly, a hospital that does not provide technical support for its doctors or adequate health care for its patients will find it more difficult to compete for the doctors and patients who might use its services and so pay for those services.

Given the central role that human resources play in organizational effectiveness, it is clear that the organization needs to employ those individuals most able to help it accomplish its goals and to remain competitive. The human resource management function in any organization must therefore have as one if its basic goals a clear understanding of how the organization competes, the kinds of human resources necessary to promote its ability to compete, and the most appropriate methods for attracting and developing those human resources.[21] This goal relates clearly to the strategic perspective developed more fully in Chapter 2.

Enhancing Productivity and Quality

A related but somewhat narrower concern for most organizations in the world today involves the issues, hurdles, and opportunities posed by productivity and quality. **Productivity** is an economic measure of efficiency that summarizes and reflects the value of the outputs created by an individual, organization, industry, or economic system relative to the value of the inputs used to create them.[22] **Quality** is the total set of features and characteristics of a product or service that bears on its ability to satisfy stated or implied needs.[23] In earlier times, many managers saw productivity and quality as being inversely related; the best way to be more productive was to lower quality and therefore costs. But today, most managers have come to realize that productivity and quality usually go hand in hand. That is, improving quality almost always increases productivity.

Organizations around the world have come to recognize the importance of productivity and quality for their ability not only to compete but also to survive. But actually improving productivity and quality takes a major and comprehensive approach that relies heavily on human resource management. Among other things, an organization that is serious about productivity and quality may need to alter its selection system to hire different kinds of workers. It will definitely need to invest more in training and development to give workers the necessary skills and abilities to create high-quality products and services, and it will need to use new and different types of rewards to help maintain motivation and effort among its employees. Thus, human resource management also has the goal in most organizations of helping to enhance productivity and quality through different activities and tasks.

Complying with Legal and Social Obligations

A third fundamental goal of the human resource management function today is to ensure that the organization is complying with and meeting its legal and social obligations. We noted earlier the impact of the 1964 Civil Rights Act and other regulations on hiring and other related human resource management practices and activities. More recently, the Americans with Disabilities Act has also had a major impact on human resource management. It is clearly important that organizations stay within the relevant legal boundaries whenever they deal with their employees. An organization that does not comply with government regulations and various legal constraints risks huge financial penalties, as well as considerable negative publicity and damage to its own internal corporate culture. This point is amply illustrated in the HR Legal Brief.

Beyond the strict legal parameters of compliance, however, more and more organizations today are also assuming at least some degree of social obligation to the society within which they operate. This obligation extends beyond the minimum

■ **Productivity** is an economic measure of efficiency that summarizes and reflects the value of the outputs created by an individual, organization, industry, or economic system relative to the value of the inputs used to create them.

■ **Quality** is the total set of features and characteristics of a product or service that bears on its ability to satisfy stated or implied needs.

Organizations demonstrate their social responsibility in a variety of ways. Brenda Dempsey, director of corporate communications for The J. M. Smucker Company, is shown here teaching students in a business-economics class at Orrville High School. Smucker offers its employees unlimited paid time off for volunteer efforts such as this. Dempsey teaches classes on decision making, business ethics, and problem solving as part of the course.

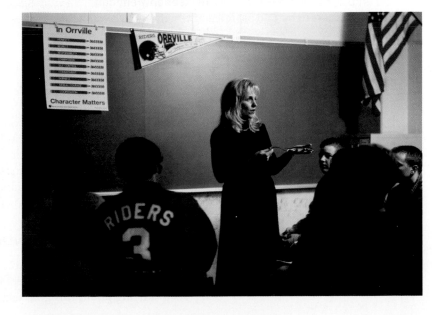

HR Legal Brief

Paying the Price

Just how important is the human resource department? Recent experiences at Rent-A-Center clearly show what can happen when a firm minimizes the importance of the human resource function. Thorn Americas, a unit of London-based Thorn EMI, had prospered as a large player in the rent-to-own industry. The firm had a large, professionally staffed human resource department and was known for its progressive hiring and employment development practices.

In 1998 Thorn merged with another large rent-to-own business, Renters Choice. The new firm was renamed Rent-A-Center, and an outsider named J. Ernest Talley was brought in to run the combined business. But Talley had some unusual views of the human resource function. Specifically, he saw human resources as an expense, bristled at the notion of government regulation, and allegedly had a strong bias against women. For example, he was quoted by one employee as saying, "Get rid of women any way you can." Another indicated that he said, "Women should be home taking care of their husbands and children, chained to a stove, not working in my stores."

Even though Rent-A-Center had 2,300 stores and 13,000 employees, Talley essentially eliminated the firm's human resource function. For example, he fired the firm's top human resource executive and dropped all training and employee relations activities. He kept only enough clerical support to handle payroll and benefits activities.

> **"Women should be home taking care of their husbands and children, chained to a stove, not working in my stores."**
>
> (Quote attributed to J. Ernest Talley by a Rent-A-Center employee*)

But his stance on women and the culture he created proved to be costly. Thousands of talented women left the company, and thousands of potentially valuable new employees were systematically blackballed. Talented males also left in droves, at least in part because they wanted no part of what Talley was trying to do.

Not surprisingly, Talley's stance soon prompted legal action. Several women charged that they had been demoted or forced to resign because of their gender. Others charged that Talley had created a hostile work environment, a key form of sexual harassment. For instance, at one national sales meeting in Las Vegas, Talley hired scantily clad go-go dancers for entertainment. Many of the men in attendance got drunk, while the women felt humiliated.

The lawsuit against Rent-A-Center represented 5,300 current and former employees, as well as approximately 10,000 rejected job applicants. One attorney involved in the case said, "I've never seen a case in which so many women and men tell the same kind of story all across the country. It's remarkable." Faced with overwhelming evidence, Rent-A-Center forced Talley to retire and settled the suit for $47 million in payments. The firm also agreed to re-establish a human resource department, hire a human resource vice president, and take numerous other steps to change its employment practices and culture.

Source: Robert Grossman, "Paying the Price," *HRMagazine,* August 2002, pp. 28–37 (*quote on p. 30).

---

activities necessary to comply with legal regulations and calls for the organization to serve as a contributing "citizen." Such efforts might include outreach programs to help attract individuals—often from minority populations—who may lack the basic skills necessary to perform meaningful jobs, or even the divestiture of holdings in countries with poor records on human rights. These activities are becoming increasingly important as financial management firms offer investment funds that specialize in socially responsible organizations, and corporate social performance (CSP) is often considered another dimension of organizational performance.

Promoting Individual Growth and Development

Finally, a fourth goal for human resource management in most contemporary organizations is to help promote the personal growth and development of its employees.[24] As a starting point, this goal usually includes basic job-related training and development activities. But in more and more organizations, it is increasingly going far beyond basic skills training. Some firms, for example, now offer basic educational courses in English, math, and science for their employees. Many organizations also include some provision for career development—helping people understand what career opportunities are available to them and how to pursue those opportunities. Formal mentoring programs are also commonly being used to help prepare women and minorities for advancement in the organization.[25]

Individual growth and development may also focus on areas that do not relate directly to job responsibilities. For example, some organizations provide stress-management programs to help their employees better cope with the anxieties and tensions of modern life. Wellness and fitness programs are also becoming more common as organizations seek new and different ways to help their employees remain physically, mentally, and emotionally fit and better prepared to manage their lives and careers. Still another common area for continuing education is personal financial planning, which may even include assistance in writing a will or retirement planning.

THE SETTING FOR HUMAN RESOURCE MANAGEMENT

As organizations continue to change and adapt to new challenges, the settings in which human resource activities take place can also change. The traditional model, where all human resource activities resided in a separate human resource department, is becoming rare. Instead, human resource activities are carried out by both line and staff managers. Furthermore, we are seeing differences in the way human resource management operates in larger versus smaller companies. We will explore some of these different settings.

Human Resource Management as a Staff Versus Line Function

Organizations historically divided their managers into two groups: line management and staff management. Human resource management was traditionally considered to be a staff function. **Line managers** were those directly responsible for creating goods and services. That is, their contributions to the organization can generally be assessed in terms of their actual contributions and costs to the organization's bottom line. The performance of a sales manager whose unit costs $500,000 per year to support (for salaries, administration, and so forth) and which generates $3.5 million per year in revenue can be evaluated this way. Operations managers, financial managers, and marketing managers were generally considered to have line functions.

Staff managers, on the other hand, were those responsible for an indirect or support function that would have costs but whose bottom-line contributions were less direct. Legal, accounting, and human resource departments were usually thought of as staff functions. Their role was to support line management's efforts to achieve organizational goals and objectives. Today, however, many organizations have blurred this distinction. New forms of organizational design and a trend toward smaller staff units have shifted traditional work arrangements, for example.[26] As a result, although human resource activities are still often seen as staff functions, it is becoming more common for line managers to have responsibility for human resource management.

■ **Line managers** are those directly responsible for creating goods and services.

■ **Staff managers** are those responsible for an indirect or support function that would have costs but whose bottom-line contributions are less direct.

Even in organizations that have kept the more traditional structure of formal human resource management departments, the kinds of work carried out by those departments and their relationships with the rest of the organization have changed in most cases. Advances in the measurement of human resource management activities have made it more feasible to evaluate these activities in much the same way as we evaluate other organizational functions.[27] Understanding how human resource management can exist in these different settings helps shed light on the way in which human resource managers interact with other managers.

Any organization that has a human resource department assigns that unit staff (or support) functions with staff (or support) responsibility.[28] The human resource department is usually given specific responsibility for certain functions and shares responsibility for other functions. The most common specific responsibility assigned to the human resource department is legal compliance. The department is expected to keep abreast of all local, state, and federal laws that affect human resource practices and to monitor court cases and decisions that might modify or extend those laws. Human resource managers are also usually expected to maintain data and records to show how the organization has attempted to maintain compliance. In larger organizations, a separate human resource unit is often created for the sole purpose of dealing with organized labor. Usually called the labor relations department, this unit handles labor contract negotiations and administers labor agreements after they have been accepted.

The human resource department also takes primary responsibility in most organizations for recruiting potential new employees for entry-level positions and for the initial screening of applicants for those positions. Similarly, human resource managers generally design the basic compensation and benefits system used by the organization. They also design the performance appraisal system, basic training and development programs, incentive and performance-based reward systems, and discipline and grievance systems. Human resource managers have also become increasingly involved with total quality management efforts and their organization's international activities.

In some organizations, human resource management departments are structured around "centers of excellence." In these cases, the human resource department is responsible for providing services only in those cases where they can provide higher-quality services than can be purchased on the outside (i.e., through outsourcing, discussed earlier). In other cases, the human resource department functions as a consulting operation within the organization. They are expected to be responsive to the needs of the other functional areas, but they have to "sell" their services to the line managers. In these arrangements, the human resource management department budget is very small, and the only way to hire and retain employees in that area is to provide services that other managers are willing to pay for (literally). Thus, the human resource management department becomes a self-funding operation, or it could even become somewhat of a profit center.

In any case, in the more modern, strategic view of human resource management, the human resource department is also responsible for coordinating the various human resource management activities and ensuring that they are consistent with corporate strategy. If those services are provided primarily internally by the human resource management department, this coordination can be fairly simple. As those activities move outside the organization, perhaps by contracting with outside vendors, the coordination problem becomes much more complex. In these cases, the human resource management department is responsible for identifying suitable vendors, monitoring the performance of those vendors, *and* ensuring that each vendor is providing services that help the organization meet its overall strategic goals.

In addition, organizations are becoming increasingly interested in ways to evaluate the effectiveness of human resource management activities, regardless of the source of those activities, and this is an additional strategic goal of the modern human resources management department. Traditionally, many experts believed that human resource management practices could not be assessed with anywhere near the objectivity that we could evaluate the effectiveness of a sales campaign, for instance. It was assumed that, if the human resource management department was functioning properly, people would generally be happier, but there was little real attempt to measure effectiveness beyond that. This view changed, first in the 1950s with the beginning of serious discussions about the utility, or value, of human resource management practices.

In the 1980s and 1990s **utility analysis** became much more sophisticated, and it became possible to determine exactly how much human resource management activities contributed to a company's bottom line.[29] The advent of high-performance work systems resulted in broader metrics for evaluating human resource management activities,[30] and as a result, it is now possible to develop fairly objective measures of the impact and/or effectiveness of human resource management practices. It remains the role of the human resource management department, however, to develop these metrics and to apply them to all human resource management activities undertaken on behalf of the organization. We will return to this topic again in Chapter 2.

> ■ **Utility analysis** is the attempt to measure, in more objective terms, the impact and effectiveness of human resource management practices in terms of metrics such as a firm's financial performance.

Despite the importance of the activities for which the human resource management department is typically responsible, the fact remains that many activities formerly carried out by the human resource management department are either subcontracted to outside firms (who can presumably carry them out more efficiently at lower cost) or performed by line managers.

Management positions that were once called line positions are more likely to be called **operating managers** today. These managers oversee the acquisition of other kinds of resources, the transformation of those resources into goods and services, and the sale and distribution of those goods and services to customers. Even in organizations that continue to have specialized human resource managers to handle some of the human resource duties, operating managers are increasingly expected to participate in the human resource management function.

> ■ **Operating manager** is an increasingly popular term for an employee previously called a line manager.

For example, operating managers are expected to recognize, appreciate, and follow the various legal constraints imposed on the organization, even though compliance may technically be the responsibility of the human resource department. For example, it is not advisable to ask a job applicant certain questions regarding personal plans or activities (i.e., "Are you planning to start a family soon?" or "What type of position does your husband/wife have?"). Such questions, even when asked innocently, may be the basis for discrimination (real or imagined) and can damage the career prospects of the applicant and cost the firm money in the form of a lawsuit or legal settlement if actual discrimination is later demonstrated. Thus, it is the responsibility of every operating manager to understand the legal framework within which they function.

In fact, in many organizations where self-managed work teams are common, almost all human resource activities are the responsibility of the team leader and the team members themselves. In such cases, a human resource manager might be asked to provide consulting help to the team design and implement necessary practices, but the human resource manager provides only help and guidance. He or she does not set or implement policy.

But even as the lines of distinction between human resource managers as staff and operating managers blur, the potential for conflict still exists between the staff

Small businesses seem to be threatened by megacorporations such as Wal-Mart, but for some of these small businesses this is simply a challenge that requires more creative solutions. For example, the Wild Rumpus Bookstore in Minneapolis had to find a way to compete with large chains such as Barnes and Noble. Owner Collette Morgan decided to try a strategy that larger organizations would never dream of. Her idea was to sell children's books, but to do so in a way that was entertaining to kids. One of her more fanciful innovations was to buy two chickens—named Elvis and Dalai—for the children to play with. The store also has cats, birds, and tarantulas. While Morgan sells books at the cover price (whereas large chains tend to discount them), she stocks titles the larger stores don't bother with and provides a more complete experience to children and their parents who buy books.

and operating managers. This conflict usually stems from their basic interdependence and the limits that each can impose on the other. Operating managers, for example, may view the myriad legal regulations for hiring new employees as unnecessary and burdensome and vent their frustrations at the human resource managers who try to get them to comply. Likewise, human resource managers may become frustrated when operating managers do not take such regulations seriously or do not follow them appropriately. And while each can be of benefit to the other, taking advantage of that benefit takes extra time. For example, a human resource manager who needs input from an operating counterpart to design a training program may become frustrated at the additional time and effort needed to get that information and perhaps wish that she or he had proceeded without going to the trouble to solicit the information from the operating manager.[31]

Clearly, then, it is necessary for human resource managers and operating managers to work closely together. Each has valuable expertise and information that can be of benefit to the other. Each is likely to need the expertise and information that the other can provide to carry out his or her own job most effectively. And finally, the two sets of managers must work closely together if they are to achieve the full and complete potential that resides in the human resources of their organization. Human resource management is truly a shared responsibility and must be approached from that perspective. When conflict does arise, both parties need to work productively to resolve it and to proceed to work together as partners with the same ultimate set of goals and objectives. In some organizations these problems are avoided by having operating managers perform human resource functions. In other organizations, these problems are avoided by outsourcing many human resource activities. But in those remaining organizations where a traditional human resource department still exists, resolution of the conflict between staff and operating managers is essential for human resource managers to become strategic partners in the organization.

The Human Resource Department in Smaller Versus Larger Organizations

As noted earlier, responsibilities for carrying out human resource functions may reside in a separate organizational unit, most often called the human resource department. Not all small organizations have such departments, however.[32]

Human resource management in smaller organizations   Most small organizations still use operating managers to handle their basic human resource functions. In the case of a franchised operation, like a single McDonald's or Pizza Hut restaurant, or an individual retail outlet such as a Gap or Limited clothing store, the store manager generally hires new employees, schedules and tracks working hours for all employees, and disciplines problem employees. The franchiser or home office, in turn, generally suggests or mandates hourly wages, provides performance appraisal forms for local use, and may handle payroll services as well.

A small independent business is generally operated in the same way, with the owner or general manager handling human resource duties. Payroll and other basic administrative activities may be subcontracted to businesses in the local community that specialize in providing such services for other local organizations. Relatively little training is provided in these small organizations, and other human resource issues are relatively straightforward. Very small organizations are exempt from many legal regulations (again, we cover this topic more fully in Chapter 3). Thus, a single manager can usually handle the human resource function in smaller firms without too much difficulty.

Human resource management in larger organizations   As the firm grows beyond a certain size, however, a separate human resource unit becomes a necessity. At first, the manager who had been handling the human resource duties may delegate them to a special assistant, or even to an individual human resource manager. But when an organization reaches a size of around 200 to 250 employees, it generally establishes a self-contained human resource department. While there is no standard approach, a firm of this size might have one full-time manager and a single secretary or assistant to function as its human resource department. These individuals handle all of the firm's human resource administration.

As the firm continues to grow, however, more assistance is needed to staff the human resource department, and so that department also grows. Indeed, in very large organizations, human resource functions are themselves likely to specialize into subunits. For example, large firms might have one department to handle recruiting and selection, one to handle wage and salary administration, one to handle training and development, and still another to handle labor relations. Figure 1.4 shows how Texas Instruments has organized its human resource function.

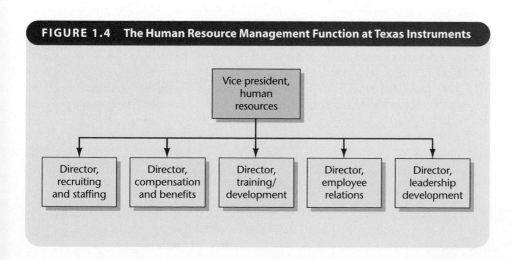

FIGURE 1.4   The Human Resource Management Function at Texas Instruments

HUMAN RESOURCE MANAGERS

Who are today's human resource managers? Given the rapid and dynamic changes that have characterized this field, it should come as no surprise that human resource managers represent a diverse set of professionals with a variety of backgrounds, experiences, and career objectives. A human resource executive today needs to understand different specialized areas, such as the legal environment, the process of change management, labor relations, and so forth. In addition, contemporary human resource executives must also possess general management skills and abilities reflecting conceptual, diagnostic, and analytical skills. It is important that they fully understand the role and importance of the human resource function for their organization.[33] Thus, both a solid educational background and a foundation of experience are necessary prerequisites for success.[34]

Consistent with these changes, it is often more useful to conceptualize human resources as a center of expertise within the organization. That is, everyone in the organization should recognize human resource managers as the firm's most critical source of information about employment practices, employee behavior, labor relations, and the effective management of all aspects of people at work. This view of human resource management is illustrated in Figure 1.5, which builds upon the systems view of human resource management presented earlier in Figure 1.2.

Professionalism and Human Resource Management

Accompanying the shifts and changes in human resource functions and importance is a greater emphasis on professionalism, reflected by a clear and recognized knowledge base and a generally understood way of doing business.[35] Human resource managers are no longer regarded as second-class corporate citizens. And

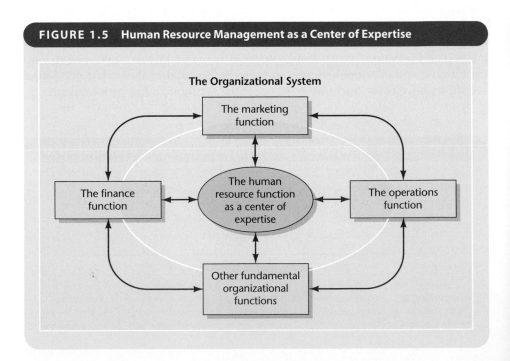

FIGURE 1.5   Human Resource Management as a Center of Expertise

more and more organizations are including a stint in human resources as a normal step on a person's way to the top. Senior human resource executives in large firms earn six-figure salaries and receive the same sorts of perquisites once reserved only for executives of operating units. Indeed, the salaries for human resource executives continue to rise at an impressive rate. Human resource departments are also being viewed more and more as cost centers, with the goal of providing clear and measurable financial benefits to the organization.[36]

Many human resource managers today belong to the Society for Human Resource Management (SHRM), the field's largest professional association. SHRM publishes professional journals that enable members to stay abreast of the newest developments in the field, sponsor workshops and conferences, and so forth. To help establish human resource management as a recognized profession, SHRM has created the Human Resource Certification Institute (HRCI). The HRCI is expected to become the recognized symbol of accreditation in much the same way that the accounting profession uses the certified public accountant (CPA) exam and credential to designate those individuals who have formally achieved basic minimal competencies in prescribed areas.

The HRCI currently has two levels of accreditation. To become a Professional in Human Resources, a manager must have four years of professional experience and pass an examination covering the basic body of human resource knowledge (having a college degree in an appropriate field such as human resource management or industrial/organizational psychology reduces the experience requirement base to two years). To become a Senior Professional in Human Resource Management, an individual must pass the same exam and have eight years of professional experience. The three most recent years of experience must be at a policymaking (senior executive) level in an organization.

Careers in Human Resource Management

How does one become a human resource manager? Career opportunities in human resource management continue to grow and expand and are expected to continue to do so. One obvious way to enter this profession is to get a degree in human resource management (or a related field) and then seek entry-level employment as a human resource manager. Alternative job options may be as the human resource manager for a small firm or as a human resource specialist in a larger organization. Some universities also offer specialized graduate degree programs in human resource management. For example, a master of science or master of business administration degree with a concentration in human resource management would likely lead to a higher-level position in an organization than would a bachelor's degree alone.

Another route to human resource management would be through line management. As described earlier, more and more firms are beginning to rotate managers through the human resource function as part of their own personal career development program. Thus, people who go to work in marketing or finance may very well have an opportunity at some point to sample central human resource management responsibilities. Regardless of the path taken, however, those interested in human resource management are likely to have a fascinating, demanding, and rewarding experience as they help their organization compete more effectively through the power of the people who comprise every organization in every industry in every marketplace in the world today.

Chapter Summary

Human resource management is a relatively new functional area in many organizations. As today's large organizations began to emerge around 100 years ago, they found it necessary to establish specialized units to handle hiring and the administration of current employees. These units were usually called personnel departments and were headed by personnel managers.

Contemporary human resource management deals with different complex and strategic issues. The basic tasks and functions of human resource managers today include adopting a strategic perspective, understanding their environmental context, staffing the organization, enhancing motivation and performance of employees, ongoing management of the existing workforce, and other challenges.

Human resource management generally has four basic goals to pursue: facilitating organizational competitiveness, enhancing productivity and quality, complying with legal and social obligations, and promoting individual growth and development.

Line (or operating) managers and staff managers (or specialized human resource managers) typically share the responsibility for effective human resource management. Both sets of managers must work to deal with the conflict that often occurs. The owner or general manager still often handles human resource management in smaller firms, but as organizations grow, they usually establish separate human resource departments.

Today's human resource managers are becoming more and more professional in both their training and their orientation toward their work. A variety of career paths are also available for people wanting to work in the human resource function.

Key Points for Future HR Managers

► Modern human resource managers must function as strategic partners. That is, they must understand the nature of the business and how human resource activities can help support and foster business goals.

► Traditionally, human resource management was not viewed in such high esteem, and those responsible for these activities were instead seen primarily as recordkeepers.

► The passage of the Civil Rights Act of 1964 and the increasing global competition of the 1980s resulted in a fundamental change in the importance of the human resource management function.

► Many traditional human resource management activities are now being outsourced, but human resource management departments are still generally responsible for tying human resource practices to a firm's strategic goals and for measuring the effectiveness of human resource management practices.

► Human resource management has become a true profession, and a career in this field typically requires formal education.

► Human resource management practices differ fairly dramatically between smaller and larger organizations.

Key Points for Future General Managers

► The effective management of a firm's human resources is probably the most important source of sustained competitive advantage for a modern organization.

► The changing legal environment has made it critical that an organization be aware of the legal requirements involved in all human resource management practices. Failure to do so can be quite costly.

► Effective human management practices support corporate strategic goals.

► Everyone who deals with people has a need to understand some basic notions of human resource management.

Review and Discussion Questions

1. Identify five examples of human resources in your college or university.

2. Summarize the evolution of the human resource function in organizations.

3. Summarize the basic ideas underlying the human resource management system concept.

4. What are the goals of human resource management?

5. Who is responsible for human resource management?

6. Why do you think human resource management (or personnel) was previously held in such low esteem in many organizations?

7. Do you think human resource management would have become more important even if laws such as the 1964 Civil Rights Act had never been passed? Why or why not?

8. Identify several consequences of an organization's failure to recognize that its human resource management practices comprise an interrelated system.

9. Do you think some human resource management goals are more important than others? Why or why not? What implications might be drawn if a particular manager felt that certain goals were indeed more important than others?

10. Do you think it might be possible for a large company today to function without a human resources department?

Closing Case

Enterprise Builds on People

When most people think of car-rental firms, the names Hertz and Avis usually come to mind. But in the last few years, Enterprise Rent-A-Car has overtaken both of these industry giants, and today it stands as both the largest and the most profitable business in the car-rental industry. In 2001, for instance, the firm had sales in excess of $6.3 billion and employed over 50,000 people.

Jack Taylor started Enterprise in St. Louis in 1957. Taylor had a unique strategy in mind for Enterprise, and that strategy played a key role in the firm's initial success. Most car-rental firms like Hertz and Avis base most of their locations in or near airports, train stations, and other transportation hubs. These firms see their customers as business travelers and people who fly for vacation and then need transportation at the end of their flight. But Enterprise went after a different customer. It sought to rent cars to individuals whose own cars are being repaired or who are taking a driving vacation.

The firm got its start by working with insurance companies. A standard feature in many automobile insurance polices is the provision of a rental car when one's personal car has been in an accident or has been stolen. Firms like Hertz and Avis charge relatively high daily rates because their customers need the convenience of being near an airport and/or they are having their expenses paid by their employer. These rates are often higher than insurance companies are willing to pay, so customers who use these firms end up paying part of the rental bill themselves. In addition, their locations are also often inconvenient for people seeking a replacement car while theirs is in the shop.

But Enterprise located stores in downtown and suburban areas, where local residents actually live. The firm also provides local pickup and delivery service in most areas. It also negotiates exclusive contract arrangements with local insurance agents. They get the agent's referral business while guaranteeing lower rates that are more in line with what insurance covers.

In recent years Enterprise has started to expand its market base by pursuing a two-pronged growth strategy. First, the firm has started opening airport locations to compete with Hertz and Avis more directly. But their target is still the occasional renter rather than the frequent business traveler. Second, the firm also began to expand into international markets and today has rental offices in the United Kingdom, Ireland, and Germany.

Another key to Enterprise's success has been its human resource strategy. The firm carefully targets a certain kind of individual to hire: its preferred new employee is a college graduate from the *bottom* half of the graduating class, and preferably one who was an athlete or who was otherwise actively involved in campus social activities. The rationale for this unusual academic standard is actually quite simple. Enterprise managers do not believe that especially high levels of achievement are necessary to perform well in the car-rental industry, but having a college degree nevertheless demonstrates intelligence and motivation. In addition, since interpersonal relations are important to its business, Enterprise wants people who were social directors or high-ranking officers of social organizations such as fraternities or sororities. Athletes are also desirable because of their competitiveness.

Once hired, new employees at Enterprise are often shocked at the performance expectations placed on them by the firm. They generally work long, grueling hours for relatively low pay. And all Enterprise managers are expected to jump in and help wash or vacuum cars when a rental agency gets backed up. All Enterprise managers must adhere to a stringent set of dress and grooming requirements. For instance, men must wear coordinated dress shirts and ties and can have facial hair only when "medically necessary." And women must wear skirts no shorter than two inches above their knees or creased pants.

So what are the incentives for working at Enterprise? For one thing, it's an unfortunate fact of life that college graduates with low grades often struggle to find work. Thus, a job at Enterprise is still better than no job at all. The firm does not hire outsiders—every position is filled by promoting someone already inside the company. Thus, Enterprise employees know that if they work hard and do their best, they may very well succeed in moving higher up the corporate ladder at a growing and successful firm.[37]

Case Questions

1. Would Enterprise's approach to human resource management work in other industries?

2. Does Enterprise face any risks from its human resource strategy?

3. Would you want to work for Enterprise? Why or why not?

Building HR Management Skills

Purpose: The purpose of this exercise is to serve as an icebreaker at the beginning of the course while simultaneously getting you to think about how human resource management will affect you personally.

Step 1: Your instructor will ask you to form small groups of four to five members each. Each member of the group should first introduce him- or herself to other group members.

Step 2: Group members should write their majors and career objectives on a sheet of paper and place the sheets in the center of the group so that everyone can read them.

Step 3: Working in concert with your group members, respond to the following questions and ideas:

1. How does human resource management affect each academic major and set of career objectives represented in the group?

2. How would group members feel about starting their careers in a human resource department?

3. How would group members feel about taking a position in human resources later in their careers?

4. What specific skills and abilities do group members believe are most important for someone who wants to work in human resources?

5. What will group members expect from the human resources department at the organization where they begin their career?

Step 4: Each group should select one member to serve as its representative. Your instructor may ask each representative to summarize the responses of her or his group to these questions either verbally or in writing.

Step 5: Reconvene with your group and discuss areas of agreement and disagreement among the various groups and group members.

Ethical Dilemmas in HR Management

Assume that you are a top human resource executive for a large, privately held company. Your specific area of responsibility is managing all aspects of compensation and benefits for the company; you report to the executive vice president of administration. This individual, in turn, is from the finance department and oversees HR, finance, and environmental regulation and shows little interest in HR per se as long as things are going smoothly.

The firm employs over 20,000 workers, has operations in fifteen countries, and has a long and stable history of growth and profitability. The owners of the firm, the descendants of the original founder, are not actively involved in management and express satisfaction with the firm's current and projected financial performance. Indeed, all components of financial performance are excellent, and the firm is widely respected for the quality of its management. The owners also have often expressed an interest in protecting their workers and maintaining as much job security as possible. The firm has not been forced to lay off any of its employees in more than twenty years.

About a year ago you read some research extolling the benefits of outsourcing. You have been quietly looking into how outsourcing might benefit your company.

Your findings are troubling, and you are now trying to decide how to proceed. Specifically, you have determined that outsourcing parts of the firm's human resource function could yield some modest cost savings for the firm. Unfortunately for you, compensation and benefits also seem to be the area most conducive to outsourcing.

On the one hand, as a manager you feel obligated to consider anything that might lower costs and/or improve the financial performance of the firm. Outsourcing does seem almost certain to improve financial performance, albeit only in relatively small ways. Thus, if you present your findings to your boss, the firm and its owners will benefit. On the other hand, if outsourcing were to be implemented, you estimate that approximately fifteen employees would lose their jobs, and your own position would be substantially diminished in importance.

Questions

1. What are the ethical issues in this situation?

2. What are the basic arguments for and against outsourcing in this situation?

3. What do you think most managers would do? What would you do?

HR Internet Exercise

Each year *Fortune* magazine publishes a list of what it calls "The Best Companies to Work for in America." The editors of the magazine base their list on extensive reviews of the human resource practices of many different firms and surveys of current and former employees.

As the first step in this exercise, use the Internet to identify the ten very best places to work as reflected in the most recent *Fortune* list. Next, visit the websites for these ten organizations and review the material at these sites through the eyes of someone looking for a job. Be sure to visit all the links to each company's different webpages at its website. Use the information you find to answer the following questions.

Questions

1. What specific information on each website most interested you as a prospective employee?

2. Based solely on the information you located, which company scores best, in your mind, as a potential employer?

3. What are the advantages and disadvantages to both employers and individuals seeking employment of using the Internet as a potential recruiting tool?

PART TWO

The Environment of Human Resource Management

2

The Strategic Human Resource Environment

CHAPTER OBJECTIVES

After studying this chapter you should be able to:

■ Describe the strategic context of human resource management.

■ Identify three types of strategies and relate each to human resource management.

■ Discuss human resource strategy formulation and relevant organizational factors.

■ Describe the process of human resource planning.

■ Discuss the processes through which human resource strategy is implemented.

■ Discuss how the human resource function in organizations can be evaluated.

For the past several years Starbucks Corporation has been the highest profile and fastest growing food and beverage company in the United States. Howard Schultz bought Starbucks in 1987 when it was still a small mail-order operation. Schultz promptly reoriented the business away from mail-order sales and emphasized retail coffee sales through the firm's coffee bars. Today, Starbucks is not only the largest coffee importer and roaster of specialty beans, but it is also the largest specialty coffee-bean retailer in the United States.

What are the keys to Starbucks' phenomenal growth and success? One important ingredient is its well-conceived and implemented strategy. Starbucks is on a phenomenal growth pace, opening a new coffee shop somewhere almost every day. But this growth is planned and coordinated each step of the way through careful site selection. And through its astute promotional campaigns and commitment to quality, the firm has elevated the coffee-drinking taste of millions of Americans and fueled a significant increase in demand. Another key to Starbucks' success is its near-fanatical emphasis on quality control and operations efficiencies. For example, milk must be heated to precise temperatures before it is used, and every espresso shot must be pulled within twenty-three seconds or else it is discarded. And no coffee is allowed to sit on a hot plate for more than twenty minutes. Schultz also refuses to franchise his Starbucks stores, fearing a loss of control and a potential deterioration of quality.

"One reason a lot of youths don't find corporate America so attractive is because of the IBM image: I'll become a blue suit. Starbucks makes you feel like a partner."

(Karen Hunsaker, Starbucks employee)*

The people who work for Starbucks have also played a major role in the firm's success. Managers at each store have considerable autonomy over how they run operations, as long as the firm's basic principles are followed. Starbucks also uses a state-of-the-art communication network to keep in contact with its employees. The firm hires relatively young people to work in its restaurants and starts them at hourly wages that are somewhat higher than most entry-level food-service jobs. The company also offers health insurance to all of its employees, including part-timers, and also has a lucrative stock-option plan for everyone in the firm. A state-of-the-art information system also allows every employee to keep abreast of what's happening in the company.

Its phenomenal growth rate notwithstanding, Starbucks is also continually on the alert for new business opportunities. One area of growth is international markets. As recently as 1996, Starbucks opened its very first coffee shops outside the United States: two in Japan and another in Singapore. By the end of 2002, 900 Starbucks stores operated in twenty-two markets outside North America. Another growth area for the company is brand extension with other companies. For instance, the firm collaborates with Dreyer's to distribute five flavors of Starbucks' coffee ice cream to grocery store freezers across the country. Starbucks also collaborates with Capital Records on Starbucks jazz CDs, which are available in Starbucks' stores. And Redhook Brewery even uses Starbucks' coffee extract in its double black stout beer![1] ■

Human resources can be an important source of competitive advantage for any organization, but it is critical that the organization understand how to use those resources to gain competitive advantage. Starbucks, the worldwide coffee company, sells high quality coffee. Some of the company's coffee buyers are shown here being trained on the taste characteristics of different types of coffee. The role of the selection process is to ensure that these employees have some coffee-tasting aptitude when they are hired. Then Starbucks must train them so that they develop an expertise in different types of coffee and are able to purchase the right beans for the tastes Starbucks' customers want.

S tarbucks has achieved undeniable success through an astute combination of strategy, control, and human resources. Under the leadership of Howard Schultz, the firm has been on a phenomenal growth and expansion pace, with everything dictated by an overarching strategy. Precise operations systems and control standards ensure consistent product quality, and highly motivated people throughout the organization keep everything running according to plan. Take away any of the three elements—strategy, operations, and motivated people—and both the company and its remarkable performance would not be the same. Indeed, more and more managers today are recognizing the important links that exist among strategy, operations, and human resource management. Further, a strategic orientation to human resource management provides a useful and effective perspective on how to create these linkages.

Thus, this chapter is devoted to the strategic human resource environment. The first section discusses the strategic context of human resource management in terms of the organization's purpose, mission, and top management team. The next section focuses on corporate, business, and functional strategies and their relationship to human resource management. We then address the increasingly important area of strategic human resource management in terms of, first, its formulation and, second, its implementation. Important organizational characteristics that affect and are affected by these processes are also described. Finally, we provide a framework for how organizations evaluate the human resource function.

THE STRATEGIC CONTEXT OF HUMAN RESOURCE MANAGEMENT

Human resource management does not occur in a vacuum but instead occurs in a complex and dynamic milieu of forces within the organizational context.[2] A significant trend in recent years has been for human resource managers to adopt

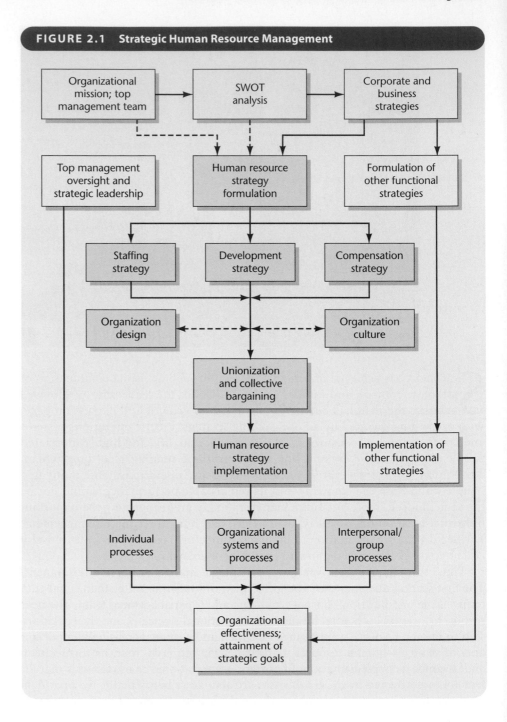

FIGURE 2.1   Strategic Human Resource Management

a strategic perspective on their job and to recognize the critical links between organizational strategy and human resource strategy. Figure 2.1 illustrates the framework we will use to describe strategic human resource management. As the figure shows, this process starts with an understanding of the organization's purpose and mission and the influence of its top management team and culminates with the human resource manager serving as a strategic partner to the operating divisions of the organization. That is, under this new view of human resource

POINT | COUNTERPOINT

Best Practices or Contingency Approach?

Strategic human resource management experts agree that human resource managers should be strategic partners and work to support the strategic goals of the organization. They disagree, however, about whether there is a set of best human resource practices that should be adopted by all organizations, or whether the choice of which practices to implement should be driven by the firm's strategic goals.

POINT ... There is one set of best practices that should be adopted by all firms because ...	COUNTERPOINT ... All practices should depend upon the firm's strategic goals because ...
Research has indicated that some practices tend to work better than others.	Research has indicated that there is no practice that always works.
Best practices lead to outcomes such as higher commitment and higher individual goals.	Desired outcomes depend on the firm's strategic goals.
It is easier to defend the use of practices that others have found successful.	What works for one firm may not work for another.
A body of sound scientific data supports the effectiveness of these practices.	It is impossible to assess effectiveness without considering organizational goals.
If there are no best practices, there are no principles to teach and there are no right answers.	There are no right answers (not any simple ones).

So ... Some human resource practices probably work better than others, but how they are applied will depend on a firm's strategic goals. Also, it does make sense for any firm to consider its own goals rather than copy someone else's practices when designing a human resource management system.

management, the human resource manager's job is to help line managers (at all levels) achieve their strategic goals. In this way, the human resource manager adds value to the organization by providing expertise concerning how to use the firm's human resources to accomplish its objectives.

But this view also has important implications for how human resource managers are trained and how human resource management courses are designed. Traditionally, managers, scholars, and textbook authors have discussed the newest—and presumably the best—ways to interview candidates or to select employees, as well as the best models for compensation and performance appraisal. But when we begin to consider the role of the human resource department as being that of a strategic partner, does it still make sense to talk about the single best way to do anything? Are there truly "best practices" that all firms should adopt, or should the practices adopted by a firm depend exclusively on the firm's specific strategic goals? The "truth" probably lies somewhere between these two extremes, but there have been loud debates within the human resource community over whether a best-practices approach or a contingency approach (based on the strategy pursued) is most logical.[3] Our Point/Counterpoint feature for this chapter addresses this controversy.

Indeed, it would seem that some general practices *are* better. If we examine fundamental human resource management practices, it seems reasonable to suggest that formal performance appraisals are better than no appraisals (see Chapter 9), for example, and that using systematic selection techniques is better than hiring based on intuition and/or some nonsystematic basis (see Chapter 7). But, within some constraints, exactly *how* these practices are implemented probably should depend on the firm's strategic goals. That is, although formal appraisals are better than no appraisals, exactly what is appraised should be consistent with a firm's strategic goals and missions and should be consistent with the other factors we will discuss throughout this chapter.

Therefore, an organization must choose human resource practices that fit its strategy and mission, and so the "best" practices for one firm may not be exactly the "best" for another firm. We will try to remind the reader of this fact throughout the book, but we recognize that this ambiguity can be a source of frustration. Students and managers alike often want to know what will work best in a particular organization. Although we will provide information and suggestions about general practices that should work (usually), the specific best solution or practice will depend on various characteristics of the organization such as strategic goals and top management values. There are few, if any, simple answers once we recognize the strategic role of human resource management.

The Influence of Organizational Purpose and Mission

■ An organization's **purpose** is its basic reason for existence.

■ An organization's **mission** is a statement of how it intends to fulfill its purpose.

An organization's purpose and mission are among the most fundamental contextual forces that define the strategic context of human resource management. An organization's **purpose** is its basic reason for existence. The purpose of a business is to earn profit for its owners; the purpose of a university is to discover and disseminate new knowledge; the purpose of a museum is to preserve artifacts and historical relics. An organization's **mission** is how its managers have decided to fulfill its purpose. That is, a mission statement specifies how the organization intends to manage itself so it can pursue the fulfillment of its purpose most effectively. A mission statement attempts to specify the unique characteristics and strengths of an organization and identifies the scope of the business's operations in particular products and markets.[4] Figure 2.2 shows the Starbucks mission statement. Note the prominence given to the firm's employees as the very first "guiding principle." This statement—and its placement—convey clearly the importance that Starbucks places on its employees.

Both its purpose and its mission affect an organization's human resource practices in some obvious ways. A university, for example, must employ highly educated faculty members to teach courses and to conduct research in specialized areas. A civil-engineering firm must employ people who understand construction and structural engineering; a natural history museum needs people who understand history and science; a marketing firm needs employees with sales expertise. But even finer gradations can be drawn within each type of organization, as defined by their respective missions. For example, an oil-exploration firm like Shell needs more petroleum engineers, while an electronics firm like Intel needs more electrical engineers, and a construction firm like Bechtel needs more civil engineers.

Mission statements often provide subtle cues about the importance that the organization places on its human resources. Many progressive firms today, like

FIGURE 2.2   Starbucks Corporate Mission Statement

STARBUCKS MISSION STATEMENT

Establish Starbucks as the premier purveyor of the finest coffee in the world while maintaining our uncompromising principles while we grow.

The following six guiding principles will help us measure the appropriateness of our decisions:

- Provide a great work environment and treat each other with respect and dignity.

- Embrace diversity as an essential component in the way we do business.

- Apply the highest standards of excellence to the purchasing, roasting and fresh delivery of our coffee.

- Develop enthusiastically satisfied customers all of the time.

- Contribute positively to our communities and our environment.

- Recognize that profitability is essential to our future success.

Courtesy—Starbucks Coffee Company.

Starbucks, refer to the importance of their human resources in their mission statement. Southwest Airlines and Wal-Mart also stress the value of their employees in their mission statements. But some firms do not explicitly refer to employees in their mission statements. While most of these firms really do, of course, value the people who work for them, the lack of specific reference to those people might be an indication that human resources are somehow not seen as being as important to the organization as other issues and goals. While mission statements make a public commitment to some course of action (such as valuing human resources), we must recognize that, in some cases, the language of a mission statement is intended to placate a group of stakeholders, such as employees, rather than to signal an organization's true priorities.[5]

The Influence of the Top Management Team

The **top management team** of an organization refers to the group of senior executives responsible for the overall strategic operation of the firm. Common organizational positions that are assumed to be part of the top management team include the chairperson of the board of directors, the chief executive officer

■ The **top management team** of an organization refers to the group of senior executives responsible for the overall strategic operation of the firm.

Whole Foods markets have become a true phenomenon. Whereas health food stores have traditionally been small and shabby, Whole Foods stores are big, bright, attractive, and, most of all, profitable. Part of the reason for Whole Foods' success is Americans' growing concerns about being overweight and unhealthy, but part of it is also due to founder John Mackey's strategic view for the company. He believes that in order for customers to be willing to pay higher prices for things such as "shade-grown coffee," they have to be educated. Therefore, pamphlets and signs are placed throughout the stores proclaiming why the products Whole Foods sells are special. He also realized that he needed to make his stores "one-stop shopping" destinations, so they are not only much larger than any other health food stores but also larger than most other supermarkets. Mackey also believes in his people. Empowerment is a big part of his human resource management strategy, and employees have a say in many of the company's policies. Through all his strategic decisions, Mackey has been willing to do things differently, and that willingness has paid off.

(CEO), the chief operating officer (COO), and the president. Other members of the top management team generally include the senior executive (usually having the title of vice president) responsible for each major functional area within the organization. For example, the senior vice presidents responsible for marketing, finance, and human resource management, respectively, are all likely to be considered part of an organization's top management team.

The top management team sets the tone for the organization and plays a major role in shaping its culture (as discussed later in this chapter). Some top management teams have a clear vision of where they want the firm to go and how they think it should get there. They also do a good job of articulating this vision throughout the organization. In this case, middle- and lower-level managers know what is expected of them and can direct their own efforts and the efforts of members of their own division, department, or team toward this common goal. Other top management teams, however, present an ambiguous, contradictory, or vague vision of where they see the organization headed. As a result, other managers in these organizations may be unsure about how to proceed and be unable to communicate effectively with their own employees.[6] In fact, views of leadership that emphasize the importance of personal charisma in leaders tend to suggest that effective leaders need both a clear vision and a means of communicating that vision. If an organization has top managers who are unable to accomplish both these goals, the organization is less likely to be successful.[7]

While top managers sometimes use speeches and proclamations to articulate the organization's vision and purpose, their actual behavior more commonly communicates their true personal values and beliefs, and thus those of the organization. Herb Kelleher, the legendary CEO of Southwest Airlines, knew many employees by name and insisted that they call him Herb. Before his death, Sam Walton personally visited every Wal-Mart store at least once a year and spoke

The Lighter Side of HR

The top management team in an organization plays a major role in determining its strategies and its culture. When top managers clearly respect the firm's employees and treat them with dignity, those employees feel valued and are likely to become more motivated and committed to the firm. But if top managers take a condescending approach to lower-level employees, the results can be disastrous. For example, as illustrated here, employees will almost certainly realize when a top manager is only pretending to be interested in their welfare.

Source: DILBERT by Scott Adams reprinted by permission of United Feature Syndicate, Inc.

with all employees via the firm's satellite telecommunications network almost once a week. Employees who work for leaders like these recognize that they are important and that their effort is valued by senior managers. In contrast, other top managers try to insulate themselves from lower-level members of the organization. They seldom visit work locations and treat their employees with disdain. James Dutt, a former CEO of a major conglomerate called Beatrice Foods, once told a subordinate that if his wife and children got in the way of his working twenty-four hours a day, seven days a week, he should get rid of them. More recently, Kenneth Lay created a culture at Enron that promoted internal cut-throat competition and a win-at-all-costs mentality. While some employees embraced this culture, others felt uncomfortable and many valuable employees left the firm.

But we should not assume from this discussion that the top management team or even the CEO will *always* have a major influence on what goes in an organization. In many cases, serious constraints restrict the power of the top management team and preclude them from having a great impact. A body of research that has examined this problem suggests that the ability of the top management team to influence the organization is constrained by the nature of the industry (an industry where commodity products are produced tends to constrain the influence of the top management team), the nature of the organization (more powerful boards of directors tend to constrain the influence of the top management team), and the nature of the individuals themselves.[8] This research, using the term *managerial discretion,* has found that the ability of the top management team to influence the organization and its success can vary a great deal as a function of these constraints.

CORPORATE, BUSINESS, AND FUNCTIONAL STRATEGIES

As indicated earlier, top managers are responsible for the strategic operations of their firms. The key to strategic operations, in turn, is developing and implementing effective strategies. These strategies may be at the corporate, business, and/or functional level, including the human resource function.[9] In addition to strategy formulation (as shown earlier in Figure 2.1), the top management team of the organization also provides oversight and strategic leadership for the organization on an ongoing basis. It should be clear by now, therefore, that functional strategies should be consistent with and supportive of corporate strategy.

SWOT Analysis and Human Resource Management

■ Strategies are typically formulated through a process involving a **SWOT analysis.** This involves identifying strengths, weaknesses, opportunities, and threats.

The first step in formulating strategy is what some managers call a **SWOT analysis.** SWOT is an acronym that stands for "strengths, weaknesses, opportunities, and threats." The idea behind a SWOT analysis is for managers in the firm to assess carefully the opportunities and threats that exist in a firm's environment and the strengths and weaknesses that exist within the organization itself. The managers then attempt to use the firm's strengths to capitalize on environmental opportunities and to cope with environmental threats. Strengths are also used to offset weaknesses within the organization. Human resources play a fundamental role in SWOT analysis because the nature and type of people who work within an organization and the organization's ability to attract new talent represent significant strengths or weaknesses. Likewise, a surplus or a scarcity of talented and capable people in the external labor market also represents important environmental opportunities and threats.[10]

■ **Corporate strategy** deals with determining what businesses the corporation will operate.

Many organizations formulate strategy at three basic levels: the corporate level, the business level, and various functional levels. **Corporate strategy** deals with determining what businesses the firm will operate. **Business strategy** deals with how the firm will compete in each market where it conducts business. Finally, **functional strategies** deal with how the firm will manage each of its major functions, such as marketing, finance, and human resources. Strategies at all three levels, however, affect the human resource management function under the strategic approach to human resource management.

■ **Business strategy** deals with how the firm will compete in each market where it conducts business.

■ **Functional strategy** deals with how the firm will manage each of its major functions, such as marketing, finance, and human resources.

Corporate Strategy and Human Resource Management

Using the results of their SWOT analysis, most organizations develop corporate strategy from one of two perspectives. One perspective focuses on a single, overarching grand strategy for the firm, while the other is based on diversification.

■ A **grand strategy** is a single, overall framework for action that the top management team develops at the corporate level.

Grand strategy   A **grand strategy** is a single, overall framework for action that the top management team develops at the corporate level.[11] It is most commonly used when a business chooses to compete in one market or in only a few closely related markets. When a business has identified a unique niche and is successfully expanding aggressively within that particular market niche, it is pursuing what experts call a *growth strategy*. As the term suggests, a growth strategy focuses on the growth and expansion of the corporation. Since 1990, for example, the Home Depot has opened about 100 new stores each year, clearly a growth strategy. Starbucks has also been using a rapid growth strategy as it continues its geographic and brand expansion, opening on average at least one new store somewhere in the world every day.

A key challenge for human resource managers when firms are using a growth strategy is recruiting and training large numbers of qualified employees to help operate growing operations. The Home Depot, for instance, hires dozens of new management trainees each year, along with hundreds of new retail associates and other operating employees to staff its new stores. Human resource managers at The Home Depot are responsible for recruiting and hiring these people, orienting and training them, and making their initial job assignments. Similarly, Starbucks hires dozens of new employees each month. The firm's human resource managers run continuous training programs to teach these new employees the precise methods for brewing coffee and maintaining quality control in all other areas of their job responsibilities. Thus, in both these firms the human resource function focuses its activities on ways to help each organization achieve its corporate goals.

We should also note that when organizations view the human resource area as a true strategic partner, they also use input from human resource managers in their initial formulation of corporate strategy. For example, when The Home Depot's top managers first decided to pursue a growth strategy, the firm's top management team likely consulted with the human resource management team to ensure that they had the capability to attract and train the large number of new employees needed to implement the anticipated growth. In other words, a true partnership requires both parties to consult with and support each other.

A growth strategy can also be pursued externally through mergers, joint ventures, or the acquisition of other businesses. A major initial challenge for human resource managers in this situation is determining how to merge two existing workforces into a single cohesive and integrated unit. In some cases, for example, there will be unnecessary duplication of employees and choices will have to be made about which overlapping employees to retain, which to transfer, and which to lay off. Similarly, it is likely that the two firms will be using different human resource philosophies for issues such as training practices, promotion policies, and so forth. Hence, human resource decision makers must decide which practices to retain and which to discard. When The Walt Disney Company acquired ABC, among the first questions that had to be answered were: (1) Who would manage various parts of the new enterprise? and (2) How would the human resources comprising the two firms be integrated into one new operation? In fact, there is reason to believe that the failure to integrate different strategies and cultures may be an important factor in the failure of some mergers and acquisitions.[12] Furthermore, because there is always a great deal of concern and speculation over what will happen to employees, it is critical that the entire merger or acquisition process be managed relative to its impact on employees. Failure to do so can result in undue stress, the loss of valued employees, and long-lasting moral problems in organizations.[13]

A second grand strategy that organizations are sometimes forced to adopt, at least in the short run, is called a *retrenchment* or a *turnaround strategy*, which occurs when an organization finds that its current operations are not effective. For example, a firm might find that its dominant products are in declining markets, its technology is rapidly becoming obsolete, or it is in some other way not performing as well as it should. Major changes are usually needed to rectify these kinds of problems. In most of these cases, organizations go through a period of *downsizing* (or *rightsizing*, as some managers prefer to call it) in an effort to get back on the right track. They close operations, shut down factories, terminate employees, and take other actions to scale back current operations and reduce their workforce. Their ultimate goal is to take the resources generated as a result of these steps and reinvest them into other more promising products and markets.

Downsizing has become a common response to competitive problems. As more employees find their jobs at risk, the traditional *psychological contract* between the organization and the employee is changing. No longer can employees feel certain of keeping their jobs as long as they perform well, and the increased uncertainty makes it more difficult for employees to commit fully to their organizations. As a result of these problems, human resource managers clearly need to be involved when the organization is eliminating jobs and/or decreasing the size of its workforce. They need to help manage the process so that employees continue to feel attached to and committed to the organization. In addition, human resource managers must help ensure that decisions about who will be let go are made for job-related reasons as opposed to reasons that might reflect or suggest bias or illegal discrimination. Similarly, human resource managers can help optimize the transition process for displaced workers through practices such as equitable severance packages and outplacement counseling. A few years ago, International Harvester declared bankruptcy and was reborn as Navistar, a much smaller operation. Human resource managers were involved in all phases of this process and in making decisions about which employees would be most valuable to the new enterprise and how best to retain them.

A final grand strategy that some firms use is a stability strategy. A *stability strategy* essentially calls for maintaining the status quo. A company that adopts a stability strategy plans to stay in its current businesses and intends to manage them as they are already being managed. The organization's goal is to protect itself from environmental threats. A stability strategy is frequently used after a period of retrenchment or after a period of rapid growth. When the firm is using a stability strategy, human resource managers play a major role in determining how to retain the firm's existing employees when the firm can offer little in the way of advancement opportunities, salary increases, and so forth.

Diversification strategy   Another widely used approach to corporate strategy is diversification.[14] A corporation that uses the diversification strategy usually makes the decision to own and operate several different businesses. For example, General Electric, one of the most successful practitioners of this strategy, owns varied businesses that manufacture aircraft engines, industrial products, major appliances, and technical products. It also owns the NBC television network and financial services and insurance businesses.

The various businesses owned by a corporation are usually related to one another in some way. This strategy is called *related diversification*.[15] The basic underlying assumption for using related diversification is that the corporation can achieve synergy among the various businesses that it owns. For example, The Limited has an ownership stake in over a dozen different retail chains, including Express, Victoria's Secret, Structure, Bath & Body Works, and Abercrombie & Fitch. A single group of buyers supply all of the firm's chains, a single development operation seeks new locations for all chains, and so forth. This type of organization often adopts a policy of rotating managers across the various businesses so they develop an overall managerial perspective on the whole firm. A manager might start out with Express, get promoted to a new position at Bath & Body

■ **A diversification strategy** is used by companies that are adding new products, product lines, or businesses to their existing core products, product lines, or businesses.

Works, and then move into yet another position with Abercrombie & Fitch. The related aspects of the businesses presumably make such cross-business transfers easier. Because the markets for each business are similar, the firm can develop relatively uniform procedures for selection, compensation, training, and so forth.

Sometimes, however, an organization decides to expand into products or markets that are unrelated to its current products and markets. This approach is called *unrelated diversification*. A firm that pursues a strategy of unrelated diversification attempts to operate several unique businesses in different, unrelated markets. General Electric, as already noted, owns businesses that compete in different unrelated areas. The basic logic behind unrelated diversification is that a company can shield itself from the adverse impact of business cycles, unexpected competition, and other economic fluctuations. Since the various businesses are presumably unrelated, a downturn or setback in one does not necessarily suggest a corresponding downturn or setback in another.

Human resource executives in a firm that uses unrelated diversification must approach the human resource function in a very different way. In most cases, managers remain within a single business unit as they progress up the corporate ladder. Because each unrelated business is likely to have its own unique hiring, compensation, and training needs—as dictated by its own competitive environment—these functions will likely be customized and decentralized for each business. Thus, while the career tracks and compensation packages for managers at Express and Victoria's Secret will likely be similar to one another, the career tracks and compensation packages for managers at NBC and GE Appliance may be quite different from one another. The NBC compensation packages, for instance, will more closely resemble those at ABC and CBS, while the GE Appliance compensation packages may be more like those at Whirlpool and Maytag.

Organizations that use the diversification approach for managing their corporate strategy must also work to ensure close coordination between their corporate human resource functions and the human resource functions within each of their businesses or divisions. Essentially, the corporate human resource group must interface with three sets of constituents. One set of constituents is the top management team, or corporate management. Second, corporate human resources can also be involved in representing the firm in its interactions with external constituents such as the government, labor unions, and benchmark companies (companies to which the organization compares itself). And third, corporate human resources can also be involved with the division management, division human resources, and the employees of each division or business owned by the corporation.[16]

Business Strategy and Human Resource Management

As noted earlier, decisions must also be made about how to compete in each market where a firm operates. This question determines business strategy. A diversified corporation must therefore develop a business strategy for each of its operating units.[17] Two different approaches can be used to develop a business-level strategy.

The adaptation model   One approach to business strategy is called the **adaptation model**.[18] This model suggests that managers in an organization should try to match the organization's strategy with the basic conditions of its environment. Different levels of environmental complexity and change are expected to be

■ The **adaptation model** is one popular approach to business strategy where a business seeks ways to adapt to its environment.

matched most appropriately with different forms of strategy. The three basic strategic alternatives from which managers should select are the defender strategy, the analyzer strategy, and the prospector strategy.

A *defender strategy* is assumed to work best when a business operates in an environment with relatively little uncertainty and risk and a high degree of stability. The goal of the defender is to identify for itself a relatively narrow niche in the market and then to direct a limited set of products or services at that niche. Although defenders may compete with other firms aggressively, their primary approach is to guard and to secure their position within an existing market. Thus, while they monitor trends and developments outside their chosen domain, they focus primarily on their existing environment. Hershey Foods is a good example of a defender. The firm concentrates almost exclusively on the confectionery market. Another good example of a defender is Wrigley, the venerable chewing gum company founded in 1891. Human resource managers in organizations using this strategy are most likely to recruit and seek to retain stable employees who exhibit high levels of commitment and loyalty to the firm.

A second type of strategy used in this approach is the prospector strategy. The *prospector strategy* anchors the other end of the continuum. This strategy works best when the environment is dynamic and growing and has considerable uncertainty and risk. Prospectors are advised to be on constant alert for discovering and capitalizing on new ideas and opportunities. They continually focus on new products and markets and try to avoid a long-term commitment to any single type of technology, using multiple technologies instead. This strategy makes it easier for the organization to shift easily from one product market to another. General Electric is a good example of a prospector. As noted earlier, the firm owns everything from a jet-engine business to a television network. For the right opportunity, the firm will buy any business that might be for sale or sell any business it currently owns. Human resource managers in organizations using this strategy may prefer to recruit and retain entrepreneurial employees who are highly flexible and who are more dedicated to their craft or profession than to the organization itself.

The analyzer strategy falls between the extremes of the defender and prospector strategies. The *analyzer strategy* is most appropriate in relatively stable conditions with a moderate degree of uncertainty and risk. An analyzer tries to identify and take advantage of new markets and products while simultaneously maintaining a nucleus of traditional core products and customers. The Walt Disney Company is a good example of an analyzer. The firm cautiously moved into television and video markets a few years ago, has expanded its movie division, and is currently investing in electronic games and virtual reality products, but it takes each step slowly and only after careful deliberation. Human resource managers in firms that pursue this strategy may seek to recruit and retain employees who might be moderately entrepreneurial and flexible, but who will also be quite dedicated and loyal to the organization.

The adaptation model also identifies a fourth strategic alternative called the reactor. The *reactor* is really seen as a strategic failure, however, and is not held up as a model that any firm should emulate. A reactor is a firm that either improperly ignores its environment or else attempts to react to its environment in inappropriate ways. During the early 1980s Kmart was guilty of using the reactor strategy. It failed to keep pace with Wal-Mart, for example, and spread itself too thin by investing heavily in specialty retailing. Human resource managers in organizations functioning as reactors may lack a clear understanding of exactly what qualities they are seeking in their employees. And indeed, this lack of understanding may contribute to the firm's poor performance.

Competitive strategies   The other dominant approach to business-level strategies identifies three **competitive strategies** that are presumed to be appropriate for a wide variety of organizations in diverse industries.[19] These strategies are differentiation, cost leadership, and focus.

A company that uses a **differentiation strategy** attempts to develop an image or reputation for its product or service that sets it apart from those of their competitors. The differentiating factor may be real and/or objective, such as product reliability or design, or it may be more perceptual and/or subjective, such as fashion and appearance. Regardless of its basis, however, a firm that can differentiate its products or services from those of its competitors can charge higher prices for those products or services, thereby earning a larger profit. Rolex and BMW are both examples of firms that have used a differentiation strategy successfully. Human resource managers contribute to the successful use of a differentiation strategy by recruiting and retaining employees who can perform high-quality work and/or provide exemplary customer service. Likewise, employee training will likely focus on quality improvement, and reward systems may be based on factors such as quality of work and customer satisfaction.[20]

A **cost leadership strategy** is one that focuses on minimizing the costs as much as possible. This strategy allows the firm to charge the lowest possible prices for its products, thereby presumably generating a higher overall level of revenue. Low cost may be achieved through production efficiencies, distribution efficiencies, or product design efficiencies. Timex and Hyundai are examples of businesses that have used a cost leadership strategy successfully. Human resource contributions here focus on recruiting and retaining employees who can work as efficiently and productively as possible. On the other hand, more experienced employees may demand higher wages, and so it might also be possible to reengineer jobs so that they require minimal skills, and then select employees who can perform the jobs but who may not remain with the organization long. Fast-food restaurants often control labor costs using an approach such as this one. In any case, training may emphasize efficient production methods, and reward systems may be based more on quantity than on quality of output. One popular approach to reducing costs today is moving production to other countries where labor costs are lower.

Finally, when an organization uses the **focus strategy**, it tries to target a specific segment of the marketplace for its products or services. This focus may be toward a specific geographic area, a specific segment of the consuming population based on ethnicity or gender, or some other factor that serves to segment the market. Within that focus, a firm may attempt either to differentiate or to cost lead its products or services. Fiesta Mart is a Houston-based grocery store chain that has prospered by focusing its marketing on the large number of immigrants, especially Hispanics, who live in the Southwest. These stores sell Mexican soft drinks, cornhusks for wrapping tamales, and many other products that are not carried in general-purpose grocery stores. The key human resource goal in this instance is recruiting and retaining employees who understand the focal market. For example, Fiesta Mart must recruit, hire, and retain employees who really understand the products they are selling and who speak Spanish, the language of most of its customers.

■ The **competitive strategies** framework suggests three basic strategies are appropriate for a wide variety of organizations in diverse industries. These strategies are differentiation, cost leadership, and focus.

■ A company that uses a **differentiation strategy** attempts to develop an image or reputation for its product or service that sets the company apart from its competitors.

■ A **cost leadership strategy** is one that focuses on minimizing the costs as much as possible.

■ The **focus strategy** is undertaken when an organization tries to target a specific segment of the marketplace for its products or services.

Functional Strategies and Human Resource Management

The third level of strategy formulation and implementation is at the functional level. Functional strategies address how the organization will manage its basic functional activities, such as marketing, finance, operations, research and development, and human resources. Thus, at this level human resource strategy formulation formally begins to take shape. It is clearly important that a human resource functional strategy be closely integrated and coordinated with corporate, business, and other functional strategies. Indeed, without such integration and coordination, organizational competitiveness will clearly suffer.[21]

Much of our discussion throughout the remainder of this text explicitly or implicitly addresses the human resource function from a contextual perspective that includes other fundamental business functions. As you saw in Figure 2.1, human resource strategy is, of course, our primary concern. Keep in mind, however, that other functional strategies are also developed and (as you saw in the figure) combine with the human resource strategy and top management strategic leadership to determine the firm's overall performance.

HUMAN RESOURCE STRATEGY FORMULATION

Using the organization's overarching corporate and business strategies as context, managers can then formally develop the organization's human resource strategy, as noted above. As illustrated earlier in Figure 2.1, this strategy commonly includes three distinct components—a staffing strategy, a development strategy, and a compensation strategy. These dimensions are shown in more detail in Figure 2.3.

Staffing refers to the set of activities used by the organization to determine its future human resource needs, to recruit qualified applicants interested in working for the organization, and then to select the best of those applicants as new employees. Obviously, however, this process can be undertaken only after a careful and systematic strategy has been developed to ensure that staffing activities mesh appropriately with other strategic elements of the organization. For example, as already noted, if the business employs a growth strategy, the staffing strat-

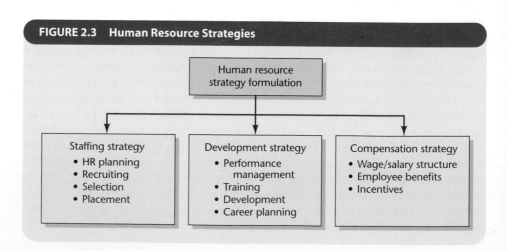

FIGURE 2.3   Human Resource Strategies

egy must be based on the aggressive recruiting and selection of large numbers of qualified employees.[22] But if retrenchment is the expectation, the staffing strategy will focus instead on determining which employees to retain and how to handle best the process of terminating other employees.

Similarly, human resource managers must also formulate an employee development strategy for helping the organization enhance the quality of its human resources. This strategy usually involves performance management, the actual training and development of employees and managers, and career planning and development for appropriate employees. As with staffing, the development strategy must be consistent with corporate and business strategies. For example, if an organization uses a differentiation strategy, the firm needs to invest heavily in training its employees to produce the highest-quality products and/or provide the highest-quality service. Performance management must also be focused on recognizing and rewarding performance leading to improved quality. But if cost leadership is the strategy of choice, the firm may choose to invest less in training (helping to keep overall costs low) and orient what training is offered toward efficiency and productivity improvement methods and techniques.

Third, the compensation strategy must likewise complement other strategies adopted by the firm. Basic compensation, performance-based incentives, and employee benefits and services—the major components of the compensation strategy, must all be congruent with their relevant strategic contexts to be effective. For example, if a firm uses a strategy of related diversification, its compensation system must be geared to, first, rewarding those employees with different skills that allow them to transition across businesses and, second, be flexible enough to facilitate those same cross-business transfers. If a manager moves from one division to another, for instance, that manager's pension plan should be readily portable to the new assignment. If the firm uses unrelated diversification, on the other hand, compensation may instead be focused on depth of knowledge and skills. Hence, the firm may choose to pay a premium salary to a highly talented expert with unusual skills relevant to one of the firm's businesses. The ability of this expert to transition across businesses is less important and thus is not likely to be a factor in compensation.[23]

Of course, these three components cannot be treated independently of each other. Each component must be tied to the overall human resource strategy, and each must consider the factors and constraints produced by the other components. A recently proposed theoretical model attempts to look at the entire array of interrelationships with employees from a strategic perspective. The model of human resource architecture suggests that not all employees possess capabilities of equal strategic value to a firm, and so they should be treated differently.[24] Specifically, the authors argue that a firm can have at least four types of employment modes, which they refer to as internal development, acquisition, contracting, and alliance, for its employees. The model suggests strategic imperatives for establishing these different relationships. (We will return to a discussion of human resource architecture in Chapter 17.)

To help explain the complexities of the interchange among these aspects of human resource strategy and corporate strategy, we can consider a situation where an organization is moving into a new line of business, or at least changing its emphasis within existing businesses. A good case in point is the major oil companies in the United States. Someone growing up in this country in the 1960s and 1970s would remember gas stations as places where someone stopped to get gas for a car and perhaps was able to buy a cold drink or a snack from a vending machine. Over time, the image of the gas station changed dramatically. Through the 1980s and 1990s oil companies expanded the services available at these stations, and many of them became minimarts offering a wider variety of food and beverages. By the beginning of the twenty-first century, many oil companies entered into alliances with fast-food chains (such as McDonald's and Kentucky Fried Chicken) so that patrons could buy a meal as well as gas.

These services were viewed as a means to get potential customers to stop at a given gas station. Although the oil companies made money from products sold at the minimarts, they did not see these products as a primary line of business. But at the end of the 1990s and in the earlier years of the twenty-first century, several large mergers occurred between major oil companies (e.g., British Petroleum and AMOCO, Exxon and Mobil), and as a result the new merged companies discovered that they owned a large number of food marts around the country. Human Resources Around the Globe describes how BP-AMOCO has sharpened its thinking regarding its human resources as a result of their merger.

When attempting to formulate the human resource strategy as well as its three basic components, human resource managers must also account for other key parts of the organization. These components are important because they affect both how strategies are formulated and how they are implemented. Three critical components are organization design, the corporate culture, and unionization.[25] A fourth component, the labor force and how it relates to human resource planning, will be discussed in more detail a bit later in the chapter.

The Impact of Organization Design

■ **Organization design** refers to the framework of jobs, positions, clusters of positions, and reporting relationships among positions that are used to construct an organization.

Organization design refers to the framework of jobs, positions, groups of positions, and reporting relationships among positions that are used to construct an organization.[26] One form of organization design used by many smaller and/or newer organizations is the *functional design* (this design is also called the *U-form organization*, with the *U* representing "unitary"). The organization groups its members into basic functional departments such as marketing, finance, and operations. For this form of organization to operate effectively, considerable coordination across departments must exist. Senior management is usually expected to provide this coordination. A U-form organization typically has a single human resource department responsible for organizationwide human resource functions and activities, and the human resource manager and department work with all other functional areas across the firm.

A second form of organization design used in some organizations today is the *conglomerate,* or *H-form design* (the *H* stands for "holding company"). A conglomerate design is used when an organization has implemented a strategy of unrelated diversification. The corporation itself is essentially a holding company that results from this unrelated diversification. Because the various businesses that comprise the organization are unrelated to the others, each functions with a high degree of autonomy and independence. A corporate-level staff usually plays a key role in coordinating the activities of the various divisions, and human resource management is a common staff function in an H-form organization. But each of the unrelated businesses within the corporation also has its own human resource department that functions with relative autonomy within that specific business. The corporate-level staff provides broad and general oversight and links business-level issues with corporate-level issues.

Blending the Multinational Mix

As the merger between British Petroleum and AMOCO was being completed in 1998, the firm's executives realized that the combined company actually owned more retail outlets than McDonald's! The business then began developing strategies to exploit these resources, and several of them related to human resource issues.

"There's no ocean wide enough to keep two oil companies apart."*

First, BP-AMOCO, as the new company was called, needed to recruit a new type of employee—a retail sales employee. Although each firm had employed many of these people in the past, their function was not central to the company's strategic goals (which focused on oil and gasoline). But if retailing was going to be a major business in the future, the company wanted to make sure they recruited top salespeople. This change also necessitated new human resource policies designed to retain the retail employees they already had and to train those employees to provide better services. This situation is also complicated by the fact that many of these retail outlets are actually franchised to other owners. Since the company traditionally focused more on employees directly involved in the drilling and refining of oil, this change required new systems and new policies.

This was only the beginning, however. If the company wanted to be a major retailing power, it needed a presence everywhere in the United States. An examination of where the company owned stations, however, indicated that it was extremely weak in California and the Pacific coast. How could it penetrate that market quickly? BP-AMOCO could obviously build new stations in California, but starting from scratch would take a long time. Instead, managers identified a target for another acquisition. ARCO was another large oil company with energy holdings in Alaska that were attractive, but with something else BP-AMOCO needed even more—most of ARCO's service stations were located on the West Coast. If BP could acquire ARCO, it would have the market penetration it needed.

In order to get the acquisition approved by the Justice Department, the company ended up having to sell ARCO's Alaskan operations but was able to retain its West Coast retailing business. Hence, BP, as the firm renamed itself, may now move even faster into retailing as a major part of its strategy and will continue to need new types of employees. The human resource function at the new company will have to work to meld the cultures of a traditional British company (BP), a Midwest-based U.S. oil company (AMOCO) and a West Coast–based oil company (ARCO). Clearly, the decision to exploit BP's retail outlets in a more meaningful way will have far-reaching implications for the firm's human resource function.

Source: Hoover's Handbook of World Business 2003 (Austin, Tex.: Hoover's Business Press, 2003), pp. 114–115(*quote on p. 114).

A third form of organization design that is fairly common today is the *divisional* or *M-form organization* design (the *M* stands for "multidivisional"). The divisional design looks similar to the H-form design except that the businesses are closely related to one another. The M-form design is especially popular because of the presumed synergies that can result from related business groupings. Coordination is usually decentralized in an M-form organization, down to the various operating companies where the work is actually being performed. While M-form organizations may have a corporate human resource staff, most of the basic human resource functions are handled within each division.[27] The primary function of the corporate-level human resource department is to facilitate synergy across businesses. Presumably, the U.S.-based oil companies discussed above are moving to this type of form.

In recent years, many organizations have been moving toward yet another form of organization design. While this new design has no precise name, the popular press often refers to it as the *flat organization,* or the *horizontal corporation.*

Such an organization is created by eliminating levels of management, reducing bureaucracy, using very wide spans of management, and relying heavily on teamwork and coordination to get work accomplished. Horizontal corporations are presumed to be highly flexible and to provide a great deal of opportunity for adaptation, fewer managers, and greater levels of empowerment on the part of subordinates. The human resource function in these organizations is likely to be diffused throughout the organization so that operating managers take on more of the responsibility for human resource activities, with a somewhat smaller human resource staff providing basic services and playing more of a consultative role.

The Impact of Corporate Culture

■ An organization's **culture** refers to the set of values that helps its members understand what the organization stands for, how it accomplishes what it wants to accomplish, and what it considers important.

The culture of the organization also affects how it formulates and implements its human resource strategy. An organization's **culture** refers to the set of values that helps its members understand what the organization stands for, how it does things, and what it considers important.[28] Culture is a complex and amorphous concept that defies objective measurement or evaluation. Nevertheless, because it is the foundation of an organization's internal environment, culture plays a major role in shaping managerial behavior and is a strong element in how the organization manages its human resources.

While there is no such thing as an ideal culture, it is important that an organization have a strong and well-articulated culture. This type of culture enables people within the firm to know what the organization stands for, what it values, and how they should behave with regard to the organization.[29] The human resource department often plays a key role in helping new employees learn about the culture through orientation and through the telling and retelling of stories and corporate history. For current organizational employees, culture can be communicated through training, consistent behavior, and other organizational activities. Sometimes something as simple as a slogan can be used to manage culture. For example, when Continental Airline's current management team took over, they touted their turnaround strategy as the "Go Forward Plan"—a signal to look ahead and not back. And when Schwinn, a 100-year-old bicycle company, changed its corporate culture ten years ago, it helped enact the change with a new slogan: "Established 1895. Re-established 1994."

While an organization's culture is shaped by several different forces, an important force is the founder of the organization. Organizations with strong-willed and visionary founders often find that the remnants of that founder's vision remain a central part of their culture today. Walt Disney's influence is still found throughout the corporation that bears his name. Even though Sam Walton died a few years ago, his values and approach to doing business will likely remain a part of Wal-Mart for decades to come. As an organization grows, its culture is modified, shaped, and refined through other forces. These forces include symbols, stories, slogans, heroes, and ceremonies. Shared experiences also play a role in determining and shaping the culture of an organization. Members of teams who work long hours together to develop a major new product, like the new Ford F150 pickup truck, or who jointly experience a major crisis, like dealing with the aftermath of September 11, 2001, often develop a common frame of reference and become a more cohesive work group.

Human resource managers may find that, depending on the circumstances, corporate culture may either facilitate or impede their work. If the firm has a strong and well-understood culture that seems attractive to people, human resource managers often find it easier to attract and retain the most qualified employees. Southwest Airlines and Starbucks fall into this category, with each of these firms receiving large numbers of applications from prospective employees. Like other managers in these firms, the human resource managers themselves have a clear understanding of what the organization stands for and how they are expected to contribute. Organizations that have strong cultures and that wish to maintain those cultures tend to select people who have values consistent with that culture. We will discuss the role of fit later in the book, but for now it is important to note that some organizations select employees not because they are necessarily the most qualified of all applicants. Instead, they might select individuals who are qualified enough to do the job but who also share the values and beliefs of the firm's culture. In other words, they select the person who best fits the organization's culture and image.

Finally, managing culture is important for the success of corporate mergers and acquisitions. As noted above, the large U.S.-based oil companies are currently struggling with the ways they can integrate very different cultures into a new corporate identity. In these cases, as in most cases, the job of integrating cultures to form one new culture is the job of the human resource department. The success of this integration (and in fact the creation of a new unique corporate culture and identity for the merged organization) is critical for the overall success of the merger or acquisition. Several scholars have noted that the failure to deal with the human resource implications of mergers and acquisitions leads to their failure far more frequently than do problems with finances.[30] An interesting example of these culture problems occurred several years ago when Philip Morris acquired General Foods. The employees of General Foods considered themselves part of a benevolent company that made family-oriented products such as Jell-O and Maxwell House coffee. Imagine their surprise when their new employers (who also owned Miller Brewing Company) continued *their* usual practice and distributed cartons of cigarettes to each employee every Friday!

The Impact of Unionization and Collective Bargaining

Other important aspects of the workforce that affect the human resource management function are unionization and collective bargaining. Labor relations is the process of dealing with employees who are represented by an employee association, usually called a union. Union membership in the United States has been declining gradually for the last several years but remains an important force in many industries. The success of the Teamsters in their strike against United Parcel Service (UPS) in 1997, as well as other high-profile strikes such as one at General Motors and the one involving West Coast shipping ports in 2002, may well encourage unions to renew efforts to organize more workers. Also, in recent years the AFL-CIO has begun linking living-wage issues to larger social movements, introducing new sources of pressure on human resource management.[31] In any case, unions can play an important role in formulating and implementing human resource strategy. For example, if management and union leaders do not work together, the union can be a major obstacle to the organization attempting to make significant workplace changes. On the other hand, a strong union can facilitate the same type of change if its leaders and the firm's management are working together productively. We cover unionization and collective bargaining in detail in Chapter 14.

HUMAN RESOURCE PLANNING AND THE WORKFORCE

■ **Human resource planning** is the process of forecasting the supply and demand for human resources within an organization and developing action plans for aligning the two.

Probably the most important factor that affects the human resource management function is the labor force or workforce. An organization may pursue a growth strategy, and the human resource manager may attempt to recruit and hire new employees, but if there are not enough people in the labor force with the required skills or background, the efforts to recruit and hire will fail and so will the overall growth strategy. Thus, the composition of the labor force is a major limiting factor in pursuing strategic goals. The successful management of this component requires what is called human resource planning, and this planning can often make the difference between organizational success and failure.[32] **Human resource planning,** illustrated in Figure 2.4, can be defined as the process of forecasting the supply and demand for human resources within an organization and developing action plans for aligning the two. This section examines that process in more detail.

Forecasting the Supply of Human Resources

An important first step in human resource planning is forecasting the future supply of human resources—predicting the availability of current and/or potential employees with the skills, abilities, and motivation to perform jobs that the organization expects to have available. Several mechanisms can be used to help managers forecast the supply of human resources vis-à-vis its current employees. By looking internally at its own records, the organization is likely to be able to draw on considerable historical data about its own abilities to hire and retain employees. In addition, the organization can glean information about the extent to which people leave their jobs voluntarily or involuntarily. All of this information, in turn, is useful in predicting the internal supply of human resources in the future.

Suppose, for example, that Atlas Industries, a regional manufacturing and supply business serving the plumbing industry, has averaged 15 percent turnover for each of the last ten years, with little variation from year to year. When Atlas's hu-

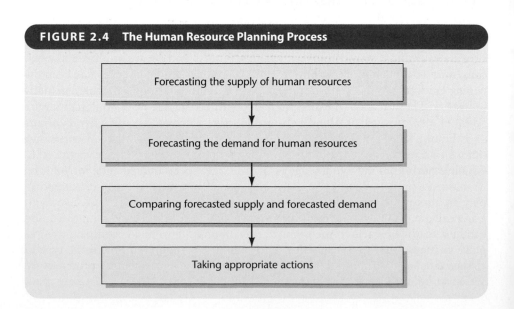

FIGURE 2.4   The Human Resource Planning Process

Forecasting the supply of human resources

↓

Forecasting the demand for human resources

↓

Comparing forecasted supply and forecasted demand

↓

Taking appropriate actions

man resource manager attempts to predict the future supply of existing workers, at least initially it seems reasonable to predict a relatively similar level of turnover for the forthcoming year. Thus, the internal supply of the human resources at Atlas will likely decline by about 15 percent during the next year. Assuming the firm plans to maintain its current operations and will need a workforce comparable to what it has today, it becomes necessary for the organization to plan to replace those individuals who will depart by recruiting and hiring new employees.

An increasingly important element in this part of the human resource planning process for most organizations is the effective use of the organization's human resource information system. While we discuss the concepts associated with human resource information systems more completely in Appendix 1, it is relevant to introduce and briefly discuss them here, particularly as they pertain to human resource planning. A **human resource information system** is an integrated and increasingly an automated system for maintaining a database regarding the employees in an organization. For example, a properly developed human resource information system should have details on every employee regarding date of hire, job history within the organization, education, performance ratings, compensation history, training and development profile, and various special skills and abilities that each employee possesses.[33]

■ A **human resource information system** is an integrated and increasingly automated system for maintaining a database regarding the employees in an organization.

Of course, the human resource manager also needs to look carefully at impending retirements and the firm's experiences with involuntary turnover. We will discuss issues of retirement later in Chapters 8 and 15, and we will discuss issues involved in organizations' attempts to manage the turnover process in Chapter 8.

Because a firm often expects to need new employees in the future, it is also important to forecast the supply of human resources outside the firm that will be potentially available for it to recruit and hire. Here it is important to consider both general trends in the population and the workforce and at the same time to generate specific data about availability as it relates to the specific firm.

Labor force trends and issues   Several changes in the labor force continue to emerge and affect human resource management. Decades ago, the labor force in the United States was primarily male and primarily white. Now, however, the workforce is much more diverse in numerous ways.[34] For example, most people once followed a fairly predictable pattern of entering the workforce at a young age, maintaining a stable employment relationship for the period of their work lives, and then retiring at the fairly predictable age of sixty-five. But today, these patterns and trends have all changed. For example, the average age of the U.S. workforce is gradually increasing and will continue to do so.

Several reasons have contributed to this pattern. First, the baby-boom generation continues to age. Declining birth rates among the post-baby-boom generation are simultaneously accounting for a smaller percentage of new entrants into the labor force. Improved health and medical care also contributes to an aging workforce. People are simply able to maintain a productive work period for a longer part of their lives today. And finally, mandatory retirement ages have been increased or dropped altogether, allowing people to remain in the labor force for a longer period of time.

Gender differences in the workforce also play an important role. More and more women have entered the workforce, and their presence is felt in more and more occupational groupings that were traditionally dominated by men. In 2000 the composition of the workforce in the United States was almost 50 percent female. Nevertheless, some critics claim that a glass ceiling still exists in some organizations. A glass ceiling refers to an invisible barrier that keeps women from progressing to higher levels in the organization. We will explore this concept and related points more fully in Chapter 3.

Changing ethnicity is also reflected in the workforce today. The percentage of whites in the workforce is gradually dropping, while the percentage of Hispanics in the workforce is climbing at an almost comparable rate. The percentage of African Americans and Asians in the workforce is also growing but at a much smaller rate. In addition to age, gender, and ethnicity, other diversity forces are also affecting the labor force. For example, country of national origin is an important diversity dimension. Physically challenged employees and employees with other disabilities are also an important part of workforce trends. And many other dimensions of diversity, such as single-parent status, dual-career couples, gays and lesbians, people with special dietary preferences, and people with different political ideologies and viewpoints are each playing an important role in organizations today. We cover diversity more fully in Chapter 16.

In addition, external data can also be used to predict the supply of labor in specific regions. Over the last several years, for example, there has been a gradual movement of population away from the northern and northeastern parts of the United States and toward the southern, southeastern, and southwestern parts of the country. Thus the supply of labor in the North and Northeast is gradually declining, while the supply of labor in the southern parts of the United States is gradually increasing. In other parts of the world, wherever immigration rules permit, workers are gradually shifting away from developing parts of the world and toward industrialized and economically prosperous regions. For instance, many workers in eastern regions of Europe continue to move into western areas in anticipation of better employment prospects.[35]

In all cases, future labor supplies are typically forecasted by developing mathematical trend models using data from the past, with appropriate adjustments for migratory trends and predictions. These models, which essentially assume that trends will continue in a linear (i.e., straight-line) fashion, are usually reasonably accurate. But they can be far less accurate when some unforeseen event or trend disrupts expectations. An example was the unexpected increase in the labor-force participation rates for women during the 1980s. Although women's participation rates had been climbing for years, statistical predictions based on simple trend lines substantially underestimated the growth rates in the 1980s. In retrospect, observers realized that new (i.e., first-time) entries by women into the labor force were being substantially supplemented by other women already in the labor force but who were previously underemployed.

Finally, we should also note the special forecasting situation generally known as executive succession. **Executive succession** involves systematically planning for future promotions into top management positions. This process is much more complicated because it is often critical that exactly the right type of person is selected for a top position, the development costs to groom this person are very high, and the actual decision may have a major impact on the firm's future. Thus, many organizations try to bring as much order and logic to the process as possible. For example, senior executives usually indicate well in advance when they expect to retire—sometimes several years in advance. The firm can then draw on its cadre of up-and-coming managers for replacement candidates. Sometimes a specific set of individuals may be moved into special high-profile jobs, with the expectation that whoever does the best job will receive the promotion when the

■ **Executive succession** involves systematically planning for future promotions into top management positions.

senior person steps down. In other cases, the most likely successor is moved into the number two spot to eliminate all uncertainties and to allow this person to concentrate on learning as much as possible about the senior position.[36]

This latter approach may be advantageous because the new person is already in line should the organization need to move more quickly than anticipated. For example, in late 1998 Procter & Gamble's board of directors realized that the firm was facing substantially greater competition than in the past and that its performance was beginning to slide. To accelerate the change in strategy, it promoted its new heir apparent to the top spot earlier than originally planned. But the reason Procter & Gamble had this option was that it had already done an effective job of succession planning.[37]

Forecasting the Demand for Human Resources

In addition to supply, strategic planning requires that human resource managers must also develop forecasts about future demand. That is, they need to ascertain the numbers and types of people the organization will actually need to employ in the future. One important ingredient in this assessment is the organization's own strategic plans regarding anticipated growth, stability, or decline, described earlier in the chapter.

But it is also necessary to consider larger, broader trends in the economy when forecasting the demand for human resources. For example, the chart illustrated in HR in the 21st Century shows how some jobs, like retail salespersons, have remained in high demand since 1900. But other jobs, like tailors, masons, tobacco factory workers, and butchers, have dropped sharply. Still others, such as nurses, hotel and restaurant managers, and moving equipment operators, have seen demand increase significantly. These general demand trends influence the availability of human resources for two reasons. First, employees for jobs in high demand will be more difficult to hire and will be more expensive to hire. In addition, students and future employees who track these demand trends often make decisions about what majors to pursue in college based on their anticipated employability. Thus, general trends like the ones described here must be part of the planning process.

HUMAN RESOURCE STRATEGY IMPLEMENTATION

After human resource managers have formulated their strategy—taking into consideration organization design, culture, technology, and the work- and labor force—they can then turn their attention to its actual implementation. As shown earlier in Figure 2.1, strategy implementation is put into operation through the actions of individual employees (as manifested through various individual processes), groups of employees (as manifested through various interpersonal and group processes), and organizational systems and processes. Figure 2.5 on page 65 illustrates these processes in more detail.

Of course, the most important driver of any implementation plan is the strategy that has been chosen. For example, as we described earlier in the chapter, organizations often adopt corporate strategies aimed at growth, stability, or retrenchment. Clearly if an organization intends to grow, it will most likely need to hire additional human resources in the future.[38] Likewise, if the organization

Easy Come, Easy Go

Managers attempting to forecast the future supply of and demand for jobs and employees face numerous uncertainties. One major uncertainty for long-term planning is the extent to which any given job may become more or less popular in the future. The following graph clearly illustrates this point. The graph rank orders the top thirty jobs (by millions of workers) for the years 1900,

1960, and 1995. Only eight job categories among the most popular in 1900 are still on the list by 1995. Some jobs, like carpenters, have consistently dropped further down the list, whereas others, such as police officers and guards, have steadily risen. But most striking is simply the array of jobs on the 1995 list that did not appear previously—jobs such as computer programmers, health technicians, and lawyers and judges.

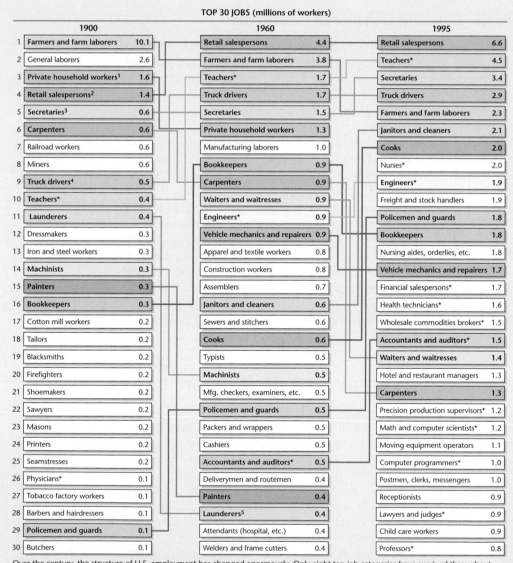

TOP 30 JOBS (millions of workers)

	1900		1960		1995	
1	Farmers and farm laborers	10.1	Retail salespersons	4.4	Retail salespersons	6.6
2	General laborers	2.6	Farmers and farm laborers	3.8	Teachers*	4.5
3	Private household workers[1]	1.6	Teachers*	1.7	Secretaries	3.4
4	Retail salespersons[2]	1.4	Truck drivers	1.7	Truck drivers	2.9
5	Secretaries[3]	0.6	Secretaries	1.5	Farmers and farm laborers	2.3
6	Carpenters	0.6	Private household workers	1.3	Janitors and cleaners	2.1
7	Railroad workers	0.6	Manufacturing laborers	1.0	Cooks	2.0
8	Miners	0.6	Bookkeepers	0.9	Nurses*	2.0
9	Truck drivers[4]	0.5	Carpenters	0.9	Engineers*	1.9
10	Teachers*	0.4	Waiters and waitresses	0.9	Freight and stock handlers	1.9
11	Launderers	0.4	Engineers*	0.9	Policemen and guards	1.8
12	Dressmakers	0.3	Vehicle mechanics and repairers	0.9	Bookkeepers	1.8
13	Iron and steel workers	0.3	Apparel and textile workers	0.8	Nursing aides, orderlies, etc.	1.8
14	Machinists	0.3	Construction workers	0.8	Vehicle mechanics and repairers	1.7
15	Painters	0.3	Assemblers	0.7	Financial salespersons*	1.7
16	Bookkeepers	0.3	Janitors and cleaners	0.6	Health technicians*	1.6
17	Cotton mill workers	0.2	Sewers and stitchers	0.6	Wholesale commodities brokers*	1.5
18	Tailors	0.2	Cooks	0.6	Accountants and auditors*	1.5
19	Blacksmiths	0.2	Typists	0.5	Waiters and waitresses	1.4
20	Firefighters	0.2	Machinists	0.5	Hotel and restaurant managers	1.3
21	Shoemakers	0.2	Mfg. checkers, examiners, etc.	0.5	Carpenters	1.3
22	Sawyers	0.2	Policemen and guards	0.5	Precision production supervisors*	1.2
23	Masons	0.2	Packers and wrappers	0.5	Math and computer scientists*	1.2
24	Printers	0.2	Cashiers	0.5	Moving equipment operators	1.1
25	Seamstresses	0.2	Accountants and auditors*	0.5	Computer programmers*	1.0
26	Physicians*	0.1	Deliverymen and routemen	0.4	Postmen, clerks, messengers	1.0
27	Tobacco factory workers	0.1	Painters	0.4	Receptionists	0.9
28	Barbers and hairdressers	0.1	Launderers[5]	0.4	Lawyers and judges*	0.9
29	Policemen and guards	0.1	Attendants (hospital, etc.)	0.4	Child care workers	0.9
30	Butchers	0.1	Welders and frame cutters	0.4	Professors*	0.8

Over the century, the structure of U.S. employment has changed enormously. Only eight top job categories have survived throughout. And many more top job categories now require substantial education.

* Requires education. [1]Servants and housekeepers in 1900. [2]Merchants and salespeople in 1900. [3]Clerks in 1900. [4]Teamsters and coachmen in 1900. [5]Launderers and dry cleaners in 1960.

Source: "Top 30 Jobs" from *Forbes*, May 6, 1996, p. 17. Reprinted by permission of Forbes Magazine. © 2003 Forbes, Inc.

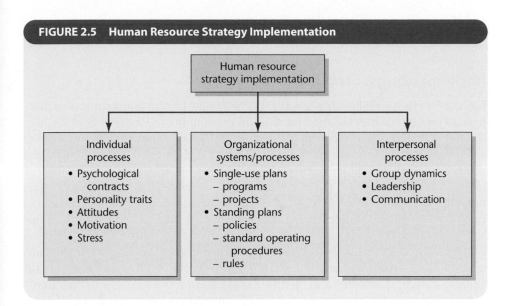

FIGURE 2.5   Human Resource Strategy Implementation

Human resource strategy implementation

Individual processes
- Psychological contracts
- Personality traits
- Attitudes
- Motivation
- Stress

Organizational systems/processes
- Single-use plans
  - programs
  - projects
- Standing plans
  - policies
  - standard operating procedures
  - rules

Interpersonal processes
- Group dynamics
- Leadership
- Communication

expects to enter a period of stability, its human resource demand is also likely to be relatively stable.[39] And finally, of course, if a period of decline or retrenchment is anticipated, then the organization may be confronting a decreased demand for human resources. We will describe implementation activities associated with each of these strategies in turn.

Implementing a Growth Strategy

A strategy of growth is indicative of growing sales, increasing demand, and expanding operations for the organization. When the organization is growing and expanding, it most likely will need to hire new employees in the future. In some cases, the organization may be able to hire employees readily without additional work. For example, if the organization is currently receiving 1,000 qualified applications per year and has been hiring only fifty of those individuals, it may be able to meet its growth rate by simply increasing the number of people that it hires. Instead of fifty, the firm may begin hiring seventy-five or 100 people a year.

In other situations, implementing a growth strategy may be more difficult. Market conditions may be such that qualified employees are hard to find. For example, if the firm is receiving 100 qualified applications per year and is currently hiring as many as ninety of those individuals, then it is unlikely that it will be able to hire dramatically larger numbers of them without taking some additional actions. The organization may have to increase its recruiting efforts to attract more job applicants and even perhaps to begin to provide additional support to apprentice or training programs. Support of various college and university programs might also be a way of increasing the supply of available labor talent in the future.

A related incident recently involved United Parcel Service (UPS), the giant delivery business. UPS is based in Louisville, Kentucky, and maintains a huge operation there. The firm recently wanted to launch a major expansion but was concerned about its ability to attract enough new workers, especially those who might be interested in working the night shift. The firm threatened to build its expansion in another state unless Kentucky would help. Facing the threat of losing such a big employer, the state passed and funded major job training legislation and programs to help it attract and develop capable workers of the type that UPS needed.[40]

Implementing a Stability Strategy

In many ways, a stability strategy may be the easiest for the human resource manager to implement because the organization presumably must do what it has been doing all along. But even here specific and subtle planning nuances must be considered. For example, the organization will naturally experience a certain amount of attrition in its employee ranks each year. As noted earlier, some people will leave for better jobs, some people will retire, some will leave because of poor performance, and others will leave for reasons such as career relocation on the part of a spouse or significant other. Thus, even an organization that is projecting a period of stability is likely to need to augment its human resource labor force to replace those individuals who leave the organization for various reasons. In such cases, the organization can implement programs such as training to upgrade the skills of current employees and therefore make them more valuable to the organization. Alternatively, the organization might implement programs designed to reduce turnover among current employees, making stability easier to maintain.

Implementing a Reduction Strategy

In some cases, an organization may find itself facing reductions. Perhaps an organization is experiencing cutbacks, such as many organizations in the United States faced in the 1980s and into the early 1990s. Organizations such as IBM, General Motors, Chrysler, and others reduced their workforce by the thousands. Levi Strauss cut over 6,395 jobs; the economic downturn that hit the United States in 1998 forced many Wall Street investment firms to lay off stockbrokers and analysts.[41] SBC Communications announced plans to cut 11,000 jobs in late 2002.

Sometimes these reductions can be handled through normal attrition processes as described above. For example, if the organization currently has 1,000 employees and it knows from experience that approximately 100 of those individuals will retire, resign, or be fired next year, and if it forecast that it will need only 900 employees following next year, then it may need to do very little. But if the actual forecast calls for only 700 employees, the organization must figure out how to eliminate the other 200 jobs in addition to the 100 that will disappear automatically. This sort of situation may call for laying people off, or terminating them, and we will discuss some important issues associated with this downsizing process in Chapter 8.

A popular alternative to terminations and layoffs, especially for managers, is early retirement. The idea is to make offers to employees to enhance their retirement benefits so that people might consider retiring at an earlier age than they would have done otherwise. Of course, this process involves costs to the organization. The organization may be forced to pay additional benefits to those employees above and beyond what they would have ordinarily expected to pay. It is also possible that the organization might lose people that it would have preferred to keep. That is, its highest-performing employees may be those who opt for early retirement. In fact, they may see early retirement as an opportunity for increasing their income by taking retirement benefits from their current employer but using their high-performance credentials to gain new employment with another organization. On the other hand, lower-performing employees are less likely to have this option and thus may be more likely to remain with the current organization.

Individual and Interpersonal Processes and Strategy Implementation

Overall strategic concerns should drive the implementation of human resource management strategy, but the manager should also be concerned with individual and interpersonal processes that can affect strategy implementation. Individual processes are especially important because of the role they play in affecting the performance effectiveness exhibited by each employee in a firm. The starting point for understanding individual processes is the psychological contract that an organization has with its employees. A **psychological contract** is the overall set of expectations held by an individual with respect to what he or she will contribute to the organization and what the organization, in turn, will provide to the individual.[42] Individuals see themselves as contributing their time, energy, effort, experience, and talent, and they expect to receive compensation, benefits, security, challenge, opportunities for promotion, and similar forms of rewards. Properly established and maintained psychological contracts are a fundamental starting point in ensuring that employees are committed to working toward organizational goals and contributing to organizational effectiveness by implementing the strategies that managers have developed. Special problems arise when the implementation of a new strategy involves a change in the terms of the psychological contract.[43] We explore psychological contracts more fully in Chapter 17.

Individual personality traits and attitudes are also important parts of individual processes in an organization. Personality is the relatively stable set of psychological attributes or traits that distinguish one person from another. Some organizations believe that one or more particular personality traits may relate to how well an employee can perform a certain job or type of job. Personality traits such as self-esteem and agreeableness may be important traits for someone who will be working in a job that requires regular interaction with the public, while conscientiousness appears to be important for performance in a wide variety of jobs.[44] Human resource managers are usually responsible for determining the best way to measure relevant personality traits in job applicants and for being able to verify that those measures—as well as the underlying traits themselves—do indeed relate to job performance.

Attitudes also play an important role in implementing strategy in an organization. If people have positive attitudes toward their work and organization, they will be more committed to making contributions to organizational effectiveness and in helping achieve strategic goals. Workers with negative attitudes, on the other hand, are less likely to make this commitment and may be more inclined to be absent frequently and/or to seek alternative employment. Human resource managers are often called on to help other managers assess the attitudes of their workers by developing attitude surveys, administering those surveys to employees, and then interpreting and evaluating the results.

Perhaps the most important individual process in organizations, however, is motivation. Motivation is the set of forces that cause people to behave in certain ways. Individual motivation is also a major determinant of individual performance, but motivation is at the heart of what causes an employee to choose to expend the effort that will support any organizational activity. Unfortunately, the process of motivating employees to behave in desired ways is quite complicated,

■ A **psychological contract** is the overall set of expectations held by an individual with respect to what he or she will contribute to the organization and what the organization, in turn, will provide to the individual.

and there is a great deal we do not understand about it. Nonetheless, theories and models of motivation attempt to explain the phenomenon, and we will discuss several in Chapter 12.

Still another important individual process in organizational settings is stress. Stress is a person's adaptive response to a stimulus that places excessive psychological or physical demands on that person. Important considerations for human resource managers include an understanding of the causes of stress, the processes by which stress affects individuals, and how organizations and individuals can cope better with stress in organizational settings. Human resource managers are increasingly being called on to help employees cope with stress, and we will discuss some of the issues involved in these efforts in Chapter 15.

Finally, since little behavior in organizations takes place in isolation, human resource managers also need to consider interpersonal processes that develop from the relationships an employee has with coworkers, supervisors, and/or subordinates. These processes are becoming even more important as organizations move more and more toward having employees work as part of a team instead of as an individual. Human resource managers must deal with various issues rising from the emphasis on teams, ranging from deciding who should be part of a team to how to evaluate the performance of team members and reward them. Clearly, in this new work environment, the management of interpersonal processes is important for implementing human resource strategy.

Leadership is also an important priority for many organizations. Most experts believe that effective leadership is vitally important to organizational success, yet they cannot agree on how to define, measure, or predict leadership. Human resource managers are expected to help identify potential leadership qualities among existing employees and then to help structure procedures for developing and enhancing those qualities. Obviously these managers must have a basic understanding of leadership to help the organization achieve its goals.

A final important interpersonal process that is directly related to the implementation of human resource strategy is communication. Communication is the process by which two or more parties exchange information and share meaning. Written communication, oral communication, and nonverbal communication are all pervasive in organizations. Electronic mail has become an especially important area of communication in recent years. In many organizations, the human resource department is responsible for coordinating communication among employees through newsletters, bulletin boards, intranets, and so forth. Clearly human resource managers need to understand how to enhance communication to make sure that their efforts are indeed helping to implement their strategies.

Human resource managers must obviously have a keen understanding of the behavioral processes that are critical in determining the relative effectiveness of various human resource functions such as compensation, rewards, performance appraisal, and training and development. All managers need to understand and appreciate these behavioral processes to understand the actions of those with whom they work. Finally, human resource managers are often charged with the responsibility of developing and implementing programs aimed at improving various behavioral processes. For example, they may be asked to overhaul the reward system to boost motivation and productivity, to develop training programs for workers to cope better with stress, or to help identify ways to improve interpersonal communication or resolve interpersonal conflict.

EVALUATING THE HUMAN RESOURCE FUNCTION IN ORGANIZATIONS

Evaluating the effectiveness of the human resource function has emerged as an important trend in recent years. Human resource management was historically seen as an organizational cost or expense. That is, the organization budgeted a certain amount of money to spend on the management of its human resource function. As long as the human resource manager stayed within this budget, and the employees seemed generally happy, everything was generally assumed to be fine. More recently, however, many organizations have become more concerned with the cost as well as with the benefits of human resource management for two seemingly contradictory reasons.

First, as we discussed in Chapter 1, many organizations are now subcontracting or outsourcing some of their human resource management functions to external vendors. A big part of the decision about whether or not to outsource a function depends on the actual cost of keeping the function in-house. At the same

Alan G. Lafley, CEO of Proctor & Gamble, sits down with Richard L. Antoine, the head of HR for Proctor & Gamble. What makes this meeting interesting is that it is taking place at Antoine's dining room table, it's Sunday night, and this is the way the two spend every Sunday evening. Lafley became CEO of P&G in 2000, and he has done a remarkable job of turning around the corporate giant. Although P&G is a legendary company, its performance before Lafley arrived had been less than legendary. Profits were down, market share was down, and most importantly, morale was down. Lafley changed all that. He made it clear that P&G must pay attention to its cornerstone products such as Tide, Pampers, and Crest; that the company would become more flexible on pricing; and that some innovations and new products would be acquired from the outside. But most importantly, he told employees that they were not the problem, but the solution, and he concentrates on developing and building staff. His weekly meeting with the head of HR—rather than the CFO or the head of marketing—is a visible sign of the importance he places on the human resources of the company.

time, many organizations are coming to view effective human resource management as a source of competitive advantage, and so they are focusing on the potential benefits of human resource management functions. In fact, these trends are not at all conflicting. Organizations are examining the costs and benefits of their human resource management functions to see which ones actually do contribute to competitive advantage and which should be outsourced. Functions that add little value are likely to be outsourced, even if they are not terribly expensive, and functions that add competitive advantage are likely to be retained, even if they are relatively expensive. Of course, the functions themselves may or may not contribute to competitive advantage, but it is the way the organization chooses to allocate its resources to manage those functions that will determine where the firm derives its competitive advantage.

In any event, different approaches are being used in an attempt to measure the costs and benefits of specific human resource functions, and (as mentioned in the previous chapter) line managers may even be allowed to decide between the corporation's human resource department or an outsider vendor when they need human resource management help. Traditionally, organizations relied primarily on indirect measures of the effectiveness of their human resource management practices. For example, high turnover or high absenteeism indicated low satisfaction with the job, and this predicament was seen as a problem with human resource management. Low levels of absenteeism and turnover and/or low costs were associated with positive human resource management practices and, as noted above, costs were not given serious consideration. Later, as we noted in Chapter 1, more sophisticated methods of utility analysis allowed organizations to put a dollar value on the contributions of various human resource management practices and forced them to consider costs as well. We will discuss utility analysis in some detail in Appendix 2, and will deal with the evaluation of specific human resource functions at the conclusion of many of the chapters throughout this book.

In addition to the evaluation of specific human resource functions, there has been a recent trend toward evaluating entire systems of human resource activities. That is, instead of determining if any one human resource management practice can produce value, this approach examines the relationship between "bundles" of practices and the overall performance of the organization in terms of factors such as profitability, stock price, and productivity. Although the specific practices that have been investigated differ somewhat from study to study, and despite issues raised about the measurement of effectiveness,[45] the evidence seems to be mounting that organizations adopting more enlightened human resource management practices actually do better than other organizations.[46] Although, as noted, we need to know exactly which practices work, these sets of practices have generally become known as **high performance work systems**, and they include practices such as those illustrated in Table 2.1.

Of course, several questions must be answered before we can fully understand the importance of these human resource management practices. For example, as we noted in the Point/Counterpoint feature earlier in the chapter, there is some question about whether these practices are truly universally effective. There are also questions about the mechanisms through which these practices lead to firm performance; clearly the practices listed in Table 2.1 (which are derived from several research studies and are typical of the work in this area) are quite broad and cover several different elements. For example, formal performance appraisals can take many different forms, as we will see later in Chapter 9. Although it may be

■ **High performance work systems** rely on a set of "best practices" to use human resources to gain a meaningful competitive advantage.

> **TABLE 2.1   Human Resource Management Practices That May Lead to Improved Firm Performance**
>
> - Self-directed work teams
> - Total quality management (TQM)
> - Contingent pay
> - Attitude surveys
> - Formal performance appraisals
> - Continuous training

better to have *some* formal appraisal than none at all, it is also likely to be true that different types of appraisal systems will lead to different outcomes. And while it might be preferable to make pay contingent on *something*, exactly what pay should be contingent on is probably important as well. In general, however, there is reason to believe that an organization can be more competitive if it adopts these practices, and this represents a new way of evaluating a firm's human resource practices.

Chapter Summary

The strategic context of human resource management plays an important role in determining the effectiveness of not only the human resource function but the entire organization as well. Understanding the organization's purpose and its mission guides human resource managers as they formulate their strategy. They must also recognize the role of the top management team.

Top managers use SWOT analysis to formulate corporate, business, and functional strategies. As part of this process, the current status of an organization's human resources can be a critical organizational strength or weakness. Corporate strategy involves decisions about which markets or businesses the firm intends to address, whereas business strategy deals with competitive issues within a particular market or business. The firm's human resource strategy itself is an important functional strategy that must be integrated with marketing, finance, operations, and other relevant functional strategies.

The actual process of formulating human resource strategy results in separate but consistent strategies for staffing, employee development, and compensation. To enact human resource strategy effectively, it must be closely coordinated with the particular form

of organization design the firm uses, the culture it creates, and the impact of unionization and collective bargaining.

Effective human resource planning can often make the difference between organizational success and failure. The human resource planning process involves forecasting the supply and demand for labor and taking appropriate steps to address projected differences. One key element in the human resource planning process is the effective use of the organization's human resource information system.

The implementation of human resource strategy requires an understanding of fundamental individual and interpersonal behavioral processes. Individual processes include psychological contracts, individual personality traits, employee attitudes, motivation, and stress. Interpersonal processes include group behavior, leadership, and communication.

Managers should attempt to evaluate the effectiveness of the human resource function and its role in helping the organization attain its strategic goals. This evaluation usually focuses on specific human resource practices. However, recent evidence suggests that bundles of so-called best practices may be a viable alternative approach.

Key Points for Future HR Managers

► All human resource management activities must be aligned with an organization's strategic goals.

► Corporate level strategy is often stated in a company's mission statements and is influenced by the firm's top management team, who sets the strategic directions.

► Human resource strategy must be consistent with corporate strategy and with the design of the organization and its technology, unionization, and culture.

► The labor force and the human resource planning process are also critical for successful strategy formulation.

► Formulating strategy is important, but the implementation of human resource strategy is even more critical for the human resource management function.

► Modeling high performance work systems may be a good start for the design of a human resource management system, but the specific policies should reflect the unique strategy and environment of the organization.

Key Points for Future General Managers

► Corporate and business strategies define how an organization will operate and compete in the market.

► Grand strategies at the corporate level include a growth strategy, a retrenchment (or turnaround) strategy, and a stability strategy.

► A diversification strategy is one where an organization decides to operate different related or unrelated businesses.

► The adaptation model of strategy suggests that organizations should match their strategy to the environment. The model includes defender, prospector, analyzer, and reactor strategies.

► Major competitive strategies include differentiation, cost leadership, and focus strategies (i.e., targeting a specific segment of the market).

► Human resource management strategy is determined by organizational level strategy as well as by organizational design, culture, technology and the workforce.

► Certain specific human resource practices may be capable of providing a competitive advantage to organizations.

Review and Discussion Questions

1. Discuss the influence of organizational purpose, mission, and the top management team on human resource strategy.

2. Distinguish among corporate, business, and functional strategies. How does each general level of strategy relate to human resource management?

3. Specify the circumstances under which a firm's human resources, as part of a SWOT analysis, might be seen as an organizational strength. Specify the circumstances under which human resources might be seen as a weakness.

4. Discuss how the specific corporate strategies relate to human resource management.

5. Discuss how the specific business strategies relate to human resource management.

6. What are the advantages and disadvantages to an individual who accepts a job as a human resource manager in a firm that is in the midst of a retrenchment corporate strategy? A reactor business strategy?

7. If you were hired as a human resource manager in a large firm where the human resource function was poorly integrated with other functional areas, what steps would you take to improve this integration?

8. Explain how organization design, culture, and unionization issues are related to human resource management.

9. How does the firm's human resource strategy interact with other functional strategies and the strategic leadership of top management to affect organizational effectiveness?

10. Why is it important for all managers to understand behavioral forces in organizations? Why might it be especially important for human resource managers to understand these forces?

Closing Case

Hiring the State of Rhode Island

Coleman Peterson is facing a mission that's almost impossible. As executive vice president of Wal-Mart Stores' "people" division, he will oversee the hiring of more than 1 million employees over the next five years. That's like hiring the entire population of Rhode Island or the city of San Antonio.

About 800,000 global new hires will be added, and other hires will take the place of current employees expected to leave because of natural turnover. That will bring Wal-Mart's total global workforce—already the largest private labor force in the United States—to more than 2 million, up from 1.3 million. That would eclipse the population of the U.S. armed forces, which was about 1.4 million in 2000.

The stumbling economy has put a chill on hiring at most companies, but that's not the case at Wal-Mart. Instead, Wal-Mart executives see the downturn as a catalyst for growth because cash-strapped consumers are likely to turn to discounters. The Bentonville, Arkansas-based company's ability to meet its ambitious hiring goal is critical to its continued dominance in the retail market, analysts say. It needs people to maintain its aggressive push into other profitable areas, such as the $680 billion retail grocery business.

But there are challenges. The mass merchandiser will have to expand quickly while still being selective about whom it hires. It will have to overcome attacks in lawsuits and from unions on its reputation as an employer. And it will face mounting wage pressures that run counter to the retailer's focus on keeping operational costs low. "The biggest challenge is the numbers," Peterson says. "The numbers are just so large. But the issue is no different than the one [founder] Sam Walton faced. We have to focus on one associate at a time."

Wal-Mart's aggressive hiring plan will seek to continue bringing in minorities and female applicants and turn part-time, college-age workers into long-term employees. Some keys to success are offering competitive salary programs that are still cost-effective and retaining workers by promoting them through the ranks. While officials won't disclose pay information, unions that have pressed the company for wage increases put front-line workers' salaries at $7 to $8 an hour. Analysts say wages may be higher in some cases because they vary by location and job position.

The plan includes:

Advancement. The goal is to move employees from part-time cashiers on up the ranks to department managers, assistant store managers, and beyond. Already, 65 percent of the company's managers began in hourly jobs. "That's the biggest draw," says Matt Loveless, a supercenter manager in Rogers, Arkansas, who joined twelve years ago. "There's the opportunity, if you want to be a buyer, you can do that. You can even do operations."

College Recruiting. Fanning out on eighty college campuses annually, recruiters at Wal-Mart are not following the lead of other companies by pulling back. One reason: college campuses provide a major opportunity to tap diversity. About 48 percent of the trainees Wal-Mart hires are minorities and 50 percent are women, which is accomplished in part by contacting minority fraternities and sororities and visiting traditionally minority-dominated college campuses. Wal-Mart is also boosting its paid college internship programs, especially in areas such as pharmacy and merchandising, where a labor shortage has competitors snapping up graduates.

Training. Wal-Mart is relying on a program allowing college students to begin management-training programs while still in school. The program has taken off in the past two years and is seen as a critical way to get college-age hires interested in careers with Wal-Mart after graduation.

Connections. Executives hope that Wal-Mart's long-standing ties with Students in Free Enterprise (SIFE) will yield valuable hires. SIFE is a nonprofit collegiate organization with chapters on more than 700 campuses. Students come up with programs and outreach efforts focusing on free enterprise. Many of the students in these programs will be recruited by Wal-Mart to serve in management and other posts. "Wal-Mart always finds the most economical way to do everything, and we're an economical way to get talent," says Alvin Rohrs, CEO of SIFE. "Some [students] like to work for Wal-Mart because they like the communities they're in. Others want to work for a large corporation."

What's at stake: Wal-Mart's ability to continue diversifying. Currently, it has more than 510 Sam's Club warehouses. They also have thirty-three Neighborhood Markets, where groceries are sold. And there are more than 1,100 supercenters selling full-line groceries and general merchandise. It also has more than 1,600 Wal-Mart discount stores.

Wal-Mart executives remain confident that the hiring needs will remain the same over the next five years. The company's net income has grown by over 10 percent per year for the last decade and even began to increase in recent years as the economy faltered. "If you study this company, we always perform best in tough economies," says Tom Coughlin, CEO of Wal-Mart stores division. As the economy gets tougher, he says, more people live paycheck to paycheck. "More and more people are looking for value."

Wal-Mart will have to grapple with ways to increase pay and benefits. It's a critical issue for the company's workers. About 60 percent of employees have told Wal-Mart in surveys that one of the main reasons they joined was because of the company's health benefits, according to information posted on Wal-Mart's website. But the company is not known as a generous spender, analysts say. Lawsuits have been filed by workers who say they were forced to work overtime for no pay, and the company keeps such a tight rein on spending that executives occasionally share hotel rooms on business trips.

The company will also have to remain selective—adding tens of thousands of workers who can deliver customer service, not just fill a hiring quota. Customer care is critical to the success of a deep discounter such as Wal-Mart. Already, that is an area where the company's image has been faltering, analysts say. "It used to be you could walk up to any Wal-Mart employee and they'd either help you or find a person who could," says David Schehr, research director at GartnerG2, a research service for business strategists, adding that the customer service has since faltered.

But Wal-Mart executives remain convinced that their multifaceted hiring approach will reap gains in the marketplace along with a growing labor pool. "How are we going to fuel this growth? The major source is internal," Peterson says. "Every time we open a Wal-Mart store or a Sam's Club, it's a recruiting outpost."[47]

Case Questions

1. What corporate and business strategies is Wal-Mart pursuing?

2. Discuss how Wal-Mart's growth plans affect and are affected by its human resource strategy.

3. What does this case illustrate about human resource planning?

Building HR Management Skills

Purpose: The purpose of this exercise is to enhance your appreciation of the links among human resource strategy and corporate, business, and other functional strategies.

Step 1: Your instructor will ask you to form small groups of four to five members each. Read the introductory scenario below and then proceed through the remaining steps in order. Develop brief, overview answers to the various questions as they are posed.

The Situation: Your group has just been hired as the top management team for a midsize firm. The firm has been floundering in recent years—market share and profits have dropped, morale is low, and the firm's stock price is at an all-time low. The board of directors has come to realize that retrenchment is needed to turn the firm around. Thus, the board fired the old team, hired your team, and gave you total responsibility for the anticipated turnaround. The facts are as follows: your firm has been making home appliances such as refrigerators, stoves, and microwaves. Ten years ago, the company had 20 percent of the market, annual revenues of $500 million, and a workforce of 15,000 employees. Today, the company has 7 percent of the market, annual revenues of less than $300 million, and a workforce of 14,500. (No new employees have been hired in three years, but few have left.) As a first step, the board wants the workforce trimmed, product quality improved, and a more effective marketing strategy developed. In the long term, the board wants the firm to diversify into other, less competitive markets.

Step 2: Identify three fundamental human resource strategy issues, challenges, and opportunities facing your firm immediately.

Step 3: Fast-forward five years: your turnaround has been successful. The firm has increased its market share to over 15 percent, sales are over $450 million, and the workforce has been trimmed. The situation is looking bright, but your team and the board believe that it is still a bit too soon to launch a diversification effort. Identify three fundamental human resource strategy issues, challenges, and opportunities facing your firm now.

Step 4: Fast-forward another five years: your firm has continued to prosper and has just launched a diversification program. The core business now has almost 25 percent of the home appliance business, sales are approaching $750 million, and the workforce has grown to almost 20,000 employees. As first steps in diversification, the firm has bought another firm that makes home-electronics products (televisions, stereos, etc.) and is starting its own new small-appliances business (can openers, coffee makers, etc.). Identify three fundamental human resource strategy issues, challenges, and opportunities facing your firm now.

Step 5: Fast-forward another five years: your firm has continued to prosper and now sees itself as a mature, diversified home-products company. In addition to the businesses noted above, your company also now owns businesses that make telephones and related communication equipment (facsimile machines, copiers, etc.), cable-related television operations (regional cable television companies, pay-per-view businesses, etc.), and related automotive accessories (CD players, portable facsimile machines, etc.). But your management team believes that the firm has now entered a period of stability. Little new growth is foreseen, for instance, and the company wants to maintain its status quo for the next few years. Identify three fundamental human resource strategy issues, challenges, and opportunities facing your firm now.

Step 6: Report your ideas and suggestions through whatever form your instructor assigns (in-class presentations, written notes to be turned in, general discussion).

Ethical Dilemmas in HR Management

Assume that you are a project manager in the human resource department for a large manufacturing business. All told, your firm's human resource department employs about 120 people. As part of a strategy calling for related diversification, the firm has recently announced a merger with one of its largest competitors. That firm has about 100 people in its human resource department. Your firm will be the dominant partner in the merger, controlling 56 percent of the new enterprise.

Your boss just informed you that you will be responsible for developing plans to integrate the two human resource departments during the merger. He estimates that the new, combined department will need about 160 people, necessitating a layoff of about sixty people. Your most critical task, therefore, will be to decide who stays and who has to leave. Your boss has given you clear and unambiguous written instructions that you are to select the best people possible from the two current departments, regardless of current affiliation. After he gave you these instructions, however, he also lowered his voice and said, "Of course, we should try to take care of as many of our own people as we can."

Questions

1. What are the ethical issues in this situation?

2. What criteria might you find it necessary to use in making your decisions?

3. What are your personal feelings about how to prioritize individual employees in a situation like this?

HR Internet Exercise

AT&T maintains what it calls a "fact-book" on the Internet. Its web address is **http://www.att.com/att/factbook.html**.

The factbook includes a wide array of information about the firm, its mission, its strategy, and other elements of its operations. It also has information about careers and jobs at AT&T. Visit the website and read and study the information that you find. Focus especially on information regarding the firm's strategy and its human resources. Use the information you find to answer the following questions:

Questions

1. What relationships, if any, do you see between AT&T's corporate or business strategies and its human resource strategy?

2. This chapter suggests that overall strategy affects human resource strategy, and that human resource strategy also affects overall strategy. Can you make any inferences about which of these two viewpoints AT&T seems to have adopted?

3. If AT&T changed its corporate or business strategies, would it necessarily have to change its human resource strategy? Why or why not?

3

The Legal Environment

CHAPTER OBJECTIVES

After studying this chapter you should be able to:

■ Describe the legal context of human resource management.

■ Identify key laws that prohibit discrimination in the workplace and discuss equal employment opportunity.

■ Discuss legal issues in compensation.

■ Discuss legal issues in labor relations.

■ Describe several emerging legal issues in human resource management.

■ Discuss the importance to an organization of evaluating its legal compliance.

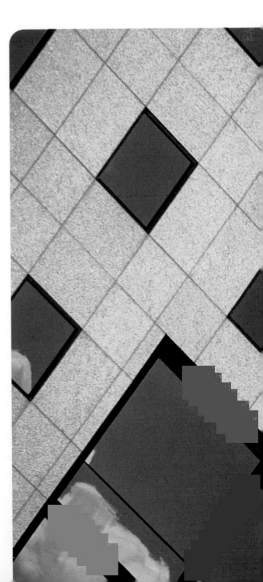

Omar Belazi, a former RadioShack store manager, recently joined legions of other disgruntled workers when he filed a lawsuit against his former employer. There were years, says Mr. Belazi, when he enthusiastically logged sixty-five-hour workweeks, stayed late to clean the store's restrooms and vacuum the floor, and worked all weekend just to meet sales goals. Regardless of the hours he worked, however, he received the same monthly salary. Belazi gradually grew tired of the burden and left RadioShack.

"It gets to be very stressful, very tiring. You just get up and go to RadioShack and go home and go to sleep."

(Omar Belazi, ex–RadioShack employee)

He eventually became part of a class-action lawsuit against RadioShack that included 1,300 current and former California store managers. Their contention was that they were managers in title only. More specifically, the lawsuit argued that all true management decisions were made at higher levels in the organization, leaving those with store manager titles to do little more than sales work. But because they had a managerial title and were paid salaries, the company did not have to pay them overtime. The lawsuit was settled in July 2002 when RadioShack agreed to pay $29.9 million to the plaintiffs.

At the heart of the argument is a decades-old law that mandates overtime payments for hourly operating workers who work more than forty hours a week but allows firms to pay salaries to professionals regardless of how many hours they work. The Fair Labor Standards Act specifically exempts those in executive, administrative, or professional jobs from overtime payments. But because so many jobs have shifted from manufacturing settings to service settings, and because the nature of so many jobs has changed, the lines between different kinds of work have blurred.

And whether intentional or not, many firms now routinely use general titles such as "manager," "administrator," or "analyst" but assign employees with those titles tasks that do not always fit the title. For instance, Mr. Belazi was not directly forced to work extra on weekends or to clean the restrooms. But if an hourly worker had been hired, that person's time would have been charged against the store's weekly labor budget. If he didn't maximize the labor hours he and his employees devoted to selling, his store's sales would drop and he would be reprimanded.

RadioShack, of course, is not the only employer who has had to confront this problem. Starbucks and SBC Pacific Bell both settled similar charges in California with payments to plaintiffs. In Louisiana, Eckerd Drugs also settled a case involving 1,100 pharmacists. In this case the pharmacists charged that their pay was docked if they worked less than forty hours per week but that they received no overtime if they worked in excess of forty hours. Eckerd denied guilt and maintained that it settled only to avoid a lengthy court battle. And Wal-Mart is currently fighting thirty-eight such lawsuits in thirty states.[1] ∎

Like almost every other organization today, RadioShack must adhere to the laws and regulations that govern its employment practices. In general, organizations try to follow such laws and regulations for several reasons. One is an inherent commitment in most organizations to ethical and socially responsible behavior. Another is to avoid the direct costs and bad publicity that might result from lawsuits brought against the organization if those laws and regulations are broken. But as the opening case illustrates, these laws and regulations are sometimes ambiguous and open to different interpretations. As we will see, failure to follow the law, even because of a well-intentioned misunderstanding, can be enormously costly to an organization.

As we noted in Chapter 1, the proliferation of laws and regulations affecting employment practices in the 1960s and 1970s was a key reason for the emergence of human resource management as a vital organizational function. Managing within the complex legal environment that affects human resource practices requires a full understanding of that legal environment and the ability to ensure that others within the organization also understand it.[2] This chapter is devoted to helping you understand the legal environment of human resource management. First we establish the legal context of human resource management. We then focus on perhaps the most important area of this legal context—equal employment opportunity—and review several key court cases that have established the law in this area. Two subsequent sections introduce legal issues in compensation and in labor relations. Various emerging legal issues are then introduced and discussed. Finally, we conclude by summarizing how many organizations today evaluate their legal compliance.

THE LEGAL CONTEXT OF HUMAN RESOURCE MANAGEMENT

The legal context of human resource management is shaped by different forces. The catalyst for modifying or enhancing the legal context may be legislative initiative, social change, or judicial rulings. Governmental bodies pass laws that affect human resource practices, for example, and the courts interpret those laws as they apply to specific circumstances and situations. Thus, the regulatory environment itself is quite complex and affects different areas within the human resource management process.[3]

The Regulatory Environment of Human Resource Management

The legal and regulatory environment of human resource management in the United States emerges as a result of a three-step process, starting with the actual creation of new regulation. This regulation can come in the form of new laws or statutes passed by national, state, or local government bodies; however, most start at the national level. State and local regulations are more likely to extend or modify national regulations than create new ones. In addition, as we will see later, the president of the United States can also create regulations that apply to specific situations.

The Lighter Side of HR

The regulatory environment of human resource management imposes numerous constraints on organizations. Laws regarding employment practices have become so complicated in recent years that many employers are unsure of their own rights when it comes to hiring or terminating employees. For example, a firm that uses discriminatory practices can be sued for not hiring someone or for firing a current employee. But the firm can also be liable if it should reject or fire someone but fails to do so! Not surprisingly, many employment decisions today are routinely reviewed by human resource experts and/or attorneys. And the opinions of these experts and attorneys often determine whether or not someone will be hired or fired.

"I've been speaking to my attorneys, Larson, and this time we think we've got you fired."

(Danny Shanahan, c/o Riley Illustration)

The second step in the regulation process is the enforcement of these regulations. Occasionally the laws themselves provide for enforcement through the creation of special agencies or other forms of regulatory groups. (We will discuss one important agency, the Equal Employment Opportunity Commission, later in the chapter.) In other situations enforcement might be assigned to an existing agency, such as the Department of Labor. The court system also interprets laws that the government passes and provides another vehicle for enforcement. To be effective, an enforcing agency must have an appropriate degree of power. The ability to levy fines or bring lawsuits against firms that violate the law are among the most powerful tools provided to the various agencies charged with enforcing human resource regulations.

The third step in the regulation process is the actual practice and implementation of those regulations in organizations. That is, organizations and managers must implement and follow the guidelines that the government has passed and that the courts and regulatory agencies attempt to enforce. In many cases, following regulations is a logical and straightforward process. In some cases, however, a regulation may be unintentionally ambiguous or be interpreted by the courts in different ways over time. Regardless of the clarity of the regulation, the actual process of implementing and demonstrating adherence to it may take an extended period of time. Thus, organizations are sometimes put in the difficult position of figuring out how to follow a particular regulation and/or needing an extended period of time to enact full compliance. The Lighter Side of HR highlights this point.

Basic Areas of Legal Regulation

Regulations exist in almost every aspect of the employment relationship. As illustrated in Figure 3.1, equal employment opportunity intended to protect individuals from illegal discrimination is the most fundamental and far-reaching area of the legal regulation of human resource management. Indeed, in one way or another, almost every law and statute governing employment relationships is essentially attempting to ensure equal employment opportunity. But equal employment opportunity has been interpreted to include protection that goes beyond ensuring that a person has a fair chance at being hired for a job for which

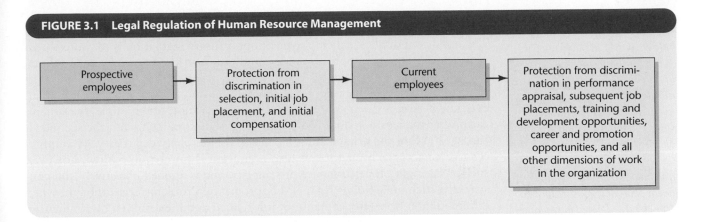

FIGURE 3.1   Legal Regulation of Human Resource Management

Prospective employees → Protection from discrimination in selection, initial job placement, and initial compensation → Current employees → Protection from discrimination in performance appraisal, subsequent job placements, training and development opportunities, career and promotion opportunities, and all other dimensions of work in the organization

the person is qualified. As illustrated in Figure 3.1, this protection extends to preventing illegal discrimination against current employees with regard to performance appraisal, pay, promotion opportunities, and various other dimensions of the employment relationship. In addition, several related legal issues warrant separate discussion as well.

EQUAL EMPLOYMENT OPPORTUNITY

Some managers assume that the legal regulation of human resource management is a relatively recent phenomenon. In reality, however, concerns about equal opportunity can be traced back to the Thirteenth and Fourteenth Amendments to the Constitution of the United States. The Thirteenth Amendment, passed in 1865, abolished slavery; the Fourteenth Amendment, passed in 1868, made it illegal for government to take the life, liberty, or property of individuals without due process of law. The Fourteenth Amendment goes on to prohibit states from denying equal protection to their residents. In recent years, the Fourteenth Amendment has also been applied to the concept of reverse discrimination, wherein white citizens argue that they have been discriminated against by agencies going too far in their efforts to provide equal opportunity to minorities. It is also important to note, however, that the Fourteenth Amendment generally relates only to so-called state actions. That is, it applies only to the actions of governments or to private groups deemed to be state agents and thus does not always apply to private employers.

The Reconstruction Civil Rights Acts of 1866 and 1871 extended protection offered to people under the Thirteenth and Fourteenth Amendments. For example, the Reconstruction Civil Rights Act of 1866 granted all persons in the United States the same property rights as then held by its white citizens. The Reconstruction Civil Rights Act of 1871 granted all U.S. citizens the right to sue in federal court if they feel they have been deprived of their civil rights. Even though these laws are over 100 years old, they still form the basis today for federal court actions that involve the payment of compensatory and punitive damages.[4]

Discrimination and Equal Employment Opportunity

Title VII of the Civil Rights Act of 1964 is probably the single most important piece of legislation affecting human resource management. President Lyndon Johnson is shown here signing the bill into law on July 2, 1964. The Civil Rights Act legislates non-discrimination at work; subsequent court decisions relating to Title VII have defined the meanings of disparate impact, job relatedness, Bona Fide Occupational Qualification, sexual harassment, and other factors. The Act continues to play a major role in corporate HR practices, and the importance of the statutes contained in the Act were reaffirmed with the passage of the Civil Rights Act of 1991.

The basic goal of all equal employment opportunity regulation is to protect people from unfair or inappropriate discrimination in the workplace.[5] However, most laws passed to eliminate discrimination do not explicitly define the term itself. It is also instructive to note that discrimination per se is not illegal. Whenever one person is given a pay raise and another is not, for example, the organization has made a decision to differentiate the first person from the second. It can be said that the organization has discriminated between these two employees. As long as the basis for this discrimination is purely job-related, however, such as basing it on performance or seniority, and is applied objectively and consistently, such an action is legal and appropriate. Problems arise, though, when differentiation between people is not job-related and the resulting discrimination is illegal. Various court decisions and basic inferences about the language of various laws suggest that **illegal discrimination** is what results from behaviors or actions by an organization or managers within an organization that cause members of a protected class to be unfairly differentiated from others. (We discuss protected classes later in this chapter.)

Although numerous laws deal with different aspects of equal employment opportunity, the Civil Rights Act of 1964 clearly signaled the beginning of a new legislative era in American business. The act grew out of the growing atmosphere of protest for equal rights in the early 1960s and contains several "titles" (or sections) that deal with different areas of application of the Civil Rights Act. Our discussion will focus on Title VII, which deals with work settings under the heading of Equal Employment Opportunity.

Title VII of the Civil Rights Act of 1964 The most significant single piece of legislation specifically affecting the legal context for human resource management to date has been **Title VII of the Civil Rights Act of 1964.** Congress passed the Civil Rights Act and President Lyndon Johnson signed it into law in 1964 as a way to ensure that equal opportunities are available to everyone. Title VII of the Civil Rights Act states that it is illegal for an employer to fail or refuse to hire, to discharge any individual, or to discriminate in any other way against any individual with respect to any aspect of the employment relationship on the basis of that individual's race, color, religious beliefs, sex, or national origin. The law also makes it illegal to segregate, limit, or classify employees or applicants for employment in any way that could deprive them or lead to their deprivation of any employment opportunities on the same bases.

The law applies to all components of the employment relationship, including compensation, employment terms, working conditions, and various other privileges of employment. Title VII applies to all organizations with fifteen or more employees working twenty or more weeks a year and that are involved in

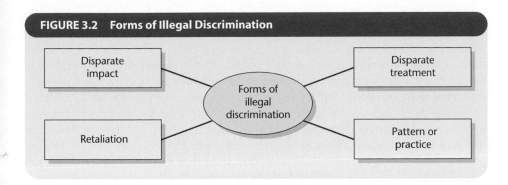

FIGURE 3.2 Forms of Illegal Discrimination

interstate commerce. In addition, it also applies to state and local governments, employment agencies, and labor organizations. Title VII also created the Equal Employment Opportunity Commission (EEOC) to enforce the various provisions of the law (we discuss the EEOC later in this chapter). Under Title VII, as interpreted by the courts, several types of illegal discrimination are outlawed. These types are discussed below and are illustrated above in Figure 3.2.

Disparate treatment Disparate treatment discrimination exists when individuals in similar situations are treated differently and when the differential treatment is based on the individual's race, color, religion, sex, national origin, age, or disability status. For example, if two people with the same qualifications for the job apply for a promotion and the organization decides which employee to promote based on one individual's religious beliefs or gender, the individual not promoted is a victim of disparate treatment discrimination. To prove discrimination in this situation, an individual filing a charge must demonstrate that there was a discriminatory motive; that is, the individual must prove that the organization took the individual's protected class status into consideration when making the decision.

One circumstance in which organizations can legitimately treat members of different groups differently is when there exists a **bona fide occupational qualification** (**BFOQ**) for performing a particular job. This condition means that some personal characteristic, such as age, legitimately affects a person's ability to perform the job. For example, a producer casting a new play or movie can legally refuse to hire an older person to play a role that is expressly written for a very young person. There are few BFOQs, however. For example, a restaurant cannot hire only young, attractive people as servers based on the argument that their customers prefer young, attractive servers. In fact, customer and/or client preference can *never* be the basis of a BFOQ. As we shall see, however, this situation can become quite complex.

To claim a BFOQ exception, the organization must be able to demonstrate that hiring on the basis of the characteristic in question (e.g., age) is not simply a preference but a **business necessity.** That is, the organization must be able to prove that the practice is important for the safe and efficient operation of the business. But what if customers at a casino would prefer female card dealers or if customers at an automobile dealership would prefer male salespersons? These customers might go elsewhere if these preferences were not satisfied, and those decisions could surely hurt the business involved. In general, neither of these cases would qualify as a BFOQ; however, reality is rarely this simple.

The case of *Diaz* v. *Pan American World Airways*,[6] for example, was filed after Celio Diaz (a male) applied for the job of flight attendant with Pan American

■ **Illegal discrimination** is what results from behaviors or actions by an organization or managers within an organization that cause members of a protected class to be unfairly differentiated from others.

■ **Title VII of the Civil Rights Act of 1964** states that it is illegal for an employer to fail or refuse to hire or to discharge any individual or to discriminate in any other way against any individual with respect to any aspect of the employment relationship on the basis of that individual's race, color, religious beliefs, sex, or national origin.

■ **Disparate treatment** discrimination exists when individuals in similar situations are treated differently and when the differential treatment is based on the individual's race, color, religion, sex, national origin, age, or disability status.

■ A **bona fide occupational qualification (BFOQ)** states that a condition like age, sex, or other personal characteristic legitimately affects a person's ability to perform a job.

■ A **business necessity** is a practice that is important for the safe and efficient operation of the business and thus is a permissible BFOQ. It indicates that an employment practice can be shown to be related to performance on the job.

Airlines (Pan Am). He was rejected because Pan Am had a policy of hiring only women for this position (as did many airlines in 1971). Diaz filed suit for discrimination, but Pan Am argued that gender was a BFOQ for the job of flight attendant. This argument was based on Pan Am's own experience with male and female flight attendants and on the fact that Pan Am's customers overwhelmingly preferred to be served by female attendants. A lower court accepted the airlines' argument that ". . . an airline cabin represents a unique [and stressful] environment in which an air carrier is required to take account of the special psychological needs of its passengers. Those needs are better attended to by females."[7] The appeals court reversed that decision, however, citing that Pan Am's data on the relative effectiveness of male and female flight attendants was not very compelling and noting that customer preference was not relevant because no evidence existed that hiring male flight attendants would substantially affect the business performance of the airlines. Although this ruling seems clear, Asian restaurants are regularly allowed to hire only Asian-American waiters because this situation adds to the authenticity of the dining experience and is therefore deemed a business necessity.

■ **Disparate impact** discrimination occurs when an apparently neutral employment practice disproportionately excludes a protected group from employment opportunities.

Disparate impact   A second form of discrimination is disparate impact. **Disparate impact** discrimination occurs when an apparently neutral employment practice disproportionately excludes a protected group from employment opportunities. This argument is the most common for charges of discrimination brought under the Civil Rights Act. For example, suppose a restaurant determined that, for health reasons, no one who had hair long enough to cover his or her ears would be hired to handle food. Although this practice would be applied to *all* applicants and would certainly result in some long-haired males not being hired, it would have a much greater impact on female applicants because they are more likely to have longer hair. As a result, even though all applicants would be treated the same, this practice would result in the rejection of many more female applicants. This situation would be an example of disparate impact discrimination because the organization, even with no direct intention of discriminating against women, is using a particular employment practice that results in discrimination against women. In this situation, intent to discriminate is irrelevant (and the proper solution is to have all employees wear hairnets).

One of the first instances in which disparate impact was defined involved a landmark court case, *Griggs* v. *Duke Power*. Following passage of Title VII, Duke Power initiated a new selection system that required new employees to have either a high school education or a minimum cutoff score on two specific personality tests. Griggs, a black male, filed a lawsuit against Duke Power after he was denied employment based on these criteria. His argument was that neither criterion was a necessary qualification for performing the work he was seeking. After his attorneys demonstrated that those criteria disproportionately affected blacks and that the company had no documentation to support the validity of the criteria, the courts ruled that the firm had to change its selection criteria on the basis of disparate impact.[8]

The important criterion in this situation is that the consequences of the employment practice are discriminatory, and thus the practice in question has disparate (sometimes referred to as adverse) impact. In fact, if a plaintiff can establish what is called a prima facie case of discrimination, the company is considered to be at fault unless it can demonstrate another legal basis for the decision.[9] This finding doesn't mean that the company automatically loses the case, but it does mean that the burden of proof rests with the company to defend itself, rather than with the plaintiff trying to prove discrimination. Therefore, it is extremely important to understand how one establishes a prima facie case. Although there are several ways, the most common approach is the so-called **four-fifths rule.** Specifically, the courts have ruled that disparate impact exists if a selection criterion (such as a test score) results in a selection rate for a protected class that is less than four-fifths (80 percent) than that for the majority group. For example, assume that an organization is considering 100 white applicants and 100 Hispanic applicants for the same job. If an employment test used to select among these applicants results in sixty white applicants (60 percent) being hired, but only thirty Hispanic applicants (30 percent) being hired, disparate impact is likely to be ruled because Hispanics are being hired at a rate that is less than four-fifths than that of whites. At this point, the organization using the test would be required to prove that its differential selection rate of whites versus Hispanics could be justified (the basis for this justification will be explained below).

But demonstrating that an organization's policies have violated the four-fifths rule can sometimes be complicated. In the case of *Wards' Cove Packing* v. *Antonio*,[10] the defendant, a salmon cannery in Alaska, had two distinct types of jobs for which people were hired. Cannery jobs were seen as skilled (administrative and engineering) while noncannery jobs were viewed as unskilled. The plaintiff's attorneys argued that since the noncannery jobs were predominantly filled by Filipino and Native Alaskans, while the cannery jobs were held predominantly by whites, the company had violated the four-fifths rule and they had therefore established a prima facie case for disparate impact. The defendant did not dispute the statistics but argued that the policies in place did not lead to apparent disparate impact and therefore there was no prima facie case. The Supreme Court agreed with the defendant, ruling that the statistical proof alone was not sufficient for establishing a prima facie case. Therefore, the burden of proof did *not* shift to the defendant but rested with the employee involved. Wards Cove won the case. In addition to illustrating the problems with establishing a violation of the four-fifths rule, the Wards Cove case was also widely seen as dealing a major blow to the enforcement of the Civil Rights Act of 1964—a topic to which we will return shortly.

Two methods are used for demonstrating disparate impact. **Geographical comparisons** involve comparing the characteristics of the potential pool of qualified applicants for a job (focusing on characteristics such as race, ethnicity, and gender) with those same characteristics of the present employees in the job. Thus, if the potential pool of qualified applicants in the labor market for the job of bank teller is 50 percent African-American, a bank hiring from that market should have approximately 50 percent African-American tellers. Failure to achieve this degree of representation is considered a basis for a prima facie case of disparate impact discrimination. This comparison depends a great deal on a clear understanding of the labor market from which the organization typically recruits employees for this job. Even within the same organization, different jobs might draw on different "relevant" labor markets with different characteristics. For instance, a university might rely on a national labor market for new faculty members, a regional labor market for professional staff employees, and a local labor market for custodial and food-service employees. It is also important to note that the definition of the "potential pool of qualified applicants" draws heavily on census data for the area.

■ The **four-fifths rule** suggests that disparate impact exists if a selection criterion (such as a test score) results in a selection rate for a protected class that is less than four-fifths (80 percent) of that for the majority group.

■ **Geographical comparisons** refer to a method to determine disparate impact. In this case, the presence of protected class employee in a company's workforce is compared with the presence of qualified members of that protected class in the geographical area from which the company draws applicants.

■ **McDonnell-Douglas test** is a basis for establishing a prima facie case. The criteria for this basis are that an applicant is a member of a protected class, is qualified for the job for which he or she applied, and was turned down, but the company continued to seek other applicants with the same qualifications.

Finally, the **McDonnell-Douglas test,** named for a Supreme Court ruling in *McDonnell-Douglas* v. *Green,*[11] is another basis for establishing a prima facie case. Four steps are part of the McDonnell-Douglas test:

1. The applicant is a member of a protected class (see below).

2. The applicant was qualified for the job for which he or she applied.

3. The individual was turned down for the job.

4. The company continued to seek other applicants with the same qualifications.

Pattern or practice discrimination   The third kind of discrimination that can be identified is pattern or practice discrimination. **Pattern or practice discrimination** is a form of disparate treatment that occurs on a classwide or systemic basis. Although an individual can bring charges of practice discrimination, the issue is that the organization engages in a pattern or practice of discrimination against all members of a protected class instead of against one particular member. Title VII of the 1964 Civil Rights Act gives the attorney general of the United States express powers to bring lawsuits against organizations thought to be guilty of pattern or practice discrimination. Specifically, Section 707 of Title VII states that such a lawsuit can be brought if there is reasonable cause to believe that an employer is engaging in pattern or practice discrimination. A good example of pattern or practice discrimination allegedly occurred several years ago at Shoney's, a popular family-oriented restaurant chain with operations and locations throughout the South. A former assistant manager at the firm alleged that she was told by her supervisor to use a pencil to color in the "o" in the Shoney's logo printed on its employment application blanks for all black applicants. The presumed intent of this coding scheme was to eliminate all those applicants from further consideration.[12]

■ **Pattern or practice discrimination** is a form of disparate treatment that occurs on a classwide basis.

To demonstrate pattern or practice discrimination, the plaintiff must prove that the organization intended to discriminate against a particular class of individuals. A critical issue in practice or pattern discrimination lawsuits is the definition of a statistical comparison group or a definition of the relevant labor market. A labor market consists of workers who have the skills needed to perform the work and who are within a reasonable commuting distance from the organization. The definition of the labor market is a major issue then in resolving lawsuits brought under pattern or practice discrimination suits.

Retaliation   A final form of illegal discrimination that has been occasionally identified in some organizations is retaliation for "participation and opposition." Title VII states that it is illegal for employers to retaliate against employees for either opposing a perceived illegal employment practice or participating in a proceeding that is related to an alleged illegal employment practice. If an employee's behavior fits the legal definition of participation and/or opposition and the organization takes some measure against that particular employee, such as a reprimand, demotion, or termination, the employee can file a lawsuit against the organization under Title VII.

Employer defense   Our discussion so far has focused on the types of illegal discrimination and the ways in which a plaintiff can establish a case of discrimination. As noted earlier, however, once a prima facie case has been established, the burden of proof shifts to the defendant. That is, the defendant has to provide evidence for nondiscriminatory bases for the decisions made. Therefore, it is critical to understand that just because a prima facie case has been established, it does not necessarily mean that the defendant (typically the company) will be found liable. The company can defend itself by providing evidence that the selection decision (or employment decision of any type) was based on criteria that are job related. That is, the defendant (usually an organization) must be able to prove that decisions were made so that the persons most likely to be selected (or be promoted, or receive a pay raise) are those who are most likely to perform best on the job (or who have already performed best on the job). This situation is also referred to as validation of the practice in question. In Chapter 7 we will discuss how one validates a selection technique and therefore establishes that it is job related. (Appendix 2 provides a more technical discussion of how one validates a selection technique.) Many of these issues are also based on the court ruling in the *Albermarle Paper Company* case, which is also discussed in Chapter 7.

Protected Classes in the Workforce

We have made several references so far to protected classes. It is now time to turn our attention to what that term means in practice. Many of the discriminatory practices described above stemmed from stereotypes, beliefs, or prejudice about classes of individuals. For example, common stereotypes at one time were that black employees were less dependable than white employees, that women were less suited to certain types of work than were men, and that disabled individuals could not be productive employees. Based on these stereotypes, many organizations routinely discriminated against blacks, women, and disabled people. Figure 3.3 depicts recruiting advertisements with explicit or implicit discriminatory connotations from earlier times. Such ads would create major problems if an organization tried to use them today.

To combat this discrimination, various laws have been passed to protect different classes or categories of individuals. While varying from law to law, a **protected class** consists of all individuals who share one or more common characteristic as indicated by that law. The most common characteristics used to define protected classes include race, color, religion, gender, age, national origin, disability status, and status as a military veteran. As we will see, some laws pertain to several protected classes, while others pertain to a single protected class. Class definition generally involves first specifying the basis of distinction and then specifying which degree or category of that distinction is protected. For example, a law may prohibit discrimination on the basis of gender—a basis of distinction—and then define the protected class as females. This distinction does not mean that an organization can discriminate against men, of course, and in some cases men could even be considered members of a protected class. But the law was almost certainly passed on the assumption that most gender-based discrimination has been directed against women and thus it is women who need to be protected in the future.

At the same time, an important issue is the extent to which an organization can give preferential treatment to members of a protected class. While exceptions can

■ A **protected class** consists of all individuals who share one or more common characteristic as indicated by a specific law.

FIGURE 3.3   Discriminatory Recruiting Ads from Earlier Times

be made in certain circumstances, by and large the intent of most equal employment opportunity legislation is to provide fair and equitable treatment for everyone, as opposed to stipulating preferential treatment for members of a protected class.[13] This interpretation becomes a bit complicated, though, and can result in charges of reverse discrimination, our next topic.

Affirmative Action and Reverse Discrimination

■ **Affirmative action** represents a set of steps taken by an organization to seek qualified applicants from groups underrepresented in the workforce.

When charges of illegal discrimination have been supported, courts sometimes impose remedies that try to reverse the effects of past discrimination. Most frequently, these remedies have taken the form of some type of affirmative action. (As we shall see below, some organizations are also required to file affirmative action plans even without charges of illegal discrimination.) **Affirmative action** refers to positive steps taken by an organization to seek qualified employees from underrepresented groups in the workforce. When affirmative action is part of a remedy in a discrimination case, the plan takes on additional urgency and the steps are somewhat clearer. Three elements make up any affirmative action program.

■ A **utilization analysis** is a comparison of the race, sex, and ethnic composition of the employer's workforce compared to that of the available labor supply.

The first element is called the utilization analysis. A **utilization analysis** is a comparison of the racial, sex, and ethnic composition of the employer's work-

One of the more controversial aspects of equal employment opportunity is the notion of affirmative action. The Civil Rights Act of 1964 does not require affirmative action, nor does the Civil Rights Act of 1991, but various executive orders do require affirmative action for federal contractors. These protestors are marching outside the Supreme Court in April 2003 as the Supreme Court was deciding the legality of two different affirmative action plans instituted by the University of Michigan. The Court upheld one plan whereby race could be considered as one factor in admissions decisions; but it struck down a different plan whereby minority applicants were given a fixed number of extra "points" in the decision process. This decision left no one completely satisfied, although it did suggest that universities could consider race as a factor in admissions decisions. Hence, the controversies around affirmative action are likely to continue.

force compared to that of the available labor supply. For each group of jobs, the organization needs to identify the percentage of its workforce with that characteristic (i.e., black, female, etc.) and identify the percentage of workers in the relevant labor market with that characteristic. If the percentage in the employer's workforce is considerably less than the percentage in the external labor supply, then that minority group is characterized as being underutilized. Much of this analysis takes place as part of the discrimination case, if one is involved, and the affected groups are defined by the specifics of the case.

The second part of an affirmative action plan is the development of goals and timetables for achieving balance in the workforce concerning those characteristics, especially where underutilization exists. Goals and timetables generally specify the percentage of protected classes of employees that the organization seeks to have in each group and the targeted date by which that percentage should be attained. It is important to recognize that these goals and timetables do not automatically constitute quotas. A quota would involve setting aside a specific number of jobs to be filled only by members of a particular protected class. Goals and timetables are considerably more flexible than quotas. The idea underlying goals and timetables is that if no discriminatory hiring practices exist, then underutilization should be eliminated over time. Nonetheless, in some instances, the courts have imposed temporary quotas on organizations to ensure that the effects of past discrimination can be eliminated.

The third part of the affirmative action program is the development of a list of action steps. These steps specify what the organization will do to work toward attaining its goals to reduce underutilization. Common action steps include increased communication of job openings to underrepresented groups, recruiting at schools that predominantly cater to a particular protected class, participating in programs designed to improve employment opportunities for underemployed groups, and taking all necessary steps to remove inappropriate barriers to employment. In some cases this third part might also include preferential hiring.

■ **Reverse discrimination**
refers to any practice that has disparate impact on members of nonprotected classes. For example, quota systems where an organization would be required to hire a certain number of black females would be considered reverse discrimination relative to white males, unless the system was dictated by a court order.

That is, given two equally qualified applicants for a job, the organization would be required to hire the member of the underrepresented group in every case until its goals and targets are met.

In the last part of the 1990s, the courts began to impose many more restrictions on what was acceptable (or required) in the way of preferential hiring and quotas. We will discuss representative relevant court decisions shortly, but the impetus for some of these decisions was the concern that affirmative action *could* in some cases appear to be a form of reverse discrimination. **Reverse discrimination** refers to any practice that has a disparate impact on members of *nonprotected* classes. Thus, charges of reverse discrimination typically stem from the belief by white males that they have suffered because of preferential treatment given to other groups.

The two most famous court cases in this area help to illustrate how complicated this issue can be. In the *Bakke* case[14] a student, Allen Bakke, had applied to medical school and was denied admission. At issue was the fact that the University of California at Davis had set aside sixteen of its 100 seats for an incoming class for minority students to promote diversity and affirmative action at the school. Bakke's attorneys argued that he was not necessarily more qualified than those admitted for the eighty-four "white" openings, but that he was more qualified than those admitted to the sixteen openings set aside for minorities. Since the school had imposed this system on its own (to correct past injustice), the Court ruled that this "set-aside" program constituted reverse discrimination because it clearly favored one race over another, and it ruled in favor of Bakke.

In the *Weber* case[15] a white male, Brian Weber, applied for a temporary training program that would lead to a higher-paying skilled job at a Kaiser Aluminum facility. He was not accepted into the program, and he sued because he claimed that African-American applicants with less seniority were admitted into the program strictly because of their race. In fact, Kaiser and United Steelworkers had agreed to a contract whereby 50 percent of the openings for these programs would be reserved for African-Americans in an attempt to address the fact that African-Americans had been systematically excluded from these programs in the past. The Supreme Court found in favor of Kaiser and the union, acknowledging that a collective-bargaining agreement such as this one was binding and was a reasonable means of addressing past discrimination.

Given these two legal decisions, one might question the current status of reverse discrimination cases. In fact, it is by no means clear. Within the space of a few years, the Supreme Court ruled against an organization giving preferential treatment to minority workers during a layoff,[16] ruled in support of temporary preferential hiring and promotion practices as part of a settlement of a lawsuit,[17] and ruled in support of the establishment of quotas as a remedy for past discrimination,[18] but it ruled that any form of affirmative action is inherently discriminatory and could be used only as a temporary measure.[19] It would appear that the future of affirmative action is unclear, suggesting that the courts will be leaning more toward interpretations in line with reverse discrimination in the future. In fact, this scenario is even more likely as the Supreme Court seems to be moving more to the right politically.

Two recent and related events seem to reinforce this view. In 1996, a circuit court judge ruled that a goal of increasing student diversity at the University of Texas was not sufficient grounds for giving preference to racial minorities in terms of admission or financial aid.[20] And in 1998 California voters ratified a proposition called the California Civil Rights Initiative, which outlawed *any* preferential treatment on the basis of race, gender, color, ethnicity, or national origin for all public employment, education, and contracting activities. However, in 2003 the Supreme Court ruled that the University of Michigan could use diversity as one of several factors in making its admissions decisions.

Sexual Harassment at Work

One final area of coverage for the Civil Rights Act that is critical for the human resource manager is sexual harassment. This area is particularly important in this context because much of the litigation and the organization's liability in these cases depend on the initial responses to charges of sexual harassment, and these responses are typically the responsibility of someone in human resources. Sexual harassment is defined by the EEOC as unwelcome sexual advances in the work environment. If the conduct is indeed unwelcome and occurs with sufficient frequency to create an abusive work environment, the employer is responsible for changing the environment by warning, reprimanding, or perhaps firing the harasser.[21]

The courts have ruled that there are two types of sexual harassment and have defined both types. One type of sexual harassment is **quid pro quo harassment.** In this case, the harasser offers to exchange something of value for sexual favors. For example, a male supervisor might tell or imply to a female subordinate that he will recommend her for promotion or provide her with a salary increase, but only if she sleeps with him. Although this type of situation definitely occurs, organizations generally have no problem in understanding that it is illegal and knowing how to respond.

But a more subtle (and probably more common) type of sexual harassment is the creation of a **hostile work environment,** and this situation is not always so easy to define. For example, a group of male employees who continually make off-color jokes and lewd comments and perhaps decorate the work environment with inappropriate photographs may create a hostile work environment for a female colleague, to the point where she is uncomfortable working in that job setting. Most experts would agree that this situation constitutes sexual harassment. But what if an employee has an inappropriate magazine in a desk drawer and a coworker sees it only when she (or he) happens to walk by when the drawer is open?

In *Meritor Savings Bank* v. *Vinson*[22] the Supreme Court noted that a hostile work environment constitutes sexual harassment, even if the employee did not suffer any economic penalties or was not threatened with any such penalties. In *Harris* v. *Forklift Systems*[23] the Court ruled that the plaintiff did not have to suffer substantial mental distress to receive a jury settlement. Hence, it is critical that organizations monitor the situation and be alert for these instances because, as noted, it is the organization's responsibility for dealing with this sort of problem.[24]

Therefore, the human resource manager must play a major role in investigating any hint of sexual harassment in the organization. The manager cannot simply wait for an employee to complain. Although the Court had ruled in the case of *Scott* v. *Sears Roebuck*[25] that the employer was not liable for the sexual harassment because the plaintiff did not complain to supervisors, the ruling in the *Meritor* case makes it much more difficult for the organization to avoid liability by claiming ignorance (although this liability is not automatic). This responsibility is further complicated by the fact that, although most sexual harassment cases involve men harassing women, there are, of course, many other situations of sexual harassment that can be

■ **Quid pro quo harassment** is sexual harassment in which the harasser offers to exchange something of value for sexual favors.

■ **Hostile work environment** is a more subtle form of sexual harassment and results from a climate or culture that is punitive toward people of a different gender.

identified. Females can harass men, and in the case of *Oncale* v. *Sundowner*[26] the Supreme Court ruled unanimously that a male oil rigger who claimed to be harassed by his coworkers and supervisor on an off-shore oil rig was indeed the victim of sexual harassment. Several recent cases involving same-sex harassment have focused new attention on this form of sexual harassment.[27] Regardless of the pattern, however, the same rules apply: sexual harassment is illegal and it is the organization's responsibility to control it. This chapter's HR Legal Brief provides additional insights into sexual harassment in a unique setting—the U.S. Army.

Other Equal Employment Opportunity Legislation

In addition to the Civil Rights Act of 1964, a large body of supporting legal regulation has also been created in an effort to provide equal employment opportunity for various protected classes of individuals. Although the 1964 act is probably the best known and most influential piece of legislation in this area, a new civil rights act was passed in 1991 and numerous other laws deal with different aspects of equal employment or are concerned with specific areas of work. These additional major laws and related regulations are discussed more fully in this section.

Executive Order 11246 Because President Johnson believed that Title VII of the 1964 Civil Rights Act was not comprehensive enough, he subsequently issued **Executive Order 11246.** This order prohibits discrimination based on race, color, religion, sex, or national origin for organizations that are federal contractors and subcontractors. Executive Order 11246 specifically states that employers who receive more than $10,000 from the federal government must take affirmative action to ensure against discrimination in their hiring and retention practices. The executive order also specifies that those organizations with contracts greater than $50,000 must develop a written affirmative action plan for each of their organizational units within 120 days of the beginning of the contract. Executive Order 11246 is enforced by the Office of Federal Contract Compliance Procedures (OFCCP), which is discussed later.

Executive Order 11478 President Richard Nixon issued **Executive Order 11478,** which requires the federal government to base all of its own employment policies on merit and fitness and specifies that race, color, sex, religion, and national origin should not be considered. The executive order also extends to all contractors and subcontractors doing $10,000 or more worth of business with the federal government.

The Equal Pay Act of 1963 The **Equal Pay Act of 1963** requires that organizations provide the same pay to men and women who are doing equal work. The law defines equality in terms of skill, responsibility, effort, and working conditions. Thus, an organization cannot pay a man more than it pays a woman for the same job on the grounds that, say, the male employee needs the money more because he has a bigger family to support. Similarly, organizations cannot circumvent the law by using different job titles for essentially the same work, such as a school district giving a man the title of assistant superintendent and a woman the title of curriculum coordinator. If the work is essentially the same, then pay differentials on the basis of difference in titles alone is illegal.

This does not mean, of course, that men and women must be paid the same if there are legitimate, job-related reasons for pay differences. That is, a man may

■ **Executive Order 11246** prohibits discrimination based on race, color, religion, sex, or national origin for organizations that are federal contractors and subcontractors.

■ **Executive Order 11478** requires the federal government to base all of its employment policies on merit and fitness and specifies that race, color, sex, religion, and national origin should not be considered.

■ The **Equal Pay Act of 1963** requires that organizations provide equal pay to men and women who are doing equal work.

Sexual Harassment in the Army

The United States Army is an instructive organization to study from a human resource management perspective. In 2001, approximately 500,000 people served full-time in the army. Of this number, approximately 75,000 were women. Among the officer corps are approximately 10,000 women. The numbers of enlisted women, and especially women officers, are lower than one would expect to find in most civilian organizations, but the army (as well as the entire military in the United States) is a male-dominated culture, and women are relative newcomers to the regular army.

"The problem remains with the leadership of the army."

(Retired Brigadier General Evelyn Foote*)

Despite these facts, the army has often portrayed itself as a model of equal opportunity. Promotions and advancement are based purely on merit, and for several years the army has had formal, zero-tolerance policies to guard against discrimination and sexual harassment. Nonetheless, in 1996, complaints at the Army Ordnance Center and School at Aberdeen, Maryland led investigators to identify over fifty victims of sexual harassment and inappropriate sexual conduct, and twenty instructors were suspended as a result of the investigation. Four of these instructors were sent to prison, including one sergeant sentenced to twenty-five years for numerous counts of rape. Follow-up investigations revealed widespread incidences of harassment and sexual misconduct in the army—mostly against women, but also against men.

The army's response was sweeping and significant. Training was upgraded, selection criteria for drill instructors were tightened, and more equal opportunity adviser positions were created. And the leadership in the army admitted that the problem was not a lack of training but a lack of strong leadership on the issues related to sexual harassment. As a result, the number of sexual harassment complaints dropped dramatically. For example, in 1997, 390 sexual harassment complaints were filed, and 128 of these complaints were substantiated. By 2000, 104 complaints were filed and forty-six were substantiated—in a workforce of over 500 million persons. Thus, it would seem that the army's swift and sweeping response did the job. Or maybe not. . . .

Outside consulting and advocacy groups argue that women (as compared to men) who have been harassed simply bypass the army when seeking remedies. Anonymous army surveys dealing with the gender climate in the army confirm this situation. For example, these surveys indicate that, in 1997 (just after the Aberdeen incident), 78 percent of women responding to the survey reported incidents of crude or offensive behavior, while 47 percent reported incidents of unwanted sexual attention, 15 percent reported sexual coercion, and 7 percent reported incidents of sexual assault. In 2001, the numbers had, in fact, changed. Now, 84 percent of women responding to the survey reported incidents of crude or offensive behavior, 51 percent reported incidents of unwanted sexual attention, 17 percent reported sexual coercion, and 8 percent reported incidents of sexual assault. These data clearly suggest the situation has not gotten better and may, in fact, have gotten worse!

What went wrong? Many soldiers report that too much time is spent on sexual harassment training, and many of them ignore the entire issue. The problem doesn't seem to be the quantity of training, but the quality of training. Also, too few people are willing to work on equal opportunity issues, and very few officers are willing to mentor women soldiers who complain about sexual misconduct. Perhaps most important, a male-dominated, "macho" culture remains in the army, and it may be difficult to change. Data suggest that enlistment by women in the army is increasing. On the one hand, this information suggests that the problems are not deterring women from joining. On the other hand, if the problems are not resolved, their impact may become more visible as the numbers of soldiers involved increases. Retired Brigadier General Evelyn Foote says that "the problem remains with the leadership in the army." Without the full and clear commitment of the top brass, the army is not likely to change its culture. Over time, it might be possible to change the culture as more women are promoted to officer ranks, but even if that were effective, it would take over forty years to get the number of female officers who could make a difference.

As our country enters more dangerous times, it is critical that we have a strong military, and sexual discrimination and sexual harassment have no place in it. It remains to be seen if the army is up to the task, but it is clear that it is concerned and that it is trying.

Source: Adapted from Robert Grossman, "It's Not Easy Being Green . . . and Female," *HRMagazine,* September 2001, Vol. 46, pp. 38–48 (*quote on p. 45).

be paid more than a woman doing the same job if there are legitimate organizational practices to support such a differential. For example, suppose a firm gives a 5 percent seniority raise every year. A man who has worked for the firm for ten years may therefore legitimately be paid more than a woman who has worked at the same firm for only five years. Of course, for these practices to be legal the organization must also be paying the woman more than it is paying another man who has worked in the organization for only two years. Other potential differences in pay might be made on the basis of merit, quantity or quality of performance, or any other work- or performance-related factor.[28]

■ The **Age Discrimination and Employment Act (ADEA)** prohibits discrimination against employees over the age of forty.

The Age Discrimination and Employment Act   The Age Discrimination and Employment Act (ADEA) was first passed in 1967 and later amended in 1986. The ADEA prohibits discrimination against employees forty years old or older. The ADEA is very similar to Title VII of the 1964 Civil Rights Act in terms of both its major provisions and the procedures that are followed in pursuing a case of discrimination. Like Title VII, enforcement of the ADEA is the responsibility of the Equal Employment Opportunity Commission.

The ADEA was felt to be necessary because of a disquieting trend in some organizations in the early 1960s. Specifically, these firms were beginning to discriminate against older employees when they found it necessary to lay people off or otherwise to scale back their workforce. By targeting older workers who tended to have higher pay because of their seniority with the firm, companies were substantially cutting their labor costs. In addition, there was some feeling that organizations were also discriminating against older workers in their hiring decisions. The specific concern here was that organizations would not hire people in their forties or fifties because (1) they would have to pay those individuals more based on their experience and salary history and (2) they would have a shorter potential career with the organization. Consequently, some organizations were found guilty of giving preferential treatment to younger workers over older workers.

One area where the ADEA has generated a fair amount of controversy relates to mandatory retirement ages. The Supreme Court has indicated that an agency or an organization may require mandatory retirement at a given age *if and only if* it could be shown that age was a BFOQ. Thus, the organization in question would have to demonstrate the inability of persons beyond a certain age to perform a given job safely. But, in several decisions, the Court has indicated that it will interpret this BFOQ exception very narrowly. In fact, in *Johnson* v. *Mayor and City of Baltimore*,[29] the Court ruled that not even a federal statute requiring firefighters to retire at age 55 constituted a BFOQ exception to the law.

In recent years, age-bias lawsuits have actually started to decline. For example, age-related claims filed with the EEOC declined from 19,809 in 1993 to 15,785 in 1997. Several explanations have been suggested for this trend. Low unemployment in the 1990s has simply forced employers to retain as many qualified employees as possible. Early in the twenty-first century, the U.S. economy was again showing signs of slowing down. It remains to be seen if changes in the employment situation will translate into renewed discrimination based on age. Evidence shows that some organizations seem to be more sensitive about age-related issues today and are thus less likely to take inappropriate or illegal actions against older workers.[30]

■ The **Vocational Rehabilitation Act of 1973** requires that executive agencies and subcontractors and contractors of the federal government receiving more than $2,500 a year from the government engage in affirmative action for individuals with disabilities.

The Vocational Rehabilitation Act of 1973   The Vocational Rehabilitation Act of 1973 requires that executive agencies and subcontractors and contractors of the federal government receiving more than $2,500 a year from the government engage in affirmative action for disabled individuals. The Employment Standards Administration of the Department of Labor was assigned the role of enforcing the Vocational Rehabilitation Act of 1973.

The Vietnam Era Veterans' Readjustment Act of 1974 The Vietnam Era Veterans' Readjustment Act of 1974 is similar to the 1973 Vocational Rehabilitation Act. This law requires that federal contractors and subcontractors take affirmative action toward employing Vietnam-era veterans. Vietnam-era veterans are specifically defined as those serving as members of the U.S. armed forces between August 5, 1964, and May 7, 1975. Enforcement of the Vietnam Era Veterans' Readjustment Act was assigned to the Office of Federal Contract Compliance Procedures (OFCCP).

> ■ The **Vietnam Era Veterans' Readjustment Act of 1974** requires that federal contractors and subcontractors take affirmative action toward employing Vietnam-era veterans.

The Pregnancy Discrimination Act of 1979 As its name suggests, the **Pregnancy Discrimination Act of 1979** was passed to protect pregnant women from discrimination in the workplace. The law requires that the pregnant woman be treated as any other employee in the workplace. Therefore, the act specifies that a woman cannot be refused a job or promotion, fired, or otherwise discriminated against simply because she is pregnant (or has had an abortion). She also cannot be forced to leave employment with the organization as long as she is physically able to work. Finally, the Pregnancy Discrimination Act also specifies that if other employees have the right to return to their jobs after a leave, then this benefit must also be accorded to pregnant women. In one high-profile case a few years ago, actress Hunter Tylo won a $5 million judgment against the producers of her television show *Melrose Place* after they used her pregnancy as a basis for writing her out of the show.[31]

> ■ The **Pregnancy Discrimination Act of 1979** was passed to protect pregnant women from discrimination in the workplace.

The Civil Rights Act of 1991 The **Civil Rights Act of 1991** was passed as a direct amendment of Title VII of the Civil Rights Act of 1964. During the twenty-five years following the passage of the original act, the U.S. Supreme Court handed down several rulings that helped define how the Civil Rights Act would be administered. But in the course of its 1989 Supreme Court session, several decisions were handed down that many felt seriously limited the viability of the Civil Rights Act of 1964.[32] In response to this development, the Civil Rights Act of 1991 was passed essentially to restore the force of the original act. Although some new aspects of the law were introduced as part of the Civil Rights Act of 1991, the primary purpose of this new law was to make it easier for individuals who feel they have been discriminated against to take legal action against organizations.

Specifically, the Civil Rights Act of 1991 prohibits discrimination on the job and makes it easier for the burden of proof to shift to employers (to demonstrate that they did not discriminate). It also reinforces the illegality of making hiring, firing, or promotion decisions on the basis of race, gender, color, religion, or national origin; it also includes the Glass Ceiling Act, which established a commission to investigate practices that limited the access of protected class members (especially women) from attaining the top levels of management in organizations.

For the first time, the act provides the potential payment of compensatory and punitive damages in cases of discrimination under Title VII. Title VII, as originally passed, was concerned primarily with compensation for back pay. But law also limited the amount of punitive damages that could be paid. Depending on the size of the organization, the allowable damage range is from $50,000 to $300,000 for each instance of violation of the law. Punitive damages can only be

> ■ The **Civil Rights Act of 1991** makes it easier for individuals who feel they have been discriminated against to take legal action against organizations and provides for the payment of compensatory and punitive damages in cases of discrimination under Title VII.

paid if the employer intentionally discriminates against someone or if the employer discriminated with malice or reckless indifference to an individual's federally protected rights. In addition, the Civil Rights Act of 1991 allowed juries rather than federal judges to hear these cases.

This law also makes it possible for employees of U.S. companies working in foreign countries to bring suit against those companies for violation of the Civil Rights Act. The only exception to this provision is the situation in which a country has laws that specifically contradict some aspect of the Civil Rights Act. For example, Moslem countries often have laws limiting the rights of women. Foreign companies with operations in such countries would almost certainly be required to abide by local laws. As a result, a female employee of a U.S. company working in such a setting would not be directly protected under the Civil Rights Act. However, her employer would still need to inform her fully of the kinds of discriminatory practices she might face as a result of transferring to the foreign site and then ensure that when this particular foreign assignment were completed, her career opportunities would not have been compromised in any way.[33]

The Civil Rights Act of 1991 has had several important consequences. Because of the potential payoff for a successful discrimination suit, it has dramatically increased the number of suits that individuals have filed against businesses. This increase in lawsuits has dramatically clogged the Equal Employment Opportunity Commission; it has several thousand pending cases that it simply does not have time to process. For example, during the three years ending September 1994, the number of backlogged, unresolved cases in the hands of the EEOC more than doubled. While this backlog has now been reduced, several thousand claims are still pending. A second effect of the Civil Rights Act of 1991 has been to make organizations even more aware than they were before of the need to avoid any instance of discrimination in the employment relationship.

■ The **Americans with Disabilities Act of 1990 (ADA)** prohibits discrimination based on disability in all aspects of the employment relationship such as job application procedures, hiring, firing, promotion, compensation, and training, as well as other employment activities such as advertising, recruiting, tenure, layoffs, leave, and fringe benefits.

The Americans with Disabilities Act of 1990   The **Americans with Disabilities Act of 1990 (ADA)** is potentially one of the most important pieces of equal employment opportunity legislation to affect human resource management. The ADA was passed in response to growing criticisms and concerns about employment opportunities denied to people with various disabilities. For example, one survey found that of 12.2 million Americans not working because of disabilities, 8.2 million would have preferred to work. Similarly, another survey found that almost 80 percent of all managers surveyed found the overall performance of their disabled workers to be good to excellent. In response to these trends and pressures, the ADA was passed to protect individuals with disabilities from being discriminated against in the workplace.[34]

Specifically, the ADA prohibits discrimination based on disability and all aspects of the employment relationship such as job application procedures, hiring, firing, promotion, compensation, and training, as well as other employment activities such as advertising, recruiting, tenure, layoffs, leave, and benefits. In addition, the ADA also requires that organizations make reasonable accommodations for disabled employees as long as the accommodations themselves do not pose an undue burden on the organization. The act initially went into effect in 1992 and covered employers with twenty-five or more employees. It was expanded in July 1994 to cover employers with fifteen or more employees.

The ADA defines a disability as (1) a mental or physical impairment that limits one or more major life activities, (2) a record of having such an impairment, or (3) being regarded as having such an impairment. Clearly included within the domain of the ADA are individuals with disabilities such as blindness, deafness, paralysis, and similar disabilities. In addition, the ADA covers employees with cancer, a history of mental illness, or a history of heart disease. Finally, the act also covers employees regarded as having a disability, such as individuals who are disfigured or who for some other reason an employer feels will prompt a negative reaction from others. In addition, the ADA covers mental and psychological disorders such as mental retardation, emotional or mental illness (including depression), and learning disabilities.

On the other hand, individuals with substance-abuse problems, obesity, and similar non-work-related characteristics may not be covered by the ADA.[35] But because the ADA defines disabilities in terms of limitations on life activities, myriad cases continue to be raised. For example, in recent years workers have attempted to claim protection under the ADA on the basis of ailments ranging from alcoholism to dental problems! These activities have led some to question whether the ADA is being abused by workers rather than serving to protect their rights.[36]

In fact, the definition of a disability and what constitutes a "reasonable accommodation" pose the greatest potential problems for the human resource manager. Individuals who are confined to wheelchairs, are visually impaired, and/or have similar physical disabilities are usually quite easy to identify, but many employees may suffer from "invisible" disabilities that might include physical problems (e.g., someone needing dialysis) as well as psychological problems (acute anxiety) and learning disabilities (such as dyslexia). Thus it is not always obvious who among a group of employees is actually eligible for protection under the ADA.[37]

One area of coverage where the courts and EEOC (the agency charged with the administration of the ADA) have taken a fairly clear position deals with AIDS and HIV in the workplace. Both AIDS and HIV are considered disabilities under the Americans with Disabilities Act, and employers cannot legally require an HIV test or any other medical examination as a condition for making an offer of employment. After an offer of employment has been extended, however, organizations can make that offer contingent on the individual taking a physical examination. If an individual is found to be HIV positive, an employer cannot discriminate against that job applicant in a hiring decision, although it might be permissible to reassign the person in certain industries such as food services.

Essentially, organizations must follow a certain set of guidelines and employ common sense when dealing with AIDS-related issues. For example, they must treat AIDS like any other disease that is covered by law, they must maintain confidentiality of all medical records, they cannot discriminate against a person with AIDS, they should strive to educate coworkers about AIDS, they cannot discriminate against AIDS victims regarding training or consideration for promotion in the organization, and they must accommodate or make a good-faith effort to accommodate AIDS victims.

While taking a fairly clear position on AIDS and HIV, the EEOC is still working to develop guidelines and interpretations to allow organizations to comply more effectively in other areas of coverage. The U.S. Supreme Court took a major step toward clarifying the ADA in mid-1999, however. In a landmark decision, the Court ruled that individuals who can correct or overcome their disabilities through medication or other means are not protected by the ADA. For example, if a worker can correct his or her vision by wearing corrective lenses but prefers not to do so, an employer no longer must make accommodation for that individual.[38]

In addition, the reasonable accommodation stipulation adds considerable complexity to the job of human resource manager and other executives in organizations. Clearly, for example, organizations must provide ramps and wide hallways to accommodate individuals confined to a wheelchair. At the same time, however, providing accommodations for other disabilities may be more complex. If an applicant for a job takes an employment test, fails the test (and so is not offered employment), and *then* indicates that he or she has a learning disability (for example) that makes it difficult to take paper-and-pencil tests, the applicant probably can demand an accommodation. Specifically, the organization would likely be required either to find a different way to administer the test or to provide the applicant with additional time to take the test a second time before making a final decision. Likewise, an existing employee diagnosed with a psychological disorder may be able to request on-site psychological support.

Recently, yet another issue involved with granting accommodations has been identified.[39] The nature of many accommodations granted to employees is such that other employees who are not disabled and who are not requesting an accommodation are unlikely to be envious or resentful about the accommodation. But this is not the case for all requested accommodations. For example, a woman claimed that having every Friday off was the only accommodation that would help to reduce her stress at work.[40] What if the organization granted her that accommodation? Surely other employees would wonder why they could not have Fridays off, especially since stress is not typically a visible disability. This situation would lead to resentment and potentially to other problems. Therefore, although the ADA does not consider coworker reactions as relevant to determining whether or not an accommodation is reasonable, the knowledgeable human resource manager will at least think about how others might react to an accommodation when trying to deal with the legal requests of employees with disabilities.

■ The **Family and Medical Leave Act of 1993** requires employers with more than fifty employees to provide up to twelve weeks of unpaid leave for employees after the birth or adoption of a child; to care for a seriously ill child, spouse, or parent; or in the case of an employee's own serious illness.

The Family and Medical Leave Act of 1993   The **Family and Medical Leave Act of 1993** was passed in part to remedy weaknesses in the Pregnancy Discrimination Act of 1979. The law requires employers with more than fifty employees to provide up to twelve weeks of unpaid leave for employees after the birth or adoption of a child; to care for a seriously ill child, spouse, or parent; or in the case of an employee's own serious illness. The organization must also provide the employee with the same or comparable job upon the employee's return.[41]

The law also requires the organization to pay the health-care coverage of the employee during the leave. However, the employer can require the employee to reimburse these health-care premiums if the employee fails to return to work after the absence. Organizations are allowed to identify key employees, specifically defined as the highest paid 10 percent of their workforce, on the grounds that granting leave to these individuals would grant serious economic harm to the organization. The law also does not apply to employees who have not worked an average of twenty-five hours a week in the previous twelve months.[42]

Clearly, a substantial body of laws and regulations govern equal employment opportunity. Many people argue, of course, that all these laws and regulations are necessary. Without them, organizations might either intentionally or unintentionally revert to former employment practices that led to illegal discrimination

POINT | COUNTERPOINT

Too Much Human Resources Regulation?

Human Resources and the Law: As should be clear to you after reading this chapter, many laws deal with the human resource management function. Since the 1960s and the passage of the Civil Rights Act, the number of new regulations and guidelines has increased, and a backlash has begun to develop against some of these regulations. Some of the criticism began when President Reagan publicly joked about OSHA safety regulations that explained how to use a ladder, and more recently many people of all races have begun speaking out against affirmative action, suggesting that it leads to reverse discrimination. Is there too much regulation in the human resource field? Do these regulations put organizations at a competitive disadvantage?

POINT ... There is too much regulation of human resources activities because ...	COUNTERPOINT ... Human resources regulations are beneficial because ...
So many individuals are members of protected classes that no one is really protected.	Everyone is protected by nondiscrimination laws, not only members of protected classes.
The laws against discrimination have already done their job, so women and minorities can compete for any job.	Women still earn less than 80 percent of what men earn (on average), and the poverty rate among African-Americans is still several times higher than it is for white Americans.
Continuing such regulations, especially in light of recent improvements, actually results in reverse discrimination. This trend is most obvious under quota systems.	Reverse discrimination is illegal. Quotas are considered reverse discrimination unless imposed by court order.
Organizations should have the right to select whomever they believe is the most qualified. Not to do so would be in violation of stockholder expectations.	Nothing in the law or in any court decision would force an organization to hire less-qualified individuals. It is important to realize that qualified means "able to do the job." A hiring system based on racism would actually be harmful to a firm's effectiveness.
No one can understand the complex regulations, which often make no sense and may even contradict each other.	The laws are complex and court decisions suggest interpretation that may be contradictory, but the same could be said for all other U.S. laws. Should we abandon them all?

So ...   There are many misconceptions about antidiscrimination legislation. Quotas and reverse discrimination are illegal under the law, although it may sometimes seem as though organizations are discriminating against majority-group applicants and employees. The law simply requires organizations *not* to discriminate against persons who are members of a protected class. In fact, such discrimination would actually result in less-qualified persons being hired. The key, however, is to focus on the level of performance predicted by a test score, not on the test score itself. When viewed in this light, the goals of the law and the goals of the organization are not in conflict.

against large numbers of people. On the other hand, some critics argue that the regulatory environment has grown too complex. They point to the myriad and occasionally contradictory rules and regulations that have created a "bureaucratic jungle" that is just too hard to negotiate. The arguments on both sides of this issue are highlighted in the Point/Counterpoint feature for this chapter.

FIGURE 3.4   Investigating and Resolving a Discrimination Complaint

MARY SMITH believes she has been discriminated against at work. She was passed over for a promotion to supervisor, and believes it was because she was a woman, rather than because she was unqualified. Specifically, all candidates for promotion must be approved by their immediate supervisor, and most of these supervisors are older white men who have been heard to say that women should not be promoted. In fact, almost no women have been promoted to supervisor in this organization. What can Mary do?

STEP 1: Mary files a complaint with her local or state EEO agency.
STEP 2: Local/state EEO agency agrees to investigate Mary's claim on behalf of EEOC, and the agency contacts Mary's employer to determine whether the claim has any merit.

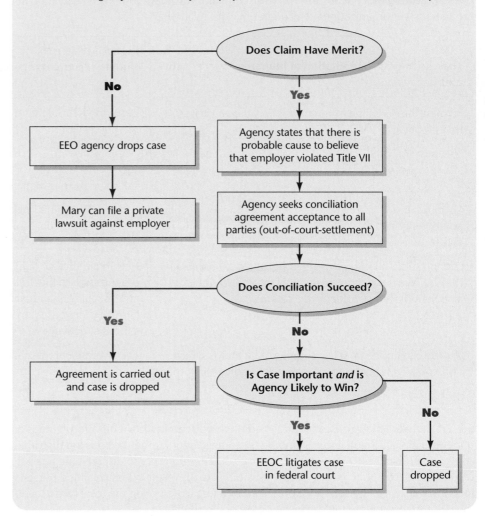

Enforcing Equal Employment Opportunity

The enforcement of equal opportunity legislation generally is handled by two agencies. As noted earlier, one agency is the Equal Employment Opportunity Commission (EEOC) and the other is the Office of Federal Contract Compliance Procedures (OFCCP). The EEOC is a division of the Department of Justice. It was created by Title VII of the 1964 Civil Rights Act and today is given specific

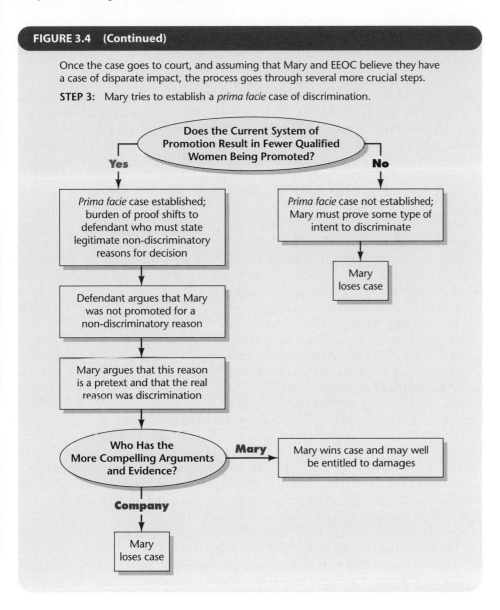

FIGURE 3.4 (Continued)

Once the case goes to court, and assuming that Mary and EEOC believe they have a case of disparate impact, the process goes through several more crucial steps.

STEP 3: Mary tries to establish a *prima facie* case of discrimination.

Does the Current System of Promotion Result in Fewer Qualified Women Being Promoted?

Yes → *Prima facie* case established; burden of proof shifts to defendant who must state legitimate non-discriminatory reasons for decision

No → *Prima facie* case not established; Mary must prove some type of intent to discriminate → Mary loses case

Defendant argues that Mary was not promoted for a non-discriminatory reason

Mary argues that this reason is a pretext and that the real reason was discrimination

Who Has the More Compelling Arguments and Evidence?

Mary → Mary wins case and may well be entitled to damages

Company → Mary loses case

responsibility for enforcing Title VII, the Equal Pay Act, and the Americans with Disabilities Act. The EEOC has three major functions: (1) investigating and resolving complaints about alleged discrimination, (2) gathering information regarding employment patterns and trends in U.S. businesses, and (3) issuing information about new employment guidelines as they become relevant.

The first function is illustrated in Figure 3.4, which depicts the basic steps that an individual who thinks she has been discriminated against in a promotion decision might follow to get her complaint addressed. In general, if an individual believes that she or he has been discriminated against, the first step in reaching a resolution is to file a complaint with the EEOC or a corresponding state agency. The individual has 180 days from the date of the incident to file the complaint. The EEOC will dismiss out of hand almost all complaints that exceed the 180-day time frame for filing. After the complaint has been filed, the EEOC assumes responsibility for investigating the claim itself. The EEOC can take up to sixty days to investigate a complaint. If the EEOC either finds that the complaint is not valid or does not complete the investigation within a sixty-day period, the individual has the right to sue in a federal court.

If the EEOC believes that discrimination has occurred, its representative will first try to negotiate a reconciliation between the two parties without taking the case to court. Occasionally, the EEOC may enter into a *consent decree* with the discriminating organization. This consent decree is essentially an agreement between the EEOC and the organization that stipulates that the organization will cease certain discriminatory practices and perhaps implement new affirmative action procedures to rectify its history of discrimination.

On the other hand, if the EEOC cannot reach an agreement with the organization, two courses of action may be pursued. First, the EEOC can issue a right-to-sue letter to the victim; the letter simply certifies that the agency has investigated the complaint and found potential validity in the victim's allegations. Essentially, that course of action involves the EEOC giving its blessings to the individual to file suit on his or her own behalf. Alternatively, in certain limited cases, the EEOC itself may assist the victim in bringing suit in federal court. In either event, however, the lawsuit must be filed in federal court within 300 days of the alleged discriminatory act. The courts follow this guideline very strictly, and many valid complaints have lost standing in court because lawsuits were not filed on time. As already noted, the EEOC has recently become backlogged with complaints stemming primarily from the passage of the newer civil rights act. One recent court case that involved the implementation of a discriminatory seniority system was settled in such a way that it helped provide the grounds for amending Title VII to provide exceptions to the 300-day deadline for filing a lawsuit.

The EEOC recently announced a new policy for prioritizing pending complaints to help clear its backlog and to provide better enforcement of the law. When a new complaint is filed, a case officer quickly reviews it and makes a judgment about its merits. Cases that appear to reflect a strong likelihood of discrimination are then given higher priority than are cases that appear to have less merit. Even higher priority is given to those cases that appear to have the potential for widespread or classwide effects.[43]

The second important function of the EEOC is to monitor the hiring practices of organizations. Every year all organizations that employ 100 or more individuals must file a report with the EEOC that summarizes the number of women and minorities that the organization employs in nine different job categories. The EEOC tracks these reports to identify potential patterns of discrimination that it can then potentially address through class-action lawsuits.

The third function of the EEOC is to develop and issue guidelines that help organizations determine whether their decisions are violations of the law enforced by the EEOC. These guidelines themselves are not laws, but the courts have generally given them great weight when hearing employment discrimination cases. One of the most important set of guidelines is the uniform guidelines on employee selection procedures developed jointly by the EEOC, the U.S. Department of Labor, the U.S. Department of Justice, and the U.S. Civil Service Commission. These guidelines summarize how organizations should develop and administer selection systems to avoid violating Title VII. The EEOC also frequently uses the Federal Register to issue new guidelines and opinions regarding employment practices that result from newly passed laws.[44] This activity has been particularly important in recent years as a result of the passage of the Americans with Disabilities Act.[45]

The other agency primarily charged with monitoring equal employment opportunity legislation is the Office of Federal Contract Compliance Procedures (OFCCP). The OFCCP is responsible for enforcing the executive orders that cover companies doing business with the federal government. Recall from our earlier discussion that businesses with contracts of more than $50,000 cannot discriminate based on race, color, religious beliefs, national origin, or gender, and they must have a written affirmative action plan on file.[46]

The OFCCP conducts yearly audits of government contractors to ensure that they have been actively pursuing their affirmative action goals. These audits involve examining a company's affirmative action plan and conducting on-site visits to determine how individual employees perceive the company's affirmative action policies. If the OFCCP finds that its contractors or subcontractors are not complying with the relevant executive orders, then it may notify the EEOC, advise the Department of Justice to institute criminal proceedings, or request that the Secretary of Labor cancel or suspend contracts with that organization. This latter step is the OFCCP's most important weapon because it has a clear and immediate impact on an organization's revenue stream.

While the EEOC and the OFCCP are the two primary regulatory agencies for enforcing equal employment legislation, it is also important to recognize that other agencies and components of our government system also come into play. The Department of Labor and the Department of Justice, for example, are both heavily involved in the enforcement of equal employment opportunity legislation. The U.S. Civil Service Commission is also actively involved for government organizations where civil-service jobs exist. The U.S. judicial systems reflected by our courts also play an important role in enforcing all human resource management legislation.

LEGAL ISSUES IN COMPENSATION

As noted earlier, most employment regulations are designed to provide equal employment opportunity. However, some legislation goes beyond equal employment opportunity and really deals more substantively with other issues. One such area is legislation involving compensation. We introduce this legislation here and return to it in Chapter 11.

Legal Perspectives on Total Compensation

Over the years the federal government has passed several laws dealing with total compensation. The most far-reaching of these laws has been the Fair Labor Standards Act. The **Fair Labor Standards Act (FLSA)**, passed in 1938, established a minimum hourly wage for jobs. The rationale for this legislation was to ensure that everyone who works would receive an income sufficient to meet basic needs. The first minimum wage was $0.25 an hour. Of course, this minimum wage has been revised many times and is currently $5.15 per hour.

The FLSA was amended in 1990 to permit a subminimum training wage equal to the greater of $3.35 per hour or 85 percent of the minimum wage. Employers are permitted to pay this subminimum wage to any new employee who is under the age of twenty for up to ninety days. The rationale for this amendment was that organizations would be motivated to hire younger employees and to

■ The **Fair Labor Standards Act (FLSA),** passed in 1938, established a minimum hourly wage for jobs.

provide them with training because they could pay them a lower wage for this initial period of time. This amendment also causes a dilemma for managers in some situations—the FLSA amendment clearly provides an incentive for hiring more young workers, yet the firm is still forbidden from discriminating against older workers because of the ADEA!

For the first time, the FLSA also formally defined the workweek in the United States as forty hours per week. It further specifies that all full-time employees must be paid at a rate of one and a half times their normal hourly rate for each hour of overtime work beyond forty hours in a week. This hourly rate includes not only the base wage rate but also components such as piece-rate payment and bonuses. Note, however, that the law makes no provision for daily work time. Thus, while a normal workday might be considered eight hours, an employer is actually free to schedule, say, ten or twelve hours in a single day without paying overtime as long as the weekly total does not exceed forty hours.

Not all employees are covered by the FLSA. Although several factors are used to determine who is covered, the primary distinguishing characteristic is the basis for payment. The FLSA primarily covers workers who are called nonexempt, which refers to occupations where individuals are paid on an hourly basis. Exempt employees (which refers to the fact that they are exempt from the minimum wage and overtime provisions of the FLSA), on the other hand, include executive, professional, administrative, and outside sales employees who are generally paid on a monthly or annual basis. The determination of exempt status depends on job responsibilities and standards. The actual determination of whether or not a job is exempt is a fairly complicated process. Several criteria are used to determine whether or not an individual's job is exempt from the FLSA. For professional employees, these criteria include consistently exercising discretion or judgment, and doing work requiring knowledge generally acquired by prolonged specialized study. For executives, these criteria include having control (or great influence) over hiring, firing and promotion, and exercising discretionary powers.

The FLSA also includes child labor provisions. Although these were much more important in earlier decades, these provisions still provide protection for persons 18 years of age and under. They include forbidding the employment of minors between 16 and 18 in hazardous occupations such as mining and meat-packing, and restrict the ability of persons under 16 years of age to be employed in work destined for interstate commerce. They also provide limits to the number of hours that persons under 16 can work.

Legal Perspectives on Other Forms of Compensation

■ The **Employee Retirement Income Security Act of 1974 (ERISA)** was passed to guarantee a basic minimum benefit that employees could expect to be paid at retirement.

Another important piece of legislation that affects compensation is the **Employee Retirement Income Security Act of 1974 (ERISA)**. This law was passed to protect employee investments in their pensions and to ensure that employees would be able to receive at least some pension benefits at the time of retirement or even termination. ERISA does not mean that an employee must receive a pension, rather it is meant to protect any pension benefits to which the employee is entitled. (This topic will be discussed in somewhat more detail in Chapter 13.) ERISA was passed in part because some organizations had abused their pension plans in their efforts to control costs or to channel money inappropriately to other uses within the organization and in part because of corruption.

Government regulations cover almost every aspect of employee compensation. All managers, therefore, need to have a basic understanding of the legal context of pay, working hours, and benefits. Human resource managers need a complete and thorough understanding of these issues.

LEGAL ISSUES IN LABOR RELATIONS

Another area of human resource management where various government regulations are extremely important is labor relations. The term *labor relations* generally refers to the formal and legal relationship between an organization and some or all of its workers who have formed and joined a labor union. We introduce these regulations here and then cover them in more direct relation to unions in Chapter 14.

Unionization and the Law

The **National Labor Relations Act,** or **Wagner Act,** was passed in 1935 in an effort to control and legislate collective bargaining between organizations and labor unions. Prior to this time the legal system in the United States was generally considered hostile to labor unions. The Wagner Act was passed in an effort to provide some sense of balance in the power relationship between organizations and unions. The Wagner Act describes the process through which labor unions can be formed and the requirements faced by organizations in dealing with those labor unions. The Wagner Act served to triple union membership in the United States and granted labor unions significant power in their relationships with organizations.

Following a series of crippling strikes, however, the U.S. government concluded that the Wagner Act had actually shifted too much power to labor unions. As a result, businesses had been placed at a significant disadvantage. To correct this imbalance, Congress subsequently passed the **Taft-Hartley Act** in 1947 and the **Landrum-Griffin Act** in 1959. Both of these acts regulate union actions and their internal affairs in a way that puts them on an equal footing with management and organizations. The Taft-Hartley Act also created the National Labor Relations Board (NLRB), which was charged with enforcement of the act.

Although the basic issues of unionization and collective bargaining have become pretty well established, some legal issues have emerged in this area. The Taft-Hartley Act guarantees these rights but also guarantees that these unions should be independent. This issue has come up in two fairly recent cases. More important for the future, in both these cases, the company was involved in setting up autonomous work teams that were empowered to make certain decisions about employees. In *Electromation* v. *NLRB*,[47] the National Labor Relations Board ruled that the company's "action committees," formed to deal with employee

Threatened strikes by employees and threatened lockouts by employers are two weapons used during the collective bargaining process. But the goal of all collective bargaining is to reach an agreement, not to strike or lockout workers. Nonetheless, sometimes things don't work out. In September 2002, after a number of rallies and protests by the International Longshore and Warehouse Union at several ports in California, the shippers called a lockout that kept the union employees from the ships and the cargo on those ships. The lockout resulted in tons of unloaded cargo, as shown here, the closing of all West Coast ports, and the loss of over $1 billion per day. The lockout lasted 12 days, and ended only when President Bush invoked the Taft-Hartley Act and ordered talks to resume and the parties to reopen the ports.

■ The **National Labor Relations Act, or Wagner Act,** was passed in an effort to control and legislate collective bargaining between organizations and labor unions.

■ The **Taft-Hartley Act and the Landrum-Griffin Act** regulate union actions and their internal affairs in a way that puts labor unions on an equal footing with management and organizations.

working conditions and staffed by employees, actually constituted a threat to the union already in place in the company. These action committees, which the NLRB ruled were dominated by management, were seen as an alternative way to deal with problems concerning working conditions and could allow the company to circumvent the union and the collective-bargaining process. As such, the company was found in violation of the Taft Hartley Act. In a similar case, *E.I. Du Pont de Nemours* v. *NLRB,*[48] the board ruled that Du Pont's safety committees were essentially employer-dominated labor organizations and thus were in violation of the Taft Hartley Act.

Collective Bargaining and the Law

Collective bargaining is the process used to negotiate a labor contract between a union and company management. Each of the laws noted above, as well as several other sets of regulations, precisely govern the steps involved in this negotiation process and carefully spell out what each side can and cannot do. Given the complexities of this process, we discuss it in detail in Chapter 14. Several important laws govern relationships between organizations and labor unions. Given both the complexities and the significance of these relationships and the importance of good labor relations, most of the larger organizations use dedicated specialists to handle union-related issues. All managers, however, need to understand the basic legal context of labor relations.

LEGISLATION AND EMPLOYEE RIGHTS

The final area of legislation that has a strong impact on the job of the human resource manager comes in the broad area of employee rights. Although the relative weight given to employee versus employer rights shifts over time, there has always been an attempt to consider the rights of both parties in legislation. We discuss employee rights and responsibilities more fully in Chapter 17, but it is important to note briefly the legal aspects of employee rights in this chapter.

Employee Safety and Health

■ The **Occupational Safety and Health Act of 1970 (OSHA)** grants the federal government the power to establish and enforce occupational safety and health standards for all places of employment directly affecting interstate commerce.

Employees also have the right to work in safe and healthy environments, and these rights continue to be important in organizations. The **Occupational Safety and Health Act of 1970 (OSHA)** is the single most comprehensive piece of legislation regarding worker safety and health in organizations. OSHA granted the federal government the power to establish and enforce occupational safety and health standards for all places of employment directly affecting interstate commerce. The Department of Labor was given power to apply the standards and enforce the provisions of OSHA. The Department of Health was given responsibility for conducting research to determine the criteria for specific operations or occupations and for training employers to comply with the act itself. OSHA also makes provisions through which individual states can substitute their own safety and health standards for those suggested by the federal government.

The basic premise of OSHA (also known as the *general duty clause*) is that each employer has an obligation to furnish each employee with a place of employment that is free from hazards that can cause death or physical harm. OSHA is generally enforced through inspections of the workplace by OSHA inspectors, and fines can be imposed on violators. Again, we will deal with these issues in more detail in Chapter 15.

Privacy Issues at Work

In the twenty-first century, issues of privacy are more important to Americans than ever before. Therefore, it is not surprising that privacy at work has become more important as well. The history of legislation dealing with privacy at work, however, actually goes back several years. The **Privacy Act of 1974** applies directly to federal employees only, but it has served as the impetus for several state laws. Basically, this legislation allows employees to review their personnel file periodically to ensure that the information contained therein is accurate. Prior to this privacy legislation, managers could place almost any information they pleased in a personnel file and only certain other managers could see those files.

But the larger concerns with privacy these days relate to potential invasions of employee privacy by organizations. For example, organizations generally reserve the right to monitor the e-mail correspondence of employees. Presumably employees should be using company e-mail only for company business, so this practice may not be a problem, but it does mean that employees who receive unsolicited e-mails from suspect vendors (such as pornographic websites) may also have that information shared with their employer. Potential invasions of privacy are also related to two other areas of employee rights that are protected by law, and these areas are discussed next.

Drugs in the Workplace

The **Drug-Free Workplace Act of 1988** was passed to reduce the use of illegal drugs in the workplace. This law applies primarily to government employees and federal contractors, but it also extends to organizations regulated by the Department of Transportation and the Nuclear Regulatory Commission. Thus, long-haul truck drivers and workers at most nuclear reactors are subject to these regulations. The actual regulations themselves are aimed at establishing a drug-free workplace and include the requirement, in some cases, for regular drug testing.

But concerns over the problems of drugs at work have also led many other companies not covered by this law to establish drug-testing programs of their own. In fact, drug testing is becoming quite widespread, even though there is little hard evidence addressing the effectiveness of these programs.[49] The issue for the present discussion is whether these testing programs constitute an invasion of employee privacy. Many opponents of drug-testing programs argue that

Drug testing is growing in popularity in the U.S., as illustrated by this sign outside a Home Depot store in Illinois. Employees who are likely to use drugs on the job (as indicated by the presence of illegal substances in their blood or urine) are also likely to cause accidents and other problems at work. Yet some opponents view drug testing as invasive and point to the fact that there are a disturbing number of cases in which an applicant tests positive for drug use even when the person has not been using drugs. Nonetheless, the practice of drug testing is likely to continue to grow in the coming years.

■ The **Privacy Act of 1974** allows employees to review their personnel file periodically to ensure that the information contained therein is accurate.

■ **Drug-Free Workplace Act of 1988** was passed to reduce the use of illegal drugs in the workplace. The regulations are aimed at establishing a drug-free workplace and include the requirement, in some cases, for regular drug testing.

drug testing is clearly appropriate for cases where there is some "reasonable" basis for suspected drug use, but not otherwise. Others argue that organizations that test for drug use often do not test for alcohol use. Of course, alcohol consumption is not illegal, but this related issue then raises the question of the purpose of drug testing. Presumably organizations are concerned about drug use on the job because they believe that it affects performance. If this belief is true, then surely alcohol consumption on the job should be of equal concern, but it is not. On the other hand, do organizations have a right to investigate the behavior of employees when they are *not* on company time if the behavior does not affect performance on the job?

There are no easy answers to these questions, and so drug testing will likely continue to be an issue of employee versus employer rights. Of course, what makes the privacy issues here even more salient is the method generally used to test for drugs on the job. Urinalysis (by far the most common method) is extremely invasive and has been known to result in a fair number of false positive tests (i.e., employees are incorrectly identified as drug users). As a result, several alternatives have begun to appear in organizations, including testing of one's individual hairs.[50] Perhaps these new technologies will reduce some of the concerns over drug testing while providing employers the protection they deserve from drug use on the job.

Employment-at-Will

■ **Employment-at-will** is a traditional view of the employment relationship in which both employer and employee have the mutual right to terminate an employment relationship at any time, for any reason, and with or without advance notice to the other.

The concept of employment-at-will dates back to employment relationships in England at the beginning of the Industrial Revolution in the eighteenth century. The basic premise of **employment-at-will** is that both employer and employee have the mutual right to terminate an employment relationship at any time for any reason and with or without advance notice to the other. Specifically, the idea is that an organization employs an individual of its own free will and can therefore terminate that employment at any time for any reason. Over the last two decades, however, some employees have begun to challenge the employment-at-will doctrine by filing lawsuits against their former employers on the grounds of what they call wrongful discharge.[51]

We will discuss employment-at-will, including the growing body of exceptions to this doctrine that have emerged in the courts, in more detail in Chapter 8. But for now, it is worth noting how employee knowledge has become an issue in discussions about employment-at-will. The courts have long held that an employee with secret and proprietary technical knowledge, such as chemical formulas for a revolutionary new fertilizer or electronic specifications for a new computer module, could not simply resign and then turn that information over to a competitor. But in recent years this issue has been extended to areas such as general organizational practices, strategies, and business plans. With the continued evolution of information technology, this issue promises to become increasingly important to human resource managers responsible for recruiting and hiring new executives.

Plant Closings and Employee Rights

■ **Worker Adjustment and Retraining Notification (WARN) Act of 1988** requires than organizations employing at least 100 employees must provide notice at least sixty days in advance of closing a facility or laying off fifty or more employees.

The **Worker Adjustment and Retraining Notification (WARN) Act of 1988** stipulates than an organization employing at least 100 employees must provide notice at least sixty days in advance of plans to close a facility or lay off fifty or more employees. The penalty for failing to comply is equal to one day's pay (plus benefits) for each employee for each day that notice should have been given. An organization that closes a plant without any warning and lays off

1,000 employees would be liable for sixty days of pay and benefits for those 1,000 employees, which could translate into a substantial amount of money. The act also provides for warnings about pending reductions in work hours but generally applies only to private employers. There are exceptions to the WARN requirements; those exceptions are related to unforeseeable business circumstances such as a strike at a major employer or a government-enforced shutdown.[52]

We will discuss other issues related to reductions in the workforce in Chapter 8, but the events of September 11, 2001, constitute a clear example of an exception to the requirements about notification. It has been clear in all cases that no business could have reasonably foreseen and planned for such an attack, and therefore there is no issue about a failure to warn employees about closings and layoffs.

Ethics and Human Resource Management

Another important and related issue for all managers, not just human resource managers, is ethics.[53] Ethics is a separate concept from the law but is closely intertwined. **Ethics** refers to an individual's beliefs about what is right and wrong and what is good and bad. A person's set of ethics is formed by the societal context in which people and organizations function. In recent years, ethical behavior and ethical conduct on the part of managers and organizations have received increased attention, a trend fueled by scandals at firms such as Enron, Worldcom, Imclone, and Tyco International. The basic premise is that laws are passed by the government to control and dictate appropriate behavior and conduct in a society. The concept of ethics serves much the same purpose because of its premise about what is right and what is wrong.

But ethics and law don't always coincide precisely. For example, it may be perfectly legal for a manager to take a certain action, but some observers might find his or her action to be unethical. For example, an organization undergoing a major cutback might be able legally to terminate a specific employee who is nearing retirement age. But if that employee has a long history of dedicated service to the organization, many people could consider termination ethically questionable. Managers from every part of the organization must take steps to ensure that their behavior is both ethical and legal. Some organizations develop codes of conduct or ethical statements in an attempt to communicate their stance on ethics and ethical conducts publicly.

There is a difference between behavior at work that is illegal and behavior that is unethical, but sometimes the two converge. The legacy of Enron is still being written, but its now infamous illegal accounting practices have helped give new meaning to corporate corruption. Evidence is still coming to light to suggest that the culture at Enron supported corruption and lying. The company went from being the darling of business school cases about the new economy and how to reward and motivate performance to the poster child for greed and the problems that come from rewarding the bottom line at all costs. Several Enron executives have been sentenced to prison and more trials are still pending. (Enron Chairman Kenneth Lay is shown here being sworn in during a Senate Commerce Committee hearing.) Hopefully, this will serve as a cautionary tale for others who believe in corporate growth and wealth at all costs.

■ **Ethics** is an individual's beliefs about what is right and wrong and what is good and bad.

EVALUATING LEGAL COMPLIANCE

Given the clear and obvious importance as well as the complexities associated with the legal environment of human resource management, it is critically important that organizations comply with the laws and regulations that govern human resource management practices to the best of their ability. The assurance of compliance can best be done through a three-step process. The first step is to ensure that managers have a clear understanding of the laws that govern every aspect of human resource management. That is, all managers must understand and be intimately familiar with the various laws that restrict and govern their behavior vis-à-vis their employees.

Second, managers should rely on their own legal and human resource staff to answer questions and to review procedures periodically. Almost all larger organizations have a legal staff consisting of professionals trained in various areas of the legal environment of business. A human resource manager or other manager with a legal question regarding a particular employment issue or practice is well advised to consult the firm's attorney about the legality of that particular action.

And third, organizations may also find it useful to engage occasionally in external legal audits of their human resource management procedures. This audit might involve contracting with an outside law firm to review the organization's human resource management systems and practices to ensure that they comply with all appropriate laws and regulations. Such an external audit will, of course, be expensive and somewhat intrusive into the organization's daily routine. When properly conducted, however, external audits can keep an organization out of trouble.

Chapter Summary

The legal context of human resource management is shaped by various forces. The first step in this process is the actual creation of new regulation. The second step is the enforcement of those regulations. The third step is the actual practice and implementation of those regulations in organizations. Regulations exist in almost every aspect of the employment relationship.

The basic goal of all equal employment opportunity regulation is to protect people from unfair or inappropriate discrimination in the workplace. Illegal discrimination results from behaviors or actions by an organization or managers within an organization that cause members of a protected class to be unfairly differentiated from others. Four basic kinds of discrimination are disparate treatment, disparate impact, pattern or practice discrimination, and retaliation. Depending on the specific law, a protected class consists of all individuals who share one or more common characteristic, as indicated by that law.

The major laws and related regulations that affect equal employment opportunity include Title VII of the Civil Rights Act of 1964, Executive Order 11246, Executive Order 11478, the Equal Pay Act of 1963, the Age Discrimination and Employment Act (ADEA), the Vocational Rehabilitation Act of 1973, the Vietnam Era Veterans' Readjustment Act of 1974, the Pregnancy Discrimination Act of 1979, the Civil Rights Act of 1991, the Americans with Disabilities Act of 1990 (ADA), and the Family and Medical Leave Act of 1993. The enforcement of equal opportunity legislation generally is handled by the Equal Employment Opportunity Commission (EEOC) and the Office of Federal Contract Compliance Procedures (OFCCP.)

The most far-reaching law dealing with total compensation is the Fair Labor Standards Act, which was passed in 1938. This law established a minimum hourly wage for jobs. Another important piece of legislation that affects compensation is the Employee Retirement Income Security Act of 1974 (ERISA).

The National Labor Relations Act, or Wagner Act, was passed in 1935 in an effort to control and legislate collective bargaining between organizations and labor unions. Congress subsequently passed the Taft-Hartley

Act in 1947 and the Landrum-Griffin Act in 1959 to regulate union actions and their internal affairs.

Several related areas of human resource management are affected by laws and associated legal issues. These related areas include employee safety and health, (especially as related to the Occupational Safety and Health Act [OSHA]), various emerging areas of discrimination law (especially sexual harassment), employment-at-will, ethics, and human resource management.

Key Points for Future HR Managers

▶ Dealing with legal issues has become the most critical part of the human resource manager's job, and it is an area where a great deal of expertise is needed.

▶ Human resource managers must balance the needs of the organization with the need to obey the law.

▶ Human resource managers are generally responsible, under the law, for communicating the duties and responsibilities of line managers to those managers and for making sure that those line managers act appropriately.

▶ The Civil Rights Act remains the single most important piece of legislation for human resource management. Title VII outlaws discrimination on the basis of race, gender, color, religion, or national origin.

▶ The Civil Rights Act outlaws disparate treatment as well as disparate impact discrimination against members of protected classes under the law.

▶ Disparate treatment cases involve policies that systematically treat members of some groups differently than members of other groups. The only clear exception is called a bona fide occupational qualification (BFOQ), which is a narrow basis for what would otherwise be disparate treatment.

▶ Disparate impact cases involve using policies that, although they are applied equally to all employees, will have a more adverse impact on employees who are members of protected classes.

▶ Three methods are available for establishing a prima facie case of discrimination: violation of the four-fifths rule, population comparisons, and the McDonnell test. Once such a case has been established, the burden of proof shifts to the defendant.

▶ Reverse discrimination occurs when a practice or policy has a disparate impact on the majority group (such as white males). The potential for reverse discrimination exists when certain voluntary quotas are implemented.

▶ Sexual harassment is an important issue in organizations. Different types of sexual harassment exist, but all involve either unwanted attention or an uncomfortable workplace. Once the management of an organization has been notified that sexual harassment has occurred, the organization is legally responsible for correcting the offending practices.

▶ The Americans with Disabilities Act outlaws discrimination against individuals with disabilities. It also requires that an organization provide a reasonable accommodation to anyone who has a disability and requests such an accommodation. The definition of disability under this law is quite broad, and so the potential liability is quite large.

▶ The Fair Labor Standards Act provides for a minimum wage and overtime provisions and establishes child-labor laws.

▶ The Employee Income Security Act (ERISA) requires that an organization guarantee employee pension rights in certain ways if the organization plans to deduct the cost of pensions from its taxes.

▶ The Taft-Hartley Act recognizes employee rights to organize and bargain collectively, and organizations must be careful not to violate those rights.

▶ The Occupational Safety and Health Act (OSHA) requires that employees work in a safe work environment. It stipulates substantial penalties if these rights are violated.

▶ Employment-at-will limits an employee's right to keep his or her job and protects the employer's right to terminate employees for cause.

▶ Employees' rights to privacy usually involve statements in personnel files but also involve other issues relating to invasions of privacy by employers.

▶ Employers' rights to administer drug tests are somewhat limited because they can clash with employees' rights to privacy.

Key Points for Future General Managers

▶ The law represents a major constraint on corporate human resource practices.

▶ The Civil Rights Act is probably the single most important piece of legislation that addresses which human resource practices are allowed under the law.

▶ Under the Civil Rights Act, policies that are applied equally to all employees but have a different (and adverse) effect on employees based on race, gender, religion, color, or national origin are potentially illegal.

▶ Sexual harassment is outlawed under the Civil Rights Act, and the scope of activities covered here is quite broad.

▶ Laws also outlaw discrimination on the basis of disability and age.

▶ Still other laws regulate how people are paid, how organizations deal with unions (or attempts to unionize), and worker safety and privacy.

▶ No human resource decision should be made without consulting someone knowledgeable about the legal implications of the action. These consultations should include a professional human resource manager as well as a lawyer.

Review and Discussion Questions

1. Describe the process through which the legal context of human resource management is created.

2. Summarize the role of the Thirteenth and Fourteenth Amendments to the U.S. Constitution in equal employment opportunity.

3. What is illegal discrimination? What is legal discrimination?

4. Identify and summarize the various forms of illegal discrimination.

5. Identify and summarize five major laws that deal with equal employment opportunity.

6. Why is most employment regulation passed at the national level, as opposed to the state or local level?

7. Which equal employment opportunity laws will likely affect you most directly when you finish school and begin to look for employment?

8. Which equal employment opportunity law do you think is most critical? Which do you think is least critical?

9. Which equal employment opportunity law do you think is the most difficult to obey? Which do you think is easiest to obey?

10. In the case of a conflict between a legal and an ethical consequence of a human resource decision, which do you think should take precedence?

Closing Case

Seinfeld and Sexual Harassment

What role can a popular television show possibly play in a major sexual harassment lawsuit? As it turns out, a pretty big one! The show in question is *Seinfeld*, one of the most popular sit-coms in television history. The event that sparked the lawsuit took place in the corporate headquarters of Miller Brewing Company and involved Jerold MacKenzie, a fifty-five-year-old, nineteen-year Miller executive, and Patricia Best, his secretary.

The incident occurred about ten years ago. The *Seinfeld* episode in question involved a story in which the show's main character, Jerry Seinfeld, meets and starts dating a woman whose name he cannot recall. But he does recall that it rhymes with a part of the female anatomy. He subsequently spends the rest of the episode running through different possible names for the woman. She dumps him when she realizes that he doesn't know her name. After she leaves, he finally remembers that her name is Delores.

Mr. MacKenzie apparently found the show to be especially funny. On the day after the show aired, he made a point of bringing it up for discussion with Ms. Best. Ms. Best indicated that she had not seen the show. As he began to describe the show for her, she indicated to him that she didn't want to discuss it. Mr. MacKenzie persisted, however, and continued to push her into discussing it with him. When he couldn't bring himself to say the name of the female body part, however, he made a photocopy of a dictionary page containing the word and gave it to Ms. Best.

Ms. Best became quite upset and reported to Miller Brewing Company's human resource department that Mr. MacKenzie had sexually harassed her. She also indicated that he had harassed her on earlier occasions. A few days later, Mr. MacKenzie was summoned to a meeting with a group of Miller attorneys and a senior human resource manager. He was asked about the *Seinfeld* incident and he acknowledged that it had happened as Ms. Best had reported. He also indicated that he saw their discussion simply as office conversation and that Ms. Best had not seemed to be bothered or upset at the time of the conversation.

The next day Mr. Mackenzie was visited by another senior corporate executive; this executive indicated that he (MacKenzie) was being terminated for unacceptable management performance. The incident with Ms. Best was identified as a major part of the final decision to terminate MacKenzie's employment with Miller, but he was also told that it was part of a pattern of poor decisions that had already attracted the attention of senior managers. Mr. MacKenzie indicated surprise but left with little argument or discussion.

As time passed, however, Mr. MacKenzie gradually began to feel that he had been mistreated. Finally, in 1997 he reached the point where he felt compelled to take some action. After consulting with his attorney, he filed a lawsuit against Miller Brewing Company, the executive who had made the decision to terminate him, and Ms. Best. Among his charges were wrongful discharge and libel. After hearing both sides of the case, a jury of ten women and two men decided that he was right. Indeed, they so strongly believed that Mr. MacKenzie was a victim rather than a sexual harasser that they awarded unusually large judgments, including punitive damages, of $24.5 million against Miller Brewing Company, $1.5 million against Ms. Best (this amount was later dropped due to a legal technicality), and slightly over $600,000 against the executive who had terminated him.[54]

Case Questions

1. Do you think Mr. MacKenzie's actions constituted sexual harassment? Why or why not?

2. Do you think Miller Brewing Company's termination of Mr. MacKenzie was justified? Why or why not?

3. What is your opinion of the jury's decision?

Building HR Management Skills

 Purpose: Affirmative action was created as a way of directly and proactively attracting more qualified members of protected classes into the workforce. While most people believe that affirmative action has served a useful function, some people now believe that it is no longer needed. Specifically, they argue that companies today recognize the importance of hiring the best people possible and will continue to seek those individuals on their own, without the pressure of formal affirmative action. Others, however, believe that affirmative action is still necessary to meet its original objectives. The purpose of this exercise is to give you additional insights into the arguments surrounding affirmative action.

Step 1: Your instructor will ask you to form groups of seven members each. Using a random procedure, divide your group into two subgroups of three members each and a moderator.

Step 2: One subgroup will work together to develop a set of arguments about why affirmative action is still a necessary and important component of equal opportunity employment. The other group will work together to develop a set of arguments about why affirmative action is no longer a necessary and important component of equal employment opportunity.

Step 3: Reconvene as a group of seven. The moderator will randomly select one side to present its case first. That group will have three minutes to make its case. The second group will then take three minutes to make its case and one additional minute to rebut the first group. Finally, the first group will have one minute to rebut the arguments made by the second group.

Step 4: The moderator will then summarize the relative persuasiveness of each group regarding the affirmative action issue. In addition, the moderator should feel free to add whether or not either group did not bring up any additional thoughts he or she had about the issue.

Step 5: Develop a brief summary of the arguments made by both groups. Using whatever format is suggested by your instructor, share these arguments with the rest of the class.

Ethical Dilemmas in HR Management

 Assume that you are a human resource manager in a large manufacturing plant. The following facts summarize an important situation:

1. A potential safety hazard has been identified in a section of the factory.

2. You strongly recommend to the plant manager that this safety hazard be corrected immediately.

3. The plant manager agrees that the problem is a priority, although not one that is as important as you seem to feel.

4. Her plans are to reduce the number of people who work in the area as much as possible, and then correct the safety hazard next month when the plant will be shut down for a week while some new technological equipment unrelated to the safety hazard is installed.

5. Trying to correct the problem now would be very expensive, adding several thousands of dollars to the costs of correcting the problem next month when the plant is closed.

This morning you went to your health club before work. You usually go in the evening, but because of a conflicting social obligation, you changed your routine and exercised before work. While getting dressed in the locker room, you inadvertently overheard a conversation between two people outside the locker area. It seems that one is an OSHA inspector. This individual told his friend that he was scheduled to make an unannounced visit to a nearby manufacturing plant later in the week for an inspection. You were not trying to eavesdrop, and you didn't hear the entire conversation. Based on what you did hear, however, you are almost certain it is your plant that will be inspected.

Questions

1. What are the ethical issues in this situation?

2. What are the pros and cons for keeping this information to yourself versus telling your plant manager what you heard?

3. What do you think most managers would do? What would you do?

HR Internet Exercise

 One of the most critical issues facing all human resource managers today is compliance with various legal regulations. The following website summarizes most current lawsuits in federal courts involving claims of various forms of discrimination: **http://www.nyper.com**.

Visit this website and select any two categories of pending lawsuits. Then visit those locations and review some of the lawsuits. Choose two lawsuits from each area that seem interesting to you (for a total of four). Write a brief description of each lawsuit. Then describe the potential implications for you as a future human resource manager for each potential outcome of the lawsuits.

Questions

1. How useful is the Internet in keeping human resource managers informed about legal actions that may affect them?

2. Does relying on the Internet for legal information pose any risks?

3. What other legal information would you like to see on the Internet?

4

The Global Environment

CHAPTER OBJECTIVES

After studying this chapter you should be able to:

■ Describe the growth of international business.

■ Identify and discuss global issues in international human resource management.

■ Discuss the human resource management function in international business.

■ Identify and discuss domestic issues in international human resource management.

■ Describe the issues involved in managing international transfers and assignments.

■ Summarize the issues in international labor relations.

One of the most significant trends in U.S. business today is the growing practice of moving production to foreign factories in an effort to capitalize on lower labor costs. General Motors (GM) has been very successful with this practice, especially in Mexico. Almost 20 percent of the firm's North American manufacturing workforce is now based in Mexico. Indeed, GM and Delphi Automotive Systems, GM's huge parts-making subsidiary, are among the most attractive—and important—employers in Mexico.

"It's the turn of the [twentieth] century all over again, now, south of the border."

(Charles Robinson, U.S. auto industry consultant)*

The benefits of producing in Mexico are clear. Local wage standards mean that Mexican workers are paid about one-tenth the pay rate of their counterparts in Flint, Michigan, GM's other big North American production center. They also expect fewer benefits, and the government imposes fewer regulations on employers. The products that come out of the Mexican plants can be exported tariff-free back to the United States.

Mexican workers also agree that they are getting a good deal. For example, while their wages may seem low by U.S. standards, most of them are actually earning far more than they would be if they were working for Mexican firms in other parts of the country. They also generally feel that they have better benefits, more job security, improved job training, and greater opportunities for advancement than if they were employed elsewhere. Indeed, some observers feel that the northern Mexico region today is very much like Detroit was

seventy years ago because it has become a magnet for motivated but undereducated workers looking for a better way of life.

One factor that continues to support GM's growing pressure in Mexico, however, is that it does indeed generally benefit both the company and its workers. Provisions of NAFTA (the North American Free Trade Agreement) provide protection for domestic workers, and GM seems to be a good employer. Unlike corporate practices in other parts of the world (some of which are discussed later), GM's human resource strategy in Mexico seems to be well-conceived and effectively implemented.

But not everything is perfect. GM's biggest union, the United Auto Workers (UAW), is seriously concerned about what GM is doing and sees it as a major threat to the long-term job security of its own members in the United States. GM's plants in Mexico experience very high turnover—as much as 50 percent a year—in large part because many of their workers leave their families behind when they come north to work and then get lonely and return home. And many of the workers are poorly educated and must first be taught to read and write before true job-related training can even begin. In the event of a long-term slowdown in the auto industry, any major job cuts by GM could seriously undermine its current reputation as a major employer of choice in Mexico. But for the present at least, it seems to be a true win-win situation.[1] ■

It's no secret that international business is booming these days. Almost every large firm located anywhere in the world is always on the alert for new business opportunities anywhere else in the world. Such opportunities include new markets where products and services can be sold; new locations where products and services can be created for lower costs; and areas where new information, financing, and other resources may be obtained. To manage international expansion effectively, firms need skilled and experienced managers and employees who understand both specific individual foreign markets (such as Japan or Germany) and general international issues (including areas such as exchange rate fluctuations, political risk, and the cost of labor). One of the fastest growing and most important concerns for human resource managers in many companies today is preparing other managers for international assignments. In reality, however, this is only one part of international human resource management.

This chapter will explore international human resource management in detail. We begin with a general overview of the growth of international business. Global issues in international human resource management are then introduced and discussed. Next we examine the human resource function in international business. Domestic issues in international human resource management are identified and described, and then we describe the management of international transfers and assignments. Finally, we summarize the basic issues in international labor relations.

THE GROWTH OF INTERNATIONAL BUSINESS

International business is not a new phenomenon. Indeed, its origins can be traced back literally thousands of years as merchants plied their wares along ancient trade routes linking southern Europe, the Middle East, and the Orient. Silks, spices, grains, jade, ivory, and textiles were among the most popular goods forming the basis for early trade. Even in more recent times Columbus's voyages to the so-called New World were motivated by the economic goal of discovering new trade routes to the Far East. Wars have been fought over issues arising from international commerce, and the British Empire was built around the financial and business interests of the British nobility. In more recent years, however, several specific trends have emerged in international business that provide a meaningful context for the study of human resource management.

It is becoming increasingly difficult to separate domestic business from international business as globalization spreads to virtually all economic sectors. These employees in Silao, Mexico, assemble cars at a General Motors plant. The cars made there are sold in Mexico as well as in the United States and various foreign markets. Hence, it is clear that "GM Built" doesn't necessarily mean "Made in the USA."

The forces that shaped today's competitive international business environment began to emerge in the years following World War II. As a result of that global conflict, Japan and most of Europe were devastated. Roads and highways were destroyed and factories were bombed. The United States was the only major industrial power that emerged from World War II with its infrastructure relatively intact. Places not devastated by the war, such as South and Central America and Africa, were not major players in the global economy even before the war, and Canada had yet to become a major global economic power.

Businesses in war-torn countries had little choice but to rebuild from scratch. They were in the unfortunate position of having to rethink every facet of their business, including technology, productions, operations, finance, and marketing. Ultimately, however, this position worked to their advantage. During the 1950s, the United States was by far the dominant economic power in the world. Its businesses controlled most major marketplaces and most major industries. At the same time, however, Japan, Germany, and other countries were rebuilding their own infrastructures and developing new industrial clout.

During the 1960s this newly formed industrial clout first began to exert itself in the world marketplace. Firms from Germany (like Siemens, Daimler-Benz [now DaimlerChrysler], and Bayer) and Japan (like Toyota, NEC, and Mitsubishi) began to take on new industrial strength and slowly but surely began to challenge the dominance of U.S. firms in markets ranging from automobiles to electronics. Firms from other parts of Europe had also fully recovered and were asserting themselves in areas ranging from petroleum and energy (e.g., Shell and British Petroleum) to food (e.g., Nestlé and Cadbury), to luxury goods (e.g., LVMH and Gucci). By the late 1970s businesses from other countries emerged as major players in the world economy, and by the 1980s many of them had established dominant positions in their industries. At the same time, many U.S. firms had grown complacent, their products and services were not of high quality, and their manufacturing and production methods were outdated and outmoded.

Eventually, U.S. firms decided that they had little choice but to start over as well. Thus, during the latter part of the 1980s and into the early 1990s, many U.S. firms practically rebuilt themselves. They shut down or renovated old factories, developed new manufacturing techniques, and began to focus renewed emphasis on quality. By the mid-1990s, global competitiveness seemed to have become the norm rather than the exception. The United States, Japan, and Germany remained the three leading industrial powers in the world. However, other western European countries such as France, England, the Netherlands, Spain, and Belgium were also becoming increasingly important. In Asia, Taiwan, Singapore, and Malaysia were also emerging as global economic powers, with China's emergence as a global power looming on the horizon. At the beginning of the twenty-first century, there has been some slowing in the economic growth rates in Southeast Asia, but China has clearly come into its own as a world economic power.

Substantial developments in Europe (which we will discuss below) have strengthened the position of countries there. In North America, Canada and Mexico also began to show promise of achieving economic pre-eminence in the global marketplaces, and many countries in South America have also begun to globalize their operations. Figure 4.1 illustrates the regions of the world that are especially significant in today's global economy, and Table 4.1 shows the world's largest industrial corporations.

But several other developments in the world have an impact on the new global economy. First, many developed countries, such as the United States,

FIGURE 4.1 **Global Business Centers**

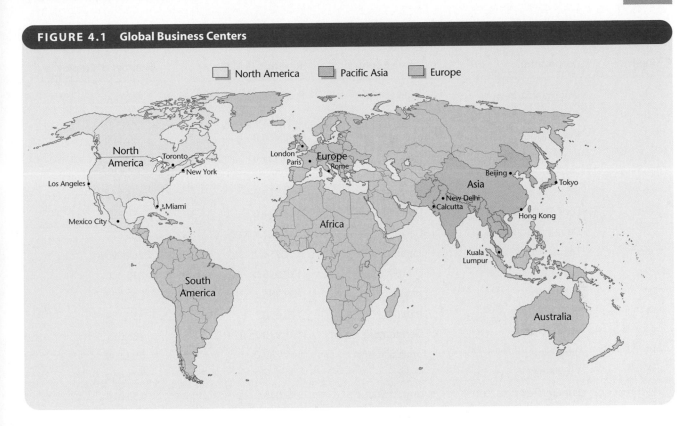

In summary, then, no business can afford to ignore the global environment.

Japan, and the countries of western Europe have experienced slowing rates of growth in their populations. This trend has implications for the demand for certain types of consumer goods as well as for the availability of individuals to work producing those goods. On the other hand, countries such as Mexico, India, Indonesia, and China (despite its one-child-per-couple policy) continue to experience rapid population growth. This growth is fueling a demand for international goods and also makes these locations attractive sites for new businesses or joint ventures. Furthermore, the collapse of the Japanese markets and the downturn in the U.S. stock market in 2002 (especially the high-tech sector) have proven how interdependent global economies really are. No global organization can ignore elections in Serbia, the independence movement in Timor, or attempts to strengthen the Japanese yen. All of these events, once seen as far removed from the concerns of American businesses, now have a strong and immediate impact on how firms in this country and other countries around the world do business. Finally, as we shall discuss below, the growth of regional economic alliances has also had a substantial impact on the global business community.

In summary, then, no business can afford to ignore the global environment. Even those businesses that do not sell their products and services in foreign markets are still likely to obtain at least some of their resources from foreign markets and most must compete with businesses from foreign countries as well. As we will see, however, businesses in today's global environment can take a wide variety of forms and they can adopt several different strategies for competing in this environment. And human resource management is a key component in each of these forms and strategies.

TABLE 4.1   The World's Largest Multinational Firms

Rank	Corporation	Home Country	Revenue ($ Millions)	Number of Employees
1	Wal-Mart Stores	United States	246,525.0	1,300,000
2	General Motors	United States	186,763.0	350,000
3	Exxon Mobil	United States	182,466.0	92,500
4	Royal Dutch/ Shell Group	Great Britain/ Netherlands	179,431.0	116,000
5	BP	Great Britain	178,721.0	115,250
6	Ford Motor Company	United States	163,871.0	350,321
7	DaimlerChrysler	Germany	141,421.1	365,571
8	Toyota Motor	Japan	131,754.2	264,096
9	General Electric	United States	131,698.0	315,000
10	Mitsubishi	Japan	109,386.1	47,370
11	Mitsui	Japan	108,630.7	37,734
12	Allianz	Germany	101,930.2	181,651
13	Citigroup	United States	100,789.0	252,500
14	Total Fina Elf	France	96,944.9	121,469
15	ChevronTexaco	United States	92,043.0	53,014
16	Nippon Telegraph & Telephone	Japan	89,644.0	207,400
17	ING Group	Netherlands	88,102.3	115,000
18	Itochu	Japan	85,856.4	39,109
19	International Business Machines	United States	83,132.0	315,889
20	Volkswagen	Germany	82,203.7	324,892
21	Siemens	Germany	77,205.2	426,000
22	Sumitomo	Japan	75,745.2	31,589
23	Marubeni	Japan	72,164.8	27,000
24	Verizon Communications	United States	67,625.0	229,497
25	American International Group	United States	67,482.0	80,000
26	Hitachi	Japan	67,228.0	339,572
27	U.S. Postal Service	United States	66,463.0	854,376
28	Honda Motor	Japan	65,420.4	126,900
29	Carefour	France	64,978.6	396,662
30	Altria Group	United States	62,182.0	166,000
31	AXA	France	62,050.8	78,142
32	Sony	Japan	61,334.6	161,100

TABLE 4.1 (Continued)

Rank	Corporation	Home Country	Revenue ($ Millions)	Number of Em...
33	Nippon Life Insurance	Japan	61,174.5	72,784
34	Matsushita Electric Industrial	Japan	60,744.3	288,324
35	Royal Ahold	Netherlands	59,454.6	270,739
36	ConocoPhillips	United States	58,384.0	57,300
37	Home Depot	United States	58,247.0	300,000
38	Nestlé	Switzerland	57,279.1	254,199
39	McKesson	United States	57,129.2	24,500
40	Hewlett-Packard	United States	56,588.0	141,000
41	Nissan Motor	Japan	56,040.8	127,625
42	Vivendi Universal	France	54,977.1	284,182
43	Boeing	United States	54,069.0	165,000
44	Assicurazioni Generali	Italy	53,598.9	59,753
45	Fannie Mae	United States	52,901.1	4,700
46	Fiat	Italy	52,612.5	189,969
47	Deutsche Bank	Germany	52,133.2	77,442
48	Credit Suisse	Switzerland	52,121.7	78,457
49	Munich Re Group	Germany	51,980.0	41,396
50	Merck	United States	51,790.3	77,300

Source: Data from http://www.fortune.com/fortune/global500 "The 2003 Global 500," July 21, 2003.

GLOBAL ISSUES IN INTERNATIONAL HUMAN RESOURCE MANAGEMENT

Various global issues in international human resource management must be addressed by any international firm. As shown in Figure 4.2, one issue is the development of an international human resource management strategy.[2] Another is developing an understanding of the cultural environment of human resource management. A third is developing an understanding of the political and legal environment of international business.

International Human Resource Management Strategy

The overall strategy of a business has to be logical and well-conceived, and so too must the effective management of a firm's international human resources be approached with a cohesive and coherent strategy. As a starting point, most

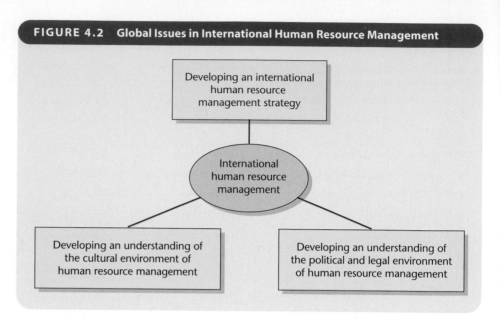

FIGURE 4.2 Global Issues in International Human Resource Management

Developing an international human resource management strategy

International human resource management

Developing an understanding of the cultural environment of human resource management

Developing an understanding of the political and legal environment of human resource management

international businesses today begin by developing a systematic strategy for choosing among home-country nationals, parent-country nationals, and third-country nationals for various positions in their organization.[3]

Some firms adopt what is called an **ethnocentric staffing model**. Firms that use this staffing model primarily use parent-country nationals to staff higher-level foreign positions. This strategy is based on the assumption that home-office perspectives and issues should take precedence over local perspectives and issues and that parent-country nationals will be more effective in representing the views of the home office in the foreign operation.[4] The corporate human resource function in organizations that adopt this mentality are primarily concerned with selecting and training managers for foreign assignments, developing appropriate compensation packages for those managers, and handling adjustment issues when the manager is reassigned back home. Local human resource officials handle staffing and related human resource issues for local employees hired to fill lower-level positions in the firm. Sony Corporation's operations in the United States follow this model. Sony Corporation of America, a wholly owned subsidiary of Sony Corporation, handles local human resource issues, but top executives at the firm's operations around the United States are Japanese managers from the firm's Japanese home office.

Other international businesses adopt what is called a **polycentric staffing model**, which calls for a much heavier use of host-country nationals throughout the organization, from top to bottom. Thus, the use of the polycentric staffing model is based on the assumption that such individuals (that is, host-country nationals) are better equipped to deal with local market conditions. Organizations using this approach usually have a fully functioning human resource department in each foreign subsidiary that is responsible for managing all local human resource issues for lower-level and upper-level employees alike. The corporate human resource function in such companies focuses primarily on coordinating relevant activities with their counterparts in each foreign operation. U.S. energy companies operating in Asia often adopt this model, especially because these op-

■ Firms that use the **ethnocentric staffing model** primarily use parent-country nationals to staff higher-level foreign positions.

■ The **polycentric staffing model** calls for heavy use of host-country nationals throughout the organization.

erations are often joint ventures between the U.S. company and one or more local companies.

Still other firms adopt what is called a **geocentric staffing model**. The geocentric staffing model puts parent-country nationals, host-country nationals, and third-country nationals in the same category. The firm then attempts to hire the best person available for a position, regardless of where that individual comes from. The geocentric staffing model is most likely to be adopted and used by fully internationalized firms such as Nestlé and Unilever.[5] In many ways, the corporate human resource function in geocentric companies is the most complicated of all. Every aspect of the human resource management process—planning, recruiting, selection, compensation, and training—must be undertaken from an international perspective. Each foreign subsidiary or operation still needs its own self-contained human resource unit to handle ongoing employment issues.

Understanding the Cultural Environment

The cultural environment of international business also poses a variety of more applied challenges and opportunities for human resource managers. A **country's culture** can be defined as the set of values, symbols, beliefs, and languages that guide behavior of people within that culture. A culture does not necessarily coincide precisely with national boundaries, but these two different constructs are sometimes similar in terms of geographic area and domain. While all managers in an international business need to be aware of cultural nuances (by definition human resource managers are concerned with people), they must be especially cognizant of the role and importance of cultural differences and similarities in workers from different cultures.

Cultural beliefs and values are often unspoken and may even be taken for granted by those who live in a particular country. When cultures are similar, relatively few problems or difficulties may be encountered. Human resource managers can extrapolate from their own experiences to understand their function in the other culture. Thus, U.S. managers often have relatively little difficulty doing business in England. Managers in both countries speak the same language and a common framework exists for understanding both commercial and personal relationships.

It is estimated that there are as many as 4 billion people in the world who earn less than $2,000 (U.S.) a year. This group represents a huge and largely untapped market for a wide variety of products. But families that earn between $6 and $7 a day are not likely to have much disposable income, and what disposable income they do have is likely to be spent on necessities. In fact, the World Bank estimates that people in low income nations, despite their large population, account for less than 4 percent of private consumption. How can companies who want to expand their markets change that picture? One way is to offer lower cost technology that can help people in poorer countries. For example, this farmer near Bangalore, India, is using a Simputer to collect information about crop prices so he can plan next year's plantings. At $200 the computer is still too expensive for many Indians, but the manufacturer plans to rent short-term access to the Simputer. Thus, many more people can afford to use the computer, and they can use it to increase their earnings. This, in turn, will allow them to buy more products.

More significant issues can arise, however, when considerable differences exist between the home culture of a manager and the culture of the country in which business is to be conducted. Thus, there is a higher likelihood of culturally related

The practice of U.S. firms' employing low wage workers and children in non-U.S. manufacturing facilities has been hotly debated. Nike is Vietnam's largest private employer. It employs 50,000 people and its plants export 22 million pairs of shoes annually. These workers are completing the assembly of Nike shoes in Cu Chi, Vietnam. Critics argue that Nike is exploiting the availability of cheap labor. But companies such as Nike argue that these workers are unlikely to find other work that pays as well or has working conditions that are as good. Is this really exploitation or a case in which Nike reduces costs while Vietnamese workers get better jobs?

■ The **geocentric staffing model** puts parent-country nationals, host-country nationals, and third-country nationals all in the same category, with the firm attempting always to hire the best person available for a position.

■ A **country's culture** can be defined as the set of values, symbols, beliefs, and languages that guide the behavior of people within that culture.

problems and difficulties between managers from, say, Canada and India. Differences in language, customs, and business and personal norms increase the potential for misunderstandings, miscommunication, and similar problems. In these instances, human resource managers must be careful to avoid overgeneralizing from their own experiences or perspectives.

Cultural differences can also have a direct impact on business practices in international situations. For example, the religion of Islam teaches that people should not make a living by exploiting the problems of others and that making interest payments is immoral. As a result, no outplacement consulting firms exist in Saudi Arabia and the Sudan (because outplacement involves charging a fee to help terminated workers cope with their misfortunes). As a result of these and myriad other cultural differences, then, managers may encounter unexpected complexities when doing business in countries where these sorts of cultural differences exist.

Language is another important cultural dimension that affects international human resource management practices. Most obviously, differences in specific languages such as English, Japanese, Chinese, and Spanish dramatically complicate the issues involved in dealing with international business. Unfortunately, U.S. managers who are fluent in different languages tend to be relatively rare. When a U.S. organization does find such an employee, that individual usually becomes a valuable asset. On the other hand, it is fairly common for Asian managers to learn English in school, and most European managers are multilingual. It is interesting to note that several years ago many U.S. colleges and universities (and especially business schools) began dropping foreign-language requirements. As it turns out, those decisions may result in some competitive disadvantage for managers educated in the United States.

Another cultural factor that is most directly related to human resource management practices has to do with roles that exist in different cultures. The United States has seen considerable change over the last few decades regarding the role of women in our society. For example, women have made considerable strides in pursuing and achieving career opportunities previously closed to them. In some parts of the world, however, the situation is quite different. In Japan, for example, women may still find it fairly difficult to launch a successful career. Similar situations exist in some European countries, as well as in almost all the countries in the Middle East. Some role differences are related to status and hierarchy. In the United States, for example, relatively little psychological distance exists between managers and subordinates, resulting in a certain degree of familiarity and informality. But in many Asian countries, this psychological distance is much greater, resulting in more formalized roles and less informal communication across levels in the organization.

Perhaps the most systematic study of national values was undertaken by a Dutch scholar named Geert Hofstede, who studied cultural differences among managers in fifty-three countries.[6] He defined five dimensions of culture:

- *Power distance* (status and authority differences between a superior and a subordinate)

- *Individualism versus collectivism* (the extent to which persons define themselves as individuals rather than as members of groups)

- *Masculinity versus femininity* (assertive, competitive, success-driven values versus quality of life, relationship-oriented values in society)

- *Uncertainty avoidance* (preference for structured rather than unstructured situations)

- *Time orientation* (emphasizing long-term values such as thrift and persistence versus short-term values such as fulfilling social obligations)

Hofstede's work has been influential in the field of international management and provides some useful general guidelines for what to expect when dealing with managers or employees from different countries.

But Hofstede's work has some limitations as well. The initial sample, although quite large (100,000), was drawn from a single organization (IBM). Thus, it is difficult to tell if some of the effects found in the study were due to country cultures or one or more elements of the corporate culture that all respondents shared. Even though the sample was large, it is still difficult to make generalizations across the entire populations of countries. For example, the United States was described as being the highest on individualism, in the middle on masculinity versus femininity and on time orientation, and quite low on power distance and uncertainty avoidance. But is this description true of all Americans? Surely not. It is not even clear that they describe the "typical" American (whoever that might be). Even within countries, for instance, regional and ethnic differences account for large differences in values. Thus, one must be careful not to overgeneralize from these results. Nonetheless, Hofstede's work provides some interesting and useful ideas about differences across cultures that are relevant to human resource managers.

Yet another significant cultural factor has to do with children. In the United States child labor is closely regulated and children traditionally attend school until they become young adults. In other countries, however, this practice may be quite different. For example, in Bangladesh it is quite common for children to be a major source of income for their families. Many children do not attend school at all and begin seeking jobs at a very young age. A business operating in an environment like Bangladesh, therefore, faces a significant dilemma. On the one hand, local cultural factors suggest that it is acceptable to hire young children to work for low wages because other businesses do the same. On the other hand,

POINT | COUNTERPOINT

Wages and Conditions in Foreign Plants

Wages and working conditions in some foreign plants are different from those in U.S. plants, even when the two plants are run by the same organization and are performing the same functions. The press has reported about the working conditions in Latin American plants that manufacture clothing for a company owned by Kathy Lee Gifford and about the working conditions in Asian plants that make the Nike sneakers touted by Michael Jordan. Why do these differences exist, and should U.S. companies be forced to do something about them?

The differences exist because of different expectations about wages and working conditions. U.S. firms simply pay workers in a third-world country what the workers there would otherwise earn, which is usually less than what U.S. workers doing the same job would earn.

POINT ... It makes sense for organizations to allow and even to encourage these difference because ...	COUNTERPOINT ... But on the other hand, this behavior is wrong, and U.S. firms should be forced to make changes because ...
Lower labor costs are exactly the reason the U.S. firm opens operations in these countries, and these savings allow the firm to be more competitive.	These jobs would otherwise be given to U.S. workers. The failure to do so leads to problems of unemployment and underemployment in the United States.
Wages are lower in these countries, so paying workers there what U.S. workers make would create inequalities.	U.S. companies could become a source of change, forcing other firms to raise wages and improve conditions for all workers.
Although wages are lower and conditions poorer, the cost of living is much lower in many of these countries, so that workers actually live fairly well.	Employees in foreign countries are often required to work under appalling conditions, and their wages are often not enough to alleviate their poverty.
Wages paid by U.S. firms and conditions in U.S.-owned operations are already much better than the alternatives for these foreign workers. Why should a company pay more or improve conditions more than it has to?	This is the basic issue—should U.S. firms have some social responsibility in the countries where they do business, or are these countries simply resources to be exploited?
U.S. firms are already helping these workers by providing jobs that otherwise would not be available.	This system deprives U.S. workers of jobs.

So ...   This issue is complex. When most Americans see how workers in Third World plants live and work, they are upset and call for change. We like to think of our country as being a source of positive change in the world, but should U.S. companies be held to a higher standard than foreign firms are in their own countries, especially if such a standard hurts competition? The answer is really a function of one's personal value system. How important is it to protect the rights and try to improve the lives of others? If one believes our country stands for something important, perhaps paying foreign workers more is a way to demonstrate it. On the other hand, if U.S. companies become less successful, they may not be in a position to help anyone. This issue is one we will continue to debate. What do you think?

this practice would be illegal and/or unethical by the standards that exist in most industrialized countries.

The human resource manager dealing with international issues thus faces two fundamental cultural challenges. One challenge is simply understanding and appreciating differences that exist in different cultures. The value of work, attitudes, orientation toward work, and common work-related attitudes and practices vary significantly from culture to culture, and the human resource manager needs to develop an understanding of these differences if she or he is to function effectively.[7]

The second challenge is more ethical in nature. On the one hand, many businesses relocate manufacturing facilities to other countries to capitalize on lower labor costs. Indeed, it is quite possible for a business from a country like Japan or the United States to set up a factory in Bangladesh, Pakistan, or other regions of the world and have minimal labor costs there. The ethical issue, however, is the extent to which this situation becomes exploitation. Many people, for instance, would agree that it is reasonable for a company to take advantage of low prevailing wage and benefit costs to achieve low-cost production. But if a company goes too far and truly begins to exploit foreign workers, problems may subsequently arise. This issue is illustrated in this chapter's Point/Counterpoint feature.

Understanding the Political and Legal Environment

It is also important for human resource managers in international businesses to understand the political and legal environment of the countries in which they do business. Figure 4.3 illustrates four fundamental aspects of the political and legal environment of international business that are of primary concern for human resource managers: government stability, potential incentives for international trade, controls on international trade, and the influence of economic communities on international trade. In addition, laws that affect the management of human resources are basic issues, but we will say more about those issues later.

Government stability can be thought of as either the ability of a given government to stay in power against opposing factions or as the permanence of government policies toward business. In general, companies prefer to do business in countries that are stable in both respects because managers have a higher probability of understanding how those governments affect their business. Recent events in the Middle East have indicated that some governments in that region may be less stable than had previously been believed because those governments face pressure from Muslim fundamentalists to establish governments more in line with the teachings of the Koran. The continuing struggles between Israelis and Palestinians threaten the stability of much of that region. Similar struggles between India and Pakistan, coupled with uncertainty over the future leadership of Afghanistan, also raise questions about stability in that region.

A major human resource issue relating to the topic of government stability is the extent to which expatriate managers, or any other representatives

Political forces are an important factor in the globalization of business. In 1959, the U.S. began a trade embargo against Cuba following the overthrow of the Batista regime by Fidel Castro. Since then, it has been illegal for U.S. companies to trade with Cuba; it is even illegal for U.S. citizens to bring Havana cigars into the United States. But politics have a way of changing, and the embargo is weakening. Fidel Castro, for instance, is shown here signing an agreement between his country and Archer Daniels Midland for almost $10 million worth of rice, soybeans, and soy oil. Nonetheless, U.S. citizens are still required to get official permission before traveling to Cuba, and Cuban cigars still cannot legally be brought into the United States!

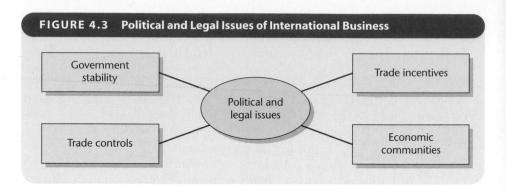

FIGURE 4.3   Political and Legal Issues of International Business

Government stability

Trade controls

Political and legal issues

Trade incentives

Economic communities

of a U.S. firm, may be put at risk as a result of political instability. For years extremist groups have targeted U.S. executives for terrorist activities. But since September 11, 2001, these fears have grown considerably. The kidnapping and assassination of journalist Daniel Pearl, for example, provided graphic evidence that U.S. employees assigned overseas can face considerable danger. In the post–September 11 world, many U.S.-based managers are more uncomfortable about traveling to parts of the world where they fear they may be threatened. Heightened security measures on planes and in airports have made these dangers salient to anyone undertaking foreign travel.

In addition, some firms continue to face situations where their managers are closely watched and/or even harassed by local government officials on the grounds that they are alleged illegal informants and/or spies for the U.S. government. Still another risk is the extent to which a business itself might become nationalized. The process of nationalization occurs when a government seizes the facilities of a company and declares them to be its own. Nationalization has occasionally occurred in the Middle East and in certain countries in South America.

Another aspect of the political and legal environment involves the incentives for international trade that are sometimes offered to attract foreign business. Occasionally, municipal governments offer foreign companies tax breaks and other incentives to build facilities in their area. Over the last few years, for example, both BMW and Mercedes have announced plans to build new assembly factories in the United States. In each instance, various state and local governments started what essentially became bidding wars to see who could attract the manufacturing facilities. Examples of incentives include reduced interest rates on loans, construction subsidies and tax incentives, and the relaxation of various controls on international trade. Some countries have also offered guaranteed labor contracts with local unions as a form of incentive designed to reduce the uncertainties an entering foreign business might face in negotiating its own initial labor contract.

A third dimension of the political and legal environment of international business consists of those very controls that some countries place on international trade. Several different controls exist. One is a *tariff,* essentially a tax collected on goods shipped across national boundaries. Tariffs may be levied by the exporting country, countries through which goods pass, and/or the importing country. The most common form of trade control, however, is the *quota,* a limit on the number or value of goods that can be traded. The quota amount is typically designed to ensure that domestic competitors will be able to maintain a predetermined market share. Honda Motors in Japan, for example, is allowed to export

Child Labor and International Business

For years, large juice distributors like Minute Maid, Tropicana, and Nestlé have bought fruit juices from suppliers in South America. But a few years ago, it was learned that many of these suppliers relied heavily on child labor to harvest oranges, lemons, and other fruit. Children as young as nine were commonly taken out of school by their impoverished parents and put to work in the citrus groves. The parents often saw no problem with this action because they themselves had also picked fruit when they were children.

In recent years, though, the situation has begun to change. For example, in 1997 the U.S. Congress amended a 1930 trade law to ban the importation of products made with child labor. Similarly, the International Brotherhood of Teamsters has also taken on a watchdog role to ensure that Brazilian exporters are held accountable for adhering to the law. Of course, critics claim that the teamsters' motivation is self-interest, but regardless of its reasons, the union is having a positive effect.

And many South American countries are also trying to stamp out child labor. For example, child advocacy groups in Brazil have helped pass a new labor code. One

"You can't take juice companies seriously about trying to eradicate child labor when they are promoting a system that clouds accountability in the workplace."

(Raimundo Limao de Mello, Brazilian attorney)*

of its provisions is a ban on child labor; another is the payment of $45 per month per child who stays in school and maintains good attendance records—the sum is about the same that the child might earn picking fruit. The juice companies themselves also claim to be imposing more stringent controls on their suppliers, although watchdog groups question their real commitment to eradicating child labor.

While it is difficult to trace accurately the activities of child fruit-pickers, most experts do agree that, slowly but surely, conditions are improving. For example, Brazilian government statistics suggest that child labor in general is down about 15 percent over the past three years. And more adults in Brazil also seem to be more aware of the importance of education and are actively discouraging fruit picking by children. But there is still a long way to go.

Sources: "U.S. Child-Labor Law Sparks a Trade Debate Over Brazilian Oranges," *Wall Street Journal*, September 9, 1998, pp. A1, A9 (*quote on p. A9); "Chile's Labor Law Hobbles Its Workers and Troubles the U.S.," *Wall Street Journal*, October 15, 1997, pp. A1, A14; "Sweatshop Police," *Business Week*, October 20, 1997, p. 39

exactly 425,000 automobiles each year into the United States. Sometimes, however, companies can circumvent quotas. Honda has built assembly factories in the United States for this purpose because the automobiles they produce within the United States do not count against the 425,000-unit quota.

For the international human resource manager, an important set of international controls involves the control of human resources. Some countries require that a foreign business setting up shop within its borders hire a minimum percentage of local employees to work there. For example, a country might require that 80 percent of the production employees and 50 percent of the managers of a foreign-owned business come from among the local citizenry. A less common but still salient factor is the control of international travel. For instance, some countries limit the number of trips that foreign managers can make in and out of their country in a given period of time. The HR Legal Brief in this chapter discusses a variation on this issue related to child labor in other countries.

A final aspect of the political and legal environment is the growing importance of the influence of economic communities. Economic communities consist of sets of countries that agree to reduce or eliminate trade barriers among their member nations. One of the most commonly cited economic communities is the

European Union (EU). The original EU members included Belgium, France, Luxembourg, Germany, Italy, and the Netherlands. Denmark, Ireland, the United Kingdom, Greece, Portugal, and Spain joined later. Austria, Finland, and Sweden have also been admitted most recently. Ten other countries, including Poland and Hungary, are under consideration for admission. For the past several years, these countries have been systematically working toward a unified market in which trade barriers and controls are gradually eliminated.

This European Union became much more formidable with the introduction of the euro, a common currency designed to eliminate exchange rate fluctuations and to make cross-national transactions easier. Twelve members of the EU (all except Denmark, Sweden, and the United Kingdom, each of whom is still considering adopting the euro in the future) officially converted their domestic currencies to the euro on January 1, 2002. These twelve countries are now called the Eurozone. From a human resource management perspective, the advent of the euro means brings up two issues: (1) individuals and employers in the Eurozone can more readily compare their compensation packages to those of their peers in other countries because they are all paid in the same currency, and (2) it is easier for firms in the Eurozone to transfer managers to other countries.

Another less comprehensive economic community was created by the North American Free Trade Agreement (NAFTA). NAFTA attempts to reduce the trade barriers that exist among Canada, the United States, and Mexico, making it easier for companies to do business in each of the three countries. Extending NAFTA to other countries in Latin America, especially Chile, has been discussed, but for now at least it remains a three-country union. No plans for a single currency have been implemented, and human resource management practices and laws remain independent. But NAFTA also includes separate labor agreements, which have the potential to affect human resource management practices dramatically. The Commission on Labor Cooperation, for example, was established to hear cases dealing with these labor agreements in areas such as child labor, occupational safety and health, and union-management relations. Some of these standards are more stringent than those imposed by U.S.-based legislation (see Chapter 3). Although it is not clear how much enforcement power the Commission on Labor Cooperation will have, it is possible that human resource managers will have to deal with an even more complex set of regulations in the future. It is interesting to note that these standards would apply not only to U.S. companies doing business in Mexico and/or Canada but also to U.S. companies doing business solely in this country.

THE HUMAN RESOURCE FUNCTION IN INTERNATIONAL BUSINESS

All basic international functions—marketing, operations, finance, and human resources—play a vital role in international business. The human resource function, for example, must deal with several general, fundamental management challenges in international business.[8] These challenges are illustrated in Figure 4.4. In addition, specific human resource management implications exist for the different forms of international business activity that firms can pursue.

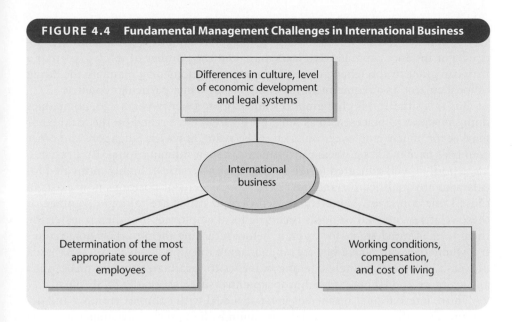

FIGURE 4.4 Fundamental Management Challenges in International Business

General Human Resource Issues in International Business

One general set of challenges relates to differences that may exist in culture, levels of economic development, and legal systems that typify the countries where the firm operates. These differences may force an international organization to customize its hiring, firing, training, and compensation programs on a country-by-country basis. A particularly difficult set of issues arises when conflict exists between the laws and/or cultures of the home country and those of the host country.

For example, as described in Chapter 3, it is illegal in the United States to discriminate in an employment relationship on the basis of gender. In Saudi Arabia, on the other hand, such discrimination is not only allowed but is expected. Women are highly restricted in their career opportunities, and a firm doing business in that country has to balance its own affirmative action efforts with the legal and cultural restrictions imposed by that country. And overt discrimination is still actively practiced in many other countries as well.[9] The Civil Rights Act of 1991 allows employees of U.S. firms working abroad to sue their employers if they violate the Civil Rights Act. But exception to this privilege exists when a country has a law that specifically contradicts the Civil Rights Act. For example, a woman could not sue a U.S. company operating in Saudi Arabia for sex discrimination because some discrimination against women is actually prescribed by law in that country. On the other hand, Japan has no laws institutionalizing such discrimination, so a woman could bring suit against a U.S. firm operating there if it were guilty of discriminatory practices.

A second fundamental human resource challenge in international business (a topic introduced earlier) is the determination of the most appropriate source of employees: the host country, the home country, or a third country. The ideal combination of employees differs according to the location of a firm's operations, the nature of its operations, and myriad other factors. A company is more likely to hire local employees, for example, for lower-level jobs with minimal skill requirements and for which there is a reasonable local supply of labor. Again, it is also necessary to consider local laws and/or customs that may limit or constrain hiring practices. For instance, immigration laws may limit the number of work visas that a firm can grant to foreigners, or employment regulations may mandate the hiring of local citizens as a requirement for doing business in a particular country.

But this situation is changing to some extent. Twenty years ago, companies doing business in places such as Singapore would have relied on the local labor market for hourly employees only. Over the years, however, Singapore and other countries have made significant investments in their human capital. As a result, a large pool of well-educated (often at western universities), highly motivated locals who are qualified for and interested in management positions now exists in these same countries. Some U.S.-based organizations are taking advantage of these relatively new labor pools by hiring local employees and then transferring them to the United States for training before returning them to their home country, where they can play a key role in managing the global enterprise. U.S.-based universities are increasingly opening branches for graduate study in places such as Singapore and China, as are European universities, especially INSEAD.

Third, international businesses must also deal with complex training and development challenges. At one level, for example, human resource managers need to provide cross-cultural training for corporate executives who are chosen for overseas assignments. In addition, training programs for production workers in host countries must be tailored to represent the education offered by local school systems. Dramatic differences in the skill and educational levels within a labor force make it necessary for international business to pay close attention to the training and development needs of all its employees in foreign markets.[10] But again, the establishment of institutions of higher education from the United States, the United Kingdom, France, and Australia has changed the face of local training and education in many countries, especially in Asia.

Yet another important international human resource management question relates to working conditions, compensation, and the cost of living. It costs more for people to live and work in some countries than in others. A general stance adopted by most international businesses is that an employee should not suffer a loss of compensation or a decrease in his or her standard of living by virtue of accepting an international assignment. Thus, human resource managers must determine how to compensate executives who accept overseas assignments and who face higher costs of living, a reduction in their quality of life, and/or unhappiness or stress because of separation from family or friends. This stance, however, can create some additional complications that we will address later when dealing with issues for expatriate managers.

Specific Human Resource Issues in International Business

Organizations can adopt a wide variety of strategies for competing in the international environment. Each strategy poses its own unique set of challenges for human resource managers. One common strategy is **exporting**, which is the process of making a product in the firm's domestic marketplace and then selling it in another country. Exporting can involve both good and services. U.S. agricultural cooperatives export grain to Russia while major consulting firms sell their services to companies in Europe and Asia. Other businesses ship gas turbines to Saudi Arabia, locomotives to Indonesia, blue jeans to Great Britain, computers

■ **Exporting** is the process of making a product in the firm's domestic marketplace and then selling it in another country.

to Japan, disposable diapers to Italy, and steel to Brazil; others sell airline service, information technology support, and various other service products.

Such an approach to international business has many advantages. First, it is usually the easiest way to enter a new market. In addition, it typically requires only a small outlay of capital. Because the products are usually sold "as is," there is no need to adapt them to local conditions. Finally, relatively little risk is involved. On the other hand, products exported to other countries are often subject to taxes, tariffs, and high transportation expenses. In addition, because the products are seldom adapted to local conditions, they may not actually address the needs of consumers in local markets, and consequently the products may not achieve their full revenue potential. The shipment of some products across national boundaries is also restricted by various government regulations. For example, textile products made in Turkey cannot be exported easily to the United States due to complex regulations developed to protect U.S. cotton producers.

If the firm functions solely as an exporter, the human resource function faces no meaningful differences in responsibilities from those in a domestic business. An exporting company usually has an export manager, and that manager likely has a staff to assist in the various parts of the exporting process. Human resource managers usually play a role in hiring people for these jobs and oversee other aspects of their employment, such as compensation and performance appraisal. But other than perhaps some exporting-specific skills required for workers in this department, these employees are treated the same as employees in the operations, sales, or finance departments. Thus, when a domestic firm begins to export to a foreign market, the human resource function may be extended to include another set of employees, but it does not change in any other meaningful way.

Another popular form of international business strategy is called **licensing**. Under this agreement, a company grants its permission to another company in a foreign country to manufacture and/or market its products in the foreign country's local market. For example, a clothing manufacturer might allow a manufacturer in another country to use its design, logo, and materials to manufacture clothing under the original firm's name. Under such an agreement, the licensing firm typically pays a royalty or licensing fee to the original firm based on the number of units it actually sells. Microsoft licenses software firms in other countries to produce and distribute software products such as Office and Windows in their local markets.

■ **Licensing** involves one company granting its permission to another company in a foreign country to manufacture and/or market the first company's products in the second company's local market.

The major advantage of this strategy is that, again, it allows the firm to enter a foreign market with relatively little risk. It also makes it possible for the firm to gain some market exposure and develop name recognition that will make it easier for it to enter the market more aggressively in the future. On the other hand, its profits are limited to those it receives from the royalty payment. Likewise, the firm must also be vigilant to ensure that its quality standards are upheld.

If a firm is involved in international business activities exclusively via licensing, the human resource function is approached in the same way as in a pure exporting enterprise. That is, no meaningful differences in the human resource function likely exist, but human resource managers need to extend their existing services and responsibilities to employees associated with the licensing activities. The human resource function itself does not really change in any meaningful way.

A third international strategy for doing business is **direct foreign investment**. A direct investment occurs when a firm headquartered in one country builds or purchases operating facilities or subsidiaries in a foreign country. That is, the

■ **Direct foreign investment** occurs when a firm headquartered in one country builds or purchases operating facilities or subsidiaries in a foreign country.

firm actually owns physical assets in the other country. Kodak, for example, constructed a research and development laboratory in Japan. This business activity represents a direct investment on the part of Kodak. Other examples of direct investment include Disney's construction of a new theme park near Hong Kong, BMW's construction of a new assembly plant in South Carolina, and Ford's acquisition of Jaguar and Volvo.

One major advantage of direct investment is that it gives the firm its own company-owned facilities in the foreign country and allows it to become truly integrated in a particular foreign market. Considerably more profit potential can be realized in direct investment because the company itself keeps all the profits its investment earns in that country. On the other hand, considerably more risk is attached to this strategy. Just as the investing firm can keep all its profits, so too must it absorb any and all losses and related financial setbacks. In addition, of course, the costs of direct investment are also quite high and are borne solely by the investing firm.

At this level of international business activity, the human resource function changes substantially from that of a domestic firm or business using a pure exporting or licensing strategy. This difference stems from the fact that in a direct investment situation, employees of the firm are working in foreign locations. Depending on the nationalities reflected in the foreign workforce (i.e., whether the firm uses a polycentric, geocentric, or ethnocentric approach to hiring), the corporate human resource function will need to extend and expand its scope and operations to provide the appropriate contributions to firm performance as determined by the philosophy used for staffing the foreign operations.

■ In a **joint venture** or **strategic alliance**, two or more firms cooperate in the ownership and/or management of an operation, often on an equity basis.

A fourth form of international strategy is a **joint venture** or **strategic alliance**. In this case, two or more firms cooperate in the ownership and/or management of an operation, often on an equity basis. A joint venture is the traditional term used for such an arrangement and describes a situation in which actual equity ownership exists. A strategic alliance might not involve ownership but still involves cooperation between firms. Joint ventures and strategic alliances are rapidly growing in importance in the international business environment. They represent a way for two or more firms to achieve synergy from working together, they reduce risk, and they provide mutual benefit to both partners. The airline industry has seen several strategic alliances. One of the largest is known as the Star Alliance. This group includes United Airlines, Lufthansa, All Nippon Airlines, Singapore Airlines, and several other airlines from all over the world. This alliance makes it easier for travelers to place reservations, purchase tickets, and make connections between any two of all the partners in the alliance. This flexibility also makes the group itself more competitive relative to nonalliance airlines.

Human resource managers in a firm that uses this strategy face an even more complex set of issues and challenges. If the new operation is a separate legal entity that functions as a semi-autonomous enterprise, the corporate human resource staff of each strategic partner needs to determine how to link and coordinate with their counterparts in both the new venture (seen as a separate entity) and their partner. If the new venture is operated within the context of one of the existing partner's organization structures, the human resource function becomes more complicated still because of the disparate relationships among the human resource staff for the new venture and its counterparts in both the partner within which it operates and the other partner (this latter relationship is somewhat more distant).

DOMESTIC ISSUES IN INTERNATIONAL HUMAN RESOURCE MANAGEMENT

Regardless of their level of internationalization, all firms dealing in foreign markets must confront three sets of domestic issues in the management of their human resources. These domestic issues, shown in Figure 4.5, are local recruiting and selection issues, local training issues, and local compensation issues.

Local Recruiting and Selection Issues

Nonmanagerial employees, such as blue-collar production workers and white-collar clerical and office workers, are usually host-country nationals in international business. Basic and fundamental economic reasons explain this pattern. Simply put, host-country nationals are usually cheaper to employ than are parent-country nationals or third-country nationals. Host-country nationals are also frequently used because local laws usually promote the hiring of locals.[11] Immigration laws, for example, may restrict jobs to citizens and legal residents of a country. Thus, an international business must develop and implement a plan for recruiting and selecting its employees in a host-country market. This plan must include assessments of the firm's human resource needs, primary sources of labor in that country, labor-force skills and talents, and training requirements. In addition, the plan should also account for special circumstances that exist in the local markets. When firms hire parent-country nationals for foreign assignments, they must obviously adhere to their home-country hiring regulations. But when hiring host-country nationals, they must also be aware of the regulations, laws, and norms that govern employment relationships within the host country. Thus, while the reliance on parent-country nationals may be less expensive, it also adds complexity to the employment relationship.[12]

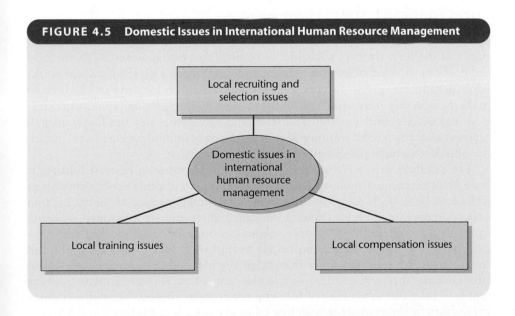

FIGURE 4.5   Domestic Issues in International Human Resource Management

Toyota Wants Only the Best

When Toyota decided to open its first automobile assembly plant in the United States several years ago, the firm knew it faced real challenges in staffing the facility. In its native Japan, many high school students go through special training programs funded by businesses to teach them various work skills. And high school graduates not heading off to college usually enroll in apprenticeship programs to develop their skills further. Because no such programs exist in the United States, Toyota realized that it would not have as large and talented a labor pool from which to hire as it did back home.

The firm initially had over 100,000 applicants for 2,700 production jobs. Many were initially screened out due to lack of education and/or experience. Most of those who remained under consideration underwent over fourteen hours of testing. Finalists from this pool then participated in various work simulations under the watchful eyes of Toyota managers. And after all this screening, only the very best were hired. All told, Toyota

> *"Those exercises are pretty close to what they'll experience on the assembly line."*
>
> (Mark Daugherty, Toyota assistant personnel manager)*

estimated that it spent over $13,000 hiring each worker for the factory.

After the plant was up and running, however, Toyota didn't slack off in its hiring rigor. Indeed, it still maintains the same high standards today. For example, applicants today who meet minimum education and experience qualifications are invited to the factory for a difficult twelve-hour assessment that the company calls the "day of work." Throughout this day, the applicants simulate work in various settings, meet with existing employees, and undergo detailed tests. The plant's managers try to make the work simulations as realistic as possible, and they hire only those employees who perform at the very highest levels. Does the hiring process pay off? Toyota managers believe that it does, and they point to the fact that product quality in the United States is comparable to what it achieves at home.

Sources: "Toyota Devises Grueling Workout for Job Seekers," *USA Today*, August 11, 1997, p. 3B (*quote on p. 3B); "Toyota Takes Pains, and Time, Filling Jobs at Its Kentucky Plant," *Wall Street Journal*, December 1, 1987, pp. 1, 29.

Local Training Issues

Human resource managers must also understand the training and development needs of the host country's workforce to help host-country nationals perform their jobs most effectively. The training and development needs of a local workforce depend on several factors. One, of course, is the location of the foreign market. In highly industrialized markets, such as England or Japan, organizations can usually find a cadre of capable employees who may need only a small amount of firm-specific training. But in a relatively underdeveloped area, training and development needs will be much more extensive.

For example, when Hilton first began opening hotels in eastern Europe, it found that restaurant waiters, desk clerks, and other customer-service employees lacked the basic skills necessary to provide high-quality service to guests. Because eastern European employees were accustomed to working in a planned economy in which they did not have to worry about customer satisfaction, they had difficulty recognizing why it was important to shift their focus. As a result, Hilton had to invest considerably more than originally planned in training employees to provide customer service. Training is also important if international business wants to take full advantage of locating production abroad. Many firms move production facilities to areas with low labor costs, such as Malaysia and Mexico, but then find that the productivity of the labor force is relatively low. Thus, they have to invest additional training and development dollars to bring the workforce up to the performance standards they expect. Some of the methods that Toyota uses both to select and to train workers in the United States are described in this chapter's HR Around the Globe feature.

Local Compensation Issues

Compensation must also be addressed at a local level for international businesses. Some countries, such as the United States, focus compensation on assessing individual performance and then compensating that individual accordingly. In other countries, however, such as Japan, the emphasis is based more on group work and less on individual performance. Dramatic differences in life styles, standards of living, and regulation also cause a wide variation in the way in which firms compensate their employees in different foreign locations.

Of course, dramatic differences in benefit packages are offered to workers in different countries as well. In countries with socialized medicine, such as the United Kingdom, firms do not have to worry as much about paying all or part of employee health-insurance premiums (although they pay higher taxes to help support the government program). In Italy, most workers expect to have several hours off in the afternoon. In Germany, most workers get six weeks of paid vacation time a year, and many work only thirty hours a week. German autoworkers earn $39 an hour in wages and benefits, compared to $25 in the United States and $27 in Japan.[13]

It is also important for international human resource managers to look at the total picture of compensation rather than on some simple index such as the hourly wage. For example, as already noted, some firms choose to move production to Mexico to take advantage of lower labor costs. While it is true that labor costs in Mexico are cheaper than they are in the United States (when compared on an hourly basis), it is also true that Mexican law requires employers to pay maternity leave to their employees, provide a Christmas bonus equal to fifteen days' pay, and provide at least three months of severance pay for workers who are terminated. Thus, lower labor costs may be at least partially lost due to these and other higher costs for other benefits.

MANAGING INTERNATIONAL TRANSFERS AND ASSIGNMENTS

Another extremely important part of international human resource management is the effective management of expatriate employees.[14] **Expatriates** are employees who are sent by a firm to work in another country and may be either parent-country nationals or third-country nationals. Particularly key areas of importance here include selecting, training, and compensating expatriates.[15]

Selecting Expatriates

Recruiting and selecting employees for an international business requires that the human resource manager address two sets of questions.[16] The first question is the

■ **Expatriates** are employees who are sent by a firm to work in another country and may be either parent-country nationals or third-country nationals.

definition of skills and abilities necessary to perform the work that the organization needs to have done. The second set of issues relates to defining the skills and abilities that are needed to work in a foreign location.

The first step, then, is to define the actual skills necessary to do the job. Different types of assignments typically require different types of skills for success. Traditionally, expatriate managers were sent abroad to provide some technical expertise that was not available in the local economy. In such cases, it is extremely important that the manager selected has the requisite technical skills and communication skills needed to work with less technically adept workers. Because these assignments are often for a limited time, however, it may be less critical that the manager possess extensive cultural skills. But multinational enterprises (MNEs) more and more often send managers overseas, not to help the overseas operation, but to help the manager. That is, they see expatriate assignments as a critical developmental opportunity that is essential for career progress.[17] Clearly, success in these assignments is based less on technical skills, and cultural skills would be far more critical because the expatriate manager is supposed to learn from his or her experience and carry this information back to the home country. Some of the more common skills and abilities assumed to be necessary in this regard include adaptability, language ability, overall physical and emotional health, relatively high levels of independence and self-reliance, and appropriate levels of experience and education. We will say more about required skills and abilities a bit later in the chapter.

The recruitment of employees for international business is an important step in the human resource management process. International businesses attempt to recruit experienced managers through various channels. One common source of recruits is the firm itself. That is, a good starting place may be to seek employees already working for the firm and in the host country who might be prepared for international assignment. In some cases, the firm may be selecting individuals for their first international assignment, but in other cases they may be selecting people for their second or third international assignment. Nestlé, for example, maintains a cadre of approximately 200 managers who are capable of and willing to accept an international assignment anywhere the firm does business.[18]

International businesses also frequently look to other organizations as a source of prospective managers. These may be home-country managers who are qualified for an international assignment, or managers already working in an international assignment for another firm. For higher-level positions in an organization, international businesses often rely on professional recruiting firms to help them identify prospective managerial candidates. These recruiters, often called *headhunters,* are recruiting firms that actively seek qualified managers and other professionals for possible placement in positions in other organizations. Headhunting has long been an accepted practice in the United States. In both Japan and Europe, headhunting was considered unethical until recently. Within the last decade or so, however, headhunting has become a more accepted practice in most industrialized countries.[19]

Increasingly, many firms are finding it necessary to hire new college graduates for immediate foreign assignment. Traditionally, this practice has been relatively unpopular because organizations believed that managers needed to develop experience in a firm's domestic operations before taking on an international assignment. Because of both the shortage of global managers and the recent emphasis that many colleges of business are placing on training international managers, however, firms are finding that they can hire younger managers and place them in foreign assignments more quickly than was the case in the past. Potential managerial candidates with foreign-language skills, international travel experience, and course work in international business or related fields are especially attractive candidates for firms in this position.[20]

After a pool of qualified applicants has been identified, the organization must then select the managers that it needs for international assignments. In general, organizations look at three sets of criteria for selecting people for international assignments: managerial competence, language training, and adaptability to new situations. It is extremely important that organizations select managers for international assignments with deliberate care. The cost of a failed international assignment is extremely high. Expatriate failure is defined as the early return of an expatriate manager to his or her home country because of an inability to perform in the overseas assignment.[21]

Experts suggest that a failed expatriate assignment for a top manager might cost the organization as much as $250,000, in addition to any salary losses. This figure includes the expatriate's original training, moving expenses, and lost managerial productivity. Failure of expatriate assignments is quite high. Estimates place the expatriate failure rate in U.S. companies at between 20 and 50 percent. Japanese and European firms appear to do a somewhat better job of selecting international managers and, as a result, experience a lower expatriate failure rate.[22]

Several factors may contribute to this pattern. One is the inability of the manager and/or the manager's spouse and family to adjust to a new location. Evidence suggests that this inability interferes with the manager's ability to adjust to the new setting and subsequently contributes to failure.[23] As a result of this pattern, some firms are beginning to pay more attention to helping spouses and children adjust to the new environment, and many other firms are placing a greater emphasis on the nontechnical aspects of a prospective manager's suitability for a foreign assignment. For example, they look closely at a person's cultural adaptability, as well as the adaptability of their families. It is also important to consider the perspective of international managers' motivation for and real interest in the foreign assignments. Some managers are attracted to foreign assignments because they relish the thought of living abroad or perhaps they see the experience as being useful in their career plans.[24] In addition, personality and international experience (of any type) also seem to be important determinants of expatriate success.[25]

Regardless of their motives in seeking international assignments, and regardless of their skills and abilities to carry out those assignments, many managers who don't have a realistic preview of what an international assignment really is become disillusioned within a few months of accepting such an assignment. Thus, it is critical that organizations prepare managers completely for what they might expect when they move overseas. It is also becoming clear that, once expatriate managers arrive at their new assignments, it is critical that they receive support and help from the host-country nationals with whom they will be working.[26] This realization is quite important because it may have far-reaching implications for other expatriate human resource policies. Specifically, as we shall see below, a great deal of attention is given to the problem of how to compensate expatriate managers. Most of the policies and practices result in expatriate managers earning considerably more than any host-country counterparts. In the past, this problem was not that serious because few local managers had the background and training of the expatriates. In fact, it was this very lack of local competence that led many organizations to assign expatriate managers. But, as noted above, organizations increasingly see expatriate assignments as helpful to the home-country manager. As a result, he or she may be assigned to a foreign post even though other host-country nationals (HCNs) are capable of doing the same job. As many countries more routinely send potential managers abroad for training and education, the HCN may well be as qualified in every way as the expatriate. To date, however, most expatriate policies dictate that the expatriate manager would earn more than the HCN doing the same or a similar job. This situation can lead to resentment on the part of the HCN and can potentially lead the HCN to withhold the help and support the expatriate needs to be successful. Does this situation mean that expatriates should not be compensated for their overseas assignments? Surely not, but it does mean that organizations may have to take a closer look at their expatriate policies and practices and evaluate them in light of the importance of obtaining HCN support for the expatriate once he or she arrives in their new assignment.[27]

Training Expatriates

Given the potential costs involved in failure, it is not surprising that organizations also spend a great deal of time and money on training expatriate managers. General Motors spends almost $500,000 a year on cross-cultural training for 150 or so U.S. managers and their families heading to international assignments. The firm reports that less than 1 percent of its expatriate assignments fail, and it attributes much of its success to its training program.[28] Training (as we will cover more fully in Chapter 9) is instruction directed at enhancing specific job-related skills and abilities and most often focuses on operating employees and technical specialists. For example, a training program might be designed to help employees learn to use a new software package as part of an international communication network. Development (we will also cover this topic more fully in Chapter 9) is general education devoted to preparing future managers for higher-level positions and/or new assignments within the organization. For example, a development program might span several months or even years and be targeted to helping managers improve their ability to make decisions, to motivate subordinates to work harder, and to develop more effective strategies for the organization.[29]

Training for expatriate managers may be as "simple" as language training (which is not very simple if it involves a completely unfamiliar language, such as Japanese for the English speaker) or it can be rather involved. For example, language-training programs and other forms of language training from cassette tapes, videotapes, and similar media are very common and fairly inexpensive.[30] In addition, it is common to have some type of classroom training dealing with the history of the country or the area and with daily living conditions (e.g., how to make a phone call or hail a taxicab). It is also typical to have some training component that deals with social manners and issues involved in social exchanges (when should you shake hands and when should you avoid shaking hands, for example, or how deeply to bow).[31]

The Cultural Assimilator is a more complex training program built around short case studies and critical incidents. It asks the manager how he or she would react to different situations, and it provides detailed feedback on the correct responses.[32] In addition, firms are more and more often sending prospective expatriates to their ultimate foreign destination for short periods of time before their permanent move. This experience allows them to become acculturated on a gradual basis and to obtain a truly realistic picture of what life will be like. But whatever the exact nature of the training, the goals of expatriate training are becoming clearer and more consistent. Increasingly, multinational organizations are recognizing that managers given overseas assignments must be able to communicate with others in the host country and must be able to adapt to different life styles and values. When we consider all the factors that seem to go into expatriate success, it becomes clearer why some have suggested that a manager given an assignment in a foreign country must possess "the patience of a diplomat, the zeal of a missionary, and the language skills of a U.N. interpreter."[33]

Compensating Expatriates

As noted above, another important issue in international human resource management is compensation. To remain competitive, an organization must provide compensation packages for their managers that are comparable to those in a given market. Compensation packages include salary and nonsalary items and are jointly determined by labor-market forces such as the supply and demand of managerial talent, professional licensing requirements, the standard of living, occupational status, government regulations, and so forth.[34]

Most international businesses find it necessary to provide expatriate managers with differential compensation to make up for differences in currency valuation, standards of living, life-style norms, and so on. When managers are on short-term assignments at a foreign location, their salary is often tied to their domestic currency and home-country living standards. Of course, these managers are reimbursed for short-term living expenses, such as the cost of hotel rooms, meals, and local transportation. If the foreign assignment is for a longer time period, however, compensation is usually adjusted to allow the manager to maintain her or his home-country standard of living. This adjustment is particularly important if the manager is transferred from a low-cost location to a high-cost location or from a country with a relatively high standard of living to one with a relatively low standard of living.[35]

Differential compensation usually starts with a cost-of-living allowance. This basic difference in salary is intended to offset the differences in the cost of living between the home country and the host country. The logic is that if managers accept a foreign assignment, they should enjoy the same standard of living as they would have enjoyed had they remained in their home country. If the cost of living in the foreign country is higher than that at home, then the manager's existing base pay alone will result in a lower standard of living. The firm may therefore need to supplement the base pay to offset the difference. On the other hand, if the cost of living at a foreign location is lower than that at home, no such allowance is needed (few companies would actually lower the manager's salary).

Occasionally, organizations might have to provide an additional salary inducement simply to convince people to accept a foreign assignment. Many employees may be relatively interested in accepting assignments to countries such as England, France, Italy, or Japan, but it may be more difficult to entice people to accept a position in Haiti, Pakistan, or Vietnam. Thus, organizations sometimes find

■ A **hardship premium** (also called a **foreign-service premium**) is an additional financial incentive offered to individuals to entice them to accept a less attractive international assignment.

it necessary to provide what is called a **hardship premium,** or a **foreign-service premium,** to induce people to accept these kinds of assignments. Total Fina Elf S.A. is a large French oil company. The firm has substantial holdings in the African country of Angola. During a recent bloody civil war in the country, however, Total pulled its employees out. When the war ended Total began to again assign managers to run its Angolan operations. But because of lingering violence and other concerns, the firm had to provide them with a 25 percent salary premium as well as numerous other incentives in order to get the desired mix of managers to agree to accept their new assignments.

Many international businesses also find that they must set up a tax-equalization system for their managers on foreign assignments. A tax-equalization system is designed to ensure that the expatriates' after-tax income in the host country is comparable to what the person's after-tax income would have been in the home country. Every country has its own unique income tax laws that apply to the earnings of its citizens and/or to earnings within its borders by foreign citizens, and companies must develop plans to make sure that the tax burden for individuals is equalized relative to the amount of salary they earn.

The other part of compensation besides salary is benefits. Most international businesses find that, in addition to salary adjustments, they must also provide benefit adjustments. Special benefits for managers on foreign assignments usually include housing, education, medical treatment, travel to the home country, and club membership. Housing benefits are usually provided as a way of helping to equalize housing expenses in different areas. Since equalizing the type of housing an executive enjoys in her or his home country may be very expensive, housing is usually treated as a separate benefit for expatriate managers. If a manager is going on a long-term or permanent foreign assignment, the organization may buy the manager's existing home and may help the manager buy a home in the host country.

Firms also find it increasingly necessary to provide job location assistance for the spouse of an executive being transferred abroad and to help cover the education costs for their children. For example, children may need to attend private schools, and the firm would pay the tuition and perhaps other school fees. Medical benefits are also often adjusted for managers on international assignment. For example, some people consider medical facilities in Malaysia to be substandard and as a result, firms that transfer employees to that country often find it necessary to agree that their employees can travel to Singapore whenever they need something other than routine medical attention.

International businesses may also provide expatriates with a travel allowance for trips back to the home country for personal reasons such as to visit other family members or to celebrate holidays. A manager and her or his family may typically be allowed one or two trips home per year for personal reasons at the company's expense. If the assignment is relatively short term and a manager's family remains at home, the manager may be provided with even more trips home to compensate for the fact that the manager and her or his family are separated.

Finally, it may be necessary to provide certain kinds of club memberships. In some cultures, for example, belonging to a specific club or participating in a particular activity is a necessary part of the business world. The Japanese, for instance, often conduct business during a round of golf. At the same time, memberships in golf clubs in Japan cost thousands of dollars, and a single round of golf costs many times more what it costs in the rest of the world. As a result, managers assigned to foreign posts in Japan may be given supplemental benefits to cover the

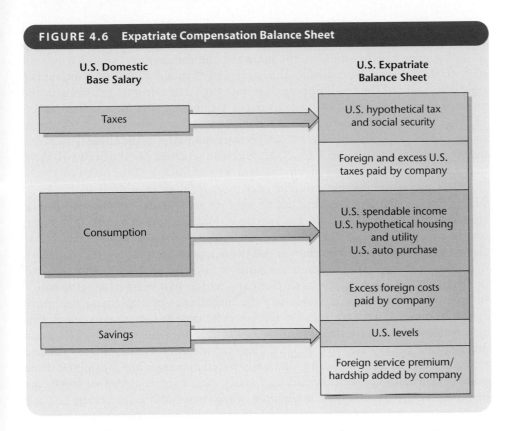

FIGURE 4.6   Expatriate Compensation Balance Sheet

U.S. Domestic Base Salary	U.S. Expatriate Balance Sheet
Taxes	U.S. hypothetical tax and social security
	Foreign and excess U.S. taxes paid by company
Consumption	U.S. spendable income U.S. hypothetical housing and utility U.S. auto purchase
	Excess foreign costs paid by company
Savings	U.S. levels
	Foreign service premium/ hardship added by company

costs of golf-club memberships and to be able to conduct business effectively.[36] When we take all these factors into consideration, it is easy to see how HCNs could become resentful about the salary and perks that expatriates receive. On the other hand, most companies believe that only by providing such inducements can they persuade qualified managers to accept overseas assignments.

Figure 4.6 illustrates how one company conceptualizes its compensation package for expatriates. The left side of its "balance sheet" summarizes what an employee is currently earning and spending in the United States, broken down into taxes, consumption, and savings. The right side of the "balance sheet" provides more detail for these categories, allowing managers to provide comparable income to managers taking international assignments. It is interesting that, although more than 85 percent of North American companies use this approach, it is not without its critics.[37] Furthermore, the high costs associated with this approach have led some to call for shorter term assignments and some forms of cost-sharing by the expatriates.[38]

Repatriation

The final step in managing the human resources of global business involves bringing the expatriate manager home. Although this issue may seem quite simple, much more is involved than simply packing up belongings and putting the manager and his or her family on a plane. A great deal of adjustment is often required (more or less depending on how long the assignment was) on both a personal and a professional level.[39]

On a personal level, the expatriate manager may have to become accustomed to living on less real income and going without perks such as club membership or an assigned car. In addition, the manager and the manager's family may all have to become reaccustomed to U.S. practices that can include driving on the right-hand side of the road, tipping at restaurants, and not trying to bargain the price of everything they buy. If the overseas assignment was for a longer period of time, the returning managers may also need to learn new styles in clothing, food, and music. For some managers who were not living in the United States before the tragedy of September 11, 2001, and who returned home afterward, there may be a need to adjust to a much different way of life.

The repatriation process could be even more difficult on a professional level. The expatriate manager has been out of sight for a while and may have lost some status within the organization. The manager's old job may not exist any longer, and he or she may be concerned about the nature of the new assignment. He or she may have questions about how much the company truly values the manager's overseas experience. Perhaps these are some of the reasons why roughly one-half of repatriated managers leave their company within two years of repatriation.[40] In any event, most experts emphasize the importance of explaining the entire expatriation/repatriation process to managers before they are sent overseas. It is also critical to stay in touch with expatriates so that they can maintain their social and network ties within the company. This step includes regular phone calls and visits, and it also means ensuring that expatriated managers are considered when other opportunities present themselves. Finally, most experts agree that some type of career counseling is helpful at the time of repatriation. It is interesting to note, however, that few companies actually follow the advice of these experts and so they fail to complete the process successfully. This is indeed interesting, since a recent survey indicated that 40 percent of expatriates leave their company within two years of repatriation because of reported poor career opportunities.[41]

INTERNATIONAL LABOR RELATIONS

Labor relations, which we will discuss more fully in Chapter 14, are the processes of dealing with employees who are organized into labor unions. Labor relations are also heavily regulated by law, as we noted briefly in Chapter 3, and the actions of management toward labor and the actions of labor toward management are heavily restricted. Different situations, however, exist in other countries. In many countries throughout the world, labor parties seek to achieve the political goals of unions in those countries, and these parties are often quite powerful. Also, in many countries, labor unions are much more concerned with social issues than they are in the United States, and so their political activism often extends beyond the wages and conditions of employment. In any case, union membership is quite large in many countries and continues to grow. In fact, over half the world's workforce outside the United States belongs to labor unions.

Different norms or expectations exist in other countries about the relationships between unions and management. In England, labor "contracts" are not really legal contracts at all but are merely understandings that can be broken at any time by either party with no penalty. And throughout Europe, temporary work stoppages are frequently used by unions in a bid for public backing of their de-

The nature of the relations between unions and management differs dramatically around the world. For example, in the European Union more workers are unionized, unions tend to be much stronger, and they tend to be much more active politically than are unions in the U.S. As a result, strikes such as the one pictured here are much more common. Here, tens of thousands of striking workers from many labor unions attended a protest in Marseille, France, in 2003. The employees were protesting government plans for pension reform that would reduce employee benefits. Workers in the U.S. might well strike for a similar cause, but one rarely sees such a widespread event as this, which affected air, train, and bus travel, garbage collection, and other services.

mands. In Paris, for example, one-day work stoppages by employees who work in the city's buses, subways, and railroads are frequently used for this purpose. In contrast to the situation in Europe, labor relations in Japan tend to be cordial. Unions are created and run by the businesses themselves. Because the Japanese culture discourages confrontation and hostility, unions and management tend to work together cooperatively. Disputes are usually dissolved cordially and through mutual agreement, and it is rare that a third-party mediator must be consulted. Strikes are also rare in Japan.

Chapter Summary

Various global issues in international human resource management must be addressed by any international firm. One issue is the development of an international human resource management strategy. Another is developing an understanding of the cultural environment of human resource management. A third is developing an understanding of the political and legal environment of international business.

The international human resource function must deal with several fundamental management challenges in international business. One major set of challenges relates to differences that may exist in culture, levels of economic development, and legal systems that typify the countries where the firm operates. A second fundamental human resource challenge in international business is the determination of the most appropriate source of employees: the host country, the home country, or a third country. Third, international businesses must also deal with different complex training and development challenges. Yet another important international human resource management question relates to working conditions, compensation, and the cost of living.

Organizations can adopt a wide variety of strategies for competing in the international environment. One strategy is exporting, which is the process of making a product in the firm's domestic marketplace and then selling it in another country. In licensing, a company grants its permission to another company in a foreign country to manufacture and/or market its products in the foreign country's local market. Direct investment occurs when a firm headquartered in one country builds or purchases operating facilities or subsidiaries in a foreign country. In a joint venture or strategic alliance, two or more firms cooperate in the ownership and/or management of an operation, often on an equity basis.

All firms dealing in foreign markets must also confront three sets of domestic issues in the management of their human resources. These domestic issues are local recruiting and selection issues, local training issues, and local compensation issues. International human resource management must also pay close attention to the various issues involved in the effective management of expatriate employees. Key areas of importance include selecting, training, and compensating expatriates.

Labor relations are the processes of dealing with employees who are organized into labor unions. In the United States, membership in labor unions has steadily declined in recent years and labor relations are heavily regulated by laws. Different situations exist, however, in other countries.

Key Points for Future HR Managers

▶ It is critical that a firm develop an international human resource management strategy for dealing with overseas business.

▶ An important part of this strategy is to determine the appropriate mix of host-country nationals (HCNs), expatriates, and third-country nationals who will staff operations in a given country.

▶ Managing cultural differences is one of the more difficult aspects of managing overseas assignments. Although cultures can differ on many dimensions, a great deal of work has been done to understand the cultural dimensions of individualism versus collectivism, power distance, masculinity versus femininity, uncertainty avoidance, and time perspective.

▶ Recruitment and selection decisions regarding managers for overseas assignments should consider factors such as technical skills but should also consider language facility, cultural sensitivity, and various personality characteristics.

▶ Spousal adjustment is one of the strongest predictors of expatriate success, and so it is critical that the company prepare the manager's spouse as well as the manager for the assignment.

▶ Successful adjustment by the expatriate manager is more likely when that manager can turn to HCNs for help and advice. Expatriate policies should be made with full consideration of this fact.

▶ Training of expatriate managers should include cultural training and should prepare the manager, as well as the manager's spouse and family, for daily life in the country.

▶ Expatriate compensation continues to be an important part of managing the expatriation process. Although the balance-sheet approach is the most common, it has some problems and is likely to result in much different compensation for expatriate managers and host-country managers.

▶ Many expatriate assignments actually fail *after* they are completed. Therefore, it is critical that the company work hard to repatriate the manager successfully once his or her assignment is over.

▶ Labor relations and the role of unions in society and organizations vary considerably around the world and these differences must be considered.

Key Points for Future General Managers

▶ It is critical that a firm develop an international human resource management strategy for dealing with overseas business.

▶ An important part of this strategy is to determine the appropriate mix of host-country nationals (HCNs), expatriates, and third-country nationals who will staff operations in a given country.

▶ It is critical for an organization to understand the cultural, political, and legal environments in a country where it is considering doing business.

▶ It is critical that a firm develop an international business strategy that includes consideration of the relative importance of exporting, licensing, direct investment, and joint ventures for doing business in a given country or region.

▶ Policies for recruiting, selecting, training, and compensating expatriate managers must consider the impact these practices have on host-country nationals because these host-country nationals must help the expatriate adjust to his or her new environment, and they may be less likely to do so if they feel resentment toward the expatriate manager.

▶ A strategic approach to expatriation must include a strategy for repatriation.

Review and Discussion Questions

1. Summarize recent growth and trends in international business.

2. What are the basic international business strategies that firms can pursue?

3. What are the basic human resource management functions in international business?

4. What are the basic human resource management issues to be addressed by an international business?

5. What are the basic domestic issues in international human resource management for the firm in its home country?

6. What are the human resource management implications of each strategy for international business?

7. What do you see as the basic similarities and differences in the human resource function between domestic and international businesses?

8. Which do you think is more critical for international human resource management: understanding the cultural environment or understanding the political and legal environment?

9. When a basic incongruence exists in the ethical context of human resource management between the foreign-country environment and a firm's home-country environment, which do you think should take precedence, the foreign-country environment or the firm's home-country environment?

10. Would you be interested in an international assignment as part of your employer's management development strategy? Why or why not? What factors would be most important to you in making such a decision?

Closing Case

Human Resources and International Mergers

Mergers and acquisitions are nothing new, of course, but a new slate of megamergers between international giants may well portend a new era in global consolidation. Two of these mergers, in particular, have the potential to reshape international competition. And each also has significant implications for international human resource practices. One megamerger involved Chrysler Corporation and Daimler-Benz. The other involved Amoco and British Petroleum.

The news about Chrysler and Daimler-Benz made headlines around the world when the deal was announced in midsummer 1998. Most experts agreed at the time that it was a good match. Chrysler made moderately priced cars and light trucks, was strong in North America but weak in Europe, and had distinctive competencies in design and product development. Daimler-Benz, on the other hand, made luxury cars and heavy trucks, was very strong in Europe, and had distinctive competencies in engineering and technology. While billed as a merger, Daimler-Benz actually bought Chrysler for $38 billion. The new company, called DaimlerChrysler AG, remained headquartered in Germany and became the fifth largest automobile company in the world.

Myriad strategic, technical, and operational systems had to be integrated before the two firms truly become one, and these problems proved to be dramatically more complex than originally thought. Indeed, integration problems persist today and the new firm has yet to capture the efficiencies and economies of scale and scope that the firm's managers intended. Blending the two firms' human resources also presented a formidable challenge. Prior to merging, Chrysler and Daimler-Benz had a combined worldwide workforce of 421,000 employees. After the merger was complete, however, not all these workers were needed. Hence, job cuts occurred at the production, technical, operations, and executive levels. But the two firms also had to deal with powerful unions, the United Auto Workers (UAW) for Chrysler in the United States and IG Metall in Germany.

Some issues were associated with employment conditions. Consider, for example, representative conditions at three plants. In Germany, prior to the merger, Daimler-Benz auto workers had an hourly wage range of from $15 to $20 per hour, got six weeks of annual vacation and twelve sick days, and worked an average of thirty-five hours a week. The Mercedes-Benz plant in Alabama, however, had substantially different conditions. Its workers earned from $14.05 to $19.20 an hour, got twelve days of vacation time and ten sick days, and worked an average of forty hours per week. At Chrysler's biggest plant, in Detroit, meanwhile, workers earned between $19.37 and $23.22 an hour, got four weeks of vacation time and five sick days, and worked an average of 50.5 hours per week (of which 10.5 hours were compensated at a rate of time and a half). Clearly,

then, integrating these disparate conditions under a single employment umbrella was a challenge.

A second big international merger was announced later the same year, this one between Amoco and British Petroleum (BP). At the time of the announcement, Amoco was the fourth largest oil producer in the United States, while BP was the third largest in the world, behind Royal Dutch/Shell and Exxon. Like the Chrysler and Daimler deal, this one was also not a true merger—BP was actually the buyer, with a 60 percent ownership stake in the new company. The firm remained headquartered in London, but all of its U.S. operations shifted to the Amoco organization and brand name.

Again, the firms had to address significant human resource issues as the integration of the two operations unfolded. BP's operations in the United States were based in Cleveland, while Amoco operated out of Chicago. BP announced that it would shut down most of its Cleveland operation, with some employees there transferred to Chicago. To make room, Amoco also indicated that several jobs in its own headquarters would be eliminated. All told, the firms cut about 6,000 of their combined 99,000 jobs. Most of these cuts were in marketing and exploration. But no one can really say for sure exactly how many cuts will eventually be made, or when full integration will be achieved. And, of course, integrating compensation, benefits, and other human resource practices will also be a complex task.[42]

Case Questions

1. What are the likely advantages and disadvantages that firms in these kinds of mergers can expect?

2. What are the advantages and disadvantages for individual workers at firms that merge with international partners?

3. What basic human resource issues, besides those mentioned in the case, must be addressed as a result of these mergers?

Building HR Management Skills

Purpose: The purpose of this exercise is to provide you with some critical insights into the complexities associated with international human resource management.

Step 1: Your instructor will divide your class into small groups of four to five members each. Begin by reading and discussing the context description that follows.

Assume that your group is the human resource management executive team of a large electronics firm. Your firm has several factories located throughout North and South America. The company has just decided to open its first Asian factory in Thailand. Plans call for the plant to open in two years. The plant will require a general manager, four associate managers, and ten other relatively high-level managerial positions (a purchasing manager, a warehouse manager, etc.). The plant will also require approximately thirty first-line supervisors, 600 operating employees, and thirty maintenance and custodial workers. Finally, approximately twenty-five office and clerical workers will also be needed.

Step 2: Your boss has asked your team to develop a staffing plan for the new plant. She wants to know where each type of employee should come from, when they should be hired, and how they should be trained. Spend about twenty minutes discussing this step as a group and outlining the basic issues that you will need to meet this request adequately. That is, your task is *not* to develop the actual plan; instead, your task is to decide what information you need to develop the plan and where you might go to get that information.

Step 3: Report the results of your group's deliberations to the entire class. Identify areas of agreement and disagreement across groups and explore why there were differences.

Ethical Dilemmas in HR Management

Assume that you are a senior human resource management executive for a large multinational firm. Your firm routinely buys products manufactured in factories in Asia, and it also operates three foreign plants itself, one each in Malaysia, Thailand, and Pakistan. The company hired a new chief executive officer (CEO) a few months ago. The CEO, in turn, has a reputation for being an outspoken advocate for the rights of foreign workers. He routinely proclaims that your company's foreign workers are treated exceptionally well, that he is proud of your firm's record in this area, and that he is willing to stake his personal reputation on the ethical and humane treatment of workers employed by both your firm and your firm's suppliers.

You recently returned from a fourteen-day inspection of your three international plants, plus four plants operated by two of your major suppliers. While you did not see any major problems, you have become quite concerned that your firm's treatment of its foreign workers is not as good as it once was. For example, the weak economy in Thailand has resulted in your plant manager there increasing work hours and withholding pay increases that had been planned. More troubling is what you saw in a supplier factory. What once was a comprehensive educational center for younger workers has been greatly reduced in scope, and you detected hints that it might be shut down altogether.

After your return, you spoke with the CEO and relayed to him your concerns. He seemed to be genuinely bothered by the news, but indicated that he wanted to delay taking any actions. He noted, for example, that your firms' annual shareholder meeting was coming up next month. If news of your concerns were to leak out, the firm's stock price might drop and the proposed slate of bonuses for senior managers, including you, might be jeopardized. He indicated that he would prefer to keep things quiet for now, but he promised to take some action to improve the situation in the foreign plants shortly after the meeting. Meanwhile, you have observed him to continue making boastful proclamations about the company's treatment of its foreign workers.

Questions

1. What are the ethical issues in this situation?

2. What are the arguments for and against following your CEO's suggested approach?

3. What do you think most managers would do? What would you do?

HR Internet Exercise

Identify five companies that are foreign owned but that have large U.S. operations. For example, Toyota, a Japanese firm, has a large U.S. subsidiary that is legally incorporated as Toyota Motor Sales, U.S.A., Inc. Nestlé, a Swiss firm, owns Carnation Foods in the United States.

Search the Internet to see if you can locate separate websites for both the parent company and its U.S. subsidiary. Next, determine the extent to which the two websites contain any information regarding human resource issues. If you can locate this informa-tion, see if you can identify any parallels, extensions, or even inconsistencies between them.

Questions

1. What role might the Internet play in helping an international business coordinate its international human resources?

2. What risks does an international business run by relying on the Internet to address human resource issues?

PART THREE

Staffing the Organization

5

Job Analysis and Job Design

CHAPTER OBJECTIVES

After studying this chapter you should be able to:

■ Describe the job analysis process.

■ Identify and discuss common job analysis methods.

■ Discuss modeling competencies and the end of the "job".

■ Describe job design in the workplace.

■ Identify and discuss motivational approaches to job design.

■ Discuss legal issues In Job analysis and job design.

Businesses today face unprecedented changes in myriad areas ranging from mergers and acquisitions to layoffs and plant closures, to globalization. Manufacturing firms have been especially hard hit by these changes, losing 1.7 million jobs in the United States between 1999 to 2002 alone. In this volatile environment companies must reduce expenses, but they also recognize that repeated cycles of hiring and firing drive workers out of the industry, costing firms more in the long run. "It's important to have a skill base and good loyal people who already know the company," says Richard Dillard, director of public affairs at Milliken & Co. To cope with hiring uncertainty, many firms are adapting by increasing job flexibility.

"It's important to have a skill base and good loyal people who already know the company."

(Richard Dillard, director of public affairs, Milliken & Co.)*

Each firm develops a customized approach to implementing job flexibility. For example, the Nestlé's plant in South Carolina keeps a roster of part-time workers who can be called to work on a daily basis. Lincoln Electric, a Cleveland-based maker of welding equipment, moves workers between manufacturing positions and even into clerical jobs, paying different rates for each assignment. Lincoln Electric's sales were down in 2001, and production supervisors moved into desk jobs. John Stropki, Lincoln Electric's president of North American operations says, "We pay them for the job they are doing, not the job they used to do." Crown Mold and Machine transfers workers between day and night shifts at its Ohio fiberglass-mold factory.

A&R Welding of Atlanta sends young, unmarried welders to out-of-state projects when local demand is slack. The Ohio plant of Blackhawk Automotive Plastics cross-trains employees so they can operate any of its plastic-forming machinery. "We're continually refining the process and reallocating people," says Clifford Croley, a Blackhawk owner. When Milliken & Co. closed a textile factory, laying off 190 employees in South Carolina, they rehired about seventy for nearby factory locations.

Employers appreciate the benefits of flexible job arrangements, including lower costs, less need for rehiring and retraining after downsizing, and greater ease in scheduling staff. For workers, the reality is not always positive. Employees appreciate more time with family and benefits continuity, but they fear the loss of seniority or pay. Rick Willard, a thirty-year Lincoln veteran, made $20 an hour until his plant was sold. Today, Lincoln is training him for a new job and he is working longer while earning 40 percent less. Willard says, "Some people resent being moved. I was just worried what type of job I would have. It's good for the company. Sometimes it's good for the employees." It remains unclear whether internal flexibility works for all firms, but it seems to work best in manufacturing organizations. Economists Peter Cappelli and David Neumark, working with the National Bureau of Economic Research in 1999, found that only in manufacturing firms did the use of job flexibility reduce turnover.

Companies will no doubt continue to look for ways to increase their adaptability to change, and that could be a plus for workers. E. Jeffrey Hill, research associate for Brigham Young University's Family Studies Department, takes a positive approach when he says, "As companies offer flexibility . . . and more individuals use that flexibility, the work-family imbalance that was problematic for employees in the twilight of the 20th century can become the balance so many seek in the 21st century."[1] ■

Companies like Nestlé, Milliken, and the others noted in the opening vignette are looking for new and more productive ways to get work done. To accomplish this goal, however, it is critical that firms have a basic and thorough understanding of the actual jobs being performed. After all, it is difficult for a manager to hire people, assign them to certain jobs, train them to perform those jobs, and later evaluate how well they are performing unless the manager is thoroughly familiar with the jobs.

With an understanding of the nature of human resource management and the human resource environment as a foundation, it is now possible to begin a more focused and detailed analysis of the specific activities and operations of the human resource management process itself, including how jobs are constructed and designed. Chapter 5 is the first of three chapters that involve **staffing**—the process of ensuring that the organization's current and future human resource needs are being filled most effectively. It addresses job analysis and job design. Chapter 6 deals with the recruitment of human resources, while Chapter 7 is devoted to the selection and placement of human resources.

In Chapter 2 we discussed the importance of human resource planning as part of a strategic approach to human resource management. This planning process is never-ending; people leave organizations for different reasons, and the jobs that the organization needs to have performed also change for various reasons. New technology, shifts in labor demand, and improved work methods, for example, can each alter an organization's human resource needs. A critical part of this planning process is job analysis. In fact, job analysis provides the basic information needed for all staffing decisions, and it is an important source of information for the design of compensation programs, appraisal programs, and training programs. A related concept, job design, also plays an important role in the development of certain types of programs designed to increase motivation on the job. Therefore, it is safe to say that job analysis is a basic building block for much of the human resource management process.

■ **Staffing** is the process of determining the organization's current and future human resource needs and then taking steps to ensure that those needs are met effectively.

JOB ANALYSIS

Job analysis is the process of gathering and organizing detailed information about various jobs within the organization so that managers can better understand the processes through which they are performed most effectively.[2] Generally, then, job analysis is an effort to study and understand specific jobs in the organization so that managers can have a full sense of the nature of those jobs and the kinds of skills and abilities necessary to perform them. As we already noted, job analysis is a fundamental input and building block of the planning process but as illustrated in Figure 5.1, it also relates to other human resource management processes.

As shown in the figure, job analysis affects selection, or hiring, decisions because the job analysis process indicates the tasks to be performed by the person to be hired. Job analysis results in assessments about the underlying skills and abilities needed to perform the job, and leads to logical and appropriate plans to recruit individuals who are most likely to have these skills and abilities. Selection techniques, for instance, can be designed and administered to determine which of the applicants recruited have the necessary skill and ability levels.

■ **Job analysis** is the process of gathering and organizing detailed information about various jobs within the organization so that managers can better understand the processes through which they are performed most effectively.

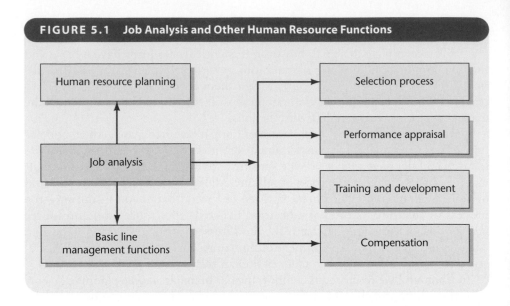

FIGURE 5.1   Job Analysis and Other Human Resource Functions

Under the Americans with Disabilities Act (ADA), job analysis has taken on an even more important role in the selection of new employees in many companies. As we noted in Chapter 3, the ADA outlaws discrimination based on disabilities. The ADA does not require an organization to hire someone who cannot perform the job in question, of course, but it does require an organization to hire a "qualified individual with a disability," specified as ". . . an individual with a disability who, with or without a reasonable accommodation, can perform the essential functions of the employment position that such an individual holds or desires" (Americans with Disabilities Act, Title 1, section 101).

The Americans with Disabilities Act (ADA) has added new urgency to job analysis. The ADA is concerned about the ability of workers to perform critical functions of the job; the definition of what constitutes a critical function is determined through job analysis. If someone can perform those functions, the organization is required to provide them with a reasonable accommodation for any disability that might interfere with their performance on the rest of the job. Many see these accommodations as critical for allowing disabled Americans to work and support themselves, but some are concerned about the cost of required accommodations. These workers are actually protesting an attempt by the State of California to have the ADA ruled unconstitutional. The protesters were successful; the ADA still stands.

Consider, for example, the implications of an organization refusing to hire a disabled applicant because a manager assumes that the individual cannot perform the job. The individual might have grounds for a discrimination claim if ambiguity exists about exactly which job elements are essential to the organization and which are less essential or optional and if the applicant can demonstrate a capacity for performing the job. Thus, it becomes more important than ever for managers to determine the essential functions of the jobs within the organization because they must identify those parts of jobs (e.g., tasks, duties) that absolutely must be carried out effectively for the person to be successful in performing the job. This information can best be obtained through job analysis.

Figure 5.1 also indicates that job analysis relates to performance appraisal. This relationship stems from the fact that it is necessary to understand what an employee should be capable of doing in a job before one can assess how well that employee is actually performing. Job analysis similarly affects training and development because it provides information that helps managers better understand the kind of training and development programs that are necessary to enhance employee competencies and capabilities so the employees can achieve ideal levels of performance. Job analysis information is also important for compensation (job analysis methods used for establishing compensation rates are often referred to as job evaluation) because work behaviors have traditionally been a primary basis for compensation. (As we will see later, however, compensation based on knowledge or competencies, rather than behaviors, is becoming more common.)

In addition to its fundamental role in human resource planning and other aspects of the human resource function, job analysis is also important to line managers for various general reasons. First, line managers must have a thorough understanding of the work-flow processes that characterize their particular work units. That is, they have to understand how work flows from employee to employee, from job station to job station, and from work group to work group. To develop this understanding, of course, they must also have a fundamental insight into the basic mechanics, character, and nature of each job. Job analysis provides this insight. Also, because line managers are often involved in hiring and appraisal decisions, they must rely on the information provided by job analysis to help determine who should be hired and how well employees are doing their jobs.

Job analysis provides fundamental input to the human resource manager by helping to define the kinds of both general work and specific jobs that the organization relies on now and will be relying on in the future.[3] Whereas the focus

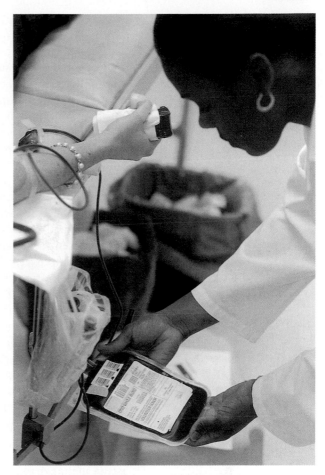

Job analysis is important if an organization is to fully understand the skills and competencies required to perform a particular job. Consider, for example, the job of a nurse at a Red Cross blood donation center. The nurse has to understand how to screen potential donors, how to actually draw their blood, how to properly document and store the donated blood, and how to monitor the vital signs of the donor for a brief period of time after the donation is complete. In addition, the nurse needs to have good interpersonal skills in order to deal with people effectively. Job analysis provides the critical information necessary to develop the right selection criteria for this job.

■ **Knowledge, skills, and abilities (KSA)** are the fundamental requirements necessary to perform a job.

■ **Job families** are groups of jobs with similar task and KSA requirements.

of job analysis is typically an individual job, in many organizations, the tasks and responsibilities on some jobs may be similar to those on other jobs. Likewise, the **knowledge, skills, and abilities (KSA)** requirements may be similar for a set of jobs. As a result, for planning purposes, organizations often try to form **job families**—groups of jobs that have task and KSA requirements that are quite similar. These job families can be quite useful in several ways. First, if the jobs within a job family have similar KSA requirements, it might be possible to train employees so that they can apply what they have learned to the entire family of jobs, making them much more flexible resources for the organization. In addition, this training for job families rather than for specific jobs can help employees remain useful to the organization even if their present jobs become obsolete.[4]

Well-conceived job families can also be used to help organizations in career planning. The jobs within a family represent jobs that have similar patterns of requirements. If they occur at different levels within an organization, those jobs can represent a typical career path for an employee. Thus, managers can plan where an employee might go as his or her career builds, and they might also discover where to find replacements when an opening occurs in a job.

Finally, job families can be used in selection decisions. For instance, once an organization has established the selection requirements for one job within a family, managers may be able to use this information to predict requirements in other jobs within the family.[5] In fact, if it is reasonable to believe that an employee will progress through all the jobs in a job family, the organization might well choose to select individuals based on the needs of the *highest* level job within the family rather than on those of the specific job for which an individual is applying. For example, suppose Texas Instruments needs to hire some technicians to support engineering work teams. The human resource manager in charge of this hiring might determine that each technician will rotate across several groups over a four-year period, performing different functions for each. The astute manager might therefore set as a hiring standard for all technicians the performance requirements for all such support roles, even though some technicians may start out in less demanding roles.

THE JOB ANALYSIS PROCESS

The job analysis process itself is generally clear and straightforward. As a starting point in this process, it is helpful first to understand the steps involved, including who is responsible for job analysis. As illustrated in Figure 5.2, the job analysis process generally follows three steps: determining information needs, determining methods for obtaining information, and determining who will collect information.[6]

Determining Information Needs

The first step is determining the organization's precise information needs. A wide range of information on various jobs may be obtained during the course of job analysis. The exact type and nature of the information obtained, however, depend on both the intended purposes of the job analysis information and various constraints, such as time and budget limitations, imposed by the organization.

FIGURE 5.2   Steps in Job Analysis

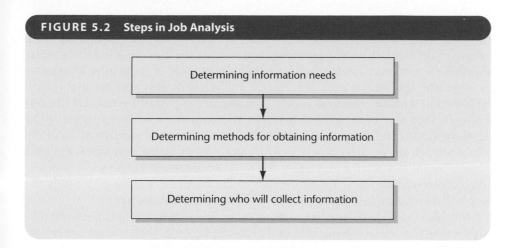

Regardless of constraints, however, the job analysis must provide enough information about what someone does on a job to allow a determination of the knowledge, skills, and abilities necessary to perform the job. If the organization lacks the time and/or resources to obtain this minimum amount of information, there is really no point in proceeding with the job analysis.

Examples of the types of job analysis information that might be gathered include general work activities (such as a description of the specific tasks that are carried out, how the job interfaces with other jobs and equipment, the procedures used in the job, behaviors required on the job, and the physical movements and demands of the job) and the machines, tools, equipment, and work aids used in the performance of the job. Other useful information that may be collected includes details regarding the job context (physical working conditions such as exposure to dust, heat, and toxic substances, the indoor environment versus outdoor environment, and so forth). Information may also be collected regarding the organizational context and social context of the job. In addition, details regarding work schedule, various financial and nonfinancial incentives, and personal requirements (job-related attributes such as specific skills, education, and training; work experience and related jobs; physical characteristics and aptitudes) are usually desirable pieces of information.[7]

Determining Methods for Obtaining Information

Once human resource managers decide what types of information are to be collected in the job analysis, the next step in the job analysis process is to determine how that information will be collected. Various methods are used to collect job analysis information. The most common include the observations of task and job behaviors, interviews with job incumbents, and the use of questionnaires and checklists. For example, the individuals who perform the job analysis, called **job analysts**, can sometimes gather the desired information on jobs simply by observing people performing those jobs. This method is especially useful for unskilled manual jobs but has less relevance for jobs involving creative thought and analytic skills. If job incumbents know that they are being observed, they might try to do the job as it was originally specified, rather than as it is actually done, for the benefit of the observer.

■ **Job analysts** are individuals who perform job analysis in an organization.

In many cases it is also beneficial to interview individuals who are performing the jobs being analyzed.[8] These individuals are in a position to explain both the nature of the work they are performing and the qualifications and credentials that they believe are necessary for the successful performance of those jobs. Of course, even though this information is both rich and relevant, it is possible that it may be biased as a result of various predispositions on the part of the individuals. For example, they may be tempted to overstate the skills and qualifications needed to perform the job and they may overstate the complexities and sophistication of the job. Although job analysis may be carried out for any number of reasons, as noted above, employees often assume that the purpose for the job analysis is to determine compensation rates. Therefore, they might believe that, by exaggerating the importance or complexity of their jobs, they will receive more pay.

It is also possible to interview others who are knowledgeable about the job, rather than the actual job incumbent. For example, a job analyst might interview the person who supervises the incumbent, assuming that the supervisor is informed about what the incumbent does and does not have an incentive to exaggerate the job in any way. Although the supervisor would probably not expect to receive more pay for supervising someone who does a more complex job, other dynamics might still compromise the honesty of the supervisor's responses. Stated simply, although it might feel good to perform a complex and important job, it might feel even better to *supervise* someone who does a complex or important job.

Other people with expertise who can be interviewed include higher-level supervisors, industrial engineers, and even human resource managers. Because these individuals are further removed from the actual job, they may have even less incentive to distort it, but they are also more likely to be mistaken or misinformed about what actually takes place on the job. As a result, if critical job analysis information must be collected through the interview process, it is important to interview multiple individuals who have different perspectives on the actual job, and then integrate or average the information collected.

Another possible way of gathering job analysis data is for the job analyst to perform the job for a long enough period of time to be able to describe the job based on actual experience. Hands-on experience may not always be feasible, however, and jobs requiring specialized training or jobs where errors are costly are not usually amenable to this form of job analysis. On the other hand, alternative methods for job analysis, such as questionnaires and checklists, may prove useful. Standardized questionnaires and checklists are widely available, but sometimes organizations choose to develop their own custom measures. We discuss these methods more fully later in this chapter.

Determining Who Will Collect Information

The third step in job analysis is determining who is responsible for collecting the information—for conducting the job analysis. In general, the responsibility of job analysis is jointly shared by three different individuals or groups. One is the line manager who is responsible for the performance of the various jobs being analyzed. For example, it is the line manager's responsibility to convey to the human resources function exactly what information is available, what information is needed, and the specific purpose of the job analysis itself. The human resource group or department is also responsible for job analysis. For example, the human resource department typically performs and/or contracts for the services necessary to perform the job analysis. Thus, the human resource department may need to buy certain job analysis instruments, such as the position analysis questionnaire (discussed later in the chapter), and/or subcontract with job analyst specialists who will conduct the job analysis itself.

And finally, the responsibility also lies partially with the job analyst or analysts. A job analyst, as already noted, is the individual who actually conducts the job analysis. Depending on the method used and the nature of the organization involved, the job analyst might be a current job incumbent (as is the case in some checklist approaches), another employee of the organization (who might be a full-time job analyst in a large organization), or someone from outside the organization (such as a consultant or professional job analyst) hired to do the job analysis. In the latter instance, the job analyst will probably have to rely on employees of the organization to learn enough about the job to conduct the job analysis, and the analyst might use any or several of the methods described above to complete the analysis.

Smaller firms may be more inclined to hire analysts from consulting firms when they need to perform job analyses, although many small firms simply do not conduct job analysis. When they need to obtain information about jobs, they may instead refer to available reference materials. Traditionally, the major source of such information was the *Dictionary of Occupational Titles* (DOT), a multi-volume publication of the Department of Labor, which provides a job description and information about required KSAs for almost every job performed in the United States. But the DOT is rapidly being replaced by O*NET, a computerized job classification system that contains all the information (updated, of course) that had formerly been contained in the DOT, as well as a great deal of additional information, which makes it quite useful to smaller firms who cannot or do not wish to rely on consultants. We will discuss the O*NET a bit later in the chapter.

JOB ANALYSIS METHODS

As we noted earlier, organizations can use several methods to perform job analyses. In this section we will discuss these methods in more detail. We will also discuss two related areas: job descriptions and job specifications.

Collecting Job Analysis Data

The primary source of data for job analysis work is usually **subject matter experts** (**SMEs**). SMEs are the individuals from whom job analysts obtain data for the job analysis; they may be existing job incumbents, supervisors, or other knowledgeable employees. For the job analysis to be successful, it is critical that the employees selected to provide the job analysis information be intimately familiar with the nature of the jobs themselves. Thus, participants in job analysis tend to be experienced and high-performing individuals who thoroughly understand the job.[9]

The job analysis information itself takes various forms. First, it is important to identify the major job dimensions that comprise a particular job. For example, suppose a human resource manager at Exxon has been asked to conduct a job

■ **Subject matter experts (SMEs)** are individuals presumed to be highly knowledgeable about jobs and who provide data for job analysis; they may be existing job incumbents, supervisors, or other knowledgeable employees.

analysis of the position of administrative assistant in a particular department. Existing data likely already indicate the basic dimensions of the job and might include keyboarding; answering a telephone; handling routine copying; arranging appointments; greeting visitors; making certain, routine administrative decisions; and handling related administrative details. If structured questionnaires or checklists are used for job analysis, these dimensions are usually already specified in the questionnaire.

If some form of narrative about the job is to be prepared instead, the various major job dimensions must then be subdivided into the specific tasks associated with each major job dimension. For example, keyboarding is a major job dimension that can take various forms. It might include tasks such as typing address labels on an envelope using a conventional typewriter, keyboarding major documents into personal computers and word-processing software, operating scanning devices to input previously prepared text and graphics, and various other specific tasks that together comprise the job of keyboarding.

Ultimately, the job analysis must also identify the basic KSAs necessary to perform the job. For example, the skills and abilities necessary to handle a keyboarding task may include skills such as familiarity with various word-processing packages, familiarity with various scanning devices, and familiarity with various computer and operating systems, in addition to physical dexterity and coordination. In some cases, the KSAs are developed, after the job analysis is completed, by the job analyst and the SMEs. When an organization uses a standardized questionnaire, these KSAs might be identified through a computer algorithm, based on the job analysis information provided. In these cases, the organization is less dependent on the decision-making skills of the job analyst.

Occasionally, job analysts go further and offer potential changes that might be forthcoming in a job. For example, if the organization is already aware of new technology that is about to be installed or is planning to implement major changes in how work is being performed, these events and circumstances may also be incorporated into the job analysis process. Some software packages today include voice recognition dictation systems that nearly eliminate the need for physical keyboarding. To the extent that job analysts believe that this technology will become commonly used in the foreseeable future, they may need to incorporate into the job analysis the ways in which this technology can alter the job being studied.

Specific Job Analysis Techniques

Several job analysis techniques can be used by an organization. The most commonly used methods are the straight narrative, Fleishman job analysis system, task analysis inventory, functional job analysis, position analysis questionnaire (PAQ), and critical incidents approach.[10]

Narrative job analysis   The most common approach to job analysis is simply to have one or more SMEs prepare a written narrative or text description of the job. These narratives can vary in terms of length and detail. To some extent the quality of the information depends on the writing skills of the job analyst. Although it is possible to specify the format and structure of these narratives, they are typically individualistic, making it difficult to compare the tasks on one job with the tasks on another. They are relatively inexpensive, however, and it generally does not require a great deal of training for someone to complete a narrative job analysis.

Fleishman job analysis system   Another popular method for job analysis is the Fleishman job analysis system.[11] This approach defines abilities as enduring attributes of individuals that account for differences in performance. The system itself relies on the taxonomy of abilities that presumably represents all the dimensions relevant to work. The taxonomy includes a total of fifty-two abilities. In general, these fifty-two specific abilities are presumed to reflect cognitive, psychomotor, and sensory abilities. Examples of the specific abilities included in the Fleishman system include oral comprehension, written comprehension, oral expression, written expression, fluency of ideas, night vision, depth perception, auditory attention, and speech clarity. The actual Fleishman scales consist of descriptions of each ability, followed by a behavioral benchmark example of the different levels of the ability along a seven-point scale. An organization using this job analysis technique relies on a panel of subject matter experts (again, incumbent workers and/or supervisors are most commonly used) to indicate how important the ability is for the job, and the actual level of ability required for a particular job. Because of its complexity, job analysts who use this method require training, but it is also much closer in operation to the notion of competency modeling, which we will discuss below.

■ The **Fleishman job analysis system** is a job analysis procedure that defines abilities as the enduring attributes of individuals that account for differences in performance; it relies on the taxonomy of abilities that presumably represents all the dimensions relevant to work.

Task analysis inventory   Another method of job analysis is the **task analysis inventory**. The task analysis inventory method actually refers to a family of job analysis methods, each with unique characteristics. However, each one focuses on analyzing all the tasks performed in the focal job. Any given job may have dozens of tasks, for example. Again relying on subject matter experts, this method requires the generation of a list of tasks performed in a job. Once the list has been developed, a job analyst—frequently the job incumbent—evaluates each task on dimensions such as the relative amount of time spent on the task, the frequency with which the task is performed, the relative importance of the task, the relative difficulty of the task, and the time necessary to learn the task.

■ The **task analysis inventory** is a family of job analysis methods, each with unique characteristics; each focuses on analyzing all the tasks performed in the focal job.

Task inventories require a fair amount of effort to develop. Once they are developed, however, they are relatively easy to use. This approach to job analysis is often used in municipal and county governments, and is also the most common form of job analysis used in the U.S. military. The information generated by this approach to job analysis is often detailed, and it is useful for establishing KSAs and training needs. The military has used these inventories to establish career paths and job families, where the jobs clustered together have a large amount of overlap in terms of the important tasks.[12] Managers then use a single task inventory to analyze all the jobs in the family. It is more difficult, though, to make comparisons across job families, and this drawback reduces the usefulness of task inventories to some degree.

Functional job analysis   One attempt to have a single job analysis instrument that can be used with a wide variety of jobs resulted in the development of functional job analysis.[13] According to this approach, all jobs can be described in terms of the level of involvement with *people, data,* and *things.* For example, employees on a job at a Halliburton manufacturing site might be said to "set up" machines (things), "mentor" people, and "synthesize" data. All are high levels of involvement and would indicate a complex job. The exact definition of each of these terms is provided to the job analyst. The Department of Labor relies on functional job analysis for some of its classifications of jobs, but it is not used widely in private industry. Nonetheless, this approach is important because it represents the first attempt to develop a single instrument that can describe all jobs in common terms.

Position analysis questionnaire   One of the most popular and widely used job analysis methods is the **Position Analysis Questionnaire (PAQ)**. The PAQ was developed by Ernest McCormick and his associates, and it is a standardized job analysis instrument consisting of 194 items. These items reflect work behavior, working conditions, or job characteristics that are assumed to be generalizable across a wide variety of jobs.[14] The items that comprise the PAQ are organized into six sections. *Information inputs* include where and how a worker gets information needed to perform his or her job. *Mental processes* represent the reasoning, decision-making, planning, and information-processing activities involved in performing the job. *Work output* refers to the physical activities, tools, and devices used by the worker to perform the job. *Relationships with other people* include the relationships with other people that are required in performing the job. *Job context* represents the physical and social contacts where the work is performed. Finally, *other characteristics* include the activities, conditions, and characteristics other than those previously described that pertain to the job. Figure 5.3 illustrates some items from the PAQ section dealing with the information inputs.

Job analysts are asked to determine whether each scale applies to the specific job being analyzed. The analyst rates the item on six scales: extent of use, amount of time, importance of the job, possibility of occurrence, applicability, and special code. Special code refers to unique and special rating scales that are used with a particular item. These ratings are then submitted to a centralized location indicated on the questionnaire where computer software compiles a report regarding the job scores on the job dimensions.

A major advantage of the PAQ is that, like functional job analysis, its dimensions are believed to underlie all jobs. This feature allows a wide variety (although probably not *all*) jobs to be described in common terms. In the case of the PAQ, this feature results from the items and dimensions of the PAQ that describe what a worker does on the job rather than what gets done. For example, a baker bakes bread and a pilot flies an airplane, but when we examine how these workers get the information they need to do their jobs, we find that they both rely heavily on dials and instruments for critical information. We do not mean to suggest that the two jobs are related, just that workers perform similar functions even on diverse jobs.

Unlike functional job analysis, the PAQ can provide information on 187 separate items, allowing a much richer picture of what happens on a job (the PAQ actually includes 194 items, but the remaining items deal with methods of pay). Finally, another strength of the PAQ is the fact that, because it has been widely used for many years, a considerable database of information exists, attesting to its validity and reliability. In general, research supports the validity and reliability of the instrument. Research also suggests that the PAQ measures thirty-two dimensions and thirteen overall job dimensions. A given job score on these dimensions can be useful in job analysis.[15] Because the instrument has been so widely used, it has also been statistically related to other measures, including the scores of job applicants on standardized selection tests, compensation rates on various jobs, and even the importance of various abilities.[16]

■ The **Position Analysis Questionnaire (PAQ)** is a standardized job analysis instrument consisting of 194 items reflecting work behavior, working conditions, or job characteristics that are assumed to be generalizable across a wide variety of jobs.

FIGURE 5.3   Job Analysis Technique—Sample Items from the Position Analysis Questionnaire (PAQ)

1	INFORMATION INPUT

1.1   Sources of Job Information

Rate each of the following items in terms of the extent to which it is used by the worker as a source of information in performing his job.

Code	Extent of Use (U)
N	Does not apply
1	Nominal/very infrequent
2	Occasional
3	Moderate
4	Considerate
5	Very substantial

1.1.1   Visual Sources of Job Information

1. __U__   Written materials (books, reports, office notes, articles, job instructions, signs, etc.)

2. __U__   Quantitative materials (materials which deal with quantities or amounts, such as graphs, accounts, specifications, tables of numbers, etc.)

3. __U__   Pictorial materials (pictures or picturelike materials used as *sources* of information, for example, drawings, blueprints, diagrams, maps, tracings, photographic films, x-ray films, TV pictures, etc.)

   Patterns/related devices (templates, stencils, patterns, etc., used as *sources* of information when *observed* during use; do *not* include here materials described in item 3 above)

4. __U__   Visual displays (dials, gauges, signal lights, radarscopes, speedometers, clocks, etc.)

37. __S__   Reasoning in problem solving (indicate, using the code below, the level of reasoning that is required of the worker in applying his knowledge, experience, and judgment to problems)

— **Code   Level of Reasoning in Problem Solving**

1   Very limited (use of common sense to carry out simple, or relatively uninvolved instructions, for example, janitor, deliveryman, hod carrier, etc.)

2   Limited (use of some training and/or experience to select from a limited number of solutions the most appropriate action or procedure in performing the job, for example, salesclerk, postman, electrician, apprentice, keypunch operator, etc.)

3   Intermediate (use of relevant principles to solve practical problems and to deal with a variety of concrete variables in situations where only limited standardization exists, for example, draftsman, carpenter, farmer, etc.)

4   Substantlal (use of logic or scientific thinking to define problems, collect information, establish facts, and draw valid conclusions, for example, mechanical engineer, personnel director, manager of a "chain" store, etc.)

5   Very substantial (use of *principles* of logical or scientific thinking to solve a wide range of intellectual and practical problems, for example, research chemist, nuclear engineer, corporate president, or manage of a large branch or plant, etc.)

3.3   Activities of the Entire Body

Code	Importance to This Job (I)		
N	Does not apply	3	Average
1	Very minor	4	High
2	Low	5	Extreme

85. __I__   Highly skilled body coordination (activities involving extensive, and often highly learned coordination activities of the whole body, for example, athletics, dancing, etc.)

86. __I__   Balancing (maintaining body balance or equilibrium to prevent falling when standing, walking, running, crouching, etc., on narrow, slippery, steeply inclined, or erratically moving surfaces, for example, walking on narrow elevated beam, working on steep roof, etc.)

Even though it is widely used, however, the PAQ also has some noteworthy shortcomings. The PAQ instrument itself is relatively complex, and an employee must have the reading level of a college graduate to be able to complete it. Although the PAQ is supposed to be applicable to most jobs, there is reason to believe that it is less useful for higher-level managerial jobs, and it less useful for describing white-collar jobs.[17] Despite these limitations, the PAQ remains the most popular standardized job analysis instrument available and is commonly used by firms such as Kodak, Nestlé USA, and Delta Airlines.

Critical incidents approach   Critical incidents are examples of particularly effective or ineffective performance.[18] When used for job analysis, the **critical incidents approach** focuses on the critical behaviors that distinguish between effective and ineffective performers. Although this approach to job analysis is most widely used in connection with the development of appraisal instruments, it is generally useful because it focuses the organization's attention on aspects of the job that lead to more or less effective performance.

The O*NET   The O*NET is technically not a job analysis procedure; it is a database that provides both basic and advanced job analysis information. As such, it can be viewed as an alternative to conducting job analysis. The O*NET presently has information for over 1000 occupations and is organized according to a system known as the standard occupational classification. For each occupation, information is provided on the relative importance of thirty-three specific knowledge areas including administration and management, mathematics, psychology, and foreign language. The O*NET also provides information about the relative importance of ten basic skills such as reading comprehension, writing, and critical thinking, as well as for thirty-six cross-functional skills such as coordination, persuasion, and time management. Information is also available about experience requirements for different jobs and the importance of various cognitive, physical, sensory, and psychomotor abilities. Links to other resources are provided, and they yield information about legal requirements, job hazards, and environmental conditions.

Although new information is being added all the time, it is still quite possible that the O*NET does not have information that an organization needs about a specific job. Also, the match between the job, as it exists in a given firm, and the job, as it is classified in the O*NET, may not be perfect. Thus, in many cases, more traditional types of job analyses are still needed. Nonetheless, the O*NET provides a valuable resource for anyone interested in doing job analysis, and it is likely to become even more important as various branches of the U.S. government move toward implementing the system.

Although these techniques are the most commonly used in industry, we should note that, in many cases, the organization simply develops its own job analysis technique or instrument. This is especially true for managerial jobs and for jobs performed by teams rather than by individuals. In both cases, no widely accepted standardized job analysis instruments are available. Regardless of which job analysis technique an organization employs, however, at some point a narrative description of the job will probably be needed. Therefore, it is important to draw a distinction between a job description and a job specification, which we discuss in the next section. The HR in the 21st Century feature for this chapter discusses an interesting related issue—job titles.

■ The **critical incidents approach** to job analysis focuses on critical behaviors that distinguish between effective and ineffective performers.

What's in a Job Title?

One often overlooked aspect of job analysis and design is the creation of job titles. Businesses tend to rely on the same titles again and again: production supervisor, administrative clerk, sales associate, vice president of accounting. These titles may seem purely functional, but often they are not. What title should be given to the only employee who can speak Arabic with the firm's Middle Eastern customers? Is it fair to call the person who controls access to the firm's chief executive officer (CEO) a secretary or an assistant? A recent business trend is to allow employees to develop their own creative job titles. These titles serve different purposes: to express workers' true contribution to the organization, to allow workers some autonomy and creative input, and to increase fun. Here are a few examples.

Chief super mom, Jill Darby Ellison, uses her network of parents and knowledge of family events to provide Web content to ActivityOne.com, a firm that provides information about community events. When asked how she obtained the title, Ellison says, "The title is a combination of what I do in my personal life and what I do in my professional life." Seth Zuckerman was hired by Ecotrust to travel the West Coast communicating with local, grassroots environmental efforts. He named his job circuit rider, after the ministers who traveled from church to church in 1800s frontier America. International Paper's division heads have titles such as prince of pine, baron of boards, monarch of mulch, and marquis of machinery. Joe Boxer founder Nicholas Graham goes by the title of chief underpants officer.

Other offbeat job titles include manager of mischief, chief privacy officer, idea ambassador, chief detonator (who provides public relations for start-ups), the truth (the guy who always says the things that people don't want to hear), and web archaeologist. Would you prefer to be addressed as queen for the day, top dog, or minister of comedy? Or perhaps as slave boy? Slave boy is Tim Cleaver of Amazing Online Marketing, who says, "Will Slave Boy be on my resumé? Sure. If a company doesn't want to hire me because I used to have a goofy title, I probably don't want to work there anyway."

> **"Will Slave Boy be on my resumé? Sure. If a company doesn't want to hire me because I used to have a goofy title, I probably don't want to work there anyway."**
>
> (Tim Cleaver, Amazing Online Marketing)*

Sources: Alison Overholt, "Slave Boy," *Fast Company*, June 2001, p. 56; Annie F. Pyatak, "The Truth," *Fast Company*, April 2001, p. 74; Christine Canabou, "Chief Detonator," *Fast Company*, July 2000, p. 64; Curtis Sittenfeld, "Chief Underpants Officer," *Fast Company*, August 1998, p. 54; Curtis Sittenfeld, "Web Archaeologist," *Fast Company*, December 1998, p. 52; Erika Dykstra, "Manager of Mischief," *Fast Company*, December 1999, p. 66; Erika Germer, "Chief Privacy Officer," *Fast Company*, July 2001, p. 50; Erika Germer, "Circuit Rider," *Fast Company*, October 1999, p. 96; Jen Grasso, "Chief Super Mom," *Fast Company*, November 2000, p. 92 (quote); Lauren Heist, "Prince of Pine," *Fast Company*, June 2000, p. 72; Nancy Einhart, "Idea Ambassador," *Fast Company*, April 2001, p. 66.

Job Descriptions and Job Specifications

A **job description** lists the tasks, duties, and responsibilities that a particular job entails. Observable actions are necessary for the effective performance of the job. The job description specifies the major job elements, provides examples of job tasks, and provides some indication of the relative importance in the effective conduct of the job.[19] A **job specification** focuses more on the individual who will perform the job. Specifically, a job specification indicates the knowledge, abilities, skills, and other characteristics that an individual must have to perform the job. Factual or procedural capabilities and levels of proficiency refer more to skills. In general, enduring capabilities that an individual possesses can be thought of as abilities. Job specifications may include general educational requirements, such as

■ A **job description** lists the tasks, duties, and responsibilities for a particular job and specifies the major job elements, provides examples of job tasks, and provides some indication of the relative importance in the effective conduct of the job.

FIGURE 5.4   Example Job Description and Job Specification

Job Title: Accounts Payable and Payroll Accountant, Johnson & Johnson Corp.

Job Description: Business partner with Accounts Payable and Payroll Departments to develop expense forecasts and commentary; prepare Accounts Payable and Payroll shared services charge-outs to affiliates; ensure Accounts Payable and Payroll inputs are posted weekly; perform account analysis/reconciliations of Cash, Liability, and Employee Loan accounts related to Accounts Payable and Payroll; submit routine reports to Corporate; identify and implement process improvements relative to all responsibilities listed above.

Job Specification: BS degree in accounting or finance; 2+ years of accounting/finance experience; sound knowledge of Integral Accounts Payable and General Ledger Systems; working knowledge of Hyperion Software, PACT; good communication skills; able to work independently at off-site location.

■ A **job specification** focuses on the individual who will perform the job and indicates the knowledge, abilities, skills, and other characteristics that an individual must have to be able to perform the job.

having a high school degree or a college degree, as well as the specifications of job-related skills, such as the ability to keyboard seventy words a minute, or the requirement that an individual be fluent in Japanese or Spanish.

Taken together then, the job description and the job specification should provide a parallel and mutually consistent set of information and details that focuses on the job itself and the individual most likely to be successful performing that job. This information should then inform all subsequent recruiting and selection decisions. Figure 5.4 illustrates an actual job description and job specification for a particular kind of accountant at Johnson & Johnson. This description and specification were created as part of a job analysis and are used to communicate to job applicants and managers what skills and abilities are necessary to perform the job.

MODELING COMPETENCIES AND THE END OF THE "JOB"

As we begin a new century, many scholars and other human resource experts have argued that the nature of work is changing so much that the concept of a "job" is becoming obsolete. Although many people will continue to have "jobs" for some time to come, in some work settings it may well be true that the traditional view of jobs and work is no longer applicable. In these settings people usually work on teams where the focus is on getting tasks accomplished rather than on specific task requirements. Also, some employees rotate tasks and responsibilities over time. In these situations there is a clear need for an alternative to traditional job analysis techniques (including the O*NET). Even in cases where people continue to perform traditional jobs, however, there is potential value in approaching the problem from the perspective of modeling competencies instead of describing jobs.

Some view competencies as being broader than abilities, while others suggest that competencies exist at a deeper level and really underlie abilities. Generally, however, experts view competencies as characteristics of employees (or teams of employees) that lead to success on the job. Thus, abilities such as decisiveness and adaptability are seen as competencies that might underlie more specific abilities such as decision making or coping with change. Whatever the definition used, competency modeling represents a dramatic shift in focus from most traditional job analysis (although it is closer to the Fleishman approach described earlier than to other traditional job analysis approaches).

The idea driving this approach is that organizations must define what people need to be successful. It is not important to know whether an employee will type letters or run a lathe. It is important in this view, however, to know that the employee needs to be adaptable. Typically, teams of top managers, working with consultants, identify the competencies necessary to compete in the future. These competencies are then described in clear behavioral terms, measures are designed, and each is rated according to its relative importance for future success. Employees who have these competencies are then sought through the recruiting and selection process, or current employees are provided training opportunities to acquire these competencies and are then rewarded when they do acquire them. (See the discussion of skill-based pay and knowledge-based pay in Chapter 12.) The critical difference is that the human resource manager no longer focuses on what is needed to be successful at one job, but instead focuses on what is needed to be successful at any and all jobs within the organization.

As we shall see in Chapter 7, this competency modeling approach has the greatest implications for selection. And as we shall see later in this chapter, this approach can lead to some potential problems with legal issues because it is harder to defend the decision to hire someone based on general competencies rather than on the specific requirements of a particular job.

JOB DESIGN IN THE WORKPLACE

Job analysis is conducted to learn more about what people do on their jobs. Human resource managers have other reasons, however, for their interest in studying jobs. Some organizations attempt to learn what happens on current jobs to create better jobs for their employees. Indeed, job design is one of the more popular strategies for improving the quality of employee work life. **Job design** is the determination of an individual's work-related responsibilities. For a machinist at Caterpillar, let's say, job design might specify what machines are to be operated, how they are to be operated, and what performance standards are expected. For a manager at Caterpillar, job design would involve defining areas of decision-making responsibility, identifying goals and expectations, and establishing appropriate indicators of success. The natural starting point for designing jobs is determining the level of desired specialization. This stems from the fact that as companies grow and as they seek new avenues to boost productivity, there are natural tendencies toward specializing jobs.

Job specialization is the degree to which the overall task of the organization is broken down and divided into smaller component parts. Job specialization evolved from the concept of *division of labor*. Adam Smith, an eighteenth-century economist, described how division of labor was used in a pin factory to improve productivity. One worker drew the wire, another straightened it, a third cut it, a

■ **Job design** is the determination of an individual's work-related responsibilities.

■ **Job specialization** is the degree to which the overall task of the organization is broken down and divided into smaller component parts.

The shift from individual production to mass production has resulted in much greater specialization for workers. Individual workers each perform relatively simple tasks—over and over—as part of a larger assembly or manufacturing process. This inspector checks Harley Davidson motorcycles as they come off the assembly line. The inspector has no part in the actual assembly of the motorcycle. He is responsible solely for ensuring that each one meets quality standards.

fourth filed the point, and so on. Smith claimed that ten workers working in this fashion were able to produce 48,000 pins a day, whereas each worker working alone would have been able to produce only twenty pins per day. The best example of the impact of specialization is the automobile assembly line pioneered by Henry Ford and his contemporaries. Mass-production capabilities stemming from job specialization techniques have had a profound impact throughout the world. High levels of low-cost production transformed U.S. society during the first several decades of the twentieth century into one of the strongest economies in the history of the world. And today examples of job specialization can be found in settings as diverse as computer assembly lines to fast-food restaurants.

Job specialization was really an outgrowth of the scientific management movement discussed in Chapter 1 and represents a mechanistic approach to job design. It has been argued that this approach to job design provides four benefits to organizations.[20] First, workers performing small, simple tasks will probably become proficient at those tasks. Second, transfer time between tasks may decrease. If employees perform several different tasks, some time may be lost as they stop doing the first task and start doing the next. Third, the more narrowly defined a job is, the easier it may be to develop specialized equipment to assist with that job. Fourth, when an employee who performs a highly specialized job is absent or quits, the manager should be able to train someone new at relatively low cost. Although specialization is generally thought of in terms of manufacturing jobs, many organizations have extended the basic elements of specialization to managerial and professional jobs as well.

On the other hand, job specialization can have negative consequences. The foremost criticism is that workers who perform highly specialized jobs may become bored and dissatisfied. The job may be so specialized that it offers no challenge or stimulation. Boredom and monotony set in, absenteeism rises, and the quality of the work may suffer. The anticipated benefits of specialization also do not always occur. For example, an early study conducted at Maytag found that the time spent moving work in process from one worker to another was greater than the time needed for the same individual to change from job to job. Thus, although some degree of specialization is necessary, it should not be carried to extremes because of the negative consequences that could result. Managers should be sensitive to situations where extreme specialization should be avoided. Even jobs that are not inherently specialized, of course, can also become tedious through constant repetition.

To counter the problems associated with specialization and repetition, managers have sought other approaches to job design that achieve a better balance between organizational demands for efficiency and productivity and individual needs for creativity and autonomy. Several other general approaches to job design have therefore been proposed and discussed. We will discuss two of these briefly here. In the next section we will focus more fully on a third alternative approach to specialization that is much more prevalent in modern organizations.

The biological approach focuses on **ergonomics,** which is the study of the interface between an individual's physical characteristics and the environmental requirements of the job. This approach leads to interventions such as providing chairs that do not put undue stress on the back and computer keyboards that support the wrists and thus help reduce the chances of developing carpal tunnel syndrome. Many automobile manufacturers have also become concerned with ergonomics in the design of cars, especially relative to the design of seats and some controls.

The perceptual-motor approach is somewhat related to the biological approach, but it is concerned with the possibility of exceeding a person's mental capabilities. Thus, lighting might be changed to prevent glare and reduce eye stress, or dials might be redesigned to make them easier to read. Helmets for fighter pilots now include digital readouts that are projected inside the helmet so that the pilot does not have to glance down to read an instrument while flying at supersonic speeds.

Many changes in the workplace environment are made to make work more "user friendly," often relying on principles from ergonomics. In 2003 Ford Motor Company unveiled a new design for a production line used to produce F150 truck cabs. With the new design, each vehicle moves on a wooden platform and a lift allows it to be adjusted to the correct height for each worker. This design should reduce fatigue and allow workers to be more efficient. The new production facility using this modified assembly line is set to open in Dearborn, Michigan, in 2004.

■ **Ergonomics** is the study of the interface between an individual's physical characteristics and the environmental requirements of the job.

MOTIVATIONAL APPROACHES TO JOB DESIGN

The third alternative approach to job specialization, known as the motivational approach, is concerned with designing jobs so that they will motivate employees to work harder. Motivation is stimulated by making the job more interesting and/or challenging. We will focus on various job design techniques that fall under this last heading, but we should note that each approach can provide benefits to the organization and that each also has its own drawbacks. An instrument (the multimethod job design questionnaire) has been designed to help an organization evaluate job design relative to all four approaches (job specialization plus the three alternative approaches).[21]

The motivational approach to job design has clearly had the greatest impact on the design of work. This approach was conceived as an alternative to job specialization, but it also focuses on trying to increase employee motivation directly through the design of work. We will discuss five motivational approaches to job design: job rotation, job enlargement, job enrichment, the job characteristics approach, and work teams. As we shall see, the use of work teams is a bit different in its intent. Although a driving consideration is still to help motivate employees to work harder, this approach is also concerned with designing more effective ways of doing a job, and it has a great deal of applicability in today's organizations.

■ **Job rotation** involves systematically moving employees from one job to another.

Job rotation involves systematically moving employees from one job to another. A worker in a warehouse might unload trucks on Monday, carry incoming inventory to storage on Tuesday, verify invoices on Wednesday, pull outgoing inventory from storage on Thursday, and load trucks on Friday. Thus, the jobs do not change; instead, workers move from job to job. For this very reason, however, job rotation has not been very successful in enhancing employee motivation or satisfaction. Jobs that are amenable to rotation tend to be relatively standard and routine. Workers who are rotated to a "new" job may be more satisfied at first, but the novelty soon wanes. Although many companies (among them American Cyanamid, Bethlehem Steel, Ford, Prudential Insurance, TRW, and Western Electric) have tried job rotation, it is most often used today as a training device to improve worker skills and flexibility.

■ **Job enlargement** was developed to increase the total number of tasks workers perform based on the assumption that doing the same basic task over and over is the primary cause of worker dissatisfaction.

Based on the assumption that doing the same basic task over and over is the primary cause of worker dissatisfaction, **job enlargement** was developed to increase the total number of tasks that workers perform. As a result, all workers perform a wide variety of tasks, presumably reducing the level of job dissatisfaction. Many organizations have used job enlargement, including IBM, Detroit Edison, AT&T, the U.S. Civil Service, and Maytag. At Maytag, for example, the assembly line for producing washing-machine water pumps was systematically changed so that work originally performed by six workers, who passed the work sequentially from one person to another, was performed by four workers, each of whom assembled a complete pump. Although job enlargement does have some positive consequences, they are often offset by several disadvantages: (1) training costs usually rise; (2) unions have argued that pay should increase because the worker is doing more tasks; and (3) in many cases, the work remains boring and routine even after job enlargement.

■ **Job enrichment** attempts to increase both the number of tasks a worker does and the control the worker has over the job.

A more comprehensive approach, **job enrichment**, assumes that increasing the range and variety of tasks alone is not sufficient to improve employee motivation.[22] Thus, job enrichment attempts to increase both the number of tasks a worker does and the control the worker has over the job. To accomplish this objective, managers remove some controls from the job; delegate more authority to employees; and structure the work in complete, natural units. These changes increase the subordinates' sense of responsibility. Another part of job enrichment is to assign new and challenging tasks continually, thereby increasing the employees' opportunity for growth and advancement.

AT&T was one of the first companies to try job enrichment. In one experiment, eight typists in a service unit prepared customer-service orders. Faced with low output and high turnover, management determined that the typists felt little responsibility to clients and received little feedback. The unit was changed to create a typing team. Typists were matched with designated service representatives, the task was changed from ten specific steps to three more general steps, and job titles were upgraded. As a result the number of orders delivered on time increased from 27 to 90 percent, the need for messenger service was eliminated, accuracy improved, and turnover became practically nil.[23] Other organizations that have tried job enrichment include Texas Instruments, IBM, and General Foods. Problems have been found with this approach, however. For example, analysis of work systems before enrichment is needed but seldom performed, and managers rarely deal with employee preferences when enriching jobs.

The **job characteristics approach** is an alternative to job specialization that does take into account the work system and employee preferences.[24] It is also one of the most widely used and widely studied approaches to job design. As illustrated in Figure 5.5, the job characteristics approach suggests that jobs should be examined and improved along five core dimensions:

1. *Skill variety:* the number of tasks a person does in a job

2. *Task identity:* the extent to which the worker does a complete or identifiable portion of the total job

3. *Task significance:* the perceived importance of the task

4. *Autonomy:* the degree of control the worker has over how the work is performed

5. *Feedback:* the extent to which the worker knows how well the job is being performed

The higher a job rates on these five dimensions, the more employees will experience various psychological states. Experiencing these states, in turn, presumably leads to high motivation, high-quality performance, high satisfaction, and low absenteeism and turnover. Finally, a variable called growth-need strength is

■ The **job characteristics approach** is an alternative to job specialization that takes into account the work system and employee preferences; it suggests that jobs should be diagnosed and improved along five core dimensions.

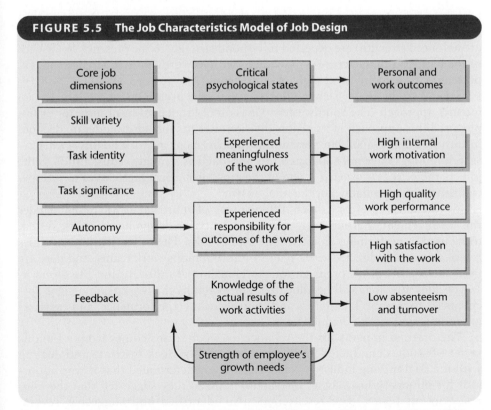

FIGURE 5.5 The Job Characteristics Model of Job Design

Source: J. R. Hackman and G. R. Oldham, "Motivation Through the Design of Work: Test of a Theory," from *Organizational Behavior and Human Performance*, Vol. 16, 1976, pp. 250–279. Reprinted with permission from Elsevier.

Teams are increasingly common in the workplace as organizations realize that certain tasks are best handled by a group of individuals working together towards a common goal. Of course, this model of accomplishing tasks has been around for a long time in other settings. For example, the yacht racing crew pictured here is a team. Although each person has a specific task to carry out, the boat will only perform well if everyone does his or her job and coordinates with every other crew member. This particular example also illustrates the advantages and potential disadvantages of working in teams. It is difficult to imagine sailing such a large boat with only one person, or with a group of people who do not work well together. Yet in the flurry of activity it is difficult to monitor behavior to ensure that each person does his or her best as part of the team. Thus it is important that each team member understand and be committed to the goals of the team in order for the team to be successful.

■ A **work team** is an arrangement in which a group is given responsibility for designing the work system to be used in performing an interrelated set of jobs.

presumed to affect how the model works for different people. People with a strong desire to grow, develop, and expand their capabilities (indicative of high growth-need strength) are expected to respond strongly to the presence or absence of the basic job characteristics; individuals with low growth-need strength are expected not to respond as strongly or consistently.

Several studies have been conducted to test the usefulness of the job characteristics approach. The Southwestern Division of Prudential Insurance, for example, used this approach in its claims division. Results included moderate declines in turnover and a small but measurable improvement in work quality. Other research findings have not supported this approach as strongly. Thus, although the job characteristics approach is one of the most promising alternatives to job specialization, it is probably not the final answer.

Work teams represent a much different way of approaching job design. Under this arrangement, a group is given responsibility for designing the work system to be used in performing an interrelated set of jobs. These groups are sometimes referred to as self-directed work teams or autonomous work teams, and they are permanent parts of the organizational architecture. In these teams, the group itself decides how jobs will be allocated. For example, the work team assigns specific tasks to members, monitors and controls its own performance, and exercises autonomy over work scheduling.

The original impetus for the reliance on work teams comes from a famous series of studies conducted in England by the Tavistock Institute and dealing with the coal-mining industry.[25] The researchers determined that it was important for miners to have social interaction, and so they suggested that the miners work in teams. The researchers also identified and suggested several changes in the actual coal-mining jobs themselves. As it turned out, the job changes were also conducive to team settings in that they increased the need for coordination. After the jobs were changed and the workers formed into

POINT | COUNTERPOINT

Should Work Be Designed for Teams?

Teams are growing in popularity, and there is a lot of talk about the importance of teamwork in organizations. But teams are not for everyone, and many challenges come with the reliance on teams to get the job done.

POINT... Teams are useful and effective because ...	COUNTERPOINT... Teams are a problem because ...
They are consistent with the way most work is done today.	They make it difficult to assess the contributions of individual employees, which in turn makes rewards, based on performance, difficult to manage.
They encourage cooperation and allow flexibility for the organization.	They require close coordination within teams and even more across teams, and it is not clear that flexibility is increased.
They allow workers to have more control over their lives.	Many workers do not really want that control because it also entails responsibilities such as scheduling.
They provide important social interactions for workers, and those interactions make jobs more motivating.	They make it easier for employees to waste time on the job.

So ... Teams can provide significant benefits to organizations, and in some cases, the nature of the work dictates that teams are how the work *should* be done. But teams bring problems and complications, so they should be used only when the nature of the work and the nature of the employees involved support their use.

---

teams, performance in the mines improved considerably, and the miners reported more satisfaction and increased motivation. Hence, in some settings, teams make a great deal of sense. But work teams are not without problems and they certainly are not the answer in all cases. The Point/Counterpoint feature above explores some of the issues associated with the use of teams at work.

LEGAL ISSUES IN JOB ANALYSIS AND JOB DESIGN

Because job analysis is a critical building block for much of the human resource management process, it should not be surprising that numerous legal issues have been raised with regard to job analysis. In fact, federal government guidelines on selection include discussion of the appropriate ways to conduct job analysis and state that any attempt to establish the job relatedness of a selection instrument must begin with a careful analysis of the jobs in question. Most of the specific cases, in fact, have been concerned more with the *failure* of an organization to perform a job analysis. For example, in *Albermarle* v. *Moody* the Albermarle Paper Company had argued that tests found to be job related for one set of jobs could be used to select employees for another set of jobs that they argued were similar.[26] The court found that, in the absence of clear job analysis information to support such a claim (and there was no job analysis information), it was unacceptable to assume that the jobs in question were the same.

The Americans with Disabilities Act of 1990 (ADA) raises additional legal issues associated with job analysis. As noted in Chapter 2, the ADA states that an employer must offer a reasonable accommodation to any employee who has a disability and who can perform the "essential functions" of the job. Basically, essential functions are those that take up a significant part of the employee's time, are performed regularly, and have consequences for other parts of the job. Organizations need to rely on careful job analysis to determine exactly what those essential functions are and thus determine if the employee is entitled to an accommodation under the law.

Finally, several issues regarding the accuracy of job analysis information have potential legal implications.[27] Perhaps the most troubling of these issues relates to potential gender discrimination in job analysis. Specifically, evidence suggests that jobs occupied primarily by male incumbents are more likely to be rated as more complex and higher level than are similar jobs occupied primarily by female incumbents.[28] One striking result that has been published relates to different job analysis information generated for the jobs of "prison guard" and "prison matron," which are simply the traditional titles for persons of different gender doing the same job (these different titles are no longer used, incidentally). Because the information from job analysis can be used for determining appraisal systems as well as compensation rates, this problem is potentially serious.

Finally, as discussed in Chapter 2, the creation of autonomous work teams has presented a new legal challenge. In the *Electromation* decision, the National Labor Relations Board (NLRB) ruled that the autonomous work teams and action committees created at the company were illegal labor organizations.[29] That is, they were labor organizations because they scheduled work, determined wages, and made selection and promotion decisions; and they were illegal because they were created and controlled by management.

Chapter Summary

Job analysis is one of the building blocks of the human resource planning process and is also a fundamental source of information for that same planning process. Job analysis involves the gathering and organizing of detailed information about various jobs within the organization so that managers can better understand the processes through which jobs are most effectively performed. Job analysis provides input to the human resource planning process by helping planners better understand exactly what kinds of work must be performed.

Job analysis itself generally follows a three-step process: determining information needs, determining methods for obtaining information, and determining who will collect information. The responsibility of analysis is jointly shared by line managers, the human resource group or department, and the job analyst(s). Commonly used methods of job analysis include the narrative approach, Fleishman job analysis system, task analysis inventory, functional job analysis, position analysis questionnaire, and critical incidents approach.

Job design is the determination of an individual's work-related responsibilities. Job specialization is the degree to which the overall task of the organization is broken down and divided into smaller component parts. Job rotation involves systematically moving employees from one job to another. Based on the assumption that doing the same basic task over and over is the primary cause of worker dissatisfaction, job enlargement was developed to increase the total number of tasks that workers perform. A more comprehensive approach, job enrichment, assumes that increasing the range and variety of tasks alone is not sufficient to improve employee motivation. The job characteristics approach is an alternative to job specialization that takes into account the work system and employee preferences. Another alternative to job specialization is work teams.

Key Points for Future HR Managers

▶ Job analysis provides critical information about what people do on their jobs.

▶ Job analysis information provides the basis for recruitment, selection, compensation, appraisal, and training.

▶ Various sources of job analysis information are available and each has advantages and drawbacks. You must match the job analyst to your needs.

▶ Several job analysis methods are available. The position analysis questionnaire is the most widely used structured instrument, but you should be aware of the strengths and weaknesses of each technique and choose a technique based on your needs.

▶ The O*NET is a potentially revolutionary approach to job analysis that may replace other job analysis techniques, especially in smaller companies.

▶ Competency modeling is a new approach to job analysis. It focuses on broader requirements and on those requirements that might be applicable for a wide variety of jobs within an organization.

▶ Job design emphasizes the creation of an optimal design for the tasks that someone does at work and includes several approaches and models. The most widely used is the job characteristics model, which attempts to design jobs so that they are more motivating for employees.

▶ Reliance on teams is a different but increasingly popular approach to the design of work, but it too has strengths and weaknesses.

▶ Job analysis (or the absence thereof) has been an important part of the legal pressures on the human resource management function, and any attempt to establish the job relatedness of a test, where the basis for the argument is not a careful job analysis, is doomed to failure in the courts.

▶ The Americans with Disabilities Act has made job analysis an even more critical part of the system because the act emphasizes the establishment of the "critical functions" on a job.

Key Points for Future General Managers

▶ Job analysis is and should be the basic cornerstone for all other human resource management functions.

▶ It is essential to understand the strengths and weaknesses of different job analysis approaches because one is not better than the others.

▶ Competency modeling is concerned with identifying broader sets of requirements that may cut across individual jobs within an organization.

▶ It is possible to design (or redesign) jobs so that employees are motivated to work harder simply because of the nature of the work they do. Although this approach does not work for everyone, it is important to realize that the design of jobs can have an important impact on productivity.

▶ Autonomous work teams can be very helpful, but they also have drawbacks.

▶ Consistent court rulings have made it clear that attempts to establish the job relatedness of tests must be based on careful job analysis.

▶ Under certain circumstances, the formation of autonomous work teams can be viewed as the formation of illegal work organizations, which violates the National Labor Relations Act.

Review and Discussion Questions

1. Identify the basic purposes of job analysis.

2. List the steps in job analysis.

3. Compare and contrast job descriptions and job specifications.

4. Compare and contrast the major techniques that organizations use for job analysis.

5. Can all jobs be analyzed? Why or why not?

6. Are there circumstances when managers might choose not to have job descriptions and/or job specifications?

7. Distinguish between job behaviors and job competencies.

8. What is the ergonomic approach to job design?

9. Compare and contrast job rotation, job enlargement, and job enrichment.

10. Summarize the basic legal issues related to job analysis.

Closing Case

Doing the Dirty Work

Business magazines and newspapers regularly publish articles about the changing nature of work in the United States and about how many jobs are being changed. Indeed, because so much has been made of the shift toward service-sector and professional jobs, many people assume that the number of unpleasant and undesirable jobs has declined.

In fact, nothing could be further from the truth. Millions of Americans work in gleaming air-conditioned facilities, but many others work in dirty, grimy, and unsafe settings. For example, many jobs in the recycling industry require workers to sort through moving conveyors of trash, pulling out those items that can be recycled. Other relatively unattractive jobs include cleaning hospital restrooms, washing dishes in a restaurant, and handling toxic waste.

Consider the jobs in a chicken-processing facility. Much like a manufacturing assembly line, a chicken-processing facility is organized around a moving conveyor system. Workers call it the chain. In reality, it's a steel cable with large clips that carries dead chickens down what might be called a "disassembly line." Standing along this line are dozens of workers who do, in fact, take the birds apart as they pass.

Even the titles of the jobs are unsavory. Among the first set of jobs along the chain is the skinner. Skinners use sharp instruments to cut and pull the skin off the dead chicken. Toward the middle of the line are the gut pullers. These workers reach inside the chicken carcasses and remove the intestines and other organs. At the end of the line are the gizzard cutters, who tackle the more difficult organs attached to the inside of the chicken's carcass. These organs have to be individually cut and removed for disposal.

The work is obviously distasteful, and the pace of the work is unrelenting. On a good day the chain moves an average of ninety chickens a minute for nine hours. And the workers are essentially held captive by the moving chain. For example, no one can vacate a post to use the bathroom or for other reasons without the permission of the supervisor. In some plants, taking an unauthorized bathroom break can result in suspension without pay. But the noise in a typical chicken-processing plant is so loud that the supervisor can't hear someone calling for relief unless the person happens to be standing close by.

Jobs such as these on the chicken-processing line are actually becoming increasingly common. Fueled by Americans' growing appetites for lean, easy-to-cook meat, the number of poultry workers has almost doubled since 1980, and today they constitute a workforce of around a quarter of a million people. Indeed, the chicken-processing industry has become a major component of the state economies of Georgia, North Carolina, Mississippi, Arkansas, and Alabama.

Besides being unpleasant and dirty, many jobs in a chicken-processing plant are dangerous and unhealthy. Some workers, for example, have to fight the live birds when they are first hung on the chains. These workers are routinely scratched and pecked by the chickens. And the air inside a typical chicken-processing plant is difficult to breathe. Workers are usually supplied with paper masks, but most don't use them because they are hot and confining.

And the work space itself is so tight that the workers often cut themselves—and sometimes their coworkers—with the knives, scissors, and other instruments they use to perform their jobs. Indeed, poultry processing ranks third among industries in the United States for cumulative trauma injuries such as carpel tunnel syndrome. The inevitable chicken feath-

ers, feces, and blood also contribute to the hazardous and unpleasant work environment.[30]

Case Questions

1. How relevant are the concepts of competencies to the jobs in a chicken-processing plant?

2. How might you try to improve the jobs in a chicken-processing plant?

3. Are dirty, dangerous, and unpleasant jobs an inevitable part of any economy?

Building HR Management Skills

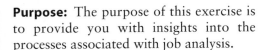

Purpose: The purpose of this exercise is to provide you with insights into the processes associated with job analysis.

Step 1: Your instructor will divide the class into small groups of four to five members each.

Step 2: Your group should select a job with which group members have some familiarity. Examples might be cook at McDonald's, retail clerk at The Gap, or a similar job.

Step 3: Based on group members' understanding of the job, outline how you would conduct a job analysis for that job.

Step 4: Draft a job description and a job specification that you think represent the job.

Step 5: Assume you are managers in the company you chose for analysis. Develop planning scenarios for growth, stability, and reductions.

Ethical Dilemmas in HR Management

Assume you are a manager for a manufacturing company. For years your low-wage workers have complained because their jobs are boring. At the same time, you also know that the highly specialized nature of each job maximizes efficiency and allows you to pay relatively low wages (because it's easy to replace anyone who leaves).

You recently interviewed for a job with another company. Even though you decided not to take the position, you did have a chance to tour and study that firm's production facilities. You learned that your firm could actually change the jobs in your factory in ways that would make them more stimulating and enjoyable for your workers. But you also know that you would lose a relatively small degree of efficiency. In addition, because the jobs would be a bit more chal-

lenging, you might have to pay higher wages.

You have two choices. One is to keep the jobs in your plant as they are currently designed (maximizing efficiency and minimizing wage costs) but keep a bored and disinterested workforce. The other is to redesign the jobs in the plant (losing some efficiency and perhaps increasing labor costs), but your workers would find their jobs more enjoyable and challenging.

Questions

1. What are the ethical issues in this situation?

2. What are the basic arguments for each course of action?

3. What do you think most managers would do? What would you do?

HR Internet Exercise

 Use the Internet to see what information you can obtain about the jobs listed below:

1. Sanitation workers

2. Coffee brewers

3. Petroleum refinery workers

4. Retail clerks

5. Restaurant cooks

Questions

1. Identify the essential skills and competencies needed to perform each of these jobs.

2. How valuable do you think the Internet is for job analysis and job design?

3. Do you need any additional information that you could not find on the Internet?

6

CHAPTER OBJECTIVES

After studying this chapter you should be able to:

■ Identify the organization's and the individual's goals in recruiting.

■ Identify and discuss the basic sources for recruiting.

■ Describe various methods for recruiting and note the advantages and disadvantages of each.

■ Discuss realistic job previews and their role in effective recruiting.

■ Identify and discuss common alternatives to recruiting.

■ Describe job choice from the standpoint of prospective employees.

■ Discuss how organizations evaluate the recruiting process.

Recruiting Human Resources

One of the many consequences of the terrorist attacks of September 11, 2001, was that the U.S. government decided to take over passenger security screening at most of the nation's commercial airports. Screening had previously been handled by various private firms hired by individual airports (at larger airports) or by airline employees themselves (primarily at smaller airports). The purpose behind the change was to bring greater control and a higher level of competence and consistency to the screening process and thus boost security and airline safety.

The Transportation Security Administration (TSA), created in response to the September 11 attacks, was assigned responsibility for hiring and maintaining a workforce of screeners at the nation's 429 commercial airports. Five airports continued to have privately employed screeners under a pilot program approved by Congress, but the other 424 were mandated to have an all-federal workforce by November 19, 2002.

When the government first tried to recruit screeners, officials found that a surprisingly high percentage of the applicants were unqualified. And there were far fewer female candidates than expected. The Transportation Security Administration had initially set a goal of filling half of all the screening positions with women. But because so few qualified women could be recruited, the agency eventually had to reduce this goal to one-third.

Officials also had to step up advertising and recruitment campaigns—job fairs were launched in various cities, for example. The Transportation Security Administration also began trying to attract more qualified applicants—and women in particular—by offering part-time positions or seasonal work. In addition, there has been more online advertising and increased listings with both private and public employment agencies.

There was even doubt for a while that the agency would be able to meet its federally mandated deadline. "Initial difficulties in hiring and training the passenger screener work force made it a challenge for TSA to meet the deadline for federalizing this work force," said Gerald Dillingham, the General Accounting Office (GAO) director of civil aviation issues. But that problem may be the tip of the iceberg. That is, given the difficulties in attracting qualified applicants to begin with, it may be even harder to attract new applicants in the future when the job market begins to improve in other sectors of the economy.[1] ■

> *"Initial difficulties in hiring and training the passenger screener work force made it a challenge for TSA to meet the deadline for federalizing this work force."*
>
> (Gerald Dillingham, the GAO's director of civil aviation issues)*

Managers at the Transportation Security Administration (TSA) face a real dilemma because they are charged with attracting qualified applicants to fill important jobs but have had difficulties in doing so. In one way or another, all organizations must address the problems and opportunities faced by the TSA—the need to recruit new people who are both interested and capable of working for them.

In this chapter we examine the recruiting process in more detail. We start by assessing the goals of recruiting. We then look at the sources and methods of recruiting. After describing the importance of realistic job previews in effective recruiting, we discuss the recruitment of part-time and temporary workers, as well as alternatives to recruiting. Finally, we briefly note how organizations evaluate the effectiveness of their recruiting efforts.

PLANNING AND RECRUITING

In Chapter 2 we discussed planning for growth strategies and planning for stability strategies. In both cases, an organization needs to attract new employees from the outside. Although recruiting is concerned with internal as well as external sources of employees, much of the strategic focus is on external recruiting. In the case of a growth strategy, the organization simply needs more employees in the future than it does now. Clearly this situation requires acquiring new human resources from the outside. As noted in Chapter 2, however, even a stability strategy requires the acquisition of new resources to replace those employees who leave and/or retire.

Except under the scenario where the organization is planning for reductions, recruiting activities are critical to the strategic goals of the organization. Even when the firm is planning for reductions, however, those reductions may not be across the board, so that the need for employees in some areas may decrease while the need for employees in other areas may increase, thus necessitating recruitment. For instance, a firm may be planning to shut down one of its operations, thus eliminating jobs at that work site. At the same time, it may be facing needs for new employees in other areas and/or employees who have skills not reflected among the employees who are laid off. So an organization may be in the paradoxical position of attempting to reduce the number of overall people it employs while simultaneously hiring new employees. Of course, it is difficult for an employee who has lost his or her job because of layoffs to realize that, at the same time employees are being let go, the company is actively seeking new employees in other areas.

Recruiting is the process of developing a pool of qualified applicants who are interested in working for the organization and from which the organization might reasonably select the best individual or individuals to hire for employment.[2] As we will see, however, and as illustrated in Figure 6.1, it is important to remember that recruiting is a two-way street. That is, just as the organization is looking for qualified job applicants, those applicants are also likely to be looking at various potential employment opportunities. Thus, both organizations and individuals have recruiting goals.[3] The best hiring opportunities for organizations and employment opportunities for job seekers emerge when these different goals match.

■ **Recruiting** is the process of developing a pool of qualified applicants who are interested in working for the organization and from which the organization might reasonably select the best individual or individuals to hire for employment.

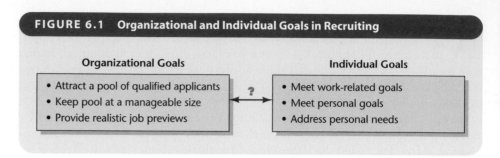

FIGURE 6.1 Organizational and Individual Goals in Recruiting

Organizational Goals		Individual Goals
• Attract a pool of qualified applicants • Keep pool at a manageable size • Provide realistic job previews	?	• Meet work-related goals • Meet personal goals • Address personal needs

The Organization's Goals in Recruiting

The most basic and fundamental goal of an organization's recruiting effort is essentially to fulfill the definition of recruiting—to develop a pool of qualified applicants. This overriding goal, however, also suggests several related goals that are important to the recruiting process.

One of these goals is to optimize the size of the pool of qualified applicants. If an organization has, say, ten openings, and somehow attracts several thousand applicants for those ten jobs, then the organization has actually created a considerably large problem for itself. Enormous amounts of time and resources will be necessary to process the large number of applicants for the positions, and if this processing is not handled effectively and efficiently, then ill will for the organization will result. Thus, the human resource department handling the recruiting process does not really want to attract a pool of applicants that is too large.

Of course, the human resource department should also have as a goal attracting a talent pool that is greater than the number of available positions. That is, the organization presumably wants to have some discretion over whom it hires. Thus, a recruiting process that generates ten applicants for ten jobs is not necessarily effective. In this case the organization is not completely sure that it has the ten best people for the ten jobs, but managers may have little choice over whom they will hire. We will touch again on this notion of optimizing rather than maximizing the size of the recruitment pool, but in a different context, in the next chapter.

The goal of the recruiting process is not necessarily to achieve fine grades of differentiation among job applicants. That concern is really part of the selection process, which we will cover in detail in Chapter 7. The goal of the recruiting process is simply to generate a reasonably large pool of qualified applicants who are interested in working for the organization and then to allow the selection process to help determine which individual applicant or which set of applicants should be hired. Notice, however, that it is necessary to have *qualified* applicants. Thus, although we are not interested at this stage in identifying the truly best potential employees, successful recruiting means generating a pool of potential employees who have a reasonable chance of being successful on the job.

A final goal of the recruiting process is to offer an honest and candid assessment to prospective applicants of what kinds of jobs and what kinds of opportunities the organization can potentially make available to them. It does no one any good to trick or mislead job applicants into thinking that they will have more challenging or higher-level jobs than are actually available or that they will be earning higher salaries than the organization is prepared to pay. Thus, the recruiting process needs to paint a realistic picture of what the potential job entails. We discuss this issue in more detail later when we discuss realistic job previews.

The Prospective Employee's Goals in Recruiting

Of course, it is also important for the organization to remember that the prospective employee in the recruiting pool also has goals that affect the process. Indeed, human resource managers must never forget that recruiting is a two-way process. Just as the organization is seeking qualified applicants who are interested in employment with the firm, so too are individuals likely to be approaching several organizations and trying to entice as many of them as possible to offer employment.[4]

Thus, the organization is attempting to develop a pool of qualified applicants and individuals are simultaneously attempting to create a pool of potentially interesting and attractive job opportunities from which they can select. As a result, it is important for the human resource manager to understand prospective employees' goals as part of their own recruiting process. During the economic downturn in 2002, many job seekers turned to creative and unusual ways to attract the attention of potential employers. Some examples are discussed in HR in the 21st Century.

In many cases a prospective employee's goals are relatively straightforward. Individuals work for several reasons, but the most common are financial income, job security, promotion opportunities, benefits, challenging work assignments, and so forth. In addition to these goals, however, individuals can also have idiosyncratic goals. For example, some people put extra emphasis on the location of a particular job opportunity. They may want to work close to their hometown, close to where they went to school, in a big city, in a small city, near family, near the ocean, or near recreational opportunities.[5]

Another goal that prospective employees may have is to optimize their personal situations. For example, in small cities with large universities, many job applicants are students or the spouses of students, thus creating a relatively unique labor market. On the one hand, an organization interested in recruiting prospective employees is likely to have a large pool from which to choose. On the other hand, because of the transient nature of students and student families, many employees recruited from such a labor pool are likely to want jobs only for a few years.

While organizations seek applicants, unemployed persons are seeking jobs. Finding creative ways to get the two groups together and get a potential employer to notice a potential employee can sometimes be more rewarding than more traditional methods of recruiting and job hunting. The man in this photo is attending a Pink Slip Party in the Silicon Valley in California. As the dot-com bust led to increased layoffs in the area, the frequency of parties where employers and the unemployed were invited to meet in a relaxed setting also increased. When times get tough for job seekers, creative approaches such as this man's sign on his back are more likely to get attention than more common approaches such as simply handing out his resumé.

Job Seekers Take Creativity to a New Level

Forget the classifieds. As the job search becomes increasingly competitive, employees are getting far more creative—and desperate—in their search for work. They're sending cakes and flowers to hiring managers; passing out resumés on street corners; and in some cases, taking jobs for no pay. The desperate measures are inspired by the persistent weakness in the job market. New jobless claims reached 426,000 in September 2002, the highest in ten years. The total number of workers receiving state employment benefits also rose to 3.6 million.

Some workers are making concessions or taking actions that would have been unthinkable a few years ago:

- Executives at Seabridge Software, a provider of customer retention software in San Francisco, California, posted an ad online offering job candidates stock options—but no pay. More than 500 resumés were received, and six employees were hired. "Some people told me, 'You won't get anybody who will work for no cash,' but I still get resumés," says founder Jamie Pardi.
- After months of looking for work, Tiffany Fox of Houston, Texas, made a sign that read, "Hire Me" and stood on a busy corner. Fox handed out information with her phone number and background. It worked: Fox wound up getting a sales job for a telecommunications firm after a manager drove by and asked, "Is this

"Desperate times call for creative measures."

(Tiffany Fox, job seeker)

for real?" "Desperate times call for creative measures," says Fox, who got more than 150 phone calls and ten interviews. "I got quite a few marriage proposals, too."

- Computer engineer Harold Robinson and product marketer Richard Sanchez made a six-by-five-foot sign emblazoned "2 Guys Looking for Work." They donned business suits and stood at a busy intersection for two weeks in July. "My wife said, 'You're going to do what?'" says Sanchez, forty-four, of Aliso Viejo, California. "We had people stop and interview us right on the corner. Starbucks came by and gave us free coffee." But their novel approach failed to land them jobs.
- Job seekers have sent hiring managers gifts such as singing telegrams, lottery tickets, and doughnuts according to a survey of 250 advertising and marketing executives by Menlo Park, California–based staffing services firm The Creative Group.

Such tactics illustrate a dramatic change from a few years ago, when employers were the ones taking creative measures, such as renting billboards and banner-flying airplanes to advertise jobs. The tables have turned because the weak economic rebound has been mostly a jobless recovery.

Source: "Job Seekers Take Creativity to New Level" from *USA Today*, September 13, 2002, p. 1B. Copyright © 2002 *USA Today*. Reprinted with permission.

SOURCES FOR RECRUITING

One fundamental decision that an organization must make as part of its recruiting strategy is whether to focus recruiting efforts internally or externally. As summarized in Table 6.1 and discussed in each section below, both internal and external recruiting have unique advantages and disadvantages.

Internal Recruiting

■ **Internal recruiting** is the process of looking inside the organization for existing qualified employees who might be promoted to higher-level positions.

Internal recruiting is the process of looking inside the organization for existing qualified employees who might be promoted to higher-level positions. This situation may not seem particularly useful for increasing the size of the workforce, but internal recruiting can play a role even in growth strategies. If the organization can

TABLE 6.1   Advantages and Disadvantages of Internal and External Recruiting

	Advantages	Disadvantages
Internal recruiting	■ Increases motivation ■ Sustains knowledge and culture	■ May foster stagnation ■ May cause a ripple effect
External recruiting	■ Brings in new ideas ■ Avoids the ripple effect	■ May hurt motivation ■ Costs more

fill higher-level openings with present employees who are ready to move up, it will have to fill lower-level positions from the outside later. These lower-level positions would presumably be easier and less costly to fill. Using this approach in an ideal situation, the organization could fill all of its needs, except those for entry-level jobs, from the inside and then recruit externally for entry-level job openings.

In any event, it is generally important that an organization always uses internal recruiting as part of its overall planning process because internal recruiting has several advantages over external recruiting. A major advantage of internal recruiting is motivation. Many employees want—and some expect—to advance and move up the organizational ladder to higher-level positions. An opportunity to do just that is likely to be seen as a viable reward and an important source of motivation for many people. Hence, an organization that routinely promotes from within through internal recruiting will usually find that it is more likely to have a committed and motivated workforce.

Another advantage of internal recruiting is that employees promoted to higher-level positions bring with them an existing familiarity and understanding of the organization: its heritage, culture, policies and procedures, strategies, and ways of doing business. As a result, their transition to higher-level positions is somewhat easier and the organization can often rely on the fact that these individuals will continue to promote and enhance the corporate culture in a positive and beneficial manner.

On the other hand, a disadvantage of internal recruiting is that it may foster stagnation and stifle creativity and new ideas. People tend to develop a certain mindset and way of doing business, and they tend to maintain that outlook as they progress in the organization. If the corporate culture is not what managers would really like, they should recognize that promoting from within is not necessarily likely to be a positive force for change.

Another disadvantage of internal recruiting is the so-called ripple effect. For example, if a person is promoted from one level of the organization to a higher-level position, then the job that that individual vacates must be filled. If that job is filled from someone still lower in the organization, an open position that the organization has to fill still exists. A relatively few promotions can sometimes result in a large-scale set of transfers and movements from position to position within the organization. As noted above, however, if an organization approaches this process strategically, only the lowest level positions will remain vacant and, at that point, the organization can turn to external recruiting.

External Recruiting

■ **External recruiting** is the process of looking to sources outside the organization for prospective employees.

External recruiting involves looking to sources outside the organization for prospective employees. Not surprisingly, external recruiting has advantages and disadvantages that are directly counter to those of internal recruiting. For example, external recruiting has the advantage of bringing in new ideas, new perspectives, and new ways of doing things. Hence, the organization can enhance its vitality, creativity, and potential ability to innovate by routinely bringing in people from the outside. External recruiting also avoids the ripple effect. In some cases, no internal employees may be able to fill new positions, thereby making external recruiting the only option.

A few years ago the managers and owners of a small software computer company in Iowa were frustrated because they could not make the major breakthroughs necessary to fuel growth for the firm. After considerable discussion, they decided that it was simply a case of no one inside the firm having the managerial skills needed to take the company to the next stage in its growth. All current managers were professional engineers, and none really had much managerial experience. Consequently, the firm decided to hire an outsider to come in and run the business. Within a couple of years, he had increased the firm's sales from $750,000 a year to over $11 million.[6]

On the other hand, external recruiting may result in motivational problems in the organization. Current employees may feel that they have been denied opportunities and that outsiders who are brought into the organization at higher levels may be less qualified than the current employees themselves. External recruiting also tends to be a bit more expensive than internal recruiting because of the advertising and other search processes that must be undertaken.

Many organizations prefer to rely on both internal and external recruiting strategies. This combined approach allows an organization to match the advantages and disadvantages of each particular recruiting effort to its own unique context. For example, during its dramatic growth period in the 1990s, Compaq Computer recruited both internally and externally. The firm wanted to ensure that current employees had ample promotion opportunity, but it also felt that it needed to hire people at a faster rate than could be accommodated by internal recruitment alone. Thus, each major hiring phase was carefully assessed and decisions were made in advance about the sources to be used. In some instances almost all recruiting was done internally, while in others only external recruiting was used. In still other cases, the firm looked both inside and outside at the same time for new recruits.

Internships: A Mixed Model

Although it is easier to think about recruiting having either an internal or external focus, it is possible to take an approach that really combines elements of the two. Many students try to obtain internships that will provide real-world experience, but internships are also quite useful from the organization's perspective. Of course, an intern is a form of temporary employee (see later in this chapter) who can help respond to work demands in the short term. But, more important, internships can be an important recruiting tool.

The intern is hired, in essence, on approval. That is, if the organization does not think that the person is someone who will be able to contribute to the organization or that the person is a good fit, the organization simply allows the internship to end. The intern is not really rejected because he or she has never really applied. On the other hand, if the intern is someone that the organization is interested in, the organization can offer the person permanent employment. Even if the intern is a student who must complete his or her studies, the organization might want to offer a contract to the person that would become effective on graduation. At that point, this contract would really become a form of internal recruiting but because the intern is not a permanent employee, it is also a form of external recruiting.

In fact, using internships to bring people into the organization and then hiring them allows the organization to obtain the best of both internal and external recruiting. The interns bring in a fresh perspective, the organization knows a lot about the intern, and the intern is somewhat familiar with the orga-

Internships help new job seekers obtain needed job experience, and they aid employers in the recruiting process. Interns are either unpaid or paid below market wages, and hiring interns allows a company to get information about how a person behaves at work and how well he or she can perform. School systems often depend upon this approach in hiring new teachers, relying on student teachers who serve as interns. Here, an experienced teacher helps a student teacher prepare the lesson for the day's class.

nization. This practice is becoming more common, and in some cases, interns who do not receive permanent job offers may even feel as if they have been rejected. Even if that feeling becomes more common among interns generally, recruiting interns on a tryout basis is an effective way of combining internal and external recruiting. HR Tech Talk discusses how some organizations have started using virtual interns.

METHODS OF RECRUITING

Internal recruiting is usually handled with one set of recruiting methods, while external recruiting typically relies on different methods.[7] In this section we will first examine methods used for internal recruiting and then look at other methods that are more likely to be used for external recruiting.

Methods for Internal Recruiting

The three most common methods used for internal recruiting are job posting, supervisory recommendations, and union halls.

Job posting Perhaps the most common method that organizations use for internal recruiting is a process called **job posting**. Job posting is a relatively simple procedure. Vacancies in the organization are publicized through various media such as company newsletters, bulletin boards, internal memos, and/or the firm's intranet. Any individual who is interested in being considered for the position

■ **Job posting** is a mechanism for internal recruiting in which vacancies in the organization are publicized through various media such as company newsletters, bulletin boards, internal memos, and the firm's intranet.

Internships Go Virtual as Firms Seek Ways to Save

 Some cost-cutting employers are trying a novel alternative to the traditional student apprenticeship: virtual internships. Companies are hiring college students to work on projects from afar rather than relocating them for short-term assignments. The programs, dubbed e-internships, represent a new way for companies and pending graduates to get connected.

Employers are experimenting with the idea because more college students have access to computers, virtual work has become more commonplace, and companies want to tap more affordable labor sources. Firms can save money because the internships may be short in duration or unpaid. For example:

> *"It tests your communication skills and shows you can work virtually."*
>
> (Dennis Joseph, virtual intern)

- At Cardinal Health in Dublin, Ohio, college students in states such as Arkansas and Ohio have been hired for virtual internships. Using school computers, they have worked on data warehousing and other projects and searched for errors on websites. The students are paired with a mentor and are paid. The company is a provider of health-care products and services. Dennis Joseph, twenty-three, is a senior at Southern Arkansas University in Magnolia who is testing applications as a virtual intern. "It tests your communication skills and shows you can work virtually," he says.
- International Truck and Engine, a maker of commercial trucks and diesel engines based in Warrenville, Illinois, has launched a virtual internship program. Last year, four students at Hiram College in Hiram, Ohio, worked

for the company and were supervised by phone and e-mail. The students, who each received $500, worked on a Web-marketing project. "We get a lot of great work at a low cost," says Jim Clarke, manager of channel development in used-truck operations. "The only thing is [that] they don't learn anything about the company culture. But it's a good recruiting tool."

- At Edwards & Hill Communications in Baltimore, Maryland, about ten college students have participated in virtual internships. Using their own computers, the students post casting notices online for the multimedia company, which runs a website that caters to the entertainment industry.

No one knows how many companies are offering virtual internships, but hiring experts say that they're a creative approach that could catch on. And even though students may never set foot in the companies that hire them, the e-internships often retain the hallmarks of traditional programs. Students often have mentors, projects to work on, and online brainstorming sessions with colleagues. "It was a pretty cool experience," says Guru Pinglay, twenty-six, a technical support analyst at Cardinal Health who previously worked as a virtual intern and was hired in June. "The communication problems were more, but that was the only disadvantage."

Source: "Internships Go Virtual as Firms Seek Ways to Save," *USA Today*, October 22, 2002, p. 1B. Copyright © 2002 *USA Today.* Reprinted with permission.

---

simply files an application with the human resource department. Some organizations that rely heavily on internal recruiting go so far as to require that jobs be posted internally before any external recruiting is undertaken. Note that a candidate hired through a job posting could be applying for a promotion or merely for a transfer. Figure 6.2 illustrates an example of a job posting.

Supervisory recommendations   Another method of internal recruiting is through supervisory recommendations. In this case, when a new position needs to be filled, a manager simply solicits nominations or recommendations for the position from supervisors in the organization. These supervisors look at the employees for whom they are responsible, and if any are particularly well suited for the new job opening, then the supervisors recommend those individuals to the higher-level manager.

FIGURE 6.2   Sample Job Posting at Xerox

Job Key-Properties			
Job Number 238570	**Job Grade** 8-9	**Post Date** 2003-12-04	**Apply Before** 2003-12-11
Location Addition	**Comp Type** NON-EXEMPT	**Job Type** Non-Manager Full Time	

Please Attach
- OJP Application
- Personal History
- Copy of last two (2) Performance Appraisals

Hiring Manager Information		
Name		**Mail Stop** 2000
E-Mail Address John.Smith@usa.xerox.com	**Intelnet Number** 8*555-5555	**External Number** (248) 555-5555

Open Job Information

Job Title	
Site Coordinator	
Organization NASG	**Job Location** [Refers to the actual city location]

Position Objectives

This position is for the expansion of the GM account. Day-to-day customer contact with the account. Coordinate production and administrative tasks performed by Account Associates. Operational responsibilities to include negotiating turnaround time for jobs, scheduling all steps of production, quality checking jobs to achieve standards of performance, documenting all customer compliments and complaints, coordinating service on equipment, ordering supplies, timely submission of data/reports, inventories as required, and maintenance of Site Manual. Assist team members on all operational processes. Maintain positive relationship with customers, peers, sales, administration and other Xerox units to ensure a smooth Document Management Services operation. Work closely with immediate manager sharing information and following-up with account activity.

Essential Functions

- Customer relationship building
- Demonstrate continuous team leadership
- Equipment administration (inventory/location, up-time, volume trends, order/manage supplies, etc.)
- Coordination of production job through-put and ensure Quality Standards/ Standards of Performance are met
- Provide guidance and direction to other Account Associates as needed
- Full knowledge of Xerox equipment, service offerings and processes
- Systems knowledge, as required

Applicant Qualifications

- 2-3 years industry-related operations experience
- AAS degree strongly preferred
- Proficient with PC and applications (i.e., MS Office: Word, Excel, PowerPoint and Access)
- Working in team environment
- Systems knowledge required including operating systems, client server networks, digital printing and document applications
- Able to work with minimal supervision
- Ability to adapt and provide customer services in a changing environment
- Data collection and analysis
- Self-starter who shows initiative

Key Messages

- This job is available to <u>any</u> organization.
- Relocation is <u>not</u> available for this job.
- The entire posting cycle generally takes between 30-60 days.

Courtesy of Xerox Corporation.

It is important, however, that supervisors give equal consideration to all potential candidates in these cases. In a landmark decision, *Rowe* v. *General Motors*, the Supreme Court found General Motors (GM) guilty of discrimination because, under a system where supervisory recommendations were needed for promotions, supervisors failed to recommend qualified black candidates as frequently as they recommended white candidates. As a result, at the time of the suit, almost no black supervisors were working at most GM facilities.

Union halls   Still another method of internal recruiting is through union halls. This method is particularly common in organizations that have strong and well-established unions. Indeed, the union contract itself may specify that union members be accorded the opportunity to apply for new positions on a priority basis. The mechanics of this approach may parallel those of job posting—job openings are listed, along with application procedures, and this information is made available to union members through various channels such as newsletters and bulletin boards.

We should also point out that, given the large numbers of layoffs and workforce reductions (from downsizing) in recent years, some potential applicants are somewhere between the classifications of internal and external candidates. Individuals who have been laid off (as opposed to terminated) are usually considered first when openings occur in the organization (and indeed this procedure may be mandated by certain union contracts). These individuals may not be active employees at the time, but they would still be considered internal candidates. On the other hand, individuals who actually lost their jobs during downsizing—that is, they were officially terminated—are technically no longer employees of the organization and so would be considered external candidates. Because they had worked for the organization previously, however, they would share more characteristics in common with internal candidates and might constitute a good source of potential applicants.

Methods for External Recruiting

Somewhat different methods are likely to be used by an organization engaged in external recruiting because the organization needs to reach potential applicants from outside the company. We will first consider three sources or types of external applicants, and then we will consider some techniques that a firm might use to attract these applicants.

■ The **general labor pool** is the local labor market from which a firm hires its employees.

■ A **referral** is an individual who is prompted to apply for a position by someone within the organization.

One major source for external applicants is the **general labor pool** from which an organization draws its employees. A labor pool is reflective of the local labor market and is generally tapped through the various techniques discussed below. A **referral** is an individual who is prompted to apply for a position by someone within the organization. For example, an employee might tell his or her neighbor or friend about an impending job opening at the organization and thus encourage that individual to apply for the position.[8] The reliance upon referrals is quite widespread, and in almost every organization, a significant number of external applicants is generated through referrals. In fact, the reliance upon referrals may even be growing. In the late 1990s, the job market had gotten so tight in some areas that organizations were providing incentives to their employees to seek out their friends as potential job candidates. For instance, employees for PriceWaterhouseCoopers, a major accounting firm, could earn bonuses of up to $7,000 if they located a new employee who accepted work and remained with the firm for six months.[9]

Direct applicants (also called *walk-ins* and *drop-ins*) are also a common external source of applicants. Direct applicants are simply individuals who apply for a position with the organization without any action on the part of the organization. In fact, the organization may not even have an opening at the time the application is made. For example, sometimes when people are looking for work, they will simply travel from prospective employer to prospective employer asking to fill out an employment application. Individuals who are seeking part-time work in retailing, for instance, may go to a shopping mall and walk from store to store, filling out application blanks as they go. As a result, the organization really doesn't need to do anything to attract these candidates.

■ **Direct applicants** are individuals who apply for a position with the organization without any action on the part of the organization.

Techniques for External Recruiting

Several techniques are commonly used for external recruiting. These techniques are summarized in the following paragraphs.

Word-of-mouth recruiting Referrals come to an organization via **word-of-mouth recruiting**. In most cases, the organization simply informs present employees that positions are available and encourages them to refer friends, family members, or neighbors for those jobs. From the organization's perspective, this method is an inexpensive way to generate a large number of applicants. In addition, if we assume that the present employees are satisfactory and that people generally associate with people who are similar to them, the organization should also have a reasonable chance of generating high-quality applicants with this method. As noted above, in most organizations, some portion of the applicants are always obtained through word of mouth. If an organization relies on this recruiting technique exclusively, however, problems may arise. If the present workforce is almost completely white and male, for example, the individuals referred will most likely be primarily white males as well, and this situation might represent discrimination in recruitment.

■ **Word-of-mouth recruiting** is when the organization simply informs present employees that positions are available and encourages them to refer friends, family members, or neighbors for those jobs.

Advertisements Advertisements in newspapers and related publications are also popular methods for external recruiting. Any local newspaper is likely to have help wanted sections ranging from perhaps a few listings to as many as several pages, sometimes organized by different kinds of job openings such as sales, health care, professional, nonprofessional, technical, and so forth. Depending on the job, these advertisements might be placed in local newspapers or national newspapers such as the *Wall Street Journal*. Figure 6.3 provides samples of newspaper advertisements placed by organizations for different kinds of job openings.

Some professional periodicals and publications also have similar kinds of spaces set aside for help wanted recruiting ads. This form of advertising tends to be relatively expensive and, perhaps surprisingly, attracts somewhat fewer qualified applicants than some of the other methods of recruiting. It does enable the organization to cast a wide net, however, in its efforts to publicize its affirmative action programs and to reach every sector of the labor market. By targeting specialized publications that might appeal primarily to members of groups that are underrepresented in the workforce, the organization might also advance its affirmative action goals. On the other hand, restricting advertisements to publications that are not widely available could be considered discriminatory.

FIGURE 6.3   Sample Newspaper Recruiting Ads

Reprinted by permission of Village Automotive Group. Reprinted by permission of Applebees.

Public employment agencies   Public employment agencies are also common sources for external recruiting. While public employment agencies have actually been around for quite some time, their activities were formalized with the passage of the Social Security Act of 1935. This law requires that anyone who is paid unemployment compensation must register that fact with a local state employment office. These state agencies work closely with the U. S. Employment Service. Their joint goal is to get unemployed individuals off state aid as quickly as possible and back in permanent jobs. The agencies start by collecting basic employment-related information about the individuals, such as their experience, aptitudes, abilities, and so forth. For example they may administer various tests to individuals to gain some insight into their abilities. The General Aptitude Test Battery is a test frequently used for this purpose.

Employers register their job openings with the local state employment agency. That agency, in turn, attempts to match the qualified individuals for whom it has documentation with jobs. For example, suppose a local construction firm needs to hire several unskilled or semiskilled workers for various construction projects. It might start by contacting the local state employment agency and explain the kind of workers it needs. The agency, in turn, may call various individuals it has on file who seem to fit the construction firm's needs. Those individuals are then referred to the firm, which processes their applications through its normal selection process, such as application blanks, interviews, and so forth. (This process is discussed more fully in the next chapter.) Two significant advantages of public employment agencies are that (1) they are free, and (2) they are a particularly useful source of job applicants for minorities, handicapped individuals, and other protected classes. Because they are state agencies, they are fully cognizant of the requirements that organizations must face and they work hard to maintain an adequate labor pool of all classes of employees.

Private employment agencies   Whereas public employment agencies tend to cater primarily to blue-collar workers, private employment agencies are more likely to serve the white-collar labor market (although some serve specialized niches such as office workers). One major difference, however, is that private employment agencies charge a fee for their services. Sometimes this fee is paid by the individual; sometimes it is paid by the organization if it hires an individual referred to it. In a public employment agency, all potential employee job applicants are currently unemployed, but many employed individuals use the services of private employment agencies in an effort to find federal work while maintaining their current job. Since private employment agencies are supported by the firms and individuals that use their services, however, they may be able to devote more resources to performing their function.

Executive search firms   An individual working for an executive search firm is also known as a **headhunter**. An organization that wants to hire a top-level manager can go to an executive search firm and explain exactly what kind of individuals it is looking for. This explanation, for example, might specify the kind of work experience the organization wants the individual to have, the degree that is necessary, the number of years of experience, and perhaps a salary profile as well. The executive search firm then attempts to locate individuals that fit this profile for the organization. Typically, the search firm screens potential candidates and then presents the organization with a small number of candidates, all of whom are highly qualified and interested.

On the other side of the coin, some highly successful executives are known to be available routinely for other jobs. They network with members of executive search firms and are receptive to any overtures made toward them. An important advantage of an executive search firm is confidentiality. The organization seeking a new employee may be able to pursue this individual in a discrete manner. Likewise, the individual who is being pursued may also be able to maintain a reasonable degree of confidentiality. Ten years ago Kodak hired Chief Executive Officer (CEO) George Fisher, who had only recently taken the position of CEO at Motorola. The executive recruiter who was in charge of the search, Gerald Roche, had been an acquaintance of Fisher's for several years. His personal relationship with Fisher played an important role in his ability to convince Fisher to leave Motorola for Kodak.[10]

On the other hand, executive search firms tend to be among the most expensive methods for external recruiting. In addition, one caveat that applies to any type of agency relates to potential discrimination. Many stories have been published in the popular press about employment agencies (both public and private) that referred individuals of one race, ethnicity, or gender for some jobs but not for others. If an organization engages the services of an employment agency that discriminates, the organization almost certainly will be held liable for the discrimination.

College placement offices   Other sources for recruiting that are particularly relevant to college students are the placement offices that most colleges and universities sponsor. Most large organizations visit college campuses every year to interview graduates for jobs within the organization. Large firms may visit many

■ A **headhunter** is an individual working for an executive search firm that seeks out qualified individuals for higher-level positions.

different colleges and universities scattered across the country, or they may choose to visit only regional or local colleges and universities.

An advantage of this method for the organization is that it can specify qualifications such as major, grade point average, work experience, and so forth. It is also a relatively inexpensive method of recruiting because the colleges and universities typically provide the facilities, schedule the appointments, and so forth. The organization sends the interviewer to the campus, and that individual sits in the interview room during the course of the day and meets prospective applicants. For students, this job search method is also quite efficient. The student can visit his or her local placement office on a regular basis, keep apprised of which companies are coming to interview, and sign up for interviews using whatever methods and protocols the college or university has established.

Microsoft relies heavily on college recruiting in its efforts to bring in new talent every year. The firm has a staff of twenty-two full-time campus recruiters who visit schools each year. These recruiters conduct half-hour interviews with thousands of prospective employees, selecting about 450 for follow-up visits to company headquarters.[11]

Electronic Recruiting

In Chapter 1 we discussed changes in technology that were affecting the human resource management process. One example is the Internet. There are few areas where the Internet has had a greater impact than on the recruiting function. In fact, many of the techniques discussed above for external and internal recruiting can now be replaced, and often are being replaced, by the Internet, and so it deserves special consideration in this chapter. The importance of electronic recruiting would be hard to overestimate. A recent article noted that in 1998, 29 percent of the *Fortune* 500 companies generated applicants through their websites, but that rate rose to 88 percent at the beginning of 2001. This same article also reported that 34 percent of these companies accepted applications only through their websites.[12] Several key reasons explain why we have experienced such an explosion in electronic recruiting.

Electronic recruiting is cost effective   This reason is one of the most important for the growth in reliance on electronic recruiting techniques. It does not cost much to post a job opening on a job board like those available at the websites **monster.com** and **hotjob.com,** and these websites are visited by literally millions of people a year. Not everyone who visits these websites is looking for a new job, and many might not be qualified for a given job, but the level of exposure offered by these services is unprecedented. In addition, professional organizations often have websites advertising jobs. The Society for Human Resource Management (SHRM), for example, contains advertisements that used to be published in their newspapers and journals. Now employees can go to the website (www.shrm.org) and search for jobs, and the companies involved can afford to run those ads for a longer period of time. Finally, many organizations are starting their own websites that include job postings. These organizations find that they can reach potential applicants and that they can use these websites as marketing tools.[13]

Electronic ads reach large numbers of applicants   Only a few years ago, the effectiveness of electronic recruiting was somewhat limited by the numbers of potential job applicants who had easy access to the Internet. Although accessibil-

From www.ibm.com/employment. Reprinted by permission of IBM.

Organizations attempt to recruit new applicants through a wide variety of sources. One source that is becoming extremely popular is the Internet. This type of recruiting is especially attractive to younger job seekers who regularly search the Internet for information about jobs. Savvy companies, especially those in the high-tech sector (such as IBM, shown here), are increasingly turning to the Internet in an attempt to attract these younger, technology-comfortable applicants.

ity varies around the world and within every country, the number of people who search the Internet is growing dramatically, and many people use the Internet when searching for jobs. Recent estimates show 160 million Internet users in the United States and 1.2 billion Internet users worldwide. In the Unites States approximately 74 percent of those with access to the Internet use it to search for jobs.[14] Thus, the Internet allows an organization instant access to a global pool of potential applicants. In this country, many organizations have reported that advertising on the Internet has also produced a more diverse group of applicants and job seekers than they had reached using more traditional methods.[15] The final bit of evidence that the Internet reaches such a large number of applicants comes from the fact that so many applicants are now posting their resumés (or "websumés") on their own home pages as a means of trying to sell themselves to companies. There is no question that the numbers of persons reached by ads on the Internet will continue to grow dramatically.

Electronic recruiting saves time   When an applicant sees an ad in a newspaper, the applicant has to call and/or write to the company to get additional information or to ask any questions. Eventually, the applicant will have to send a resumé or otherwise apply for the job, often via snail mail. On the other hand, electronic recruiting allows for e-mail questions and answers as well as electronic submission of resumés—all in a matter of minutes. This time savings is another reason why electronic recruiting is replacing many of the more traditional approaches to external recruiting and why it is also growing in importance for internal recruiting. For example, at Gillette Co. all current employees can read the company philosophy, learn about openings within the company, and apply for the jobs for which they are qualified in a few minutes on the company intranet. Office workers can do so on their work computers, while manufacturing employees can do so at computer kiosks located around the shop floor.

Limitations of Electronic Recruiting

By now you should have realized that there are no easy solutions to any of the challenges that face human resource managers. Therefore, it should not be surprising to learn that, although electronic recruiting offers many advantages, some costs are involved. The obvious problem with reaching a broad set of potential applicants is that many people may apply for a job when they are not really qualified. We discussed this issue earlier in the chapter, noting then that generating large numbers of unqualified applicants can be costly. In fact, nearly one-third of the human resource managers in a recent survey indicated that Internet recruiting caused additional work because staff members had to sift through resumés from unqualified people and had to respond to the barrage of e-mail messages that some job postings can generate.

As noted above, many companies are pleased with the increased diversity that electronic recruiting seems to provide, but differences in access to computers and the Internet still exist in the United States. A study by the Department of Labor notes that fewer Hispanic-American and African-American applicants have regular access to computers, and as a result, members of these groups are more likely to rely on more traditional sources of job information.[16] It is not clear what the impact of this differential access is if companies continue to post ads in both traditional and electronic sources, but it is an issue to consider when deciding whether to move to electronic recruiting.

Although electronic recruiting can offer a company many advantages, it seems that potential job seekers who visit company websites do not always come away happy. Many users report that company websites are difficult to navigate or are sloppy, while others complain that it is difficult to apply for a job at the website.[17] It is important for organizations to recognize that, in this electronic age, a company website may actually be the first point of contact for an applicant. The potential applicant should find the experience pleasant because this first positive impression will make the company seem more attractive as an employer. On the other hand, if the experience is a frustrating one, many potentially valuable applicants could be lost.

REALISTIC JOB PREVIEWS

■ A **realistic job preview** is an effective technique for ensuring that job seekers understand the actual nature of the jobs available to them.

Many organizations today find it increasingly important to provide prospective employees with what is called a **realistic job preview**. In the past, many recruiters were guilty of painting a glowing picture of what a particular job might entail. They made the job sound glamorous, exciting, fun, challenging, and rewarding in different ways. Once employees accepted the job, however, they found just the opposite: the job they were hired to fill proved to be boring, tedious, monotonous, and routine. Because their expectations were set so high, and because the reality they faced

The socialization of new employees contributes to successful recruitment, and Realistic Job Previews (RJPs) are an important part of this socialization process. Here, new hires at Sony watch a slide show illustrating what they can expect as they start their new jobs. In order to be effective, RJPs should portray both the positive and negative aspects of the new job. Research indicates that newcomers who receive such honest training typically have an easier time coping with their new jobs and as a result tend to be more satisfied and tend to remain in their jobs longer.

proved to be so different, they were extremely dissatisfied with their work and consequently were prone to high turnover. These problems can be partly minimized, however, if recruiters paint a more realistic picture of the job. If the job is relatively routine, then prospective job applicants should be told that fact. The idea is simply to present as realistic a preview of the actual job and its working conditions as possible without glossing over some of the more unpleasant characteristics of the job or the working conditions for that job.[18]

One relatively straightforward method for providing a realistic job preview is to provide job applicants with an opportunity to observe others performing the work. Job applicants can go to the job site and watch people work or they can watch a videotape of people performing the job. If neither of these alternatives is feasible, then at a minimum the recruiter should describe in as realistic terms as possible the job itself and the circumstances under which it will be performed.

Disney has found that using realistic job previews has greatly improved its recruiting and selection processes. At its vast Disney World complex, the firm has an employment office it calls its casting center. Before being interviewed or asked to complete a job application, people who visit the center seeking employment are instructed to watch a videotape. The video informs job seekers about the firm's strict appearance guidelines and the difficult and rigorous working conditions. The goal is to provide a candid and realistic introduction to the working conditions at Disney.[19]

Considerable research has been done to document the benefits of realistic job previews. If applicants are given realistic previews before they make a decision, some potential applicants will be discouraged and withdraw from consideration.[20] At the same time, however, those who know what to expect and still choose to join the organization generally are more successful. The results of this research include, among other things, the fact that newly hired employees who have received realistic job previews have a higher rate of job survival than those who are hired without realistic previews. Those newcomers who received a realistic job preview reported higher levels of job satisfaction, higher levels of trust in the organization, and a more realistic set of expectations about the job. A recent meta-analysis of several studies of realistic job previews reported that they are generally associated with higher performance and lower turnover.[21] Not only do realistic job previews seem to work, their effectiveness has been demonstrated with jobs as diverse as bank teller,[22] army recruit,[23] and prison guard![24]

Nonetheless, realistic job previews represent a much different approach to traditional recruiting. For that reason, some people have argued that they are not the best way to recruit new people. The Point/Counterpoint feature for this chapter discusses some of the pluses and minuses of realistic job previews.

ALTERNATIVES TO RECRUITING

Thus far our discussion of the recruiting process has focused on the organization that needs to acquire new human resources and is engaged in activities aimed at hiring job applicants for permanent positions. Organizations should also explore various alternatives to recruiting whenever feasible. Neither the organization nor the employees benefit if the organization hires, only to find later that it has to fire the employees or lay them off because of the downturn in work. Thus, if the organization is not fully committed to a long-term employment relationship, or if the organization is not sure that it can find exactly the kinds of people that it wants to hire for the long term, it might find it beneficial to use various alternatives to traditional recruiting methods.

Overtime

■ **Overtime** is an alternative to recruiting in which current employees are asked to work extra hours.

One alternative to recruiting is **overtime**, which simply means asking current workers to put in longer hours. This alternative is especially beneficial when the increased need for human resources is short term. For example, a manufacturing plant facing a production crunch might ask some of its production workers to work an extra half-day, perhaps on Saturday, for two or three weeks to get the work done. This method has two basic advantages. One is that it gives employees the opportunity to earn extra income. Some employees welcome this opportunity and are thankful to the organization for making it available. In addition, it keeps the organization from having to hire and train new employees. Since the existing employees already know how to do their work, the organization does not have to provide them with additional training.

On the other hand, overtime has some disadvantages. Labor costs per hour are likely to increase. The Fair Labor Standards Act (described earlier in Chapter 3) stipulates that employees who work over forty hours a week must be compensated at a rate of one and a half times their normal hourly rate. Thus, if an employee is making $10 an hour for a normal workweek, the organization may have to pay that same individual $15 an hour for the extra hours beyond forty each week. Another disadvantage of relying on overtime relates to the potential problems for conflict and/or equity considerations. For example, the organiza-

POINT | COUNTERPOINT

Using Realistic Job Previews

As noted in the text, a reasonable amount of research suggests that using realistic job previews can be an effective means of recruiting. Yet some obvious problems can arise with this approach, and in some situations, these problems might actually cause an organization to avoid realistic job previews.

POINT ... Organizations should use realistic job previews for recruiting because ...	COUNTERPOINT ... Realistic job previews in recruiting should be avoided because ...
Realistic job previews allow the new employees to prepare for what is to come on the job.	Realistic job previews put an organization at an unfair disadvantage when everyone else is touting the positive aspects of their jobs.
Realistic job previews allow new employees to set more realistic expectations about the job, and these expectations are more likely to be met.	Realistic job previews discourage potential employees who *could* learn to adapt to the problems.
Realistic job previews develop feelings of trust in the organization.	Realistic job previews focus too much attention on the negative aspects of the organization.
Realistic job previews may discourage some applicants, but they reduce turnover in the long run.	In tight labor markets, an organization cannot afford to discourage *any* qualified applicants.

So... Although realistic job previews are generally effective, organizations may be more reluctant to use them during times when qualified people are scarce. It is also true that an organization using realistic job previews may lose potentially successful employees to an organization that does a good job of selling itself. On balance, however, realistic job previews seem to be more effective in most situations and should be considered.

tion may not really need all the members of a work group for overtime, and it may face a complicated situation in deciding who gets to work the overtime. Unionized organizations often have contracts that specify the decision rules that must be followed when offering overtime. Yet another problem is the potential for increased fatigue and anxiety on the part of employees, particularly if the overtime is not particularly welcome and if they have to work the overtime for an extended period of time.

Corning has a small ceramics plant in Blacksburg, Virginia. Because the plant is quite small, Corning is reluctant to add new workers whenever production requirements increase temporarily. As a result, the firm routinely offers overtime to its employees. While not everyone is eager to accept this offer, enough employees do accept so that the firm can function effectively. For example, one of its employees, Joe Sizemore, routinely works between sixty and seventy hours a week. He points out that the extra income has allowed him a better life style. Corning, meanwhile, keeps a highly productive worker happy and avoids having to hire a new employee.[25]

Temporary Workers

Another increasingly popular alternative to the recruitment of full-time employees is a growing reliance on **temporary employees**. The idea behind temporary employment is that an organization can hire someone for only a specific period of time. A major advantage of temporary employment to the organization is that such workers can usually be paid a lower rate, although they are now more likely to be entitled to the same benefits as full-time workers.[26] Considerable flexibility comes from the fact that employees themselves realize their jobs are not permanent and therefore the organization can terminate their relationship as work demands mandate.[27] On the other hand, temporary employees tend not to understand the organization's culture as well as do permanent employees. In addition, they are not as likely to be as productive as are permanent full-time employees of the organization.

Employee Leasing

Another increasingly popular alternative to the recruitment of permanent full-time workers is **employee leasing**. In this circumstance the organization pays a fee to a leasing company that provides a pool of employees to the leasing firm. This pool of employees usually constitutes a group or crew intended to handle all or most of the organization's work needs in a particular area. For example, an organization might lease a crew of custodial and other maintenance workers from an outside firm specializing in such services. These workers appear in the organization every day at a predetermined time and perform all maintenance and custodial work. To the general public, they may even appear to be employees of the firm occupying the building. In reality, however, they work for a leasing company.

The basic advantage of this approach to the organization is that it essentially outsources to the leasing firm the human resource elements of recruiting, hiring, training, compensating, and evaluating those employees. On the other hand, because the individuals are not employees of the firm, they are likely to have less commitment and attachment to the organization. In addition, the cost of the leasing arrangement might be a bit higher than if the employees have been hired directly by the firm itself.

Part-time Workers

A final alternative to recruiting permanent workers is to rely on part-time workers. **Part-time workers** are those individuals who routinely expect to work less than forty hours a week. Among the major advantages of part-time employment is the fact that these employees are usually not covered by benefits, thus lowering labor costs, and the organization can achieve considerable flexibility. That is, the part-time workers are routinely called on to work different schedules from week to week, thereby allowing the organization to cluster its labor force around peak demand times and have a smaller staff on hand during down times. Part-time workers are common in organizations like restaurants. Wait staff, bus persons, kitchen help, and other employees of such an organization might be college students who want to work only fifteen or twenty hours a week to earn spending money. Their part-time interest provides considerable scheduling flexibility to the organization that hires them.

Each of the groups of employees described above can be considered part of the **contingent workforce**. The contingent workforce includes all temporary, part-time, and leased employees who are employed by organizations to fill in for permanent employees during times of peak demand. Thus, these contingent workers are considered alternatives to recruiting, but usually as alternatives that are less desirable. Some recent views of staffing take a more strategic perspective, however, and suggest that there may be situations where it would be preferable to hire temporary or contingent workers instead of permanent employees.[28] In fact, in this view, whenever a firm requires additional human resources who are not related to its core competencies or who are required to have skills or knowledge that is generally available in the marketplace, it may be to the firm's competitive advantage to add resources through some other arrangement besides permanent hires. We discuss some of these issues in more detail in Chapter 17.

■ The **contingent workforce** includes all temporary, part-time, or leased employees who are employed by organizations to fill in for permanent employees during times of peak demand.

JOB CHOICE FROM THE PROSPECTIVE EMPLOYEE'S PERSPECTIVE

Up to now, we have been focusing on ways in which organizations try to attract interested job seekers to apply for their jobs. Earlier in this chapter we discussed briefly the goals of the prospective employee in this process. We now return to that perspective because ultimately it is up to applicants whether or not they will accept an offer of employment from an organization. That is, once an organization attracts a recruit and subsequently decides to offer a job to that person, the prospective employee still must decide whether or not to accept the job. The actual selection process is the subject of the next chapter, but the recruitment process has a great deal of influence over whether a person accepts a job once it is offered.[29] Specifically, the messages sent to a potential employee during this process will provide him or her with much of the information needed to make a decision.

From the outset, the recruiter plays a large role in this decision. At the simplest level, the recruiter is probably the first real contact the potential employee has with the company. If the recruiter doesn't seem competent or acts rudely or inappropriately, the potential employee will form a negative impression of the organization as a whole and will be less likely to accept a job. Also, as we noted earlier in the chapter, many potential employees make decisions about which job to take based on beliefs about which job will meet their needs or desires best. And this information, in turn, is usually communicated during the recruitment process.

There is reason to believe that more complex signaling also takes place during the recruitment process. Although potential employees are clearly attracted to an organization because they believe it can provide valued outcomes, they are also attracted to organizations where they feel they can fit in. That is, potential employees seem more likely to accept jobs from organizations that the applicant perceives as having similar values and style.

Considerable research suggests that organizational characteristics can attract applicants who feel they would fit in, and so organizations can try to signal certain values as a way of attracting certain types of applicants.[30] For example, the U.S. Marine Corps advertisements are meant to attract individuals who believe they can be one of the "few and the proud." U.S. Army advertisements are

The Lighter Side of HR

Job applicants and recruiters must always keep in mind that recruiting is a two-way street—both parties are trying to sell themselves to the other. But as illustrated in this cartoon, people occasionally come across as being arrogant, rude, or abrupt. And when this happens, the chances for a successful matching of applicant and employer go down significantly.

targeted at individuals who see military service as providing work experience and money for college.

Thus, through recruiting materials or recruiter behavior, organizations signal that they are family friendly, that they are concerned about the environment, or that they value competitive people. Prospective employees read these signals and use them as important determinants of their job choice. But these attempts to attract certain types of applicants are not always successful.[31] In fact, a recent study found that advertisements stressing the availability of flextime and telecommuting were not attractive to all applicants. Instead, potential applicant interest depended on the nature of the flextime arrangements and the level of work-family role conflict.[32] As we shall see in the next chapter, organizations are also beginning to consider fit between the applicant and the organization in their selection decisions, but it is clear that perceived fit is important from the potential applicant's perspective as well.

Job seekers and job applicants must remember, however, that recruiters and organizations are also forming impressions of them. The manner in which a person dresses and behaves, for example, is often an important consideration for a recruiter. And just as recruiters can make a bad impression if they are rude or inappropriate, so too can a job seeker be offensive or rude. The Lighter Side of HR clearly illustrates this situation.

EVALUATING THE RECRUITING PROCESS

Because recruiting is such a vital part of the human resource management process for most organizations, it stands to reason that the organization will periodically evaluate the effectiveness of its recruiting process. Essentially, an effective recruiting process is one that results in a reasonable pool of qualified employees who are available to the organization and from which the organization can hire people whom it wants to perform various jobs. This recruiting process needs to be executed at relatively low cost. Thus, if an organization is having a difficult time attracting job applicants or if too many people are applying for its jobs, then the organization's recruiting effort might well be seen as ineffective. Similarly, if the recruiting expenses incurred by the organization are excessive or higher than they should be for the kinds of employees being recruited, then the organization should look carefully at its recruiting methods to see if efficiencies or cost savings might be justified.

In addition, it is possible and often useful to assess the advantages of different recruiting sources. This approach could involve simply calculating the yield, or the number of applicants generated by each source. In fact, a number of studies have found that applicants who learn about the organization through some sources are more likely to accept jobs and remain in those jobs than are applicants who learn about the jobs through other sources. Unfortunately, the results of these studies are inconsistent as to which specific sources produce the best results, so that it is difficult to say much for certain beyond the fact that it is best if the applicant learns about the organization through a combination of formal and informal (e.g., newspaper ads and word of mouth) sources.[33] Nonetheless, they suggest that it may be possible for an organization to target recruiting efforts at those sources that seem to yield the best applicants.

Chapter Summary

Recruiting is the process of developing a pool of qualified applicants who are interested in working for the organization and from which the organization might reasonably select the best individual or individuals to hire for employment. Organizational goals in recruiting are to optimize, in various ways, the size of the pool of qualified applicants and to offer an honest and candid assessment to prospective applicants of what kinds of jobs and opportunities the organization can make available to them. Individual goals in recruiting include satisfying personal work goals, various idiosyncratic goals, and perhaps optimizing personal situations.

Internal recruiting is the process of looking inside the organization for existing qualified employees who might be promoted to higher-level positions. The advantages of internal recruiting are employee motivation and continuity. The disadvantages include stifling creativity and new ideas and creating a ripple effect.

External recruiting involves looking to sources outside the organization for prospective employees. The advantages of this approach include bringing in new ideas, new perspectives, and new ways of doing things and avoiding the ripple effect. On the negative side, external recruiting may result in motivational problems in the organization and a lack of continuity.

The three most common methods used for internal recruiting are job posting, supervisory recommendations, and union halls. Job posting involves publicizing openings through various media such as company newsletters, bulletin boards, and internal memos. Supervisory recommendations involve soliciting nominations or recommendations from supervisors in the organization. Using union halls involves notifying local union officials about job openings.

Different methods are likely to be used by an organization engaged in external recruiting. These methods include using the general labor pool, direct applicants, referrals, advertisements, employment agencies, and colleges and universities.

Many organizations today are finding it increasingly important to provide prospective employees with what is called a realistic job preview. Realistic job previews involve providing job applicants with an opportunity to observe others performing the work.

While the organization is trying to attract applicants, those potential employees must eventually decide which jobs to accept. Although these decisions are based largely on factors such as which company pays more or meets other needs better, these decisions are also based on perceptions of fit. That is, potential employees often choose organizations which they believe share their values and approaches.

If the organization is not fully committed to a long-term employment relationship or if the organization is not sure that it can find exactly the kinds of people that it wants to hire for the long term, it might engage in various alternatives to traditional recruiting methods. Alternatives include overtime, temporary workers, employee leasing, and part-time workers.

Key Points for Future HR Managers

▶ Recruitment is the process by which qualified applicants are attracted to the organization.

▶ Although it is important to have more applicants than openings, it is *not* helpful to have too many applicants per opening.

▶ Recruitment from within is preferable because of the motivational value.

▶ External recruitment is necessary for entry-level jobs and brings new ideas into the organization.

▶ Internal recruiting techniques include job postings, supervisory recommendations, and reliance on union halls.

▶ External recruiting techniques include word of mouth, advertisements, public and private employment agencies, college placement offices, and executive search firms.

▶ Electronic recruiting is having a major impact on both internal and external recruiting because it al-

lows companies to reach a wider range of applicants and it is cost-effective, but it does come at a cost in terms of administrative burdens and the fact that not everyone has access to a computer.

▶ Realistic job previews involve telling people the truth about the job before they begin. Realistic job previews have been found to increase performance and reduce turnover.

▶ Overtime, temporary workers, leased employees, and part-time workers can all serve as alternatives to hiring full-time employees. Sometimes these alternatives may be preferable.

▶ Potential applicants are attracted to companies that meet their needs and those where they feel they will fit in. As a result, companies can try to attract certain types of applicants through the nature of their ads.

▶ Evaluation of the recruiting function depends on performance as well as turnover measures.

Key Points for Future General Managers

▶ The goal of recruiting is to generate qualified applicants for jobs.

▶ Recruiting can be either internal or external, and each has advantages and disadvantages.

▶ Decisions about the best methods for external (or internal) recruiting should be based on the kind of applicants the firm wants to attract.

▶ Electronic recruiting is revolutionizing the recruiting field. It is cost-effective and allows the firm to reach a broad range of applicants, but it can increase administrative costs.

▶ Realistic job previews involve telling applicants both the positive and negative aspects of the job. Some applicants may be frightened by this information, but these are people who would not have been successful anyway. The use of realistic job previews has been linked to more positive attitudes about the job, higher performance, and lower turnover rates for a wide variety of jobs.

▶ Alternatives to adding permanent workers to the workforce include overtime and the use of contingent workers (which include temporary, part-time, and leased employees). The decision about the group to draw from should be made strategically.

▶ Applicants decide which jobs to apply for and to accept based on the extent to which they feel they will fit with the company (in addition to consider-

ing basic issues such as compensation, benefits and terms of employment).

▶ Recruiting efforts can be assessed by examining data on satisfaction, absenteeism, turnover, and performance.

Review and Discussion Questions

1. Summarize organizational and individual goals in the recruiting process.

2. Compare and contrast the advantages and disadvantages of internal versus external recruiting.

3. Identify and describe the basic methods used by organizations for external recruiting.

4. What is a realistic job preview? What function does it serve?

5. What alternatives to recruiting can organizations use?

6. What goals do you expect will play the biggest role in your own job search process?

7. How would you feel if you thought you deserved to be promoted, but instead the organization hired someone from outside and made that person your boss? What would you do?

8. Which recruiting methods are most likely to attract your attention?

9. Do you think the Internet will become a major recruiting tool in the future? Why or why not?

10. Assume that you are talking to a high school senior who is thinking about going to your college or university. Apply the principles of a realistic job preview to this situation. What details about the college or university would you provide?

Closing Case

Give and Take

During the economic boom just a few short years ago, it seemed that workers were in the driver's seat. A general labor shortage, combined with an acute shortage of knowledge workers and other skilled employees, made it a true seller's market for those looking for work. Most top college graduates had multiple offers waiting for them as they walked across the graduation stage, and skilled technical workers could take their pick of jobs. While low inflation helped keep wages and salaries from escalating too much, business after business lavished a growing list of new benefits, perquisites, and incentives on its employees as a way first to attract and then to retain the best and the brightest.

For example, SAS Institute, a major software firm in North Carolina, offered its employees unlimited sick days; an on-site childcare facility; flexible work schedules; and free coffee, tea, and juice. Garden.com, a now defunct Internet firm in Austin, Texas, provided on-site massages and free yoga and stress-management

classes. BMC Software in Houston, Texas, greeted its employees each morning with a pianist in the lobby and provided fresh vegetables at lunch from the firm's own garden. Other benefits available from some employers included concierges, laundry pickup and delivery, and on-site pet-care centers. And some companies offered the most highly sought-after recruits a cash signing bonus or a new car.

But as the economy slowed in 2001 and 2002, the situation began to change dramatically. Whereas workers had been able to drive hard bargains before, the advantage now shifted to employers. Throughout the 1990s, as it turns out, companies had used technological advances ranging from robotics to the Internet to reduce costs in areas like advertising, production, and purchasing. And when the economy turned sour, most companies realized that they had wrung out as many costs as possible from most areas of their operations. But with the ever-increasing pressure to reduce costs further and now facing a shrinking economy, a lot of firms have started searching for the next area for cost-saving measures. Many firms have turned to their labor force for the next round of cuts.

As a start, many corporations have reduced or stopped hiring, while the hardest hit corporations have started layoffs. This trend stems in part from the realization that workers simply have fewer options for employment. This realization, in turn, reduces employer fears that employees will leave to seek jobs elsewhere just because the situation isn't as good as it was before. "This may sound bad, but there are not a lot of good choices around," says Tom Newman, vice president at Teradyne Inc.

One of the first areas hit was perquisites ("perks"). Among the lost amenities: closing the employee bowling alley at an Austin-based high-tech firm, no more free massages at the desks of Wall Street bankers, and Xerox's firing of the plant caretaker (employees now must water their own office plants). And many of the dot-coms, among the most aggressive employers in terms of new and innovative benefits, have disappeared altogether. Don't be fooled into thinking these issues are trivial, though. "There is a huge dent in morale when you take anything away from employees, no matter how miniscule it may look," says one workplace consultant, Sharon Jordan-Evans.

Next in line are the more traditional employee benefits. For instance, many firms have either reduced their contributions to some employee benefits or eliminated them altogether. Ford Motor Company and Lucent Technologies are just two of the many organizations paying less for employee health insurance or retirement plans. Bonuses, sick leave, and vacation time are also being squeezed. As a last resort, some firms are asking workers to accept pay cuts. Agilent Technology workers' pay declined 10 percent, while Disney lowered some pay rates up to 30 percent. "This was a cost structure that had gotten out of hand," claims Thomas Schumacher, referring to the $1 million earned by the studio's star animators.

Some firms today have reduced or frozen hiring, and some are also reducing or eliminating benefits and perquisites. These firms are seeking ways to lower their costs and have found that current economic conditions give them more flexibility than was the case just a few years ago. But while these actions may lower costs and protect profits in the short term, firms who follow this path may face problems when the economy rebounds. That is, they may find that they have tarnished their reputation as an employer and they may find it more difficult to attract workers when they need them again.

The hazards of cutting incentives too much include low morale, reduced productivity, or worse. When the Indiana Social Services Administration left job vacancies unfilled in 1990, the state led the country in the number of welfare fraud cases. And the effects can be long-lasting. One executive whose company instituted pay cuts says, "People are lying low, but when the economy improves they'll be out of here." Workers complain that they should not bear a disproportionate share of the cost cutting. Studies verify that median CEO compensation rose 7 percent in 2001, while worker pay rose just 3 percent and company profits fell 35 percent.

The good news for struggling firms is that some incentives are effective. The most powerful and least expensive perk can be time off from work. Experts suggest, for example, that up to 20 percent of workers would work fewer hours for lower pay. Siemens, a German electronics firm, offers workers a year-long "time-out," with reduced pay and a guaranteed job when they return. "It's a possibility for us not to lose good workers despite bad times," says Siemens's spokesperson Axel Heim. Firms are also finding that technology workers and professionals, who need to stay on the leading edge, want more training and increased job responsibilities. Patti Wilson, founder of a high-tech career-management firm, asserts, "Someone will jump jobs to learn more or stay if they feel that they're being challenged."[34]

Case Questions

1. What are the fundamental human resource issues reflected in labor-force reductions and other human resource cutbacks?

2. Aside from laying off workers, what other costs might be cut from an organization's labor force?

3. What other incentives besides benefits might a company offer its best workers to retain them?

Building HR Management Skills

Purpose: The purpose of this exercise is to give you insights into effective and ineffective recruiting via advertisements.

Step 1: Obtain a section of a newspaper (no longer than one page) that contains numerous recruiting ads. Working alone, identify the one ad that you think is most effective and the one ad that you think is least effective. Jot down on a piece of paper your reasoning for each choice.

Step 2: Form pairs with your classmates. Exchange ad pages with the student in your pair. Pick two ads from the student's paper, the ones that you think are most and least effective. Again, jot down your rationale.

Step 3: Each of you should next reveal your own choices for most and least effective recruiting ads, along with your rationales for your choices.

Step 4: This step is optional. Your instructor may ask for a few examples of particularly effective and less effective ads to be shared with the entire class.

Ethical Dilemmas in HR Management

Assume that you are a midlevel human resource manager in a major diversified corporation. For years your company has aggressively recruited on the basis of opportunities for advancement. That is, your advertising and other recruiting materials have stressed that the company only promotes from within and that highly motivated employees can expect to advance rapidly into increasingly responsible and higher-paid positions. An internal study done about ten years ago found that the average promotion time for top performers was about 1 to 1.5 years per promotion. Your interviewers have continued to emphasize this finding when they meet with prospective employees.

Over the past few years, your firm has gone through some major organizational changes that have resulted in a much flatter organization design. You have begun to suspect that the firm now has fewer opportunities for meaningful advancement. You recently submitted a proposal to the head of corporate human resources for a new promotion study to see if promotion cycles have slowed. You believe that they have slowed, and that the company should soften its statements about advancement.

The top assistant for the corporate human resources director just called and left you this voice message: "Hi Pat, this is Bill. Listen, I've read through your proposal about the promotion study, and think you should just let this die. I think we all know that promotion cycles aren't what they used to be, but who wants to step forward and really prove it? It can't do anything but hurt us. And anyway, the really sharp people still move up, and maybe one day things will go back to how they used to be. My reading is that the top brass want to carry on like we always have, and taking a real look at this might cause some real problems. If I don't hear from you within the next few days, I'll just put your proposal in the circular file [trash container]. But if you really want to stick your neck out, let me know."

Questions

1. What are the ethical issues in this situation?

2. What are the basic arguments for and against proceeding with your proposal?

3. What do you think most managers would do? What would you do?

HR Internet Exercise

Several Internet sites are dedicated to employment opportunities for job seekers. Use a search engine to locate the addresses for three different sites of this type. As you visit each site, try to place yourself in the role of a job seeker looking for employment in each of the following three areas:

1. Production manager in a manufacturing plant

2. Sales representative for a consumer products group

3. Restaurant manager

Questions

1. Are there any differences in ease of use and perceived value for job searches among the three sites?

2. Are there any differences in ease of use and perceived value for each of the three kinds of jobs being searched?

3. Identify the basic quality requirements in such sites to maximize their potential value to a job seeker.

7

Selecting Human Resources

CHAPTER OBJECTIVES

*After studying this chapter you should
be able to:*

■ Describe the steps in and responsibilities for the selection process in
organizations.

■ Identify and summarize basic selection criteria that organizations use in
hiring new employees.

■ Discuss popular selection techniques that organizations use to hire
new employees.

■ Discuss reliability and validity and
note the importance of multiple
predictors.

■ Discuss the selection decision itself.

■ Identify and summarize the basic
legal issues in selection.

■ Discuss the importance to an organization of evaluating its selection
activities.

In the few short years since it opened, the Bellagio resort in Las Vegas, Nevada, has become one of the gambling mecca's most popular destinations. But before the resort opened, and behind the scenes, the Bellagio also gave human resource managers new insights into how to staff an organization. The task facing the resort's human resource executives was daunting—they had to hire 9,600 workers in twenty-four weeks, and everyone had to be trained and on the payroll when the first customer walked through the door. The firm's human resource team not only pulled this feat off without a hitch—they did it without using a single sheet of paper!

"For us, hiring 9,600 people was like Desert Storm."

(Arte Nathan, vice president of human resources, Bellagio)*

With the precision of a full-scale military operation, the Bellagio team designed and implemented one of the most sophisticated human resource selection systems ever created. To apply for a position, applicants first called for an appointment. They were then scheduled in batches to arrive at the resort's hiring center, where they filled out an application at a computer terminal. One hundred terminals were kept busy twelve hours a day, six days a week. As applications were submitted, employees at the checkout desk conducted an unobtrusive assessment of the applicants' communication skills and overall demeanor, thus eliminating about 20 percent of the applicants.

Next came 27,000 interviews. For example, a hiring manager could sit at a personal computer and call up the highest-rated desk-clerk candidates. The database system would rank-order the candidates according to predetermined criteria. The manager could then, say, call in three applicants for face-to-face interviews. The interviews themselves consisted of a set of structured questions. During the interviews the manager would discreetly evaluate the responses to each question on a hidden keypad. These data were then fed back into the database.

If a manager wanted to hire a particular applicant, he or she could use a screen to check "conduct background check." A team of investigators would then verify employment, military, and education history; some jobs also required a mandatory drug test. About 8 percent of the applicants were rejected at this stage because of falsified or inaccurate information on their applications.

Finally, if the manager was ready to offer a job to a particular individual, another screen was used to check off this information. Applicants who made it this far were then invited to a job-offer meeting where they were offered actual jobs. If they accepted, they completed various required documents—again, in electronic form—for benefits and income-tax purposes. They were also scheduled for relevant training sessions. And when the big day came and the Bellagio officially threw open its doors, 9,600 new employees were in place and ready to work.[1] ■

Like all organizations, the Bellagio wants to hire individuals best suited for the work that needs to be performed. And like other organizations, the Bellagio has to manage its selection process efficiently and fairly. Organizations can use several basic indicators and criteria to improve the likelihood that they are hiring the best possible employees.

As we noted in Chapter 6, the recruiting process is designed to develop a pool of qualified applicants interested in employment with the organization. The premise is that the organization can then select the specific individuals whom it wants to employ from among the members of that pool. Thus, the **selection process** is concerned with identifying the best candidate or candidates for jobs from among the pool of qualified applicants developed during the recruiting process.

This chapter is concerned with the selection process. After presenting an overview of this process, we then look at basic selection criteria. Next we introduce and discuss various popular selection techniques that many organizations use. Special selection methods and techniques used for managers are then described. Reliability and validity, important attributes of effective selection techniques, are then described. Finally, we describe the selection decision itself and the determination of initial job assignments.

■ The **selection process** is concerned with identifying the best candidate or candidates for jobs from among the pool of qualified applicants developed during the recruiting process.

THE SELECTION PROCESS

Almost every organization establishes its own unique selection system; however, basic common characteristics are reflected in most selection systems. It is also important to establish who in the organization has the responsibility for selecting new employees.

Steps in Selection

At a general level, the selection process involves three distinct steps (see Figure 7.1).[2] The first step is to gather information about the members of the pool of qualified recruits (as created by the recruiting process discussed in Chapter 6). This information is gathered through several methods and techniques, most of which will be discussed later. In general, the information relates primarily to determining the levels of requisite knowledge, skills, and abilities (KSAs) possessed by an applicant. Information about factors such as education and experience is objective in nature. Other information, such as the attitudes of the individuals toward work and the impressions of current managers about the individual's likelihood of succeeding in the organization, is much more subjective and

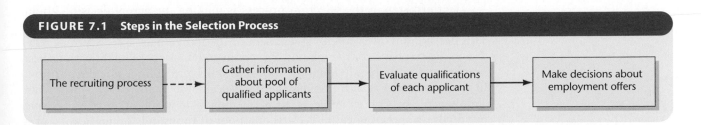

FIGURE 7.1 Steps in the Selection Process

The recruiting process ---→ Gather information about pool of qualified applicants → Evaluate qualifications of each applicant → Make decisions about employment offers

Interviews are a fairly common method for selecting among job applicants. They allow organizational representatives to see the applicant and interact with him or her, and they allow the applicant to ask questions and learn about the company. In the U.S. interviews are usually scheduled for one applicant at a time, and there may be a sequence of multiple interviews for each applicant. Employers at this job fair in Shanghai use a different approach. Job applicants stand in line for a chance to be interviewed. The interview is conducted on the spot, and applicants are contacted about results soon after.

perceptual. As we will discuss later, information about specific skill levels possessed by the individual or the individual's personality may be relatively objective but still open to subjectivity and interpretation.

The second step in the selection process is to evaluate the qualifications of each applicant from among the recruiting pool. This evaluation process occurs through the application of explicit or implicit standards to the information gathered in step 1. For example, if the standard for hiring is that the person must be able to keyboard seventy words per minute, a manager can give each applicant a keyboarding test and compare applicants' scores to that standard. Similarly, if the standard calls for a certain personality type, a manager can give personality tests, interpret test scores based on test norms, and then assess how closely the individual fits the desired profile.

But sometimes applying standards is not so straightforward. For example, if the standard is ten years of relevant work experience, someone must make the decision about whether or not people who exceed that standard are more qualified than individuals who simply meet it. For example, is an applicant with fifteen years of experience a more desirable candidate than another applicant with ten years and one month experience, or are these two candidates to be treated as equal on this dimension because they each meet the standard? We will discuss some important implications of decisions such as this one later in the chapter.

The third step in the selection process is making the actual decision about which candidate or candidates will be offered employment with the organization. This decision involves careful assessment of the individuals' qualifications relative to the standards of the job and the extent to which those qualifications best prepare and give an individual the requisite skills and abilities for the position. In some cases, an organization may need to select large numbers of people to hire simultaneously. For example, a firm opening a new factory may be hiring hundreds of operating employees from a pool of thousands of applicants, or a rapidly growing restaurant chain may need to hire dozens of management trainees to assume management positions in new restaurants in a year or two. In both cases the manager doesn't necessarily have to make fine gradations between, say, candidate number 11 and candidate number 12. The only decision is determining the extent to which a candidate is in the set of desirable people to hire or is outside that set because of job-relevant characteristics.

But if the selection decision involves hiring a specific single individual for a specific position in the organization, such as a new director of marketing or a vice president of human resources, then one individual must be selected. It is sometimes helpful at this point to rank-order the candidates who are being considered for the job. If the organization does not succeed in hiring its top choice for the job, then decisions will have already been made regarding the relative acceptability of candidate number 2, candidate number 3, and so on. In some cases, for example, if the recruiting process has been handled effectively, the organization may want to hire more than one qualified applicant in the pool. Thus, it may be helpful to develop a backup plan in case the top choice cannot be employed.

Selection Errors

Later in this chapter we will discuss various techniques available for selecting employees. We will also discuss some concepts that deal with the accuracy of the decisions made on the basis of those techniques. But no selection system is perfect, and an organization will always make at least an occasional selection error. An organization or a human resource manager can make two basic types of selection errors: **false positives** and **false negatives.**

In each case the decision maker examines the information he or she has about the applicant and then tries to predict whether the applicant will ultimately succeed or fail on the job. If the human resource manager predicts that the person will be successful, a decision may then be made to hire the person. But if the human resource manager predicts that the person will fail, then a decision is made to reject (not hire) the person. In each case, some of the predictions are correct and others are incorrect; these situations are illustrated in Figure 7.2.

■ **False positives** are applicants who are predicted to be successful and are hired but who ultimately fail.

■ **False negatives** are applicants who are predicted to fail and are not hired, but if they had been hired, they would have been successful.

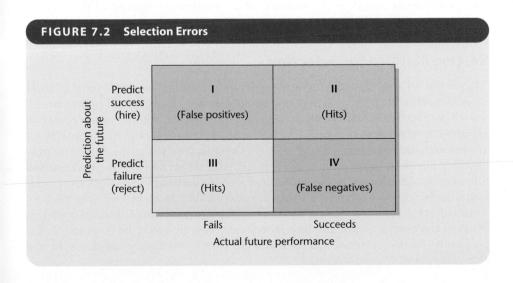

FIGURE 7.2   Selection Errors

	Fails	Succeeds
Predict success (hire)	I (False positives)	II (Hits)
Predict failure (reject)	III (Hits)	IV (False negatives)

Prediction about the future

Actual future performance

The figure shows that some of the people predicted to be successful and who are hired will in fact succeed. These are "hits" (shown in quadrant II) because the right decision was made. The bottom left quadrant (quadrant III) also shows hits. These people are rejected; if they were hired, they would fail. But the other two quadrants illustrate the two types of selection errors. Quadrant I represents the false positives: the applicants who are predicted to be successful and who are therefore hired, but who ultimately fail. Quadrant IV represents the false negatives: the applicants who are predicted to fail and so are not hired. If they *had* been hired, however, they would have been successful.

We will return to some of the ideas in Figure 7.2 later in the chapter when we discuss how to evaluate the selection system. Selection systems that minimize selection errors will obviously be more effective for the organization. We will also see later that the relative distribution of cases in these four quadrants has important implications for establishing whether a selection technique is job related. For now it is useful to think about the implications of the two types of errors. False positives (quadrant I) represent people who are hired and who fail. These cases are visible to the organization as a whole, and it is desirable to keep this number to an absolute minimum. But how exactly do managers accomplish this goal? The easiest way is to be a lot tougher in making predictions about success, that is, using more rigorous tests or more challenging interviews to make selection decisions. Indeed, the organization may set its standards for selection so high it may rarely hire anyone who fails.

However, such stringent requirements come at a cost. False negatives are people the organization should have hired but didn't. Thus, false negatives are missed opportunities and are therefore not nearly as visible as false positives. But note that if managers make selection decisions based on more and more stringent criteria, they may reduce the number of people they hire who fail, but they will also hire fewer people overall and will miss many opportunities to hire good employees. Thus, a tradeoff exists between the two types of errors: relatively modest selection standards can ensure that the organization never misses an opportunity but will hire many failures, while relatively tough selection standards may ensure that the organization hires few failures but will also pass over many qualified applicants. There is no right answer to dealing with this dilemma, but it is important to realize the nature of this tradeoff as you go through the rest of the chapter. Each organization must decide for itself which type of error is more costly.

Responsibilities for Selection

Who in the organization has the responsibility for hiring new employees? In most cases responsibilities for selecting new employees are jointly shared by human resource managers and operating managers. For example, following the center of expertise model (see Chapter 1), human resource managers in an organization are responsible for designing the selection system and for gathering basic preliminary selection data, such as experience, education, and similar background information. Employees in the human resource department may then screen out individuals who do not meet those standards. While in theory this process should have happened during the recruiting process, sometimes people slip through the cracks. Thus, the human resource function may be responsible for providing relatively objective assessments of the various candidates in the recruiting pool.

Operating managers also play a major role in this process, however. For example, in most organizations today operating managers conduct most of the interviews with applicants and they must make decisions about the relative likelihood of a given applicant fitting into the organization's culture, the existing work group, and so forth. Thus, operating managers are likely to be asked to make more subjective and personal assessments about the relative qualifications of a given employee.

In some cases, operating employees and potential colleagues of the prospective applicant may also play a role in the selection process, especially in organizations that rely heavily on teams. Coworkers will be working with the individual, and some organizations find it appropriate and effective to solicit their input about the relative attractiveness of various candidates being considered for the job. When hiring new managers, Trammell Crow Real Estate Investors conducts candidate interviews with two or three other managers and a secretary or a young leasing agent. This approach helps the firm assess how the prospective manager relates to nonmanagers. Chaparral Steel Company relies heavily on work teams in its mill. Team members interview and make recommendations about various applicants for a job on their team.

In smaller organizations that lack a full-time human resource manager or self-contained human resource department, responsibilities for selection may fall on a single individual, usually the owner/manager of the organization. This person may handle the recruiting process, develop a pool of applicants, interview each applicant, and then select whom she or he wants to hire. Many smaller retailing stores located in shopping malls, such as The Gap and Foot Locker, operate this way.

BASIC SELECTION CRITERIA

On what basis does a manager or an organization try to select a given individual from a pool of qualified applicants? As we discussed in Chapter 5, a major outcome of the job analysis process is the generation of job specifications, or requisite KSAs. KSAs are the individual characteristics that the organization feels are necessary for people to be able to perform specific jobs. They might include attributes such as education and experience, specific skills and abilities, and personal characteristics.

Education and Experience

Education and experience are relatively straightforward to assess. In a selection context, **education** refers to the formal classroom training an individual has received in public or private schools and in a college, university, and/or technical school. Some jobs require that people have a high school diploma, other jobs require a two-year associate degree from a community or junior college, while still other jobs require a four-year college education. Sometimes the educational fields (a person's major) are open; in other cases they must be within a specified area, such as mechanical engineering, French, or human resource management. Occasionally, jobs may require advanced degrees, such as a master's degree or perhaps even a doctorate in a specific field of study. In some cases a technical certification

■ **Education** refers to the formal classroom training an individual has received in public or private schools and in a college, university, and/or technical school.

may also be a good indicator of education in a particular field of study. Many vocational and technical schools offer certificates when they train people for craft work such as electrical work, mechanical work, plumbing, and so forth.

In the last few years U.S. automobile manufacturers have started placing a higher premium on education when hiring new assembly workers. Managers at these firms have realized that a more educated workforce will be more open to new training and learning and will better appreciate the importance of product quality. At Ford, for example, about 80 percent of the firm's total number of production workers has a high school degree. However, the percentage of workers hired since 1991 who have high school degrees is 97 percent. As less-educated workers retire or leave for various reasons, the overall educational level of the company's workforce will gradually increase under this new policy.[3]

■ **Experience** is the amount of time the individual has spent working, either in a general capacity or in a particular field of study.

Experience refers to the amount of time the individual may have spent working, either in a general capacity or in a particular field. Experience is presumably an indicator of an individual's familiarity with work and his or her ability to work, and a surrogate measure of a person's competencies as an employee. In some cases it may be necessary that the individual have a predetermined level of experience in a certain field of study. For example, if a large organization is looking to hire someone to be director of advertising, it will quite likely expect applicants to have substantial experience in the advertising field. In other cases, however, the experience requirement may be more general. Simply having a certain number of years' experience in full-time work activities might be sufficient evidence of an individual's employability. And some entry-level jobs may require no experience at all.

Skills and Abilities

■ **Skills and abilities** relate precisely to the specific qualifications and capabilities of an individual to perform a specific job.

Other selection criteria are skills and abilities. **Skills and abilities** relate more precisely to the specific qualifications and capabilities of an individual to perform a specific job.[4] For example, even though an individual may have a college degree and a wealth of work experience, she or he may not have effective skills and abilities regarding spatial relations (the ability to manipulate three-dimensional objects in one's mind). If the organization needs someone who has high levels of spatial relations (which would be the case for many assembly-line jobs), an applicant who lacks that skill would not be an attractive candidate for the organization.

As organizations move toward teamwork and team-based operating systems, many of them are also putting more emphasis on hiring individuals with the skills necessary to function effectively in a group situation.[5] Recall, for example, the earlier example of Chaparral Steel's use of existing team members to help hire new members. The rationale for this practice is that current team members are in a position to assess a given individual's ability to fit in and become an effective member of the team.

Personal Characteristics

In some jobs it is also important to an organization to assess the personal characteristics of individual job applicants. These personal characteristics are believed to reflect the individual's personality and may be an important factor in certain kinds of jobs. For example, a department store manager may believe that effective salespeople are individuals who have an outgoing and pleasant personality. Thus, this manager, when interviewing prospective job applicants, might look closely at their friendliness, their ability to converse, and the extent to which they are comfortable dealing with various circumstances. In contrast, a person who is more introverted, shy, and less willing to talk to people might not be a match for this particular kind of job.

When basing a selection decision on personal characteristics, the organization must be able to demonstrate a clear, performance-related basis for this decision. For example, if the department store manager cannot demonstrate empirically that an outgoing individual will be a more productive salesperson than would a shy and introverted individual, then that qualification may be of questionable legality. As we will discuss later, personal characteristics are among the most complex and sensitive selection criteria to assess and to validate.

In recent years, a real shift has occurred in the focus of selection instruments designed to measure these personality variables. A great deal of attention has been paid to instruments that measure the **big five personality traits**. These five personality traits tend to be more behavioral than cognitive or emotional, and recent research has suggested that they are likely to be more important for job performance than are more traditional personality traits.[6] The big five traits are *neuroticism* (disposition to experience states like anxiety and guilt rather than being better adjusted emotionally), *extraversion* (tendency to be outgoing, sociable, and upbeat), *openness to experience* (tendency to be imaginative and intellectually curious), *agreeableness* (tendency to be altruistic and cooperative), and *conscientiousness* (tendency to be purposeful and dependable and to pay attention to detail).

■ The **big five personality traits**, which tend to be more behavioral than cognitive or emotional, are likely to be more important for job performance than are more traditional personality traits. These traits are *neuroticism, extraversion, openness to experience, agreeableness,* and *conscientiousness.*

Hiring for "Fit"

The bases for selection discussed thus far tend to focus on matching individual applicants with specific jobs, although this issue is a bit broader when we consider personal characteristics. This approach is consistent with the discussion of traditional job analysis methods in Chapter 5. But in that chapter we also discussed the growing importance of competency modeling as an alternative to traditional job analysis. Competencies refer to relatively broad capabilities that are necessary for effective job performance, and their importance might well extend beyond a specific job. Because it is more common now for employees to rotate from one job to another, to share jobs, or to work in teams, this competency approach applied to selection is becoming even more popular.

The idea is that, rather than hiring someone who is a good fit for a specific job, an organization might instead hire someone who is a good fit for the larger organization. Thus, rather than hire someone for a programming position because of his or her computer skills alone, the firm might consider hiring persons whose personal values or personality fit with the rest of the organization. Note that the firm likely would not hire an unqualified person simply because of fit, but from among a group of reasonably qualified persons, the company would select the person who it thought would fit in best. (This concept is similar to banding, which will be discussed later in the chapter.)

But we should also note that in some cases organizations believe that the requisite skills and abilities can be taught to people once they are on the job, and so selection decisions are made almost exclusively on the basis of fit. Again, we are

It is becoming more popular for organizations to make a decision to hire an applicant based primarily on the applicant's ability to "fit" in the organization. Sometimes the notion of fit refers to personal values; sometimes it refers to personality. The man in this picture is Roy Snider, the official pep rally cheerleader for Stew Leonard's, a small and somewhat quirky supermarket chain. Snider's job is to inspire customers to say "wow," boost employee morale, and build team spirit. His official title is "Director of Wow." What does a person need to do this job? Snider says that a positive attitude and the ability to love the job are crucial. This is clearly a case in which finding someone who fits is essential.

referring to fit with the organization rather than fit for a specific job, which is more likely to depend on KSAs.[7] This trend has developed into a growing controversy in selection today. Human resource managers traditionally believed that they should hire the person with the best set of job-specific skills relative to the work that needed to be performed, but today many argue that the best hires are those who fit into the overall organization based on personal characteristics, values, and so forth.[8] The Point/Counterpoint feature for this chapter outlines some of the arguments on both sides of this controversy.

POPULAR SELECTION TECHNIQUES

Organizations use different techniques for gathering information that reflects an individual's education and experience, skills and abilities, and personal characteristics. Indeed, most organizations rely on a comprehensive system involving multiple selection techniques to ensure that they gather all the relevant data and that they assess this data rigorously, objectively, and in a nondiscriminatory fashion. In the sections that follow we will identify and discuss some of the more popular and commonly used selection techniques. Logic may underlie the sequence in which organizations use these techniques, but at the same time many organizations vary the order to fit their own particular needs, circumstances, and beliefs. Figure 7.3 on page 222 illustrates one example selection sequence that an organization might employ.

POINT | COUNTERPOINT

Selecting for Fit Versus Skill

The basis for a selection decision has traditionally been whether or not a person can do the job. That is, organizations would identify the knowledge, skills, and abilities (KSAs) needed to do a job and then select the best-qualified candidate(s). More recently, organizations have begun basing selection decisions on whether or not a person fits with the organization. That is, the decision is based on whether the applicant seems to share values and personality traits with the organization as a whole. We don't want to suggest that KSAs have become irrelevant; they are simply of secondary importance.

POINT... Organizations should select people primarily on the basis of fit because ...	COUNTERPOINT... Organizations should select people primarily on the basis of KSAs because ...
Even if they are qualified, people who don't fit in the organization will probably never succeed.	No matter how well someone fits in, he or she will never perform as well as someone who is more qualified.
A strong organizational or corporate culture depends on hiring people with consistent values.	Organizations that rely on fit simply hire more of the same kind of people.
Teams are easier to form and are more likely to be successful when all team members share some basic values.	Lack of diversity in backgrounds and interests can result in fewer ideas and less originality, and perhaps can even lead to discrimination.
People will be more attracted and committed to organizations with which they believe they share values.	Diverse populations will be committed to organizations that value diversity.
It is easier to determine whether or not an applicant is "one of us."	Determinations of fit are always subjective, whereas determinations of KSAs can be more objective and thus less biased.

So... Organizations will always use both factors to some extent, but the issue is which one is given precedence. As long as all persons selected are reasonably qualified, there would seem to be no problems with selecting people on the basis of fit, and such an approach would surely reap some benefits. The biggest potential downside to a reliance on fit is that is can lead to the exclusion of people who are different (on the base of race and/or gender), which is illegal. Of course, a tolerant, diverse culture might be exactly the culture the organization is trying to foster.

Applications and Background Checks

One of the first steps in most selection systems is to ask applicants to complete an employment application or an application blank. An **employment application** asks individuals for various facts and information pertaining to their personal background. Commonly asked questions on an employment application include details such as name, educational background, personal career goals, experience, and so forth.

Of course, all questions on an employment application must relate to an individual's ability to perform the job. For example, an employment application

■ An **employment application** asks individuals for various bits of information pertaining to their personal background.

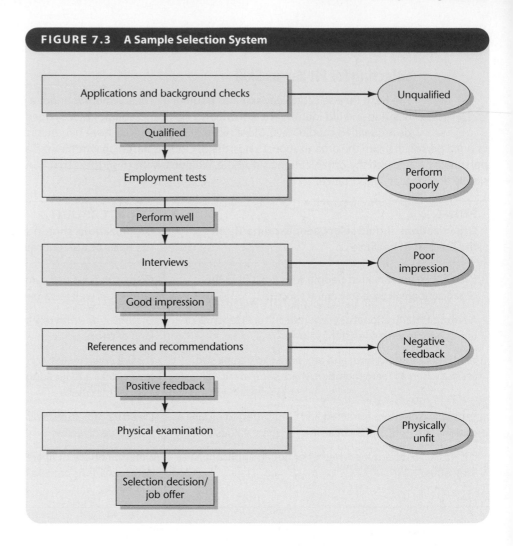

FIGURE 7.3   A Sample Selection System

cannot ask for a person's gender, age, or marital status because these questions have no bearing on that person's ability to perform specific jobs. Such questions could even serve as a basis for applicants' claims of discrimination on the basis of age or gender. An organization may need this information after someone is hired, but it is illegal to make selection decisions based on these variables and they should be avoided on application blanks. Figure 7.4 presents an example of an application blank.

One advantage of an application blank is that it provides a quick and inexpensive mechanism for gathering several kinds of objective information about an individual and information of a type that can be easily verified. As discussed in HR Tech Talk, some organizations today are even using electronic screening devices to review applications. Even on a traditional paper application, however, if an individual states that she has a bachelor's degree in electrical engineering from a given university, the organization can verify this information with a simple call to that university's registrar's office.

Likewise, the application provides a convenient barometer for measuring the extent to which a person meets the basic selection criteria. For example, suppose

FIGURE 7.4 Sample Employment Application

SEARS

APPLICATION FOR EMPLOYMENT
PLEASE PRINT REQUESTED INFORMATION
USE ONLY BLACK OR BLUE INK

Date ☐☐ / ☐☐ / ☐☐☐☐

Sears, Roebuck and Co. (hereinafter "Sears") is an Equal Opportunity/Affirmative Action Employer and does not discriminate in any aspect of employment on the basis of race, color, religion, gender, age, national origin, disability, citizenship status, sexual orientation, veteran status, marital status, ancestry, pregnancy or any other legally protected status in accordance with the requirements of federal, state and local law.

Sears maintains a drug-free workplace and therefore strictly prohibits the illegal manufacture, distribution, possession or use of drugs or controlled substances on Sears premises or while conducting company business. All applicants must take and pass a drug test after receiving an initial offer of employment. Any failure or refusal to take the test at scheduled times will disqualify the applicant from employment. Job offers for certain job categories may also be conditioned upon the results of a post-offer medical examination. Applicants' rights to confidentiality and privacy will be observed in accordance with the law.

NOTE: Sears will consider your completed and signed application active for 60 days.

PERSONAL INFORMATION

First Name | M.I. | Social Security Number ☐☐☐ - ☐☐ - ☐☐☐☐

Last Name

CURRENT ADDRESS

	Street	City	ST	Zip Code	County	Telephone No.
1						

PREVIOUS ADDRESSES

If you have not lived at your current address for 7 years, please list all prior residential addresses (most recent first) for the 7 years before the date this application is submitted. (Note: If more space is needed, use page 4 of this application.)

	Street	City	ST	Zip Code	County	Dates (From: mm/yy To: mm/yy)
2						
3						
4						

I AM INTERESTED IN THE FOLLOWING POSITION CHECKED BELOW (check one only):

Sales:
- ☐ Commission
- ☐ Non-Commission

Automotive (other than Sales or Support):
- ☐ Mechanic/Technical
- ☐ Tire/Battery Installation

Store Support:
- ☐ Asset Protection
- ☐ Facilities/Maintenance
- ☐ Replenishment/Mdse Handling
- ☐ Visual/Store Presentation
- ☐ Office/Clerical
- ☐ Technician

Other:
(Specify) ____________

Management/Salaried Position:
(Specify) ____________

I am seeking (check one and enter hours available in block to the right):
- ☐ Seasonal employment (one season, e.g. Christmas)
- ☐ Regular employment (employment for indefinite period of time)

If seasonal, indicate dates available:
____

I am available for:
☐ Part-time Work ☐ Full-time Work

If part-time, indicate maximum hours per week ____________.

HOURS AVAILABLE TO WORK	
Sun.	to
Mon.	to
Tues.	to
Wed.	to
Thurs.	to
Fri.	to
Sat.	to

(#10534 - FLS Application Rev. 09/2001)

13532

Source: The Sears Employment Application within this book is reprinted by arrangement with Sears, Roebuck and Co., and is protected under copyright. No duplication is permitted. Reprinted courtesy of Sears, Roebuck and Co.

the organization has determined that it wants to hire someone with five years' work experience and a bachelor's degree. If an applicant applying for the job indicates that he has three years' experience and only one year of college education, the organization has reasonable cause to exclude that person from further consideration. If an applicant specifies that she has a master's degree and fifteen years' experience, the organization may conclude that that individual is overqualified for the job.

In recent years, some organizations have experimented with new and more sophisticated versions of the traditional employment application. For example,

Using Computers to Hire People

Traditionally job seekers started exploring an employment opportunity by completing an application blank or submitting a copy of their resumé to the employer's human resource department. A clerk or human resource manager reviewed the applicant's credentials and made a preliminary judgment about whether the applicant met basic employment requirements. If the applicant met these basic requirements, he or she advanced to more thorough selection activities. If he or she did not, the individual was informed that the company did not have anything available for which the applicant was qualified.

In today's fast-paced and high-tech world, however, companies are increasingly using electronic screening mechanisms to make initial decisions about applicants. Among the pioneers in this area are Sony, Coca-Cola, IBM, Paine Webber, NationsBank, Avis, Microsoft, Pfizer, and Shell. The process usually starts in one of two ways: applicants are instructed to submit their application or resumé electronically, or else paper media are scanned into a firm's human resource database. At this point, the firm's human resource information system often takes over. For example, one pass through the system might eliminate any and all applicants who do not meet the basic qualifications that the firm requires of all its employees—U.S. citizenship, for example, or a high school education. In this case, the system itself may then generate and mail a rejection letter to the applicant.

For those individuals who make the preliminary cut, the information system may take another pass through an individual's electronic records, seeking out certain key-

> *"It's just another bit of machinery that gets in the way of the human-touch process."*
>
> (Steve Stahl, cofounder of Golden Handshakes, a Virginia-based support group for unemployed managers and an outspoken critic of electronic employment screening)*

words, criteria, or qualifications. For instance, a software firm like Microsoft may have its system flag those job seekers who indicate expertise in a specific programming language such as Java or HTML. Those individuals are highlighted for human resource managers, who can follow up with them on a more personal level.

Other records are stored for later review by managers seeking new employees. For example, a manager seeking to hire a new sales representative may indicate any number of specific qualifications, such as education, experience, type of experience, and so forth; query the system for applicants who meet those qualifications; and then obtain copies of the application materials for everyone in the system who is qualified. The manager may also request information about a predetermined set of applicants—say, five or ten—who most closely meet the qualifications.

Of course, these kinds of systems are not without their shortcomings. Some critics argue that electronic selection systems further depersonalize larger employers. Others believe that these systems may open the door for savvy people who know how to work the system and that they increase the odds a strong applicant may not be considered because certain buzz words were not included on that person's application materials. Still, electronic screening seems like it's here to stay, so critics may need to get used to it!

Sources: "Sir: Your Application for a Job Is Rejected; Sincerely, Hal 9000," *Wall Street Journal*, July 30, 1998, pp. A1, A12 (*quote on p. A1); Linda Thornburg, "Computer-Assisted Interviewing Shortens Hiring Cycle," *HRMagazine*, February 1998, pp. 73–78.

■ A **weighted application blank** relies on the determination of numerical indices to indicate the relative importance of various personal factors for predicting a person's ability to perform a job effectively.

one experimental method is the so-called **weighted application blank.**[9] A weighted application blank relies on the determination of numerical indices to indicate the relative importance of various personal factors for predicting a person's ability to perform a job effectively. Using information gathered from current high and low performers in the organization, it may be possible to determine whether various specific levels of education, experience, and so forth, are related to a person's ability to perform a job effectively.

Another recent innovation is the **biodata application blank**. Biodata applications focus on the same type of information found in a regular application, but they also go into more complex and detailed assessments about that background.[10] For example, in addition to asking about an applicant's college major, a biodata application might ask questions about which courses the applicant enjoyed most and why a particular field of study was chosen. As with weighted application blanks, responses to these questions are then studied for groups of good and poor performers. Responses to items that seem to differentiate between those who do well and those who do poorly are then used to predict the expected future performance of new applicants.

■ **Biodata applications** focus on the same type of information that is found in a regular application but go into more complex and detailed assessments about that background.

Note that weighted and biodata applications focus on responses that help predict performance on the job. For example, an organization would not be interested in why individuals who collected stamps as a child performed better than other applicants, and the organization would certainly not suggest that collecting stamps led to better performance. The organization cares only that certain patterns of responses seem to be associated with high performance and so seeks applicants with these patterns.

Employment Tests

Another popular selection technique used by many organizations is an employment test.[11] An **employment test** is a device for measuring the characteristics of an individual. These characteristics may include personality, intelligence, or aptitude. Although employment tests are generally traditional question-and-answer exercises that applicants complete on paper or online, the courts consider any device used to make an employment decision, including interviews, to be a test. Typically, though, employment tests per se are either paper or computer-administered. For a paper test the organization scores the employment test itself or sends it to the agency from which it acquired the test for scoring. For a computer-administered test the applicant sits at a computer and enters answers to questions using the keyboard or mouse. Figure 7.5 shows samples from several popular employment tests.

Different types of employment tests are commonly used. Before identifying them, however, we should make the distinction between aptitude and achievement tests. These terms often refer to how the test is used rather than the nature of the test. Aptitude tests focus on predicting future performance, while achievement tests focus on the mastery of some set of learned skills. For example, keyboarding tests are usually seen as achievement tests because they focus

Paper and pencil tests are popular selection techniques. They are best suited for assessing mental abilities and general knowledge, and they are more objective than interviews. Here, a group of individuals take the civil service exam in Washington, D.C. This exam is required for anyone who wants a job in civil service, whether the job is letter carrier or manager for the postal service. This system was implemented as a fair way to determine who should receive government jobs. Paper and pencil tests are used for the same reason in the private sector.

■ An **employment test** is a device for measuring the characteristics of an individual, such as personality, intelligence, or aptitude.

FIGURE 7.5   Sample Items from an Employment Test

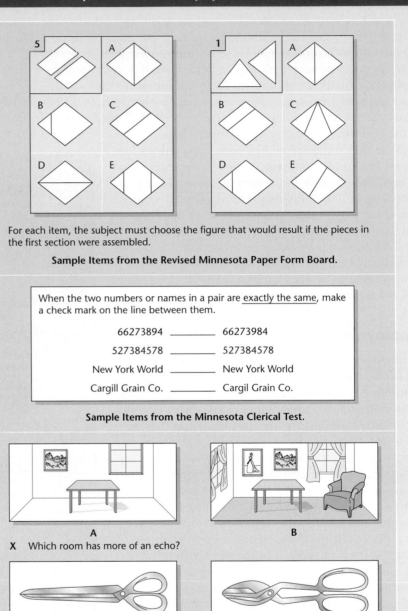

For each item, the subject must choose the figure that would result if the pieces in the first section were assembled.

Sample Items from the Revised Minnesota Paper Form Board.

When the two numbers or names in a pair are <u>exactly the same</u>, make a check mark on the line between them.

66273894 _____ 66273984

527384578 _____ 527384578

New York World _____ New York World

Cargill Grain Co. _____ Cargil Grain Co.

Sample Items from the Minnesota Clerical Test.

X   Which room has more of an echo?

Y   Which would be the better shears for cutting metal?

Sample Items from the Bennet Mechanical Comprehension Test.

on whether or not the applicant has basic proficiency or mastery in using a keyboard. Cognitive ability tests are seen as aptitude tests because they focus on the question of whether the person will be able to perform some specific task in the future. The Lighter Side of HR illustrates how *not* to complete an aptitude test!

Cognitive ability tests measure mental skills. The applicant is not required to do anything physical, only to demonstrate some type of knowledge. Therefore, knowing how a specific tool is used reflects a cognitive ability, while being able to use the tool is a psychomotor ability (which we will discuss below). An extremely important cognitive ability is intelligence. General intelligence, or *g*, refers to reasoning, or problem solving skills, but is typically measured in terms of the information one learns in school. The Scholastic Aptitude Test (SAT) is a test of general intelligence. Scores on these tests can be expressed in terms of intelligence quotient (IQ). The way these quotients are computed is beyond the scope of this discussion, but it reflects performance on a test relative to other people of the same age.

Two important facts make the use of intelligence tests in selection controversial. First, IQ is related to performance on a wide variety of jobs because more intelligent people perform better.[12] This feature makes the use of intelligence tests in selection procedures popular and is consistent with the ideas discussed earlier about the value of a more educated workforce. The second fact is that, on average, black Americans tend to score lower on these tests than do white Americans. Therefore, using intelligence tests as selection criteria will likely result in disparate impact. Many explanations have been offered about why these differences exist and what they should mean for selection.[13] Among the most common explanations are bias in test construction and fundamental cultural differences that result in different frames of reference. The key point vis-à-vis our discussion is simply that intelligence tests are potentially useful but controversial tests of a special cognitive ability.

Other cognitive abilities include vocabulary and reading comprehension (verbal ability) and mathematics (quantitative ability), clerical ability (such as the ability to put names in alphabetical order and to recognize when two names are alike or different from each other), and spatial relations (defined earlier). These cognitive abilities are important for performance on a wide variety of jobs, and they are widely used in selection settings. As noted earlier, auto manufacturers are seeking to improve the general intelligence of their workers. Ford and Chrysler both now rely on cognitive ability tests to assess basic reading and mathematical abilities.

Psychomotor ability tests measure physical abilities such as strength, eye-hand coordination, and manual dexterity. These abilities can be practiced and perfected, and the tests to measure them are usually some type of performance test. For example, the O'Connor Tweezer Dexterity test requires an applicant to

The Lighter Side of HR

Aptitude testing is a common practice in organizations today. In general, test scores are supposed to predict with reasonable accuracy the individual's performance levels in the future. The higher the test score, therefore, the more likely the job applicant will become a high performer in the future. As shown in this cartoon, however, applicants sometimes may provide more information than they intend when they complete an aptitude test for a prospective employer!

Frank and Ernest

APTITUDE TESTING

TURN IN TESTS HERE →

I FILLED OUT THE WRONG SIDE. I HOPE THAT DOESN'T COUNT AGAINST ME.

THAVES

© 1988 Thaves/Reprinted with permission. Newspaper dist. by NEA, Inc.

■ **Cognitive ability tests** measure mental skills.

■ **Psychomotor ability tests** measure physical abilities such as strength, eye-hand coordination, and manual dexterity.

■ **Personality tests** measure traits, or tendencies to act, that are relatively unchanging in a person.

pick up and move small parts with a pair of tweezers (eye-finger coordination). (The popular children's game Operation requires the same essential skills as those tapped by this test.) Psychomotor tests are popular because they apparently measure what is important for performance on the job (human resource experts say that these tests have high "face validity"). In addition, they often measure skills that are important for jobs (e.g., eye-hand coordination is important for any job requiring someone to drive a vehicle), and little evidence of disparate impact occurs when they are used.

Personality tests measure traits, or tendencies to act, that are relatively unchanging in a person. Some tests are designed to measure a wide spectrum of personality traits or dimensions; as noted earlier, however, measures of the big five personality dimensions have become extremely popular in recent years and seem useful for predicting who will do well on jobs. Personality can be measured in two ways: self-report inventories and projective techniques.

■ A **self-report inventory** is a paper-and-pencil measure where an applicant responds to a series of statements that might or might not apply to the applicant.

A **self-report inventory** is a paper-and-pencil measure in which an applicant responds to a series of statements that might or might not apply to that applicant. The most commonly used personality inventories include the Minnesota Multiphasic Personality Inventory (MMPI) and the California Psychological Inventory (CPI). Although both have been used widely in selection settings, the MMPI measures what we would consider "abnormal" personality traits, such as schizophrenia, paranoia, and psychopathology. Therefore, the test is more appropriate with clinical populations (i.e., persons who are being treated for psychological disorders) and is probably best used in selection settings as a means of screening out potentially dangerous job applicants. The CPI, on the other hand, was designed to measure more "normal" personality traits, such as introversion versus extraversion, dominance, and masculinity versus femininity. Instruments designed to measure the big five personality traits are also growing in popularity.[14]

■ The **projective technique** involves showing an individual an ambiguous stimulus, such as an ink blot or a fuzzy picture, and then asking what he or she "sees."

The other type of personality measure is known as a **projective technique**. This approach involves showing an individual an ambiguous stimulus, such as an ink blot or a fuzzy picture, and then asking what he or she "sees." Since there isn't really anything to see, whatever the applicant reports is presumed to be reflective of his or her personality. The best-known projective technique is the Rorschach Ink Blot Test, which requires trained clinicians to interpret the results. The Thematic Apperception Test asks applicants to look at an ambiguous picture and then to write a story describing the people and what they are doing. This instrument can be scored relatively objectively (with a scoring key) and yields scores on personality traits such as need for achievement (which is a need to excel at all tasks).

The evidence regarding the relative effectiveness of measurement devices for the big five personality traits notwithstanding, personality tests are not without their critics.[15] Some disagreement exists over whether cognitive ability tests (especially intelligence tests) or personality tests provide the most useful information for selection decisions.[16] Regardless of the merits of these arguments, however, both personality and cognitive ability remain popular criteria in selection techniques, as do all employment tests in general.[17] Later in the chapter we will discuss issues of reliability and validity, which are critical for choosing which tests to use. Because they are relatively objective and easy to interpret, however, there is little question that employment tests will remain an important part of most organizations' selection systems.

■ **Integrity tests** attempt to assess an applicant's moral character and honesty.

Other increasingly used forms of employment test are designed to assess an individual's honesty or integrity. **Integrity tests** attempt to assess an applicant's moral character and honesty. Most of these tests are fairly straightforward and include questions such as "Do you think most people would cheat if they thought they could get away with it?" and "Have you ever taken anything that didn't belong to you at work?" Other tests are less obvious and are based more on personality measures. Note that on many personality tests, items such as the second example above ("Have you ever taken anything that didn't belong to you at work?) are included as a type of check. That is, the assumption is that most people *have* taken something from an employer that didn't belong to them, even if it was just a pen. Therefore, when someone replies that she or he disagrees with this item (i.e., she or he hasn't taken anything), it is interpreted as an indication that the person is not being totally honest about her- or himself. However, when the same item appears on an integrity test, a person agreeing with the item (i.e., she or he *has* taken something) is assumed to be dishonest and not to be trusted.

The use of integrity tests is growing dramatically, with several million administered annually in the United States.[18] The likelihood is that the number will continue to increase as the cost of employee theft rises.[19] Despite their popularity, however, integrity tests raise serious questions when they are used in selection. First, evidence about their accuracy is supplied almost entirely by the publishers of the tests, which raises the possibility of conflict of interests. Second, these tests may do a good job of identifying potential "thieves," but many other individuals not identified by the tests steal and simply do not get caught. Finally, some applicants find these tests invasive and respond negatively to them.[20]

Work Simulations

Work simulations (sometimes referred to as **work samples**) are similar to tests, but instead of providing paper-and-pencil responses to printed questions, the prospective employee is asked to perform tasks or job-related activities that simulate or represent the actual work for which the person is being considered. For example, suppose an organization needs to hire a new data-entry specialist. The organization has determined that the data-entry specialist must be proficient with Microsoft Office software and must be capable of keyboarding seventy-five words a minute. A relatively easy method for assessing a candidate's qualifications, then, is to seat the individual at a computer, ask him or her to perform various data-entry tasks and activities using Microsoft Office software, and then keyboard a letter or document to measure how quickly the person can keyboard. Other jobs for which work simulations are appropriate might be machinist jobs, where the individual can work on the machine under close supervision, a driving test for taxi drivers or school-bus drivers, and an audition for a performing-arts organization such as a musical group. **In-baskets**, which consist of collections of hypothetical memos, letters, and

■ **Work simulations (or work samples)** involve asking the prospective employee to perform tasks or job-related activities that simulate or represent the actual work for which the person is being considered.

■ **In-baskets** are special forms of work simulations for prospective managers. They consist of collections of hypothetical memos, letters, and notes that require responses.

For some jobs, work samples are a better way to evaluate applicants than either interviews or paper and pencil tests. For example, if a potential employee will be required to operate a specific piece of equipment that requires a great degree of manual dexterity, a simulated assignment that requires manual dexterity is appropriate. Such is the case with the applicant shown here. The manager is timing the applicant's performance to ensure that he will be able to perform the required operations in a timely fashion.

notes that require prioritization and responses, are sometimes used as part of management simulations.

Personal Interviews

While tests are popular, the most widely used selection technique in most organizations is the employment interview. **Interviews** are face-to-face conversations between prospective job applicants and representatives of the organization.[21]

Kinds of interviews   Three types of interviews are common: structured, semistructured, and unstructured interviews. A fourth type, the situational interview, is also growing in popularity.

In a *structured employment interview,* the interviewer either prepares or is given by others a list of standard questions to be asked during the interview. All interviewers ask the same questions of each candidate to achieve consistency across interviews. Also, since the questions are presumably prepared based on a careful study of the job, these questions are more pertinent than are those that many interviewers would generate on their own. In some cases, after the questions are determined, potential answers are also devised and given scores. In these instances the questions are often forced-choice, where the answer is yes or no, or a number, such as number of years or salary expectations. The interviewer then simply reads the questions in sequence, records the answer on the interview protocol, and assigns scores according to a key.

The *semistructured employment interview* involves advance preparation of major or key questions to be asked. This method provides a common frame of reference for all people who are interviewed for a job and requires that they all answer a predetermined set of specific questions. However, the interviewer is also given the prerogative to ask additional follow-up questions to probe specific answers that the interviewee provides, and so forth. For example, a popular strategy used in some firms today, especially high-tech firms, is to ask challenging and unusual questions designed to assess creativity and insight. For example, Microsoft interviewers sometimes ask applicants "Why are manhole covers round?" This question has four different, relatively correct answers, each of which allows the interviewer to probe more in different areas.[22]

Finally, the *unstructured employment* interview involves relatively little advance preparation. The interviewer may have a general idea about what she or he wants to learn about the job applicant but has few or no advance questions that are formally constructed and ready to be asked. Thus, the interview is likely to be more spontaneous, to be more wide ranging in its focus, and to cover a wide variety of topics.

In addition to these basic types of interviews, another has been gaining popularity. A *situational interview* asks the applicant questions about a specific situation to see how the applicant would react. For example, an interviewer might ask the applicant something like:

> Think back to a situation where a personal conflict between a supervisor and a subordinate was interfering with the work of both parties. How did you deal with this conflict? Was the problem resolved?

In other cases, rather than ask about something that has already happened, the interviewer might ask the applicant to imagine a situation that has not yet occurred. In such cases, the interviewer might ask something like:

Suppose you had a subordinate who you knew had the abilities to perform his or her job but who simply chose not to exert any effort on the job. How would you approach this problem? What kinds of approaches might you try?

Research results indicate that these types of interviews are more likely to be predictive of future job performance than are more traditional interviews.[23] They also change the focus of the interview more explicitly from a KSA approach to a job-fit approach.

In general, interviewers prefer unstructured interviews because they view their role in the structured interview as simply a recorder of information. Thus, they believe they lose a lot of the richness and value that is presumably associated with interviews. But this reaction is based in part on interviewers' beliefs that they can make good employment decisions on their own and so don't require the structure. In fact, however, evidence suggests that structured interviews are much better predictors of subsequent job performance (i.e., they are more valid) than are unstructured interviews, and situational interviews are even better at predicting future job performance.[24] These predictive relationships, or validities, tend to be a bit lower than those for tests, but only interviews are effective at assessing KSAs such as interpersonal skills. Also, interviews of all types are generally effective at allowing organizations to decide who fits best in the organization. Therefore, interviews will continue to be a popular and useful means for making selection decisions. It is important to note, however, that the Supreme Court, in *Watson* v. *Forth Worth Bank,* ruled that interviews used for making selection decisions had the same requirements concerning demonstrating job relatedness as did any other selection technique.[25] As we already noted, establishing the fact that interviews are job related is a bit more difficult than with some other selection techniques. A major reason is that interview decisions are prone to a certain number of decision errors.

Interview errors   Relying on interviews for making selection decisions is accompanied by several problems that are more or less unique to the interview. For example, one type of error is the *first impression error*.[26] Interviewers who make this mistake are those who tend to make a decision early in the interview process. For example, the candidate being interviewed might arrive a minute or two late or might have a few awkward moments at the beginning of the interview. This situation, in turn, may cause the interviewer to make a negative decision about that individual, even though later evidence in the interview may have been more positive.

The *contrast error* occurs when the interviewer is unduly influenced by other people who have been interviewed. For example, suppose an interviewer meets with one candidate who is extremely good or extremely bad. The next person interviewed may suffer or benefit by the contrast with this person. That is, if the previous candidate was extremely good and the second candidate is only slightly above average, the interviewer may be prone to provide a lower evaluation for the second person than would have otherwise been the case. Similarly, if the previous candidate is poor and unacceptable to the interviewer, the next candidate, who again may be about average, may appear to be even better in the eyes of the interviewer and receive a more positive evaluation than is warranted.

A *similarity error* occurs when the interviewer is unduly influenced because the interviewee is similar to the interviewer in one or more important ways. For example, consider the case of a person who was graduated from a particular college or is from a certain town and who interviews someone who was graduated from the same college or who is from the same hometown. As a result of the perception of similarity, the interviewer may be more favorably disposed toward the candidate than the candidate's credentials warrant.

Another type of error that interviewers can make is that of *nonrelevancy*. For example, the interviewer may be inappropriately influenced by an individual's posture, dress, or appearance. An interviewer may rely too heavily on the extent to which an interviewee can maintain eye contact for an extended period of time. The interviewee may be shy or bashful or simply doesn't want to seem too aggressive. By not maintaining eye contact with the interviewer, however, the individual may create a false impression that she or he isn't assertive enough to do the job.

A final type of error that is common in interview situations has to do with the interviewer's knowledge of the job. Some organizations do not pay adequate attention to selecting appropriate interviewers. They may select employees to interview candidates for a particular job even though the interviewers know little or nothing about that job. Thus, the interviewer may base her or his assessment of the individual's abilities to perform the job on incomplete or inaccurate assessments of the nature of that job.

These problems exist, to a greater or lesser extent, in all interviews. Their effects can be minimized, however, with proper training of interviewers. Experience itself is not a good substitute for training, and this training should focus on the occurrence of the problems outlined above, making the interviewer aware of what he or she says and does. In addition, the training should provide interviewers with the means to replace behaviors that lead to errors with behaviors more likely to lead to their deciding on the best person for the job.

References and Recommendations

Another popular and widely used selection technique is the use of references and recommendations. The job applicant is usually asked to provide either letters of recommendation or the names and addresses of individuals who may be contacted to write such letters. Presumably, the organization can use this information as a basis for knowing about a person's past experiences and work history.

References and recommendations are often of little real value. If a job applicant selects the people to write recommendations, the individual is likely to pick people who she or he knows will write positive letters of recommendation. For example, a student is more likely to ask a professor who gave him an A for a recommendation than a professor who gave him a D. Likewise, a former boss who gave the individual high performance evaluations is a more likely reference than is a former boss who gave the individual average or below-average recommendations. Thus, the organization must be somewhat skeptical about a set of glowing recommendation letters that a job applicant submits for consideration.

A related problem is a growing concern about legal liability in the preparation of recommendation letters. Job applicants have sued someone who wrote a negative letter of recommendation that was, in turn, the basis for the individual subsequently not being offered employment. Organizations themselves have sued people who wrote favorable recommendations for job candidates who were then found to be highly unsuitable. As a result of these legal concerns, many individuals have begun to take the position that they will provide only objective information about a job candidate as part of a reference letter. Thus, they might be willing to verify dates of employment, salary, history, job title, and so forth, but they may be unwilling to provide any assessment regarding the person's performance, capabilities, or the likelihood for success in a new setting.[27]

Physical Examinations

Another popular selection technique is a physical examination. Few organizations require all applicants to submit to a physical examination; instead, they may ask only those finalists who are most likely to receive an offer of employment to take a physical examination. A primary reason for requiring a physical exam is to ascertain the extent to which the person may have the appropriate levels of stamina and physical conditioning for performing hazardous or strenuous jobs. As we discussed in Chapter 3, the Americans with Disabilities Act prohibits discrimination against prospective employees on the basis of physical abilities. As a result, many organizations have stopped using physical exams prior to an offer of employment; instead, they may require a physical or medical exam only after a job offer has been made.

A related type of physical examination that some organizations rely on is drug testing. Drug testing is an increasingly common selection technique. Like other types of physical examinations, drug tests are most commonly given to people to whom the organization is prepared to offer employment. Of course, as with all selection techniques, reliance on a drug test as a condition of employment requires that the organization be absolutely sure the administered test is valid and reliable (see below for details). That is, the organization must be prepared to demonstrate that the test is conducted under rigorous conditions and that the results are true and verifiable. Finally, as noted in Chapter 3, the organization must be sensitive to perceptions that these tests constitute an invasion of privacy.

Organizations continue to seek new and better predictors of future job performance to integrate into their selection systems. HR in the 21st Century discusses one interesting approach. Other techniques that some organizations have tried include credit history (as an indicator of overall stability), interviews with the applicant's customers, and psychological assessments by trained therapists. The owner of a tax-consulting firm in Florida even inspects an applicant's car because he believes that a dirty and messy car is indicative of a disorganized person who lacks the ability to do technical accounting work.[28] Regardless of the implicit connection (or lack thereof) of the predictor, however, it is important that human resource managers be able to demonstrate how any given predictor actually forecasts future job performance.

Assessment Centers

While companies may use any or all of the methods discussed above when selecting managers, special selection methods may also be appropriate. One fairly common special method for selecting managers is the assessment center.[29] An **assessment center** is not a physical location but is instead an approach to selecting managers based on measuring and evaluating their ability to perform critical

■ An **assessment center** is an approach to selecting managers based on measuring and evaluating their ability to perform critical work behaviors.

HR in the 21st Century

The Fine Print: Hiring Through Handwriting Analysis

 Some employers are taking their search for letter-perfect employees literally: they're analyzing job candidates' handwriting for personality clues. Despite skepticism, this unconventional approach is slowly gaining acceptance.

"It's almost uncanny," says Jack Parker, a certified public accountant in Dallas who asks hires to submit to the analysis. "At first, I thought it was a nice thing to do at a party. But it's so accurate."

It's also called graphology or document examination, a controversial practice long popular in parts of Europe. Employers in the United States, however, often have dismissed it as unscientific.

But not all agree. A spokesperson for high-tech firm Cognex says that all hires are asked to submit handwriting. "We give them the handwriting analysis so we have more pieces of the picture," says Kathy Bedrosian at the Natick, Massachusetts–based firm. "People have generally been open to it, and occasionally they're even enthusiastic because it's something different."

Job seekers may be asked to write on a blank page. Their prose is faxed or sent to handwriting experts, who prepare a personality profile. Some give consultations based on their findings.

> *"By the time we're done, we know everything about them except their underwear size."*
>
> (Mark Hopper, president of Handwriting Research, a Phoenix, Arizona–based firm)

Many handwriting experts have their own analysis styles and charge from $75 to $250 per person. Some say that those who cross their *t*'s low may have low self-esteem. A line of writing that slants upward suggests optimism. Large letters hint at extraversion.

"By the time we're done, we know everything about them except their underwear size," says Mark Hopper, president of Handwriting Research, a Phoenix, Arizona–based firm. "We do everything from *Fortune* 100 companies to health spas."

Not everyone is sold. Some say that the practice is akin to using tarot cards to make hires. Others say that firms using it may be vulnerable to legal challenges. "It's just not fair," says Lewis Maltby at the American Civil Liberties Union. "People are entitled to be judged by the quality of their work." But supporters argue that's what critics once said about drug and personality tests, which are now widely used.

Source: "The Fine Print: Hiring Through Handwriting Analysis" from *USA Today*, July 21, 1998, p. B1. Copyright © 1998 *USA Today*. Reprinted with permission.

work behaviors. Individuals participating in an assessment center are likely to be either current managers who are being considered for promotion to higher levels or a pool of external recruits such as upcoming college graduates whom the firm is considering hiring for management positions.

The individuals to be assessed are brought together in a single place such as the company's training headquarters or perhaps a conference facility at a hotel. While there, they undergo a series of tests, exercises, and feedback sessions. A normal assessment-center schedule lasts two to three days and involves about ten to fifteen individuals at any one time. During the assessment-center schedule, these individuals may undergo experiential exercises; group decision-making tasks; case analyses; individual employment tests, such as personality inventories and so forth; role-playing exercises; and other methods for assessing their potential skills and abilities.

A panel of current line managers from the organization likely attends the assessment center in the role of evaluators. These individuals oversee the conduct of the assessment center and provide evaluations about the suitability of each attendee for various management positions within the organization. At the conclusion of the assessment center, each of these evaluators provides an in-depth evaluation of each person attending the assessment center. These evaluations are then screened by other managers who are responsible for making the actual selection decisions. Among the items considered during an assessment center are the individual's abilities for performing a particular kind of work, the extent to which the evaluators believe the individual will be successful in the organization, the extent to which the individual will be a candidate for further promotion in the firm, how the individual functions in groups, and the kinds of training and development that may be necessary to help the individual develop more fully.

AT&T is among the companies that makes widespread use of assessment centers. Indeed, AT&T was one of the first companies in the United States to use the assessment-center concept, and since 1956 over 200,000 of its employees have attended various assessment centers. AT&T's evaluation of its assessment centers suggests that this method for selecting managers is a fairly effective technique for differentiating between those who are more and those who are less likely to be successful in the organization.

Assessment centers do have some disadvantages, however. Among the most significant is cost. For example, it takes a considerable amount of time to bring the panel of candidates together. The organization typically must pay for their transportation, lodging, meals, and other expenses, and in addition it must provide the same expense coverage for the line managers who are conducting the evaluations. Those managers themselves are away from their workstations, and thus lost productivity must also be considered.[30]

As noted earlier, in the eyes of the courts [and also the Equal Employment Opportunity Commission (EEOC)] (as discussed in Chapter 3), any technique used to make an employment decision is considered a test. If the use of any such test results in disparate impact, the organization must prove that it is not using the test to discriminate by demonstrating that the test is job related (we will discuss this topic in the next section). Therefore, from a legal perspective, these different selection techniques are interchangeable. From a practical perspective, however, an organization must decide which KSAs it wishes to measure and then determine which selection technique is best suited to measure each one. Therefore, in practice, organizations will typically use several of the techniques discussed here in some combination.

SELECTION TECHNIQUE RELIABILITY AND VALIDITY

Regardless of which technique or techniques an organization chooses to use for its selection decisions, it must ensure that those techniques are reliable and valid. Without such evidence, the organization is exposing itself to the possibility of discrimination. As noted above (and in Chapter 3), the organization must prove it is not discriminating when evidence of disparate impact exists. Managers can make their case by demonstrating that the selection technique is job related. In practice, they must prove that the selection technique is a valid predictor of performance on the job. As we shall discuss below, however, even without laws concerning discrimination, an organization is wasting its resources if it uses an invalid selection technique. We begin with reliability because a test that is not reliable can never be valid. (Refer also to Appendix 2, Data and Research in Human Resource Management.)

Reliability

■ **Reliability** refers to the consistency of a particular selection device.

Reliability refers to the consistency of a particular selection device. Specifically, it means that the selection device measures whatever it is supposed to measure, without random error. Systematic error may be present, though, so reliability is not the same as accuracy. For example, suppose you get on your bathroom scale in the morning, and the scale shows that you weigh 137 pounds, but in reality you weigh 135 pounds. The next day, suppose you still weigh 135 pounds, but now the scale shows that you weigh 134 pounds. Finally, on the third day, you still weigh 135 pounds, but now the scale actually shows that you weigh 135 pounds. In this case, you have an unreliable scale. It is unreliable not because the scale is usually not accurate, but because the amount and direction of error are random—on the first day the error is +2 pounds, on the second day it is –1 pound, and on the third day the error is zero. If the scale indicated your weight was 2 pounds more than it actually was every single day, your scale would still be inaccurate, but now it would be reliable—it is always off by 2 pounds in the same direction. In fact, you could always learn your true weight by simply subtracting 2 pounds from the weight indicated on your scale.

All measures that organizations use in selection have error, and all measures are less than perfectly reliable. In our bathroom scale example, notice that the actual weight is the biggest contributor to the weight indicated on the scale, with only a small amount due to the measurement error. We can imagine cases, though, where the error component is much larger—so large in fact that it wouldn't make any sense to use the scale to weigh yourself. In a selection context, this large error might mean that, although person A scores higher on an arithmetic test than person B, the differences are due solely to random error rather than to the fact that person A is actually better at arithmetic. Managers responsible for selecting new employees should always learn what part of a given score on a selection technique is due to error and what part is due to the underlying phenomenon they are trying to measure. Reliability, then, can be viewed as that part of a score that is not due to random error.

Reliability can be assessed in different ways. One common method of assessing the reliability of a selection technique is called *test-retest reliability*. In this case, the same individual or individuals are subjected to the selection technique at two points in time. If a high positive correlation exists between their scores or evaluation between the two time points, then reliability can be inferred. That is, test results seem to be consistent over time and thus are reliable. Any random error component would change over time, resulting in inconsistencies, so the degree of consistency is an indication of how much of the score is due to what is being measured rather than error. Another method of establishing reliability, particularly for employment tests, is called *alternate-form reliability*. In this case, the organization develops multiple forms of the same instrument and these multiple forms are administered to samples of individuals. To the extent that the alternative forms of the instrument yield the same score, reliability can be inferred again using the same logic as above. In this case, however, reliability is demonstrated across alternate forms and not over time.

Validity

Validity refers to the extent to which a measure or indicator is in fact a real reflection of what it is assumed to be. For example, an organization would be ill advised to use a keyboarding test as a measure of a person's potential ability as a truck driver. The ability to keyboard would have no obvious predictive relationship with an individual's ability to be an effective truck driver, and thus the measure of keyboarding skill lacks validity relative to the job of driving a truck.

The first condition for a measure to be valid is that it be reliable, as described above. If a test is measuring pure error, it cannot be measuring what it is supposed to measure. Beyond this condition, various kinds of validity are relevant to the selection process. One type of validity is content validity. *Content validity* is the extent to which a selection technique such as a test or interview measures the skills, knowledge, and abilities necessary to perform the job. A keyboarding test would, in fact, be a content valid test for the job of secretary. This test replicates conditions for a secretarial job and provides a true reflection of a person's capabilities for performing that job.

Content validity is relatively easy to demonstrate for operating jobs because the performance measures for those jobs are generally objective and verifiable. Hence, bricklaying, manufacturing work, and construction work are all jobs that can be predicted using work sample tests and other measures that have content validity vis-à-vis that particular job. When a student complains that an exam in class is not fair because there were questions on the test not covered in the book or in class, the student is really complaining about the content validity of the exam. In these cases, content validity is usually assessed by expert judgment. That is, experts indicate that the items on the test are reasonable samples of what was covered in class or what is needed on the job.

A second kind of validity is called construct validity. *Construct validity* is the extent to which a relationship exists between scores on the measure and the underlying trait the measure is supposed to tap. For example, if an organization wanted to measure the conscientiousness of applicants but was not happy with existing measures, it might develop its own measure of this personality trait. The question would be whether the measure that was developed really assessed conscientiousness—this issue is fundamental in construct validity.

How would an organization demonstrate that it was really measuring conscientiousness? The organization can use several methods, all of which would provide evidence of construct validity. (Construct validity is never really proven; instead, inferences can be drawn based on information suggestive of construct validity.) One method would be to administer the new measure along with an established and recognized measure to a group of employees. High correlations between the two measures would constitute evidence of construct validity. The organization might also believe that people who are high in conscientiousness would be more likely to stay late at work and would be less likely to leave jobs unfinished. If they found that individuals scoring higher on the new measure did in fact also tend to stay later and did not leave jobs unfinished, this finding would provide additional evidence of construct validity. Basically, then, human resource managers provide evidence for construct validity by thinking about characteristics that should and should not be related to a measure *if it were tapping what was wanted*. The more these relationships are borne out, the more confident managers can be that they are really measuring what they intend to measure.

■ **Validity** refers to the extent to which a measure or indicator is in fact a real reflection of what it is assumed to measure.

A third kind of validity that is relevant to selection decisions is criterion-related validity. Although construct validity may be the most difficult type of validity to establish, criterion-related validity is most critical to the selection process. *Criterion-related validity* is the extent to which a particular selection technique can accurately predict one or more elements of performance. Criterion-related validity is most typically demonstrated by establishing a correlation between a test or measured performance in a simulated work environment with measures of actual on-the-job performance. In this approach, the test or performance measure represents a predictor value variable, and the actual performance score itself is the criterion. If this correlation is meaningful (i.e., statistically significant), a relationship exists between test scores and performance, and the test is job related.

It is important to note that even if establishing criterion-related validity were not important in civil rights cases, it would still be critical for organizations that wanted to be sure of the relationship between scores on their selection devices and performance on the job. If this relationship were not present, it would mean that persons selected using the selection device did *not* perform any better on the job than persons who would not have been selected. That is, the selection device was not helping to select better performers. Another way of stating this is to say that if organizations selected individuals merely on the basis of chance (e.g., the flip of a coin), they would produce a workforce that was as effective as that selected using the test. Because it costs time and money to administer any selection device, the company would be throwing away money on a selection system that produced no benefits in terms of performance.

Single Versus Multiple Predictor Approaches

No selection technique is perfectly reliable and valid. Hence, most organizations choose to rely on several selection techniques and, in fact, may use all or most of

In many organizations there are several steps a candidate must go through in order to be hired. For example, it is typical for a candidate to submit references, take a paper and pencil test, and have at least one interview. The idea is that each step in the process allows the employer to identify different strengths and weaknesses. By using multiple predictors of success, the organization is more likely to form a complete picture of the candidate. Here, an applicant for a job at an ad agency presents her portfolio to an interviewer. She submitted her portfolio in advance so that the ad agency could review it before deciding to interview her. After the successful interview, the employer asked for references from past employers before deciding to hire the woman.

the selection techniques discussed above. Hence, a person who applies for a job may be subjected to a preliminary screening interview to make sure that she meets the minimum qualifications necessary for the job. Then she may have to complete an application and be subjected to background checks, followed by employment tests and/or work simulations. For example, almost all of the 100 best companies to work for in America (as determined by *Fortune* magazine), ranging from Southwest Airlines to The Container Store, rely heavily on multiple predictors when making hiring decisions.[31]

Assuming that an individual performs well on these various selection techniques, she may then be subjected to more in-depth interviews, followed by reference and recommendation checks. Finally, physical examinations might be used for those applicants who are about to be offered employment. For candidates seeking management positions, assessment centers and personal contacts may be used in addition to these other approaches. By using multiple approaches, the organization is presumably able to counterbalance the measurement error in one selection technique against another. For example, if a particular candidate for the job scores well on all selection techniques except one, the organization may either choose to ignore the results of that one selection technique or try to learn more about why the individual didn't perform better. Thus, the basic reasoning behind multiple predictor approaches is to enhance the validity and reliability of the overall selection process by taking advantage of a wider variety of information.

THE SELECTION DECISION

After subjecting the pool of qualified applicants to the organization's selection process, it will then be necessary to make the actual selection decision. In some cases, the selection decision may be relatively simple. If the organization is seeking to hire only one individual for a particular position, then the top-ranked candidate from the pool of applicants is the person who is likely to be hired. On the other hand, if the selection process involves hiring dozens or perhaps hundreds of employees for similar kinds of positions, the selection decision may simply consist of choosing where to draw the line between those who qualify for employment and those who do not.

But the person ranked highest in the pool might not always be the person who scored highest on a particular selection device (or even on a combination of such devices). As noted earlier, an organization might select a person who has "acceptable" levels of the requisite KSAs but who is a better "fit" with the culture and style of the organization. It is also common for organizations to cluster applicants who may differ somewhat in terms of KSAs but who don't differ enough from each other to be critical. Thus, the organization could use any decision rules they wished to select among the people in such a cluster without sacrificing performance on the job. This procedure, known as **banding**, allows an organization to select an applicant, for example, from some underrepresented group in the organization while still ensuring high performance standards. A variation on this approach can also be used to ensure that candidates selected because they fit can also perform the jobs in question.

■ **Banding** involves creating clusters of job applicants who do not differ substantially from one another, thus allowing an organization to select an applicant from an underrepresented group in the organization while still ensuring high performance standards.

■ The **screening process** involves a series of decisions,
each resulting in some candidates being eliminated and
others being kept for continued
consideration.

In some cases, the selection decision is a multistep process. That is, decisions are made at various steps to eliminate certain candidates from consideration, while others continue to be considered. We usually refer to this method as a **screening process.** It involves a series of decisions, each resulting in some candidates being eliminated and others being kept for continued consideration. In this case, it is typical early in the process to use less expensive selection techniques, which are easier to administer to a large number of applicants. An example would be the use of application blanks, discussed earlier in the chapter. As the process continues, more sophisticated and more expensive selection techniques would be used because fewer applicants would remain, and it should be more difficult to differentiate among the remaining applicants.

LEGAL ISSUES IN SELECTION

In Chapter 3 we discussed the Civil Rights Act and the various pieces of legislation dealing with discrimination in the workplace. Although this legislation covers the full range of employment decisions, you may have noticed in that discussion that most of the cases involved discrimination in selection. There is little doubt that an organization faces the greatest legal liability in this area, and therefore, it has received a great deal of attention. We also noted in Chapter 3 that an organization faced with a prima facie case of discrimination must prove that the basis for the selection decision was job related. The organization must demonstrate that persons scoring higher on the selection instrument are those who are most likely to perform best on the job.

Establishing this relationship is essentially what the validation process is about. In fact, the courts have made it clear in a series of key decisions that validating a selection instrument is the way to establish job relatedness.[32] Since the *Griggs* decision, the courts have become less lenient about how validation studies should be conducted and thus found acceptable.[33] Therefore, it is critical that the human resource manager understand the process of validating a selection instrument and the importance of carrying out this process in all cases, rather than just those cases with evidence of disparate impact.

Helping the organization defend itself in discrimination cases is one of the most important areas where a human resource manager can make a contribution to the firm. It is just as critical, however, for the human resource manager to help the organization avoid legal problems in the first place. Table 7.1 illustrates some critical questions that the human resource manager should ask concerning any selection system when trying to select the best employees and still work within the law.

EVALUATING SELECTION ACTIVITIES

Clearly a great deal is involved in the process of establishing and maintaining a selection system. Once such a system is set up, however, it is just as important to evaluate its effectiveness. Several techniques are available to help in this evaluation.

To begin with, recall Figure 7.2, which illustrated the two types of selection errors. If you also referred to Appendix 2 at that point in the chapter discussion,

TABLE 7.1   Critical Questions to Ask About a Selection System

1. Was a job analysis conducted to determine the functions of the job and the requisite KSAs?

2. Once job requirements were established, were selection techniques (or predictors) chosen that adequately assess the degree to which applicants possess these abilities?

3. Are other equally useful selection techniques available that have been found to have less disparate impact?

4. Are good performance measures, also based on careful job analysis, available?

5. Are there data relating scores on the predictors to performance on the job (or some other valued outcome)?

6. Are there data relating scores on the entire selection system to performance on the job?

7. Were these validity studies (used to determine the relationships between scores and performance) conducted using accepted and well-established practices?

8. Is there any evidence that any of these relationships differ as a function of the age, race, or gender of the people involved?

The answer to all of these questions should be yes except for question 3, which should be answered no. If the questions don't elicit these answers, then the potential for incurring legal problems exists. Question 8 has no "right" answer. If the relationships obtained DO vary as a function of any of these characteristics, there will be a need to examine exactly how this affects the decisions that will be made. If the answer is no, the situation will be much simpler. The human resource manager must be able to help the organization change the system and thus avoid legal problems.

it might have occurred to you that the number of selection errors is minimized (and the number of hits maximized) when the relationship between scores on a predictor and performance on the job is at its strongest. That is, the greater the validity of a predictor, the fewer the selection errors we make. Another way of looking at this situation would be to imagine that half the selection decisions were errors. More specifically, imagine that half the people selected turned out to be unsuccessful and half the people rejected would have been successful. This outcome is exactly what we would expect if we selected applicants purely on the basis of chance (the flip of a coin, for example). If the relationship between the predictor and job performance grew stronger, the number of errors would decrease. But saying that the predictor was valid (i.e., we were doing better than chance) doesn't tell us how much better than chance we are doing or what that situation is worth to the organization.

Utility analysis is an attempt to determine the extent to which a selection system provides real benefit to the organization. This method assesses the practical payoff for any selection system. Although the use of any valid predictor should increase the hit rate to better than what would happen if selections were left to chance, other factors must be considered in assessing utility. First, the organization must consider the cost. A firm might be able to increase its hit rate by 10 percent by using a selection system that costs $100,000 per applicant to implement.

■ **Utility analysis** is an attempt to determine the extent to which a selection system provides real benefit to the organization.

But is this selection system worth it? The simple answer appears to be no, but it's actually more complicated. What if the job in question were an airline pilot? What would it be worth it to you, as a consumer, to be 10 percent more comfortable that the person flying your plane was really capable of doing so? Therefore, an organization needs to consider *both* the cost of the selection system and the cost of a selection error.

The firm also needs to determine a definition of success and then estimate what percentage of applicants would be successful under different scenarios. In fact, for many low-level jobs the probability of success for a random group of applicants is probably much higher than 50 percent. In such cases, it may be difficult to increase the hit rate significantly for the selection system, and it may be relatively inexpensive to make a selection error. Therefore, many selection systems, even though they are valid, might have little utility. More detailed information about utility analysis and some formulas available for computing utility are available in Appendix 2. You may not be interested in understanding the formula, but it is important that all human resource managers understand that they must be able to justify the expense of the systems they create by showing how the improved selection system contributes to the bottom line. Whether the system is evaluated in terms of decreased accidents and turnover or increased productivity, human resource managers must demonstrate utility.

Chapter Summary

The selection process involves three clear, distinct steps: gathering information about the members of the pool of qualified recruits, evaluating the qualifications of each applicant from among the recruiting pool, and making the actual decision about which candidate or candidates will be offered employment with the organization. The responsibilities for selection are shared by human resource managers and operating managers.

The basic selection criteria that most organizations use in deciding whom to hire are education and experience, skills and abilities, and personal characteristics. The job specification determines which criteria apply to any given situation. Firms must also decide whether to focus on fit or skills.

Organizations use various techniques for gathering information about job candidates. The most common are employment applications and background checks, employment tests, work simulations, employment interviews, references and recommendations, and physical examinations. Each of these techniques has its unique strengths and weaknesses, but each can also play an important role in selection. Candidates for management positions are likely to be subject to any or all of the selection methods, and assessment centers are also common for these positions.

Regardless of which technique or techniques an organization chooses to use in making selection decisions, it must ensure that those techniques are reliable and valid. Reliability is the consistency of a particular selection device. Validity refers to the extent to which a measure or indicator is in fact an accurate reflection of what it is assumed to measure. Most organizations choose to rely on several selection techniques and, in fact, may use all or most of the selection techniques discussed in this chapter.

After subjecting the pool of qualified applicants to the organization's selection process, it is then necessary to make a final selection decision. The job offer itself must be extended and appropriate negotiations must be undertaken. Those candidates not selected must also be informed. Another important part of the selection process is the placement of an individual in his or her first job in the organization. It is also important that the organization evaluate its selection and placement activities periodically.

- Selecting qualified employees for available jobs is one of the most important aspects of the human resource manager's job.

- There are two basic types of selection errors: (1) selecting someone who ultimately fails and (2) failing to select someone who would have been successful. Both are problematic, and tradeoffs between the two types of errors exist.

- Potential criteria for selection include education, experience, skills, abilities, personal characteristics, and fit.

- Techniques available for selection include application blanks, employment tests (including cognitive ability tests, psychomotor tests, personality tests, and integrity tests), work simulations, interviews, personal recommendations, and physical examinations. Several of these techniques are now available via computer and the Internet.

- Assessment centers are used for management positions. They are settings where each candidate is evaluated on multiple criteria by multiple judges—usually higher-level managers. Although assessment centers are effective at predicting future performance, some issues are involved and they are expensive.

- Selection is one of the most important functions carried out by the human resource department.

- No selection system is perfect, and decisions must be made about which types of errors are the most and the least costly.

- Selection systems should be based on careful job analysis information.

- The basis for selection decisions must be determined. It is especially important to decide the extent to which people should be selected on the basis of their fit with the organization.

- Many techniques are available for selecting individuals. Each has some advantages and some

Key Points for Future HR Managers

- Reliability indicates the extent to which a measure is free from random error. It is critical that all selection techniques are reliable. Reliability can be assessed by computing test-retest reliability, alternate forms of reliability, or internal consistency reliability.

- Validity is the extent to which something measures what it is supposed to measure. It is also critical that any selection technique be valid. If a measure is not reliable, it cannot be valid. Validity can be assessed through content validity, construct validity, or criterion-related validity.

- Criterion-related validity is assessed by demonstrating a relationship between scores on the selection device and scores on a criterion measure of interests such as performance on the job. Establishing the criterion-related validity of a selection device is the most common method for establishing that a selection device is job related, as required by law.

- Selecting employees is one of the most important functions of the human resource manager. The success of these activities can be evaluated by conducting a formal utility analysis, which can assess whether the costs associated with the selection process can be justified by cost savings and/or productivity gains.

Key Points for Future General Managers

drawbacks. An ideal system would combine several of these techniques into a single system. There is no one best way to select people, however, and when any technique, including an interview, is used for making a selection decision, it is treated as a test for legal purposes and must be validated.

- Using tests that are not valid (and not reliable) is irrational and can lead to serious legal problems.

- Several methods, all falling under the general category of utility analysis, can assess whether the costs of a selection system are justified by increased productivity or decreased costs.

Review and Discussion Questions

1. What are the general steps in the selection process?

2. What are the most common selection criteria that organizations use when making selection decisions?

3. What are the meanings of the terms *false positive* and *false negative?* What are the advantages and disadvantages if an organization commits too many of either?

4. What does the phrase "hiring for "fit'" mean?

5. Identify and describe several popular selection techniques.

6. What is an assessment center? How is it used?

7. What do reliability and validity mean with respect to selection techniques?

8. Can you identify various kinds of jobs where experience is more important than education? Where education is more important than experience?

9. Which selection techniques do you feel most confident using? Least confident using? Why?

10. What are the major risks involved when human resource managers rely too heavily on networks and contacts to hire a new manager?

Closing Case

Hiring High-Risk Employees Can Pay Off for Business

When most people think of new employees starting to work for an organization, they most likely imagine only the brightest, most highly motivated, and most upstanding and respectable applicants being chosen for employment. But with surprising frequency, these new employees may in fact be former drug addicts, alcohol abusers, welfare recipients, and homeless people. What could prompt a business to hire from these ranks as it expands its workforce? The reasons run the gamut from absolute necessity to social conscience. Regardless of the organization's motive, however, many managers report that with a little extra attention and caution, new employees chosen from what might be considered high-risk labor pools can actually pay big dividends.

One example is Candleworks, a small candle-making company based in Iowa City, Iowa. The firm's owners, Lynette and Mike Richards, didn't want to hire high-risk employees at first. Instead, they tried to follow the conventional wisdom of hiring only the best and the brightest. The problem, however, was that they simply couldn't find enough "qualified" workers from this pool who were interested in working long hours for relatively low wages. Unfilled jobs and high turnover eventually forced the owners to look elsewhere for employees and, in near-desperation, they took a big chance on hiring one applicant who was undergoing treatment for alcohol abuse.

As it turned out, because this employee had few other opportunities, he greatly valued his job and was very appreciative of the trust placed in him by the Richardses. He eventually became a highly committed and valuable employee. Because of this positive experience, the Richardses subsequently began to recruit and hire high-risk employees systematically and routinely, and these individuals are now the foundation of the workforce at Candleworks.

Ken Legler, owner of Houston Wire Works, a Texas-based enterprise, has also experienced a major labor shortage. Legler's solution has been to tap into a works program sponsored by the Texas Department of Corrections. Depending on the situation, convicts may be bused to and from a work site, or work may instead be shipped to and from a prison. Convicts receive training in how to perform the necessary work and are paid (usually at the minimum wage rate) for their work.

But not all employers use high-risk employees purely out of necessity. For example, Microboard Processing, Inc. (MPI), a small New England electronics firm, makes giving troubled people a second chance a basic part of its business philosophy. MPI is owned and managed by Craig Hoekenga. Hoekenga has always had a strong sense of social responsibility and believes that his best way of making a contribution to society is by offering second chances to high-risk employees.

Indeed, almost one-third of MPI's employees today might be classified as high-risk. They include former welfare recipients, people who have never held a steady job, convicted felons, and former drug addicts. Hoekenga insists that at least 10 percent of the firm's new hires each year be from one of these high-risk categories. While the firm also hires plenty of "conventional" employees—those with respectable backgrounds and solid work histories—Hoekenga considers his high-risk workers to be the backbone of the company.

For example, Ruth Tinney recently applied for employment at MPI. At the time of her application, she had not worked for several years and had spent the three previous years on welfare. Hoekenga gave her a two-week trial, and now she has a regular position as an assembly-line worker. He can also point to numerous other success stories throughout his business, and he can describe many former employees who were essentially rehabilitated while working at MPI but who then left for other jobs—for advancement opportunities, relocation to another part of the country, and so forth.

But not all of his new hires succeed, of course. He estimates that about two or three employees out of every ten he hires eventually fail. For example, one former drug addict who had worked at the firm for over a year returned to drug abuse and went back to jail. Hoekenga points out that he has to give newly hired, high-risk employees a while to learn the ropes. Many, for example, have never held a steady job and do not understand or appreciate the need for regular and prompt attendance. Consequently, they may come in late for work and/or not show up regularly.

Therefore, MPI allows them considerable latitude in absenteeism and tardiness during the first few weeks. Each instance of tardiness or absenteeism is followed by a conversation with Hoekenga or a supervisor. In these conversations, Hoekenga and his supervisors stress the need for punctual and regular work schedules and focus on the need for improvement. Their goal is to teach their high-risk employees proper work habits during the first six months of employment. After that time, the firm takes a much harder line and cuts people less and less slack. But the ones who make it feel an especially strong sense of loyalty and appreciation toward Hoekenga and his company and make enormous contributions to the firm's continuing profitability and growth.[34]

Case Questions

1. What do you see as the major advantages and disadvantages of hiring high-risk employees?

2. What differences in employment strategies exist between firms like Candleworks and MPI?

3. The examples cited in this case involve smaller businesses. How might a big corporation like IBM or Ford try to hire high-risk employees?

Building HR Management Skills

Purpose: The purpose of this exercise is to provide you with insights into the strengths and weaknesses of the employment interview as a selection technique.

Step 1: Your instructor will ask you to form groups of three members each. If there are one or two extra students, they can join another group.

Step 2: The members of each group should select a job with which they all have some basic familiarity. Examples of jobs include a counterperson at a fast-food restaurant such as McDonald's, a retail clerk at an apparel store such as The Gap or The Limited, or an attendant at a convenience store.

Step 3: With your team members, discuss the basic selection criteria that the organization is most likely to use in selecting someone to perform the job identified in step 2.

Step 4: Randomly select (by tossing coins, drawing names from a cap, etc.) one person to play the role of manager, one to play the role of job applicant, and one to be the observer. If a group has four members, there will be two observers.

Step 5: The manager should conduct a brief interview (about ten minutes long) with the job applicant. The manager should attempt to focus on assessing the applicant regarding the criteria identified in step 3. The applicant can provide hypothetical answers but should attempt to be realistic and consistent while answering questions.

Step 6: At the end of the interview, the observer(s) should first comment on his or her perceptions of the effectiveness of the interview, noting the quality of the questions asked and the appropriateness of the answers elicited. Then the manager and applicant should provide their own comments regarding how they felt about the interview.

Ethical Dilemmas in HR Management

Assume that, after working for several years, you have returned to graduate school to take some advanced courses and earn a master's degree as a way of improving both your specific job skills and your overall prospects for career advancement. While your degree program is relatively technical in nature, you did take a course in industrial psychology. One of the topics covered in this course was personality testing and measurement. As a term paper for this course, you studied and reviewed thoroughly the most popular personality tests used by companies as selection techniques.

You completed your degree and are now looking for a new position. You are especially interested in working for one particular company, and this firm is also actively considering you. As part of its selection process, the firm has requested that you complete a battery of tests, including some personality measures. Because you understand these tests so well and have a good understanding of the type of person the firm is looking for, you know that you can answer the questions in the personality measure so that you will be a near-perfect candidate for the job. On the other hand, you also know that the personality traits the company is seeking, and on which you can score highly, are not exactly descriptive of your own personality. But you also believe that you are so highly motivated that you will excel if given the right opportunity.

Questions

1. What are the ethical issues in this situation?

2. What are the basic arguments for and against "cheating" on the personality tests?

3. What do you think most job seekers would do? What would you do?

HR Internet Exercise

Assume that you are interested in seeking a new job. Identify five large companies for which you think you might like to work. If you don't want to work for a big company, simply select five major companies with which you have some basic familiarity and then role play a job seeker who might be interested in them. Next, write a brief description of how you envision seeking and gaining employment with each firm through traditional methods—writing the firm, scheduling an appointment for an interview, etc.

Next, visit the firms' websites and see how they deal with employment opportunities. (Do not actually submit application materials to any of the firms unless, of course, you are genuinely interested in working there!) Go as far as you can, however, into their application/pre-employment options and menus and learn as much as you can about their Internet-based recruiting and selection methods and techniques.

Questions

1. As a job seeker, which approach—traditional or Internet-based—made you feel more interested in each firm?

2. As a job seeker, what are the relative advantages and disadvantages of each approach?

3. From the company's perspective, what do you see as the relative advantages and disadvantages of each approach?

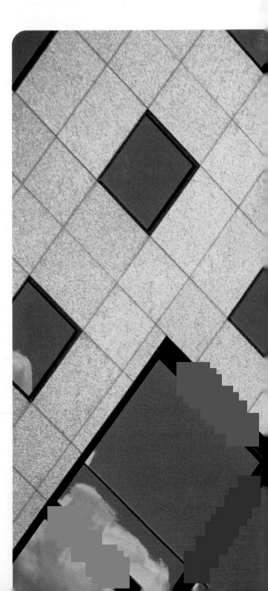

8

CHAPTER OUTLINE

CHAPTER OBJECTIVES

After studying this chapter you should be able to:

■ Understand the concept of right-sizing and describe organizational strategies for rightsizing.

■ Discuss the effectiveness of down-sizing in organizations.

■ Discuss termination options and issues.

■ Describe the issues associated with employment-at-will.

■ Identify the major reasons for voluntary turnover in organizations.

■ Understand the determinants of job satisfaction and how satisfaction relates to turnover.

■ Discuss how organizations can evaluate rightsizing strategies.

Rightsizing, Termination, and Retention

With a stalled economy, a depressed technology sector, and the continuing economic fallout resulting from the terrorist attacks on September 11, 2001, U.S. companies need all the help they can get. To lower expenses, managers are turning more often to firing employees (also called terminating, downsizing, rightsizing, or getting the pink slip).

"A lot of us are unhappy, but what are we going to do—go somewhere else?"

(A long-time Dell employee)*

A quick review of recent business headlines conveys a bleak picture for workers: "American Airlines Cuts 7,000 Jobs," "United Slashes 9,000 Jobs in Bid for Solvency," "IBM Laid Off 15,600 in Second Quarter." Indeed, almost 1.5 million workers were laid off in 2002. And these layoffs came on top of 1.96 million terminations in 2001. While layoffs slowed in 2003, few companies seemed eager to begin replacing jobs they had eliminated. Industries such as telecommunications and auto production were especially hard hit, with lower-paid workers suffering the most. Surveys also indicated that many firms planned to make additional layoffs, and few planned to increase hiring dramatically.

The job cuts, coupled with higher productivity and better use of automation, have made U.S. firms more efficient. But at what price? The remaining workers, who must learn new tasks and work harder to replace their laid-off colleagues, are prone to stress. Hamilton Beazley, a management consultant, calls such additional duties ghost work. He describes ghost work as challenging for employees, saying, "It can be totally demoralizing and can cripple the individual as well as the organization."

Not surprisingly, most workers are not pleased with having to pick up the slack for laid-off coworkers. Some workers refer to ghost work as speed up because each remaining worker has to work harder, or stretch out because they have to put in longer hours. Land Windham, a labor spokesperson, says, "*They* call it productivity," referring to management.

Given the shaky job market today, however, most workers are willing to endure the stress and discouragement of ghost work. Computer maker Dell laid off 6,000 of its 40,000 workers in 2001, allowing the firm to cut personal computer (PC) prices and increase sales and profits. A long-time employee says, "A lot of us are unhappy, but what are we going to do—go somewhere else?" The danger for employers is that, if the job market improves, many disgruntled workers may do just that.[1] ■

In Chapter 2 we discussed the human resource planning process and noted that an organization may forecast growth, stability, or reductions in its workforce needs. As described in Chapters 6 and 7, growth and stability scenarios require the organization to recruit and hire more employees for the future. But the reduction scenario essentially means that the organization will need fewer workers in the future than it does at present. In all three cases, therefore, it is essential that the organization, through the human resource management function, manage the size of its workforce effectively. This process is called rightsizing. More specifically, **rightsizing** is the process of monitoring and adjusting the composition of the organization's workforce to its optimal size.

Managing the size of the workforce, in turn, may involve layoffs or early-retirement programs to reduce the size of the workforce or it may involve retention programs to maintain the size of the workforce. In either case, it is also essential that the organization take care to retain the "right" people. That is, reduction or retention strategies must target the specific types of employees the organization would like to eliminate or keep. For the most part, organizations choose to retain highly committed, highly motivated, and productive employees and would prefer to lose less committed and less productive employees. How an organization achieves this goal while staying within the limits of the law will be the focus of this chapter.

■ **Rightsizing** is the process of monitoring and adjusting the composition of the organization's workforce to its optimal size.

RIGHTSIZING THE ORGANIZATION

Over the past two decades people in the United States have witnessed firsthand the cyclical nature of economic forces. In the 1980s numerous layoffs and workforce reductions occurred at U.S. firms, primarily as the firms adjusted to increased global competition. Both academic researchers and the popular press discussed at length the best ways to manage layoffs and the challenges of dealing with the survivors of layoffs. Then, in the 1990s, the economy began to grow at an unprecedented rate, and expert opinion began to focus more on recommendations for recruiting and retaining valuable employees. Then came September 11, 2001, and its aftermath—the economy slowed and workforce reductions began again. By the middle of 2002, the Dow Jones Industrial Average had its sharpest decline since the Great Depression, and layoffs and reductions were again the order of the day. This time, however, most organizations took a more strategic approach than they had in the 1980s.

Thus, organizations face a real challenge in managing the size of their workforces as a way to deal with their current needs and potential future economic realities. Some organizations rely on temporary workers or other contingent workers as a way of dealing with this uncertainty. We discussed some of the issues involved in managing this type of workforce in Chapter 6. These contingent workers help provide a buffer for the organization. When facing declining needs for employees, the organization can simply decide not to renew the contracts of temporary workers or end their relationship with contingent workers in other ways. But these tactics are simply buffers. When a more serious reduction in the size of the workforce is needed, more extreme measures are often necessary.

Many people have lost their jobs in many industries since the economic slowdown that began in 2001. However, in the case of Enron the reason for massive layoffs was quite different. After it became clear that the company had engaged in fraudulent accounting procedures, the company filed for bankruptcy protection, and almost the entire workforce was let go. Enron faces thousands of legal complaints from former investors and employees, and has sold almost every asset. Soon after this picture was taken the company even sold the tilting "E" pictured here in front of the Houston headquarters. Enron had been hailed as a model for the "new economy," but it is now used as a case study about greed and fraud. In the end, it is the former Enron employees who have paid the highest price for the company's wrongdoings.

Planning for Declines and Early Retirement

When it is possible to plan systematically for a gradual decrease in the workforce, it may also be possible to manage that reduction through early retirements and natural attrition. That is, in some cases organizations can conduct planning exercises that suggest the need to reduce the size of the workforce over the next few years. This reduction may be due to anticipated changes in technology or customer bases or even to anticipated changes in corporate or business strategies. The organization can attempt to manage the reduction first by simply not replacing workers who leave voluntarily and/or by providing incentives for other employees to retire early.

Clearly, in any mature organization a certain number of employees will retire every year, and the organization can reduce the size of the workforce by simply not replacing those retired employees. But what if normal retirement rates are not expected to be enough to produce the necessary reductions? In those cases, the organization can offer certain types of incentives to convince some employees to retire earlier than they had planned.

For example, in organizations that have a defined benefit retirement plan (see Chapter 13), the pension that an employee earns at retirement is a function of (among other things) the number of years that person has worked and her or his salary. An organization could simply announce that anyone who is thinking about retiring will automatically have, say, three years added to their years of service if they make a decision to retire by a certain date. As a result, an employee could feel comfortable about retiring three years earlier than he or she had planned. An organization could also increase the rate at which it matches employee contributions to 401K plans (also discussed in Chapter 13) or in some other way make it financially more attractive for employees to retire early.

Some organizations plan for early retirement in other ways. IBM, for example, provides programs for all new managers in the area of wealth accumulation. That is, the company provides experts who counsel managers on ways to build their personal wealth (i.e., increase their net worth). If there is some pressure on managers to retire early, the company can feel comfortable knowing that those managers will not be hurt by an early retirement. Traditionally IBM also offered retiring managers consulting arrangements in which the managers could be hired on a contingent basis as needed after their retirement.

It is critical to remember, however, that these plans must truly be voluntary or the organization may encounter legal problems. By definition early-retirement plans target older workers, so any attempt—real or perceived—to coerce them into leaving can be construed as age discrimination. As noted in Chapter 3, age discrimination toward older workers is illegal.

Strategies for Layoffs

Early retirement may not always be a sufficient way to reduce the size of an organization's workforce, however. In some situations the need for a reduction may arise too fast to be managed systematically through retirement of employees, or the need may be greater than originally forecasted. In these cases it is usually necessary to reduce the workforce through layoffs.

People often react badly when they are told they will no longer have jobs. Some may decide to sue, for instance. Wrongful termination suits involve employees who believe that the organization acted illegally in terminating the employment relationship. Sometimes these suits revolve around contracts but more often they revolve around potential discrimination. For example, in many cases layoffs tend to have a greater impact on older employees, which can be in violation of the Age Discrimination in Employment Act.

Aside from legal complexities, many employees who have lost their jobs develop negative feelings toward their former employer. These feelings usually manifest themselves through negative comments made to other people or refusing to conduct personal business with their former employer. For example, employees laid off by a struggling retailer such as Kmart may avoid shopping there themselves and they might encourage their families and friends to take all their business to a competitor such as Target or Wal-Mart. Sometimes, tragically, an employee who has been laid off reacts by attacking the manager and/or coworkers perceived to be responsible. Hundreds of such attacks occur each year, and several dozen result in the loss of life. Therefore it is critical that any layoffs be carried out humanely and carefully.

Much of people's reactions to layoffs are determined by perceptions of the justice involved in the layoff process. Three types of justice seem to be related to reactions to layoffs. **Distributive justice** refers to perceptions that the outcomes a person faces are fair when compared to the outcomes faced by others. This type of justice

In recent times, when organizations talk about rightsizing they are usually talking about getting smaller. In some cases it even means closing offices or plants. Here we see the headquarters of Silicon Graphics Inc., a computer firm located in Mountain View, California. The sign outside the building advertises extra space that is being offered for lease. The space is available because in 2003 the firm reduced its workforce by 1000, or 25 percent. This reduction in workforce was a direct result of the need to reduce costs in the face of declining revenues.

■ **Distributive justice** refers to perceptions that the outcomes a person faces are fair when compared to the outcomes faced by others.

is often important in determining an employee's reactions to pay decisions, for example. Most experts believe that these perceptions are based on both the actual outcomes faced (e.g., how much I am paid, whether or not I lose my job) and the perceptions of what others have contributed.[2] For example, a person may be paid less than his coworker, but if he can see that she contributes more to the company than he does and that the difference in the pay is proportional to the difference in contributions each makes, he can still view the outcome as fair. Others argue, however, that unequal outcomes alone lead to perceptions of low distributive justice and when someone loses his or her job and someone else does not, it is difficult to see how this difference in outcome can be linked to differences in contribution.[3]

Nonetheless, someone who loses his or her job may still react reasonably as long as he or she feels that the organization has not also violated another type of justice. **Procedural justice** refers to perceptions that the process used to determine the outcomes was fair. Thus, an employee who loses his or her job may be less angry if everyone in a department also lost their jobs or if layoffs were based on objective and accepted criteria. Several models of procedural justice have been proposed, and these models have yielded the dimensions of procedural justice presented in Table 8.1.

It is also clear, however, that an employee (or anyone) will judge a process to be fair when it leads to an outcome that is favorable.[4] This perspective explains why most students generally consider fair tests to be the ones they perform best on. It is also why employees who do not lose their jobs are more likely to view the basis for layoff decisions as being more just (see, however, the discussion on survivor guilt).

Finally, a third dimension of justice, **interactional justice**, refers to the quality of the interpersonal treatment people receive when a decision is implemented.[5] Thus,

■ **Procedural justice** refers to perceptions that the process used to determine the outcomes was fair.

■ **Interactional justice** refers to the quality of the interpersonal treatment people receive when a decision is implemented.

TABLE 8.1   Critical Dimensions of Procedural Justice

Voice: The perception that the person had some control over the outcome, or some voice in the decision.

Consistency: The perception that the rules were applied the same way to everyone involved.

Free from Bias: The perception that the person applying the rules had no vested interest in the outcome of the decision.

Information Accuracy: The perception that the information used to make the decision was accurate and complete.

Possibility of Correction: The perception that some mechanism exists to correct flawed or inaccurate decisions.

Ethicality: The perception that the decision rules conform to personal or prevailing standards of ethics and morality.

Representativeness: The perception that the opinions of the various groups affected by the decision have been considered in the decision.

Source: Adapted from Jason Colquitt, Donald Conlon, Michael Wesson, Christopher Porter, and K. Yee Ng, "Justice at the Millennium: A Meta-Analytic Review of 25 Years of Organizational Justice Research," *Journal of Applied Psychology*, 2001, Vol. 86, pp. 425–445.

a person losing his or her job will feel that the decision was more just if the decision is communicated to them in a considerate, respectful, and polite manner. In fact, scholars have proposed more recently that there are two separate dimensions to interactional justice. The first deals with the extent to which the person was treated with respect and dignity when he or she was told about the decision, while the second refers to the extent to which the decision maker provides information about the decision rules used and how they were applied. These two dimensions have been called interpersonal justice and informational justice, respectively.[6]

The human resource manager who has to deal with layoffs should consider these justice issues. Basically, they suggest that when layoffs are necessary, they should be implemented using a well-formulated strategy that can be communicated to and understood by the employees and that follows the rules implied by the dimensions of procedural justice in Table 8.1. Finally, the decisions should be communicated in a way that conveys respect and caring for the people involved.

Of course, the actual strategy used for determining who will be laid off must also be reasonable. As noted above, a layoff strategy that targets older workers is probably illegal and would rarely be considered as fair. Thus, if layoff decisions are to be made on the basis of seniority, it should be the *least* senior employees who are let go, even though the most senior employees are probably the highest paid and the organization could thus save the most money if they were no longer employed. Also, layoff decisions are often made on the basis of performance. That is, the organization decides to lay off its poorest performers. But how does an organization decide who are the poorest performers? Typically, this decision is based on past performance appraisals, and we will discuss the important issues associated with performance appraisals in the next chapter. But performance appraisals are far from perfect (as we shall see in the next chapter), and they are prone to various biases. When layoff decisions are based on performance ratings, those ratings take on the role of employment tests. In other words, because the organization is making a decision based on the performance ratings, the courts consider the performance ratings to be employment tests, as discussed in Chapter 3. Thus if there is evidence of disparate impact in the layoffs, the organization will need to demonstrate that the performance ratings are job related or valid. This process is not always simple, as we shall discuss below.

Finally, the layoff strategy must also include some plan for call backs if the demand for labor increases again. For example, will the first to be laid off also be the first to be called back? This option doesn't have to be followed by the organization, but it is most likely to be perceived as a fair strategy. It is also likely that the demand grows in some areas before it does in others, and so call backs could be based on organizational needs. Decisions must also be made about whether an employee continues to receive benefits when he or she is laid off and how long those benefits last. Thus, a strategy for layoffs must include rules for who is let go as well as rules for who is called back.

Legal Issues in Layoffs

When employees who lose their jobs in a layoff perceive that the decision was unjust (using the rules discussed above), they are more likely to take some type of action. As noted above, if the layoff strategy produces some form of disparate impact (i.e., members of protected classes are more likely to lose their jobs) legal actions can become problematic. Decisions to lay off more senior employees cannot be based on stereotypes about older workers and their ability to perform the job. In fact, many advocates of older workers argue that decrements in performance associated with aging actually take place at a much slower rate than most people believe. Therefore, strategies that have a greater impact on older workers are generally difficult to defend. In fact, Storage Technology was sued in late 1990 for age discrimination when employees charged that layoffs were targeted toward employees over the age of forty. The company paid $5 million in a settlement.

Strategies based on performance can also be difficult to defend. We discussed ways to establish the job relatedness of selection techniques, but it is more difficult to establish the job relatedness of a performance appraisal system. As we shall see in the next chapter, many organizations use a single appraisal instrument to rate all employees. As a result, the content of the appraisal system does not always reflect the nature of the job in question. This method makes a content validity approach difficult. A criterion-related validity approach also requires the organization to demonstrate a relationship between performance ratings and job performance. But job performance is typically measured using performance ratings, so this approach requires the organization to develop a separate measure of job performance to carry out the validation process. If the organization could develop a separate measure of job performance, however, it would probably be using that measure instead of performance ratings. Thus, it is critical for the layoff strategy to appear fair, and to minimize disparate impact to avoid legal problems.

Finally, as noted in Chapter 3, when an organization is about to undertake a large-scale layoff or site closure, it is necessary to announce this step far enough in advance to allow employees (and others) to take some action to adjust to the coming changes. The Worker Adjustment and Retraining Notification (WARN) Act requires at least sixty days' notice for a facility closure or a mass layoff (see Chapter 3 for a more precise definition of *mass layoff*). Failure to provide this notification can result in serious financial penalties, especially for a firm facing pressure to reduce costs. From the organization's perspective, however, some potential costs come with announcing planned layoffs. Once this plan is made known, many employees will seek alternative employment to avoid being out of work (which is the intention of the law). The employees most likely to find alternative employment are the best employees, however, and the firm is most likely to want to retain these employees. It is difficult to balance the requirements of the law (and of the individual employees) with the needs of the organization that desires to retain its top talent. Additional legal issues may arise in the future if the current trend toward exporting jobs to foreign countries continues to expand. This issue is discussed in HR Around the Globe.

Is Downsizing Effective?

Given the prevalence of downsizing as a response to pressures to reduce labor costs and make a firm more efficient, it would seem that a lot of support would be forthcoming for the effectiveness of downsizing as a strategy. Why else would so many firms turn to this strategy as a means of becoming more competitive? The data on the effectiveness of downsizing is rather mixed, however, and most of the data suggest that downsizing is *not* an effective strategy.

A major study of the effects of downsizing was conducted in the 1990s.[7] The authors compared several groups of companies that were tracked from 1980

Exporting Jobs?

American workers have become used to the fact that large organizations will occasionally downsize their workforce and some people will lose their jobs. But in recent years, workers in the United States have also had to deal with the fact that some of the jobs that are lost are actually being exported to other countries where workers expect and are paid much less than their American counterparts. Quite recently, however, this problem has spread to groups of workers that have not been affected by the exportation of jobs in the past.

Specifically, many Americans are aware of the fact that a person who receives an M.B.A. from a reasonable program can earn a great deal of money. In fact, a typical M.B.A. with three years experience will earn about $100,000 per year. But, of course, that is for someone who earns an M.B.A. from a school in the U.S. and who works in the U.S. In India, an M.B.A. with three years of work experience earns an average of $12,000 a year. Although this may sound like a good reason to pursue an M.B.A. in the U.S., many American workers are finding that this salary differential is turning into a serious disadvantage.

For a quite a few years, U.S.- and European-based companies have been exporting low-level manufacturing jobs to Latin America and Asia. Everything from designer polo shirts to cars are often manufactured for U.S. (or European) companies at some offshore location, and then shipped back here for sale. But now, while US companies are continuing to export low-paying, semiskilled jobs overseas, they are also beginning to export white-collar jobs overseas as well. In 2000, it was estimated that the U.S. exported white-collar jobs that generated $4 billion in payroll. In the next 15 years, it is expected that the U.S. will export 3.3 million white-collar jobs and $136 billion in wages abroad.

Large U.S. companies are in fact leading this trend, with companies such as IBM, Microsoft, and Proctor and Gamble exporting thousands of white-collar jobs to lower-wage markets. The types of jobs that are being exported cover a wide range. As already noted, for instance, manufacturing jobs have been exported for a number of years; in recent years many call center jobs have also

"In the next 15 years, it is expected that the U.S. will export 3.3 million white-collar jobs and $136 billion in wages abroad."

been exported overseas. But now, jobs such as financial analysts, architectural drafters, and accountants are being exported as well. For example, data from the Department of Labor indicate that in the year 2000, there were essentially no management jobs being sent overseas but that by 2005 there will be almost 40,000 such jobs that will have been lost to American workers. This is in addition to the over 100,000 computer jobs and almost 300,000 office jobs expected to be exported by 2005. This is outsourcing on a huge global scale, and not surprising, many people are upset about it.

Of course, workers themselves are worried. Halfway through the fiscal year of 2003 the unemployment rate in the U.S. was 6.2 percent, which fueled worker concerns about the loss of their jobs and actually led to higher unemployment rates. Even when companies are growing and can assure workers that exporting some jobs will not affect them in any way, workers worry about the future. Organized labor is also concerned about this trend, which they argue is a threat to the American middle-class workforce. As a result, unions such as the Communications Workers of America have actually called for a congressional investigation into the large-scale exporting of these jobs. It will be interesting to see how this trend and the labor movement's reactions to it might translate to gains in unionization among white-collar workers in the future.

The reason for exporting these jobs is actually quite simple. The wage differentials between workers in the U.S. and workers in countries such as India are huge. Yet Indian workers are well-educated and highly motivated and, with a little training, can speak colloquial American English quite well. The combination is one that is difficult for many firms to resist. Clearly, if they can provide quality goods and services at a lower cost, they can increase sales and profits as they increase their competitive stance relative to other firms in this country and abroad.

Although some experts claim that the real threat to American jobs is not great and that it will become more apparent as the economy improves, others see it as a real problem and have actually refused to send jobs overseas even though they can save money. It is difficult to see any reason why this trend should slow down in the future, unless there is much more pressure from legislative bodies and groups of workers (organized labor and others). Without such pressure we must assume that the problem will become more serious and we will have to see exactly what the impact is on the American workforce and American economy.

Sources: "USA's New Money-Saving Export: White-Collar Jobs," *USA Today*, August 5, 2003, pp. 1B–2B; *Hoover's Handbook of World Business 2003* (Austin, Tex.: Hoover's Business Press, 2003).

through 1994, but our discussion will focus on only three. "Stable employers" were defined as those firms where changes in employment throughout these years fell between plus and minus 5 percent. (This was the largest group in the study.) "Employment downsizers" were firms where the decline in employment was more than 5 percent during this time *and* the decline in plant and equipment was less than 5 percent during the same period. "Asset downsizers" were defined as firms where the decline in employment was less than 5 percent during this time, but the decline in plant and assets was at least 5 percent greater than the decline in employment. They examined the impact of these strategies over time on two indices of performance: return on assets (a financial index of profitability) and common stock prices. The results are plotted in Figure 8.1.

As you can see in the figure, employment downsizers had the lowest levels of return on assets over time and also did quite poorly on stock price. In both cases, the asset downsizers produced the greatest performance over the period. Most of the pressure on management to downsize the workforce comes from stockholders, who believe that this method is a good way to cut costs and increase profitability. But the results of this study suggest that firms facing increased competition or some other need to downsize should consider reducing plants and assets rather than their workforce.

A new reality for employers in the U.S. is the exporting of white-collar jobs. India has become a favored location for these jobs since Indian workers tend to be well educated, highly motivated, and willing to work for lower wages. Here, an Indian woman works at a call center for a U.S. firm. It is increasingly common for a customer in the U.S. to call a U.S.-based computer manufacturer to ask for help and speak to someone in India. Usually the customer does not even realize they are speaking to someone in another country. The trend of outsourcing jobs to other countries has contributed to the reduction of U.S. jobs and will likely slow new job growth in this country.

Other studies have also reported negative effects on stock prices and other financial indexes as a result of downsizing.[8] Given these findings, why do firms continue to downsize as a reaction to the need to cut costs? Some evidence suggests that, in the short run, the stock market reacts positively to these cuts, and so man-

FIGURE 8.1 Effects of Three Employment Strategies on Firm Performance

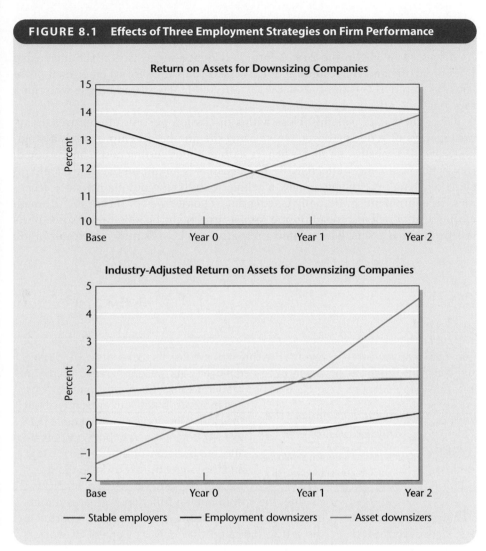

Return on Assets for Downsizing Companies

Industry-Adjusted Return on Assets for Downsizing Companies

— Stable employers — Employment downsizers — Asset downsizers

Source: Wayne Cascio, Clifford Young, and James Morris, "Financial Consequences of Employment Change Decisions in Major U.S. Corporations," from *Academy of Management Journal*, 1997, Vol. 40, pp. 1175–1189. Copyright © 1997 by Academy of Management. Reprinted by permission of Academy of Management via Copyright Clearance Center.

agers are reinforced for their decisions. But other potential costs, not only potential direct financial costs, are also associated with downsizing.

Earlier in this chapter we emphasized issues that can occur in conjunction with those employees who lose their jobs in a layoff, but issues related to those who avoid losing their jobs in the layoff also crop up. A phenomenon known as survivor syndrome can counteract many of the presumed cost savings that led to the layoffs in the first place.[9] This syndrome describes employees who feel guilty over keeping their jobs (that is, they survived) when others lost their jobs. Their morale and commitment to the organization drops dramatically. In fact, according to a study of firms implementing layoffs through the 1990s, almost 70 percent of the human resource managers surveyed reported declines in employee morale, more than 40 percent reported increased voluntary turnover, and over

10 percent reported an increase in disability claims—all within the first year of the layoff.[10] These data may underestimate the total costs of increased layoffs. As discussed in HR in the 21st Century, evidence suggests that the increasing rates of layoffs and the resulting joblessness are causing serious emotional problems for employees—both those actually affected by layoffs and those who think they *might* be affected by layoffs.

Given these data, we must close with a discussion of some alternatives to layoffs as ways of reducing costs. Downsizing the number of employees is a tangible way of demonstrating that a firm is serious about cutting costs, but as noted, it may not be the most effective. Reducing assets is an alternative. This could include reducing investments in new machinery, stretching out maintenance schedules for equipment, or actually getting out of some lines of business. Although closing plants will also result in job loss, a firm might be able to sell some of its less productive assets. Thus, some alternatives to layoffs may also result in job

HR in the 21st Century

The Hidden Costs of Layoffs

The economic downturn of the early twenty-first century has resulted in many organizations facing tough times and laying off more employees. Those employees who have lost their jobs, as well as their families, face increased financial hardships, but a growing body of evidence suggests that financial hardship is not the only cost incurred during these layoffs.

Some of the evidence is frightening. For example, in 2001, New Mexico faced the largest increase in the jobless rate from the previous year of any state. That same year New Mexico also saw the number of suicides reach an all-time high. Also in 2001, calls to employee assistance providers (EAPs) in the state were up 10 percent, and a pharmacy management firm reported that the use of antidepressants was up almost 13 percent.

The National Mental Health Association has conducted a study showing a strong link between depression and losing one's job, and the use of antidepressants has also been tied to job loss. In addition, about 15 percent of those suffering from severe depression commit suicide, and data from twenty years ago indicate that the economic downturn in the 1980s was associated with at least 900 additional deaths from suicide.

But the evidence suggests that employees actually laid off are not the only ones to suffer from the increased

"Sleep and alcohol are the only escapes for me."

(Kenneth Kott, high-tech employee laid off after seventeen years)

layoffs. The threat of job loss has taken its own toll, and seven of ten employees in a recent survey reported a great deal or a moderate amount of stress on their jobs, and most attributed it to insecurity about their jobs. Men appear to suffer more than women, but members of both genders are affected by actual or threatened job loss, and the longer the exposure to the stress, the more serious the potential problems.

Thus, the cost in human suffering is great and is expected to grow even more. Another survey reported in the article indicated that only 11 percent of workers polled responded that the economy and unemployment had no real effect on them, 55 percent responded that it increased overall stress and made them insecure about the future, 18 percent said that it made them focus on living for today, and 16 percent said that it caused them to restructure the time they spent at work. But one should not overlook the more concrete costs associated with stress related to layoff. The National Mental Health Association estimates that stress, manifested by absenteeism, lost productivity, and actual treatment expenses, costs the economy nearly $44 billion annually. It is clear that we cannot easily overestimate the cost of large-scale layoffs as a means of rightsizing organizations.

Source: Stephanie Armour, "Layoffs Deliver Storm of Emotional Troubles," *USA Today*, Oct. 29, 2002, pp. 1B–2B.

loss, but that outcome isn't a foregone conclusion. Some firms find even more productive ways to reduce costs. Some years ago, one of the authors of this textbook learned about a DuPont plant that was facing layoffs or closure because of high labor costs. The plant manager (subsequently promoted several times) asked the employees to get involved in the decision about reducing costs. The employees suggested a combination of job sharing, salary reductions (the plant was nonunion), early-retirement plans, and part-time work, which resulted in almost no employees losing their jobs. At the same time, the plant became extremely profitable and the employees developed a loyalty to the company that was the envy of the manufacturing sector.

TERMINATION

Rightsizing or downsizing refers to strategies designed to reduce the overall size of the workforce. The size of the workforce can also be reduced in other ways. Later, we shall talk about the voluntary turnover problem, where (presumably) valuable employees decide to leave the organization and seek employment elsewhere. But sometimes the organization wants to sever the employment relationship, not with a large number of employees but with specific employees. We turn our attention now to the various issues involved in terminating employees whose services are no longer desired.

Managing Involuntary Turnover

Effective human resource practices are supposed to ensure that most employees perform their job satisfactorily. Recruitment and selection practices are aimed at attracting people who can perform the jobs to which they are assigned, and training and development activities are designed to achieve the same goals. Nonetheless, sometimes an employee is simply not performing up to acceptable standards or presents enough of a disciplinary problem that he or she must be terminated.

Anytime an employee is terminated, however, it represents a failure of some part of the human resource system. It can also be costly because the firm must then seek to recruit, hire, and train a replacement. Therefore, in all the situations we will describe in this section, we should view termination as the last resort. Before terminating an employee, we must try everything reasonable to salvage the situation. These attempts begin with trying to ascertain the reasons for poor performance.

The most common reason for an employee failing to perform up to standard is that the employee simply does not know how or cannot perform at that level. It may be a problem due to a lack of ability, for example. That is, the employee should never have been hired for the job because he or she is simply not capable of performing it effectively. A simple example would be the case where someone was hired to be a reporter but he or she cannot write effectively. The original decision to hire the person was an error, and in such cases it is in everyone's best interests for the employee to leave the company or to be reassigned to another job.

In other cases, the person might have the potential to perform effectively but he or she was never properly trained. Perhaps the training program was ineffective or the employee has never been properly supervised. In these cases, a lot can be done to bring the employee's performance up to standard, such as retraining or reassignment to a supervisor who is better at developing employees.

In still other cases, the employee may be suffering from various physical or psychological problems. Perhaps the employee is suffering from too much stress on the job or outside the job. It is also possible that the employee is suffering from severe psychological problems or is abusing drugs or alcohol. Finally, it is possible that the employee is suffering from a physical ailment that is interfering with work. Obviously, in each of these cases the organization should seek to help the employee deal with the problems.

Most organizations have some type of employee assistance program (EAP) designed either to help the employee directly or to refer the employee to competent professionals who can provide that help. Originally, many EAPs focused on alcoholism, but more recently they have expanded to deal with drugs and more general problems of mental health.[11] Considerable evidence suggests that effective EAPs can help employees and reduce the costs associated with lost workdays and poor productivity.[12] These plans can also save costs by serving as gatekeepers for employee health plans because they determine what types of services are best suited for each employee.[13] But, more important, these programs make it possible for potentially valuable employees to be brought back to productive levels, thus ensuring their continued employment and yielding savings for the organization.

In still other cases, poor performance is due to motivational problems, not to personal or ability problems. For whatever reasons, the employee chooses not to perform at expected levels, even though he or she is capable of doing so. In such cases, organizations typically resort to some type of disciplinary action in an attempt to convince the employee to improve his or her performance. (In the next chapter we will discuss a more positive approach to improving employee performance.)

Progressive Discipline

Most organizations try to correct problems of poor performance (broadly defined to include tardiness, absenteeism, dishonesty, or any other problems on the job), through the use of punishment. **Punishment** simply refers to following unacceptable behavior with some type of negative consequences. **Discipline** refers to the system of rules and procedures for how and when that punishment is administered and how severe the punishment should be. Note that in all cases the goal of the disciplinary program is to convince the employee to stop the ineffective or undesired behavior and to engage in more accepted or desired behavior. As we shall discuss a bit later, some have argued that disciplinary programs may be effective at getting the employee to drop the undesired behavior, but they are generally less effective at getting the employee to adopt more desired behavior.

We refer to these programs as **progressive disciplinary plans** because, almost invariably, the severity of the punishment increases over time or across the seriousness of the problem. (We will define each of the steps in more detail below.) For example, if an employee is late for work one day, a supervisor may simply issue a verbal warning. After several more infractions, the supervisor might issue a written warning, which will be added to the employee's personnel file. Continued tardiness could result in suspension and eventually in dismissal or termination. Other types of problems, however, might incur more severe penalties from the outset. For example, it is common in manufacturing facilities to have rules

■ **Punishment** simply refers to following unacceptable behavior with some type of negative consequences.

■ **Discipline** refers to the system of rules and procedures for how and when that punishment is administered and how severe the punishment should be.

■ **Progressive disciplinary plans** are organizational disciplinary programs where the severity of the punishment increases over time or across the problem.

about sleeping on the job. The penalty for an infraction is always quite severe, but in many organizations an additional distinction is made. If an employee simply falls asleep at his or her workstation, the penalty might be two weeks' suspension without pay for the first infraction. But if the employee "makes a bed"—that is, the employee leaves the workstation and lies down to sleep somewhere else—the penalty is immediate dismissal for the first infraction.

What types of problems can be specified in a disciplinary program? Typical examples are provided in Table 8.2. Each infraction, as well as the schedule of penalties, should be spelled out clearly to employees, both in the form of an employee handbook and orally at employee orientation. Whatever the infractions, the steps in the disciplinary process are almost always the same.

The first step in most progressive disciplinary programs is verbal warning. **Verbal warnings** are cautions conveyed to the employee orally rather than in writing. The supervisor or manager should keep a written record of the fact that a verbal warning was given to document the fact that all required steps were taken in dealing with an employee. **Written warnings** are more formal and are the second step in the process. Here, the supervisor gives the warning to the employee in writing and provides a copy to the human resource department. As a result, a written warning becomes part of the employee's permanent record.

At each of these steps, the manager should discuss with the employee ways for the employee to correct the problem. In some cases this discussion might be quite simple, but in others it might include a recommendation that the employee

■ **Verbal warnings**—the first step in most progressive disciplinary programs—are cautions conveyed orally to the employee.

■ **Written warnings**—the second step in most progressive disciplinary programs—are more formal warnings. They are given to the employee in writing and become part of the employee's permanent record.

TABLE 8.2 Typical Disciplinary Problems

Problems with performance	■ Failure to complete work on time
	■ Errors in work products
	■ Work products that do not meet established tolerances
Problems with attendance	■ Repeated unexcused absences
	■ Tardiness
	■ Leaving work early
Problems with ethics or honesty	■ Taking credit for the work of others
	■ Falsifying records
	■ Soliciting and/or accepting bribes or kickbacks
Other behavior problems	■ Gambling
	■ Vandalism
	■ Use of drugs or alcohol on the job
	■ Sexual harassment
Problems that could lead to immediate termination	■ Major theft
	■ Sleeping on the job
	■ Selling narcotics on the job

■ **Suspension** refers to a temporary layoff and is usually a second step in progressive disciplinary plans.

■ **Termination** is the final step in progressive disciplinary plans in which the employee is actually fired.

■ **Employment-at-will** is the only real legal perspective on employee termination and is based on a nineteenth-century common-law rule. This view asserts that because an employee can terminate an employment relationship at any time (i.e., quit a job), the employer should have similar rights. Therefore, employment-at-will states that an employer can terminate any employee, at any time, for any reason (good or bad), or for no reason at all.

seek additional help such as referral to the EAP. **Suspension**, or a temporary layoff, is the next step in the process. The suspension could last a day or a few weeks; it is rare for a suspension to last as long as a month. In some cases, the employee is suspended with pay, but this step is usually taken when an ongoing investigation involves the employee, such as the case where the employee is charged with theft. More typically, suspension is without pay. This step is meant to impress on the employee the organization's willingness to punish the infraction involved. The final step in the process is **termination**. At this point, the organization faces potential legal problems as well as potentially violent reactions by the employee. This final step should be taken only after serious consideration and the decision that the employee is not salvageable.

Employment-at-Will

It is not always easy to terminate an employee, no matter how problematic he or she may be. Considerable publicity has surrounded the issue of employees suing organizations for wrongful termination, and so you might suspect that the formal law dealing with this issue is quite complicated. It might be surprising, therefore, to learn that the only real legal perspective on employee termination is a nineteenth-century common-law rule known as **employment-at-will**. Basically, this view asserts that, because an employee can terminate an employment relationship at any time (i.e., quit a job), the employer should have similar rights. Therefore, employment-at-will states that an employer can terminate any employee, at any time, for any reason (good or bad), or for no reason at all. This view differs dramatically from the situation in many European countries, where employees can be terminated for criminal behavior only.[14]

As noted earlier in Chapter 3, in the United States companies are relatively free to terminate employees anytime they wish; thus, in most cases the employee has no legal recourse if he or she is terminated. Several important exceptions to the employment-at-will doctrine exist. These exceptions define situations where an employee who was discharged can sue for wrongful termination and thus get his or her job back. These exceptions are important to keep in mind and are presented in Table 8.3.

The first exception is the existence of a law forbidding termination for a specific reason. For example, it would be a violation of the Civil Rights Act to terminate an employee because he or she is an African-American, and it is a violation of the Taft-Hartley Act to terminate an employee because he or she advocated joining a labor union. Most regulations dealing with the workplace also forbid termination of employees who are whistle blowers. That is, a firm cannot dismiss an employee because he or she informs the government or law enforcement agencies about a violation that has occurred in the company.

Another exception exists when someone has a contractual right to his or her job. Therefore, an organization cannot terminate someone with a valid contract (unless the organization is willing to pay off the contract). Following this logic, in some cases, courts have actually stated that some employees are protected because they have an implied contract. An implied contract might exist, for example, if a contract employee had his or her contract renewed every year for the past twelve years and was told that his or her performance was good, but he or she was still terminated. It is also possible for a discussion about an annual salary to be construed as

TABLE 8.3   Exceptions to the Doctrine of Employment-at-Will

1. **The Termination Would Violate a Specific Law:** Various laws forbid termination for a specific reason. Some of the most common reasons are termination based on gender or race (violates the Civil Rights Act) or termination because of union activity (violates the Taft-Hartley Act).

2. **The Employee Has a Contractual Right to His or Her Job:** The contract might be a formal contract or an implied contract guaranteeing or implying a guarantee of employment.

3. **The Employee's Rights of Due Process Have Been Violated:** For example, if an employee is accused of theft, the employee has the right to know of the charges and to refute those charges—in a court of law if necessary.

4. **Public-Policy Exception:** This exception has been less common but involves cases where an employee is discharged for refusing to commit a crime or for reporting a crime or unethical or unsafe behavior on the part of the organization. Thus, whistle blowers are protected under this exception.

5. **Breach-of-Good-Faith Exception:** The most difficult exception to establish because it involves a breach of promise, such as terminating an employee to avoid promised commissions or bonuses.

Note: These exceptions have been cited in various court cases, but there is no guarantee that any specific state will recognize any one of these exceptions in its jurisdiction.

an implied contract for one year. In one of the more interesting cases, an employee sued after being terminated, asserting that he had been promised he could remain with the company until retirement as long as his performance was satisfactory.[15] Since his subsequent dismissal was not for cause (e.g., poor performance), the court ruled that it was improper, and the employee was given his job back.

Another exception exists when a person's rights to due process have been violated. Most often, this situation means that the organization has failed to follow all the steps in its progressive disciplinary program before terminating the employee. This situation explains why it is so critical that managers and supervisors follow all the steps in the disciplinary process *and* document the fact that each step has been followed.

Yet another exception that has been used in some cases is the public-policy exception. Under this exception, an organization cannot terminate an employee because of failure to obey an order that could be considered illegal or because of failure to take a bribe, even though the company may lose important business. In one case, a nurse at a plant in South Carolina was terminated because she complained that the company was pressuring her to send injured workers back to work before they were ready. The court found that the company's behavior was a public-policy violation because it would be better for society if organizations did *not* try to force injured workers back to their jobs prematurely.

Finally, a breach-of-good-faith exception is the most difficult to prove because it involves a breach of promise. In one of the best-known cases, an employee claimed that he was terminated after twenty-five years of employment so that the company could avoid paying him his sales commission.[16]

These exceptions vary so much from state to state that it is easier for employers to terminate an employee in some states than it is others. In any case, the exceptions to the employment-at-will doctrine signify a substantial limit on the organization's ability to terminate employees. It is important to note that, even with these exceptions, employers can terminate employees for cause. That is, if the employee violates a rule or is a poor performer, he or she can always be terminated.

The key to successful termination of an employee is documentation. An organization can terminate any employee at any time, but if the employee claims that the termination was wrong, the employer may have to prove otherwise. If an employee is dismissed for poor performance, it may be necessary to document that most (if not all) of the employee's recent performance appraisals were poor or below standard. If in fact the employee has received generally acceptable evaluations, it will be extremely difficult to terminate the employee for poor performance. Thus, supervisors must understand that if they give overly lenient ratings to a poor employee, the employee cannot be terminated later.

If an employee is terminated because of a rule violation, a written record should be made of all the steps taken along the way. If the company has a progressive disciplinary program, it will be necessary to prove that each step was followed before the employee was terminated. If an employee is terminated because of theft, the organization must prove that an honest investigation was held and that clear evidence demonstrated the employee's guilt before he or she was terminated.

If an employer does not follow the proper steps and document each one, the employee may well get his or her job back. This situation may be annoying to the employer, but it is actually far more serious than annoyance. Progressive discipline can work only if the employee truly believes that he or she will be fired without improvement in performance. If the threat of termination is not a credible one, either because procedures were not followed correctly or because of some other reason (perhaps the employee is a civil-service employee), it is extremely difficult to correct a problem employee. The credible threat of termination is actually an important part of the process through which an organization can turn a poorly performing employee into a productive one.

Some organizations have begun to adopt an approach referred to as positive discipline, which has a somewhat different orientation.[17] This approach integrates discipline with performance management. (We will discuss this topic in the next chapter.) Positive discipline emphasizes positive changes rather than punishment. Typically, the process is still somewhat progressive in nature, with warnings leading to eventual termination if the problem is not corrected. The major difference, however, is that a great deal of counseling and problem solving are integral to the process. Therefore, the employee is given as much help as is reasonable to help him or her identify the behaviors desired by the organization and to eliminate undesirable behaviors.

As we noted at the beginning of this section, most discipline systems have the following shortcoming: they can help eliminate undesired behavior but they do not help the employee to understand what he or she should be doing instead. Thus, positive discipline seems to represent a real advantage over more traditional systems. It is not clear, however, whether or not the performance management aspect of the system needs to be an integral part of the disciplinary system or if it can work just as well on its own. In any case, aligning disciplinary practices with performance management may be an important approach to remember.

EMPLOYEE RETENTION

Our emphasis thus far has been on the issue of involuntary turnover. That is, the employee does not necessarily want to leave the organization, but the organization no longer wants to retain the employee either because of excess labor supply or because of poor performance. Managing the flow of human resources would be relatively easy if the only employees who left were the people we wanted to see leave and who left when it was most convenient for the organization. Sometimes, however, employees we would like to retain decide to leave, perhaps because of a better offer, a spouse's job, or a sick parent. In some of these cases, the human resource manager can do little. But, in most cases, employees leave voluntarily because they are unhappy with some aspect of their working environment. Therefore we turn our attention now to the problems of retaining valued employees and managing the voluntary turnover process.

■ **Job dissatisfaction** is the feeling of being unhappy with one's job. It is a major cause of voluntary turnover.

Managing Voluntary Turnover

As noted above, managers cannot always control who leaves the organization or why they leave, but they should not assume that all turnover is negative, even in the case of voluntary turnover. In fact, although the organization does not want to force someone out, management may not be totally disappointed that the person left, and a certain amount of voluntary turnover is probably healthy for the organization.[18] Yet it is important to manage this turnover as much as possible. High rates of turnover cost the organization a great deal in terms of the expense associated with employee replacement, and such turnover can hurt the organization's reputation as a good place to work. Some of the positive and negative aspects of turnover are discussed in this chapter's Point/Counterpoint feature.

To manage turnover, it is important to understand why people leave. A major cause for turnover is **job dissatisfaction**, or being unhappy with one's job.[19] We will discuss some causes for job dissatisfaction later in the chapter (we will also discuss some additional consequences of dissatisfaction later in the chapter), but for now it is enough to say that the human resource manager plays a major role in ensuring that employees remain reasonably satisfied with their jobs. It is also the role of human resources to help reduce turnover and retain valued employees. As we shall see, job dissatisfaction is often the key to turnover. Different views explain why dissatisfied workers decide to leave.

Although many industries face continued layoffs, there are settings in which it is especially important to retain valued employees. At the cosmetics firm Avon Products, CEO Andrea Jung has revitalized the company by finding new ways to increase the company's sales force. As a result the company's profits have grown more than 11 percent during 2002 and 2003, which is almost twice the historic rate of growth for the company. The secret is a multilevel employment program called "Leadership." Under this program some 25,000 Avon sales reps function as independent contractors who are paid a commission on the products they sell, and are also paid a commission on the sales made by the new reps they hire and train. Although this program has produced some spectacular results, there is also a problem. Turnover rates among the newly recruited sales reps has been quite high. Avon is now taking steps to train the recruiters to help make their recruits more successful, earn more commissions, and hopefully remain with Avon longer.

POINT | COUNTERPOINT

Employee Retention

We usually assume that an effective human resource manager works to retain employees who are performing well. We also assume that poor performers are given enticements to leave and that it is desirable to retain all other employees. But this situation is not always clear, and there are some arguments for *not* retaining employees who might be interested in leaving.

POINT ... **Organizations should seek to retain employees because ...**	COUNTERPOINT ... **Organizations should not seek to retain employees because ...**
It is expensive to replace employees.	Keeping dissatisfied employees can cost more if they "infect" other employees.
High turnover reduces general morale in the organization.	Morale could go up if troublesome employees leave.
Experienced employees are better able to contribute to the organization.	New employees can bring fresh ideas to the organization.
A shortage of qualified employees can result in decreased efficiency.	Turnover creates new opportunities for advancement for those who stay.

So... The key is to manage the turnover process because some turnover is definitely healthy for the organization. Of course, some employees are more difficult to replace than others, but a certain amount of turnover ensures that new ideas can be introduced into the organization.

Models of the Turnover Process

The basic reason why people leave their jobs is because they are unhappy with them. Thus, the simplest view of the employee turnover process would suggest that, if we increase job satisfaction, we will decrease turnover. Although this basic view is correct, the processes involved are somewhat more complex.

First, the economy and the labor market play a role. It has been noted that the prevailing unemployment rate is as big a factor in whether or not a person leaves a job as is the level of dissatisfaction.[20] Clearly, this explanation makes a great deal of sense. Even if an employee is extremely dissatisfied, he or she is not likely to quit without real prospects of finding another job.

Recognizing this fact, several turnover models emphasize the role of dissatisfaction in the decision to look for alternatives, and it is seen as a necessary (but not sufficient) first step in the decision to quit. At least two major streams of research have proposed models incorporating these ideas, and the basic concepts of these models are present in Figure 8.2.[21] As you can see in the figure, the process begins with factors leading to job dissatisfaction (which will be discussed below). Job dissatisfaction causes the employee to begin thinking about quitting, which leads to a search for alternatives. Only if those alternatives look better does the employee decide that he or she will quit, a decision first manifested by an intention to quit.

FIGURE 8.2 A Model of the Turnover Process

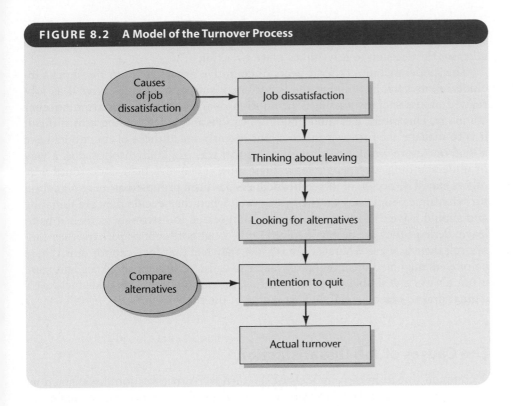

Of course, the implication of this type of model is that managers should re-duce the sources of job dissatisfaction. It is best to stop the turnover before the employee begins searching for alternatives because he or she might find an alter-native that is more attractive. Once an employee begins searching for alterna-tives, it may still be possible to retain the employee by convincing him or her that the present job really is better than the alternatives. In fact, the search for alter-natives sometimes leads to increased satisfaction on the present job after the em-ployee discovers that the alternatives were not as positive as once believed.

Other models have proposed similar mechanisms but have also suggested that job dissatisfaction must reach a critical level before anything happens and, at that point, it may be too late to do anything. In other words, this approach sug-gests that, as levels of job dissatisfaction increase, there is little change in the employee's intentions to leave. Those levels of job dissatisfaction finally reach a critical level, however, and the intention to leave becomes so strong that the em-ployee is almost guaranteed to leave.[22]

Another interesting model that deviates a bit from the basic model in Figure 8.2 revolves around the notion of "shocks" to the individual.[23] First, this model proposes that several paths can lead to turnover, and they do not all require shocks. Nonetheless, the major focus is on a shock—an event that can be either positive or negative but is so profound that it causes the employee to think about the organization, the job, and how he or she fits with both. This model begins with shock and not with job dissatisfaction. In fact, the dissatisfaction occurs only because the employee started thinking about the job in response to the shock. The decision to leave is largely based on the perception that the employee does not really fit with the company—that is, the present job in the present company is not consistent with the image the employee has of him- or herself. In some cases, the employee will leave without even considering alternatives, but in all cases the decision to leave takes place over time.

The model includes other aspects of cognitive processing, but the shocks include events such as winning the lottery or losing a loved one, as well as job-related events such as missing a promotion or receiving an offer from another company. This model has interesting implications for understanding how difficult it is to manage the turnover process, but recently the authors of the model have added one more wrinkle. Although the model was originally proposed as a way of understanding why people leave their jobs, it can also help understand why others stay. The notion of **job embeddedness** has been proposed as an explanation for why some people stay on their jobs, even when they decide they are unhappy and should leave.[24] Some employees are simply tied too strongly to their jobs to leave. Perhaps they are deeply involved in the neighborhood, or perhaps they cannot sell their houses. Whatever the reason, they feel that they cannot quit. These employees may be quite unhappy, which can cause resulting problems. This state is not always a desirable state. Nonetheless, the notion of job embeddedness adds a great deal to our potential understanding of the turnover process.

> ■ **Job embeddedness** refers to the fact that some people stay on their jobs, even when they decide they are unhappy and should leave. Other ties in the community or obligations keep the employee on the job.

The Causes of Job Dissatisfaction

A common thread in these models of the turnover process is job dissatisfaction. Wherever and however in the process the dissatisfaction occurs, reducing job dissatisfaction is likely to reduce turnover. Therefore it is important to understand the causes of job dissatisfaction. Although most of the sources of job dissatisfaction that have been studied are related to the job, some of the more creative approaches have focused on factors that have little or nothing to do with the job.

One interesting line of research has focused on the study of pairs of identical twins. Identical twins are a useful source of data because they are identical genetically, although they may well work at very different types of jobs. In one particular study, the authors found that identical twins reported quite similar levels of job satisfaction, regardless of the jobs they had. Although the authors have interpreted their results with due caution, these results raise the distinct possibility that a certain component of job satisfaction may be genetic.[25]

Others have suggested a similar but less radical approach, suggesting that some individuals are simply disposed toward being satisfied, while others are disposed toward being dissatisfied. Thus, they argue that individuals differ in their tendencies to be happy and unhappy and, although conditions on the job play a role, these tendencies are potentially as important in determining the levels of job dissatisfaction an employee will experience and report.[26] As a result, for some individuals, the organization can do little to make them happy; for other individuals, the organization can do little that will make them unhappy. More typical approaches to job dissatisfaction, however, tend to focus on job-related factors.

Nature of the work One of the most important sources of dissatisfaction on the job is the nature of the work that a person does.[27] In Chapter 5 we discussed issues of job design and job enrichment, and these approaches developed largely as a reaction to the importance of the work done as a determinant of job satisfaction. For example, a consistent relationship exists between job complexity (and job challenge) and job satisfaction such that employees with more complex and challenging jobs are more satisfied.

In addition, job satisfaction tends to be higher when the job is less physically demanding. We don't want to suggest that a boring job is preferred—quite the contrary—but a job that requires constant physical exertion and strain tends to lower levels of job satisfaction. Also, jobs that help employees achieve something of value tend to result in higher levels of job satisfaction. That is, if an employee feels that he or she is accomplishing some good on the job, satisfaction tends to be higher. In addition, if an employee values status, and a job provides him or her with more status, levels of satisfaction are also likely to be higher.[28]

Pay and benefits Perhaps not surprisingly an employee's level of satisfaction on the job is affected by the extent to which the employee is satisfied with pay and benefits. In general, higher levels of pay and more attractive benefits tend to result in greater satisfaction, and we will discuss issues of both compensation and benefits in Chapters 11 and 12, respectively. But other considerations also determine satisfaction with pay. Earlier in the chapter, we discussed issues of fairness and justice relative to decisions about laying off employees. We noted that distributive justice was concerned with the level of outcomes received, and although we discussed processes underlying distributive justice perceptions earlier, we need to elaborate a bit on those perceptions now.

An important factor in determining satisfaction with an outcome such as pay is what other people are making, and not just anyone, but other employees who are at similar levels in the organization. In fact, the models of distributive justice suggest that we compare our pay with another "comparison person." We note not only what each of us makes but also what we make relative to what we contribute. Contributions might include years on the job, education, performance, or some combination of these and other factors. We assess our own contributions relative to what we are paid. And we compare the ratio of contribution to pay to the contributions that our comparison person makes relative to his or her pay. Note that we are making all the judgments, and the judgments may be incorrect. Nonetheless, if our input/outcome ratio (the ratio of contribution to pay) is the same (or better) than the comparison person's ratio, we will be satisfied with our pay. If our ratio is not high, then we will be dissatisfied.

Supervisors and coworkers Supervisors and coworkers represent two additional potential sources of job dissatisfaction. An employee may be satisfied (or dissatisfied) with coworkers for several reasons. An important one is that the employee believes that he or she shares certain values and attitudes with coworkers. This perception that everyone has some shared vision of the world and can work together as a team is an important determinant of job satisfaction.[29] Clearly, the impression that coworkers do not share values and attitudes can lead to dissatisfaction. In addition, coworkers can be seen as sources of social support, which can also lead to increased job satisfaction

Employees can be satisfied with supervisors for many of the same reasons. That is, shared values and social support can be important determinants of satisfaction with a supervisor as well as with a coworker. In addition, an employee can be satisfied (or dissatisfied) with a supervisor's leadership ability. How a supervisor leads (i.e., his or her leadership style) and the effectiveness of the work group are important determinants of satisfaction with the supervisor.[30]

Each of these sources of job dissatisfaction can be measured and thought of independently or as part of a whole. That is, studying and considering satisfaction with pay in its own right has some value, while others consider it simply as one source of overall satisfaction with the job. We will return to this issue below when we discuss methods of measuring satisfaction. Before turning to that topic, however, we turn our attention to some of the outcomes of dissatisfaction on the job.

The Effects of Job Dissatisfaction

We began our discussion of job satisfaction by noting that it is a major determinant of voluntary turnover and thus our major reason for discussing job satisfaction, but it is worth noting that job dissatisfaction can have other negative effects. Furthermore, some of these effects are related to topics we will discuss later in the text.

For now our primary concern with job dissatisfaction is that it leads to increased voluntary turnover. As noted earlier, job dissatisfaction is a major determinant of turnover, but it is also predictive of other types of withdrawal behavior. For example, a strong relationship exists between job dissatisfaction and absenteeism.[31] Part of this relationship is due to the fact that employees who are dissatisfied may not always be able to leave their jobs (because of a lack of alternatives), and so they choose to withdraw partially, by being absent. In addition, it is possible to withdraw even more gradually (or partially) by simply being late. HR in the 21st Century presents an interesting view of the causes of absenteeism—a view that considers several issues discussed elsewhere in this chapter.

A more subtle form of withdrawal that doesn't involve being away from the job is a reduction of commitment to the organization. **Organizational commitment** is the degree to which an employee identifies with an organization and is willing to exert effort on behalf of the organization.[32] Employees lacking organizational commitment are excellent candidates for turnover when a workable alternative presents itself. They are also unlikely to exert extra effort or even to encourage others to join the organization.

Dissatisfied employees are also more likely to join unions. Several studies support this relationship and, although the process of joining a union is fairly complex, job dissatisfaction has consistently been found to be a good predictor of who joins unions.[33] We will discuss the implications of this relationship in more detail in Chapter 14.

Finally, dissatisfied employees are less likely to engage in behaviors on the job known broadly as organizational citizenship behaviors,[34] sometimes called contextual performance.[35] **Organizational citizenship behaviors (OCBs)** include those behaviors that are beneficial to the organization but are not formally required as part of an employee's job. These behaviors include activities such as volunteering to carry out extra tasks, helping and cooperating with others, following rules even when such behavior is inconvenient, and endorsing and supporting organizational goals. We will discuss contextual performance further in the next chapter, but clearly the organization benefits when employees engage in these types of behavior, and dissatisfied employees are simply less likely to do so.

In addition, considerable evidence suggests that job dissatisfaction imposes a different type of cost on an organization. Job dissatisfaction has been found to be strongly linked to stress (discussed more fully in Chapter 15), job burnout (the con-

■ **Organizational commitment** is the degree to which an employee identifies with an organization and is willing to exert effort on behalf of the organization.

■ **Organizational citizenship behaviors (OCBs)** include employee behaviors that are beneficial to the organization but are not formally required as part of an employee's job.

HR in the 21st Century

Absenteeism as an Entitlement

Earlier in the chapter, we discussed the notion of distributive justice; that is, people must believe they are getting their fair share in any relationship. As organizations become leaner through downsizing, however, they are forced to do more with fewer employees. As a result, some companies are cutting back on vacations and paid sick days. In fact, a survey conducted by the Society for Human Resource Management indicates that only 91 percent of firms offered paid vacations in 2001 versus 95 percent in 1999. In addition, they found that companies offering personal days (in addition to sick and vacation days) dropped from 57 percent to 46 percent during the same period. Finally, some evidence suggests that more companies are telling employees that if they don't use their vacation days by the end of the fiscal year, they will forfeit those days.

One result of the various trends and policies is a sharp increase in unscheduled absenteeism. In fact, the cost of unscheduled absenteeism is expected to rise 30 percent above the levels for 2000. There is reason to believe that

> *"Employers have gotten stingier about [granting] time off, so people are thinking, 'I'll take it anyway.'"*
>
> (Jennifer Gwaltney, laid-off conference planner in Virginia Beach, Virginia)

employees feel they are entitled to these extra days off because the company has not kept its end of the bargain or because of the extra stress at work. Unscheduled absences because of personal reasons rose 21 percent in 2002 alone, and 20 percent of employees in another recent poll indicated that they have tried to take more vacation days than they were entitled to.

Although these trends may simply be a different manifestation of job dissatisfaction, they seem to go beyond that simple explanation. Employees feel that they are being shortchanged by their employers and that those employers are too demanding. One of the few ways they can seek to restore equity without losing their jobs is to be absent. Should organizations clamp down even tighter or should they allow this form of equity restoration? What would be the consequences if employees did not feel they could take this time off? This issue will remain an interesting challenge for human resource managers over the next few years.

Source: Stephanie Armour, "Faced with Less Time Off, Workers Take More," *USA Today,* October 29, 2002, p. 1A.

---

dition of physical, emotional, and mental exhaustion on the job[36]), and (through the first two processes) employee health.[37] Thus, happier workers are healthier workers. Dissatisfied employees are more likely to be absent for health reasons.

The most intriguing possibility, however, is the link between job satisfaction and productivity. The notion that happy workers may be productive workers has attracted scholars for almost 100 years. Although there are cases where performance and satisfaction have common determinants, and even cases where the most productive employees are also the most satisfied, no consistent causal relationship between job satisfaction and performance has been found. Thus, higher levels of job satisfaction do not necessarily lead to higher levels of performance, and an organization should not target increases in job satisfaction in the hope of raising productivity.

Measuring and Monitoring Job Satisfaction

As should be clear by now, job satisfaction is extremely important for managing the size and the effectiveness of the workforce. As a result, organizations spend a fair amount of time and effort monitoring the levels of job satisfaction among their employees. This monitoring is done primarily through the use of attitude surveys that are distributed to employees once or more a year. The responses from these surveys are used to track changes in employees' attitudes—such as job satisfaction—so that the organization can respond to them before they become problematic.

Although many organizations design their own attitude surveys (or hire consulting firms to design them), some widely used measures of job satisfaction often show up as part of these surveys. By using standard measures of job satisfaction, an organization not only tracks changes in its employees' levels of satisfaction, it can also compare satisfaction levels with other organizations that use the same measures.

The job descriptive index (JDI) is the most commonly used measure of job satisfaction.[38] It measures satisfaction with specific aspects of the job such as pay, the work itself, and supervision; however, it does not have a single overall measure of job satisfaction (although it is easy to assess overall satisfaction using the JDI). For each aspect of the job, a series of descriptors might apply. For example, for the work itself, adjectives such as *routine* and *satisfying* are listed, among others. Employees are asked to indicate if each adjective "describes your work," "does *not* describe your work," or if the employee "can't decide." The employee indicates the level of agreement by placing a Y, N, or ? next to each item. The instrument is scored so that agreement with a positive adjective (e.g., satisfying) is given a 3, disagreement with a positive item is given a 0, and the question mark is given a 1 (indicating a moderate level of dissatisfaction).

Other instruments do include direct measures of job satisfaction, and some include questions about the levels desired versus what is experienced. One instrument, known as the faces scale, presents a series of faces that are either happy or sad, and the employee is instructed to check the face that best reflects his or her feelings about the job.[39]

Whatever the measure, most organizations are interested in changes in the levels of job satisfaction over time. Before leaving this discussion, it is important to make a final note. The primary reason for measuring job satisfaction is because dissatisfied employees tend to quit their jobs. Thus, over time, employees who are the most dissatisfied will quit the soonest. The next time the organization surveys its employees, the survey will not include those employees who have already quit. As a result, it is quite likely that the overall levels of job satisfaction will go up, even if the organization does nothing to improve job satisfaction, because only the more satisfied employees are still on the job. The others have already left, indicating a serious problem that the organization *could* overlook if managers are not paying attention.

Retention Strategies

The purpose of discussing job satisfaction is to provide some insights into how to manage voluntary turnover. At the simplest level, one could say that the way to manage turnover is to increase the levels of satisfaction among employees. But the key is in understanding exactly how to do that. First, when an organization learns of a potential problem, most likely through a survey, it is important that *something* be done. Employees are less likely to respond honestly to survey questions if they feel that no one will respond to their concerns. More specifically, two other types of interventions (both discussed previously in different contexts) have been found to increase levels of job satisfaction.

Job enrichment, discussed in Chapter 4, has been consistently linked with higher levels of job satisfaction. By making the work more challenging and meaningful, and by granting employees more autonomy and more opportunity to use their skills, the work itself becomes both motivating and satisfying (and more satisfied employees are also more productive). These employees are also more likely to find the work itself more satisfying, which in turn reduces turnover rates.

Realistic job previews (RJPs), which were discussed in Chapter 6, are also a useful intervention for increasing retention. As noted in that chapter, RJPs are pre-employment previews providing accurate and realistic information to the job applicant. They can also be used with new employees as a means of socializing them in their new job roles. RJPs are effective in reducing turnover for several reasons. First, because potential employees have more complete information about the job (including the nature of the work, supervision, pay, etc.), those who are more likely to be dissatisfied with the job characteristics are less likely to accept the jobs. Therefore, RJPs help ensure that the people on the job are those most likely to be satisfied and thus remain. In addition, when new employees are made aware of potential sources of dissatisfaction prior to encountering them, the employees can prepare themselves (psychologically or even physically) so that, when they encounter the problem, they are ready to deal with it. In fact, when employees learn that they can cope with various problems on the job by preparing, this knowledge can be a source of job *satisfaction* and thus promote retention.

In the late 1990s the battle for talented employees in high-tech industries heated up (this battle had cooled considerably by early 2002). It was fairly common for one firm to lure away the employees of a competitor by offering more money and better working conditions. To retain valued employees, many firms began trying new strategies. One strategy that became fairly popular was the use of stock options. Stock options are reasonably standard components of executive pay packages. They give the employee the right to purchase a certain number of shares of stock at a given price. That stock option price is often just slightly lower than the selling price of the stock when the option is issued. If the stock appreciates in value (like it did at Dell), these options can become very valuable. The employee exercises the option, buys the stock at an option price that is lower than the present selling price for the stock, and then can sell the stock for an immediate profit (some firms don't even require the employee to purchase the stock at that point but simply pay out the profit). This practice became quite controversial after the fall of Enron and other firms, especially because the organization does not typically carry the value of the options as a liability.

During the competitive days of the late 1990s, companies such as Dell and Microsoft added a new wrinkle to retain employees. Although the employee was issued stock options early in the employment relationship, the options were restricted so that the employee could not exercise the options for five (or so) years. If the stock was climbing (as it was for Dell and Microsoft), the employee who left before he or she had completed five years of employment would forgo potentially large profits because he or she would not be able to exercise the stock options.

■ **Realistic job previews (RJPs)** are pre-employment previews that provide accurate and realistic information to the job applicant. They can also be used with new employees as a means of socializing them in their new job roles, and they are effective in reducing turnover.

This retention plan worked quite well with successful high-tech firms during the 1990s and is essentially a sound approach to retaining valued employees. This technique is clearly less effective when the stock prices fall (as they generally did in 2001–2002). In fact, if the stock price falls below the option price, the option is said to be under water, and there is no reason to exercise the option. Thus, the incentive to remain with the company is lost.

EVALUATING THE RIGHTSIZING PROCESS

Organizations increase or decrease the size of the workforce in response to changes in markets. As discussed in Chapter 2, this process should be the result of continuous strategic planning. Therefore, if the process is effective, the organization should never be seen as doing anything out of the ordinary. That is, the organization should be projecting increases or decreases in the need for labor and addressing these projections in the most painless ways. Early-retirement plans and estate-planning programs make it easier for older employees to ease out of the company and either make room for new employees or obviate the need for cutbacks. Managing the voluntary turnover process (as well as the involuntary turnover process) is another way to reduce the size of the workforce without taking drastic measures.

When a downturn (such as the general downturn in the U.S. economy following September 11, 2001) simply cannot be anticipated, an organization must conduct layoffs in ways that are compassionate, recognizing that the affected employees are now unemployed, and perceived as fair. A critical part of the entire process, though, is the retention of valued employees. It is difficult to tell, however, how well a company is doing in retaining employees until the employees decide to leave, and then it is a bit too late. It is possible, and advisable, however, to conduct exit interviews of all employees who leave voluntarily. An exit interview is simply a formal discussion with an employee who has announced his or her decision to quit. Because the employee will no longer be working with the company, he or she will presumably be honest about the reasons for leaving. Individuals leave their jobs

Layoffs continue as firms become more efficient and rely more on outsourcing to supply basic operational needs. Recent layoffs have hit younger workers quite hard. In fact, by 2003 workers under age thirty-five experienced a higher unemployment rate than workers forty-five to fifty-four years and even those over age fifty-five. As a result, younger workers are being forced to find new positions, often at lower pay. Such is the case with Karen Levine, a Wharton M.B.A., who went from jobs at General Mills, Unilever, and Deloitte Consulting to working for $8 an hour at Pottery Barn.

for a wide variety of reasons, so it is always useful to learn why any individual decided to quit. More important, if several employees quit and most of the people leaving cite the same or similar reasons for leaving, the organization can get a good idea of the problem that needs to be fixed.

Chapter Summary

Organizations strive to maintain the right number of employees, often through strategies or tactics designed to reduce the size of the workforce (also known as downsizing). Organizations achieve these reductions through early retirement and plans to encourage early retirement, or they achieve them through layoffs. Layoffs can bring legal problems (especially concerning potential age discrimination), and the survivors of layoffs often experience guilt. Furthermore, evidence suggests that downsizing is not an effective strategy. A final way to reduce the size of the labor force is through termination—that is, some people can be fired. Although employment-at-will is the law, there are enough exceptions to this doctrine that organizations are often sued for wrongful termination.

While organizations seek to eliminate some employees, they must also strive to retain valued employees. This process involves reducing voluntary turnover and requires an understanding of the causes of voluntary turnover. The major determinant of voluntary turnover is usually job dissatisfaction, or being unhappy on one's job.

Several models of the voluntary turnover process exist, but these models usually focus on helping us to understand how job dissatisfaction results in turnover. One model, however, focuses on job embeddedness and helps understand, instead, why some dissatisfied employees choose to remain on their jobs.

In addition to relating to turnover, job satisfaction can lead to other outcomes, and it is therefore a major concern for organizations that seek to monitor levels of employee satisfaction and dissatisfaction. For example, higher levels of employee satisfaction are related to higher levels of employee commitment and a greater frequency of behaviors known as organizational citizenship behaviors (OCBs). OCBs are behaviors that are not required of an employee but are important for the functioning of the organization.

Finally, it is important that an organization evaluate its rightsizing activities relative to employee satisfaction and productivity.

Key Points for Future HR Managers

▶ Rightsizing usually involves a reduction in the workforce.

▶ A rightsizing strategy involves a combination of early retirement, natural attrition, and possibly layoffs.

▶ Layoffs are potentially the most troublesome means of reducing the workforce. They bring potential legal problems, and evidence suggests that they are not effective in the long run.

▶ Terminating employees can also bring legal problems, and the exceptions to the concept of employment-at-will can result in wrongful termination suits.

▶ Retaining valued employees is just as important for rightsizing as is workforce reduction.

▶ Several models of the voluntary turnover process exist, but if we want to reduce voluntary turnover, the best single place to focus on is job satisfaction.

▶ Increasing job satisfaction can also improve employees' organizational commitment and the occurrence of extra-role behaviors typically referred to as organizational citizenship behaviors.

Key Points for Future General Managers

▶ Rightsizing of the workforce often involves downsizing, or the reduction of the workforce.

▶ When possible, reductions should be made by relying on natural attrition and early retirement rather than on layoffs because layoffs can lead to legal problems and have been shown to be relatively ineffective at reducing costs.

▶ Although employment-at-will is the common-law rule, it is not acceptable to terminate employees without cause. The various exceptions to employment-at-will can result in serious legal problems.

▶ While trying to reduce the workforce, it is also necessary to retain valued employees. The best way to retain valued employees is to monitor and improve job satisfaction.

▶ Job satisfaction is related to absenteeism and turnover, but it is also related to organizational commitment.

▶ Job satisfaction is also related to organizational citizenship behaviors. These behaviors are not the responsibility of employees; if someone does not carry them out, however, the organization suffers.

Review and Discussion Questions

1. Explain how organizations can use early-retirement programs to facilitate rightsizing.

2. Identify and discuss examples of distributive, procedural, and interactional justice that you have experienced.

3. Summarize the basic legal issues involved in layoffs.

4. Distinguish between involuntary and voluntary turnover.

5. Discuss the process of progressive discipline and explain its importance to organizations.

6. What is employment-at-will? Comment on the positive and negative characteristics of this concept.

7. What are the basic causes of job dissatisfaction?

8. Discuss the fundamental issues of validity as they relate to measures of job satisfaction.

9. What are the basic consequences of job dissatisfaction in the workforce?

10. Describe realistic job previews and comment on their role in rightsizing.

Closing Case

Retaining the Best Employees

Discussions and articles about employee retention focus most often on relatively glamorous high-tech employees such as programmers, engineers, and scientists. But many employers face similar challenges at the other end of the spectrum. Restaurant workers, retail clerks, and clerical workers, for instance, are often in low supply. And employers face a double bind when competing for such workers—market conditions necessitate relatively low wages because most job skills are relatively easy to teach, but the large number of jobs makes worker mobility fairly easy. The hotel industry provides a good case in point.

Annual turnover in the lodging industry generally runs as high as 160 percent. Complicating the situation even further, wages are often very low, job mobility is very high, and people who do this work must possess strong interpersonal skills. Little wonder, then, that hotels are working aggressively to figure out new ways to hire and retain the very best people.

The Four Seasons chain is considered one of the best in the industry at employee retention. When the chain opened a new hotel in Scottsdale, Arizona, a few years ago, it discovered that the public bus system took forty-five minutes to transport people from nearby Phoenix, where many of its employees lived, and then dropped them 2 miles from the hotel. As a result, many Four Seasons workers were always on the alert for jobs closer to home. The firm's response? It launched its own bus service for employees without cars. The Four Seasons also aggressively promotes from within. As a result, its annual turnover rate is only about 25 percent.

Other chains are also creatively engaged in employee retention programs. Orient-Express Hotels enables any employee to train for a job in another department for three weeks at full pay, even if no jobs are open in that department. The program allows employees to learn new skills and to experience new job settings. It also enables the firm to be more flexible because it often already has employees trained in the area where new jobs are opening.

Classic Hospitality, a consortium of five boutique hotels in Washington, D.C., works hard to attract motivated and personable employees, but the firm also encourages those employees to alert their manager when they are interested in new opportunities.

This approach allows the firm to tailor new opportunities for those employees deemed to be most valuable. Of course, not every employee moves to a new job on request, but many of those employees are less effective and do not particularly create problems if they leave.

Other chains offer incentives that range from bonuses to innovative reward programs, to extra paid time off, to their very best employees. Programs such as this one, human resource managers argue, go a long way toward helping them keep their most valuable employees.[40]

Case Questions

1. How are low-wage jobs unique with respect to turnover and retention issues?

2. What role might job satisfaction and dissatisfaction play in the hotel industry?

3. When can a hotel chain not worry too much about retention?

Building HR Management Skills

Purpose: The purpose of this exercise is to help you develop a better understanding about how experts retain valuable employees.

Step 1: Working with a small group of your classmates, select a local employer to serve as a hypothetical client. An example might be a neighborhood Italian restaurant, a family-owned discount store, or an independent coffee shop.

Step 2: Assume that your group represents a consulting firm specializing in employee retention. You have been approached by the client identified in step 1. The problem is that a large national firm is planning to move in across the street. (Examples might be Olive

Garden, Target, or Starbucks for the three businesses noted earlier.)

Step 3: Your client is only somewhat concerned about business competition with the new firm because of its large and loyal customer base. However, the client is more concerned about the new business luring away its best employees. You are asked to develop a retention plan.

Step 4: Develop answers to the following questions:

1. What information will you need to help your client?

2. Where can you obtain this information?

3. What kinds of retention ideas come to mind first?

Ethical Dilemmas in HR Management

Assume that you are working as the human resource manager for a large manufacturing firm. An area supervisor terminated an employee recently for poor

performance, and this employee has threatened to take legal action. The employee maintains that she was terminated because she had attended a meeting of employees who were thinking about a union organization campaign. The supervisor claims that the union organization meeting had nothing to do with the termination and that he had documented poor performance over a period of almost six months. When you spoke to the supervisor, he showed you the documentation, and he also made it clear that he *did* know the employee had attended the union meeting. He stated that she had been a "troublemaker" all along. You have been told to resolve this situation as quickly as possible.

Questions

1. What are the ethical issues in this situation?

2. Do you believe that the termination was due to poor performance alone?

3. How important is the fact that the company lawyers have suggested this case is a sure win for the company?

HR Internet Exercise

Assume that you are the human resource manager for a large telecommunications company. Your firm plans to reduce its workforce by approximately 10,000 workers (out of a total workforce of 140,000). Use the Internet to locate details about at least three recent major downsizing programs in your industry and/or in related industries.

Questions

1. What, if anything, can you learn from the experiences of the firms that you researched?

2. Do you think it is better to model a layoff plan after other firms or to develop your own? Why?

3. In what ways is it easier and in what ways is it harder to lay off people when other firms in your industry are doing the same thing?

PART FOUR

Enhancing Motivation and Performance

CHAPTER **9**

Appraising and Managing Performance

CHAPTER **10**

Training, Development, and Organizational Learning

9

Appraising and Managing Performance

CHAPTER OBJECTIVES

After studying this chapter you should be able to:

■ Describe the purposes of performance appraisal in organizations.

■ Summarize the performance appraisal process in organizations.

■ Identify and describe the most common methods that managers use for performance appraisal.

■ Discuss the limitations of performance appraisal in organizations.

■ Describe how performance feedback should be provided by managers.

■ Identify and discuss frequently used performance appraisal follow-up measures.

■ Identify and describe the basic legal issues in performance appraisal.

What do AT&T, Allied Signal, du Pont, Honeywell, Boeing, Intel, Texaco, UPS, Xerox, and FedEx have in common? They were among the first adopters and are today comprehensive users of a new method for evaluating the performance of managers. This approach is generally called 360-degree feedback.

Until just a few years ago, an individual's performance was evaluated in most companies by the employee's direct supervisor. Adhering strictly and narrowly to this approach tended to focus on only one perspective of performance—the perspective of the supervisor—and it was conducted in an autocratic and controlling manner. But several companies, including those identified above, began to recognize the shortcomings of the standard approach and started seeking better alternatives. All eventually ended up with an approach relying on evaluation and feedback from all sides of the employee's position in the organization: above, below, beside, and sometimes even outside the organization.

Because this network of evaluators essentially "surrounds" the individual's position, it was quickly labeled 360-degree feedback. At first, most companies that adopted this new approach made it a secondary part of their formal performance appraisal systems. Indeed, the most common method was to continue to use traditional supervisory evaluations as the formal performance appraisal mechanism but to provide the 360-degree feedback to glean purely developmental information. In most cases, for example, only the individual saw this information.

More recently, however, some firms have started going beyond straightforward employee development with their 360-degree feedback programs and now include more of an evaluative component. AT&T and Boeing, for example, now make 360-degree feedback a major part of their performance appraisal systems. Other firms have experimented with different approaches to incorporating 360-degree feedback into performance appraisal. One common method used today is to rely on the 360-degree process to identify those at the extremes—the very best and the very worst performers. Employees in the middle are not differentiated. The traditional supervisory appraisal is then used to differentiate among these individuals.

But some firms go still further with the 360-degree approach. At FedEx, for example, any manager who receives a total score on his or her 360-degree evaluation below a specified cutoff in two consecutive rating cycles is relieved of supervisory responsibilities. While this approach might strike many managers as a bit extreme, it clearly illustrates the various philosophies that companies use when trying to find better ways to assess the performance of their employees and managers.[1] ■

> *"The 360-degree feedback process holds the potential to deepen employees' understanding of their own performance."*
>
> (Bruce Pfau and Ira Kay, business writers)*

Many major corporations—indeed, a veritable who's who of corporate America, including an estimated 90 percent of *Fortune* 1000 corporations—seem enamored with 360-degree feedback. This fact clearly underscores the importance of feedback in general and performance feedback in particular. This feedback serves various purposes and makes potentially significant contributions to companies and individual employees alike. Indeed, we can almost think of performance-related feedback as being like a ship's navigational system. Without such a system, the ship's captain would have no way of knowing where the ship was, where it had come from, and where it was heading. Similarly, without an effective performance management system, organizations and individual employees would have no way of knowing how well they were doing or where improvements might be needed. This chapter is about performance management systems in general and its key component, performance appraisal, in particular.

Performance appraisal is the specific and formal evaluation of an employee to determine the degree to which the employee is performing his or her job effectively. Some organizations use the term *performance appraisal* for this process, while others prefer to use different terms such as *performance evaluation, performance review, annual review, employee appraisal,* or *employee evaluation.* The outcome of this evaluation is some type of score or rating on a scale. These evaluations are typically conducted once or twice a year. **Performance management** refers to the more general set of activities carried out by the organization to change (improve) employee performance. Although performance management typically relies heavily on performance appraisals, performance management is a broader and more encompassing process and is the ultimate goal of performance appraisal activities. Performance management should occur all the time on the job.

■ **Performance appraisal** is the specific and formal evaluation of an employee conducted to determine the degree to which the employee is performing his or her job effectively.

■ **Performance management** is the general set of activities carried out by the organization to change (improve) employee performance.

WHY ORGANIZATIONS CONDUCT PERFORMANCE APPRAISALS

Most people involved in performance appraisals tend to be dissatisfied with them. This tendency is true for both the person being rated and the person doing the rating. We will discuss some of the major reasons for this dissatisfaction in this chapter. But the fact that performance appraisals are so widely used in spite of this dissatisfaction is a strong indicator that managers believe that the performance appraisals are important and that they have a meaningful role to play in organizations. In fact, managers conduct performance appraisals for several different reasons. Organizations also hope to achieve several goals with performance appraisals.[2]

The Importance of Performance Appraisal

As just noted, most managers may be unhappy with various facets of the performance appraisal process, but most would agree that they are nevertheless very important. One reason why appraisals are so important to organizations is that they provide a benchmark for assessing the extent to which recruiting and selection processes are adequate. Recall from earlier chapters that the organization endeavors to recruit and select high-quality employees who are capable of working effectively toward the accomplishment of the organization's goals. Performance appraisal helps managers assess the extent to which they are indeed recruiting and selecting the most appropriate employees. When this information is used in conjunction with performance management techniques, described later in the chapter, it can lead to real improvements in the performance of individual employees. Ultimately, organizations try to use this improvement at the level of the individual, and translate it into improvements in the performance of the entire organization.

In addition, performance appraisal also plays an important role in training, as we will see in Chapter 10. Organizations frequently find it necessary and/or beneficial to invest in their employees by providing them with additional training and development opportunities. This training and development is intended to help them improve their performance. Performance appraisal is therefore needed, first, to assess the current level of performance exhibited by employees and, second, to determine the extent to which this level of performance improves or increases as a result of the training and development. That is, if managers assume that training and development improve the performance of those employees who participate, information from performance appraisals is helpful in verifying if—and by how much—performance does indeed improve as a result of training and development.

Performance appraisal is also important because it is—or at least should be—fundamentally linked to an organization's compensation system. In theory, organizations prefer to provide greater rewards to higher-performing employees and lesser rewards to lower-performing employees. To provide this compensation on a fair and equitable basis, however, it is important that the organization can differentiate between its higher- and its lower-performing employees. Managers want to know that they are giving the appropriate rewards to employees for appropriate reasons. Performance appraisal plays a big role in this process.

Performance appraisal is also important for legal reasons. Organizations must be able to demonstrate that their promotions, transfers, terminations, and reward allocations are based on merit (or the lack thereof), as opposed to some discriminatory factor such as gender or race. Performance appraisal, therefore, is the mechanism by which the organization can provide this documentation. Managers must be able to rely on performance appraisal information to demonstrate that all of their important employment-related decisions have been based on the actual performance of those affected by the decisions. Without proper performance appraisal, an organization is subject to concerns or charges that there is at least the impression that promotions and other rewards may be based on a factor or factors other than actual performance.

Performance appraisal also plays an important role in employee motivation and development. Most people want to know how well they are doing so that they can correct their deficiencies, capitalize on their strengths, and improve their overall contributions to their jobs. Again, performance appraisal provides this information to employees. An individual who is told that he or she is doing well on three dimensions of his or her job performance but needs to improve on a fourth dimension recognizes how managers see him or her and knows where to allocate additional developmental work and effort in the future.[3]

Finally, performance appraisal provides valuable and useful information to the organization's human resource planning process. Recall from our discussion in Chapter 2 that assessing the current supply of human resources is an important element in human resource planning. The supply of human resources is most effectively conceptualized, however, from the standpoint of the quality of those human resources. For example, from the standpoint of the actual number of employees needed, an organization may have enough people on its payroll to satisfy its staffing needs. But if many of those individuals are doing a poor job, the organization may need to take a much different approach to its future recruiting and selection activities than if all employees are doing an excellent job. Likewise, knowing the distribution of qualified employees within the organizational system is an important factor for managers to know. And performance appraisal helps provide this information to managers.

Goals of Performance Appraisal

Given the importance of performance appraisal, as documented in the preceding section, the goals of performance appraisal are almost self-evident. For example, a basic goal of any appraisal system is to provide a valid and reliable measure of employee performance along all relevant dimensions. That is, the appraisal results should reflect the true picture of who is performing well and who is not, and they should indicate the areas of specific strengths and weakness for each person being rated. We should note, though, that it is extremely difficult to assess the extent to which an appraisal system accomplishes these goals. Furthermore, it is probably most important that employees have confidence in the reliability and accuracy of the appraisals. In other words, because managers cannot be absolutely sure that appraisals reflect true levels of performance, organizations should not forget the importance of the perceptions of accuracy and fairness. We assume that if appraisals were accurate and meaningful, they would be perceived as such, but the perceptions probably matter the most![4]

In addition, another goal of appraisals is to provide useful and appropriate information for the organization with regard to human resource planning, recruiting and selection, compensation, training, and the legal context. This information can help the organization avoid discrimination against employees on the basis of some irrelevant factor such as gender, age, or ethnicity. Therefore, this goal of performance appraisal specifically and most directly relates to the organization's ability to document any employment-related decisions based on supposed or presumed performance.

The ultimate goal for any organization using performance appraisals, however, is to improve performance on the job. This goal has two parts. First, the organization needs to be able to use performance appraisals for decision making. The relevant decisions might include determining who gets fired, who gets promoted, and how much money employees are paid. The second part of this goal relates to motivation. That is, the appraisal should provide employees with information about their strengths and weaknesses so that they can work to become more effective on the job. These two considerations

Improving employee performance requires more than simply completing a rating form that evaluates the employee's performance. It also requires a formal performance review in which the manager discusses with the employee the employee's strengths and weaknesses, and together they formulate goals for the future. Here, a manager ends a performance review with a smiling employee who now has a better understanding of what she needs to do during the next evaluation period.

serve the larger goal of improving performance by affecting motivation. Managers can generally assume that when employees get feedback about areas that need improvement, they will be motivated to make these improvements if they recognize that improving their performance will improve their chances for a promotion, pay increase, or some other important outcome or benefit. At the same time, employees should also gain a clear understanding of where they stand relative to the organization's expectations of them vis-à-vis their performance.

THE PERFORMANCE APPRAISAL PROCESS

Several tasks are necessary for the performance appraisal process to be successful. Some should be done by the organization, some by the rater(s) (the individual[s] who will be conducting the performance appraisal), and in many organizations by the ratee (the individual whose performance is evaluated). In addition, follow-up and discussion should accompany the process. Although some of this follow-up and discussion may be more accurately considered performance management rather than performance appraisal per se, it is still an integral part of how organizations manage the entire process. Figure 9.1 illustrates the actual performance management system of one major corporation. While some firms might make minor modifications to reflect their philosophies more closely, these general steps are almost always followed. The *performance appraisal* part of this overall process is highlighted and will be the framework for much of the discussion that follows. In later sections of this chapter, we will address and discuss the remaining parts of the process.

The Role of the Organization

The organization, primarily through the work of its human resource function, develops the general performance appraisal process for its managers and employees to use. One of the first considerations relates to how the information gained from performance appraisals is to be used. For example, will it be used for developmental feedback only? Or will decisions about merit pay and/or other outcomes be based on these ratings as well? It is obviously important that everyone understand exactly what the ratings are to be used for and exactly how they will be used. The organization also generally determines the timing of the performance appraisals. Most organizations conduct formal appraisals only once a year, although some organizations conduct appraisals twice a year or even more frequently for new employees. However frequent the appraisals, the organization and its human resource managers must decide when they will be conducted. The most common alternatives are for appraisals to be done on the anniversary date of each individual employee's hiring or for all appraisals throughout the organization to be conducted during a specified period of time each year.

Conducting appraisals on employment anniversary dates means spreading the appraisals over the entire year. Under this system, supervisors may always have some appraisals to conduct, but they are not necessarily required to complete an excessive number of appraisals at any one time. On the other hand, spreading the appraisals over the year may make it more difficult to make comparisons among

FIGURE 9.1   The Performance Management Process in a Typical Organization

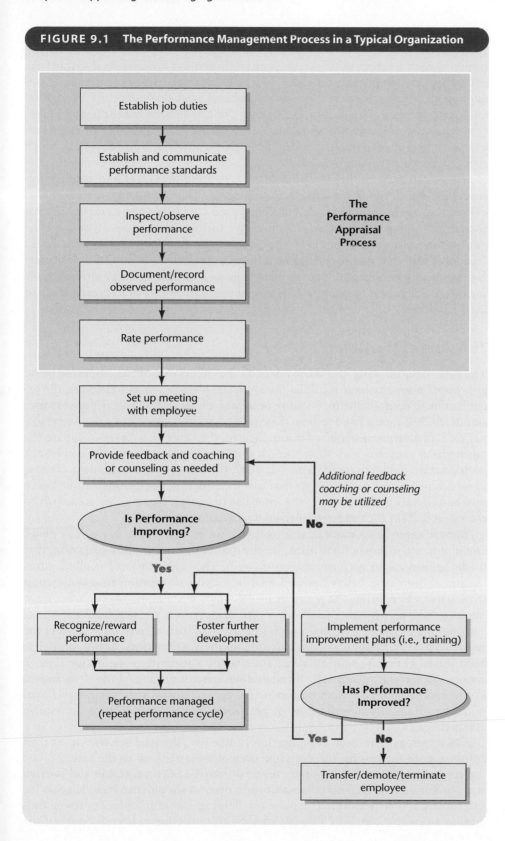

employees. Unless managers budget their salary dollars carefully over the entire year, those employees who reviewed earlier in the year may have a greater opportunity to earn a larger salary increase than those who are reviewed toward the end of the year simply because there may be fewer salary dollars remaining. Conducting all appraisals at the same time (probably near the end of the fiscal year) avoids problems of having to ration salary dollars quite as carefully and makes comparisons among employees easier. But requiring a large number of appraisals at one time may also make it more likely that a rater will not devote as much time as desired to each appraisal.

The organization is also responsible for ensuring that clear and specific performance standards are available to managers. The organization should also ensure that these standards are communicated carefully to the employees. Although this step involves those individuals performing the ratings as well, the organization must ensure that everyone rates performance using the same set of standards and that employees know what is expected of them. Otherwise, performance appraisal cannot accomplish its goals and the organization may have serious problems by creating a disgruntled workforce and/or exposing itself to legal liabilities.

The Role of the Rater

The rater (traditionally and most typically the supervisor of the employee being appraised) plays the largest role in the appraisal process. As noted above, the organization is responsible for making sure that all raters have clear performance standards, but raters have to help develop and learn those standards. As performance information is acquired about a ratee, the rater also has to compare the information acquired with these standards as a way of evaluating the employee's performance. When making these decisions, the rater must consider the context in which performance occurs so that any extenuating conditions can be taken into consideration. In addition, the rater has to communicate those standards to the ratees so that each individual will know what is expected.

But the rater has a more critical role to play as well. On a day-to-day basis, an employee behaves, or performs, on the job and exhibits many behaviors that might be relevant to performance on that job. The rater's task is to collect information about those behaviors and translate that information into the ratings themselves. Therefore, the rater truly becomes a decision maker who must observe ratee performance and process the information gleaned from the observations. Because most formal appraisals are conducted only once a year, the rater must also somehow store this information in memory, recall what has been stored at the appropriate time, and use the information to provide a set of ratings. This task is potentially difficult and time consuming.[5] Indeed, as shown in The Lighter Side of HR, managers may very well distort their appraisals based on the most recent observations of performance rather than on a long-term perspective.

Once ratings have been completed, it is also usually the rater who must then communicate the results and consequences of the appraisal to the ratee. When the results are somewhat negative, this task may be uncomfortable and is often stressful for managers. This communication process should also include goals for the future and a performance plan for helping the employee improve, thus adding a positive element. This set of activities, of course, is really part of the

The Lighter Side of HR

A major drawback of annual performance reviews is that some managers tend to be biased by recent behaviors. That is, they remember recent events more clearly and may have fuzzier memories of employee behaviors that are several months old. Consequently, when these managers do performance appraisals of their subordinates, they may rely more heavily on recent behaviors than on older ones. While few managers will be as blatant as the one shown in the cartoon here, they should recognize that milder forms of this behavior can indeed occur, and they should try their best to take a longer and more complete perspective on the appraisal process.

performance management process. Finally, the rater is ultimately responsible for preparing the employee to perform at desired levels. That is, the supervisor must be sure that the employee knows what is required on the job, has the needed skills, and is motivated to perform at the level desired.

The Role of the Ratee

Although attempts to improve appraisals often focus on the organization or the rater, the ratee also has responsibilities in the appraisal process. First, for performance appraisals to work most effectively, a ratee should have a clear and unbiased view of his or her performance. Problems can occur during the appraisal process if there is disagreement between the rater and the ratee, so it is essential that both parties have all the information they can collect about the ratee's performance. This approach may require the ratee to acquire information about the performance of coworkers and requires the ratee to gain an understanding about how his or her behavior affects performance. This approach should also allow the ratee to be more receptive to feedback from the rater (especially if it is somewhat negative), which in turn makes it more likely that the ratee will change his or her behavior in response to that feedback.

Who Performs the Performance Appraisal?

Another important aspect of performance appraisal is the determination of who conducts the appraisal and what information will be used. The most common appraisers are shown in Figure 9.2.

As noted earlier, the individual's supervisor is the most likely rater. Supervisors are perhaps the most frequently used source of information in performance

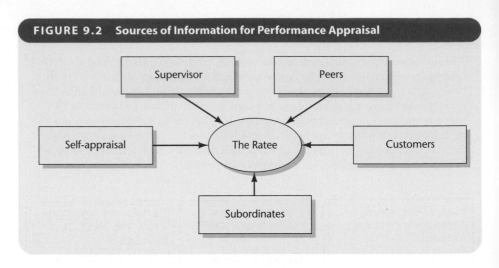

FIGURE 9.2   Sources of Information for Performance Appraisal

appraisal. The assumption underlying this approach is that supervisors usually have the most knowledge of the job requirements and they have the most opportunities to observe employees performing their jobs. In addition, the supervisor is usually responsible for the performance of his or her subordinates. Thus, the individual supervisor is both responsible for employees' high performance and accountable, perhaps, for their low performance.[6]

At the same time, it should also be recognized that supervisors are not necessarily a perfect source of information. A supervisor may not have as much in-depth job knowledge as might be expected. For example, if the job has changed dramatically over the last few years because of new technology or other factors, the supervisor might not be as familiar with the job as in the past. Likewise, a supervisor may have been promoted from another part of the organization and thus may have never performed the jobs that she or he is supervising. In addition, in some job settings the supervisor may not really have an adequate opportunity to observe the employee performing his or her work. This situation is especially true in outside sales, where sales representatives spend much of their time working alone with customers in the field, out of view of their supervisor.

But these limitations all relate to the supervisor's *ability* to provide a meaningful appraisal. In addition, we must also consider the question of the supervisor's *motivation* to provide such ratings. Motivational issues are involved regardless of who does the appraisal, but it is especially important to realize that supervisors are not always motivated to give the most accurate ratings they can. For example, there is always the possibility that the supervisor is biased (either for or against) the person being rated. Only mixed evidence of systematic bias against members of identifiable groups based on race,[7] age,[8] gender,[9] and disability exists.[10] Nonetheless, a supervisor may be negatively or positively biased toward various workers because of personal liking, attitudes, personal relationships, and so forth. As a result favoritism and/or negative bias may be possible.

Supervisors might also choose to be inaccurate in their ratings because they feel threatened by a particular subordinate and want to prevent him or her from getting ahead, or because the supervisor wants to get rid of a problem subordinate and tries to do so by getting her or him promoted into a different department. In addition, supervisors may be concerned about team member relations and decide to rate all team members the same, regardless of what they deserve, to avoid jealousy or conflict. These and other motivational factors that affect supervisory ratings are discussed in depth by Kevin R. Murphy and Jeanette N. Cleveland,[11] but the main point here is to appreciate that supervisors may choose to be inaccurate in their ratings for a wide range of reasons.

Peers, colleagues, and coworkers represent other potential sources of information for performance appraisal systems. An advantage of using peers in a performance appraisal process is that, by definition, they have expert knowledge of job content and they may also have more of an opportunity than does the supervisor to observe the performance of a given worker on a day-to-day basis. Peers also have a different perspective on the performance of their work: they really understand their own opportunities and limitations regarding performance. Merck and 3M Corporation both use peer evaluations as a major component of their performance appraisal process.

Of course, friendship, group norms, and other personal factors may intervene in this situation. And individuals may see their own performance as being significantly different than others perceive it in the group.[12] Also, in some situations, coworkers might be competing with each other for a promotion (or some other reward), which may affect their motivation to be accurate in their peer evaluations. Because peers or coworkers remain in an ongoing relationship with each other, someone who received poor ratings from his or her coworkers may try to retaliate and rate those coworkers poorly during subsequent evaluations.[13] Nevertheless, peer evaluation is particularly useful in professional organizations such as law firms, architectural firms, academic departments, and so forth. As more and more organizations begin to use work teams for production work, peer evaluations are becoming more widely used in those contexts as well.

A third source of information in the performance appraisal process is subordinates of the individual being appraised. Subordinates are an especially important source of information when the performance of their own manager is being evaluated, and this information is perhaps most useful when the performance appraisal is focused on the manager's leadership potential. That is, if top-level managers in an organization are appraising the performance of a certain middle manager on the basis of his or her leadership potential, then the subordinates of that manager are perhaps the best source of information for evaluating that person's performance. Of course, a major problem with using subordinates as input to the performance appraisal process is that this approach may influence the manager's behavior in the sense that she or he may be more focused on making workers happy and satisfied than in making them perform at a high level.[14] Nonetheless, there has been a great deal of recent interest in so-called upward appraisals and in the ways to make them more effective.[15]

Another source of information in a performance appraisal process is self-evaluation. In many professional and managerial situations, individuals may frequently be asked to evaluate their own performance. The rationale for this approach is that, more than any other person in the organization, an individual is in the best position to understand his or her strengths and weaknesses and the extent to which he or she has been performing at an appropriate level. Of course, the biggest negative aspect of using self-ratings is the tendency on the part of many people to inflate their own performance.

A final source of information in the performance appraisal system is customers. Because of the dramatic increase in the service sector of the U.S. economy in recent years, the use of customers as a source of information in performance appraisal has received much more attention. The inclusion of customers might be accomplished through techniques such as having customers fill out feedback forms or respond to mail surveys whenever they use the services of an organization. Some restaurants, like Red Lobster and Chili's, put brief feedback forms on the table when the customer receives his or her meal check. These forms ask the customer to rate the server, the cook, and so forth, on various characteristics relevant to the meal just consumed. The advantage of this method is that customers are the lifeblood of an organization and it is very helpful to managers to know the extent to which customers feel that employees are doing a good job. On the other hand, this method may be expensive and may be able to tap only certain aspects of an employee's job.

One important detail for any manager to recognize is that each source of performance appraisal information is subject to various weaknesses and shortcomings. As a result, many organizations find it appropriate and effective to rely on different information sources when conducting a performance appraisal. That is, they may gather information from not just supervisors or peers, but both. Indeed, some organizations gather information from all the sources described in this section. This approach, the basis for the chapter-opening vignette, has even gained a new term in the management literature: *360-degree feedback*.

■ **360-degree feedback** is an approach to performance appraisal that involves gathering performance information from people on all sides of the manager—above, beside, below, and so forth.

Organizations that use **360-degree feedback** gather performance information from people on all sides of the manager—above, beside, below, and so forth.[16] By focusing on 360-degree feedback, they obtain information on a person's performance from all perspectives. This approach allows them to match the strengths and weaknesses, the benefits and shortcomings, from each perspective and thus gain a more realistic, overall view of a person's true performance.[17] It is important to recognize, however, that the feedback from the different sources could be inconsistent. Otherwise, there is no value in obtaining evaluations from different sources. But this approach means that the manager has to reconcile different feedback and that the organization probably needs to use these ratings for feedback and development purposes *only*. If decisions are to be based on these evaluations, the organization would have to decide how to weight the ratings from the different sources.[18] The Point/Counterpoint feature for this chapter provides more details about the strengths and weaknesses of this approach to performance appraisal. While it is not a panacea (and in fact few studies have evaluated its effectiveness), variations on 360-degree appraisal systems are likely to continue to be popular for some time.

Regardless of who conducts the appraisals, another important issue to consider when conducting effective appraisals is that organizations typically conduct them once a year. Therefore, the rater who is evaluating a ratee's performance should consider the entire year's performance as part of the evaluation. Thus, the rater must observe and then remember the relevant performance information that occurred over that time.[19] But memories are not perfect. Raters forget what happened, especially if it happened some time ago. Rater memory is therefore a critical factor, limiting the accuracy and effectiveness of performance appraisals. If a rater cannot remember a performance incident, he or she cannot rate it. Note that, although most of the research on rater memory has focused on the supervisor as rater, this issue is important for any rater.

What can be done to address this problem? Several organizations and studies have found a rather simple solution: having raters keep performance diaries (or performance logs) can help.[20] Performance diaries or electronic records of the

POINT | COUNTERPOINT

360-Degree Feedback

A system of evaluation and feedback in which different groups of people evaluate a specific employee is called 360-degree feedback. Typically, an employee might receive ratings and feedback from peers, supervisors, subordinates, and customers or clients. Organizations differ in how they summarize and/or present these data to the employee, and they also differ on whether the ratings are used for feedback only (to be seen only by the employee for his or her personal development) or whether they are used for decision making as well. In either case the logic is that the employee can learn more about how he or she is viewed by a wider range of people, providing a more complete picture.

POINT... Evaluation systems based on 360-degree feedback are useful because ...	COUNTERPOINT... But such systems cause problems because ...
They provide ratees with information about how they are viewed by other employees.	The ratee then has to determine how to deal with all of this information.
They provide more information for development—working toward improvement or addressing weaknesses—than any other tool.	They are useful for providing a more complete picture, but the amount of information transmitted can be overwhelming.
They recognize that different groups of employees are likely to have different perspectives and thus have different views.	These differences must then be reconciled somehow. Whose view does the ratee rely on primarily if the recommendations conflict? This situation is especially problematic if the appraisals are to be used for decision making.
Ratings and feedback from different groups can be obtained in areas where each group has special insights (e.g., asking customers about the employee's dealings with customers).	Most organizations ask all raters to rate the ratee in all areas.
Ratees tend to view the appraisals as useful and helpful.	Employees probably need help and guidance (e.g., a coach) in figuring out what to do with the potentially conflicting information.
Important organizational decisions can be based on input from multiple sources.	The original proponents of the system recommended that the ratings be used for feedback only, and we have little data on how effective the data are when they are used for decision making. If evaluations conflict, whose recommendations does the organization rely on for making decisions?

So... Appraisal systems based on 360-degree feedback are potentially helpful, especially when they are used for feedback purposes only. When organizations first implement these systems, they are often meant to be used for feedback only. As time goes by and important decisions must be made, however, many organizations begin to use these appraisals for decision making as well. In any case the different perspectives are likely to result in different evaluations, and so 360-degree systems are most likely to be effective when the employee has a coach to help interpret and sort out the evaluations. We should note, however, that although these systems are becoming extremely popular, their effectiveness is still not known.

relevant performance information for a ratee are recorded at the time the behavior occurs. For example, if a supervisor observes an especially effective interaction between a salesperson and a customer, the supervisor notes the salesperson's name, the date, and the time, and then writes a brief description of the interaction. Keeping such diaries for all ratees (and writing down incidents of both good and poor performance when they occur) has at least three important advantages:

1. Raters do not have to rely on their imperfect memories to provide ratings; they can consult their diaries.

2. Raters can provide detailed feedback about the basis for the ratings they give, which should increase the perceptions of procedural fairness.

3. If an employee is discharged for poor performance and the employee subsequently sues the organization, these diaries can serve as the documentation of performance that the organization needs to defend itself in court.

What Gets Rated?

Another important decision to make regarding the design of appraisal systems is what should be rated. The choice of appraisal instruments (discussed below) is related to this issue because some systems are clearly designed to measure some aspects of performance rather than others. But the decision of what to rate should be based more on the needs of the organization than on the choice of rating instrument. Although the decision about what to rate can probably include many factors, three choices are most commonly encountered. All are related to task performance, which will be distinguished from contextual performance later.

It is most common for organizations to rate traits in conducting appraisals. Traits are abstract properties of individuals that generally cannot be observed directly but can be inferred from behavior. For example, many organizations rate employees on their attitude and their initiative. We may or may not agree on what these terms mean, but we can never truly observe something like a person's attitude. Instead, we infer it from his or her behavior. Thus, a rater might believe that an employee who is always smiling has a good attitude, but that may or may not be the reason for the employee's smiling. Rating traits allows an organization to use the same appraisal instrument for all or most employees, and this approach is based on the assumption that similar traits underlie effective performance for all jobs. It should be noted, however, that an analysis of court cases involving performance appraisals suggests that trait-based appraisals are the most difficult to defend because the courts tend to see them as more subjective than other systems.[21] Also, feedback concerning rating traits is often less instructive and helpful than other types of feedback.

In some cases, organizations base their appraisals on behaviors. These appraisals tend to be based on job analysis, and they tend to be tailored for specific jobs. For example, a ratee may be evaluated on how well he or she follows up on sales leads. These appraisals are still subjective, but they require the rater to evaluate behaviors that he or she can physically observe and therefore they seem more objective. Reliance on behaviors can also lead to an emphasis on processes underlying effective performance. In the example above, one might assume that following up sales leads is part of the process of being an effective salesperson. Providing feedback about behaviors and processes can be instructive and useful because it can help employees to understand how to improve their performance.

The final commonly encountered option is to rate performance based on outcomes. For example, rather than evaluating whether the salesperson has a good attitude or whether the salesperson follows up on leads, an organization could simply tally actual sales. Focusing on outcomes has the advantage of emphasizing the most objective measures of performance available. Also, when these systems are used, they are usually tied to specific goals, which have added benefit (discussed below). Feedback can be relatively straightforward and easy to interpret (i.e., you did or you didn't meet your sales goal), although feedback is even more useful if it includes information on how to improve future performance. Goals can be stated in terms of absolute amounts or in terms of improvement (e.g., increase sales by 10 percent over last year). It is important to set the right goals (goals that help the organization to achieve its objectives), and it is important to monitor the means by which employees meet their goals (i.e., to make sure they act ethically and legally). Appraisal systems built around outcome measures are a reasonable alternative for organizations to consider.

Who Should Be Rated?

A final issue to consider is exactly who should be rated in the appraisal process. Specifically, this issue is connected with the use of work teams. With work teams, the organization must decide whether to evaluate individual performance or team performance, and this issue can become quite complicated.

If individuals are rated and rewarded based on their individual performance, they have less reason to cooperate with other team members to accomplish the team's goals. In some cases, this situation might be desirable. For example, although the Ryder Cup in golf is considered to be a team competition, the team's performance is simply the sum of the scores of individual team members. Therefore, having team members seek to maximize their own performance helps the team as well. In other team settings that are structured in a similar manner, the team leader or fellow team members can provide ratings as well.

But in other team settings, it is critical that team members work together toward a common goal. In these cases, it is critical that performance be measured and rewarded only at the team level. One person's performance should not be considered except as part of the whole. Some employees are uncomfortable with this kind of system and believe that they should be recognized for their individual efforts. Also, in such settings, it is possible for one employee to relax and let the other team members carry the workload. This free-rider problem is a real challenge to work teams. Nonetheless, if the team functions as a team rather than as a set of individuals, it is essential that the team's performance is appraised and rewarded.[22]

METHODS FOR APPRAISING PERFORMANCE

Different performance appraisal methods and techniques are used in organizations. By their very nature, most appraisals are subjective. That is, we must rely on a rater's judgment of an employee's performance. As a result performance appraisals are also prone to problems of bias (some of which were discussed above) and rating errors (which will be discussed later in this chapter). Raters tend to be uncomfortable passing judgment on employees, and employees generally don't care to be judged in this way. The question then becomes: Why do we rely on these subjective evaluations? Why not rely instead on objective performance information and rate employees on outcome achievement alone?

Several reasons explain why subjective evaluations are far more common than objective performance measures. The biggest reason, however, is relatively simple: for most jobs, and for all managerial jobs, straightforward objective measures of performance do not exist. Even in cases where easy outcome measures might be available, there are often complications. For example, it would seem a relatively simple matter to measure the performance of the manager of a bookstore by calculating total sales or sales per square foot. But a bookstore in an upscale shopping village is more likely to sell a lot of higher-priced hardcover books than is a bookstore in a rural or economically depressed area. If the manager of either store had played a role in choosing the location, this approach might be relevant. But for large chains such as Barnes and Noble or B. Dalton, the corporation chooses the store location. As a result, a major determinant of sales volume is really outside the control of the manager, and so sales figures alone do not provide a good source of information about the manager's performance. A careful evaluation will almost always result in the acknowledgment that many so-called objective measures of performance are based on factors outside the control of the person being evaluated, and so they are not really effective measures of individual performance.

Of course, objective data that do reflect conditions under the control of the individual employee are sometimes available. These data could be sales figures for outside sales employees. In other cases, a rater could measure outcomes such as reductions in complaints. These examples are best suited for outcome-based appraisal methods. In many other cases, however, organizations have no choice but to rely on judgments and ratings. Therefore a great deal of effort has been spent in trying to make these subjective evaluations as meaningful and as useful as possible. Some of the methods that have been proposed are based on relative rankings, while others rely more on absolute ratings.

Ranking Methods

One method of performance appraisal is the **simple ranking method**, which involves having the manager simply rank-order, from top to bottom or from best to worst, each member of a particular work group or department. The individual ranked first is presumed to be the top performer, the individual ranked second is presumed to be the second-best performer, and so on. Ranking is generally global or based on overall performance.

An advantage of the ranking method is that it is relatively simple. It also provides specific performance-rated information for employees. That is, an individual who is ranked second out of five knows exactly where she or he stands relative to the other four members in her or his work group. On the other hand, the ranking method also suffers from some difficulties. One is that it is difficult to use with a large number of employees. Another shortcoming of the ranking method is that the basis for the ranking is often subjective and difficult to define. That is, because it is an overall and general measure of global performance, it does not generally make any allowances for specific attributes or characteristics of

■ The **simple ranking method** involves having the manager rank-order, from top to bottom or from best to worst, each member of a particular work group or department.

performance. As a result, ranking methods are acceptable for making decisions, but they do not provide useful feedback to employees.

A variation on the ranking method is the **paired comparison method** of performance appraisal, which involves comparing each individual employee with every other individual employee, one at a time. The individual in each pair that is presumed to be the higher performer is given a 1 for that particular paired comparison, and the other employee is given a 0. When all possible comparisons have been made, the manager adds the number of points that have been allotted to each individual. The individual with the most points is deemed to be the top performer in the group, the individual with the second highest number of points is the second-best performer, and so on. One advantage of this method is that it allows the manager to compare people in a simple and straightforward manner, that is, one person against another. On the other hand, with a large number of people being evaluated, the number of comparisons that are necessary increases rapidly.

Another type of performance appraisal technique is the forced distribution, a method that has been in practice for many years.[23] The **forced distribution method** involves grouping employees into predefined frequencies of performance ratings. Those frequencies are determined by the organization in advanced and are imposed on the rater. For example, a decision might be made that 10 percent of the employees in a work group can be grouped as outstanding, 20 percent as very good, 40 percent as average, 20 percent as below average, and the remaining 10 percent as poor. The manager then classifies each employee into one of these five performance classifications based on the percentage allowable. For example, if the manager has twenty employees, then two of those employees can be put in the top and bottom categories, four employees can be put in the second from the top and second from the bottom categories, and the rest will fit into the middle category. The forced distribution method is familiar to many students because professors who grade on a so-called bell or normal curve are using this method.

An advantage of this system is that it results in a normal distribution of performance ratings, which many people see as inherently fair. Also, from the organization's perspective, if employees are to receive merit pay increases, a forced distribution ensures control over how much money is spent on merit pay. On the other hand, the distribution that is being imposed may have no relationship to the true distribution of performance in the work group. For example, many more employees than 10 percent may deserve to be rated as outstanding, and so the forced distribution may result in perceptions of unfairness and may even result in employees losing motivation. It might also be that *all* the employees are performing at acceptable levels, but the forced distribution methods, as well as the other ranking methods, force the rater to make distinctions that might not really be meaningful. The HR Legal Brief feature for this chapter discusses another potential pitfall regarding the forced distribution approach (called the ABC employee evaluation system in the feature). As a result, most organizations rely instead on some type of absolute judgments and employ a system of performance ratings rather than rankings.

Rating Methods

One of the most popular and widely used performance appraisal methods is the graphic rating scale. A **graphic rating scale** simply consists of a statement or question about some aspect of an individual's job performance. Following that

■ The **paired comparison method** of performance appraisal involves comparing each individual employee with every other individual employee, one at a time.

■ The **forced distribution method** involves grouping employees into predefined frequencies of performance ratings.

■ A **graphic rating scale** consists of a statement or question about some aspect of an individual's job performance.

HR **Legal Brief**

Goodyear Stops Labeling 10 Percent of Its Workers as the "Worst"

 A few years ago Goodyear adopted what was then an increasingly popular approach to performance appraisal that relies heavily on the forced distribution method. But the firm then announced that it would abandon the system which had asked managers to identify the 2,800 employees who make up the worst-performing 10 percent of the company's salaried workforce. What forced the about-face? The tire maker became the target of an age discrimination lawsuit that claimed that it singled out too many older employees as bad workers.

Goodyear became the latest company to put the brakes on so-called ABC employee evaluation systems, which had gained favor with large companies eager to weed out underperforming workers. In March 2002, Ford Motor Company quit handing out C's to its bottom 10 percent and paid $10.6 million to settle an age discrimination suit filed by the same law firm taking on Goodyear.

As is typical of ABC systems, Goodyear gave A's to the top 10 percent of workers, B's to the middle 80 percent, and C's to the bottom 10 percent. Spokesperson Keith Price says that the system was not discriminatory and that the suit filed by Michigan law firm Pitt Dowty McGehee & Mirer had no influence over Goodyear's decision.

As in the Ford case, the Goodyear case gained momentum when the American Association for Retired Persons (AARP), an advocacy group for older Americans (you must be at least 50 years old to be a member) committed itself to provide legal resources to those suing the tire company. The lawsuit named eight plaintiffs

> *"It's pretty blatant that they're trying to get rid of older employees."*
>
> (John Van Hoose, fifty-nine, Goodyear employee who recently got a C)*

aged fifty-five to fifty-nine, whose annual salaries ranged from $48,700 to $71,700. The lawsuit claimed that hundreds of workers in more than ten states could join if the case was granted class-action status.

Jim Skykora, fifty-five, the youngest and best-paid plaintiff, said in an interview that he designed tires for General Motor's vehicles and has had all eleven of his projects approved in the past four years. He was graded a B– a year ago, then was downgraded to a C and told that he was at risk of being fired.

The plaintiffs' lawyers plan to go ahead with their lawsuit to find out if a disproportionate number of older workers have been fired or denied raises and bonuses during the eighteen months that Goodyear's system was in place. Goodyear's Price says that even if the company was inadvertently discriminating, the human resources department would have seen statistics showing that too many older workers were being singled out. That is not the case, Price says.

Plaintiff lawyer Megan Bonanni says that the discovery process will show if that's true. Judging by the C workers who have come forward, it is a "sea of white hair," she says.

While some companies are retreating from ABC appraisal systems, General Electric (GE) remains an outspoken advocate and has no plans to abandon it. Spokesperson Gary Sheffer says GE has never been sued over it.

Source: "Goodyear to Stop Labeling 10% of its Workers as Worst" from *USA Today,* September 11, 2002. Copyright © 2002 *USA Today.* Reprinted with permission. *Quote from John Russell, "Goodyear Backs Down," *Beacon Journal,* September 12, 2002, p. A15.

statement or question is a series of answers; the rater must select the one that fits best. For example, one common set of responses to a graphic rating scale is *strongly agree, agree, neither agree nor disagree, disagree,* and *strongly disagree.* These descriptors or possible responses are usually arrayed along a bar, line, or similar visual representation, and this representation is marked with numbers or letters that correspond to each of the descriptors.

Figure 9.3 illustrates a graphic rating scale. One of the appealing features about graphic rating scales is that they are relatively easy to develop. A manager simply needs to brainstorm or otherwise develop a list of statements or questions that are presumably related to indicators of performance relevant to the organization. A

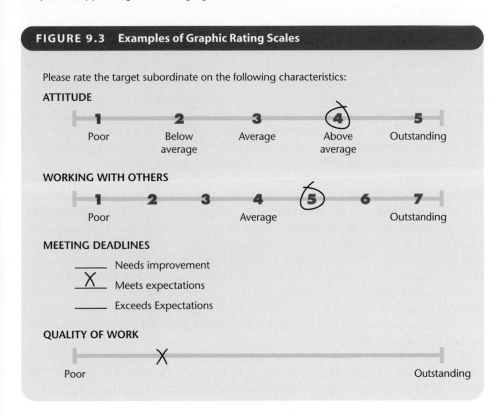

FIGURE 9.3   Examples of Graphic Rating Scales

Please rate the target subordinate on the following characteristics:

ATTITUDE

1   2   3   4   5

Poor   Below   Average   Above   Outstanding
       average   average

WORKING WITH OTHERS

1   2   3   4   5   6   7

Poor   Average   Outstanding

MEETING DEADLINES

_____ Needs improvement

__X__ Meets expectations

_____ Exceeds Expectations

QUALITY OF WORK

       X

Poor   Outstanding

wide array of performance dimensions can be tapped with various rating scales on the same form. Each of the descriptors on the rating form is accompanied by a number or a letter for responses. Most graphic rating scales have ranges of 1 to 5 or 1 to 7, although occasionally a scale may use only 1 to 3 or perhaps as many as 1 to 9 alternatives.

To develop a performance measure, the manager simply adds the points for a particular employee's graphic scale items to obtain an overall index of performance (which is why these scales are sometimes referred to as summated ratings). For example, if an appraisal instrument contains five graphic rating scales and each has a possible range of 1 to 5, then the potential performance scores for an individual can range from a minimum of 5 (when the individual receives an evaluation of 1 on each item) to a maximum of 25 (when the individual receives a 5 on each dimension). The specific dimensions measured by graphic rating scales should be based on job analysis, but this approach is not typically taken. Instead, to have a single instrument that can be used with all or most employees in an organization, graphic rating scales typically measure performance relative to traits or behaviors such as initiative or problem-solving capabilities or even attitudes. Also, in some cases, the organization might add an overall performance scale in addition to scales for the specific dimensions.

Although they are popular, graphic rating scales have problems. Managers may tend to go down the list of items and circle all the points at one end or the other of the scale. As we will see later, this pattern results in errors of what is called leniency or severity. On the other hand, some managers tend to circle primarily midpoints on the scale. This approach results in what is called central tendency. In all these cases, the real problem is a range restriction. It has also been suggested that graphic rating scales are particularly prone to the problem where an evaluation in one area or a general impression about the ratee influences ratings on all scales. This problem, which will also be discussed later in the chapter, is usually called halo error. Another shortcoming of the graphic rating scale is the tendency for managers to attribute perhaps too much precision and objectivity to them. That is, because numbers can be added and divided, a person may end up with a score such as 4.25 or 3.65. Thus, people may believe that the results are more objective and precise than they are in reality.

■ The **critical incident method** relies on instances of especially good or poor performance on the part of the employee.

A somewhat different type of rating instrument involves the use of the **critical incident method.** (Recall from Chapter 4 that this method can also be used as a job analysis technique.) A critical incident is simply an example or instance of especially good or poor performance on the part of the employee.[24] Organizations that rely on this method often require raters to recall such instances on the job and then describe what the employee did (or did not do) that led to success or failure. Thus, this technique provides rich information for feedback to the employee and defines performance in fairly clear behavioral terms. In other cases, managers are asked to keep a log or diary in which they record examples or critical incidents that they believe reflect good and bad performance on the part of individual employees.[25]

For example, a critical incident illustrating good performance by a gasoline station attendant might be as follows: "On Monday, January 15, you were observed to have fully restocked certain merchandise counters in the store without being instructed to do so. And you also illustrated very pleasant and service-oriented behavior when dealing with three customers. You handled each quickly and efficiently but gave each customer the prompt and courteous attention that each one wanted." On the other hand, a critical incident to illustrate less effective performance for the same job might be: "On Thursday, February 15, you were observed to be sitting behind the counter reading a newspaper when merchandise inventory stocking needed to be done. You were also observed to be curt and blunt with several customers. You processed their purchases quickly, but you did not really give each customer any personal attention."

An advantage of the critical incident method is that it allows managers to provide individual employees with precise examples of behaviors that are believed to be effective and less effective performance. On the other hand, the critical incident method requires considerable time and effort on the part of managers because they must maintain a log or diary of these incidents. In addition, the method may make it difficult to compare one person with another. That is, the sample of behaviors developed from one employee may not be comparable to the sample of behaviors acquired for another. In any event, maintaining such diaries or logs may help raters in making evaluations and providing clear feedback regardless of how they use the information from the diaries.[26]

■ **Behaviorally Anchored Rating Scales (BARS)** are appraisal systems that represent a combination of the graphic rating scale and the critical incident method.

Another method for appraising performance involves the use of **Behaviorally Anchored Rating Scales (BARS).**[27] BARS appraisal systems (also known sometimes as behavioral expectation scales) represent a combination of the graphic rating scale and the critical incident method. They specify performance dimensions based on behavioral anchors associated with different levels of performance. Figure 9.4 presents an example of a BARS rating scale. As shown in the figure, the performance dimension has different behavioral examples that specify different levels of performance along the scale.

FIGURE 9.4 Behaviorally Anchored Rating Scales

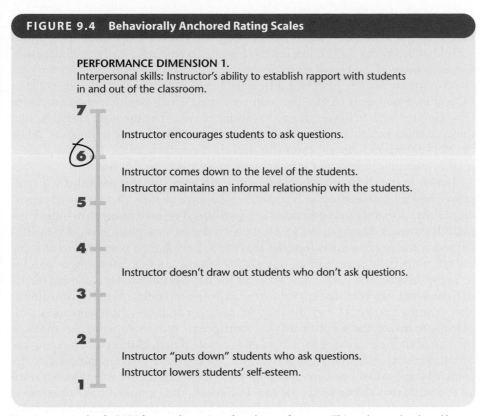

PERFORMANCE DIMENSION 1.
Interpersonal skills: Instructor's ability to establish rapport with students in and out of the classroom.

7

Instructor encourages students to ask questions.

6

Instructor comes down to the level of the students.
Instructor maintains an informal relationship with the students.

5

4

Instructor doesn't draw out students who don't ask questions.

3

2

Instructor "puts down" students who ask questions.
Instructor lowers students' self-esteem.

1

Here is an example of a BARS for one dimension of teacher performance. This scale was developed by one of the authors with the students in his class.

Developing a BARS is a complicated and often expensive process. Generally these scales are developed by the same managers who eventually use them to evaluate employees. First, the managers must develop a pool of critical incidents that represent various effective and ineffective behaviors on the job. These incidents are then classified into performance dimensions, and the dimensions that the managers believe represent a particular level of performance are used as behavioral examples, or anchors, to guide the raters when the scales are used. At each step, an incident is discarded unless the majority of managers can agree on where it belongs or what level of performance the incident illustrates.[28] The manager who then uses the scale has to evaluate an employee's performance on each dimension and determine where on the dimension the employee's performance fits best. The behavioral anchors serve as guides and benchmarks in helping to make this determination.

A significant advantage of BARS is that they dramatically increase reliability by providing specific behavioral examples to reflect effective and less effective behaviors. Because the managers themselves develop the scales, they tend to be more committed to using them effectively, and the process of developing the scales helps raters develop clearer ideas about what constitutes good performance on the job. The process of developing truly effective BARS is extremely expensive and time-consuming, and so they are rarely used in their pure form. Instead, some modified BARS procedures are often adopted in an attempt to reap some of the benefits without incurring the costs.

■ **Behavioral Observation Scales (BOS)** are developed from critical incidents like BARS but use substantially more critical incidents to define specifically all the measures necessary for effective performance.

A related measure of performance is the **Behavioral Observation Scale (BOS)**.[29] Like BARS, a BOS is developed from critical incidents. Rather than using only a sample of behaviors that reflect effective or ineffective behavior, a BOS uses substantially more of the behaviors to define specifically all the measures necessary for effective performance. A second difference between a BOS and a BARS is that a BOS allows managers to rate the frequency with which the individual employee has exhibited each behavior during the rating period. The manager then averages these ratings to calculate an overall performance rating for the individual. While the BOS approach is an improvement over the limitations of the BARS approach, it takes even more time and can be even more expensive to develop.

Earlier in the chapter, we noted that it might be reasonable to evaluate an employee based on outcomes. In fact, another popular method of appraising performance that does focus on outcomes is a **goal-based** or **management-by-objectives (MBO)** system.[30] *Management by objectives* is the most popular term used for this approach, although many companies that use it develop their own label to describe the system in their organization. In an MBO system, a subordinate meets with his or her manager and together they set goals for the subordinate for a coming period of time, often one year. These goals are usually quantifiable, objective, and almost always written down. During the year, the manager and the subordinate meet periodically to review the subordinate's performance relative to attaining the goals. At the end of the year, a more formal meeting is scheduled, During that meeting the actual degree of goal attainment is assessed. The degree of goal attainment then becomes the individual's performance appraisal. That is, if an individual has attained all the goals that she or he set for her- or himself, then employee performance is deemed to be very good. On the other hand, if not all goals were accomplished and the individual is directly responsible for that performance deficiency, then her or his performance is judged to be less than adequate or acceptable.

■ A **goal-based** or **management-by-objectives (MBO)** system is based largely on the extent to which individuals meet their personal performance objectives.

Goal-based systems are often seen as the best alternative available for rating performance, but care must be taken when these systems are used. Specifically, the kinds of behaviors specified in the goal-setting process are exactly what the employee will tend to focus on. Therefore it is critical that the organization really wants to encourage these particular behaviors. For example, if a sales representative's goals are stated in terms of dollar volume of sales, he or she might exert a lot of pressure on customers to increase the dollar volume of merchandise they're ordering in a coming period to boost his or her performance measures. At the same time, however, the sales representative may also hurt the firm's relationship with the customer if too much pressure is applied or if the customer ends up ordering more merchandise than is really needed. Thus, an important long-term goal may be sacrificed for the achievement of a short-term goal. The only solution to this type of potential problem is to emphasize the need for care in setting goals.

One relatively new innovation in performance appraisal methods is the use of computer monitoring. It is now possible to monitor electronically how employees are spending their time and how productive they are. These systems are now used widely with customer-service representatives and reservations clerks. In fact, you may have heard a telephone recording (after you pressed the right numbers to get the service you wanted) stating, "This call may be monitored for quality purposes." This recording is an indication that electronic monitoring is taking place. For example, it is possible to track how many calls an employee receives, how long each call takes, and (with minimal input) the outcome of those calls. It is also possible to track when an employee is not at his or her phone station, which has caused some people to raise serious questions about invasion of privacy.[31] Although only a limited number of studies have investigated the effectiveness of this method, it seems as though the approach can be effective without triggering negative reactions on the part of employees—at least under certain circumstances.[32] While we need to know a great deal more about the effects of computer monitoring on individuals, the fact remains that this approach is being used with growing frequency in the workplace, and it is likely to become even more popular in the future.[33]

Which System Is Best?

Despite the time and effort that have gone into developing and improving performance appraisal systems, it is difficult to find much advantage for any one system over the others.[34] We shall discuss issues of rating errors later in the chapter, and much research has focused on the susceptibility of different types of rating instruments to different types of errors. But this research has been inconclusive, and it is somewhat misguided. As noted at the beginning of this chapter, the ultimate reason for conducting performance appraisal is to improve performance. Therefore, it is difficult to suggest which system is best because it is difficult to predict how a set of employees will react to a given system. The human resource manager must take what is known about each type of system and decide how well the system fits into the culture and operations of the organization.

Thus, performance appraisal systems are neither good nor bad; these systems work or they don't for a particular organization. It is probably advisable to have some employees and supervisors involved in the development of any system so that they feel a sense of ownership. But the critical issue is how the organization uses the information collected in the performance appraisal. In fact this issue is at the heart of the performance management process, and we shall discuss it in more detail later. For now, though, it is safe to say that when employees perceive the appraisal system as fair and just, they work harder to make it work and they respond more constructively to the ratings they receive, thus making the system work.

UNDERSTANDING THE LIMITATIONS OF PERFORMANCE APPRAISAL

We noted earlier that all the participants in the appraisal process tend to be dissatisfied with the process. Several problems with appraisals contribute to this dissatisfaction, and we will discuss some of these problems below. Over the last few years, however, a different type of issue has emerged relative to performance appraisal; this issue may represent a more basic deficiency in most appraisal systems.

Typically, performance appraisal systems assess performance on aspects of one's job. That is, the areas for which the employee receives ratings are those areas the employee has been told are part of his or her job. Recently, a great deal of interest has focused on what has been termed contextual performance, which brings a different dimension to the question of what should be appraised.[35] **Contextual performance** refers to tasks an employee does on the job that are not required as part of the job but that nevertheless benefit the organization in some way (we introduced this topic in the previous chapter). These behaviors might include staying late at work, helping coworkers get their work done, and any of the behaviors that benefit the general good of the organization. These behaviors are often referred to as organizational citizenship behaviors.[36] Because these behaviors are never stated

■ **Contextual performance** refers to tasks an employee does on the job that are not required as part of the job but that still benefit the organization in some way.

Organizations are increasingly concerned with contextual performance as well as with the more traditional task performance. Whereas task performance refers to the assigned tasks and responsibilities that come with the job, contextual performance refers to things an employee does for the good of the organization that go above and beyond job requirements. Dr. Larry Nathanson, an Emergency Room doctor at Boston's Beth Israel Deaconess Medical Center is an excellent case in point. Although his primary job is to provide emergency care for patients who come to the emergency room, he realized that the usual dry-erase board was an ineffective tool for keeping track of ER patients. He initiated an effort to replace the board with a new system called an "electronic dashboard," which electronically monitors patients and their needs. Hospital officials estimate that this new system saves thirty minutes in processing time for each patient, which is important given that 60,000 patients visit the hospital's emergency room each year.

as formal requirements of the job, the employee is never formally told that he or she is expected to do these tasks. They might be told informally, however, that such behaviors are valued by the organization in general and/or the manager in particular. In any event, they *do* benefit the organization and raters *do* consider them when conducting employee evaluations.[37]

How important are contextual performance behaviors in determining the overall ratings an employee receives? A recent study indicates that, although they are important, they are not as important as task behaviors (or even as important as counterproductive behaviors), but they do matter.[38] The next question is, How important *are* these behaviors? Clearly, the organization benefits if someone engages in these behaviors, and therefore they represent part of an employee's overall contribution to the organization. On the other hand, they are not required of anyone. Some, especially union members, argue that it is inherently unfair to evaluate someone on something that is not part of his or her job. Perhaps that assertion is true, but it seems that, consciously or not, raters *do* take these behaviors into account. We can speculate about whether or not reliance on contextual performance behaviors can serve to discriminate unfairly against certain groups of employees. For example, a single parent may not be able to volunteer for overtime. Should he or she be penalized for this situation?

Of course, one potential solution would be to include these contextual performance dimensions as part of the formal appraisal. Then these behaviors would no longer reflect citizenship behavior but would simply reflect someone doing his or her job. As such, they can be part of any appraisal decision. But would that solution really solve the more basic problem? In all likelihood, some employee will always be willing to do something extra for the organization. It is not reasonable, however, to expect extra work from every employee and, regardless of how exhaustive a list we construct, outstanding employees will always find a way to make an extra contribution. We clearly need to learn a lot more about the role of contextual performance in the appraisal process, but this line of inquiry raises some basic questions about the premise for ratings and the importance of behavior at work that is not required.

In addition to the issue of contextual performance, almost all performance appraisal techniques suffer from other limitations. Thus, it is important to recognize that no performance appraisal system is perfect. All performance measurement techniques and appraisal approaches are subject to one or more weaknesses or deficiencies.[39] One deficiency is known as projection. **Projection** occurs when we tend to see in others characteristics that we ourselves have and that we think contribute to effectiveness. That is, we tend to judge people like ourselves to be higher performers than we do people who are less like ourselves. The basis for similarity may be demographic characteristics (for example, race, gender, or age) or other characteristics (for example, the college the individual attended or his or her personal appearance, life style, etc.).

Another performance deficiency is contrast error. **Contrast error** occurs when we compare people against one another instead of against an objective standard. For example, suppose a particular employee is a good performer but not an outstanding one. If that individual happens to work in a group of people where everyone else is a relatively weak performer, the "average" individual may appear to be a better performer than he or she really is. Likewise, if the same person works in a group of exceptionally strong performers, the person may be seen as a poorer performer than might otherwise be the case.

Managers who conduct performance appraisals are also prone to make what is called distributional errors. A **distributional error** occurs when the rater tends to use only one part of the rating scale. Sometimes the distributional error may be *severity,* which occurs when the manager gives low ratings to all employees by holding them to an unreasonably high standard. The opposite error is *leniency,* which occurs when a manager assigns relatively high or lenient ratings to all employees.[40] A *central tendency* distributional error occurs when the manager tends to rate all employees as average, using only the middle part of a rating scale.

A final type of error that may occur is what is known as either halos or horns. A **halo error** occurs when one positive performance characteristic causes the manager to rate all other aspects of performance positively. For example, suppose a given employee always comes to work early and is always full of energy and enthusiasm at the beginning of the workday. The manager may so appreciate this behavior that he or she gives the employee a high performance rating on all other aspects of performance, even when those other aspects may be only average or merely adequate.[41] The opposite of a halo error is a **horns error**. In this instance, the manager tends to downgrade other aspects of an employee's performance because of a single performance dimension. For example, the manager may feel that a given employee does not dress appropriately and views that characteristic negatively. As a result, the manager may also give the individual low performance ratings on other performance dimensions when higher ratings are justified.

But there is one additional point that should be discussed relative to these rating errors. Using the term *error* implies that there is a correct rating and that the observed rating in some cases is incorrect. So, for example, when we discuss leniency error, we observe that the ratings are "too high." That implies that we know how high the ratings really should be—but we don't. We really never have correct answers (sometimes referred to as "true scores") when we look at a set of ratings, so we really don't know whether a rating or set of ratings reflect reality or a rating error. Therefore, what we observe might be leniency or it might simply mean that the employee is really good. This fact makes it difficult to suggest that organizations take extraordinary measures to reduce "errors."

- **Projection** occurs when we tend to see in others characteristics that we ourselves have and that we think contribute to effectiveness.

- **Contrast error** occurs when we compare people against one another instead of against an objective standard.

- A **distributional error** occurs when the rater tends to use only one part of the rating scale.

- A **halo error** occurs when one positive performance characteristic causes the manager to rate all other aspects of performance positively.

- A **horns error** occurs when the manager downgrades other aspects of an employee's performance because of a single performance dimension.

Nonetheless, these rating "errors" such as leniency and halo sometimes make it difficult to differentiate between different employees, or to accurately identify the strengths and weaknesses of a given employee. Furthermore, employees (ratees) might be less likely to perceive a set of lenient ratings as accurately reflecting their performance, and so may not be willing to work to improve their performance. As a result, organizations often do work to reduce rating error. One method for error reduction is to train managers to overcome these weaknesses. For example, sometimes pointing out to managers their tendency to commit distributional errors or contrast errors may be sufficient to enable those managers to do a better job. A related method for improving the accuracy of performance evaluations is the so-called rater accuracy training. This approach (also called frame of reference training) attempts to emphasize for managers the fact that performance is multidimensional in nature and to train those managers with the actual content of various performance dimensions.[42]

As noted earlier in the chapter, even if a rater can be trained to avoid errors and to provide accurate ratings, he or she may simply choose to be inaccurate in the ratings he or she gives. Therefore it is critical that organizations do whatever they can to reward raters for doing a good job in performance appraisal by reinforcing the fact that these appraisals are important. It may also be important to punish raters who do not take the task seriously. It is important to realize that a rater who really wants to be inaccurate or unfair can probably find a way to do so, whatever systems an organization puts in place. That is why it is so important for the organization to do what it can to convince raters that it is in their own best interests to do the best job they can in appraising employee performance.

PERFORMANCE MANAGEMENT AND PROVIDING FEEDBACK

As noted at the beginning of this chapter, performance appraisal is part of a broader process called performance management. As we saw in Figure 9.1, after performance appraisal is completed, the next major activity is the provision of feedback, coaching, and counseling. Many managers do a poor job in this area, in part because they don't understand how to do it properly and in part because they don't enjoy it. Almost by definition, performance appraisal in many organizations tends to focus on negatives and, as a result, managers may have a tendency to avoid giving feedback because they know an employee who hears negative feedback may be angry, hurt, discouraged, or argumentative. But clearly, if employees are not told about their shortcomings, they have no reason to try to improve and have no guidance concerning how to improve. Therefore, it is critical that a rater follow up the appraisal by providing feedback to the employee. The rater can do several things to improve the performance feedback process.

The Feedback Interview

One method of improving performance feedback is to provide feedback on a regular basis via feedback interviews. Instead of providing feedback annually, in tandem with the annual performance appraisal interview, it might be more appropriate for managers to provide feedback on an ongoing basis. Feedback might be provided on a daily or weekly basis, depending on the nature of the job, and should focus on various characteristics of performance, including both effective and ineffective performance.[43] In fact, if managers remember that the goal of performance management is changing employee behavior, they should also recognize the fact that they clearly are more likely to effect change with more frequent feedback.

Another useful method for improving performance feedback is to have the individual appraise his or her own performance in advance of an appraisal interview. This method involves having employees think about their own performance over the rating period and helps sensitize them to areas where they have done both a good and an ineffective job. This method also lends efficiency to the process because the manager and the subordinate may be able to focus most of their time and effort in a performance appraisal interview on those areas of performance assessment where they disagree. That is, if the manager and the subordinate both agree that certain elements of the subordinate's performance are very good and that certain other elements need improvement, it may be possible to spend little time discussing those elements and to focus more energy on the performance areas that are in disagreement.

It is also important during a performance feedback interview to encourage participation and two-way communication. Some managers are prone to lecture a subordinate on the outcome of the performance appraisal interview. The basic nature of the meeting, then, involves the manager telling the subordinate how he or she has been evaluated and then concluding the interview. As a result, the subordinate may feel threatened and that she or he had no voice in the process. Participation and two-way dialogue, however, allows the individual to express her or his own feelings and opinions about job performance and to provide other kinds of feedback as appropriate.[44]

It is also important for the manager to try to balance positive and negative feedback. As already noted, many managers tend to focus on the negative. In reality, however, employees are likely to have many positive characteristics related to performance as well. Thus, while the manager must clearly address the negative performance characteristics noted in the appraisal, these negative attributes should be balanced against praise and recognition of the positive aspects of the employee's performance.

Also, throughout the interview and the performance management process, it is essential that the manager take a developmental and problem-solving orientation to the process. That is, it is important not to focus on the individual as a person by saying things like, "You are a bad employee." Instead, the focus should be on providing developmental feedback targeted at behavior, not on the individual him- or herself. A simple distinction between saying things like, "You are a poor performer" versus "Your performance is not acceptable" can help keep the focus on behavior and not on the individual.

The performance appraisal interview should conclude with a future-oriented discussion of what will happen next. This discussion often includes topics such as

The performance review is the place for a manager to provide feedback for the employee, but it is also the place for the employee to promote his or her accomplishments during the evaluation period. As Dana Hall, a managing director of hedge fund Lighthouse Partners, discovered, women such as herself often have difficulty communicating clearly their own accomplishments and overall value to a company. Since realizing this difficulty was holding her back in her career, she worked to improve it. Now she helps other women executives manage their careers better by teaching them how to be more effective self-promoters.

setting goals for correcting performance deficiencies and discussing the possibility of pay raises, promotion prospects, and similar kinds of awards. Of course, if performance is judged to be deficient, the feedback interview may focus on topics such as the establishment of a probationary period (after which employment may be terminated), the development of a training strategy for improving performance, and so forth. Regardless of the level of present performance, this interview setting should provide a time when the rater and the employee discuss future performance goals for the employee. If the organization uses a goal-based appraisal system, this discussion may be automatic. Even if a different type of appraisal model is used, it is helpful for the employee to have clear and specific goals for improving future performance. These goals, along with continued and regular feedback, should constitute the critical part of any performance management program.

Even with these recommendations, feedback is not always as effective as we would like to believe. Many of today's recommendations and practices are based on the assumption that, if done properly, they will provide employees with feedback about their job performance. Several years ago, however, a study reviewed the research on the effectiveness of feedback interventions, beginning with early studies from the nineteenth century.[45] This study found that, although feedback was effective in almost two-thirds of the cases, feedback was not effective in the rest. In fact, in a large number of cases, providing feedback to employees actually lowered subsequent performance. This result was independent of the nature of the feedback (i.e., whether the feedback was positive or negative), which suggests that any feedback can, under certain conditions, have a negative effect on subsequent performance.

The study found that feedback was more likely to have a negative effect when the employee was new to a job, the job was extremely complex, ways to improve performance were not discussed, or goals for the future were not considered. The study also reported that feedback must focus the employee's attention on the task at hand. When feedback is provided so that the employee can take it personally, the feedback is much more likely to interfere with rather than enhance subsequent performance. Thus, the recommendations above will help ensure that feedback has the desired effect.

Archiving Performance Appraisal and Management Results

The organization must develop a system for archiving performance appraisal results. That is, the results of the performance appraisal should be stored so that the records can be easily attained and referred to at a later point. For example, if the individual is put on probation and told that he or she will be terminated if performance doesn't improve over the next six months, it is important that the manager have access to this information when the next performance appraisal is completed. This safeguard is especially important if the manager who did the performance appraisal is promoted or otherwise reassigned, and someone else must follow up with the employee.

Archiving performance appraisal results is also important in terms of equal employment opportunity issues. An organization must be able to demonstrate, beyond reasonable doubt, that an individual employee was sanctioned, rewarded, punished, terminated, or remanded for training on the basis of performance rather than on the basis of factors such as gender, race, and so forth. Figure 9.5 provides an example of one method used to archive performance appraisal

FIGURE 9.5 Forms for Archiving Performance Appraisal Information

Lansdale

hrly EMPLOYEE PERFORMANCE APPRAISAL _____ 90-DAY _____ ANNUAL _____ PROB.

Employee Information

Name:
Position:
Department:

Reviewer:
Current Review Period:
Next Review Date:

Rate the individual in each category below from one to four with four being the highest. Provide supporting comments for all categories.

Category	Rating	Supporting Comments
Quality of Work The extent to which work produced is accurate, thorough and effective	1 2 3 4 ☐ ☐ ☐ ☐	
Job Knowledge The level of understanding of assignments and requirements in order to perform the job duties.	1 2 3 4 ☐ ☐ ☐ ☐	
Team Work The level of cooperation and contribution to a team effort within the department or with other departments. The extent to which the employee makes an extra effort in a rush operation.	1 2 3 4 ☐ ☐ ☐ ☐	
Productivity The volume of work regularly produced. Speed and consistency of output.		
Initiative The degree to which the employee seeks new tasks, makes improvements or suggestions, accepts new responsibilities and strives for self-improvement.		
Safety Adherence to safety procedures, suggestions for safety improvements, helps to minimize risk to self and others and any downtime due to failure to follow procedures.		
Attendance and Availability Available for overtime; reliable attendance record. _____ Days absent _____ Days tardy _____ Days left early		

Overall Rating = _____ (Add score total and divide by 8)

List General Areas of Strength:

Identify Areas to Target for Improvement:

List Goals and Areas to Focus On:

Supervisor's Additional Comments/Summary:

Employee Comments:

This form has been reviewed and discussed with me by my supervisor. My signature acknowledges that I read it and noted any exceptions and additional comments above.

Employee Signature: _____ Date: _____

APPROVALS
Reviewer/Supervisor: _____ Date: _____

Source: Courtesy of Lansdale, Inc.

results. The document includes not only the performance appraisal scales but also other information, including the action plan for performance improvement. At the end of each appraisal cycle, this form is added to the individual employee's file. Thus, in the future, managers can refer to previous evaluations and have a more complete perspective on the employee's previous performance.

PERFORMANCE MANAGEMENT AND FOLLOW-UP MEASURES

Effective performance management typically involves some type of reward to employees who meet goals or improve their performance. There are many types of rewards that can be used in this context, including plaques and extra time off. But traditional rewards also work well. Here an employee smiles as he receives a bonus check for his outstanding performance during the previous quarter.

A typical outcome of the performance feedback interview is the development of an action plan for the future. If the employee's performance has been good, average, or some similar categorization, the plan typically addresses how the employee can maintain that level in the future. It also identifies areas where improvements can be made. It is also likely that some reward, usually a pay increase commensurate with acceptable performance, is given at this time. If the person's performance has been outstanding, exemplary, or some similar categorization, the plan may focus more on potential development opportunities that can lead to promotion and advancement. In this case, the employee will likely be awarded a larger pay increase and may receive, in addition, one-time rewards such as a bonus and/or award. As noted at the beginning of the chapter, these performance management activities, in conjunction with performance appraisal, should allow the organization to work towards improving the performance of individual employees. Well-designed performance management programs should also help the organization to transform the improvement in individual performance into improvements in corporate performance.

In many cases, however, the employee's performance will be deficient in one or more areas and actions will be outlined for correcting those problems. Training and development efforts are among the most common. Sometimes the development efforts may be self-imposed. For example, if a sales representative is deemed to be deficient in one aspect of his performance, simply alerting him to that fact and suggesting that he work on doing a better job may be enough. If the problem relates to being late for too many sales calls, he might, on his own initiative, start being more efficient in setting appointments and making a greater effort to be on time. In other situations, however, the deficiency may be associated with job-related skills and abilities. For example, suppose a recently promoted engineering supervisor is seen by some of the engineers in her group as being too controlling. Her previous technical education and training may not have included any management courses, so she might be sent to a management seminar dealing with delegation and participative management techniques. If the individual's performance is judged to be significantly lower than desired, however, more extreme measures might be required. These disciplinary actions were discussed in the previous chapter.

EVALUATING THE PERFORMANCE APPRAISAL AND MANAGEMENT PROCESSES

At the beginning of this chapter, we noted the strategic importance of the performance appraisal system. Clearly the organization must monitor the extent to which it is conducting its performance appraisals effectively, adequately, and appropriately. As with selection, performance appraisal must be free from bias and discrimination.

Beyond these stipulations, however, the performance appraisal system must also help the organization identify its strongest performers so that they can be appropriately rewarded and efforts can be made to retain them. It should also identify low performers so that their performance deficiencies can be remedied through training or other measures. Periodic audits of the performance appraisal system by trained professionals can be an effective method for assessing the effectiveness and appropriateness of the performance appraisal process used by the organization.

Because performance appraisal feeds into the performance management process, and because the ultimate goal of this process is to improve performance on the job, managers should be able to see real improvements in organizational performance if the process is working. This improvement may take the form of fewer errors in production, fewer returns in sales, improved performance appraisals, or lower levels of absenteeism or turnover. In the long run, however, these outcomes are not critical to the organization unless they translate into some improvement in overall firm performance. That is, if performance appraisal and performance management systems are doing what they were designed to do, the organization as a whole should perform better.

A management system that attempts to tie together several of these pieces is available. The Productivity Measurement and Evaluation System (ProMES) incorporates ideas from goal setting to feedback, and includes incentives for improvement.[46] More important, it includes a method for tying performance at the individual and group level to organizational productivity. The system requires the designation of "contingencies," which describe the relationship between performance in an area and overall effectiveness, and it requires objective measures of effectiveness and performance. The system has been widely adopted (especially in Europe) and has been quite successful. Its success relies largely on aspects of performance management, coupled with clear goals, so that employees are told exactly where and how to exert their efforts, which ultimately lead to organizational productivity. This connection is important because there is actually little data that relates performance appraisal or performance management techniques to organizational effectiveness.

LEGAL ISSUES IN PERFORMANCE APPRAISAL

When performance appraisals are used as the basis for human resource decisions (as in the case of merit pay or promotion decisions), they are considered the same as any other test under the law. This designation includes decisions about layoffs based on performance. Therefore, appraisals that show evidence of disparate impact must be validated the same as any selection technique. This principle was first established in *Brito* v. *Zia Company*,[47] and was reinforced as part of the decision in the *Albermarle Paper Company* case discussed earlier in the text (both in Chapter 3 and in Chapter 7).

As noted above, performance appraisal decisions are known to suffer from various types of biases and problems. Also noted earlier in the chapter was the fact that ratings based on traits tend to have ambiguous standards, and so they are probably more prone to these biases. It is difficult to validate appraisal decisions using the methods described in Chapter 7 (i.e., content validity, construct validity, and criterion related validity). Therefore it is critical that the organization can demonstrate that the ratings provided are in areas that are "job related," that raters can observe the behaviors they are rating, and that raters received some training to help them do a better job with rating performance. It is worth noting that, if an appraisal system is used for providing feedback *only*, it is not subject to these same legal requirements.

Chapter Summary

Performance appraisal is the specific and formal evaluation of an employee conducted to determine the degree to which the employee is performing his or her job effectively. Performance management refers to the more general set of activities carried out by the organization to change (improve) employee performance.

Performance appraisals are important because they ensure that recruiting and selection processes are adequate, play an important role in training, can help link performance with rewards, demonstrate that important employment-related decisions are based on performance, and can promote employee motivation and development. They also provide valuable and useful information to the organization's human resource planning process. The ultimate goal for any organization using performance appraisals is to improve performance on the job.

The organization, primarily through the work of its human resource function, develops the general performance appraisal process, including issues of timing, for its managers and employees to use. The organization is also responsible for ensuring that clear and specific performance standards are available to managers and employees.

Both the rater and the ratee have specific responsibilities. Raters can include the supervisor, peers, colleagues, coworkers, subordinates of the individual being appraised, the individual him- or herself, and customers and clients. When all of these raters are used, the appraisal is called 360-degree feedback.

Several methods can be used to assess performance. Ranking techniques include the simple ranking method, the paired comparison method, and the forced distribution method. Rating techniques include graphic rating scales, the critical incident method, Behaviorally Anchored Rating Scales (BARS), Behavioral Observation Scales (BOS), and goal-based or management-by-objectives systems.

All performance measurement techniques and appraisal approaches are subject to one or more weaknesses or deficiencies. The most common problems include projection, contrast errors, distributional errors, halo errors, and horns errors. Organizations can take steps, including training and awareness, to reduce rating error.

After performance appraisal is completed, the next major activity is the provision of feedback, coaching, and counseling. One method of improving performance feedback is to provide feedback on a regular basis via feedback interviews. Another useful method for improving performance feedback is to have the individual appraise his or her own performance in advance of an appraisal interview. It is also important during a performance feedback interview to encourage participation and two-way communication and to try to balance positive and negative feedback. Care must be taken to ensure that the feedback is having the desired effect on performance. Results of appraisals should also be stored for future reference.

A typical outcome of the performance feedback interview is the development of an action plan for the future. This plan should specify what the organization expects the employee to do in the future regarding performance and how the organization is likely to respond. It is also important that the organization monitor the extent to which it is conducting its performance ap-

praisals effectively, adequately, and appropriately. As with selection, performance appraisal must be free from bias and discrimination. Finally, it is important to find ways to relate performance appraisal and performance management activities to firm-level outcomes.

- ▶ Performance appraisal serves several purposes in organizations, but the primary purpose for conducting appraisals is to improve employee performance and thus improve organizational effectiveness.

- ▶ The rater in the appraisal process has the ultimate responsibility for how well an appraisal system works, and raters can and do distort appraisals.

- ▶ Raters can be chosen from several sources, but ideally the person best able to assess performance in an area should be the person to conduct the appraisal.

- ▶ Multisource or 360-degree appraisals combine ratings data from multiple sources. Although these appraisals are potentially useful for feedback purposes, they are problematic when used for decision making, and no evidence exists to suggest that these appraisals are more effective than alternative methods. It is clear, however, that 360-degree appraisals are more costly to conduct.

- ▶ Performance appraisals can focus on behaviors, traits, or outcomes. Although each can provide useful information, appraisals designed around outcomes, stated in terms of goals, may be more useful than others.

- ▶ Teams provide a real challenge for performance appraisals, and in some cases it is best to assess the team. In other cases, it is best to assess individual team members.

Key Points for Future HR Managers

- ▶ Many alternative methods are available for the actual design of an appraisal system. Years of research have indicated no clear advantage to any of these methods, with the possible exception of goal-based appraisals.

- ▶ It is important to consider the role of contextual performance in the appraisal context. Although this approach refers to behaviors that are not formally evaluated, they are also behaviors that are critical for the organization.

- ▶ Several appraisal errors, such as halo error, are commonly discussed, but it is no longer clear that these are truly errors, or that organizations should exert a great deal of effort to reduce them.

- ▶ Regardless of the appraisal system used, performance management is critical to achieve the most important goal for the process—the improvement of performance. Performance management systems such as ProMES are available. They are designed specifically to enhance organizational performance.

- ▶ Feedback does not always work as intended. Sometimes providing feedback can hurt subsequent performance.

- ▶ When appraisals are used for decision making, they are subject to the same legal requirements as are selection tests.

- ▶ Appraisal systems should always be designed so that they have the greatest likelihood of improving individual and organizational performance.

- ▶ Raters must be convinced that it is in their best interests to be fair and accurate in appraisals. No type of system can replace rater motivation to do a good job.

Key Points for Future General Managers

- ▶ Although 360-degree appraisals are popular, evidence does not support their effectiveness relative to other, less expensive methods, and it is problematic to use 360-degree appraisals for decision making.

- ▶ In team settings, decisions must be made about whether appraisals and feedback should focus on the whole team or on individual members.

▶ Contextual performance refers to those behaviors that we do not evaluate formally but that must occur for the organization to function effectively. Decisions have to be made about how to treat contextual performance.

▶ Clear evidence shows that one appraisal system is not more effective than any other type of appraisal system, although there is some reason to believe that goal-based systems may offer some advantages over the alternatives.

▶ The key to improving organizational effectiveness is more likely to lie with performance management systems than with performance appraisal systems.

▶ Feedback does not always have the desired effect on performance. Sometimes providing feedback can hurt subsequent performance.

Review and Discussion Questions

1. Distinguish between performance appraisal and performance management.

2. Identify and briefly describe the basic steps in performance appraisal.

3. What are the basic goals of performance appraisal?

4. Summarize the roles of the organization, the rater, and the ratee in performance appraisal.

5. Who are the most common raters in the performance appraisal process?

6. Identify and critique the basic methods for performance appraisal.

7. What are the basic limitations and weaknesses of performance appraisal? Relate each to the specific technique(s) it is most likely to characterize.

8. From the standpoint of the rater, what can you do specifically to ensure effective performance appraisals?

9. From the standpoint of the ratee, what can you do specifically to increase the chances of a more effective performance appraisal?

10. How might feedback interviews and meetings be conducted most effectively?

Closing Case

Accelerated Performance Reviews May Improve Retention

Most organizations have traditionally conducted performance appraisals for everyone on a routine schedule, either once a year near the anniversary of each employee's hiring date or during one common period when everyone was evaluated. A schedule was especially true for new employees, who were told at the start of their employment when their first review would be. Part of the logic underlying this system was that newcomers were considered to be on probation until their first review. In addition, organizations felt that new employees might need an extended period of time to learn their jobs and to have a reasonable time in which to establish their capabilities.

From the standpoint of the newcomers themselves, they often saw value in the recognition that they had

ample time to learn their jobs before they would be evaluated. On the other hand, they also knew that, because increased compensation and/or promotions are usually tied to performance appraisals, they had little opportunity to seek a pay raise or to be given greater job responsibilities until that first review had been completed. Thus, the standard review cycle had both pluses and minuses for new employees.

In recent years, though, this cycle has been gradually altered in some firms. And this change has come about in large part because of the tight labor market in certain areas, especially rapidly growing high-tech firms. Because the highly skilled workers these firms need are well aware of their value to prospective employers, some of the more enterprising and self-assured candidates have started requesting—or in some cases demanding—promises of earlier reviews to have an opportunity to ratchet up their salaries more quickly. The practice of early reviews has also started spreading outside the high-tech environment to include areas such as banks, accounting firms, and insurance companies.

These firms are finding that by offering earlier reviews, they have a better chance of landing the top prospects. A guaranteed review after six months is rapidly become an expectation in the eyes of some of the most promising recruits. For example, one recent survey of executive search firms found that over 27 percent of new management positions currently being filled come with the assurance of an initial six-month review. But one factor that is often overlooked in this trend is that the recruit still has to ask for the earlier performance review. If he or she does not, the company is likely to stick with its normal one-year cycle.

So, can the cycle take place any faster? Absolutely. For example, consider the case of software programmer David Parvin, a recent college graduate courted by Cougar Mountain Software, a Boise, Idaho, company. Parvin learned that Cougar Mountain provided performance reviews of its new hires after thirty days. But Parvin wanted it even faster, so he demanded a two-week review. And sure enough, during his first two weeks on the job, he so impressed his bosses that they gave him a 7.1 percent pay raise. During his first eighteen months on the job, he continued to request frequent reviews, earning a total of six raises and one major promotion.

While this cycle may seem extreme, one reason it has worked is that Cougar Mountain has a history of rapid reviews. Indeed, about 10 percent of its new hires get a raise after thirty days, and almost all get a raise within three months. The firm's managers also believe that this practice helps Cougar Mountain retain its most valuable employees. In an industry with extremely high turnover, Cougar Mountain's turnover among all its employees is only about 10 percent; among its very best employees, it is an incredible 1 percent.

Of course, this approach can also create some problems. In addition to the extra administrative time and expense needed to manage an organic performance appraisal and salary adjustment system, potential morale problems can occur with other employees. To address this concern, some companies require those who will be getting frequent reviews to keep their arrangement a secret in the hope of avoiding problems with other employees. But word is still likely to get out, especially if more than just a few new employees are getting this special attention.

For the future, there seems to be a difference of opinion about whether or not this practice will continue. Some experts predict that as soon as the tight labor market begins to loosen (for example, when firms stop adding new jobs), firms will quickly move to drop the frequent review process. Others believe just the opposite will occur, and that firms may well come to value the flexibility that this system affords and will want to apply it to everyone. That is, as long as they review and reward their highly valued workers on an accelerated schedule, they may be able to slow the process for less valued workers. Thus, a well-established worker with a history of being judged as adequate may be evaluated even less frequently—and get fewer raises—than is the case today.[48]

Case Questions

1. What do you see as the advantages and disadvantages of frequent performance appraisals?

2. Under what circumstances would you envision wanting more frequent reviews? Under what circumstances would you prefer just the opposite?

3. What is your prediction about the future of rapid performance appraisal cycles?

Building HR Management Skills

Purpose: The purpose of this exercise is to help you develop insights into the process of developing performance appraisal methods and systems. As background, conceptualize how performance appraisal works in a typical course such as the one you are taking now: the instructor is the rater and the students are the ratees. Instructors generally use some combination of exams, tests, papers, cases, and/or class participation as the basis for evaluation and then provide the formal appraisal in the form of a letter grade.

Step 1: Your instructor will ask you to form small groups of four to five members.

Step 2: Working with your group members, develop three alternative methods that an instructor might use to evaluate your performance. Try to match your methods to those discussed in this chapter whenever possible.

Step 3: Evaluate each method you developed in terms of its potential usefulness. Identify the strengths and weaknesses of each method relative to the traditional system.

Step 4: Discuss and develop responses for the following questions:

1. What barriers might exist to the adoption of one of the new methods you developed?

2. What limitations characterize the traditional system? Do any of your methods overcome these limitations?

3. At your school, do students evaluate instructors? If so, how might the current method be improved?

4. Does 360-degree feedback have any relevance in the classroom?

Ethical Dilemmas in HR Management

Assume that you are a marketing executive in a major corporation. You need to hire a new staff member to fill a position that has just been created. The members of your current staff are not interested in the position, do not have the requisite skills for the position, or already have comparable or better positions. Thus, the person you select will come from outside your work group.

You have asked the human resource department to help identify three possible candidates from inside the organization. You have met with each of these people and thoroughly reviewed their educational backgrounds, experience, performance appraisals, and other qualifications. You have eliminated one person because of lack of fit, but you now face a complicated decision between the other two. Specifically, you see them as relatively equal in terms of potential. The real problem, however, is one of diversity and equal opportunity.

One candidate is a black female. You are personally committed to equal opportunity for minorities and have a reputation for helping members of protected classes whenever appropriate. You are familiar with this candidate's current boss. You see that the candidate has received performance appraisals consistently in the range of 3.8–4.2 on your firm's 5-point rating scales. But because of your knowledge of her boss, you know that these numbers really mean that her performance has been in the range of 4.2–4.6 (her boss rates everyone on the low side—in your opinion, about 0.4 point below where others would rate them).

The other candidate is a white male. This individual's performance appraisal ratings have been in the range of 4.0–4.4. You also know this person's boss very well, and believe that these scores are pretty accurate as is because his boss always does a fair, objective, and equitable job in her performance appraisals.

Your dilemma is whether to select the white male on the basis of the numbers or to select the black female on the basis of what you think the numbers really mean. While you have the authority to make this decision yourself, you also want to make sure that you can defend it in the event that the individual not selected questions how and why you chose the other individual for the position.

Questions

1. What are the ethical issues in this situation?

2. What are the basic arguments for and against selecting each candidate?

3. What do you think most managers would do? What would you do?

HR Internet Exercise

Many different human resource consulting firms offer services in the area of performance appraisal, including advice on how to install systems, how to use 360-degree feedback, forms to use, and so forth. Assume that you have just taken the position of senior human resource executive for a large manufacturing business and believe that its current performance appraisal system is inadequate. Your plan is to scrap the current system and replace it with a new one. Because you are both quite busy with other problems and also have little direct experience with performance appraisal yourself, you are interested in engaging the services of a consulting firm to help.

Using a search engine, search the Web for the following key terms: *performance appraisal, performance assessment, performance management,* and any other version of the term that you think is appropriate. Locate several consulting firms that might offer the services you need. Review each site thoroughly, and then narrow your list to the three most promising. Finally, list the additional information you want to have before selecting one.

Questions

1. What role does the Internet serve when selecting a consulting firm for a purpose such as the one described above?

2. How realistic do you think the information on the Web is for reviewing and selecting a service provider for the purpose described above?

3. Compare notes with your classmates and see if any of you chose some of the same firms. Compare your evaluations of each.

10

Training, Development, and Organizational Learning

CHAPTER OBJECTIVES

After studying this chapter you should be able to:

■ Identify and describe the purposes of training and development.

■ Discuss new employee orientation.

■ Describe how training and development needs are assessed.

■ Discuss common training and development techniques and methods.

■ Discuss the unique considerations in management development.

■ Discuss how organizations, as well as individuals, can learn and develop.

■ Describe how organizations can evaluate the effectiveness of their training and development programs.

I n today's competitive business environment, customer service is often a key ingredient in both attracting new customers and retaining existing ones. Indeed, surveys show that poor customer service is the leading complaint—even ahead of price—cited by customers who stop buying a company's products or services. A surly hotel desk clerk, an uninformed retail clerk, or an argumentative customer-service representative can all cost a business substantial current and future earnings by alienating even the most loyal customers.

American Express clearly recognizes this problem and goes to great lengths to ensure that its customer-service representatives are properly trained and rewarded for providing high-quality service to the firm's cardholders and other customers. Indeed, the firm's customer-service representatives must be knowledgeable about a wide array of financial services. They must also be knowledgeable about the highly regulated financial industry in which they operate. And they must always be polite and respectful when talking to customers on the telephone.

To help maintain a properly trained workforce, American Express relies on a combination of classroom and Web-based training. Some instructional material is presented in the form of half-hour e-learning modules that employees can view on their computers. But the firm also understands the importance of classroom training, especially in areas associated with providing high-quality customer service.

While some firms outsource their training to other companies, American Express handles all its training in-house. Managers argue that only in-house experts can provide the quality of training that the firm requires. They also point out that most trainers started out as customer-service representatives, which demonstrates that opportunities for advancement exist in the company. The firm also focuses heavily on training assessment. All training participants are surveyed routinely to determine their perceptions of the quality and value of the training they receive. And American Express also prides itself on monitoring the actual performance changes that result from training. For instance, if a training program is intended to shorten telephone calls with customers by teaching representatives how to use the firm's information systems more efficiently, tests are done to see if the length of telephone calls actually drops after the training is completed.[1] ■

"It costs ten times more to get a new customer than to maintain an existing customer. You really want to keep existing customers happy."

(Diane Durkin, president of
Loyalty Factor, a training company)*

Training and development together represent yet another major human resource function that managers need to address. American Express and most other major corporations recognize the importance of this vital human resource function. Training and development represent a fundamental investment in the employees who work for an organization, and the overall goal is to improve their ability to make contributions to the firm's effectiveness. This chapter will cover different perspectives on employee training and development. First, we outline more specifically the purposes of training and development. Next, we discuss a special form of employee training and development: new employee orientation. We examine how organizations assess their training and development needs. Then we discuss the actual development of training development programs. Training and development techniques and methods are then introduced and discussed. Finally, we look at learning and development at the organizational level, focusing on organizational development and learning.

PURPOSES OF TRAINING AND DEVELOPMENT

Employee training can be defined as a planned attempt by an organization to facilitate employee learning of job-related knowledge, skills, and behaviors. **Development**, on the other hand, usually refers to teaching managers and professionals the skills needed for both present and future jobs. Thus, each has a slightly different orientation.[2] These differences are discussed below.

The Nature of Training

Training usually involves teaching operational or technical employees how to do their jobs more effectively and/or more efficiently. Teaching telephone operators to help customers more efficiently, showing machinists the proper way to handle certain kinds of tools, and demonstrating for short-order cooks how to prepare food orders systematically are all part of training. Responsibilities for training are generally assigned to the human resource function of an organization, although many larger firms separate training departments or units within the human resource department. But in keeping with the spirit of the human resource function as a center of expertise, human resource managers in general and training managers in particular must fully integrate their activities with operating managers and units throughout the organization.

In general, training is intended to help the organization function more effectively. For example, suppose that a small manufacturing company has a workforce of machinists and other operating employees who are currently capable of working at 85 percent of plant capacity. That is, the space, equipment, and technology in the plant may be potentially capable of producing, say, 100,000 units of output per day; the existing workforce, however, can turn out only 85,000 units per day. Because of anticipated growth in product demand, managers want to be prepared to meet this demand when it occurs by boosting the plant's level of potential performance. That is, they want their workforce to be able to produce more without having to hire new employees or invest in new equipment or technology. As a first step, the organization might want to work toward achieving

■ **Employee training** is a planned attempt by an organization to facilitate employee learning of job-related knowledge, skills, and behaviors.

■ **Development** refers to teaching managers and professionals the skills needed for both present and future jobs.

95 percent of capacity—or 95,000 units per day—using existing employees and facilities. Thus, these existing employees will need to be trained in more efficient work methods, with the ultimate goal of making them more productive.

Of course, for this approach to be effective, two conditions must exist. First, managers must be relatively sure that productivity *can* be increased through training. That is, in some situations employees may already have the requisite skills to increase their productivity, but they simply do not see any reason to increase their effort enough to do so. In that case, the problem would be one of motivation, and a training program would probably not help. But if managers assume that employees are working as hard as they (reasonably) can and that they would be motivated to produce more if they knew how, training aimed at improving employee productivity would be a reasonable undertaking. The second condition is that managers should have reason to believe that productivity gains are possible with existing resources. That is, if a plant is already working at maximum efficiency—as constrained by its technology, equipment, work flow, or similar considerations—training is not likely to improve productivity.

Some training is focused on existing conditions and circumstances, as illustrated in the preceding example. That is, the training focuses on changing the behaviors of current employees as they perform their current jobs. Other training deals more specifically with accommodating changes in the work environment. For example, when new machines are placed in an organization, new software is added to computer networks, new production methods become available, and/or new organizational procedures and systems are implemented, employees must be trained in the proper use of those procedures and systems.

The Nature of Development

Rather than focusing on specific job-related skills, such as using new software or performing certain specific task and job functions, development is more generally aimed at helping managers better understand and solve problems, make decisions, and capitalize on opportunities.[3] For example, managers need to understand how to manage their time effectively. Thus, some management development programs have a component dealing with time management. Other management development programs may help managers better understand how to motivate employees (for example, to get the employees discussed above to exert extra effort). Thus, managers do not necessarily return from development programs with a specific new operational method for doing their job more effectively. Instead, they may return with new skills that may be of relevance to them in a general sense at some point in the future. They may have a better understanding of how to work more effectively, how to motivate their employees better, and how to make better decisions, and they may possess a more complete understanding of how the overall organization functions and their role within it. Development is often considered a human resource function in most organizations, but because of its strategic nature and importance, one or more senior executives are usually given specific responsibility to ensure that management development is approached systematically and comprehensively.

Learning Theory and Employee Training

Even though obvious differences exist between training and development, they nevertheless share a common underlying foundation—learning. **Learning** is a relatively permanent change in behavior or behavioral potential that results from direct or indirect experience. Technically, only individuals can learn, although we will discuss the topic of organizational learning later in the chapter. The intention of training and development, then, is for employees to learn more effective behaviors. Thus, it is necessary that managers interested in training development understand the basic fundamentals of learning theory as they apply to training and development. In addition, some organizations have begun to pay particular attention to the importance of learning in the last few years, and some have even gone so far as to attempt to redefine their organizations as learning organizations. A **learning organization** is one whose employees continuously attempt to learn new information and to use what they learn to improve product or service quality. That is, such an organization and its employees see that learning is not a discrete activity that starts and stops with the conduct of a specific training program; rather, it is an ongoing, fundamental, and continuous part of the organization and employee work relationship.[4]

Beyond this general and fundamental strategic approach to learning, however, several more specific learning techniques and principles also relate to employee training and development. These techniques and principles are illustrated in Figure 10.1. One basic learning principle has to do with motivation. Specifically, people will not learn unless they are motivated to learn. That is, the individual has to want to acquire the knowledge that the trainer or developer is attempting to impart.

Second, the learning that occurs during training and development must be reinforced in the organization. Suppose an employee learns how to do a new job in a way that takes a bit more effort but that provides a dramatic improvement in output. When the employee takes this behavior back to the workplace and attempts to put it into practice, it is helpful if the manager responsible for the employee recognizes the new behavior and provides some sort of reinforcement or reward, such as praise and positive comments. To the extent that the manager

■ **Learning** is a relatively permanent change in behavior or behavioral potential that results from direct or indirect experience.

■ A **learning organization** is one whose employees continuously attempt to learn new information and to use what they learn to improve product or service quality.

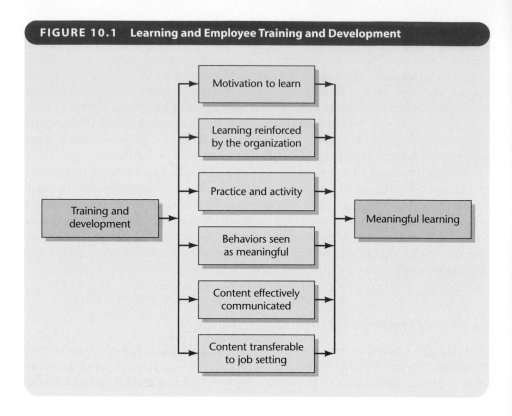

FIGURE 10.1   Learning and Employee Training and Development

ignores the new behavior or, even worse, questions or challenges it, then it will not be reinforced and will likely not be repeated in the future.[5]

Another important learning principle related to employee training and development is the notion of practice and activity. It takes time for people to internalize fully what they have learned in training and development. They need time to practice it, to use it, and to see how it affects their work performance. Once a new behavior has been learned and continues to be practiced, experts say that it has been *overlearned*. Practicing something until overlearning has occurred is a good way of ensuring that it is not forgotten, regardless of how long it has been since it was learned. This helps explain the traditional wisdom that once people learn to ride a bicycle or to swim, they never forget.

In addition, the behaviors that the individual is attempting to learn must be meaningful. That is, the individual who is undergoing the training and development must recognize the behavior and its associated information as being important and relevant to his or her job situation. Even if the material *is* meaningful and important, if this fact is not communicated effectively to the trainee, he or she will not work hard to master the material, which will presumably cause problems later. Many graduate students in business administration, for example, learn too late that it was essential to master the calculus they were taught as undergraduates.

In addition, it is important that the training materials be communicated effectively. That is, the individual must be able to receive the information being imparted and must respond favorably to that material. To a large extent, this goal depends on matching the training technique (discussed later) with the material to be transmitted. For some types of information, lectures may be quite acceptable; for others, it may be critical that some active or experiential learning be part of the training. Failure to recognize such differences, along with the inability to use the training technique in question effectively, results in major obstructions to communication of information.

Finally, the material being taught must be transferable to the job setting of the individual employee. Mastering material in a training setting is rather pointless unless the trainee can then take the material learned and apply it on the job. Two important considerations can facilitate this *transfer of training*. First, the training setting, or at least the setting in which the new behavior or skill is practiced, should resemble the actual job setting as closely as possible. Learning to assemble a piece of oil-drilling equipment in a warm, well-lit environment may not help the employee who is then asked to assemble the equipment in an Alaskan oil field during the winter. Of course, managers cannot always know all the settings in which the material will be applied, but it is nonetheless important to try to anticipate the actual conditions on the job and replicate them in training.

Training is also facilitated if the behaviors learned in training are close to those that will be required on the job. That is, it would be pointless to teach employees to do a job on one machine if they will be using a different machine that requires different procedures when they return to the job setting. In fact, this approach would result in *negative transfer,* which would interfere with performance on the job. Over time, however, machines change and so procedures learned for one machine might no longer apply if new equipment is introduced. In this situation it is important to retrain the employees to avoid problems of negative transfer.

NEW EMPLOYEE ORIENTATION

One important part of an organization's training and development program is new employee orientation. **Orientation** is the process of introducing new employees to the organization so that they can become effective contributors more quickly. Effective orientation can play a very important role in employee job satisfaction, performance, retention, and similar areas.[6] On the other hand, poor orientation can result in disenchantment, dissatisfaction, anxiety, turnover, and other employee problems.

■ **Orientation** is the process of introducing new employees to the organization so that they can become effective contributors more quickly.

Goals of Orientation

An orientation program generally has a clear and specific set of goals. One important goal is to reduce anxiety and uncertainty for new employees. When newly hired individuals come to work for the first time, they are likely to experience considerable anxiety and uncertainty. For example, they may be unfamiliar with basic issues such as how often they get paid, where the human resource department office is located, where the company cafeteria is located, where they are supposed to park, normal work hours, who will provide their job-related training, and so forth. An effective orientation program provides answers to these questions efficiently and effectively for new employees. In many organizations, new employees are briefed on their benefit options and choices and they enroll in various benefit programs during orientation.

A related goal of orientation is to ease the burden of socializing newcomers for supervisors and coworkers. In the absence of orientation, an organizational newcomer has little choice but to direct his or her questions to a supervisor or coworkers, and those individuals thus spend considerable time answering questions and providing information to new employees. Some of this informal indoctrination is inevitable, of course, and may serve the beneficial purposes of helping new people get better acquainted and integrated into their work group. But if this method were the only vehicle for orientation, supervisors and coworkers would have to spend a disproportionate amount of time answering questions. Newcomers might not always get complete or accurate answers to their questions because other employees are not likely to be completely up to date on every detail of the employment relationship with the organization.

Another goal of orientation is to provide favorable initial job experiences for new employees. In Chapter 8 we described the importance of realistic job previews as a way to avoid problems of disenchantment and disappointment when people encounter jobs that are different from what they expected. An effective orientation program can complement and reinforce this process by making sure that a new employee's initial job experiences are positive and effective. The orientation program, for example, helps newcomers feel like part of a team; allows them to become introduced to their coworkers, their supervisor, and other new employees; and in various ways eases the transition of a person from outsider to insider.

Basic Issues in Orientation

In planning an orientation for new employees, human resource managers must deal with different basic issues. These issues include the content of the orientation, the length of the orientation, and the decision about who will conduct the orientation. A sample orientation agenda showing how one company approaches these issues is depicted in Figure 10.2. The content of the orientation is of obvious importance. Most organizations try to provide their employees with a set of basic understandings of organizational policies and procedures that are relevant to that particular employee. For example, hourly workers who are expected to punch a time clock or sign a time card must be educated in how these items are handled, how to fill them out, where they are located, and so forth.

Similarly, the orientation should also provide information about issues such as hours of work, compensation, and schedules and should direct the individual to the appropriate offices and managers to answer various questions. For example, an orientation program might alert new employees to the fact that if they have a question or issue regarding potential discrimination, they should direct the question to the firm's equal employment opportunity (EEO) officer.

Some organizations also find it appropriate to include a general overview and introduction to the business itself as part of their orientation. This introduction would include information such as the firm's history, its evolution, its successes, and perhaps even some of its failures. Organizations that have a strong corporate culture are especially likely to include this information as part of the orientation process. It helps impart information quickly and efficiently about the firm's culture to its newly hired employees, which makes it easier for them to understand

FIGURE 10.2   Sample New Employee Orientation Schedule

PACIFIC LABORATORIES

A LIFE-LABS
COMPANY

9:00   Welcome and overview of the day (with refreshments)

9:30   Introduction to the company

10:00   Overview of the employment relationship
- wage and salary policies
- work schedules
- parking
- training opportunities
- performance appraisal policies
- discipline procedures
- grievance procedures

11:00   Overview of benefit options

12:00   Lunch

1:00   Benefit enrollment

2:00   Tour of the workplace

3:00   Introduction of supervisor and coworkers

that culture and know how to function within it. At Southwest Airlines, for example, newcomers used to watch a video featuring the firm's legendary chief executive officer (CEO), Herb Kelleher, welcoming them to the team and explaining the firm's approach to doing business. But the real message was perhaps best conveyed by the format of the video—Kelleher delivered his "speech" in the form of rap music, backed by a team of other Southwest employees!

In many cases, the duration or length of an orientation program is a function of what the organization intends to impart during that orientation. Obviously, the more material that it wants to convey to new employees, the longer the orientation will need to last. In some cases, a firm may attempt to handle orientation in only an hour or two. More typically, however, orientation is likely to take a half-day or perhaps even a full day. And occasionally firms may provide an initial orientation and then have a brief follow-up a few days or weeks later to answer questions or deal with remaining issues that have arisen after employees have had a brief opportunity to experience life in the organization.

Finally, the organization must decide who will conduct the orientation session. In many situations, several different individuals are part of the orientation process. For example, one or more human resource managers are likely to be involved in new employee orientation. In some cases, operating managers are also involved. Union officials are occasionally involved in orientation when a company's workers are represented by a strong labor union. Sometimes organizations use current operating employees to facilitate the orientation program as well.

Some organizations are experimenting with retired employees performing the orientation. For example, Hewlett-Packard uses retired employees to coordinate and run the orientation process in several of its manufacturing plants around the United States. The company has found this strategy to be particularly effective because it helps convey the idea to new employees that the organization must clearly be a good place to work if these individuals are willing to come back and help orient newcomers after they retire.

ASSESSING TRAINING AND DEVELOPMENT NEEDS

Orientation is generally a one-shot activity for employees. That is, they undergo orientation when they first join the organization, but then that process is complete. Beyond orientation, however, most organizations find it appropriate and effective to continue training and development on a regular basis. That is, employees must be continually trained and developed to enhance and otherwise improve the quality of the contributions they are making to the organization. The starting point is to assess training development needs. As Figure 10.3 shows, this process generally involves consideration of three issues: needs analysis, the establishment of training and development goals, and decisions regarding in-house training versus outsourced training.

Needs Analysis

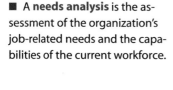

■ A **needs analysis** is the assessment of the organization's job-related needs and the capabilities of the current workforce.

The starting point in assessing training and development needs is to conduct a **needs analysis**. That is, human resource managers responsible for training and development must determine the organization's true needs vis-à-vis training. This analysis generally focuses on two issues: the organization's job-related needs and the capabilities of the current workforce. The organization's needs are determined by the nature of the work that the organization needs to have performed. That is, what knowledge, skills, and abilities must the organization's workforce have to perform the organization's work most effectively?

As part of this analysis, the manager must carefully assess the company's strategy, the resources it has available for training, and its general philosophy regarding employee training and development. By "philosophy," we mean the extent to which the organization views training as a true investment in human resources or simply as a necessity to alter or change a specific outcome or criterion measure. Workforce analysis involves a careful assessment of the capabilities, strengths, and weaknesses characterizing the organization's current workforce. That is, it is important to understand the extent to which the organization's workforce is skilled or unskilled, motivated or unmotivated, committed to the organization or not, and so forth.

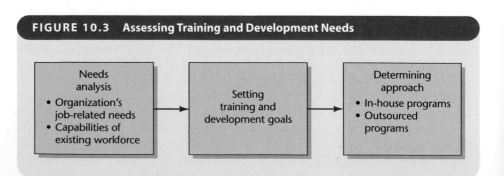

FIGURE 10.3   Assessing Training and Development Needs

Needs analysis
• Organization's job-related needs
• Capabilities of existing workforce

→ Setting training and development goals

→ Determining approach
• In-house programs
• Outsourced programs

The information for this analysis can be gathered from different sources. For example, managers may learn a great deal by observing current employees to see how they appear to be working. In addition, the manager may also ask employees directly what they view as their strengths and weaknesses and in what areas they believe further improvement is necessary. Third, the manager may ask supervisors of current employees to provide information about what training she or he would like employees to have. Fourth, the manager might also evaluate the kinds of problems and difficulties that employees encounter. For example, if the firm seems to be experiencing a lot of work-related accidents, training aimed at improving safety might be an important activity. Finally, the organization may also ask its customers to provide input vis-à-vis the kinds of training its employees need to have.

But an additional issue must be considered in determining training needs. Decisions must be made about training employees for their present jobs versus training them for the jobs they might have in the future. Obviously, the more certain we can be about those future jobs, the more attractive it might seem to provide training for those jobs. But even if we can predict future needs, arguments on both sides of this issue arise, as is illustrated in this chapter's Point/Counterpoint feature.

Setting Training and Development Goals

One of the most important steps in any program is the establishment of training and development goals. That is, for the organization to ensure that it is managing its investment properly, it is important that the organization know in advance what it expects of its employees prior to training. For example, suppose employees are producing at a level of 80 percent of capacity before training; after undergoing training designed to boost productivity, they are only producing at a level of 85 percent. An appropriate question to ask is, How effective was the training? It is surprisingly difficult to answer this question, however, if the organization had no predetermined goals or expectations. Thus, the human resource manager responsible for planning the training must look at the current state of affairs, decide what changes are necessary, and then formulate these changes into specific training development goals.

For example, consider the case of an insurance claims office. Assume that claims adjusters are processing insurance claims at an average rate of six business days per claim. Responses and feedback from customers suggest that some customers are becoming unhappy because they would like to have their claims processed more quickly. Using this information and other relevant data, the human resource manager—working in conjunction with operating managers—might decide that an appropriate and reasonable goal would be to cut the average processing time from six days down to four days. Thus, a "four-day processing average" becomes the goal of this particular training endeavor.

For some people and organizations the concept of training has moved far beyond the development of skills and competencies. For example, many professional athletes and teams are realizing the benefits of yoga training as part of their physical regimen. Tennessee Titans running back Eddie George practices yoga for physical strength, endurance, and flexibility. He has been practicing with a trainer for several years and it seems to be working for him—he has not missed a game due to injury since he started. Managers in traditional white-collar jobs are also turning to yoga as a means of relaxation to help them deal with the stress of their jobs.

POINT | COUNTERPOINT

Training for Future Jobs

We usually think about training needs in terms of present jobs, but sometimes it is possible to anticipate the needs that employees will face in the future. In these cases, it would be possible to design training programs so that they provide employees with the skills they need today *and* the skills they will need later. Problems sometimes crop up, however, with training employees in areas that will not be important for their jobs until some point in the future.

POINT... **Training programs should be designed to meet future needs as well as present needs because ...**	COUNTERPOINT... **Training programs should be designed to meet present needs only because ...**
Jobs change and old skill sets can become obsolete.	It is not always clear that an employee will remain with the organization long enough to use those additional skills.
It is easier for an employee to move up a career ladder if he or she is trained to perform all the jobs involved.	The jobs may change even more and require a different set of skills in the future.
Training for future jobs also allows maximum flexibility for staffing.	The employee can take these additional skills and move to a new organization, and *that* organization would reap the benefits.
It is simply more efficient to do all the training at one time.	An employee may have to absorb too much material at one time.

So... Clearly some risk is associated with training for future jobs. Although several potential benefits present themselves, the decision should be based on the best information possible concerning the future needs on the job, the probability that the employee will remain long enough to apply the extra training, and the chances that the extra training will make the employee more attractive to competitors.

The human resource manager should make every reasonable effort to write training program goals that are objective, verifiable, and specific. For example, a vague and general goal such as "improving employee performance" or "enhancing employee attitudes" is very difficult to evaluate. On the other hand, specific objectives and verifiable goals such as "increasing performance by 10 percent," "cutting turnover by 5 percent," "cutting customer complaints by 3 percent," and "improving accuracy or quality by 8 percent" are all likely to be effective goals for a training and development program, at least in terms of the manager's abilities to evaluate the effectiveness of the training.

In-House Versus Outsourced Programs

■ An **in-house training** or **development program** is one that is conducted on the organization's premises primarily by the organization's employees.

Another initial decision that human resource managers must make when designing training and development programs is the extent to which they want training and development to be conducted in-house or to be outsourced. We discussed the general notion of outsourcing in Chapter 1, but the decision whether to outsource each human resource function can be different. An **in-house training** or

development program is one that is conducted on the premises of the organization primarily by the organization's employees. Many larger organizations, such as Texas Instruments and ExxonMobil, have large training staffs. These training staffs consist of individuals who are familiar with the company, its jobs, and its employees. These individuals are also experts in designing and conducting training programs. Thus, the organization itself assumes the responsibility for training and developing its employees.

In-house training and development has several obvious advantages. The major advantage is that the organization can be assured that the content of its training and development efforts are precisely and specifically tailored to fit the organization's needs. That is, by definition a close working relationship exists between line managers and the training and development staff as the various training and development programs are planned and conducted for current employees. Another advantage is flexibility, particularly regarding scheduling, because the training and development programs can be taught at times that are most conducive to the organization's needs. If an employee needs to reschedule a training and development activity, it can usually be handled with relatively little difficulty.

The alternative approach of training and development is to use an outsourcing strategy. An **outsourced training** or **development program** is one that involves having people from outside the organization perform the training. Perhaps employees are sent to training and development programs at colleges and universities, a consulting firm's headquarters, or similar locations. The primary advantage of outsourced programs is cost. Because the organization does not have to maintain its own training and development staff or even its own training and development facilities, it can deliver training and development at a cost that is typically lower than would be possible if it were doing the training and development itself.

Another advantage is quality assurance. While an organization has reasonable control over its own training and development staff, it is still possible that the individuals who are assigned the responsibility of doing the training and development might not be particularly skilled trainers or educators. Thus, the effectiveness of the training and development effort might be compromised. Professional trainers, however, are almost always highly trained themselves and are also skilled educators. On the other hand, outsourced programs may be more general and even generic, and thus have less applicability and direct relevance to the organization's needs.

Most small to midsized firms rely strictly on in-house or outsourced training. Most large organizations, however, are likely to rely on a combination of in-house and outsourced training. For example, even firms like ExxonMobil that have a large in-house training and development operation are still likely to use outside trainers and developers occasionally to assist in specialized areas. And some firms are even experimenting with outsourced training provided solely in-house. That is, an independent contractor, usually a consulting firm, may take over a company's training and development function but continue to operate and conduct the training inside the company.

Finally, a special form of outsourced training and development involves partnerships between business and education. Many leading business schools such as Harvard, Northwestern, and Michigan run highly regarded management development programs that attract participants from major corporations around the

■ An **outsourced training** or **development program** is one that involves having people from outside the organization perform the training.

world. These programs may be generic, customized by industry or firm size, or even created for a single company. Many other major public and private universities also offer various programs of this type for business. And even regional schools and community colleges are moving into this area by providing basic training and development for first-line supervisors and entry-level technical employees.[7]

DESIGNING TRAINING AND DEVELOPMENT PROGRAMS

The actual design of programs, of course, is the foundation to effective training and development. Without solid and relevant content, training and development efforts are pointless. The usual approach to content development starts with outlining program content, then expanding that outline into fully formed programs. Selecting the most appropriate instructors completes the process.

Outlining and Defining Training and Development Program Content

The first step in creating training and development programs is to write a detailed outline of the intended program.[8] This outline should include topics such as a recapitulation of the training objectives, a specification of the intended audience for the training, a specification of the proposed content of the training, and estimates of the amount of time necessary to conduct the training. In addition, the outline should specify topics such as evaluation criteria, cost estimates, and whether the training can be conducted in-house or should be outsourced.

Once the training and development program has been outlined, the next step is to define its content. The definition of content would seem, at a superficial level, to be a relatively straightforward undertaking. In reality, however, defining the content of a training and development program is both extremely important and quite difficult. Simply stated, the content of a training and development program specifies the material that is intended to be taught. An example of how training and development programs are outlined and the content specified for managers heading for international assignments is described in HR Around the Globe.

Another way to approach this issue is to focus on what is to be learned. For example, consider a training and development program designed to prepare employees to use a certain word-processing package. The content specification would need to describe fully those parts of the word-processing package that are intended to be taught. Thus, the definition should specify all the parameters of the program, including what kinds of machines are appropriate, intended uses of the software, and the indicators that provide an assessment of the degree of mastery of the material.

From the perspective of what is to be learned, however, we get a much different picture. Before discussing the word-processing example from this viewpoint, it is helpful to consider a model of instructional content that was originally proposed several years ago.[9] The learning categories proposed by Robert M. Gagne are presented in Table 10.1 on page 334.

Using this framework, the learning goals of the training program for word processing would include the intellectual skills needed to understand how the

HR Around the Globe

Teaching Language Skills for a Global Workforce

Defining content is a critical part of training and development. One of the fastest growing areas of training and development today involves language skills. Because of the burgeoning global marketplace and the blurring of national boundaries, more and more companies are finding it necessary to provide language training for managers assigned to posts in foreign countries. If a U.S. company is sending a manager to work in Canada, Australia, or South Africa, language is generally not a problem. But if the manager is being sent to China, Brazil, or France, language suddenly becomes a major issue.

"We're confident you'll be able to master Chinese in the six months before you leave."

(Unidentified vice president of a Midwest industrial company, speaking to a plant manager)*

In the case of language training, of course, defining content is relatively straightforward—the content of the training consists of skills in the language that needs to be learned. Thus, the content of the language training for a manager being sent to Germany is the German language itself. It is generally useful, however, to establish more specific content guidelines than simply the language itself. For example, it is almost always easier to teach reading and writing language skills than to teach verbal skills. Depending on the nature of the work assignment, training content in this case may be further specified as including reading, writing, and/or verbal language skills.

It is also generally useful to take the situation into account. For example, if a manager is being sent for a short-term assignment to a foreign operation that is already well established and that is fully staffed by local managers, language skills may be less important than if the manager is being sent for a long-term assignment to launch a new operation where it will be necessary to interact with local government and labor officials. Thus, consideration should be given to the degree of fluency needed. Similarly, human resource managers defining training content for managers being sent abroad will likely need to look beyond language skills per se and also provide training about local customs and related lifestyle issues, and they may also include the manager's family in the training program.

Human resource managers must also avoid taking an overly simplistic approach to defining content for language training. For example, simply defining training content as Chinese isn't nearly precise enough because dozens of different dialects are spoken within mainland China. It is quite important, therefore, to know exactly where in China a manager is being sent. And even languages such as English may not be as straightforward as one might think. For example, while managers in the United States take "elevators" in their buildings, ship their products on "trucks," check the oil in their cars by looking under the "hood," and snack on "potato chips," their British counterparts use "lifts" to travel between floors, ship products on "lorrles," look under the "bonnet," and munch on "crisps."

Sources: John Freivalds, "Self-Study Programs Aid Language Training," *HRMagazine*, January 1997, pp. 57–60 (*quote on p. 57).

---

software will be used, the cognitive strategies needed to know how to apply the knowledge about the programs, and the motor skills needed to operate the machines. Therefore, when designing training programs, it is useful to approach the design both from the perspective of what is to be taught as well as from the perspective of what is to be learned.

Of course, more complex training and development programs require a more complex definition of content and of learning goals. For example, a program aimed at enhancing the decision-making capabilities of managers would need to specify fully the range of decisions that must be addressed, the circumstances under which those decisions are most likely to be made, and various other factors associated with the decision-making process. Because decision making is an

TABLE 10.1 Gagne's Learning Categories

1. *Intellectual skills* include concepts, rules, and procedures; they are often referred to as *procedural knowledge*.

2. *Verbal information* enables the individual to state something about a subject; it is also referred to as *declarative information*.

3. *Cognitive strategies* enable a learner to know when and how to use intellectual skills and verbal information.

4. *Motor skills* include basic human physical activities such as writing, lifting, and using tools.

5. *Attitudes* are learned preferences for different activities.

Source: Robert M. Gagne, "Learning Outcomes and Their Effects: Useful Categories of Human Performance," *American Psychologist,* 1984, Vol. 39, pp. 377–385.

inherently more complex undertaking than using a particular piece of software, the content of such a program would need to be more abstract and to tap into a higher level of cognitive ability.

Selecting Training and Development Instructors

Another important aspect of creating training and development programs is the selection of instructors to deliver the material. Effective instruction is an important ingredient in the success of any training and development program. Effective instructors are those individuals who deliver the content of a training or development program so that learning is facilitated; ineffective instructors, in contrast, serve as barriers or impediments to learning.

The most common choices regarding instructors are whether to use full-time professional trainers (who might be hired from an external firm or are part of an in-house training staff) or to use operating managers. The primary advantage to using operating managers or related employees is expertise. These individuals presumably understand the organization and the task to be performed and are thus extremely qualified to present instructional material aimed at those skills and requirements. On the other hand, such individuals, while they may be experts on the task to be taught, may be poorly trained as instructors. Thus, they may do a poor job of developing training materials, may not be able to deliver those materials effectively, and may otherwise do an inadequate job of classroom instruction.

The other choice is to use a professional trainer. The primary advantage of this approach is that professional trainers are likely to be qualified instructors. They understand the importance of instructional goals, can deliver the material in an effective and interesting manner, and are otherwise capable of facilitating the learning process. On the other hand, these individuals may lack the technical expertise associated with the task being taught. Thus, while they might be able to deliver the material in a straightforward manner, they may be inadequately prepared to answer in-depth questions or to deal with unexpected issues that might arise during the training program.

TRAINING AND DEVELOPMENT TECHNIQUES AND METHODS

Depending on both the content of the program and the instructor(s) selected to present it, several techniques and methods can be used for the delivery of information. We examine some of the more popular techniques in this section.

Work-Based Programs

One major family of training and development techniques and methods consists of various work-based programs. **Work-based programs** tie the training and development activities directly to performance of the tasks. The most common method of work-based training is **on-the-job training**. Some experts suggest that as much as 60 percent of training in the United States occurs on the job. In this situation, the employee works in the actual job situation and is shown how to perform the task more effectively by the supervisor or a current experienced employee.

The primary advantage of on-the-job training is that the organization begins to achieve a return on the labor cost of the employee almost immediately, assuming that the individual is capable of performing at a minimal level of competency. The employee is learning the task itself; thus, he or she should become increasingly proficient with practice and avoid problems of learning transfer. Finally, direct training costs may be lower because the organization may not need to hire dedicated trainers or send employees to training programs.[10]

On-the-job training has some disadvantages, however. One significant disadvantage is that the employee may learn only a relatively narrow approach to performing the task. That is, she or he may be able to master task performance precisely as it is being taught by the other employee, but she or he may be unable to generalize or to extend performance to other tasks or to other job settings in the organization because only the narrowly defined task is being learned.[11] This problem can be addressed if the training is combined with a rotation plan, which is discussed below. In a related vein, the individual being trained is also likely to pick up the bad habits and less effective performance techniques that might be inherent in the performance of the employee or supervisor doing the training.

Another disadvantage of on-the-job training is the potential cost to the organization of having work performed by an inexperienced employee. For example, in a restaurant, an inexperienced waitperson who is being trained through on-the-job methods may deliver poor-quality service to customers and consequently hurt the restaurant's reputation.

Another work-based program for training is apprenticeship training. **Apprenticeship** involves a combination of on-the-job training and classroom instruction.

■ **Work-based programs** tie the training and development activities directly to the performance of the task.

■ **On-the-job training**, the most common method of work-based training, involves having employees learn their job while they are actually performing it.

■ **Apprenticeship** involves a combination of on-the-job and classroom instruction.

In most cases, formal apprenticeship programs involve a coordinated effort by the employing organization, trainers in the workplace, one or more government agencies, and a skilled trade union. The government regulates apprenticeship programs closely. In general, an apprentice entering a particular occupation must agree to a period of training and learning that may take as little as two years or as much as ten years.

For example, the job of an electrician is usually learned through a period of four to five years of apprenticeship. During this period, the individual works under the tutelage of a licensed or master worker. The licensed or master worker earns a predetermined level of compensation, while the apprentice earns a lower wage. At the end of the formally defined apprenticeship program, the apprentice takes a test or must pass other qualifications to achieve his or her own license or certificate of mastery.

Another work-based program for training and development is vestibule training. **Vestibule training** involves a work-simulation situation in which the job is performed under a condition that closely simulates the real work environment. For example, a recent American Airlines television commercial portrays airline pilots regularly reporting to a flight simulator for updating and assessment. This ad shows a form of vestibule training because the flight simulator is designed to resemble as closely as possible the actual cockpit of a jet. Similarly, machine operators might be trained by using simulated equipment that is comparable to what they would use in the actual job setting.

Another work-based training program is **systematic job rotation and transfer**. This method is most likely to be used for lower-level managers or for operating employees being groomed for promotion to a supervisory management position. As the term suggests, the employee is systematically rotated or transferred from one job to another. The employee is supposed to learn a wider array of tasks and abilities and to develop a more integrative perspective on the overall task or work of the organization or the particular subunit.

Instructional-Based Programs

The second major family of training and development techniques and methods involves various **instructional-based programs**. The most commonly used instructional-based program is the **lecture or discussion approach**. In these situations, a trainer presents the material to those attending the program in a lecture format. Just as a college professor presents lectures to her or his students, a trainer in the organization lectures and presents the material to the trainees. Depending on the situation and the size of the training class, this method may be a pure lecture, or a discussion with the various trainees in attendance at the session may also occur. Sometimes the lectures may be videotaped or audiotaped, allowing various individuals in the organization to receive the same training at different times and/or at different locations. Although lectures continue to play a role in most training programs, there is evidence that their use has been declining, and they are being replaced with training outside the classroom, primarily using electronic technologies.[12]

Southwest Airlines uses lecture and discussion training programs to help its reservations specialists cope with new federal guidelines regarding food allergies. The U.S. Department of Transportation has been pressuring airlines to accommodate passengers with certain food-related allergies, especially allergies

■ **Vestibule training** involves a work-simulation situation in which the job is performed under a condition that closely simulates the real work environment.

■ **Systematic job rotation and transfer** involves the employee being systematically rotated or transferred from one job to another.

■ **Instructional-based programs** approach training and development from a teaching and learning perspective.

■ The **lecture or discussion approach** involves a trainer presenting the material to those attending the program of the trainees in a descriptive fashion.

involving peanuts. Although such allergies are rare, they are dangerous. Southwest Airlines decided to use lecture and discussion training programs because they seemed to be the most cost-effective.[13]

Another instructional-based program for training and development is **computer-assisted instruction**. In this situation, a trainee sits at a personal computer and operates software that has been developed specifically to impart certain material to the individual. A keyboard or mouse is used by the individual trainee to interface with the computer. The training materials themselves are stored on the computer's hard drive, a CD-ROM, or a website. One major advantage of this method is that it allows self-paced learning, and immediate feedback can be given to the trainee.[14] HR in the 21st Century provides an example of how one firm uses this approach. It is likely that the market for computer-based and web-based training will continue to grow dramatically. A recent study predicted that the market for this type of training, in the U.S., should grow from approximately $2 billion in 2000, to almost $15 billion by 2004.[15]

Another method that involves basic instruction as a training device is **programmed instruction**. In this instance, the material to be learned is prepared in a manual or training booklet. The individual takes the manual or booklet and studies at his or her own pace. Generally a series of self-assessments follow each section or chapter in the training materials, and the individual can thus self-test her or his learning. Of course, a more formalized testing or assessment system is commonly used at the completion of the training. (We should note that programmed instruction is increasingly being computerized. However, it remains distinguished from computer-assisted instruction per se in terms of both complexity and sophistication.)

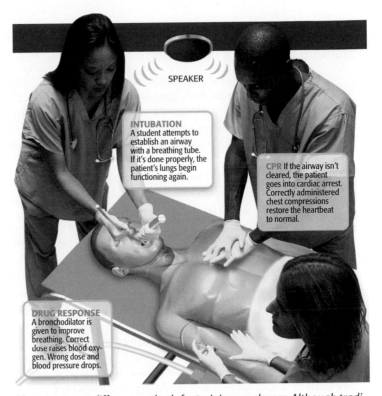

SPEAKER

INTUBATION
A student attempts to establish an airway with a breathing tube. If it's done properly, the patient's lungs begin functioning again.

CPR If the airway isn't cleared, the patient goes into cardiac arrest. Correctly administered chest compressions restore the heartbeat to normal.

DRUG RESPONSE
A bronchodilator is given to improve breathing. Correct dose raises blood oxygen. Wrong dose and blood pressure drops.

There are many different methods for training employees. Although traditional methods such as lecture can be effective, many organizations are moving toward more innovative and engaging ways to train employees. UCLA's Medical Center has begun using "The Human Patient Simulator" to train first year medical school students in crisis management. Here, students practice working on a "patient" with a blocked airway. The simulator is programmed to respond the same way a living person would, and the system tracks the students' decisions during treatment. In addition, the entire procedure is observed by a supervisor and videotaped. After the "crisis" is over, the training supervisor reviews the tape with the students to critique their performance and offer suggestions for improvement.

■ In **computer-assisted instruction,** a trainee sits at a personal computer and operates software that has been developed specifically to impart certain information to the individual.

■ In **programmed instruction,** the material to be learned is prepared in a manual or training booklet; the individual takes the manual or booklet and studies at his or her own pace.

Training Technology

In recent years the technology used for training has changed dramatically. Up until just a few years ago, almost all training involved paper and pencil, individual instruction, and mechanical reproduction of tasks. In recent years, however, new technology has reshaped the way many companies deliver training to their employees. As already noted, for example, computer-assisted instruction has become more popular in recent years. Obviously, computer-assisted instruction was impossible before the advent of computers. Indeed, it has only been within the

HR in the 21st Century

Training for the MTV Generation

Marc Prensky, vice president of human resources for Bankers Trust, had a problem. For as long as anyone could remember, the firm's derivative traders were trained by studying two-inch thick manuals and sitting through endless dry lectures and videos. But the firm's newest and youngest traders balked at this approach, using every excuse in the book to skip training sessions or leaving halfway through. Finally, Prensky hit upon the answer—because the firm's young traders had grown up as part of the MTV and video-game generation, why not use a new approach to training that would be more exciting to the traders?

After getting enthusiastic approval from top management, Prensky assembled a team and went to work. Soon, they had replaced Bankers Trust's traditional training materials and methods with a new set of materials, including board games and online quizzes using contemporary and sometimes even irreverent language and graphics. But the centerpiece of the new training model is a computer game called Straight Shooter!, patterned after the enormously popular video game Doom.

In Straight Shooter!, participants travel in cyberspace from New York to London to Hong Kong. They navigate around an electronic world filled with menacing characters (bulls and bears in New York, werewolves in London, tigers in Hong Kong) representing problems and uncer-

"In effect, we gave them depressants and then we wondered why they were bored."

(Marc Prensky, Bankers Trust vice president of human resources)*

tainties. The traders destroy the problems, resolve the uncertainties, and earn points by shooting dartlike "ideas" from their cell phones.

After players earn enough points, they encounter prospective investors who ask them questions and pose investment problems. If the trader can answer the questions and solve the problems correctly using the firm's preferred methods, the investor becomes a client and the trader earns more points. But when traders make mistakes, they may be fined or told by the investor, "Go back to business school" or "Don't call me, I'll call you." As traders earn certification, they begin competing with their colleagues around the world in an even more advanced version of the game.

Prensky says that the new training methods have been enormously successful. The derivative traders who have participated rave about both the fun and the value of the training. In addition, Bankers Trust finds this training method faster and cheaper than the previous approach. Indeed, Prensky's only real questions are, Why didn't the firm think of this approach sooner? and Why aren't more companies doing the same thing?

Sources: Jeffrey Rothfeder, "Training the 'Twitch' Generation," *Executive Edge,* September 1998, pp. 30–36; Mark Bernstein, "The Virtual Classroom: A Promising Solution for Teaching Technology," *HRMagazine,* May 1998, pp. 30–34+; "Training Takes a Front Seat at Offices," *USA Today,* January 19, 1999, p. 6B.

last few years, with the widespread adoption of personal computers, that computer-assisted instruction has become widely used.[16]

Video teleconferencing is also increasingly useful to companies. A trainer in a centralized location delivers material live via satellite hookup to remote sites in different locations; the training can thus be delivered effectively but without the travel costs necessary in transporting people to a common training site. In the early days of video teleconferencing, communication tended to be one-way. That is, the trainer presenting the material and those trainees in attendance simply saw the material being presented on a monitor. Now, however, considerably more interaction exists between trainers and trainees. The trainees usually have the capability of verbal interaction or electronic interaction via a keypad.

Another new method of training technology is interactive video. Interactive video is essentially a combination of standard video and computer-based instruction. The material is presented via video technology on a monitor from a central serving mechanism, DVD, CD-ROM, or website. The trainee interacts with the system via a mouse or keyboard. Feedback can be provided when inadequate responses or improper answers are given, and the trainee can skip material that has already been learned.

The final new aspect of training that has become increasingly popular in recent years is various team-building and group-based methods of training. Because more and more organizations are using teams as a basis for getting work done, many companies are finding it effective to develop training programs specifically designed to facilitate cooperation among the members of a team. One popular approach involves various outdoor training exercises. For example, some company programs involve a group going through a physical obstacle course using ropes, climbing, crawling, and other physical activities. Outward Bound and several other independent companies specialize in offering these kinds of programs, and their clients include firms such as General Foods, Xerox, and Burger King.[17]

A recent extension of this model involves other team-based activities such as cooking classes.[18] Wells Fargo Bank and Genentech are among the firms using this approach. Regardless of the actual task or setting, these activities are structured so that each person can be more effective with the aid of the other group members. The idea is that group members learn to trust one another and to perform more effectively together.[19] Of course, as shown in The Lighter Side of HR, not all employees see the value of these approaches!

The Lighter Side of HR

Team-building exercises centered around outdoor activity courses are popular today. The idea is that a company can send a group of employees to these programs and they can participate in various activities, all intended to help the group become a more cohesive team. Each person presumably learns to trust his or her teammates and to understand better the importance of working together. As illustrated in this cartoon, if such programs are to have any real chance for success, both the manager who plans the activity and the team members who will participate must agree on both the goals and the potential value of the programs.

MANAGEMENT DEVELOPMENT

While training and management development have the same basic goal of learning, they have significant differences. In this section we focus more specifically on management development needs and techniques.

Special Needs for Management Development

Many of the training and development issues and topics covered up to this point are applicable to both standard training and development programs. Management development has some specialized needs. Recall from our earlier discussion that management development involves more generalized training for future managerial roles and positions in the organization, as opposed to specific and immediately relevant tasks. Thus, rather than attending a single training program, managers may need to participate in different programs that span a long time.

In general, management development may also be subject to somewhat different opportunities and limitations regarding materials, training methods, and modes of instruction. For example, while the lecture method of instruction might be effective for certain kinds of learning and training activities, it is much less likely to be effective if the effort is designed to help managers learn how to make more accurate decisions. Thus, the learner needs to be a more active participant in a development program than is the case for many training programs.[20]

Special Techniques for Management Development

Several specialized techniques are widely used for management development. One method or technique for management development is the so-called *in-basket exercise*. In an in-basket exercise, the individual is confronted with a hypothetical in-basket of letters, memos, reports, phone messages, and e-mail messages associated with a particular manager. The individual trainee must then play the role of that manager by reading and evaluating each of the materials, jotting down how he or she would handle each one, and prioritizing them. Useful feedback can then be given to help the trainee understand correct and incorrect prioritization and time-management efforts on the individual's part.

Another popular management development technique is the *leaderless group exercise*. In this situation, a group of trainees are placed together in a group setting and told to make a decision or solve a problem. No individual in the group, however, is appointed as the chair or group leader. It is up to the group itself to realize that a leader must be appointed; then it is up to that individual to initiate the leadership actions appropriate for helping a group accomplish its goal effectively.

ORGANIZATIONAL DEVELOPMENT AND LEARNING

As noted earlier in the chapter, learning is a process that occurs only at the level of the individual. That is, technically, only individuals can change or learn, and so it makes little sense to talk about these phenomena at any other level. But, in fact, there are some processes that can occur at the level of the organization that are related to learning and development. Although the actual changes involved may take place in individuals, collections of individuals can change in such a way that it does make sense to talk about learning and development at the organizational level as well. We will begin with a discussion of organizational development since this involves the use of techniques that are similar to those discussed above.

Organization Development

A special form of management training that some organizations use extensively is organization development. Organization development is generally targeted at changing attitudes, perceptions, behaviors, and expectations. **Organization development** is an effort that is planned systemwide and managed from the top of the organization to increase its overall performance through planned interventions; the technique relies heavily on behavioral science technology. Note that, although organization development targets the individual, the purpose of these programs is to ultimately change the way the entire organization operates.

Organization development (OD, as it is popularly called) assumes that employees have a desire to grow and to develop, that they have a strong need to be accepted by others in the organization, and that the organization itself and the way it is designed will influence the way individuals and groups within the organization behave. As a result, collaboration between managers and employees is necessary to take advantage of the skills and abilities of the employees and to eliminate aspects of the organization that limit employee growth, development, and group acceptance. OD is a personal experience; as a result, large organizations that want to use OD generally have one or more full-time OD consultants to implement and manage their OD programs.

Different OD techniques are widely used. *Diagnostic OD* activities involve the analysis of current conditions in an organization using questionnaires, opinion or attitude surveys, interviews, and meetings. The results of this diagnosis generate a profile of the organization that is used to identify problem areas in need of correction.

Survey feedback OD involves having employees respond to questionnaires that measure perceptions and attitudes such as job satisfaction and assessments of supervisory style. Everyone involved in the survey, including the supervisor, then receives the survey results. The purpose of this approach is usually to change the behavior of supervisors by demonstrating for them how their subordinates view them. After the feedback has been provided, it is common to conduct workshops to help evaluate results and to suggest constructive changes.

Sometimes OD is undertaken to solve specific problems, such as interpersonal conflict in the organization. *Third-party peacemaking,* for example, is a common OD technique with this goal. A third party, often an external OD consultant, comes into the organization, listens to both sides of the issues, and helps the parties arrive at a mutually satisfactory solution or agreement. Different negotiation and communications have become popular in this approach. These include instructing people on "win-win" negotiation techniques (also known as integrative bargaining), where both sides can gain valued outcomes, and active listening, where participants are trained to pay attention to nonverbal as well as verbal communications.

Another common OD technique is called *process consultation*. In process consultation, the OD consultant observes managers in the organization to

■ **Organization development** is an effort that is planned systemwide and managed from the top of the organization to increase the organization's overall performance through planned interventions; the technique relies heavily on behavioral science technology.

develop an understanding of their communication patterns, decision-making and leadership processes, and methods of cooperation and conflict resolution. The consultant then provides feedback to the involved parties about the processes she or he has observed. The goal of this approach is to improve the observed processes, but it has, at times, led to criticism of this type of training. The issue is whether or not improved communication processes are a worthwhile goal in their own right. Although we will touch on this issue again in the next section, it is worth noting here as well. In any event, for quite a few years, some have argued that, while these programs are often successful at changing communication patterns, they rarely lead to any improvement in organizational effectiveness.[21]

Organizational Learning

Organizational learning refers to a process rather than to a technique or set of techniques. **Organizational learning** refers to the process by which an organization "learns" from past mistakes and adapts to its environment. Over time, rules and procedures change based on experience, but this change is still based on individual learning. That is, individuals learn how to adapt and change, and then interact with each other, so that the new information gained can be shared and distributed throughout the organization. As a result, a shared vision and interpretation of the information is developed throughout the organization, and the change permeates the entire organization. At this point the organization can be said to have "learned" how to be more effective.

A few points are important to remember. First, the process begins with individual learning and change. If there is no individual learning, there can be no organizational learning. Second, whereas the individual learning process is a cognitive one, organizational learning depends more upon social processes and sharing of information. Thus, individual learning is a necessary but not sufficient condition for organizational learning to occur.[22]

The process of organizational learning, then, involves the acquisition of new knowledge by the organization. Again, it is not enough that individuals acquire this knowledge. They must then communicate with other organizational members to insure that this knowledge is available throughout the organization. And the organization must use this information to adapt. There is a strong belief that organizations that can manage this change—that is, organizations that can acquire information and adapt—can gain significant competitive advantage versus their competitors.[23]

For example, large conglomerates such as General Electric or Viacom typically grow by acquiring other firms. Each time these firms make an acquisition, they must figure out how to best integrate the new employees into the firm, and how to marry the culture of the acquired firm with the culture of the parent firm. Presumably, these large conglomerates made mistakes over the years in both the targets for their acquisitions, and how they managed the acquisition after it was completed. But they also probably learned from their experience and got better at it over time. This is a case of organizational learning and, learning how to better target and manage acquisitions would clearly give the conglomerate an advantage over its competitors.

Furthermore, a firm can gain important new knowledge as a result of a merger or acquisition. Thus, for example, a large firm may be contemplating entering a new market in China, but the firm lacks the expertise (or knowledge) on

■ **Organizational learning** refers to the process by which an organization "learns" from past mistakes and adapts to its environment.

how to enter that difficult market successfully. The large firm (Company A) could acquire the needed information by sending key employees to some source where they can learn the needed skills, or it can acquire those skills directly by acquiring individuals who already possess the needed skills. That is, the large firm can look for another firm (Company B) that has already mastered the China market. Then Company A can either try to hire the experts away from Company B or, if the expert knowledge is widely held throughout the Company B, it can access the expertise throughout the firm via a merger, a joint venture, or a complete acquisition of Firm B.

Finally, we should note the concept of organizational memory and the role it plays in organizational learning. **Organizational memory** refers to the collective, institutional record of past events. In order for an organization to "learn" from past events, it must be possible to "recall" those events in some way. Some of these things are written down or stored electronically, so that there is a physical record of the events surrounding a recent merger, or some change in legislation, or any other event from which someone might learn a lesson. These physical records then serve as the organizational memory. But there are also many cases where this information is not formally recorded. Instead, one or more people, who were there when the event happened, become the organizational memory. These individuals are the repository for information that can help the organization to learn from experience and to avoid repeating mistakes.

■ **Organizational memory** refers to the collective, institutional record of past events.

Thus, there are a variety of ways through which an organization can gain access to new information. Once this information is shared and distributed throughout the organization so that all employees now share a view of what this information means and how it can be used to change, organizational learning is said to have occurred. When this information, and its interpretation also become part of the organizational memory, change and adaptation can continue for some time. This type of learning, and the adaptation that it involves, will clearly be critical to firms as they try to compete effectively in the twenty-first century.

EVALUATING TRAINING AND DEVELOPMENT

While it is common to evaluate all elements of human resource management, the evaluation of training and development has perhaps the longest history and is among the most important. Unlike many other aspects of human resource management, the evaluation of training and development is comparatively easy. That is, because the purpose of training and development is to enact a fundamental change in performance behavior or other outcome variable, the intent and outcome of the training and development program should be amenable to a clear assessment and evaluation.[24]

For example, consider the case of a routine training program for an organization that has recently bought new copy machines for its administrative facilities. The training program might be conducted to teach all relevant employees how the copy equipment works. For example, it would be useful to know how to change paper and toner cartridges, how to set the machine for various jobs, and how to do routine problem solving and troubleshooting in case of a minor machine malfunction. Assuming that the training program has been properly

Does training employees pay off? The answer is certainly "yes." In fact, the cost of not training employees can be very high. Tom Farmer arrived at a hotel where he had a "guaranteed" reservation. It was two o'clock in the morning and the hotel was fully booked, leaving Farmer without a room. He insisted that the hotel clerk find him another room, but the clerk refused. When he returned home, Farmer sent an e-mail message to the hotel manager and to some of his friends. He named the hotel and stated simply "Yours is a very bad hotel." Within days the e-mail was being forwarded around the world, and the hotel chain's executives were extremely concerned. They contacted Farmer and asked what they could do. His response was simple: "Train your hotel's workers."

designed (that is, instructional goals and content have been clearly specified), then it should be a relatively straightforward undertaking to determine whether or not the training has worked. Thus, when the training program has been completed, all target employees should be able to demonstrate that they are capable of changing paper and toner cartridges and so forth. Asking individuals to perform this task under the supervision of the trainer should provide a clear indication of the success (or lack thereof) of the training program.

Several issues must be understood, however. The most fundamental issue has to do with being able to assess change. Thus, it is important to understand a priori what behaviors and skills currently exist so that the evaluator will be able to determine whether or not changes have been effected. For example, if the evaluator wants to know if training has enhanced an employee's ability to operate a particular piece of equipment at a faster pace, it is necessary to have some basis for understanding the pretraining level of performance. Thus, some premeasure is generally necessary. Premeasures are taken before the training program begins. After the training, the same variables are measured again. Statistically significant positive changes are usually understood to indicate that the training program has resulted in the appropriate outcome.

Evaluating management development programs is also important, but this kind of evaluation is a bit more complex. Because the development program is intended to prepare managers for future jobs, the payoff or outcome of specific development programs may take an extended period of time to manifest itself. Management development programs also tend to have more complex goals in terms of what is to be learned than do more basic types of training programs. Nevertheless, the organization should not let this difficulty keep it from attempting to evaluate management development programs.

Organizations often take several approaches when trying to evaluate these programs. Organizations can rely on evaluations completed by the trainees after a particular training program. This practice is common even when other evaluation techniques are used because it is always useful to know how participants reacted to the training. Therefore, following the training, an organization might have the trainees in a management development program complete an instrument on which they indicate the extent to which they found the program to be useful, relevant, interesting, appropriate, and so forth.

A confound in this method, however, is that it is subject to bias based in part on the nature of the experience the trainees received as opposed to the content of the experience itself. For example, if the trainer was amusing, humorous, and well organized and thus made the session interesting, positive bias may show up in the evaluation, even though the content of the training program may have been inadequate. On the other hand, an individual may have delivered an effective training program but received less positive evaluations because she or he was less interesting or didn't have as much "pizzazz" in the program.

Even if this potential bias does not affect the responses of trainees, this approach to evaluation has an additional and perhaps more serious limitation. Whether or not the participants feel the content of the training program is adequate may have little impact on whether they actually change the way they behave on the job. Thus, trainees might be extremely pleased with the training program and how it was delivered, but because of problems with design or other conditions on the job, the training may still have no detectable impact on their behavior. Even if behavior does change in an area such as communication patterns with subordinates, this change may still not address the longer-term needs of the organization when it instituted the management development program.

Ultimately, the evaluation of management development needs to focus on overall organizational effectiveness. For example, if an organization institutes a management development program that focuses on communication skills, it would be beneficial if the participants reported that the training was useful. It would also be beneficial if fewer arguments were observed and fewer subordinates filed grievances based on interactions with managers. But the ultimate test of the effectiveness of the program would be if these changes resulted in lower turnover rates among employees who were now more satisfied with their supervisors and were perhaps more willing to exert effort on the job for those supervisors.

We will consider one final point in the evaluation (and to some extent, in the design) of training programs. All training content can be characterized as being either *specific* or *general* in content. **General training** involves providing trainees with skills and abilities that can be applied in any organization. Examples would be sending a management employee to a program designed to improve writing skills or to a general-education program that provides the manager with a skill or with some information that he or she can carry to any other organization. In fact, the manager is now "worth" more to other organizations because of this training. As a result, turnover rates often rise when organizations provide general training. Therefore, although the development program may be accomplishing the goals set out by the organization (i.e., improving communication patterns), it might hurt long-term effectiveness by resulting in other firms hiring valued employees away from the organization.

Specific training makes turnover more difficult. In these cases, the organization provides the manager (or other employee) with skills or information that is of use only to the present organization. For example, training a manager to use the new accounting procedure introduced in the organization will not make that manager more attractive to a competing firm. In Chapter 11 we discuss recent trends towards skill- and knowledge-based pay in organizations. An organization embarking on and designing training to support such a program should consider the potential costs associated with providing general training as opposed to the costs of designing specific training programs and rewarding employees for acquiring specific skills (even if those specific skills might be less critical in the future).

Some organizations rely indirectly on other firms to do their management development for them. That is, some firms, such as General Electric, Arthur Andersen,

■ **General training** involves providing trainees with skills and abilities that can be applied in any organization.

■ **Specific training** involves providing the trainee with skills or information that is of use only to the present organization.

and Motorola, are known in their respective industries to be outstanding developers of management talent. Thus, other organizations may look to these firms as a source of professionally groomed and developed managers. Instead of doing their own management development work, an organization might allow other firms to do it for them and then hire managers away once they have reached a certain point in the organization. Thus, the "training" organization bears the costs of the training and some of the benefits; the "other" organization may have to pay more to lure away the needed management talent, but it is able to reap many of the benefits without incurring any of the direct costs of the training.

Chapter Summary

Training usually involves teaching operational or technical employees how to do the jobs for which they were hired more effectively and/or more efficiently. Development is more generally aimed at helping managers better understand and solve problems, make decisions, and capitalize on opportunities. Learning is fundamental to both, however, and must always be considered when planning, conducting, and evaluating training and development programs and activities.

One important part of an organization's training and development program is new employee orientation. An orientation program generally has a clear and specific set of goals. In planning an orientation for new employees, human resource managers must deal with various basic issues, including the content of the orientation, the length of the orientation, and the decision about who will actually conduct the orientation.

The starting point in employee training per se is to assess training and development needs. This process generally involves the consideration of three factors: needs analysis, the establishment of training and development goals, and decisions regarding in-house training versus outsourced training and development.

The actual design of programs is the foundation for effective training and development. The first step in creating training and development programs is to write a detailed outline of the intended program. The

next step in the development of the program is to define its content and focus on what is to be learned. Finally, the organization must select instructors to deliver the material.

Several techniques and methods can be used for the delivery of information. Work-based programs tie the training and development activities directly to performance of the task. The second major family of training and development techniques and methods involves various instructional-based programs. New technology also plays a key role in training and development today.

Management development programs have specialized needs. In general, management development may also be subject to somewhat different opportunities and limitations regarding materials, training methods, and modes of instruction. Several specialized techniques are also widely used for management development. A special form of management training that some organizations use extensively is organization development. In addition, there is the larger issue of organizational learning where an organization develops a shared view of the world and adapts based on this new view.

Organizations need to evaluate the effectiveness of their training and development activities. Because the costs of such activities are quite high and because their effectiveness can often be measured somewhat easily, there is little reason to neglect this important activity.

► The ultimate purpose of employee training is to improve organizational effectiveness.

► Effectiveness is enhanced in settings where everyone can benefit from the training received by any employee. Such settings are referred to as learning organizations, and the goal in these settings is constant improvement.

► New employee orientation is a special kind of training in which an employee is supposed to become socialized into the organization while reducing his or her uncertainty and anxiety.

► Needs analysis should be the first step in any training program. The outcome of this analysis should result in a set of training goals.

► Tradeoffs between in-house and outsourced training programs exist.

► Work-based training techniques allow the organization to reap some benefit from the training almost immediately. These programs include on-the-

Key Points for Future HR Managers

job training, apprenticeship training, vestibule training, and systematic job rotations and transfers.

► Instructional-based training programs are the most common form of training; they include lectures, computer-assisted training, and programmed instruction.

► Management development is more concerned with generalized training for future roles rather than the mastery of specific information or skills.

► Organizational development is a large-scale intervention designed to change attitudes, perceptions, behavior, and expectations in organizations. This can also be seen as a form of organizational learning.

► Organizations must decide on the criteria for evaluating the effectiveness of training before the training begins. This decision is especially important when deciding between specific and general training.

► The ultimate goal of all training and development is increased organizational effectiveness.

► Needs analysis should precede the design of any training programs, and decisions about training goals and the criteria for evaluation should also be determined before the training begins.

► Organizations, as a whole, can also learn and adapt over time. Many organizational development activities are designed to change organiza-

Key Points for Future General Managers

tions, and organizational learning refers to shared views of events that also lead to adaptation and change.

► Organizational memory refers to information about past events that can be used to guide future decisions. This information can reside in written records, or in the memory of individuals.

► All training and development activities should be evaluated carefully.

Review and Discussion Questions

1. What are the basic differences between training and development?

2. How does learning theory relate to training?

3. What are the basic goals of orientation?

4. In what ways are training and orientation similar? In what ways are they different?

5. Discuss the role and importance of needs analysis as part of employee training.

6. What are the advantages and disadvantages of in-house training relative to outsourced training?

7. Describe the basic steps and processes through which training and development programs are developed.

8. Identify and discuss the basic training and development techniques and methods discussed in the chapter.

9. What are the special techniques often used for management development?

10. What is organization development? What basic methods for organization development are used by many organizations?

Closing Case

Boeing Trains for the Future

IntraGlobal Airlines is a company going nowhere: its sales are flat, its passengers complain about dirty airplanes, and the company is canceling more and more flights because its old Boeing 747s break down so often. Managers responsible for fixing the ailing airline face an array of tough decisions. For example, they know they need to buy new planes, but they don't know which models to buy or how to pay for them. They also know they need to change their route structure, but abandoning a city that's been loyal to the company will no doubt be bad public relations. And the firm's image is so bad that managers believe they may even need a new name for the carrier, along with a new logo and color scheme for its planes.

But what makes IntraGlobal especially interesting as a business is that it doesn't even exist! It is simply the product of some fertile minds at Boeing, the largest aircraft manufacturer in the world. IntraGlobal is a case study that serves as the centerpiece of an intense two-week management development seminar that Boeing runs quarterly for airline executives around the world. To date, about 1,000 airline employees have taken part in the program. And it is booked for at least the next year.

IntraGlobal was developed to mirror as closely as possible the real problems that once existed at airlines such as Pan American and National, before they ceased operations, and Continental, before its recent dramatic turnaround. Because the simulation isn't based on any single airline's problems or experiences, however, executives attending the seminar can't simply mimic what other managers did in the past. Instead, they have to study closely IntraGlobal's fictitious management structure, balance sheets and other financial indicators, route map and structure, and in-

ternal memoranda that are provided by the seminar's instructor.

Many senior managers from U.S. airlines such as American, Delta, and Continental and international airlines like Lufthansa and JAI have already completed Boeing's seminar. The most recent audience was comprised primarily of managers from small and mid-sized airlines in Latin America and eastern Europe. Most who attend are already specialists in one or more aspects of airline management, such as route management or finance. They come to Boeing to deepen their knowledge and to learn about other functions involved in effective airline operations.

And almost everyone who attends the seminar walks away having learned new information. For example, in one recent session most attendees were surprised to learn that engineers can change the maximum power capabilities of an airplane engine. Others were surprised to hear that filling all the seats on planes is not always a plus—full planes mean uncomfortable and disgruntled passengers and often drive customers to other competitors. And still others learn to appreciate for the first time the importance of factors such as mission statements and the decor of an airplane.

So how much does Boeing charge airlines for presenting this program to airline executives? Nothing! The only constraints imposed by Boeing are that no single airline can send more than two individuals to any given training session and that those who attend are senior managers. Boeing argues that it runs the training to provide a service for the industry. In addition, its managers claim that by interacting with different airline executives and hearing about what does and does not work for them, the firm learns how to build better airplanes. Of course, executives who go through the training program may be more inclined to favor Boeing the next time their airline needs to order new jets.[25]

Case Questions

1. What are the benefits and weaknesses of Boeing's training program from the standpoint of the airlines that send their executives to attend?

2. What are the pros and cons of the training from Boeing's point of view?

3. What other companies in different industries might consider providing training of the sort offered by Boeing?

Building HR Management Skills

Purpose: The purpose of this exercise is to give you more insights into the processes associated with effective training and development activities.

Step 1: Select a job with which you have some familiarity: maybe a job you are currently performing or have performed in the past. It could also be a job that you have had ample opportunity to observe—service station attendant, fast-food employee, hair stylist, and so forth.

Step 2: Assume that you are responsible for developing a training program to improve the job skills and performance of people currently doing the target job. Outline each of the steps you would go through, and be as specific as possible for the job itself. Pay special attention to the steps of setting goals, selecting training methods, and evaluation.

Step 3: If you used an example of a job that you have performed in the past, compare your training program with whatever actual training the organization used. Another option is to interview a manager in the organization you used for the target job and learn how the organization conducts its training. Ask the manager to critique your plan.

Questions:

1. How easy or difficult did you find this activity? What about the job made the exercise easier or harder than you expected it to be?

2. How important do you think it is for a trainer to have personal experience in performing a job before trying to teach others how to do it?

Ethical Dilemmas in HR Management

Assume that you are a senior manager for a midsized company. Your firm recently merged with two other companies to create a much larger firm. The integration of the three firms is almost complete. Your functional area will now be led by a team of nine managers, three each from the three original firms. You are the senior manager on the team. The new company is now trying to figure out how to complete the integration, especially with regard to creating trust and a spirit of cooperation among the various sets of people who have little or no experience working together.

One team member has suggested that you all go through an outdoor adventure program together. She has already done some homework and suggested a

company that conducts one-week survival-type team-building programs involving white-water rafting, rope climbing, and other similar activities. You know that she has already discussed her idea with her two colleagues from her former company and they are also enthusiastic about the idea.

You are concerned about one issue, however: one of your team members from the other firm is confined to a wheelchair and is mobility impaired. He also needs supplemental oxygen periodically. While the outdoor adventure company claims that it can accommodate all disabled participants, you still have serious doubts. This individual has heard the rumors about the trip and has already spoken to you. He has urged you to go ahead with the idea, but feels that he should not participate. Specifically, he doesn't really want to go and isn't sure if he is physically up to it. You sense that you can talk him into going, but that he really doesn't want to go.

You are unsure how to proceed. On the one hand, rejecting the suggestion made by your new team member might alienate her and her two colleagues. On the other hand, going ahead with her idea might prevent the disabled team member from being fully integrated into the team and might cause him to feel left out. While you haven't consulted them, you also worry that his colleagues might resent the team doing something from which he is being excluded. Thus, you see the following options: (1) going on the one-week outdoor survival program with everyone except the disabled team member; (2) going on the survival program and convincing the disabled team member to come as well; (3) eliminating the survival program as an option and seeking another, more inclusive activity, with you making the decision yourself; (4) eliminating the survival program as an option but allowing the group itself to develop a new alternative; or (5) not doing anything and assuming that team building will occur naturally as the new group members begin to work together.

Questions

1. What are the ethical issues in this situation?

2. What are the basic arguments for and against the different options available to you?

3. What do you think most managers would do? What would you do?

HR Internet Exercise

 As noted in the chapter, computer-assisted training is becoming more and more popular today. And this training is increasingly being provided via the Internet. As a first step, search the Web to see what information you can find about Internet-based training. See what you can find in terms of actual Internet-based training, consulting support for managers interested in Internet-based training, and so forth. Next, respond to the following questions.

Questions

1. What do you see as the primary advantages and disadvantages of Internet-based training and development?

2. Are certain kinds of jobs more and less amenable to Internet-based training? On what do you base your answer?

3. Do you think Internet-based training might someday replace all or most other forms of training? Why or why not?

4. If you were interested in a career as a trainer for a major corporation, what Internet skills do you think would be most beneficial to you personally? How might you learn these skills most effectively?

11

Managing Basic Compensation

CHAPTER OBJECTIVES

After studying this chapter you should be able to:

■ Describe the basic issues involved in developing a compensation strategy.

■ Discuss how organizations develop a wage and salary structure.

■ Identify and describe the basic issues involved in wage and salary administration.

■ Identify and describe basic legal issues in compensation.

■ Describe the importance to an organization of evaluating its compensation policies.

In 1938 the U.S. Congress passed the Fair Labor Standards Act (FLSA). Among its other provisions, the FLSA mandated that hourly employees working in excess of forty hours a week must be paid a premium wage of 1.5 times their normal hourly rate for those additional hours. The FLSA also specified that, because of the nature of their work, managerial and professional employees were exempt from this regulation. That is, because these individuals are paid salaries rather than hourly wages, they receive the same pay regardless of the number of hours they work during any given period.

"Many companies have explicit policies that limit overtime. But they have management systems that absolutely dictate too many tasks for the amount of time allotted."

(John Frazier, U.S. Department of Labor)*

While it is up to the organization to determine which jobs are exempt and which are not, several legal standards have traditionally been used in making these distinctions. Recently, however, the distinctions have become blurred in some organizations. For example, some people charge that businesses reclassify some of their wage-based, lower-level jobs as managerial positions and then refuse to pay overtime to individuals holding those jobs. Even more extreme are charges that some organizations today are pressuring hourly employees to work "off the clock"—to work when they are not being paid at all! Sometimes this practice is legal, but other times it's not.

Because of corporate downsizing programs in the last several years, some firms assume that the remaining employees can carry a greater workload. In general, this situation means working harder and being more productive. But it may also mean working longer hours. In some cases, it's a matter of work spilling over into what used to be free time. At AT&T, for example, workers are encouraged to participate in the firm's Ambassador Program by selling AT&T products to their friends, relatives, and neighbors during nonwork hours. Employees can win prizes for their efforts, but they earn no additional income.

But other cases are more troubling. In the state of Washington, for example, a jury ruled that Taco Bell was guilty of pressuring its employees to do paperwork such as timesheets and schedules at home. And workers were sometimes asked to do some food preparation after arriving at work but before clocking in. Mervyn's, a chain of discount stores, was sued by a group of its lower-level managers called "team coordinators." These managers charged that they were routinely ordered to work through their lunchtime and to take paperwork home. And Albertson's, the nation's fourth largest grocery chain, has been charged with pushing employees to work past their assigned quitting time without receiving additional wages.

Sometimes, of course, individual employees might simply be misinterpreting events and suggestions from their boss. In other situations companies charge that unions are distorting the picture. And even in cases where the law is being broken, the actions might be the isolated tactics of only one or a few managers working outside formal organizational policies to get a bit more productivity out of their employees. Regardless of the circumstances, however, it does seem that some organizations today are seeking ways to get more and more work out of fewer and fewer people. Although achiev-ing this goal can be done in various legitimate ways, some managers may be crossing the line in the methods they use to get more from their employees—without having to give anything in return.[1] ∎

The basic issue in the cases at Taco Bell, Mervyn's, and Albertson's involves payment to employees in relation to their time spent working for the respective company. Organizations clearly have the right to expect their employees to perform their jobs to the best of their abilities and to be as productive as possible during the time they are being paid to work. But individual workers also have the right to be fairly, legally, and appropriately compensated for their work. Ensuring that the financial arrangements between the organization and its employees are legal, ethical, fair, and appropriate is generally the responsibility of the organization's human resource function.

Compensation is the set of rewards that organizations provide to individuals in return for their willingness to perform various jobs and tasks within the organization. As we will see, compensation includes several different elements, such as base salary, incentives, bonuses, benefits, and other rewards. In this chapter we cover basic compensation. We start by examining how compensation strategies are developed. Next, we look at how wage and salary structures are created. Issues associated with wage and salary administration are then introduced and discussed. Finally, we conclude by noting how organizations evaluate their compensation and benefits policies. Chapter 12 covers compensation linked to performance; employee benefits, another important component of compensation, is the subject of Chapter 13.

∎ **Compensation** is the set of rewards that organizations provide to individuals in return for their willingness to perform various jobs and tasks within the organization.

DEVELOPING A COMPENSATION STRATEGY

Compensation should never be a random decision but instead the result of a careful and systematic strategic process.[2] Embedded in the process is an understanding of the basic purposes of compensation, an assessment of strategic options for compensation, knowledge of the determinants of compensation strategy, and the use of pay surveys.

Basic Purposes of Compensation

Compensation has several fundamental purposes and objectives. First, the organization must provide appropriate and equitable rewards to employees. Individuals who work for organizations want to feel valued and want to be rewarded at a level commensurate with their skills, abilities, and contributions to the organization. In this regard, an organization must consider two types of equity. These two types relate to two different comparison groups an employee might refer to in

The year 2003 was noteworthy for a lot of reasons. One unfortunate reason was that in the first quarter of the year median weekly earnings (adjusted for inflation) fell 1.5 percent—the largest drop since 1991. Some of this drop was due to the decline of Internet euphoria. But many experts were concerned that these drops in real wages are permanent as firms try to hold the line on salaries in order to compete better globally. In addition, bonuses and benefits have been cut in many organizations. Mike Leone is a pilot for American Airlines. He learned recently that he would have to take a 23 percent pay cut in order to keep his job. To the frustration of Leone and other American Airlines workers like him, at about the same time many employees were facing pay cuts, AMR, the parent company of American Airlines, announced pension guarantees totaling $14 million for its top executives.

■ **Internal equity** in compensation refers to comparisons made by employees to other employees within the same organization.

deciding if he or she is paid equitably. In addition, compensation serves a signaling function. Organizations signal to employees what they feel is important for the employee to focus on (and what they feel is less important) by paying for certain kinds of activities or attributes and not for others. As we shall discuss in more detail in the next chapter, compensation can serve as an incentive to employees to increase their efforts along desired lines. We turn first to the issues of fairness and equity.

Internal equity in compensation refers to comparisons made by employees to other employees within the same organization. In making these comparisons the employee is concerned that he is equitably paid for his contributions to the organization relative to the way other employees are paid in the firm. For example, suppose a department manager learns that all the other department managers in the firm are paid more than he is. He subsequently looks more closely at the situation and finds that they all have similar experience and responsibilities. As a result, he becomes unhappy with his compensation and likely requests a salary increase. On the other hand, he might discover that he has much less work experience and fewer responsibilities than the other managers and thus concludes that there is no equity problem. Problems with internal equity can result in conflict among employees, feelings of mistrust, low morale, anger, and perhaps even legal action if the basis for inequity is perceived to result from illegal discrimination.

External equity in compensation refers to comparisons made by employees with similar employees at other firms performing similar jobs. For example, an engineer may experience internal equity relative to her engineering colleagues in her work group because she knows they are all paid the same salary. But if she finds out that another major employer in the same community is paying its engineers higher salaries for comparable work, she might be concerned about external equity. Problems with external equity may result in higher turnover (because employees will leave for better opportunities elsewhere), dissatisfied and unhappy workers, and difficulties in attracting new employees.

Both types of equity are clearly important, but there is one additional consideration concerning internal equity. The Equal Pay Act of 1963 stipulates that men and women who perform essentially the same job must be paid the same. Generally speaking, internal equity problems occur when employees on one job feel that they are being undercompensated relative to employees on some other job or jobs within the organization. However, it is illegal to pay a woman less than a man (or vice versa) for performing the same job when no objective basis for such a differential exists. If the organization can prove that such differences are based on differences in performance and/or seniority (see below), the organization can probably avoid litigation, but it takes only the *perception* by a woman that she is being paid less than a man doing the same job for problems to begin. Also, if some jobs in the organization are performed mostly by men and others mostly by women, differences in pay between the two jobs (real or perceived) must be attributable to differences in job demands or, again, the organization might face legal problems.

It is also important that compensation serve a motivational purpose. By "motivational purpose" we mean that individuals should perceive that their efforts and contributions to the organization are recognized and rewarded. Individuals who work hard and who perform at a high level should be compensated at a level higher than are individuals who do just enough to get by and who perform at only an average or below average rate.[3] If everyone perceives this situation to be true, employees will believe that the reward system is fair and just and that internal equity exists, and they will be more motivated to perform at their highest level.

Organizations must adequately and effectively manage compensation. Compensation to employees is one of the major expenses in most organizations. On the one hand, it is important that employees be appropriately and equitably rewarded. On the other hand, it is important that the organization control its compensation costs. For example, it should be careful not to overpay individuals for the value of their contributions (which could lead to problems with internal equity) or to provide excess or superfluous benefits or rewards.[4] Thus, the ideal compensation system would be one that reflects an appropriate balance of organizational constraints, costs, budgets, income, and cash flow relative to employee needs, expectations, and demands.

The fundamental purpose of compensation, then, is to provide an adequate and appropriate reward system for employees so that they feel valued and worthwhile as organizational members and representatives. Compensation represents more than the number of dollars a person takes home in her or his pay envelope. Instead, it provides a measure of the employee's value to the organization and functions indirectly as an indicator of his or her self-worth.[5]

> ■ **External equity** in compensation refers to comparisons made by employees to others employed by different organizations performing similar jobs.

Wages Versus Salaries

Fundamental to understanding compensation is the distinction between wages and salaries. **Wages** generally refer to hourly compensation paid to operating employees; the basis for wages is time. That is, the organization pays individuals for specific blocks of their time. Most organizations calculate wages on an hourly basis. If an individual works eight hours, he or she earns eight hours times the hourly wage rate. But if an individual works only 4.5 hours, then she or he make 4.5 times the hourly wage rate. Individuals who are paid on an hourly basis typically receive their income on a weekly or biweekly basis. Most of the jobs that are paid on an hourly wage basis are lower-level and/or operational jobs within the organization.

Rather than expressing compensation on an hourly basis, the organization may instead describe compensation on an annual or monthly basis. For example, many college graduates compare job offers on the basis of annual salary, such as $42,000 versus $45,000 a year. Sometimes salaries are quoted on the basis of a monthly rate. In general, salaries are paid to professional and managerial employees within an organization. Plant managers, product managers, and professional managers in areas such as marketing and finance and accounting, for example, are all likely to be paid on an annual basis. The idea of a **salary** is that

> ■ **Wages** generally refer to hourly compensation paid to operating employees; the basis for wages is time.

> ■ **Salary** is income paid to an individual on the basis of performance, not on the basis of time.

■ A **maturity curve** is a schedule specifying the amount of
annual increase a person will
receive.

an individual is compensated not for how much time they spend in the organization but for their overall contributions to the organization's performance. On a
given day, if a manager leaves work a couple of hours early or works a couple of
hours late, that time has no bearing on the individual's compensation. She is not
docked for leaving early, nor does she get overtime pay for working extra.

Strategic Options for Compensation

Most organizations establish a formal compensation strategy that dictates how
they will pay individuals. Several decisions are embedded within this strategy.
The first decision relates to the basis for pay. Most organizations traditionally
based pay on the functions performed on the job. But more recently organizations have begun to rely on skill-based pay and pay-for-knowledge programs. In
this way, organizations signal to their employees the relative importance of what
someone does on the job versus what they bring to the job.

A second decision in developing a compensation strategy focuses on the bases
for differential pay within a specific job. In some organizations, especially those
with a strong union presence, differences in actual pay rates are based on seniority. That is, with each year of service in a particular job, wages go up by a specified amount. Therefore, the longer one works on the job, the more that person
makes, regardless of the level of performance on the job. Most public school systems use a seniority system to pay teachers—they get a base salary increase for
each year of service they accumulate. And as already noted, unions have historically preferred pay based at least in part on seniority.

Sometimes the relationship between seniority and pay is expressed as something called a maturity curve. A **maturity curve** is simply a schedule specifying
the amount of annual increase a person receives. This curve is used when the annual increase varies based on the actual number of years of service the person has
accumulated. Organizations that use maturity curves might argue that a new
person tends to learn more (in part because there is more to learn) than more
experienced employees and thus may deserve a larger increase. Meanwhile more
senior people may already be earning considerably higher income anyway and also
have fewer new tasks to learn. In any event, the assumption under a seniority-
based pay system is that employees
with more experience can make a more
valuable contribution to the organization and should be rewarded for that
contribution. These systems also encourage employees to remain with the
organization.

The minimum wage continues to
be a controversial subject in the
United States. Advocates for an
increase in the minimum wage
argue that higher wages would
allow workers to better support
their families, but opponents argue that higher wage costs
would make firms less competitive and less likely to hire unskilled workers. In other parts of
the world discussions about minimum wages also go on—but the
stakes are sometimes substantially different. Wellington Casas
is a mine worker at the Muzo
emerald mines in Colombia,
South America. Colombia is the
largest producer of emeralds in
the world, and most say that
Colombian emeralds are the
finest in the world. Yet Casas
earns a minimum wage of $130
for twenty days work. He works
around-the-clock shifts, breaking
only for meals and sleep.

In other organizations, differences
in pay are based on differences in performance, regardless of time on the
job. These systems are generally seen as
rewarding employees who are good
performers rather than those who simply remain with the organization. For
such systems to succeed, however, the
organization has to be certain that it
has an effective system for measuring

performance. Most major companies base at least a portion of individual pay on performance, especially for managerial and professional employees. Performance-based incentives will be discussed in more detail in Chapter 12.

A third decision in developing a compensation strategy deals with the organization's pay rates relative to going rates in the market. As shown in Figure 11.1, the three basic strategic options are to pay above-market compensation rates, market compensation rates, or below-market compensation rates.[6] This decision is important because of the costs it represents to the organization.[7]

A firm that chooses to pay above-market compensation, for example, will incur additional costs as a result. This strategic option essentially indicates that the organization pays its employees a level of compensation that is higher than that paid by other employers competing for the same kind of employees. Of course, it also anticipates achieving various benefits. Some organizations believe that they attract better employees if they pay wages and salaries that are higher than those paid by other organizations. That is, they view compensation as a competitive issue. They recognize that high-quality employees may select from among several different potential employers and that they have a better chance of attracting the best employees if they're willing to pay them an above-market rate. Above-market pay policies are most likely to be used in larger companies, particularly those that have been performing well.

In addition to attracting high-quality employees, an above-market strategy has other benefits. Above-market rates tend to minimize voluntary turnover among employees. By definition, above-market rates mean that an employee who leaves a company paying such wages may have to take a pay cut to find employment elsewhere. Another reason that paying above-market rates might be beneficial is that it can create and foster a culture of elitism and competitive superiority.

For example, Wal-Mart has a policy that none of its employees will be paid the minimum wage. The company doesn't want employees to feel that they are worth only the minimum amount the company could get away with paying. Thus, they pay a bit more for entry-level positions than do certain competitors such as Kmart, which is more likely to pay the minimum wage for employees. Cisco Systems, a Silicon Valley computer company, also pays higher-than-average salaries specifically as a way of retaining its valued employees in an industry where turnover and mobility are high.

FIGURE 11.1   Strategic Options for Compensation

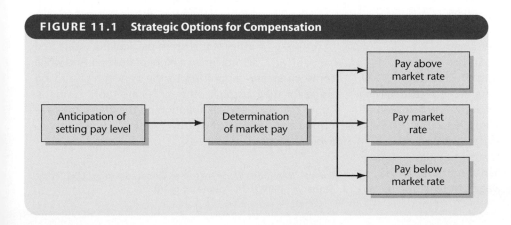

The downside to above-market compensation levels, of course, is cost. The organization simply has higher labor costs because of its decision to pay higher salaries to its employees. Once these higher labor costs become institutionalized, employees may begin to adopt a sense of entitlement, coming to believe that they deserve the higher compensation and thus making it difficult for the organization to be able to adjust its compensation levels down to lower levels. The HR in the 21st Century feature for this chapter highlights some of the issues associated with minimum-wage compensation when state or local governments impose minimums that are higher than the federal minimum. This situation involves people being paid higher wages and knowing that their wages are better than those earned in many other states.

Another strategic option is to pay below-market rates. The organization that adopts this strategy is essentially deciding to pay workers less than the compensation levels offered by other organizations competing for the same kinds of employees. Thus, it is gambling that the lower-quality employees it is able to attract will more than offset the labor savings it achieves. Organizations most likely to pursue a below-market rate are those in areas with high unemployment. If lots of people are seeking employment and relatively few jobs are available, then many people are probably willing to work for lower wages. Thus, the organization may be able to pay lower than the market rate and still attract reasonable and qualified employees. Again, the benefit to this strategy is lower labor costs for the organization.

HR in the 21st Century

Minimum Wage . . . or Minimum Wages?

Most people are aware of a minimum hourly wage in the United States, currently set at $5.15. But fewer people are aware of the fact that some states actually set a higher hourly minimum wage for their in-state workers. The current highest hourly minimum is Oregon's, at $6.50 an hour. Other states that also have higher minimum wages include California, Washington, Alaska, Connecticut, Hawaii, Massachusetts, and Vermont, as well as the District of Columbia. Oregon's latest jump went into effect January 1, 1999, and was the third of three such increases phased in starting in 1996. The goal of Oregon's initiative was to help workers catch up with cost-of-living increases during the 1970s and 1980s, when wages failed to keep pace with inflation.

In another recent development, some cities and counties, especially in high-cost urban areas, have started imposing their own minimum wages, at least for certain

"The idea was to catch up with the cost-of-living increases in the 1970s and 80s."

(Oregon state representative Diane Rosenbaum)*

kinds of jobs. For example, the city of San Jose, California, mandates that construction workers be paid either $9.50 an hour plus health benefits, or $10.75 an hour without health benefits. While this trend is just starting to attract national attention, experts are divided on whether it will grow in popularity or fall by the wayside. For example, while the states with higher minimum wages seem basically satisfied with their arrangements, few other states seem particularly interested in moving to a higher rate level. And while some cities are committed to the concept of a living wage for their citizens, other cities are more cautious. Some that try it end up abandoning the idea if they see businesses moving to nearby locations or suburbs to avoid the higher wage levels.

Source: "Minimum-Wage Increases Debated Anew," *USA Today,* January 6, 1999, p. 3A (*quote on p. 3A).

On the other hand, the organization will also experience several negative side effects. Morale and job satisfaction might not be as high as the organization would otherwise prefer. Individuals are almost certain to recognize that they are being relatively underpaid, and this situation can result in feelings of job dissatisfaction and potential resentment against the organization. In addition, turnover may also be higher because employees will be continually vigilant about finding better-paying jobs. Compounding the problem even further is the fact that the higher-performing employees are among the most likely to leave, and the lower-performing employees are among the most likely to stay.

Finally, a third strategic option for compensation is to pay market rates for employees. That is, the organization may elect to pay salaries and wages that are comparable to those available in other organizations, no more and no less. Clearly, the organization that adopts this strategy is taking a midrange perspective. The organization assumes that it will get higher-quality human resources than a firm that takes a below-market strategy. At the same time, it is willing to forego the ability to attract as many high-quality employees as the organization that takes an above-market strategy.

The advantages and disadvantages of this strategy are also likely to reflect midrange comparisons with the other strategies. That is, the organization will have higher turnover than a firm paying above-market rates but lower turnover than an organization paying below-market rates. An organization that adopts a market-rate strategy is likely to believe it can provide other intangible or more subjective benefits to employees in return for their accepting a wage rate that is perhaps lower than they might be paid elsewhere. For example, job security is one important subjective benefit that some organizations provide.

Employees who perceive that they are being offered an unusually high level of job security may therefore be willing to take a somewhat lower wage rate and accept employment at a market rate. Universities frequently adopt this strategy because they believe that the ambiance of a university environment is such that employees in such organizations do not necessarily expect higher salaries or higher wages. Microsoft also uses this approach. It offsets average wages with lucrative stock options and an exceptionally pleasant physical work environment.

Determinants of Compensation Strategy

Several different factors contribute to the compensation strategy that a firm develops. One general set of factors has to do with the overall strategy of the organization itself. As detailed in Chapter 2, a clear and carefully developed relationship should exist between a firm's corporate and business strategies and its human resource strategy.[8] This connection, in turn, should also tie into the firm's compensation strategy. Thus, a firm in a high-growth mode is constantly striving to attract new employees and may find itself in a position of having to pay above-market rates to do so. On the other hand, a stable firm may be more likely to pay market rates, given the relatively predictable and stable nature of its operations. And finally, an organization in a retrenchment or decline mode may decide to pay below-market rates because it wants to reduce the size of its workforce anyway.[9]

In addition to these general strategic considerations, several other specific factors determine an organization's compensation strategy. One obvious factor is simply the organization's ability to pay. An organization with a healthy cash flow and/or substantial cash reserves is more likely to be able to pay above-market wages and salaries. On the other hand, if the organization suffers from a cash flow crunch, has few cash reserves, and is operating on a tight budget, it may be necessary to adopt a below-market wage strategy. Thus, the organization's ability to pay is an important consideration. During the economic downturn of 2002 and 2003, many firms found themselves in this predicament. In response, several major companies reduced the pay increases they granted to their employees.[10]

In addition, the overall ability of the organization to attract and retain employees is a critical factor. For example, if the organization is located in an attractive area; has several noncompensation amenities; and provides a comfortable, pleasant, and secure work environment, then it might be able to pay somewhat lower wages. But if the organization is located in, for example, a high-crime area or a relatively unattractive city or region, and if it has few noncompensation amenities that it can provide to its employees, it may be necessary to pay higher wages simply as a way of attracting and retaining employees.

Another important determinant of a firm's compensation strategy is its legal context. As we discussed in Chapter 3, laws and other government regulations affect what an organization can pay its employees and how various benefits must be structured. For example, the Fair Labor Standards Act of 1938 establishes a minimum wage; thus organizations must pay at least that wage to hourly employees (since September 1, 1997, the minimum wage has been $5.15 an hour). The same act also defines exempt versus nonexempt employees, which has implications for overtime compensation for employees as well.

Union influences comprise another important determinant of an organization's compensation strategy. If an organization competes in an environment that is heavily unionized, such as the automobile industry, then the strength and bargaining capabilities of the union influence what the organization pays its employees. On the other hand, if the organization does not hire employees represented by unions or if the strength of a particular union is relatively low, then the organization may be able to pay somewhat lower wages and the union influence is minimal or nonexistent.

Pay Surveys and Compensation

The critical source of information that many organizations use in developing compensation strategies is the pay survey. **Pay surveys** are surveys of compensation paid to employees by other employers in a particular geographic area, industry, or occupational group. Pay surveys provide the information an organization needs to avoid problems of external equity. Some wage surveys are conducted by professional associations, especially for managerial and professional jobs. For example, the Society for Human Resource Management conducts annual salary surveys for human resource executives every other year. This information is then made available to all society members. The society and the organizations it represents can then use the information in making wage and salary decisions within the human resource area. Organizations should also keep in mind that their employees scan for information about external wages and salaries. Indeed, as discussed more fully in HR TechTalk, the Internet is making this practice increasingly common and easy today.

Other organizations also routinely conduct wage surveys. Business publications such as *Business Week, Fortune,* and *Nation's Business* routinely publish

■ **Pay surveys** are surveys of compensation paid to employees by other employers in a particular geographic area, industry, or occupational group.

Negotiating Salaries on the Web

Back in the "old days" (probably up to the final years of the twentieth century, in fact) negotiating wages and salaries was typically handled in a meeting between the employee and his or her manager. This same approach was used both for individuals who were being offered their first job with the company and for existing employees who felt they deserved a raise. But in both cases, the manager and the organization usually had the upper hand. This situation stemmed from the fact that both prospective and current employees generally had relatively little knowledge about prevailing wage and salary levels. They usually did not know what others in the firm were being paid, for example, or what similar companies were paying for similar jobs in different parts of the region or country.

But the Internet is rapidly changing all that. Several large websites now provide salary information for interested parties. Among other information, these sites include salary survey data, job listings with specified pay levels, and even customized compensation analyses. Armed with such detailed information, more and more

> *"The Internet has become the big level playing field for everyone [by exposing businesses that] are way below everyone else as far as pay is concerned."*
>
> (Brian Krueger, consultant)*

people today are negotiating better deals for themselves with their employers.

Sometimes the Web can provide even more insights, especially for crafty negotiators. For example, some people have been known to use Internet bulletin boards to track down other individuals who have recently been offered employment with a particular firm, find out how much they were offered, and then use that information as leverage in their own negotiations.

In another unforeseen development, the big-time recruiting firm of Korn/Ferry recently set up its own salary site called Futurestep. But the firm faced internal negotiations when some of its own employees used the site to determine that they themselves were being underpaid! On balance, then, it seems like the Internet will be play a major role from now on in the kinds of wages and salaries that employees expect and that companies pay.

Source: "Web Transforms Art of Negotiating Raises," *Wall Street Journal,* September 22, 1998, pp. B1, B16 (*quote on p. B16).

---

compensation levels for various kinds of professional and executive positions. In addition, the Bureau of National Affairs and other government agencies routinely conduct wage surveys within certain occupational groups, certain regions, and so forth. The Bureau of Labor Statistics is also an important source of government-controlled wage and salary survey information.

In general, the idea behind a wage and salary survey is simply to ask other organizations what they pay people to perform various jobs. The motivation for most organizations to participate in such surveys is that they gain access to the data themselves. For example, a consortium of eight large electronics companies in the United States routinely survey one another to determine what each pays new engineers and other professional employees who are hired directly out of college. They rotate the responsibility for conducting the surveys from year to year, and then each organization shares its results with the other members of the consortium. Similar arrangements exist in the petroleum industry and in certain segments of the construction industry.

Designing a wage and salary survey is a much more complex process than one might think. For example, it is necessary to identify and name various jobs and job families so that anyone who reads the survey and responds to it has the same frame of reference and the same understanding regarding what is being asked. For this reason, it is common for organizations to rely on consulting firms and other outside groups to plan and conduct wage and salary surveys on their behalf. This approach allows them to take advantage of the expertise available in such firms and to minimize their own risk and the prospects of making a significant error or mistake in the conduct of the survey.[11] Figure 11.2 presents a sample section from a pay survey.

DETERMINING A WAGE AND SALARY STRUCTURE

After human resource managers have developed their compensation strategy, they are prepared to establish a wage and salary structure for their organization. The starting point in this effort has traditionally been job evaluation. We will describe this more traditional method first and then introduce a relatively new but increasingly popular approach to creating wage and salary structures.

Job Evaluation and Job Worth

One of the basic building blocks of an effective compensation system is job evaluation. Job evaluation should not be confused with job analysis, which was discussed in Chapter 5. Recall that the purpose of job analysis is to help managers better understand the requirements and nature of the job and its performance so that appropriate individuals can be recruited and selected for that particular job.

FIGURE 11.2 Example of a Pay Survey

Organization: ABC Trucking
Location: Dallas, TX

Benchmark Jobs	No. of workers (this title)	No. of workers (total)	Average weekly hours	Base Pay			Median total compensation (base pay + benefits)	Industry			
				25th %-tile	50th %-tile	75th %-tile		Mfg.	Trans.	Utilities	Trade
File clerk	10	300	40	$15,000	$20,000	$25,000	$28,000		√		
Order clerk											
Accounting clerk											

A survey such as this one is sent to other organizations in a given region. In this case, the survey would go to organizations in various industries, but other surveys might be targeted to a specific industry. The jobs that are the focus of the survey should be benchmark jobs, where everyone understands the nature of the job, the content is fairly stable, and the job is likely to be found in a wide variety of organizations. In some surveys, specific benchmark jobs are coded to ensure that everyone reacts to the same job. Also, some surveys ask more specific questions about other areas of compensation. Data from surveys such as this one are then summarized for each job.

Job evaluation is a method for determining the relative value or worth of a job to the organization so that individuals who perform that job can be compensated adequately and appropriately. That is, job evaluation is mostly concerned with establishing internal pay equity. Several job evaluation techniques and methods have been established.[12] Among the most commonly used are job ranking, factor comparison, classification, a point system, and a regression-based system. We will discuss each of these methods for job evaluation in more detail in the following sections.

Job ranking   One of the most basic job evaluation systems is **job ranking**.[13] Job ranking is most likely to be used in relatively small and simple organizations with a small number of different jobs. In using the job-ranking method, the manager essentially rank-orders jobs, based on their relative importance to the organization, from most important to least important. The premise then is that the most important job is compensated at the highest level, the next most important job is compensated somewhat below this level, and so forth, down to the least important job, which is accorded the lowest level of compensation in the organization.

Job ranking does not work effectively when many different jobs exist in the organization. It becomes difficult to differentiate among large numbers of jobs in the same way that it is possible to differentiate among relatively few jobs. Another shortcoming of the job-ranking method is that the amount of the differential to allow between jobs ranked at different levels is not always clear. For example, the most important job and the second most important job might be differentially compensated at an amount of, say, $5,000. However, the differential between the second and the third most important job might need to be substantially greater or substantially less than this dollar figure. The ranking system alone does not provide adequate information for making these decisions.

Classification system   Another popular method of job evaluation is the **classification system**.[14] An organization that uses a classification system attempts to group sets of jobs together into classifications, often called *grades*. After classifying is done, each set of jobs is then ranked at a level of importance to the organization. Importance, in turn, may be defined in terms of relative difficulty, sophistication, or required skills and abilities necessary to perform that job. A third step is to determine how many categories or classifications to use for grouping jobs. The most common number of grades is anywhere from eight to ten, although some organizations use the system with as few as four grades and some with as many as eighteen.

The U.S. postal system is a good example of an organization that uses the classification system. The U.S. postal system has sixteen job grades, with nine pay steps within each grade. Once the grades have been determined, the job evaluator must write definitions and descriptions of each job class. These definitions and descriptions serve as the standard around which the compensation system is built. That is, once the classes of jobs are defined and described, jobs that are being evaluated can be compared with the definitions and descriptions and placed into the appropriate classification.

A major advantage of the job classification system is that it can be constructed relatively simply and quickly. It is easy to understand and easy to communicate to employees. It also provides specific standards for compensation and can easily accommodate changes in the value of various individual jobs in the organization. On the other hand, the job classification system is more complicated

■ **Job evaluation** is a method for determining the relative value or worth of a job to the organization so that individuals who perform that job can be compensated adequately and appropriately.

■ **Job ranking** is a job evaluation method requiring the manager to rank-order jobs, based on their relative importance to the organization, from most important to least important.

■ The **classification system** for job evaluation attempts to group sets of jobs together into clusters, often called grades.

The classifications system for job evaluation is used in the U.S. federal government and thus applies to jobs in the postal service. Each postal job has a general service (GS) classification, which determines the range of pay for that job. In such a system, everyone understands what aspects of the job are compensated, and while the system is extremely structured, it is easily understood and accepted. George Lacap, a mail sorter (GS–5), is shown here sorting the mail at the San Francisco Processing Center in early December, the busiest time of the year for the postal service.

■ The **point system** for job evaluation requires managers to quantify, in objective terms, the value of the various elements of specific jobs.

■ **Compensable factors** include any aspect of a job for which an organization is willing to provide compensation.

than simple ranking. It is based on the assumption that a constant and inflexible relationship exists between the job factors and their value to the organization. Because of this shortcoming, some organizations find it necessary to group jobs that do not necessarily fit together very well. Figure 11.3 presents an example of a job classification system.

Point system   The most commonly used method of job evaluation is the **point system**.[15] The point system is more sophisticated than either the ranking or the classification system and is also relatively easy to use. The point system requires managers to quantify, in objective terms, the value of the various elements of specific jobs. Using job descriptions as a starting point, managers assign points to the degree of various **compensable factors** that are required to perform each job. Compensable factors include any aspect of a job for which an organization is willing to provide compensation. For instance, managers might assign points based on the amount of skill required to perform a particular job, the amount of physical effort needed, the nature of the working conditions involved, and the responsibility and authority involved in the performance of the job. Job evaluation simply represents the sum of the points allocated to each of the compensable factors for each job.

Point systems typically evaluate eight to ten compensable factors for each job. It is important that the factors chosen do not overlap one another, that they immediately distinguish between substantive characteristics of the jobs, that they are objective and verifiable in nature, and that they are well understood and accepted by both managers and employees. Not all aspects of a particular job may be of equal importance, so managers can allocate different weights to reflect the relative importance of these aspects to a job. These weights are usually determined by summing the judgments of various independent but informed evaluators. Thus, an administrative job within an organization might result in weightings of required education, 40 percent; experience required, 30 percent; predictability and complexity of the job, 15 percent; responsibility and authority for making decisions, 10 percent; and working conditions and physical requirements for the job, 5 percent.

Because the point system is used to evaluate jobs, most organizations also develop a **point manual**. The point manual carefully and specifically defines the degrees of points from first to fifth. For example, education might be defined as follows: (1) first degree, up to and including a high school diploma, 25 points; (2) second degree, high school diploma and one year of college education, 50 points; (3) third degree, high school diploma and two years of college, 75 points; (4) fourth degree, high school education and three years of college, 100 points; and (5) fifth degree, a college degree, 125 points. These point manuals are then used for all subsequent job evaluation.

FIGURE 11.3   Job Classification System

Grade GS–1

Grade GS–1 includes those classes of positions the duties of which are to perform, under immediate supervision, with little or no latitude for the exercise of independent judgment:

    A. the simplest routine work in office, business, or fiscal operations; or

    B. elementary work of a subordinate technical character in a professional, scientific, or technical field.

Grade GS–6

Grade GS–6 includes those classes of positions the duties of which are:

    A. to perform, under general supervision, difficult and responsible work in office, business, or fiscal administration, or comparable subordinate technical work in a professional, scientific, or technical field, requiring in either case–
        1. considerable training and supervisory or other experience;
        2. broad working knowledge of a special and complex subject matter, procedure, or practice, or of the principles of the profession, art, or science involved; and
        3. to a considerable extent the exercise of independent judgment; or

    B. to perform other work of equal importance, difficulty, and responsibility, and requiring comparable qualifications.

Grade GS–10

Grade GS–10 includes those classes of positions the duties of which are:

    A. to perform, under general supervision, highly difficult and responsible work along special technical, supervisory, or adminstrative lines in office, business, or fiscal administration, requiring–
        1. somewhat extended specialized, supervisory, or administrative training and experience which has demonstrated capacity for sound independent work;
        2. thorough and fundamental knowledge of a specialized and complex subject matter, or of the profession, art, or science involved; and
        3. considerable latitude for the exercise of independent judgment; or

    B. to perform other work of equal importance, difficulty, and responsibility, and requiring comparable qualifications.

Source: U.S. Office of Personnel Management.

Job classification systems require clear definitions of classes and benchmark jobs for each class. The most widely known example of a job classification system is the General Schedule (GS) system used by the federal government. This system has eighteen grades (or classes). Most federal employees fall into one of fifteen grades, while the top three grades have been combined into a single "supergrade" that covers senior executives.

The information above outlines the descriptions of three grades from the GS system. An example of a job classified as a GS–1 would be a janitor; an example of a GS–6 job would be a light truck driver; and an example of a GS–10 job would be an auto mechanic. Within each grade are ten pay steps based on seniority, so that the range of salaries for a GS–6 starts at just under $20,000 a year and goes up to over $25,000 a year.

Factor comparison method   A fourth method of job evaluation is the **factor comparison method.** Like the point system, the factor comparison method allows the job evaluator to assess jobs on a factor-by-factor basis. At the same time, however, it differs from the point system because jobs are evaluated or compared against a standard of key points. That is, instead of using points, a factor

■ The **point manual,** used to implement the point system of job evaluation, carefully and specifically defines the degrees of points from first to fifth.

■ The **factor comparison method** for job evaluation assesses jobs, on a factor-by-factor basis, using a factor comparison scale as a benchmark.

comparison scale is used as a benchmark. Although an organization can choose to identify any number of compensable factors, commonly used systems include five job factors for comparing jobs. These factors are responsibilities, skills, physical effort, mental effort, and working conditions.

Managers performing a job evaluation in a factor comparison system are typically advised to follow six specific steps. First, the comparison factors to be used are selected and defined. The five universal factors are used as starting points, but any given organization may need to add factors to this set. Second, benchmark or key jobs in the organization are identified. These jobs are typically representative of and common in the labor market for a particular firm. Usually, ten to twenty benchmark jobs are selected. The third step is to rank the benchmark jobs on each of the compensation factors. The ranking itself is usually based on job descriptions and job specifications determined by a job analysis.

The fourth step is to allocate part of each benchmark's job wage rate to each job factor. This allocation is based on the relative importance of the job factor. Each manager participating in the job evaluation might be asked to make an independent allocation first, without consultation with other managers. Then the managers would meet as a group to develop a consensus about the assignment of monetary values to the various factors. The fifth step in the factor comparison system is to prepare the two sets of ratings based on the ranking and the assigned wages and thus determine the consistency demonstrated by the evaluators. Sixth, a job comparison chart is developed to display the benchmark jobs and the monetary values that each job received for each factor. This chart can then be used to rate other jobs in the organization as compared to the benchmark jobs.

The factor comparison system is a detailed and meticulous method for formally evaluating jobs. Thus, it provides a rigorous assessment of the true value of various jobs, which is one of its advantages. It also allows managers to recognize fully how the differences in factor rankings affect the dollars that the organization allocates to compensation for various jobs. On the other hand, the factor comparison method is also extremely complex and difficult to use. Therefore, it is time consuming and expensive for an organization that chooses to adopt it. A fair amount of subjectivity is involved, and it is possible that people whose jobs are evaluated with this system may feel that inequities have crept into the system either through managerial error or through politically motivated oversight.

Hay and Associates is a well-known compensation consulting firm that often does job evaluations for large organizations. Hay and Associates uses a factor comparison system based on three factors: know-how, problem solving, and accountability.

Regression-based system A regression-based system utilizes a statistical technique called multiple regression to develop an equation establishing the relationship between different dimensions of the job and compensation. Although any job analysis technique that allows direct comparisons across jobs can be used in such a system, the position analysis questionnaire (PAQ; as discussed in Chapter 5) has been frequently used as the basis for such a system. To develop the job evaluation system, it is necessary to collect job analysis data on each of a wide

■ A **regression-based system** for job evaluation utilizes a statistical technique called multiple regression to develop an equation that establishes the relationship between different dimensions of the job and compensation.

variety of jobs. These data should be in the form of scores on some common metric, and the job dimensions underlying the PAQ are perfectly suited for this approach. Next, for each job in the sample, managers obtain data on the current rate of compensation. The multiple regression technique then allows the organization to model how the presence or absence of different job dimensions, in different amounts, is related to compensation.

Notice that the resulting equation simply tells us that jobs with certain characteristics tend to be paid a certain amount. The method doesn't say that people doing these jobs should be paid this amount, simply that they are being paid the amount at present. Therefore, this approach to job evaluation captures and retains the present compensation system and does not present an ideal system. Once the equation is developed, managers can determine what any new job should be paid simply by conducting a job analysis, plugging the scores for the new job into the equation, and then letting the equation indicate what the job should be paid. Although the equation can be adjusted for market factors, this approach to job evaluation is more concerned with internal equity issues and, as noted above, assumes that the jobs in the sample are being compensated fairly.

Establishing Job Classes

Once the job evaluation has been completed, the next step in the development of a wage and salary structure is the establishment of job classes. Job classes represent gradations of responsibility and competence regarding the performance of a specific job. For example, in an assembly factory, one job that may be crucial to the conduct of the firm's business is that of a mechanic. A mechanic might be the individual responsible for maintaining and repairing various pieces of equipment and technology.

However, different levels of competence can exist among different mechanics. For example, one mechanic might be relatively inexperienced; while technically proficient at his or her job, that mechanic may be capable of repairing only a small percentage of the total number of machines or pieces of equipment in the factory. Other mechanics may be capable of maintaining and repairing all of the equipment within the factory.

It seems reasonable, then, that the organization would differentiate among people with these different competencies. As a result, the organization might create a series of job grades for this class of job. For example, Mechanic I might be the entry-level position for an individual with relatively little experience and capabilities regarding only a certain number of machines. At the other extreme, Mechanic V might be for an individual who is capable of performing a wide variety of mechanical tasks and is capable of repairing all machines within a particular factory. In between, of course, would be Mechanics II, III, and IV.

Recall from our discussion of job evaluation methods in the previous section that the job classification or grading system results in groups of jobs being identified. Organizations that use this method of job evaluation essentially establish their job classes as part of the job evaluation process itself. But organizations that use job rankings, the point system, or the factor comparison system are still likely, once those job evaluations are complete, to take the additional step of creating job classes as described above.

Establishing a Pay Structure

The final traditional step in the development of a wage and salary structure is the establishment of a pay structure. A pay structure must accomplish two tasks. First, it has to specify the level of pay the organization will provide to each job class as described in the previous section. Second, it must also identify the pay differentials to be paid to individuals within each job class. An example of a pay structure is shown in Figure 11.4.

The determination of compensation for different job classes is based on the organization's assessment of the relative value of each of those job classes to the organization itself. Thus, a logical rank-ordering of compensation levels should be set up for the most to the least valuable job class throughout the organization. Of course, the organization may also find it appropriate and necessary to group some job classes together. That is, two or more classes of jobs are valued relatively equally by the organization and thus should be compensated at approximately the same level. For example, using the five grades for mechanic discussed earlier, the organization might see little difference between Mechanic II and Mechanic III, and thus might pay a small increase when a person progresses from the lower grade to the higher one.

FIGURE 11.4   A Sample Wage Structure

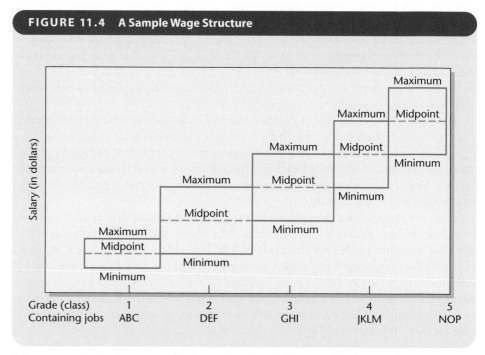

Jobs are grouped into classes or grades that are based on similar responsibilities or similar scores from a job evaluation. All jobs within a grade should be paid the same. As illustrated above, a range of pay exists within each class or grade, and overlap exists among grades so that the highest paid person in any grade is paid more than the lowest paid person in the next highest grade. This overlap allows for easier pay adjustments when someone is promoted, but the exact degree of overlap can vary from organization to organization.

A related issue is the determination of the differential in pay to be accorded to different job classes. For example, two job classes that are relatively close together in a ranking sense may still be so fundamentally different in terms of their importance to the organization that the differential in compensation is substantial. On the other hand, other job classes are relatively close to one another in both importance and ranking and, as a result, the pay differential may be modest. Second, as noted, it is also important to establish pay ranges to be applied to different jobs within a particular job class. Recall, for example, the job classification system ranking Mechanics I to V. The organization has to decide both the minimum and the maximum pay for an individual within each pay category.

Pay-for-Knowledge and Skill-Based Pay

The steps, decisions, and processes outlined above still apply to most jobs in most organizations, but recent proposals have suggested a whole different approach to compensation: employees should be rewarded for what they know rather than what they are specifically required to do on the job. The relative advantages and disadvantages of these two philosophies are summarized in the Point/Counterpoint feature for this chapter.

Pay-for-knowledge involves compensating employees (usually managerial, service, or professional employees) for learning specific material. For example, this approach might include paying programmers for learning a new programming language or rewarding managers who master a new manufacturing system. These systems can also be designed to pay for learning supervisory skills or for developing more in-depth knowledge about a topic relevant to the organization. Pay-for-knowledge systems reward employees for mastering material that allows them to be more useful to the organization in the future and are based on mastering new technology or mastering information that relates to global issues. These systems tend to be fairly expensive to start because the organization needs to develop methods for testing whether the employee has mastered the information in question. Once the systems are in place, however, the costs are usually not excessive. In addition, these plans have the potential to clash with more traditional incentive systems (see Chapter 13) because employees might choose to perfect and apply knowledge they already have rather than learn new material.[16]

Skill-based pay operates in much the same way as pay for knowledge, but these plans are more likely to be associated with hourly workers. Instead of rewarding employees who master new material, employees are rewarded for acquiring new skills. Under such a plan, for example, a secretary would be paid for learning how to use a new word-processing program. The skills involved can either be for the same job (or in the same job family) or they can be relevant for other jobs in the organization. For example, in manufacturing plants, it is often useful for employees to be cross-trained so that they have the skills to do several different jobs in the plant. This approach affords management a great deal of flexibility in scheduling, and it benefits employees because they can rotate through different jobs (providing some variety) and they acquire skills that may increase their market value if they choose to seek another job.

■ **Pay-for-knowledge** involves compensating employees for learning specific information.

■ **Skill-based pay** rewards employees for acquiring new skills.

POINT | COUNTERPOINT

What Should Be the Basis for Compensation?

The basis for compensation in most organizations is the set of job requirements. That is, employees who are expected to perform more complex, difficult, or dangerous tasks or even numerous tasks are generally paid more than other employees. Thus, the basis for compensation is the set of tasks that are required, and these tasks are usually spelled out in a job description. It has been argued, however, that this set of tasks is not the best basis for compensation. Instead, critics say that we should pay for knowledge, skill, or competency. In other words, we should not pay a person for what he or she does but for what he or she knows. Under these systems an organization specifies the knowledge bases or skills it is willing to pay for; as employees acquire this information and can demonstrate mastery, their compensation increases. We refer to this alternative as knowledge-based pay.

POINT... **We should base compensation on what a person is required to do on his or her job because...**	COUNTERPOINT... **We should base compensation on what a person knows because...**
Assessing what a person does (or should do) is easier than assessing what she or he knows.	Developing a system to certify whether employees have mastered some skill or knowledge base is relatively easy.
Most employees see this approach as a fair basis for compensation, and they can easily see the basis for compensation differences.	The organization pays people for what they can contribute in terms of special knowledge or expertise—employees are paid for what they are worth to the company.
All employees know what is expected of them and how they will be rewarded.	All employees focus on growth and the accumulation of new knowledge or skills as the means to rewards.
Paying people for what they actually do makes sense.	Paying people for what they bring to the job that is useful to the organization makes sense.
What do we do when everyone has mastered all the knowledge bases or skills specified?	Under such a system employees will strive to improve themselves, and the organization will gain flexibility as well as a more knowledgeable workforce.

So... Knowledge-based systems reward people who learn more and acquire more skills that are relevant to the job. In the long run this plan is likely to benefit the company as it tries to grow and react to changes in the environment. However, few data exist either to support or to refute this position. In addition, many bureaucratic systems must be in place to determine requisite skills and to certify mastery of those skills and knowledge bases. It is possible for an employee to master all the specified skills or knowledge bases and, at that point, have the compensation decision become complicated. Nonetheless, if knowledge-based systems can be implemented, they seem to have the potential for aiding long-run competitiveness.

WAGE AND SALARY ADMINISTRATION

■ **Wage and salary administration** is the ongoing process of managing a wage and salary structure.

Once a wage and salary structure has been developed through the job evaluation process and the establishment of job classes and pay structure, that wage and salary structure must be administered on an ongoing basis. Most organizations call this process **wage and salary administration,** or compensation administration.

Managing Compensation

As we noted at the beginning of this chapter, compensation and benefits expenses are among the costliest that any organization incurs. Thus, it stands to reason that all managers must be sensitive to these costs and must be vigilant about managing them properly. If an organization pays excess wages and salaries, then it incurs unnecessary expenses. On the other hand, if the organization does not pay sufficient wages and salaries to its employees, then it will likely experience turnover and other negative consequences.

The ongoing management of compensation and benefits is a critical part of effective wage and salary administration. In addition to monitoring costs, however, the organization needs to maintain an ongoing assessment of how well it is managing the compensation and benefits system. For example, organizations may occasionally need to change their compensation strategies. As described earlier, some organizations pay above-market rates, while other organizations pay at or below market rates. As organizational circumstances and needs change, however, it may also be necessary for the organization to change or modify its compensation strategy. Likewise, job evaluation is not a one-time operation. While job evaluations need not be conducted monthly or even yearly, it is still worthwhile for the organization to reevaluate its jobs periodically to ensure that it has an appropriate worth attached to each job, that job classes are valid, and that the pay structure of the organization is fulfilling its purpose.

Determining Individual Wages

Organizations must also develop a policy toward the determination of individual employees' wages. Regardless of the job evaluation results, most firms find it necessary and appropriate to provide differential compensation for individuals performing the same job. For both ethical and legal reasons, the basis for differential pay should not be a non-job-related factor such as gender or race. It is perfectly appropriate and indeed desirable, however, for the organization to reward people with differential compensation based on job-related qualifications.

As noted earlier, for instance, the organization might want to reward seniority by paying people who have been with the organization for a long time a higher wage or salary than individuals who are relative newcomers to the organization. Likewise, the organization may also want to reward people on the basis of performance. Thus, high performers may be paid more than those individuals who are only average or low performers, even though they are all assigned to the same job. Such an arrangement provides an effective motivational framework for

Everyone talks about the high salaries that are paid to professional athletes, especially when one considers all the performance bonuses they can earn. Coaches at major universities can also earn quite a bit, such as the $250,000 base salary earned by Bobby Knight, head basketball coach at Texas Tech University. But in 2003 Knight's team ended with a very disappointing 16–11 regular season record. What did the often-controversial Coach Knight do in response? He gave his salary back to the university. Knight still had earnings from other parts of his compensation package (such as his radio show), but Knight did what few athletes or managers in any industry are willing to do—he refused to take money for what he thought was poor performance.

the organization, but again it is important that the basis for differential pay be based on true job-related factors, such as performance or seniority, as opposed to non-job-related factors.

Pay Secrecy

■ **Pay secrecy** refers to the extent to which the compensation of any individual in an organization is secret or the extent to which it is formally made available to other individuals.

Another important aspect of wage and salary administration is pay secrecy. **Pay secrecy** refers to the extent to which the compensation of any individual in an organization is secret or the extent to which it is formally made available to other individuals. Each approach has some merit. On the one hand, advocates of pay secrecy maintain that what an individual is paid is his or her own business and it is not for public knowledge. They also argue that if pay levels are made known to everybody else, then jealousy and/or resentment may result. Indeed, most businesses practice pay secrecy, sometimes to the point of formally forbidding managers from discussing their pay with other people.

On the other hand, some organizations adopt a more open pay system where everyone knows what everyone else makes. The logic behind this strategy is that it promotes equity and motivation. If high performers are known to make more money than low performers, it follows logically that people throughout the organization will be motivated to work harder, under the assumption that they too will be recognized and rewarded for their contributions. Many publicly funded organizations such as state universities and public schools have open pay systems whereby any interested individual can look at budgets or other information to determine how much any employee is being paid. This issue is given an amusing slant in The Lighter Side of HR.

The Lighter Side of HR

Pay secrecy is a long-standing practice in many companies today. But some companies seem to be willing to consider open pay systems. At the same time, however, organizations that are interested in open pay systems should be prepared for cries of favoritism, politics, and worse! As shown in this cartoon, for example, workers who are paid less than they think they deserve will likely find reasons to criticize the pay of others, especially upper-level managers whose salaries are likely to be relatively high.

Pay Compression

A problem that some organizations must confront occasionally during wage and salary administration is pay compression. **Pay compression** occurs when individuals with substantially different levels of experience and/or performance abilities are being paid wages or salaries that are relatively equal. Pay compression is most likely to develop when the market rate for starting salaries increases at a rate faster than an organization can raise pay for individuals who are already on the payroll.

For example, suppose that an organization hires a new engineer one year at a starting annual salary of $35,000. The next year the organization wants to hire another engineer in the same field. Overall market conditions demand that such engineers are now worth $37,000 a year, and the organization finds that it has to pay that salary to attract a new engineer. Presumably, the first engineer hired has acquired a year of experience, is performing at a reasonable level in the organization, and ought to be paid more than someone who is just starting. If the organization has the resources to adjust the existing employee's salary up beyond the $37,000 level, then it is likely to avoid any major problems. On the other hand, if internal budget constraints and other considerations limit the organization's ability to adjust the compensation of its existing employees, then pay compression may result.

Indeed, it may even be possible for a newcomer starting in an organization to be paid a higher salary than an individual who has been working for the organization for a year or two. If other employees are aware of this situation, then, again, the possibility for resentment and disappointment is likely to increase. Organizations sometimes have little remedy in the event of pay compression. On the one hand, they have to respond to market shifts if they want to continue to hire at a competitive level. At the same time, their internal resources may limit their ability to maintain pay increases at the same rate that the market rate is increasing. In this case the organization may find it necessary to try to provide other kinds of rewards, such as intangible benefits and recognition, or simply face the consequences of disgruntled employees leaving because they feel they are being underpaid relative to newcomers in the organization.

> ■ **Pay compression** occurs when individuals with substantially different levels of experience and/or performance abilities are being paid wages or salaries that are relatively equal.

LEGAL ISSUES IN COMPENSATION

The major legal issues involved in compensation were discussed in Chapter 3, but we will review them briefly here. The Fair Labor Standards Act includes provisions for the minimum wage, overtime, and child labor. The first two topics are rather straightforward in most cases, but some issues arise in both areas. One of these issues may be more social than legal, but it certainly has legal implications.

As noted in Chapter 3, not every employee in every organization receives "the" minimum wage. In fact, several minimum wages exist, such as the minimum wage for agricultural jobs, and various states have also established higher minimum wages than the national limit (also, see HR in the 21st Century). Even if an employee receives the minimum wage, some argue that it is difficult to live on the minimum wage in the United States in the twenty-first century. If an employee works forty hours a week at $5.15 an hour, he or she earns $206.00 a week, or just under $11,000 a year *before* taxes, social security, and any insurance or pension deductions. Is this really a living wage in this country? Perhaps not. But raising the minimum wage unilaterally is not so simple. Surely employees are hired because they are willing to work for low wages. In economic terms, their marginal productivity level is equal to their marginal wage rate. In simpler terms, they are worth exactly what the company is paying them. If the firm were forced to pay a higher rate, they simply would not hire these individuals.

It is surely within our power, as a country, to raise the minimum wage. We could raise it to $10.00 an hour and ensure that everyone who has a full-time job can truly support him- or herself. The counterargument that this increase will result in people losing their jobs, however, makes this matter extremely complicated.

The other issue relates to overtime. The laws concerning overtime pay seem straightforward. Employees who work more than forty hours a week must be paid time and half for all hours in excess of forty, unless they are considered exempt. As explained in Chapter 3, the term *exempt* means that the employee is literally exempt from the overtime provisions, and this term usually applies to managers and professionals. In some organizations, however, employees who are asked to work more than forty hours during a week are not paid overtime but are given time off instead. This time off is referred to as *comp time* and is considered compensation for overtime. Thus, someone who has to work forty-five hours one week might be assigned only thirty-five hours the next week but still receive full pay. Comp time is often not as beneficial to the employee, who would otherwise earn more in total pay, but it is more cost efficient for the organization. And it does give employees something that many of them value—time away from work.

EVALUATING COMPENSATION POLICIES

Given the enormous cost to an organization of compensation packages, it is clearly important that managers carefully assess the benefit of these packages for the organization. On the one hand, it is important that the organization provide reasonable compensation and appropriate benefits to its employees. At the same time, it is in the best interests of the stockholders and other constituents of the organization that the firm manage its resources wisely. Thus, it is important to assess this topic periodically to ensure that costs are in line. One method of assessment is through the use of wage surveys, as noted earlier in this chapter. Similar comparisons can also be made for wage structures, benefit packages, and so forth. Any organization can learn the average insurance premium costs, for example, that other organizations are paying. While the organization may not be able to match these premiums, particularly if it has a history of accident claims, illnesses, and so forth, it can nevertheless learn how close its costs are to those of other firms.

Some organizations might find it necessary to audit their overall compensation programs to determine whether or not they are providing a competitive package. As part of the recruiting process, it is necessary, of course, that the organization is viewed as an attractive place to work if it wants to hire high-quality human resources. Part of this strategy involves considering the total compensation package, including employee benefits, a topic we will discuss in Chapter 13.

Chapter Summary

Compensation has several fundamental purposes and objectives. One fundamental purpose of compensation is to provide an adequate and appropriate reward system for employees so that they feel valued and worthwhile as organizational members and representatives. The three basic strategic options are to pay above-market compensation rates, market compensation rates, or below-market compensation rates. Several different factors contribute to the compensation strategy that a firm develops. The critical source of information that many organizations use in developing compensation strategies is pay surveys.

After human resource managers have developed their compensation strategy, they are then prepared to establish a wage and salary structure for their organization. The starting point in this effort is job evaluation, a method for determining the relative value or worth of a job to the organization so that individuals who perform that job can be compensated adequately and appropriately. Several job evaluation techniques and methods have been established. Once the job evaluation has been completed, the next step in the development of a wage and salary structure is the establishment of job classes. The final step is the establishment of a pay structure. Increasingly popular alternative approaches to compensation include pay-for-knowledge and skill-based pay.

Once a wage and salary structure has been developed through the job evaluation process and the establishment of job classes and a pay structure, then that wage and salary structure must be administered on an ongoing basis. The ongoing management of compensation and benefits is a critical part of effective wage and salary administration. Organizations must also develop a policy toward the determination of individual employees' wages. Another important aspect of wage and salary administration is pay secrecy. A problem that some organizations have to confront occasionally during wage and salary administration is pay compression.

Given the enormous cost to an organization of its compensation packages, it is clearly important that managers carefully assess the effectiveness of the firm's compensation structure to ensure that organizational and employee interests are optimized.

Key Points for Future HR Managers

▶ Compensation includes the total set of rewards an organization provides an employee in return for his or her work. Thus, it is more than just a weekly or monthly paycheck.

▶ For compensation programs to be effective, they must account for both external equity (comparisons with employees at the same job at different organizations) and internal equity (the relative pay of employees within the same organization at different jobs).

▶ A critical strategic decision in designing compensation is what exactly the organization is willing to pay for. For example, it is possible to base pay on seniority, performance, or knowledge, among other things.

▶ Another critical strategic decision is whether the organization will pay at, above, or below the market wage for a job.

▶ Pay surveys are the most common way to collect market information about compensation rates.

▶ Job evaluation is the method for determining the relative pay for different jobs within the organization. Systems for job evaluation include ranking, classification, point system, factor comparison system, and regression-based system.

▶ Pay-for-knowledge programs and skill-based pay systems are newer systems for determining compensation based on what the employee knows rather than on job duties. Under these systems the employee can increase his or her compensation by acquiring new knowledge that is valuable to the organization.

▶ Pay compression is a problem in many organizations. It occurs when the difference between lower-paying and higher-paying jobs shrinks. It is most likely to occur when market rates are rising quickly, and senior employees are paid only slightly more than new hires.

▶ The laws regarding minimum wage, overtime, and child labor are quite specific, although the issue of comp time sometimes clouds the subject of overtime.

Key Points for Future General Managers

▶ Critical strategic decisions relate to determining what should be paid to employees and what that rate should be relative to market rates.

▶ The decision concerning what to pay employees for is probably the most critical, and new pay systems such as pay for knowledge and skill-based

pay advocate paying employees for what they know rather than what they do.

▶ All decisions to pay wages and salaries at rates below, above, or at the going market rate should be made with full knowledge of the implications of each decision.

Review and Discussion Questions

1. What is compensation?

2. What are the basic differences between wages and salaries?

3. What are the basic strategic options an organization has for its compensation policies?

4. What role do pay surveys play in compensation?

5. Identify and summarize the basic methods of job evaluation.

6. Why are job classes needed? How are they developed?

7. How does an organization create a pay structure?

8. What are the basic issues involved in determining individual wages?

9. What are the advantages and disadvantages of open versus secret pay information?

10. How does pay compression develop? Why is it a problem?

Closing Case

Working by the Hour at General Motors and Wal-Mart

Hourly workers—people who are paid a set dollar amount for each hour or fraction of an hour they work—have long been the backbone of the U.S. economy. But times are changing, and so is the lot of the hourly worker. Like all change, of course, some is for the better, but some is clearly for the worse, at least from the workers' standpoint. And nowhere are these differences more apparent than the contrasting conditions for hourly workers at General Motors (GM) and Wal-Mart.

General Motors, of course, is an old, traditional, industrial company that, up until recently, was the nation's largest employer. For decades, its hourly workers have been protected by strong labor unions like the United Auto Workers (UAW). These unions, in turn, have forged contracts and working conditions that almost seem archaic in today's economy. Consider, for example, the employment conditions of Tim Philbrick, a forty-two-year-old plant worker and union member

at the firm's Fairfax plant near Kansas City. He has worked for GM for twenty-three years.

Philbrick makes almost $20 an hour in base pay. With a little overtime, his annual earnings top $60,000. But he is far from the highest paid factory worker at GM. Skilled-trade workers like electricians and toolmakers make $2 to $2.50 an hour more, and with greater overtime opportunities, they often make $100,000 or more per year. Mr. Philbrick also gets a no-deductible health insurance policy that allows him to see any doctor he wants. He gets four weeks of vacation per year, plus two weeks at Christmas and at least another week in July, when the plant is closed. In addition, he gets two paid twenty-three-minute breaks and a paid thirty-minute lunch break per day. He also has the option of retiring with full benefits after thirty years.

GM estimates that, with benefits, its average worker makes more than $43 an hour. Perhaps not surprisingly, then, the firm is always looking for opportunities to reduce its workforce through attrition and cutbacks, with the goal of replacing production capacity with lower-cost labor abroad. The UAW, on the other hand, is staunchly opposed to further workforce reductions and cutbacks. And long-standing work rules strictly dictate who gets overtime, who can be laid off and who can't, and myriad other employment conditions for Philbrick and his peers.

But the situation at GM is quite different—in a lot of ways—from conditions at Wal-Mart. Along many different dimensions Wal-Mart is slowly but surely supplanting General Motors as the quintessential U.S. corporation. For example, it is growing rapidly, is becoming more and more ingrained in the U.S. life style, and now employs more people than GM did in its heyday. But the hourly worker at Wal-Mart has a much different experience than do hourly workers at GM.

For example, consider Nancy Handley, a twenty-seven-year-old Wal-Mart employee who oversees the men's department at a big store in St. Louis. Jobs like Handley's are paid between $9 and $11 an hour, or about $20,000 a year. About $100 a month is deducted from her paycheck to help cover the costs of benefits. Her health insurance has a $250 deductible; she then pays 20 percent of her health-care costs as long as she uses a set of approved physicians. Her prescriptions cost between $5 and $10 each. She also has dental coverage; after her $50 deductible, she pays 20 percent of her dental costs. During her typical work-

day, Handley gets two 15-minute breaks and an hour for lunch, but she has to punch out at the time clock and doesn't get paid during these times.

But Handley doesn't feel mistreated by Wal-Mart. Far from it; she says that she is appropriately compensated for what she does. She has received three merit raises in the last seven years, for example, and has considerable job security. If she decides to try for advancement, Wal-Mart offers considerable potential. For example, several thousand hourly workers a year are promoted to the ranks of management. While the amount of time they must work during their work-week increases, so too does their pay. And Handley is clearly not unique in her views—Wal-Mart employees routinely reject any and all overtures from labor unions and are among the most loyal and committed employees in the United States today.[17]

Case Questions

1. Compare and contrast hourly working conditions at GM and Wal-Mart.

2. Describe the (apparent) wage structures at GM and Wal-Mart.

3. Summarize the basic issues in wage and salary administration that managers at GM and Wal-Mart most likely face.

Building HR Management Skills

Purpose: The purpose of this exercise is to help you better understand the impact of hourly wages on operating costs and profit margins.

Step 1: Working alone or with a group (your instructor will specify which), identify a local small business that likely depends heavily on hourly employees and whose owner or manager is willing to help students with a class project. Good examples might be a fast-food restaurant like McDonald's or Taco Bell, a dry cleaning establishment, or a specialty retailer.

Step 2: Interview the owner or manager of the business and obtain as much of the following information as possible:

■ Total number of hourly employees

■ Total number of labor hours needed per week

■ Average hourly wage currently being paid

■ Approximate annual revenues

■ Approximate profit margin

(*Note:* If the owner or manager will not or cannot provide some of this information, ask for general or approximate figures or ranges that might characterize a similar business.)

Step 3: Assume that because of an increase in the minimum wage, increased competition or demand for hourly workers, mandated increases from the home office, or some similar factor, hourly wages have to be increased. Calculate the following for wage increases of $0.10, $0.25, and $0.50 an hour:

■ Total annual labor cost increases for each level of hourly wage increase

- The effect of each increase on current profit margins

- The necessary increase in annual revenues needed to maintain current profit margins for each level of wage increase

Step 4: Respond to the following questions:

1. What other costs and profit factors are affected by wage increases?

2. How would you incorporate salaries into this problem?

3. In larger firms, union contracts might be the catalyst for increased wages. How similar or different would this sort of analysis be for a much bigger company?

Ethical Dilemmas in HR Management

Assume that you are the manager of a company-owned fast-food restaurant. While you have a few permanent full-time employees, your workforce consists primarily of older retirees working to supplement their social security benefits and college students working to help cover their educational expenses. Altogether, you employ ten retirees and twenty-five students. Each employee works an average of fifteen hours per week and earns the minimum wage.

A recent mandated increase in the minimum wage has cut into your profit margins, however, and the home office has dictated that you must lower labor costs. While you know that everyone will have to work harder, you also recognize that you can still manage the business effectively with fewer labor hours per week.

Your analysis has indicated that any one of four options will work. One is to terminate four of the retirees. A second option is to terminate four college students. A third option is to terminate two retirees and two college students. The final option is to retain all of your current workers but to cut their average hours from fifteen down to twelve per week.

Questions

1. What are the ethical issues in this situation?

2. What are the basic arguments for and against each of the four options?

3. What do you think most managers would do? What would you do?

HR Internet Exercise

Search the Internet for sites devoted to wages and/or salaries. Visit at least six such sites. Two especially good ones are:

http://jobsmart.org/tools/salary

http://www.careerbuilder.com/JobSeeker/CRC/Salary Information.htm

Learn as much as possible about each site and then respond to the following questions:

1. How might you, as a job seeker, use these kinds of websites to ensure that you are paid an equitable wage or salary?

2. How might you, as a human resource manager, use these kinds of websites to ensure that your firm is paying an appropriate wage or salary?

3. What information seems to be common to all the sites you visited?

4. Did you expect to find or would have liked to find certain information that did not appear on the site?

12

Incentives and Performance-Based Rewards

CHAPTER OBJECTIVES

After studying this chapter you should be able to:

■ Summarize the purposes of performance-based rewards.

■ Discuss merit compensation systems and their limitations.

■ Identify and discuss forms and limitations of incentive compensation systems.

■ Identify and describe forms and limitations of team and group incentive reward systems.

■ Discuss both standard and special forms of executive compensation and summarize criticisms of recent trends in executive compensation.

■ Summarize new approaches to performance-based rewards in organizations.

■ Understand basic concepts underlying a compensation strategy as applied to incentives and performance-based pay.

It seems like only yesterday that desperate employers were almost throwing cash at prospective new employees and going to great lengths to retain even average employees already on their payroll. But the sharp economic downturn in 2002 and early 2003 rapidly shifted the situation from a "labor sellers' market" to a "labor buyers' market" as employers cut hiring and offered people they did hire much smaller compensation and incentive packages than had been necessary only a short time before.

> *"Companies are aggressively managing their compensation dollars toward their best performers. That means that some people will get zero."*
>
> (Rick Beal, compensation consultant)*

Many companies have also taken a new look at how they distribute pay raises to their current employees. A few years ago, for example, the norm at many companies was to provide almost all employees with at least an annual cost-of-living adjustment. Those companies using merit systems tended to distribute pay across a fairly small distribution. For instance, if the average merit raise was to be, say, 4 percent, the high performers might have received as much as 6 or 7 percent, many average workers may have received 4 percent, and low performers may have received 2 or 3 percent. A very small number of employees might get a bit more, and extremely low performers, a bit less. But almost everyone got something.

But that pattern has started to change at some companies. As managers have come to appreciate the importance of their very best workers and recognize how easily they can replace average workers, these firms have started to impose a much wider distribution of merit pay raises. Part of the goal is to make their current jobs so attractive to the very best employees that they will not look elsewhere. And if average workers leave, the firm knows it can hire new people for the same—or perhaps even less—money.

So if a firm adopts this strategy, it will allocate merit dollars differently than it may have in the past. For instance, if the same firm described above can give 4 percent pay increases again this year, it may give its very top employees 9 or 10 percent, its very good employees 5 or 6 percent, its average employees 2 percent, and its lower performers nothing.

At least for the time being, this approach is likely to prove beneficial to employers in several ways. Firms will perhaps communicate more clearly than they did in the past the links between performance and rewards. They will likely keep more of their top performers. And even their average employees may stay because they have fewer options. Finally, if low performers choose to leave, the firm is likely to be able to hire better performers to replace them.

But this approach has its risks. Morale among the people who get smaller raises but remain with the firm may suffer. Long-term employees who have perhaps toiled in the best interests of the firm at the cost of their own career mobility will likely be resentful. If the firm's performance appraisal systems are flawed, then at least some of the wrong people may stay and others may leave. That is, a true high performer not recognized as such and an average performer who is evaluated more highly will each receive an incorrect signal from the organization. And when the economy rebounds, firms may again have to revert to their earlier models for distributing merit pay and other incentives.[1] ■

As we explained in detail in Chapter 11, organizations must provide basic compensation to all their employees. This basic compensation is intended to satisfy fundamental human needs and to fulfill the organization's component of the psychological contract regarding pay. Specifically, the basic compensation strategies discussed in Chapter 11 focus on the simple and straightforward compensation that people receive for performing their jobs at a satisfactory level. But many organizations find it useful to go even further with the compensation they provide and to tie at least some of the rewards that individuals receive to the individuals' performance or to the performance of the group to which the individuals belong. Indeed, rewarding employees for their performance is clearly not a new idea. As long ago as the days of Frederick Taylor (the early years of the twentieth century), scientific management experts advised managers to use piece-rate pay (paying workers for each unit produced) systems to compensate employees in proportion to their productivity. But as indicated in the chapter-opening vignette, companies today are still striving to find the best kinds of incentives and rewards to offer to their most valued employees.

This chapter will explore the role of incentives and performance-based rewards in organizations. First, we will examine the various purposes of performance-based rewards. Then we will describe merit compensation systems, followed by incentive compensation systems, group incentive reward systems, and executive compensation. Finally, this chapter will conclude with a discussion of new approaches to performance-based rewards, and a general discussion of the strategic decisions underlying approaches to performance-based compensation.

PURPOSES OF PERFORMANCE-BASED REWARDS

Performance-based rewards play several roles and address various purposes in organizations. The major purposes involve the relationship of rewards to motivation and to performance. Specifically, organizations want employees to perform at relatively high levels and need to make it worth it for them to do so. When rewards are associated with higher levels of performance, employees will presumably be motivated to work harder in the effort to achieve those awards. At that point, their self-interests coincide with the organization's interests. Performance-based rewards are also relevant to other employee behaviors.

Rewards and Motivation

It is important that organizations motivate employees to exert effort aimed at accomplishing organizational goals. As illustrated in Figure 12.1, rewards play a fundamental role in how motivation occurs in organizations.[2] For example, one of the most important theories of motivation is expectancy theory. Expectancy theory essentially suggests that people are motivated to engage in behaviors if they perceive that those behaviors are likely to lead to outcomes that they value. Thus, if pay and other performance-based rewards are of value to individual employees, it follows logically that if employees believe that their hard work will lead to the attainment of those rewards, they will be more likely to engage in behavior directed at hard work.

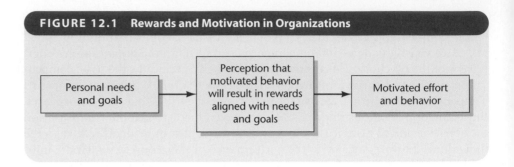

FIGURE 12.1   Rewards and Motivation in Organizations

Notice, though, that this theory also illustrates what can go wrong with performance-based pay systems. Rewards are typically based on performance, not on hard work or effort itself. Therefore, if employees feel that their hard work will *not* result in increased performance (perhaps because the job is too difficult or they believe that they are not properly trained), then they have no reason to increase effort, even though the employees can see that increased performance will be rewarded. Clearly, if employees don't see that rewards are tied to increased performance (e.g., when all pay raises are given across the board), or when some outcomes associated with increased performance are *not* attractive (e.g., the expectation of ever higher levels of performance in the future), they have little reason, again, to work harder.

Another important viewpoint on individual motivation in organizations is reinforcement theory. Reinforcement theory is based on the assumption that behavior is a function of its consequences. That is, if employees choose to engage in behaviors and they achieve a desirable outcome (such as a pay raise) as a result, then they are more likely to choose that same behavior in the future. But if they choose a behavior that results in less pleasant outcomes (perhaps increased stress), then they are less likely to choose that behavior in the future.

Therefore, if an employee works hard and receives a reward such as a pay increase or praise from the supervisor in charge as a direct result of that hard work, then the individual is more likely to work hard in the future. But if the employee works hard and receives no additional reward or no praise from the supervisor and has only fatigue and stress to show for her or his hard work, then that employee is less likely to work hard in the future. This scenario does not sound very different from expectancy theory, which was described above. In fact, although the details of the theories differ regarding the mechanisms underlying decisions to work hard on the job, in practice, the two theories bring us to the same conclusion: people will work harder if the link between that hard work and obtaining desired outcomes is strong.

■ **Agency theory** is concerned with the diverse interests and goals held by the organization's stakeholders, including its employees and managers, and the methods through which the organization's reward system can be used to align these diverse interests and goals.

Another important perspective on reward and motivation is a relatively new approach to understanding organizations. **Agency theory** is concerned with the diverse interests and goals that are held by the organization's stakeholders, including its employees and managers, and the methods through which the organization's reward system can be used to align these diverse interests and goals. Agency theory derives its name from the fact that those employees in control of most modern corporations (i.e., the managers who run the company) are not the principal owners of the organization but are instead agents that presumably represent the owners' interests.

Agency theory highlights three fundamental differences that may exist and helps explain how managers as opposed to company owners approach compensation.[3] The owners of a corporation might be more inclined to focus on minimizing cost as a way of maximizing their personal wealth. But their agents, or the managers who are running the business, might be more inclined to spend a larger percentage of the organization's resources on activities that do not contribute directly to owner wealth.

A second point derived from agency theory has to do with risk. Managers depend on the success of their organization for their income, so they may be less inclined to accept risk. And the agents of an organization may have a fundamentally different time horizon than do the owners of the firm. These agents, for example, may tend to focus more on the short run because it is easier to maximize performance over a shorter period of time than it is over a longer period of time and because their tenure with the organization may also involve a shorter period of time. We will consider the role of agency theory and employee compensation at several points later in this chapter.

Rewards and Performance

Rewards in an organization may also have a direct impact on performance both at the individual level and at the group and organizational level.[4] From one perspective, this relates primarily to the relationship between performance and motivation. Most people suggest that an individual's performance in an organization is determined by three factors: the ability to perform, the environmental context of performance, and the motivation to perform. Rewards and performance from this perspective are highlighted in Figure 12.2.

Ability to perform is handled primarily through the organization's selection and training mechanisms. That is, the organization should ensure that it hires only those people who have the ability to perform at the expected level. And for those individuals who may be deficient in ability, training and development activities may be undertaken to improve their ability. The environmental context includes factors such as equipment, machinery, materials, information, and other support factors. For example, individuals who are required as part of their work to perform spreadsheet calculations need computers with adequate memory and software to allow them to conduct spreadsheet analyses.

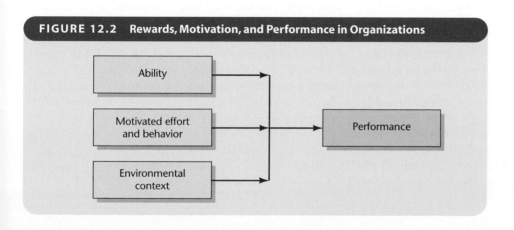

FIGURE 12.2   Rewards, Motivation, and Performance in Organizations

Ability

Motivated effort and behavior

Environmental context

Performance

Motivation is the third important ingredient in performance. As described in the preceding section, properly designed incentive- and performance-based reward systems can be significant contributors to employee motivation. Thus, if a manager wants to motivate people to perform at their highest level, she or he should structure a reward system so that people who are motivated to perform at high levels of job performance will attain rewards in exchange for achieving those high levels of performance. HR in the 21st Century describes an interesting new approach to linking rewards and performance at United Airlines. The most significant element of this plan is the fact that performance is measured in many areas.

Rewards and Other Employee Behaviors

Rewards can also be used to influence other kinds of employee behaviors. One of the most significant employee behaviors is turnover. If employees believe that their basic compensation is adequate and if they also believe that their performance is recognized and rewarded beyond the basic compensation levels, then they are likely to want to remain a member of the organization. On the other hand, if

---

HR **in the 21st Century**

Pay for Morale?

Linking pay to performance is a long-standing practice in many organizations. Compensation programs based on this link generally measure performance from a relatively objective perspective, such as sales or revenues, stock price, productivity gains, and so forth. But this practice may be ending—or least broadening in scope—to include "softer" and more subjective indices of performance. The most significant example of this effort in recent times is embedded in labor contracts recently negotiated at United Airlines (UAL). The unions were able to push for a major new approach in part because they own 60 percent of UAL's stock.

Under the terms of the agreement, more than half of the bonus pay received by the top 625 UAL managers will be determined by three new criteria—on-time performance, customer satisfaction, and employee satisfaction. While on-time performance is clearly an objective measure of performance (and a standard in the airline industry), customer and employee satisfaction are both less objective and more unusual. Indeed, only a small handful of other firms use satisfaction to determine

> *"I don't think most managers would be enthusiastic about giving employees a chance to say anything about them."*
>
> (Graef Crystal, compensation expert)*

executive pay. For example, at Eastman Kodak, employee satisfaction determines 20 percent of executive bonuses.

Of course, satisfaction has to be measured and evaluated before the new plan at UAL can be implemented. Under the terms of the agreement, an outside survey firm will be hired to perform the annual attitude surveys for both customers and employees. The results of these surveys will be shared throughout the company. Thus, everyone will know how customers and employees feel about the airline. And the firm's top managers will see their own compensation directly affected as a result. Meanwhile, the same labor unions own significant portions of the stock at Northwest Airlines and Trans World Airlines and indicate that they hope to implement the same kind of satisfaction-based incentive systems in those firms as well. Will this trend continue and become widely used, or will it remain the exception? Only time, of course, will tell.

Sources: "UAL: Labor Is My Co-Pilot," *Business Week*, March 1, 1999, p. 38 (*quote on p. 38); *Hoover's Handbook of American Business 2003* (Austin, Tex.: Hoover's Business Press, 2003).

employees believe that their performance is not recognized or that it has no impact on the rewards that they receive from the organization, then these individuals may be more likely to leave the organization and seek a more attractive job elsewhere.

Absenteeism and attendance are also affected by incentives and performance-based rewards. For example, if an organization wants to improve employee attendance, one strategy is to tie a reward to high levels of attendance. One strategy used by some companies is to provide people with a financial bonus if they exceed certain minimal levels of attendance expectations. A company using this strategy might reward employees with, say, an extra day's pay if employees miss only one or two workdays per year. Another related strategy that some organizations use is to provide premium pay to people who do not use their sick days. Some companies pay individual employees time and a half for unused sick time that is not used by the end of the year.

MERIT COMPENSATION SYSTEMS

Merit compensation systems are one of the most fundamental forms of performance-based rewards. In this section we examine merit-pay plans first and then turn our attention briefly to some of their limitations.

Merit-Pay Plans

Merit pay generally refers to pay awarded to employees on the basis of the relative value of their contributions to the organization. Employees who make greater contributions are given higher pay than those who make lesser contributions. **Merit-pay plans**, then, are formal compensation plans that base at least some meaningful portion of compensation on merit.

The most general form of the merit-pay plan is to provide annual salary increases to individuals in the organization based on their relative merit. Merit, in turn, is usually determined or defined based on the individual's performance and overall contributions to the organization. Recall that, in Chapter 9, we discussed various methods for evaluating employee performance. We noted in that chapter that performance appraisal had the most meaning to employees if it was subsequently connected with a reward such as a salary increase.

An organization using such a traditional merit-pay plan might instruct its supervisors to give all their employees an average pay raise of, say, 4 percent. But the individual supervisor is also instructed to differentiate among high, average, and low performers. Under a simple system, for example, a manager might give the top 25 percent of her employees a 6 percent pay raise, the middle 50 percent of her employees a 4 percent or average pay raise, and the bottom 25 percent of the employees a 2 percent pay raise.

Of course, it is important for the organization to have valid and reliable measures for merit. Merit generally refers to performance, but for the plan to have motivation and performance effects, people throughout the organization must have a clear understanding of what the firm means by the term *merit*. It is also necessary that the organization's performance management systems are rigorous

■ **Merit pay** is pay awarded to employees on the basis of the relative value of their contributions to the organization.

■ **Merit-pay plans** are compensation plans that formally base at least some meaningful portion of compensation on merit.

enough to make valid and appropriate differentiations among levels of performance. For example, if the system does not break out many performance classifications, it may be difficult to distribute merit raises in any sort of meaningful way.

Limitations of Merit Compensation Systems

While merit compensation systems are widely used and serve several valuable purposes in organizations, they also suffer from some relatively important limitations. One major limitation of most merit pay systems is that they focus almost exclusively on individual performance. But in some cases, an individual's performance might be determined by factors beyond her or his control. For example, coworkers, resources, and information may all play a role in determining whether or not an employee can perform at a high level.

Another basic limitation of merit systems is that they are based primarily on performance appraisal systems, which may themselves be subject to error and mistakes. Again, in our earlier discussion of performance management in Chapter 9, we noted many of the drawbacks and shortcomings that might be associated with performance appraisal techniques. As a result, it is not unusual for employees to disagree with the performance ratings they receive (regardless of whether or not they are accurate). These problems are magnified when pay increases are based on the ratings given, which has led some scholars to recommend that merit-pay plans be abandoned completely.[5]

Another important limitation of merit-pay systems is that they may be prone to focusing on too broad a period of performance. That is, individual performance might vary significantly from day to day, from week to week, and from month to month. Merit systems award salary increases on the basis of overall performance spanning a full year. Thus, they may fail to account for short-term variation and fluctuations in individual performance.

Finally, merit systems are also subject to considerable disagreement among employees and may lead to perceptions of favoritism and unfairness. Stated differently, if people in an organization disagree with their supervisor about the relative merits of the performance of different individuals, they will similarly disagree with rewards that are awarded to individuals on the basis of that level of performance.

A final limitation of merit compensation systems is that, under most such arrangements, the increases given to individuals become a permanent part of their base pay. For example, an individual who performs at an exceptionally strong level in a year that the organization has a lucrative salary budget might receive a significant merit-pay raise of, say, 10 percent or higher. That increase becomes part of the individual's base pay for the rest of her or his career with the organization. Thus, the individual might reflect a much more average level of performance for the next several years but still maintain that 10 percent pay increase that was awarded to her or him during the one especially strong year. Over the course of a twenty-, thirty-, or forty-year career, merit pay increases given during the early years of a person's tenure with the organization can amount to substantial amounts of money.

Skill- and Knowledge-Based Pay Systems and Merit

Although these systems are usually not viewed as merit-pay or incentive-pay systems, it is worth noting how skill-based pay or knowledge-based pay systems, discussed in Chapter 10, focus employee attention on different areas but still use similar motivational processes. Under these systems, instead of rewarding employees for increased performance, they are rewarded for the acquisition of more skills or knowledge. More traditional merit-pay systems reward employees for achieving some level of performance, but this performance is defined by what the organization needs (or wants) right now. In the future, different types of performance may be needed, requiring effort focused on different areas. Changing the requirements for merit pay could be confusing or even demoralizing.

Skill-based pay systems reward employees for the acquisition of job-related skills, not for any specific level of performance. Presumably, as the employee acquires more and more of these skills, he or she becomes more valuable to the organization. Because the focus is on skill acquisition rather than performance, it should be easier for the organization to shift direction or focus, without causing problems for the employee. In fact, because the employee now has these additional skills, he or she should be able to adapt to a wider variety of situations and demands, thus increasing the organization's flexibility.

Although problems are associated with these systems and their administration, they offer an alternative to more traditional merit-pay systems and provide a more strategic long-term focus for the organization.[6] In addition, they allow the organization to move employees toward focusing on more than just basic productivity.[7]

INCENTIVE COMPENSATION SYSTEMS

Incentive compensation systems are among the oldest forms of performance-based rewards. For example, as noted earlier, some companies used individual piece-rate incentive plans over 100 years ago.[8] Under a **piece-rate incentive plan**, the organization pays an employee a certain amount of money for every unit she or he produces. For example, an employee might be paid $1.00 for every dozen units of product that she or he completed successfully. But such simplistic systems fail to account for factors such as minimum wage levels, and they rely heavily on the assumptions that performance is under an individual's complete control and that the individual employee does a single task continuously throughout his or her work time. Thus, most organizations that try to use incentive compensation systems today use more sophisticated methods.

■ A **piece-rate incentive plan** involves the organization paying an employee a certain amount of money for every unit she or he produces.

Incentive Pay Plans

Generally speaking, **individual incentive plans** reward individual performance on a real-time basis. That is, rather than increasing a person's base salary at the end of the year, an individual instead receives some level of salary increase or financial reward in conjunction with demonstrated outstanding performance in close proximity to when that performance occurred. Individual incentive systems are most likely to be used in cases where performance can be objectively assessed, in terms of number of units of output or similar measures, rather than on a subjective assessment of performance by a superior.

Some variations on a piece-rate system are still fairly popular. Although many of these systems still resemble the early plans in most ways, a well-known piece-rate

■ **Individual incentive plans** reward individual performance on a real-time basis.

Steve Bennett is CEO of Intuit, a software manufacturer that sells financial programs such as Turbo-Tax and Quicken. Bennett, shown here, is a true believer in incentive pay and employee recognition programs. In fact, the company spends about 1.5 percent of its total compensation budget on employee recognition programs. In a company of over 6,000 employees, this represents a major investment. For example, employee Alan Hampton designed and built a data center for the company. He received a thank you e-mail that linked him to a website where he learned that the appreciation included an all expenses paid weekend trip with his wife to Monterrey Bay, California.

■ A **sales commission** is an incentive paid to salespeople.

system at Lincoln Electric illustrates how an organization can adapt the traditional model to achieve better results. For years Lincoln's employees were paid individual incentive payments based on their performance. However, the amount of money shared (or the incentive pool) was based on the company's profitability. A well-organized system allowed employees to make suggestions for increasing productivity. Motivation was provided in the form of a reward equaling one-third of the profits (another third went to the stockholders and the last third was retained for improvements and seed money). Thus, the pool for incentive payments was determined by profitability, and an employee's share of this pool was a function of his or her base pay and rated performance based on the piece-rate system. Lincoln Electric was most famous, however, because of the stories (which were apparently typical) of production workers receiving a year-end bonus payment that equaled their yearly base pay.[9] In recent years, Lincoln has partially abandoned its famous system for business reasons, but it still serves as a benchmark for other companies seeking innovative piece-rate pay systems.

Perhaps the most common form of individual incentive is the **sales commission** that is paid to salespeople. For example, sales representatives for consumer products firms and retail sales agents may be compensated under this type of commission system. In general, the person might receive a percentage of the total volume of attained sales as her or his commission for a period of time. Some sales jobs are based entirely on commission, while others use a combination of base minimum salary with additional commission as an incentive. Notice that these plans put a considerable amount of the salespersons' earnings at risk. Although organizations often have drawing accounts to allow the salesperson to live during lean periods (the person then "owes" this money to the organization), if he or she does not perform well, he or she will not be paid much. The portion of salary based on commission is simply not guaranteed and is paid only if the employee's sales reach some target level.

Other Forms of Incentives

Occasionally organizations may use other forms of incentives to motivate employees. For example, a nonmonetary incentive such as additional time off or a special perk might be a useful incentive. A company might establish a sales contest in which the sales group that attains the highest level of sales increase over a specified period of time receives an extra week of paid vacation, perhaps even at an arranged place such as a tropical resort or a ski lodge.[10] The Lighter Side of HR illustrates one humorous example of how such incentives might be used to attract new employees.

The Lighter Side of HR

Organizations often use incentives to attract and retain workers. As shown in this cartoon, however, managers need to remember that because people have different needs, the same incentives do not always work for everyone. For example, some people may want a bigger office, while others might want greater flexibility over working hours and conditions. And someone may even occasionally be motivated by something such as control of the office thermostat! (Cathy © 1998 Cathy Guisewite. Reprinted with permission of Universal Press Syndicate. All rights reserved.)

A major advantage of incentives relative to merit systems is that incentives are typically a one-shot reward and do not accumulate by becoming part of the individual's base salary. Stated differently, an individual whose outstanding performance entitles him or her to a financial incentive gets the incentive only once based on that level of performance. If the individual's performance begins to erode later on, then the individual may receive a lesser incentive or perhaps no incentive in the future. As a consequence, the employee's base salary remains the same or is perhaps increased at a relatively moderate pace; he or she receives one-time incentive rewards as recognition for exemplary performance. Because these plans, by their very nature, focus on one-time events, it is much easier for the organization to change the focus of the incentive plan. At a simple level, for example, an organization can set up an incentive plan for selling one product during one quarter, but then shift the incentive to a different product the next quarter, as the situation requires. Automobile companies like Ford and General Motors routinely reduce sales incentives for models that are selling well and increase sales incentives for models that are selling below expectations or are about to be discontinued.

Limitations of Incentive Compensation Systems

As with merit systems, incentive compensation systems have some shortcomings and weaknesses. One major shortcoming is that they are practical only when performance can be measured easily and objectively. Most managerial work does not fit this pattern and, in fact, is often characterized by ambiguous performance indicators that are difficult to assess. Thus, it may be much more difficult to provide valid and appropriate incentives for these individuals. Another important limitation of incentive systems is that they are often an administrative burden. That is, it may be a major challenge for the organization to evaluate performance continuously, to recognize the level of performance that warrants additional rewards, and then to provide those rewards on a fair and timely basis.

Another problem with individual incentives is that they are likely to focus attention on only a narrow range of behaviors, perhaps at the expense of other behaviors. Consider, for example, a sales representative in a department store. This sales representative may be able to maximize his or her pay by greeting every customer aggressively, trying continually to sell them items that they may or may not need, and overlooking deficiencies or shortcomings in the product offered for sale. In such cases, sales representatives sometimes make grandiose claims that have no basis in reality and may stretch the truth to the point of creating totally inaccurate expectations. Thus, the individual sales representative may maximize her or his income in the short term, but at the cost of poor morale among other less aggressive salespeople and increasingly dissatisfied customers.

TEAM AND GROUP INCENTIVE REWARD SYSTEMS

The merit compensation and incentive compensation systems described in the preceding sections deal primarily with performance-based rewards for individuals. A different set of performance-based reward programs are targeted for teams and groups. These programs are particularly important for managers to understand today because of the widespread trends toward team- and group-based methods of work and organizations.[11] The Point/Counterpoint feature for this chapter underscores some of the basic issues between individual and team-based incentive systems.

Team and Group Pay Systems

Two types of team and group reward systems are common. One type used in many organizations is an approach called gainsharing. **Gainsharing programs** are designed to share the cost savings from productivity improvements with employees. The underlying assumption of gainsharing is that employees and the employer have the same goals and thus should share in incremental economic gains.[12]

■ **Gainsharing** is a team- and group-based incentive system designed to share the cost savings from productivity improvements with employees.

In general, organizations that use gainsharing start by measuring team- or group-level productivity. It is important that this measure is valid and reliable and that it truly reflects current levels of performance by the team or group. The team or work group itself is charged with attempting to lower costs and otherwise improve productivity through any measures that its members develop and that its manager approves. Resulting cost savings or productivity gains that the team or group is able to achieve are then quantified and translated into dollar values. A predetermined formula is used to allocate these dollar savings between the employer and the employees themselves. A typical formula for distributing gainsharing savings is to provide 25 percent of the dollar savings to the employees and 75 percent to the company.

■ The **Scanlon plan** is a type of gainsharing plan in which the distribution of gains is tilted much more heavily toward employees and across the entire organization.

One specific type of gainsharing plan is an approach called the Scanlon plan. This approach was developed by Joseph Scanlon in 1927. The **Scanlon plan** has

POINT | COUNTERPOINT

Team Versus Individual Incentives

Incentives are meant to shape employee behavior in some desired direction. For example, if organizations want employees to produce more units, they would pay them for each additional unit (over some minimum) that they produce. Under such a system, employees learn to maximize their rewards by behaving in a way desired by the organization. But as organizations increase the extent to which work is done by teams, the incentive situation becomes more complex. Should organizations reward the behavior of individual team members as if they were independent employees, or should they focus on team behaviors instead? In the latter situation, organizations would reward behaviors exhibited by the team as a whole, rather than behaviors exhibited by any individual team member.

POINT... Organizations should base incentives on individual behavior because...	COUNTERPOINT... Organizations should base incentives on team behavior because...
Individual effort is the easiest to monitor, and individual behaviors are the easiest to specify.	They are ultimately interested in changing the behavior of the team when work is done by teams.
Any team performance must be a function of the effort and performance of individual team members.	Team effectiveness requires more than just the efforts of individuals to perform their own jobs. It also requires people to be concerned with team spirit and communication.
If individuals are not rewarded for their effort, they will be less motivated to exert effort.	If team members are rewarded for individual performance, each member will seek to maximize his or her own performance, even to the detriment of team effectiveness.
If individuals are not responsible for achieving performance goals, there is a good chance that no one will feel responsible.	Individuals will not exert effort to maintain effective team functioning unless they are rewarded, and this effort can be rewarded only at the team level.
There will always be free riders who will not exert effort if the job is being done by others, and anything but individual-based incentives will unjustly reward these free riders.	The free-rider problem can be addressed by the rest of the team, which can exert group pressure on nonperforming members.

So... As organizations move more toward team work, they must establish incentives so that team-level goals and objectives are accomplished. Efforts to do so by implementing individual-based incentives will almost certainly fail because individual goals may be independent of or even in conflict with team goals. Nonetheless, if organizations ignore rewards for individual efforts, team performance levels are likely to drop. The key, then, is to combine the two. One possibility is to implement team-level incentives and then to allow the team, as a group, to provide incentives to individual team members for their individual efforts.

the same basic strategy as gainsharing plans because teams or groups of employees are encouraged to suggest strategies for reducing cost. However, the distribution of these gains is usually tilted much more heavily toward employees, with employees usually receiving between two-thirds and three-fourths of the total cost savings that the plan achieves. The cost savings resulting from the plan are

Chester Cadieux II (left) is the co-founder and chair of QuickTrip, a convenience-store chain based in Tulsa, Oklahoma. He started with one store and now has 406 stores in several states. Almost every top manager started with the firm by working in a store, including president and CEO Chester "Chet" Cadieux III (right). This philosophy of learning the business from the ground up and appreciating the importance of work done at every level is evidenced in the firm's compensation policies. QuickTrip pays better than its competition and even part-time employees receive health benefits. And employees evaluate their store managers. But the defining aspect of the compensation system at QuickTrip is that the employees own one-third of the privately held company.

not given just to the team or group that suggested and developed the ideas, but are instead distributed to the entire organization.

Other Types of Team and Group Rewards

Whereas gainsharing and Scanlon plans are among the most popular group incentive reward systems, other systems are also used by some organizations. Some companies, for example, have begun to use true incentives at the team or group level. As with individual incentives, team or group incentives tie rewards directly to performance. And like individual incentives, team or group incentives are paid as they are earned rather than being added to employees' base salaries. The incentives are distributed at the team or group level, however, rather than at the individual level. In some cases, the distribution may be based on the existing salary of each employee, with incentive bonuses being given on a proportionate basis. In other settings, each team or group member receives the same incentive pay.

Some companies also use nonmonetary rewards at the team or group level. These rewards come most commonly in the form of prizes and awards. For example, a company might designate the particular team in a plant or subunit of the company that achieves the highest level of productivity increase, the highest level of reported customer satisfaction, or a similar index of performance. The reward itself might take the form of additional time off (as described earlier in this chapter) or a tangible award such as a trophy or a plaque. In any event, however, the reward is given to the entire team and serves as recognition of exemplary performance by the entire team.

Other kinds of team- or group-level incentives go beyond the contributions of a specific work group. These incentives are generally organizationwide. One long-standing method for this approach is **profit sharing**. In profit-sharing, some

■ **Profit sharing** is an incentive system in which, at the end of the year, some portion of the company's profits is paid into a profit-sharing pool, which is then distributed to all employees.

portion of the company's profits is paid at the end of the year into a profit-sharing pool that is distributed to all employees. This amount is either distributed at the end of the year or put into an escrow account and payment is deferred until the employee retires.

The basic rationale behind profit-sharing systems is that everyone in the organization can expect to benefit when the company does well. During bad economic times, however, when the company is perhaps achieving low or no profits, then no profit sharing is paid out. This situation sometimes results in negative reactions from employees who come to feel that the profit sharing is really part of their annual compensation.

Employee stock ownership plans (ESOPs) represent another group-level reward system that some companies use. Under the employee stock ownership plan, employees are gradually given a major stake in the ownership of a corporation. The typical form of this plan involves the company taking out a loan, which is then used to buy a portion of the company's own stock in the open market. Over time, company profits are then used to pay off this loan. Employees, in turn, receive a claim on ownership of some portion of the stock held by the company based on their seniority and perhaps their performance. Eventually, each individual becomes an owner of the company.

■ **Employee stock ownership plans (ESOPs)** are group-level reward systems in which employees are gradually given a major stake in the ownership of a corporation.

Limitations of Team and Group Reward Systems

While group reward systems can be effective in some situations, they are also subject to difficulties. For example, not every member of a group may contribute equally to the group's performance. But if the group incentive system distributes rewards equally to group members, then people may feel that some factors beyond individual performance dictate the distribution of rewards. Also, for incentive plans based on firm profitability, employees may not see how their efforts lead to increased profits (often referred to as a line-of-sight problem). In fact, many factors that are beyond the employees' control can affect profitability. Thus, the links among effort, performance and outcomes, as specified by expectancy theory, are often quite weak, thus resulting in little motivation. Finally, a limitation noted earlier in our discussion on profit sharing is that employees may come to view the group-level incentive as a normal part of their compensation and consequently be unhappy or dissatisfied if that reward is withheld one year.

EXECUTIVE COMPENSATION

The top level executives of most companies have separate compensation programs and plans. These programs and plans are intended to reward the executives for their performance and for the performance of the organization. In this section we will describe both standard and special forms of executive compensation and note some of the current criticisms of executive compensation.

Standard Forms of Executive Compensation

Most senior executives receive their compensation in two forms. One is a **base salary**. As with the base salary of any staff member or professional member of

■ The **base salary** of an executive is a guaranteed amount of money that the individual will be paid.

CEO compensation has been the source of a great deal of controversy. Many experts complain that CEO pay goes up regardless of how well the company is doing. But until fairly recently few critics complained about the salary paid to Jack Welch, former CEO of General Electric. Although Welch was very well paid, he was deemed to deserve it because he helped guide GE to financial success and renown. But in late 2002, Welch's wife filed for divorce. Documents submitted as part of the divorce proceedings indicated that GE was providing incredible perks for Welch, even after he retired. These perks included a $15 million Manhattan apartment, cell phones and computers, security service at each of the Welch's six homes, a Mercedes, and a limousine service. Although Welch pointed out that the terms of his retirement had been public all along, few had bothered to read the fine print. It seems that, at least in some cases, the pay and perks that a CEO receives can continue beyond retirement.

an organization, the base salary of an executive is a guaranteed amount of money that the individual will be paid. For example, in 2001 Coca-Cola paid its chairperson and chief executive officer (CEO), Douglas Daft, $4,200,000 in base salary.[13]

Above and beyond this base salary, however, most executives receive one or more forms of incentive pay. The traditional method of incentive pay for executives is in the form of bonuses. Bonuses, in turn, are usually determined by the performance of the organization. Thus, at the end of the year, some portion of a corporation's profits may be diverted into a bonus pool. Senior executives then receive a bonus expressed as a percentage of this bonus pool. The chief executive officer and president are obviously likely to receive a larger percentage bonus than a vice president. The exact distribution of the bonus pool is usually specified ahead of time in the individual's employment contract. Some organizations intentionally leave the distribution unspecified so that the board of directors has the flexibility to give larger rewards to those individuals deemed most deserving. Douglas Daft of Coca-Cola received a $1,000,000 bonus in 2001.

Special Forms of Executive Compensation

Many executives receive other kinds of compensation beyond base salary and bonuses. One form of executive compensation that has received a lot of attention in recent years has been the stock option and all its variations. Incidentally, in several organizations, these types of plans are being "pushed down" so that they apply to a broader group of managers than they did in the past. In any case, a **stock-option plan** is established to give senior managers the option to buy the company stock in the future at a predetermined, fixed price. The basic idea

■ A **stock-option plan** is an incentive plan established to give senior managers the option to buy the company stock in the future at a predetermined fixed price.

underlying stock-option plans is that if the executives contribute to higher levels of organizational performance, then the company stock should increase. Then the executive can purchase the stock at the predetermined price that, theoretically, should be lower than its future market price. The difference then becomes profit for the individual. Coca-Cola's Douglas Daft received various stock options potentially worth as much as $49,900,000.

Stock options continue to grow in popularity as a means of compensating top managers. Stock options are seen as a means of aligning the interests of the manager with those of the stockholders, and if they don't cost the organization much (other than some possible dilution of stock values), they will probably be even more popular in the future. In fact, a recent study by KPM Peat Marwick indicates that for senior management whose salary exceeds $250,000, stock options represent the largest share of the salary mix (relative to salary and other incentives). When we consider all of top management (managers with an annual salary over $750,000), stock options comprise a full 60 percent of their total compensation. The KPM Peat Marwick report also indicates that, even among exempt employees at the $35,000-a-year level, stock options represent 13 percent of total compensation. The HR Legal Brief for this chapter notes some of the current legal and regulatory issues surrounding stock-option plans.

Agency theory arguments are often cited as the rationale for stock-option plans. The owners of the firm (typically the stockholders) want to increase firm profitability, but the CEO does not necessarily have any incentive to work toward maximizing profits. By basing a considerable portion of the CEO's compensation on stock, however, the interests of the CEO are presumably aligned more closely with the interests of the owners, and everyone works toward the same goal. Some critics have noted that these interests are not really aligned, however, until the CEO or executive actually exercises the stock option. Up to that point, the executive might have an incentive to lower stock prices in the short run, in the hope of being offered more options at the lower price of the stock.[14]

But recent events have raised serious questions about the use of stock options as incentives for executives. For example, several executives at Enron (allegedly) withheld critical financial information from the markets, cashed in their stock options (while Enron stock was trading at $80 a share), and then watched as the financial information was made public and the stock fell to less than $1 a share. Of course, these actions (if proven) are illegal, but they raise questions in the public's mind about the role of stock options and about the way organizations treat stock options from an accounting perspective. Most organizations have *not* treated stock options as liabilities, even though that's exactly what they are when they are exercised. By not carrying stock options as liabilities, the mangers can overstate the value of the company, which, of course, can help raise the stock price. Finally, when stock markets generally fell during the middle of 2002, many executives found that their options were worthless because the price of the stock fell below the option price. When stock options go "under water" in this way, they have no value to anyone.

In recent years, in part due to the problems just noted, alternative forms of stock-based rewards are being explored. General Electric, for instance, recently decided to ban stock options as part of the compensation package for its chairman and CEO (currently Jeffrey Immelt). Essentially, Mr. Immelt now has a substantial portion of his compensation expressed as "performance share units" and tied to a number of specific financial performance indicators. These performance

HR Legal Brief

Stock Options as Incentives

Given the recent interest in stock options, it is perhaps not surprising that the government pays close attention to stock options. Indeed, the federal government started passing legislation regulating the use of stock options as part of compensation in the 1920s and has continued doing so ever since. Although a more detailed review of these efforts is beyond the scope of this discussion, several points are worth noting.

The government first regulated stock options as compensation in 1923. In that year, the U.S. Treasury ruled that when an employee exercised a stock option, it would be taxed as income. Specifically, the employee would be taxed on an amount equal to the value of the stock at the time the option was exercised, less the cost of the option. In 1939, the Internal Revenue Service (IRS) modified this view somewhat, stating that stock options would be treated as income only if the company *intended* the option to be compensation at the time it was issued. Stock options intended as gifts, on the other hand, would be treated as gifts (i.e., they would not be taxed). By 1945, however, the IRS dropped this distinction and taxed options as income regardless of the intent of the parties involved.

In 1934 the Securities Exchange Act required "insiders" to reveal information about their stockholdings and also restricted profits that were based on privileged information. The Revenue Act of 1950 first recognized the nature of "restricted" options, which could be sold only after a certain period of time had elapsed. In deciding that profits from the sale of these restricted stocks would not be taxed as regular (current) income but as long-term capital gains (taxed according to a schedule across multiple years), Congress moved in favor of stock options as a form of managerial compensation. Nonetheless, over the next two decades Congress began to reverse its position and by 1969 all stock options would be treated the same for tax purposes, and all profits would be taxed as income.

But as the government tightened legislation regulating stock options, the stock market itself stagnated. By 1970 long-tem incentives (such as stock options) accounted for only about 15 percent of executive compensation. The market remained sluggish through 1980 and

> *"CEOs who[se firms] underperformed the market and yet made $20 million or $30 million from options."*
>
> (Graef Crystal,
> compensation expert)*

stock options lost their popularity. But when the stock market began to regain its vitality in 1981, stock options were once again an important part of compensation. Both the Economic Recovery Act of 1981 and the Tax Reform Act of 1986 included major provisions regulating stock options.

Stock options became even more popular in the 1990s, and legislation through the 1990s lowered many tax rates. Nonetheless, in 1994, while the average compensation for a worker in the United States increased by 2.0 percent, the average income for a *Fortune* 100 firm increased by 16 percent. As a result, Congress became very interested in executive compensation and thus in stock options. Consequently, from 1994 until 1996 a series of laws reduced some of the benefits of stock options for both the manager and the organization. That trend ended in 1996, however, as Republicans took control of both houses of Congress. Legislation since that time has made it easier for companies to give stock options to their employees (since these transactions were no longer subject to as many regulations) and reduced the maximum tax rate on long-term capital gains to 20 percent.

But all this appeared to be at risk during 2000–2002, when several highly publicized bankruptcies occurred. Enron, for example, declared bankruptcy while its CEO Ken Lay enjoyed the gains from the stock options he had recently exercised. Similar tales from other companies led to a strong belief for many that something should be done about how stock options were treated. Specifically, the Financial Accounting Standards Board (FASB) recommended that forms be required to carry stock options on corporate balance sheets as liabilities. That is, corporations would be forced to share information about exactly what those stock options were worth (which is itself open to some controversy) and to list these items as real liabilities that affect the firm's bottom line.

Political pressure in the Republican-dominated Congress apparently caused the FASB to back down from its position. This move is highly unusual because the FASB is supposed to be removed from politics. Nonetheless, the result is that no changes in how stock options are reported have been implemented. Some business leaders (especially those interested in stockholder rights) have complained, and these complaints may make executives more reluctant to exercise stock options under some circumstances. For the present, however, it is likely that stock options will continue to be a popular ingredient in executive compensation packages.

Sources: "Corporate Coffers Gush with Currency of an Opulent Age," *Wall Street Journal*, August 10, 1998, pp. B1, B8; "CEO Pay Outpaces Companies' Performance," *USA Today*, March 30, 1998, p. 1B (*quote on p. 1B); Wayne Grossman and Robert Hoskisson, "CEO Pay at the Crossroads of Wall Street and Main: Toward the Strategic Design of Executive Compensation," *Academy of Management Executive*, 1998, Vol. 12, No. 1, pp. 43–57.

indictors include both short-term and long-term components. If he and the company meet the targets, the performance share units are converted into regular stock. But if the targets are not met, then Mr. Immelt's compensation remains simply his base salary plus the possibility of a straight financial bonus. Microsoft has adopted a similar approach.[15]

Aside from stock-option plans, other kinds of executive compensation are used by some companies. Among the more popular are such perquisites as memberships in private clubs, access to company recreational facilities, and similar kinds of benefits. Some organizations occasionally make low- or no-interest loans available to senior executives. These loans are often given to new executives that the company is hiring from other companies and serve as an incentive for the individual to leave his or her current job to join a new organization.

Criticisms of Executive Compensation

Executive compensation has recently come under fire for various reasons. One major reason is that the levels of executive compensation attained by some managers simply seem too high for the average shareholder to understand. It is not uncommon for a senior executive of a major corporation to earn a total income from his or her job in a given year of well in excess of $1 million. Sometimes the income of chief executive officers can be substantially more. Coca-Cola's Douglas Daft earned a total of $55 million in 2001 from all sources combined. Thus,

Dick Grasso was chair of the New York Stock Exchange for many years. During his time in that role he helped the stock exchange to open only two weeks after the World Trade Center disaster, and he has been one of the leading critics of corporate greed on Wall Street. In fact, in 2002 Grasso very publicly called for more accountability among major firms and reasonably open records about the compensation paid to top managers. As a result, the New York Stock Exchange decided to disclose the compensation packages for its own top executives, even though as a private firm it was not required to do so. Unfortunately for Grasso, this disclosure revealed among other things that in September 2003 he took $140 million from his accrued pension accounts. As a public outcry began, Grasso announced that he would forgo an additional $48 million in deferred compensation, which, to many, made him appear guilty of the corporate greed he had publicly opposed. He soon resigned from his position, suggesting that people in glass houses really shouldn't throw stones.

just as the typical person has difficulty comprehending the astronomical salaries paid to some movie stars and sports stars, so too would the average person be aghast at the astronomical salaries paid to some senior executives. Table 12.1 summarizes the compensation packages for the twenty highest-paid CEOs in the United States in 2001.

TABLE 12.1 The Twenty Highest-Paid CEOs

Rank	Company	Executive	Salary and Bonus ($ million)	Long-Term Compensation ($ million)*	Total Pay ($ million)
1	Oracle	Lawrence Ellison	0	706.1	706.1
2	JDS Uniphase	Jozef Straus	0.5	150.3	150.8
3	Forest Laboratories	Howard Solomon	1.2	147.3	148.5
4	Capital One Financial	Richard Fairbank	0	142.2	142.2
5	IBM	Louis Gerstner[†]	10.1	117.3	127.4
6	Computer Associates International	Charles Wang[‡]	1.0	118.1	119.1
7	Lehman Brothers	Richard Fuld, Jr.	4.8	100.4	105.2
8	Scientific-Atlanta	James McDonald	2.1	84.7	86.8
9	Apple Computer	Steve Jobs[§]	43.5	40.5	84.0
10	Yahoo!	Timothy Koogle[‖]	0.2	64.4	64.6
11	Applied Biosystems Group	Tony White	1.7	60.2	61.9
12	Applied Micro Circuits	David Rickey	0.9	58.6	59.5
13	Maxim Integrated Products	John Gifford	0.3	57.7	58.0
14	Emulex	Paul Folino	0.9	55.3	56.2
15	Coca-Cola	Douglas Daft	5.1	49.9	55.0
16	Philip Morris	Geoffrey Bible	5.6	44.3	49.9
17	Rational Software	Michael Devlin	1.0	46.3	47.3
18	KB Home	Bruce Karatz	7.5	36.9	44.4
19	Citigroup	Sanford Weill	18.7	23.9	42.6
20	Carnival	Micky Arison	2.2	38.3	40.5

* Long-term compensation includes exercised options, restricted shares, and long-term incentive payment; it does not include the value of unexercised option grants.
† Retired as CEO in March 2002.
‡ CEO until August 2000.
§ Amounts represent payments in fiscal 2001 toward purchase of an airplane given to Jobs as a bonus in fiscal 2000. A $90 million bonus previously reported for the same plane was not made.
‖ Stepped down as CEO in May 2001.

Source: Reprinted from the April 15, 2002 issue of Business Week by special permission. Copyright © 2002 by The McGraw-Hill Companies, Inc.

Executive compensation in the United States also seems far out of line with that paid to senior executives in other countries. For example, compensation for foreign CEOs has only recently crept into the seven-figure range, their annual bonuses are much smaller, and they seldom participate in lavish stock-option plans like those enjoyed by their U.S. counterparts. Looking at the total package clouds the compensation comparisons a bit. For example, Figure 12.3 shows the complete package of executive perquisites for seven countries. While U.S. executives clearly top the list, their counterparts tend to receive more vacation and sick time, plus a car or car allowance.

FIGURE 12.3   Senior Executive Perquisites in Different Countries

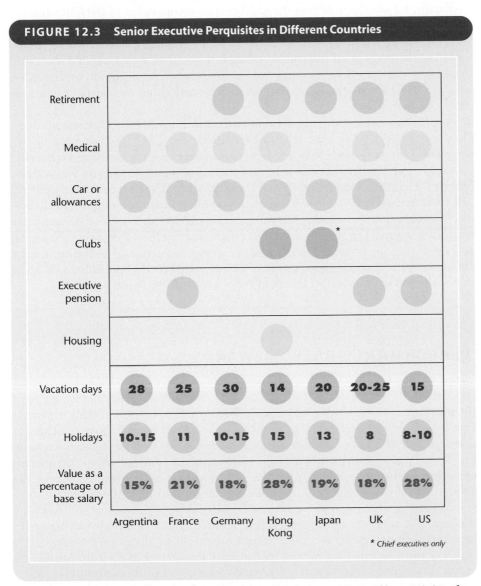

	Argentina	France	Germany	Hong Kong	Japan	UK	US
Retirement			●	●	●	●	●
Medical	●	●	●	●		●	●
Car or allowances	●	●	●	●	●	●	
Clubs				●	●*		
Executive pension		●				●	●
Housing				●			
Vacation days	28	25	30	14	20	20-25	15
Holidays	10-15	11	10-15	15	13	8	8-10
Value as a percentage of base salary	15%	21%	18%	28%	19%	18%	28%

* Chief executives only

Source: "How Perks Stack Up Worldwide" from *Forbes,* May 19, 1997, p. 162. Reprinted by permission of *Forbes* Magazine © Forbes, Inc., 1997.

Compounding the problem created by perceptions of executive compensation is the fact that little or no relationship seems to exist between the performance of the organization and the compensation paid to its senior executives.[16] Certainly if an organization performs at an especially high level and its stock price is increasing consistently, then most observers would agree that the senior executives responsible for this growth should be entitled to attractive rewards.[17] However, it is more difficult to understand situations when executives are paid huge salaries and other forms of rewards when their companies are performing at only a marginal level, yet this fact is fairly common today. For example, in 2002 Oracle's CEO Lawrence Ellison pocketed over $700 million from the sale of previously granted stock options, but the value of Oracle stock dropped by 57 percent.

Finally, we should note that the gap between the earnings of the CEO and the earnings of a typical employee is enormous. First, the very size of the gap has been increasing in the United States. In 1980, the typical CEO earned forty-two times the earnings of an ordinary worker, but by 1990, this ratio had increased to eighty-five times the earnings of an ordinary worker. In Japan, on the other hand, in 1990 a typical CEO made less than twenty times the earnings of an ordinary worker.[18]

Another concern is the impact this differential has for the typical employee. On the one hand, he or she may not believe that the CEO is making eighty-five times the contribution made by the typical employee, or at least that no one could be working eighty-five times as hard. This perception may lead to resentment and other problems on the job, and evidence suggests that such large dispersions result in decreased satisfaction, willingness to collaborate, and overall productivity.[19] On the other hand, the typical employee may view this huge salary as a prize worth aiming for. From this perspective, pay structures are seen as tournaments, and the bigger the prize, the more intense the competition, and so the greater the effort and productivity. Some evidence in fact supports this position, indicating that managers cannot really be sure of the effects of these income gaps.[20]

NEW APPROACHES TO PERFORMANCE-BASED REWARDS

Some organizations have started to recognize that they can leverage the value of the incentives that they offer to their employees and to groups in their organization by allowing those individuals and groups to have a say in how rewards are distributed. For example, a company could go so far as to grant salary-increase budgets to work groups and then allow the members of those groups themselves to determine how the rewards will be allocated to the various members of the group. This strategy appears to hold considerable promise if everyone understands the performance arrangements that exist in the work group and everyone is committed to being fair and equitable. Unfortunately, it can also create problems if people in a group feel that rewards are not being distributed fairly.

Organizations are also getting increasingly innovative in their incentive programs. For example, some now offer stock options to all their employees rather than just the top executives. Regardless of the method used, however, it is also important that managers in an organization communicate effectively what rewards are being distributed and the basis for that distribution. That is, if incentives are distributed on the basis of perceived individual contributions to the organization, then members of the organization should be informed of that fact. This approach will presumably enable them to understand the basis on which pay increases and other incentives and performance-based rewards have been distributed.

A Strategic Perspective on Incentives and Performance-Based Rewards

It should be clear that there are a variety of plans and proposals to relate rewards and compensation to some indicator of performance. Hopefully, it is also clear that each plan has advantages and disadvantages so that we cannot easily point to one such approach and suggest that it is "best." So how should an organization decide what type (or types) of plan should be adopted? It depends on the organization's strategy and what kinds of outcomes it hopes to improve. Our closing case, for instance, discusses how Continental Airlines focused on "on-time performance" as it struggled (successfully) to improve, but this is just an example of what it means to be strategic in designing incentive and reward plans.

For example, it is fairly common among restaurant chains to reward store managers for their performance. What is interesting, however, is how that performance is measured and rewarded. It would seem obvious that a manager should be rewarded (somehow) on the basis of sales. Surely, a restaurant that sells more hamburgers or sandwiches or tacos is performing better than a restaurant that sells fewer of these items. If not sales directly, perhaps the manager should be rewarded for profitability, since that is literally the "bottom line." But, in fact, it is more typical for restaurant chains to reward managers on the basis of cost. That is, some chains (such as Steak and Ale) traditionally opened some restaurants without much hope of making money, but more as a form of real estate investment. Thus, it would not make sense to reward the manager for sales or profits. In fact, some chains open company-owned (as opposed to franchised) restaurants at locations simply because the competition opened a restaurant there. There may not be enough business for both restaurants to be profitable and the move is strictly defensive.

Also, in the case of many chains, especially those that franchise locations, the restaurant is required to buy all the basic food from the corporation, and the prices charged are set for all restaurants by the corporation. In such a case, profits are quite restrained. In these cases, the only way for a restaurant to "make money" is to control costs. That is, if a manager can reduce overhead (by hiring fewer staff) and maintenance costs (by delaying repairs), the restaurant will be able to contribute more to corporate profits. As a result, an index of "controllable costs" is often calculated, and incentive pay is tied to reducing these costs.

In other industries, customer-service representatives are rewarded based on the number of customers they help during a week or month. We are aware of an appliance store chain that has determined that it can make more money by financing appliances than by actually selling them. As a result, incentives are based not on the number of units sold, but on the number of finance contracts sold. A series of successful lawsuits during 2003 revealed that some stockbrokers were being rewarded not for simply selling stocks, but for selling stocks that the investment firm had a financial interest in.

In every case, whether the plan is wise or not, or even legal or ethical, these plans reflect a strategic perspective on incentive pay. The organization decides what it needs in order to compete more effectively, and then sets up a reward system that it hopes will provide incentives to employees so that they work for the desired outcomes. Thus, the "best" type of plan is the one that gets the organization the kinds of behaviors and outcomes it seeks.

Of course, an organization must be very careful about setting up this type of incentive plan. There is often a danger that the plan is also incenting other behaviors and outcomes that the organization might want to avoid. For example, in the case of the restaurant incentives to control cost, it is possible that such a system could hurt business in the long run. Reducing overhead may result in slower, poorer service, which might cause customers to go elsewhere. Delayed repairs may also reduce the enjoyment of the dining experience and drive customers away. In the case of customer-service representatives, rewarding them for the number of customers they serve may lead them to spend less time with each customer, and so reduce overall customer satisfaction. Finally, stock incentive plans might lead top managers to engage in behaviors that drive up stock prices in the short run, but lead to long-term disaster.

Incentive pay plans, if properly designed, can be powerful tools for changing behavior, but it is important that an organization understand all of the behaviors that a particular plan might lead to, before implementing the plan. Furthermore, the organization must insure that it is rewarding the kinds of behaviors it needs to be successful.

Chapter Summary

Performance-based rewards play several roles and address various purposes in organizations. The major purposes involve the relationship of rewards to motivation and to performance. Rewards can also be used to influence other kinds of employee behaviors, such as turnover, absenteeism, and attendance.

Merit compensation systems are one of the most fundamental forms of performance-based rewards. Merit pay generally refers to pay awarded to employees on the basis of the relative value of their contributions to the organization. The most general form of merit-pay plan is the provision of annual salary increases to individuals in the organization based on their relative merit. Of course, it is important for the organization to have valid and reliable measures of merit. While merit compensation systems are widely used and serve numerous valuable purposes in organizations, they also suffer from some relatively important limitations.

Individual incentive plans reward individual performance on a real-time basis. Some variations on the piece-rate system are still fairly popular. Perhaps the most common form of individual incentive is the sales commission that is paid to salespeople. Occasionally organizations may also use other forms of incentives

to motivate people. A major advantage of incentives relative to merit systems is that incentives are typically a one-shot reward and do not accumulate by becoming part of the individual's base salary. As with merit systems, incentive compensation systems also have some shortcomings and weaknesses.

A different set of performance-based reward programs are targeted to teams and groups. These programs are particularly important for managers to understand today given the widespread trends toward team and group-based methods of work and organizations. Two types of team and group reward systems are common. One type used in many organizations is an approach called gainsharing. Another is the Scanlon plan. Whereas gainsharing and Scanlon plans are among the most popular group incentive reward systems, other systems are also used by some organizations. Profit sharing is used in many organizations, and employee stock-ownership plans are also growing in popularity. While group reward systems can be effective in some situations, they can also be subject to difficulties.

The top level executives of most companies have separate compensation programs and plans. Most senior executives receive their compensation in two forms. One form is a base salary. Most executives also receive one or more forms of incentive pay above and beyond this base salary. The traditional method of incentive pay for executives is in the form of bonuses. Bonuses, in turn, are usually determined by the performance of the organization. A form of executive compensation that has received a lot of attention in recent years is the stock option, which comes in many variations. In recent years, executive compensation has come under fire for various reasons.

Finally, any type of incentive plan is only effective if it produces the behaviors and outcomes that are needed by the organization. Thus, different situations require much different types of plans. Unfortunately, many incentive plans not only motivate employees to exhibit desired behaviors; they may also (unknowingly) lead to undesired behaviors as well. It is critical that organizations examine the results of their incentive plans very closely to make sure that they are getting what they need from those plans.

Key Points for Future HR Managers

▶ Motivation theories such as expectancy theory and agency theory are useful for understanding how rewards can lead to changes in behavior and performance.

▶ Merit-pay plans provide clear links between performance and rewards, but they are tied to subjective performance appraisals and this can lead to perceptions of favoritism.

▶ Skill-based and knowledge-based pay provide incentives for employees to acquire more knowledge and skill, but may not always lead to improved performance.

▶ When performance is a function of a team (or group) then the rewards should be team based.

These systems often result in weaker links between individual effort and reward, however.

▶ Executive compensation is much more complex and much of the compensation is based on performance measured in some way. There is a great deal of controversy over the compensation of some top managers.

▶ All incentive and performance-based reward plans must be evaluated carefully to insure that they lead to desired behaviors and outcomes rather than undesired behaviors.

Key Points for Future General Managers

▶ Incentives and performance-based rewards can be useful ways to motivate employees to exhibit desired behaviors.

▶ It is critical, however, that the desired behaviors and outcomes be clearly defined and the incentive plans designed so that they produce the desired results.

▶ Merit-pay plans reward performance as defined by performance appraisals. Incentive plans can motivate employees to behave in a way that is consistent with organizational goals. Skill-based and knowledge-based pay systems motivate employees to become more valuable by acquiring additional knowledge and skills.

▶ Any of these plans can be effective if these are the outcomes that are desired.

▶ In some case, rewards and incentives should be based on the performance of a team, rather than an individual, but these plans may weaken individual motivation to improve.

▶ Executive compensation is extremely costly and controversial. Many plans are designed simply to compete with the plans of other firms, and many critics argue that CEOs, especially, are rewarded for good performance but are never punished for poor performance.

Review and Discussion Questions

1. Explain the relationships among rewards, motivation, and performance.

2. Put yourself in the role of employee. In your present job or the next job you anticipate having, identify the rewards that are most important to you and how you think you can most likely attain them.

3. Refer to your answer to Question 2. How do you think your own absenteeism and attendance are or might be affected by incentives and other rewards?

4. Compare and contrast merit and incentive compensation systems.

5. Can merit and incentive compensation be used together? Why or why not?

6. Should all compensation be based on merit or performance? Why or why not?

7. What are the basic differences between incentive systems for individuals and incentive systems for teams and groups?

8. Which is harder to use: incentive systems for individuals or incentive systems for teams and groups? Why?

9. What are your views on the extemely high levels of executive compensation?

10. Assume that you are head of public relations for a big company that just gave its CEO a huge bonus. Outline a plan for justifying the bonus to the press.

Closing Case

Continental's Remarkable Turnaround

In 1994 Continental Airlines posted net losses (pretax) of $202 million, was ranked last among all major airlines in customer satisfaction (according to J. D. Powers and Associates), scored below its competitors on all major performance factors (such as load factor and revenue per mile flown), and had a market value of only $175 million. The firm had almost no cash reserves, and its creditors closely scrutinized every move the company made. Its employees were demoralized and few expected to remain with the company for long—even if it survived.

In 1999, however, Continental was consistently posting big profits, had twice been rated *first* in customer satisfaction by J. D. Powers, and had a cash balance in excess of $1 billion and a market value in excess of $4 billion. In addition, Continental scored above-industry averages on every important performance indicator and actually led the industry on several indicators. Continental was rated among the 100 best companies to work for by *Fortune* magazine and had a motivated, loyal, and committed workforce. It has continued to be rated as one of the best companies to work for every year since then.

How did Continental accomplish such a dramatic turnaround in only five years? Many factors helped, but one that was clearly critical was Chairman Gordon Bethune's belief that "what gets measured and rewarded gets done." As a result, shortly after Bethune took over in 1994, Continental introduced a series of incentives for employees who helped the airline meet critical goals. For example, the "old" Continental had one of the worst on-time records in the industry. A new incentive plan rewarded employees for on-time performance. The plan was actually simple. Bethune calculated what the airline saved (in hotels, meals, and rebooking charges) when flights were on time. He divided this amount by the number of employees. The total was about $100. Bethune then announced that every month that Continental was in the top five in the industry in on-time performance, each employee would receive $65, and each employee would receive a check for $100 for any month that Continental was in the top three. Continental has now distributed over $100 million in on-time bonuses.

Continental also realized that employee absenteeism was costly, both in terms of overtime payments and peak service. Therefore, every employee who had a perfect performance record for six months was entered in a drawing for eight Eddie Bauer Edition Ford Explorers (plus a check to cover the taxes). Since the program began in 1996, the company has given away thirty-eight Explorers worth $1.5 million. Also, the number of eligible employees (with perfect attendance for six months) has more than doubled and overall absenteeism has dropped 31 percent.

In addition, the airline reports a reduction in turnover (since 1994) of 52 percent and a drop in on-the-job injuries of 48 percent. Clearly, then, the incentive programs seem to be achieving the desired goals. As profits have risen, so has the price of Continental's stock: $3.25 a share in January 1995 to over $48 a share by the beginning of 1999. As a result the airline has been able to buy new planes, dropping the average fleet age of Continental's planes to 7.2 years, one of the lowest anywhere.

Finally, to be certain that Continental's employees are fully recognized for their contributions to the airline's recovery, the airline created a announced plan for bringing salaries up to the industry standard. And in 1998, Continental distributed $105 million in profit sharing to its employees—a figure representing 7 percent of total annual wages. Again, many factors have surely contributed to Continental's improved performance, but the fact that the airline decided to target specific behaviors for incentives must be seen as one of the most important and successful parts of that turnaround.[21]

Case Questions

1. What role have incentives played in Continental's success?

2. What problems or roadblocks might arise in the future to limit Continental's continued success and effectiveness?

3. Why don't more companies use Continental's approach?

Building HR Management Skills

Purpose: The purpose of this exercise is to help you better understand the opportunities and limitations in using performance-based rewards in organizations.

Step 1: Form small groups with three to four of your classmates.

Step 2: Select three different jobs with which people in your group have some familiarity. These might be jobs that people in the group perform and/or jobs that you come into contact with on a regular basis (i.e., retail salesclerk, bus driver, fast-food clerk, etc.).

Step 3: Develop a performance-based reward system for each of the three jobs you selected. For each job, specify the precise behaviors that you want to reward and the types of reward you propose to link to those behaviors.

Step 4: Compare and contrast the three different models.

Step 5: Respond to the following questions:

1. How easy or difficult is it to tie performance-based rewards to various kinds of jobs?

2. What are the major challenges in developing performance-based rewards?

3. What job characteristics or attributes make some jobs easier than others to reward on the basis of performance?

4. Can a performance-based reward system accommodate every job?

Ethical Dilemmas in HR Management

Assume that you are a senior manager in a regional warehouse and distribution center for a large national retailer. Since the center was first opened several years ago, everyone working there has been paid on either a straight hourly basis or a standard salary basis. This year, however, corporate management has unveiled a sweeping new compensation system for the entire firm. Under the terms of this plan, all employees will be eligible for annual bonuses based on unit performance. All of the employees at the center are excited about this new plan, and it seems that everyone is committed to working harder than ever to help the center's workforce get a big bonus.

Today is January 5, and the new system has just been announced and implemented. Unfortunately, you have some serious concerns. Specifically, you have heard some rumors that sometime during the next nine months the firm is likely either to sell the distribution center to a competitor or else close it down altogether. Because the center is not unionized, you suspect that if the center is closed, all the lower-level workers will simply be terminated and none of them will receive any sort of bonus. While you are reasonably certain that you and the other senior managers will be transferred to another location, you don't know if you will be involved in the new bonus system because the center will not have any year-end performance statistics on which to base a bonus.

You have tried to broach this subject with the center's general manager on several occasions but have received only vague answers. For example, she has said things like "Don't worry, the company will take care of everyone," "No one really knows what might happen,

so we shouldn't get too worked up about it," "No decisions have been made about anything yet, so we should stop trying to guess what's going to happen," and "Even if that were to happen, I'm sure the managers would be taken care of." You also suspect that her next move will be to a corporate-level job. You are troubled about the situation, though. If you tell too many people about your concerns and rumors start flying, morale will plummet. Even if the center remains open, performance will not improve. But if you remain silent and the center does close, your conscience will bother you.

Questions

1. What are the ethical issues in this situation?

2. What are the basic arguments for and against keeping quiet versus continuing to ask questions?

3. What do you think most managers would do? What would you do?

HR Internet Exercise

Put yourself in the role of a manager contemplating the implementation of a new incentive system for a major corporation. Search the Web and look for topics such as *incentives*, *merit compensation*, and *gainsharing*. Then respond to the following questions:

1. How useful do you think the Internet would be to a manager in this position?

2. What are the advantages and disadvantages of using the Internet for this kind of activity?

3. What advice would you give to other managers interested in the same issues?

13

Indirect Compensation and Benefits

CHAPTER OBJECTIVES

After studying this chapter you should be able to:

- Identify and discuss basic considerations in indirect compensation.

- Discuss legally mandated protection plans as employee benefits.

- Describe various optional protection plans as employee benefits.

- Discuss paid time off as an employee benefit.

- Identify and discuss various other benefits that some organizations provide for their employees.

- Describe cafeteria approaches to benefits.

- Identify and discuss basic legal issues in indirect compensation and benefits.

- Discuss how indirect compensation and benefits plans are evaluated by organizations.

Businesses have traditionally offered their employees various forms of indirect compensation, more commonly known as benefits. Common examples include subsidized insurance, paid vacation, paid sick time, and so forth. For years the basic benefits package provided for employees followed a "one size fits all" mindset. That is, all employees had the same insurance options, the same number of sick days, and so forth. And even though vacation time might increase with seniority, it nevertheless followed a fixed model.

Several years ago companies began using so-called cafeteria benefits plans whereby employees could have somewhat more choice and flexibility for trading off different benefits options. For instance, a dual-career couple working for different employers might be offered family health insurance at a sharp discount by each employer, but only one may actually need the coverage because it would extend to that person's spouse. Under a cafeteria model, one spouse might be allowed to forego the insurance coverage altogether and apply the company contribution to another benefits category such as more paid time off.

Recently, though, some forward-looking companies have begun to personalize their benefits program even more. Using more sophisticated data analysis tools and concepts, they are striving to personalize employee benefits to get better value for the costs of those benefits and to tailor benefits options to individual needs. One option, for example, might allow a worker to take a 20 percent pay cut in exchange for a three-month sabbatical every two years. Another might allow workers to select their own training activities rather than attend standardized corporate programs.

Among the firms experimenting with this model are Quest Diagnostics, FleetBoston Financial, and First Tennessee. These firms find that they can achieve two seemingly contradictory objectives at the same time—they can make their benefits packages more attractive to their employees while simultaneously reducing the costs they are paying for those benefits.[1] ∎

> *"This will only breed greater inequality, even for people in the same educational cohort."*
>
> (Peter Cappelli, Wharton Business School compensation expert)*

Most employees are accustomed to receiving more than just a paycheck from their employer. Indeed, to many employees the additional benefits that their employer provides are almost as important as their pay. And while companies have a long history of providing certain "standard" benefits such as insurance and vacation time, some organizations, like those in the chapter-opening vignette, are finding that it also pays to continue to provide new and unusual benefits. And it may pay even more to maximize the amount of flexibility in those benefits.

In the last two chapters we discussed basic compensation issues as well as various merit-based and incentive pay systems. The remaining part of most employees' total compensation consists of indirect compensation and benefits. Although some of these benefits are mandated by law, modern organizations are increasingly looking to indirect compensation and benefits as a means of attracting certain groups of employees. We will review the legal considerations in the administration of benefits programs and then discuss the most common types of benefits and the features of each. Next, we will discuss variable benefits programs where the benefits given to an employee can be tailored to his or her needs. Finally, we will discuss some issues associated with the evaluation of benefits and indirect compensation programs.

BASIC CONSIDERATIONS IN INDIRECT COMPENSATION AND BENEFITS

In addition to wages and salaries, most organizations provide their employees with an array of other indirect compensation and benefits. **Benefits** generally refer to various rewards, incentives, and other items of value that an organization provides to its employees beyond their wages, salaries, and other forms of direct financial compensation. Because these benefits have tangible value but are not generally expressed in financial terms, they essentially represent a meaningful form of compensation, even if they are indirect compensation. Benefits should be more than just a laundry list of specific benefit entitlements. Ideally, they should be well-developed packages of benefits and benefits options that best serve the needs and preferences of employees and the organization.

These benefits were once called *fringe benefits,* and a few people still use this expression today. When managers began to realize that they were spending perhaps more than one-third of wages and salaries in additional expenses on benefits, however, they decided that the word *fringe* might have been understating to employees the true value of these benefits. Hence, most organizations today no longer use the term *fringe benefits* but instead refer to employee benefits or simply benefits.

In fact, data from the U.S. Chamber of Commerce provides some insights into the composition of the total compensation paid to a typical employee in the United States. According to these figures, the typical employee costs the company almost $47,000 a year in total compensation. Of this amount, roughly $32,000 is paid for time worked, while the remaining $15,000 is paid for other than time worked and includes vacation time, mandated benefits, pensions, insurance, and so forth.[2]

■ **Benefits** generally refer to various rewards, incentives, and other things of value that an organization provides to its employees beyond their wages, salaries, and other forms of direct financial compensation.

It is quite clear that organizations are spending huge amounts of money on benefits. It also appears that many organizations are trying to hold the tide, or even reverse it, by asking employees to bear some of the costs of these benefits, but surely benefits costs will continue to be a large part of labor costs in the United States. The Lighter Side of HR illustrates this point—to the extreme! It is also interesting to note that, despite these figures, the United States actually ranks rather low in terms of the relative costs of benefits around the world.

These global differences are due almost entirely to the number of mandated benefits, which are based on the different social contracts (guarantees made by the government in return for higher taxes) in place in the respective countries, and they are substantial. For example, the German workweek is 37.6 hours (on average). The German worker works 1,499 hours per year, has forty-two days off, and has mandated benefit costs *alone* that equal almost 30 percent of wages. For comparison purposes, the average U.S. worker spends forty hours a week at work, spends 1,847 hours a year working, has twenty-three days off a year, and has mandated benefits costs equal to about 10 percent of wages.

Indeed, when Ford first announced its purchase of the Swedish automobile maker Volvo, Volvo workers immediately started to express their concerns about the potential loss of their relatively lavish benefits. For example, Volvo's main manufacturing plant in Gothenburg, Sweden, has a sprawling health complex that includes an Olympic-size swimming pool, tanning beds, and tennis courts. The firm spends over $600,000 a year to maintain the center. While Ford's U.S. workers enjoy a strong benefits program, it pales in comparison to the program at Volvo.[3] HR Around the Globe sheds additional light on some of the issues associated with benefits in international companies.

As you can see, the exact benefits offered differ substantially from one country to the next, but in each case the benefits are designed to meet the specific needs (relative to balancing work and family) in the host country. For example, in Egypt, resorts are quite expensive and offering short vacations for the family to spend together is helpful. Because Muslims are expected to make the pilgrimage to Mecca at least once during their life (if at all possible), vacation time is a valuable benefit. In Norway, Trinidad, and the United Kingdom, operations tend to be off-shore or in rather remote regions of the country. As a result, employees do not see their families every day and do not generally live at home. Under these circumstances, compressed workweeks are extremely important to employees, as are other benefits such as family days, where families are brought to work sites for visits at company expense.

The Lighter Side of HR

Many human resource managers are studying ways to lower the costs of the benefits they provide to their employees and/or to improve the effectiveness of the benefits they currently provide. While few managers would resort to the level of cost reduction illustrated by the human resource manager in this cartoon, it nevertheless demonstrates the mindset that some managers adopt!
(The New Yorker Collection 1995 Leo Cullum from cartoonbank.com. All Rights Reserved.)

"Before I forget, Detrick, here's the dental plan."

HR Around the Globe

Global Benefits: Similarities and Differences

Even before its recent merger with BP, Amoco was already a major multinational firm with operations in dozens of countries. One of the more challenging issues that Amoco's human resource executives have long had to confront, therefore, has been juggling the legal, cultural, and social forces dictating and reinforcing the needs for different benefits programs.

For example, in the United States, Amoco offers insurance, vacation and sick leave, alternative work schedules, childcare centers, employee assistance programs, and referral services. Indeed, its array of benefits is strong enough for Amoco to be the only oil company on *Working Mother's* list of the best companies for working mothers.

In Egypt, however, Amoco offers some different benefits. Among the more prominent is a one-time Haj pilgrimage allowance (the Haj is the required pilgrimage to Mecca that every Muslim male is required to make once during his life) and two annual subsidized trips to Egyptian resorts. In the Netherlands, the emphasis is

"You have to tailor your benefits to the unique situation in each country where you do business."

(James Yates, Amoco executive)

on flexibility—parents can take up to three months of unpaid leave after their child is born, and all employees can opt for part-time employment anytime they want, for as long as a year at a time.

Amoco's U.K. employees get much the same benefits as their U.S. counterparts, but they also get five bereavement days per year following the death of a family member and two days a year if they need to move out of their personal residence. In Norway, fathers of newborns get five days of paid leave. In addition, Amoco employees in Norway get perhaps the most unusual benefit of all. Because the country has an especially high marginal tax rate, employees are often looking for benefits that companies can provide tax-free. Those who work for Amoco, therefore, get seven free magazine subscriptions a year—the most allowed under Norwegian law!

Source: James Yates, "Work-Family Practices at Amoco," Presentation at Texas A&M University Center for Human Resource Management Conference, The Family-Friendly Organization, October 24, 1997.

Purposes of Indirect Compensation and Benefits Programs

Even though U.S. companies spend a great deal of money on benefits, they are nowhere near the top in this area relative to the rest of the world, and especially relative to European countries. Nonetheless, U.S. companies *do* spend a great deal of money on benefits, and there must be an explanation. As illustrated in Figure 13.1, indirect compensation and benefits serve various basic purposes.

First, many believe that organizations willing to spend more money on compensation are able to attract better-qualified people and/or to convince employees to work harder. The general concept underlying this approach is known as *efficiency wage theory*. This theory suggests that firms can actually save money and become more productive if they pay more because they attract employees who are better or who would be willing to work hard. Little data exists to support or refute this position, but some organizations appear to view wages and benefits as a means of attracting better applicants.

Most organizations would also argue that money spent on benefits has an impact on job satisfaction and subsequent turnover. That is, even if employees do not work harder in response to better benefits, they are more likely to remain with a firm that provides better benefits and are more satisfied with that firm. In part, an employee's reactions to specific benefits programs reflect that individual's

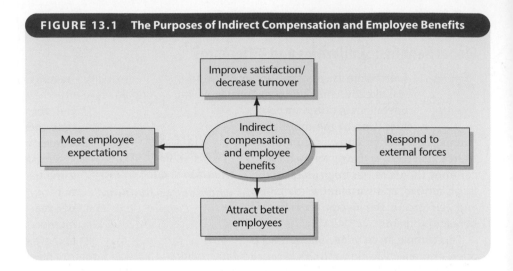

FIGURE 13.1　The Purposes of Indirect Compensation and Employee Benefits

belief about the value of benefits at the present company as compared with the value of benefits at other companies. As a result, the need to remain competitive with other firms in an industry is a major force driving up the price of benefits. Just as when one airline in a market lowers fares and all others follow suit, once one visible organization in an industry starts offering a given benefit, it is usually not long until its competitors offer similar benefits.

In addition, various social, cultural, and political forces may facilitate the introduction of new and broader benefits programs. For example, increases in the number of women in the workforce and the rising costs of health care have each affected benefits programs in recent times. Because of the growth in the numbers of female workers, more and more companies offer on-site daycare, dual-parent leave for the birth of a child, and other benefits that make it easier for people to work and have productive careers. Likewise, the health-care environment has prompted growth in benefits programs including health maintenance organization (HMOs), managed health care, and so forth.

Finally, employee expectations are a driving force in determining what benefits a firm must offer. For example, an organization is not legally required to offer *any* vacation time. But because this benefit is so desirable and has become common, almost every person who accepts a new job expects that he or she will be given some vacation time. Indeed, most people today would be unlikely to accept a permanent full-time job without this basic benefit. A major implication of these issues, then, is the strategic importance of employee benefits. Their costs are high and their impact is great. Thus, careful planning, monitoring, and communication about benefits are of paramount importance.

Legal Considerations

Vacation time is not mandated in the United States, but several other benefits *are* mandated by law and we will discuss them shortly. Clearly, those benefits stem from some specific legislation, but in addition laws govern various aspects of benefits administration without actually mandating a specific benefit. The major laws are listed on the following page:

1. Tax Reform Act of 1997—The law has numerous provisions, some of which affect employee benefits directly. For example, the law created a special new form of individual retirement account (the Roth IRA). In addition, it increased the amount that self-employed individuals can deduct for health-insurance premiums. It also relaxed the rules for home-office deductions.

2. Tax Reform Act of 1986 and Revenue Reconciliation Act of 1993—Both of these legislative acts have basically the same purpose. They set limits on how much an employee (and an employer) can contribute to tax-exempt retirement funds (qualified pension plans) such as 401K plans. These limits have the intent of ensuring that lower-paid employees are treated the same as higher-paid employees relative to tax-exempt pension contributions. These acts also stipulate that, for top executives, pay over $1 million a year cannot be exempt from taxes unless it is a performance-related bonus.

3. Family and Medical Leave Act of 1993—This act requires all organizations with at least fifty employees to grant any employee who has worked for the organization for at least one year an *unpaid* leave of up to twelve weeks for childbirth, the adoption of a child, the care of any family member with a serious health problem, or a health problem of the employee him- or herself. All health benefits must remain intact, and the employee must return to the same or an equivalent job after the leave.

4. Economic Recovery Tax Act of 1981—This act was the first to allow employees to make a tax-deductible contribution of up to $2,000 to a pension plan, savings account, or individual retirement account. The act also provides mechanisms that make it easier for companies to finance employee stock-ownership plans (ESOPs).

5. Pregnancy Discrimination Act of 1978—This act protects a woman from being fired because of a pregnancy. It has been reported that about 4 percent of employees who become pregnant (about 8,000 women a year) are fired for that reason.[4] Recent court decisions have also suggested that all related health benefits must be extended to the spouses of male employees as well.

6. Employee Retirement Income Security Act of 1974—This act does *not* require companies to set up pension funds for employees. However, if a firm does elect to have a pension fund and wishes to deduct contributions to that fund, it must follow certain guidelines. These guidelines restrict the company's freedom to take money out of pension funds as needed, restrict how those pension funds are invested, and generally attempt to ensure that an employee will

The Family and Medical Leave Act gives employees the right to take up to twelve weeks of unpaid leave to care for a newborn or a sick family member. In some states activists are now pushing for financial subsidies to make it easier for people to actually take these leaves. Indeed, twenty-eight states are currently considering such measures. Over 75 percent of those eligible for leave under the law cannot afford to take it; financial subsidies would make it easier for families to take care of sick relatives or young children like this newborn.

have money for retirement when the time comes. The act also provides formulas for vesting (when the employee has a right to the employer's contributions to the fund) and portability (the employee's ability to transfer funds to a different retirement account).

Clearly, then, the legal context plays a major role in how organizations structure the benefits programs and options that they offer to their employees.

MANDATED PROTECTION PLANS

■ **Protection plans** are benefits designed to provide protection to employees when their income is threatened or reduced by illness, disability, death, unemployment, or retirement.

Protection plans are benefits designed to provide protection to employees when their income is threatened or reduced by illness, disability, death, unemployment, or retirement. Several of these benefits are required by law but others are optional. We will first discuss those plans that are required or mandated by law.

Unemployment Insurance

One mandated benefit is unemployment insurance. Unemployment insurance was created in the United States as part of the Social Security Act of 1935. The rationale for the act was to protect those people who were experiencing the high levels of unemployment that were pervasive in the United States during the 1930s.

■ **Unemployment insurance,** a mandated protection plan, is intended to provide a basic subsistence payment to employees who are between jobs.

Unemployment insurance is intended to provide a basic subsistence payment to employees who are between jobs. That is, it is intended for people who have stopped working for one organization but who are assumed to be seeking employment with another organization. Employers pay premiums to the unemployment insurance fund. In addition, in the states of Alabama, Alaska, and New Jersey, the employees also pay a contribution to the fund. The premium payment is increased if more than an average or designated number of employees from the organization is drawing from the fund at any given time.

Unemployment insurance and related systems for certain former government workers cover almost 65,000,000 employees in the United States. Major categories that are excluded from coverage include self-employed workers, employees of very small firms with less than four employees, domestic employees, farm employees, state and local government employees, and employees of nonprofit organizations such as hospitals.

To be covered by unemployment insurance, an individual must have worked a minimum number of weeks, must now be without a job, and must be willing to accept a suitable position if one is found through the State Unemployment Compensation Commission. A critical variable in determining when an employee is qualified for receipt of benefits is the circumstances under which he or she became unemployed. In general, if the employee is out of work through no fault of his or her own, then benefits start almost immediately. For example, if an employee is laid off because the organization cuts back its workforce or shuts down operations altogether, then the employee isn't to blame for this circumstance.

On the other hand, if the employee quits of his or her own free will or is fired because of poor performance or other legitimate circumstances, then states might mandate a somewhat longer period of time before the individual becomes qualified for unemployment benefits. Regardless of the starting time, however, compensation is available for only a limited period. This period of time is usually twenty-six weeks, although in some states an extension beyond this term can be granted if there is an emergency situation, such as high unemployment rates.

The payment provided is intended to represent about half of what the individual might have been earning had he or she retained the former job, although an upper limit is placed on the benefit paid. As noted above, this program is funded through employer contributions. The tax for this program is 6.2 percent on the first $7,000 earned by each employee. Each state administers this program in its own fashion; however, considerable variation exists in how the laws and provisions are interpreted.

Social Security

A second mandated benefit is **social security**. The social security system was also established in 1935. What most people think of as social security is officially the **Old Age Survivors and Disability Insurance Program**. The initial purpose of this program was to provide some limited income to retired individuals to supplement their own personal savings, private pensions, part-time work, and so forth. The program is funded through employee and employer taxes that are withheld on a payroll basis.

At the present time, the percentage of payment is 7.65 percent. Individuals are eligible for partial benefits when they reach the age of sixty-two or full benefits when they reach the age of sixty-five. Effective in 2027, however, individuals will not be able to retire with full benefits until they reach age sixty-seven. If an employee dies before reaching retirement age, a family with children under the age of eighteen receives survival benefits, regardless of the employee's age at the time of her or his death. In addition, an employee who becomes totally disabled before the age of sixty-five is also eligible to receive insurance benefits; in fact Medicare benefits are also provided under this act.

The amount of money any individual is eligible to be paid from the social security system is a function of the average monthly wage that individual earned, weighted toward the latter years of a person's career. In addition, an individual has to have worked a minimum period of time and made a minimum amount of contributions to the system to be eligible to draw full benefits.

In recent years considerable concern has been raised in the United States about the long-term future viability of the social security system. In particular, with longer life expectancies, the increased risk of suffering disability in older age, new work patterns, and new family norms, the demands placed on the social security system have increased significantly. Indeed, the system is paying out more money than it is taking in. Thus, the government must intervene and make some manipulation or adjustment in the system to maintain its viability. In 1998, President Clinton vowed to use any budget surplus to strengthen the social security system and thus ensure its viability for years to come. He failed in his bid to do so, however. Several proposals have been offered for privatizing the system or for allowing employees to invest their own pension funds in the stock market. It is clear that social security will continue to be an issue for the coming years.

■ **Social security** (officially the **Old Age Survivors and Disability Insurance Program**), another mandated program, was originally designed to provide limited income to retired individuals to supplement their personal savings, private pensions, part-time work, and so forth.

Workers' compensation is an important legally mandated benefit available to most employees. However, benefits payable to employees injured on the job have not always kept pace with the cost of living. These construction workers in Florida are rallying to lower workers' compensation insurance rates and increase benefits that are paid to injured workers.

Workers' Compensation

■ **Workers' compensation,** another mandated protection program, is insurance that covers individuals who suffer a job-related illness or accident.

A final mandated benefit is workers' compensation. **Workers' compensation** is insurance that covers individuals who suffer a job-related illness or accident. Employers pay the cost of workers' compensation insurance. The exact premium paid is a function of each employer's past experience with job-related accidents and illnesses. Almost 90 million workers in the United States are protected under the Workers' Compensation Insurance Program.[5]

OPTIONAL PROTECTION PLANS

Another major category of employee benefits consists of various optional protection plans. These plans provide protection in the same areas as those discussed above, except that organizations are not mandated by law to provide them. It is therefore the organization's option whether or not to offer the specific benefit. As noted in the section on legislation, though, in some cases, if the organization *does* elect to offer the benefit, it may be required by law to follow certain guidelines.

Insurance Coverage

Perhaps the most common optional protection plan that many organizations provide to their full-time employees is insurance coverage. Insurance coverage is not mandated but has become such a standard benefit that most organizations elect to provide it. In some cases the organization pays all or at least a major portion of the insurance premiums. It is also common, however, for employees to bear a considerable portion of the load themselves.

Different kinds of insurance are available. Health insurance, of course, is the most common. Because of the dramatic escalation of medical costs over the last several years, this benefit has become increasingly expensive and complicated for many organizations to provide and to maintain. It is estimated that, in the United States, between 85 and 90 percent of all health-insurance coverage is purchased by employers as group plans covering their employees.[6]

While basic health insurance is the norm, some organizations also provide special programs for prescription drugs, vision-care products, mental-health services, and dental care. For example, today about one-fourth of all employees in the United States at least have the opportunity to purchase dental insurance through their employers. **Health maintenance organizations (HMOs)** are also a growing trend in health-insurance coverage. An HMO is a medical organization that provides medical and health services to employees on a prepaid basis. That is, rather than billing patients or companies for specific services rendered, the initial premium paid to the HMO provides the employee with prepaid coverage of all expenses he or she might incur for health care.

A growing trend toward cost containment strategies by organizations has been developed to reduce the huge outflow of funds for medical benefits. These

■ **Health maintenance organizations (HMOs)** are medical organizations that provide medical and health services to employees on a prepaid basis.

Pension and retirement plans are optional benefits provided to employees by many companies, especially larger ones. Problems can arise, however, when such benefit plans are not properly managed. Indeed, this was a central issue in the public relations fiasco of the Enron collapse. Employees of the firm were heavily invested in Enron stock, in part because senior managers were so optimistic about the firm's future; and restrictions kept most employees from pulling their money out even after the firm faltered. When Enron collapsed many former employees such as these women lost most—if not all—of their retirement savings.

strategies include coordinating benefits across plans and cost sharing. Unfortunately for the employee, cost sharing simply means that he or she has to bear a greater part of the cost of the insurance.

In addition, some organizations have become self-funded or self-insured. In most such cases, an organization contracts with an insurance company to provide health benefits, but some companies have been trying to fund their own health-insurance plans. They believe that this arrangement gives them greater control over costs and helps them to avoid state insurance regulations.

Other kinds of insurance coverage include life insurance, long-term disability insurance, and so forth. Life insurance, of course, provides payment to the survivors of an individual who has died or been killed. Disability insurance is designed to supplement workers' compensation insurance and provide continued income in the case of employee disability.

Private Pension Plans

■ **Private pension plans** are prearranged plans administered by the organization that provide income to the employee at her or his retirement.

In addition to the pension benefits guaranteed under the Social Security Act, many companies elect to establish **private pension plans** for their employees. These prearranged plans are administered by the organization that provides income to the employee at her or his retirement. Contributions to the retirement plan may come from either the employer or the employee, but in most cases are supported by contributions from both parties. Different retirement plans are available, including individual retirement accounts (IRAs) and employee pension IRAs. In addition, a 401K plan allows employees to save money on a tax-deferred basis by entering into salary deferral agreements with their employer. HR in the 21st Century discusses the details of a new model currently adopted for private pension plans.

■ **Defined benefit plans** are private pension plans in which the size of the benefit is precisely known and is usually based on a simple formula using input such as years of service.

■ **Defined contribution plans** are private pension plans in which the size of the benefit depends on how much money is contributed to the plan.

There are two basic types of pension plans: **defined benefit plans** and **defined contribution plans**. Under defined benefit plans, the size of the benefit is precisely known and is usually based on a simple formula using input such as years of service. This type of plan is often favored by unions and is closely monitored under ERISA. Although the employee may contribute to these plans, the amount of the contribution has no bearing on the benefits. Under defined contribution plans, the size of the benefit depends on how much money is contributed to the plan. This money can be contributed by either the employer alone (noncontributory plans) or the employer and the employee (contributory plans). Most new pension plans are contributory, defined contribution plans.

As we shall see a bit later in the chapter, legal protection dictates how the funds in pension plans are invested. Nonetheless, Enron required its employees to invest the vast majority of their 401K funds in Enron stock if Enron were to match their contributions. When Enron declared bankruptcy, the company's stock became almost worthless, which wiped out the retirement savings of many of Enron's employees.

PAID TIME OFF

Many organizations also provide their employees with some amount of time off with pay. No U.S. laws mandate this type of benefit, but most employees now expect it. One major type of paid time off is the paid holiday. Most full-time employees receive about ten paid holidays per year. The most common holidays

Taking It with You

Traditional pension plans were set up to reward those workers who stayed with the same employer for their entire career—that is, for thirty-, forty-, or even fifty-year veterans. Workers who left after only a few years typically had not accumulated a substantial balance and had to wait until at least age fifty-five—and usually age sixty-five—before they could start drawing a pension check.

The 401(k) retirement plan has made portability much easier. The employer and the employee each make contributions to an investment account, often on a pretax basis, and the employee can move the account to a new employer whenever necessary. But the risk to the employee is much greater because her or his pension balance is usually invested in securities markets.

But some big employers have begun offering a hybrid pension called a cash-balance plan. Under this arrangement, the employer pays a set amount, usually 5 to 7 percent of the employee's gross pay, into the individual's cash-balance account. The account itself has a guaranteed growth rate of about 6 percent per year. The employee receives quarterly statements showing the account value. And if the individual leaves, usually after a vesting period averaging about five years, the account is his or hers to take to the next job.

For companies, this arrangement serves as an effective recruiting tool for new employees, cuts record keeping for long-term workers, and limits liability. Little wonder, then, that companies such as AT&T, Bell Atlantic, Cigna, Cincinnati Bell, and Xerox have adopted this system. Indeed, cash-balance plans look like the model pension program for the twenty-first century.

> *"With cash-balance accounts, not only do they know what they have, they're not in pension jail until [age] 65."*
>
> (Michael Gulotta, president of ASA, a benefits management and consulting firm)*

Source: "Companies Switching to Portable Cash Pensions," *USA Today,* July 20, 1998, p. B1 (*quote on p. B1).

---

for which workers are paid without having to work include New Year's Day, Memorial Day, Independence Day, Labor Day, Thanksgiving Day, and Christmas. In addition, many other holidays are scheduled to abut a weekend so that people can have a three-day weekend. These additional holidays include President's Day in February, Memorial Day in May, Columbus Day in October, and Veteran's Day in November.

Religious holidays (in addition to Christmas) are also often given. Organizations have to be careful with this practice, however, because growing diversity in the workplace is accompanied by an increasingly diverse set of religions and thus religious holidays. An organization has to be sensitive to the fact that it can create problems if it gives time off for some religions but not others. For example, Christianity is the most common religion in the United States. Judaism is second, but Islam is on track to soon become number 2. Each of these three religions has different holidays, both in terms of numbers and dates. An organization that seeks to accommodate members of one or two religions but not all is asking for problems. But accommodating all religions creates other complications. Thus, organizations need to have clear policies and to enforce those policies in a fair and equitable manner.[7]

Paid vacations are also common but are likewise not required by law. Paid vacations are usually a period of one, two, or more weeks when an employee can take time off from work and continue to be paid. Most organizations vary the amount of paid vacation according to an individual's seniority with the organization. For example, it is typical to give an employee one week of paid vacation a year if he or she has three or less years of service with the organization. Following a third anniversary, however, the vacation benefit may increase to two weeks a year. At a later point, perhaps after ten years, it might be increased to three weeks of vacation a year. For the firm's most senior employees, such as those with perhaps twenty or twenty-five years of experience, the benefit may be increased to four weeks of paid vacation a year.[8]

Organizations administer vacation pay in very different ways. Some require employees to take their accumulated vacation time each year. Others are willing to pay employees time and a half for their vacation time if they continue to work instead of taking the time off. Some also allow employees to roll vacation time over into the next year (i.e., to save it for at least some period of time).

Earlier in the chapter, we mentioned that German workers had more extensive benefits than the typical U.S. employee. One area with considerable difference is in the number of days off per year. Although the number of days off is not mandated in the United States or the European Union, many European countries *do* mandate a minimum annual vacation. Table 13.1 illustrates some of the differences from country to country.

Yet another common paid time off plan is sick leave. This benefit is provided when an individual is sick or is otherwise physically unable to perform his or her job duties. Most organizations allow an individual to accumulate sick time on the basis of some schedule, such as one sick day per month worked. Some organizations require that employees submit a doctor's note verifying illness in the event the employee wants to draw sick pay. Other organizations take a more egalitarian approach, however, and require no such documentation, relying instead on employee honesty. One interesting wrinkle in sick-leave policies is that some organizations require the employee to use his or her allocation of sick days

---

TABLE 13.1 Minimum Annual Vacation by Law in Different Countries

Country	Minimum Vacation Time
Belgium	4 weeks
Denmark	36 days
France	36 days
Greece	4 weeks
Ireland	3 weeks
Italy	National Collective Bargaining Agreement*
The Netherlands	4 weeks
Portugal	21–30 days

* Unions and the Italian government negotiate minimum annual vacation periods as part of each collective bargaining agreement

Source: Reprinted from G. Milkovich and J. Newman, *Compensation*, 5th ed. (Chicago: Richard D. Irwin, 1996). Copyright © 1996 by The McGraw-Hill Companies. Reprinted with the permission of The McGraw-Hill Companies.

or lose them. Under such a system, it would seem illogical for an employee *not* to take all the sick days allocated during the year.

A final common method of paid time off is personal leave. Sometimes an organization allows an employee to take a small number of days off for personal business. Examples include funerals, religious observances, a marriage, a birthday, or simply a personal holiday. Organizations are usually also required to allow an employee to miss work if he or she is called for jury duty.

OTHER TYPES OF BENEFITS

In addition to protection plans and paid time off, some organizations offer various other kinds of benefit programs. For example, Clif Bar is a small company that makes energy bars; its headquarters building in California contains a rock climbing wall that employees can use. In this section we will describe several of the more common of these kinds of benefits. Figure 13.2 also illustrates recent trends among some of the more intriguing new benefits.

As noted earlier, many organizations are struggling with ways to reduce healthcare costs. In addition to the attempts described earlier, these efforts have also resulted in a different type of benefit known as **wellness programs**. Wellness programs concentrate on keeping employees from becoming sick, rather than simply paying expenses when they do become sick.[9] In some organizations, these programs may be simple and involve little more than organized jogging or walking during lunch breaks. More elaborate programs might include smoking cessation programs, blood pressure and cholesterol screening, and stress-management programs. Some organizations have full-fledged health clubs on site and provide counseling and programs for fitness and weight loss. Although these programs typically take place after work hours (or before), the companies often provide the services for free or at a low cost.

> ■ **Wellness programs** are special benefit programs that concentrate on keeping employees from becoming sick rather than simply paying expenses when they do become sick.

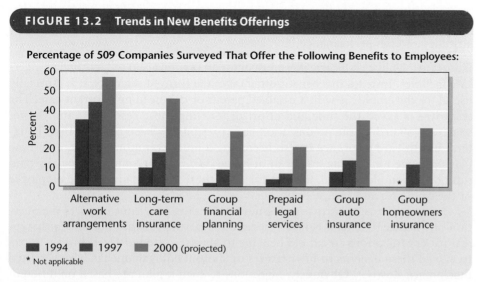

FIGURE 13.2   Trends in New Benefits Offerings

Percentage of 509 Companies Surveyed That Offer the Following Benefits to Employees:

■ 1994   ■ 1997   ■ 2000 (projected)
* Not applicable

Source: "What About Benefits?" from *Time*, November 9, 1998. Copyright © 1998 *Time* Inc. Reprinted by permission.

Some employers seem to be getting increasingly flexible and creative in the kinds of benefits they offer to their employees. Take Electronic Arts for example, a growing maker of electronic games. The firm offers its employees access to this labyrinth outside its corporate headquarters and encourages them to wander through it to relax and recharge their creative energies. Electronic Arts also provides free espresso, sponsors volleyball and basketball games, and even grants seven-week sabbaticals to employees after seven years with the firm.

Not only are these plans attractive to employees who appreciate the ease and low costs, but they are usually seen as an excellent investment by the organization. Specifically, many case studies indicate that these programs reduce the number of sick days, reduce medical costs, and improve productivity because the organization gains a more physically fit workforce.[10]

An additional group of benefits are often referred to collectively as **life-cycle benefits**. The most common are childcare and eldercare benefits. Thus, these benefits are targeted at different stages in an employee's life.

Childcare   Childcare benefits are becoming extremely popular. In fact, any organization that wants to be considered a family-friendly organization must have some type of childcare benefits, at a minimum. A claim of being family-friendly is increasingly viewed as a competitive advantage.[11] These plans might include scheduling childcare help, referrals to various types of

■ **Life-cycle benefits** are based on a person's life cycle and include childcare and eldercare benefits.

childcare services, or reimbursement accounts for childcare expenses. In many cases, however, they include company-paid daycare. For example, BP-AMOCO International's headquarters in Houston, Texas, has an on-site, freestanding daycare facility. The building had been intended for another use and then had been abandoned. The management at BP-AMOCO purchased the building and contracted with an outside firm to provide daycare services, which are heavily discounted rates for employees. Such a program has a strong impact on employee attitudes and job performance.[12]

Eldercare   Unlike childcare, it is unusual for an organization to have on-site eldercare facilities. Instead, this benefit often takes the form of referrals. It is especially useful for the employee with a disabled parent or one needing constant care. The employee is saved the time and effort of locating these resources, and the resources provided by the organization have presumably been checked first. Long-term health-care insurance is also becoming a more common benefit, and these plans provide for nursing homes or at-home care. The premium is typically paid fully by the employee and, at least for now, these benefits are for the employee or the employee and spouse only.

One of the most controversial issues for benefits programs involves the question of whether to extend benefits to same-sex partners. It has become fairly typical for organizations to extend benefits to spouses of employees, but the move to extend these benefits to life partners or spousal equivalents has been accepted much more slowly.[13] Obviously, objections to such a plan are based on different points of view, but more organizations are coming to believe that it is simply fair to extend benefits to same-sex partners. Chevron's corporate headquarters is located in San Francisco, California, and, in an attempt to be fair and to remain competitive for employees in the local market, the company decided to extend all health and insurance benefits to same-sex partners. Although this move was applauded in San Francisco, employees at headquarters for the firm's production company located in Houston, Texas, were less enthusiastic. The company made it clear, however, that *the provision of these benefits* is company policy and that they believed that gay and lesbian partners deserved equal treatment on the job, and they invited employees who could not live with this policy to seek employment elsewhere. HR Legal Brief discusses this issue in more detail.

In addition, organizations sometimes provide various additional services for their employees. These services may include relocation services and help with mortgage financing, although these benefits are typically available for senior-level employees only. In the late 1970s, IBM preferred managers to retire earlier than at age sixty-five. The company realized, in turn, that one constraint many people faced when thinking about early retirement was money. Therefore, they offered estate-planning and wealth-accumulation programs for their management employees. An employee might have to pay for these kinds of services him- or herself if they were not provided by the company, so they are rather attractive to employees.

A somewhat different type of service is contained in what are referred to as **employee assistance plans (EAPs)**. These programs are designed to assist employees who have chronic problems with alcohol or drugs or who have serious

■ **Employee assistance plans (EAPs)** are designed to assist employees who have chronic problems with alcohol or drugs or who have serious domestic or personal problems.

HR Legal Brief

Legislating Domestic Partner Benefits?

It has long been customary for firms to extend benefits such as insurance coverage to an employee's husband or wife. But what if the employee is not married to her or his domestic partner? Or if they are the same sex? More and more companies are extending benefits to their employees' unmarried and/or gay partners, sometimes because of legal pressure, sometime because of competitive pressure, and sometimes because of both. (Of course, some firms have adopted this practice just because they think it's the right thing to do.)

One major impetus for the growth in partner benefits is an ordinance passed by the city of San Francisco in California. The ordinance simply says that any firm doing business with the city has to extend benefits to unmarried and/or gay partners. The oil giant Chevron-Texaco is headquartered in San Francisco. It changed its policies to be compliant with the San Francisco ordinance, but it did so nationwide for all 26,000 of its employees. Shortly thereafter, both Shell and Amoco followed suit—not because they do business in San

"The market is very, very tight for good people, and we want to do anything we can to attract and retain them."

(Alison Jones, Chevron-Texaco spokesperson)*

Francisco but to remain competitive with Chevron-Texaco in a tight labor market.

Sometimes, this practice can have unexpected repercussions. For example, one major factor cited in a religious boycott of Disney was that the entertainment giant extended benefits coverage to its employees' unmarried and/or gay partners. One of the major reasons why Disney offered this benefit was that competitors such as Universal, Paramount, Sony, and Warner Bros. had already done so.

This practice has not increased costs for insurers. These newly insured couples tend to be younger and thus in better health. Their pregnancy rates are also lower. Over one-quarter of U.S. companies with more than 5,000 employees have revised their benefits to include unmarried and/or gay domestic partners. And if a few more cities follow the lead of San Francisco, this percentage will certainly take a big jump.

Source: "Domestic Partner Benefits on Rise," *USA Today*, October 14, 1997, p. 8B (*quote on p. 8B).

domestic problems. An increase in the number of programs for mental problems and stress, as well as for bereavement, has also been a recent trend.[14] These programs are typically voluntary and referrals are confidential. Yet the needs of the organization (especially when the personal problem is causing performance problems on the job) must be balanced with the needs of the individual to avoid any stigma attached to having the specific problem.[15]

■ A **perquisite,** or perk, as it is more informally known, is an extra benefit that may or may not have any direct financial value but is considered to be an important reward by employees.

Finally, employee perquisites are sometimes provided. A **perquisite,** or perk, as it is more informally known, is an extra benefit that may or may not have any direct financial value but is considered an important reward by employees. A perk might include a bigger office, a company car, membership in a country club, stock-purchase options, premium insurance coverage, and so forth. Perquisites are usually made available only to members of top management or to certain especially valuable professionals within the organization.

Sometimes organizations provide special perquisites that might be available to all employees. For example, some firms might provide the cost of uniforms for a company softball team, a health club on site that all members of the organization can use, a car-pooling service for employees who live some distance from the organization, and similar kinds of perquisites.

CAFETERIA-STYLE BENEFITS PLANS

■ **Cafeteria-style benefits plans** allow the employee to choose those benefits he or she really wants.

Most benefits programs are designed for all the employees in an organization. Although the exact benefits may vary as a function of level in the organization, within those levels the plans are generally "one size fits all." **Cafeteria-style benefits plans** allow the employee to choose the benefits that he or she really wants. Thus, under these plans the organization typically establishes a budget indicating how much it is willing to spend per employee on benefits.[16] The employee is then presented with a list of possible benefits and the cost of each. Employees are then free to choose the benefits in any combination they wish. Such an approach should maximize the effectiveness of the benefits program for achieving the organizational goals that we discussed at the beginning of the chapter, and some evidence suggests that cafeteria-style benefits programs can lead to increased satisfaction and reduced turnover.[17]

Not surprisingly, perhaps, these plans come with variations. In some cases, the cafeteria menu includes only basic levels of coverage, and the employee must pay (or substitute for other types of coverage) for enhanced coverage. In other cases, the employee is allowed to keep the money not spent on benefits. In yet other plans, the cost to the employee of each benefit is structured so that the employee is rewarded for choosing more cost-effective benefits (e.g., HMO versus more traditional medical plans).

Two serious problems limit the willingness of organizations to adopt cafeteria-style benefits plans, however. The first is the cost of administration. Because every employee has a potentially unique set of benefits, someone has to keep track of what benefits each employee has chosen. It is often typical for the employee to be able to change his or her choices, so the administrative task is further complicated by the fact that the package of benefits can change on an employee-to-employee basis.

The second problem stems from the presumably rational choices an employee makes. For example, if an employee has children who are at the age where children typically need dental braces, the employee will most likely select a dental plan that includes coverage for braces. Because the recipients of this plan are those employees most likely to use it, the provider will charge relatively high prices to both the employee and the organization. And because the employee will probably drop this coverage for a different benefit when his or her children get older, the costs of coverage cannot be amortized across less frequent users. This problem, known as *adverse selection,* can be costly for the organization.

One final consideration in the design of cafeteria-style benefits plans is that employees are *not* always rational in their choices. A younger employee may elect to contribute less to his or her retirement because retirement seems like a distant future event and wait until later in life before increasing the contribution. But given the power of compounding interest, a larger contribution early in life, followed by a smaller contribution later, is actually worth much more at retirement age than a smaller contribution made early in life, followed by a larger contribution made later. Therefore it is extremely important for employees to have full information about the available benefits, and in some cases it may be necessary for the organization to mandate minimum benefits levels in some areas.

As a result of these problems, some experts have suggested that organizations avoid cafeteria plans and simply determine what benefits are most likely to be attractive to most employees. Our Point/Counterpoint feature for this chapter addresses this debate.

LEGAL ISSUES IN INDIRECT COMPENSATION AND BENEFITS

Several general legal issues relate to benefits administration. One important consideration for an organization is to make sure that its benefits plan is qualified. A **qualified benefit** plan is one where (1) the employer receives an immediate tax deduction for any contributions made, (2) the employee does not incur a tax liability at the time of the employer deduction, and (3) investment returns (such as from stocks and bonds) are accumulated tax-free. Although the requirements for qualification differ for different types of benefits plans, it is critical that the plan be nondiscriminatory: the plan cannot disproportionately favor employees with higher income levels.[18]

■ **A qualified benefit** plan is one where the employer receives an immediate tax deduction for any contributions made, and the employee does not incur a tax liability on the amount deducted or on any investment returns

Of course, the most important legal issue in this area deals with the Employee Retirement Income Security Act (ERISA) of 1974. We introduced this law in Chapter 3, but it deserves additional attention here. As noted earlier, this law was passed to protect employees who had contributed to their pensions but were unable to collect those benefits later. This situation occurred primarily because of the restrictions that the organizations had placed on employees before they could receive retirement benefits. Specifically, organizations required that employees remain with the company as long as thirty years before they were vested. (**Vesting rights** are guaranteed rights to receive pension benefits.) For example, before 1974 a sixty-year-old employee with twenty-nine years of service would *not* be entitled to pension benefits if he or she left the company—or even if he or she died—before his or her thirty-year anniversary. Under ERISA, however, vesting rights become operational after six years *at the most,* and employees with less service are still usually eligible to receive some portion of their retirement benefits.

■ **Vesting rights** are guaranteed rights to receive pension benefits.

ERISA also provides protection for the funding underlying the pension plan. The Pension Benefit Guaranty Corporation oversees how pension plans are

POINT | COUNTERPOINT

Should Organizations Adopt Cafeteria Plans for Benefits?

The purpose behind cafeteria-style benefits plans is to allow employees to select those benefits they see as most useful and valuable. But some have argued that these plans are difficult and expensive to maintain and, for various reasons, employees can actually be worse off if they are allowed to make these choices themselves. Of course, most employees believe they should be able to choose. But it's possible that they would be better served if the organization made the choices for them.

POINT... **Organizations should use cafeteria-style benefits plans because...**	COUNTERPOINT... **Organizations should *not* use cafeteria-style benefits plans because...**
Employees like the idea of choice.	The amount of information an employee needs to consider is overwhelming.
These plans allow employees to choose the specific benefits that they prefer.	Employees make poor choices that can deprive them of basic coverage.
These plans allow an organization to use benefits as a reason for an employee to remain with the company.	Employees need to change their benefits as their circumstances change.
These plans allow maximum flexibility because one set of benefits is not likely to fit all employees.	These plans are expensive to administer (because they require extensive record keeping) and expensive to maintain (because employees are most likely to select the benefits they will use most).

So... Cafeteria-style benefits plans are probably not for everyone. Such plans have clear advantages, but they are also quite costly and can actually harm the employees in the long run. The more heterogeneous the workforce, the more important it is to have a cafeteria-style benefits plan but, in all cases, it is critical to provide complete information to employees so that they can make informed decisions.

funded and can seize corporate assets to support underfunded plans. In addition, ERISA allows an employee to carry a portion of his or her benefits to another job. This notion of portability is especially important when employees change jobs frequently. ERISA also imposes some minimum requirements for how pension plans are communicated to employees. If an organization does not follow ERISA guidelines, its pension plan will not be qualified as defined above.

EVALUATING INDIRECT COMPENSATION AND BENEFITS PLANS

Given the enormous cost of benefits packages to an organization, it is clearly important that managers carefully assess the advantages of those packages for the organization. On the one hand, it is important that the organization provide appropriate benefits to its employees. On the other hand, it is in the best interest of the stockholders and other constituents of the organization that the firm manages its resources wisely. Thus, it is important to assess periodically the extent to which costs are in line. One method of assessment is through the use of the wage surveys, which were discussed in Chapter 11. Although these surveys typically ask about wages for specific jobs, questions about benefits can also be included. Any organization can learn the average insurance premium costs, for example, that other organizations are paying, and even if it cannot match these premiums, the company can nevertheless get a better feel for how close its costs are to those of other firms.

Some organizations might find it necessary to audit their benefits programs to determine whether or not they are providing a competitive package. As part of the recruiting process, it is necessary, of course, that the organization be viewed as an attractive employer if the firm wants to hire high-quality human resources. Thus, if other organizations in the labor market are providing special benefits that the organization is not providing, it might have to reconsider its policy. On the other hand, the organization may be providing more benefits than its competitors are providing, and it might be possible to scale back in some areas as a way of controlling costs.

One final issue must be considered relative to evaluating benefits programs. In many cases, these programs are not as effective as they might be simply because the organization has not communicated effectively with employees about those benefits. Figure 13.3 illustrates that many employees are not fully informed about their benefits. For example, some evidence suggests that awareness about benefits could be increased through communication via several media and that,

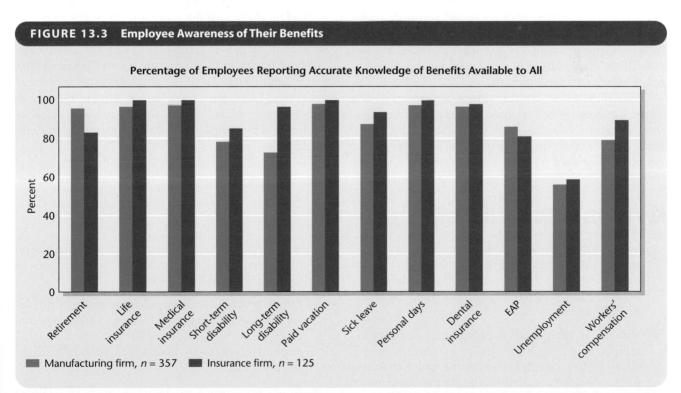

FIGURE 13.3   Employee Awareness of Their Benefits

Percentage of Employees Reporting Accurate Knowledge of Benefits Available to All

Manufacturing firm, $n = 357$ Insurance firm, $n = 125$

Source: Andrew Muonio, "How Aware Are Employees of Their Benefits?" *HRMagazine,* May 1997, p. 53; James Danehower and William Lust, *Benefits Quarterly,* Fourth Quarter 1996.

as awareness increased, so did satisfaction with benefits.[19] The reason for this relationship is underscored by the results of another study, where employees were asked to estimate the value of the employer's contribution to their benefits. When asked about family coverage, the average estimate was only 38 percent of the actual cost of those benefits to the employer.[20] It seems clear that an organization can never expect to appreciate the full advantage of its benefits program when employees underestimate the cost of their benefits by such a large amount.

Chapter Summary

Benefits take up an ever-larger portion of employers' total labor costs. Organizations sustain these costs because they believe that competitive benefits packages attract better applicants and help the company retain the employees they have already hired. Although benefits costs are high in the United States, levels of mandated benefits are much higher in Europe and elsewhere. The kinds of benefits that are attractive or appropriate to employees around the world differ considerably. Several laws provide guidelines for how benefits plans should be administered.

Additional laws mandate that all employees must have certain benefits, such as social security, unemployment insurance, and workers' compensation. In addition, many organizations offer optional protection plans such as health and dental insurance coverage and private pension plans.

Paid time off is another important benefit. The most common forms of paid time off are vacation time, holidays, religious days, sick leave, and personal time. This benefit, in particular, varies widely from country to country.

Organizations are also becoming more likely to offer benefits in areas such as wellness programs, childcare, eldercare, and employee assistance programs. Finally, some benefits provided by organizations are services and perks that the employee would otherwise have to pay for.

Because needs and preferences differ, some organizations offer cafeteria-style benefits plans in which the employee gets to pick and choose the benefits desired. These programs are expensive to run, but they result in employees getting exactly what they want, which makes the benefits program more cost effective.

Given the enormous cost to an organization of compensation and benefits packages, it is clearly important that managers carefully assess the advantages of those packages to the organization. One key factor in the administration of benefits programs is communications. Employees often underestimate the cost of the benefits provided for them, and this lack of understanding reduces the effectiveness of any benefits package.

Key Points for Future HR Managers

▶ Indirect compensation and benefits represent a significant portion of the total compensation paid to employees in the United States. Yet these portions are generally lower here than in many European countries.

▶ The rise in the cost of benefits is the result of attempts to attract high-quality employees during times of low unemployment, the belief that employees might respond to the provision of more attractive benefits by working harder, and by employee expectations about benefits.

▶ A substantial portion of the benefits paid to employees today are mandated by law and cannot be reduced without legislation.

▶ Other benefits, such as pensions and medical insurance, are not mandated but are surely expected by employees. The cost of some of these benefits (especially medical insurance) is rising at an alarming rate.

▶ Many other optional benefits, such as wellness programs and eldercare, started as a source of competitive advantage but, while costly, they are also becoming part of employee expectations at larger firms.

▶ Cafeteria-style benefits plans allow for the possibility of using benefits dollars so that they have the greatest positive impact on employee satisfaction. These plans have several disadvantages,

however, and so they require careful study before they are implemented.

▶ It is difficult to assess the effectiveness of indirect compensation plans, but it is critical that the organization communicate clearly to employees what benefits those employees are receiving.

▶ Indirect compensation and benefits represent a large portion of total compensation costs. Many of the benefits are required by law; others (such as vacations and medical insurance) have become such a strong part of employee expectations that they cannot easily be eliminated.

▶ Cafeteria-style benefits plans may allow the company to spend its benefits dollars so that the plan

Key Points for Future General Managers

has the greatest impact on employee satisfaction, although these plans have some disadvantages.

▶ Communications is a key part of the indirect compensation strategy, but the link between indirect compensation and any organizational-level outcomes is unclear.

Review and Discussion Questions

1. What are the basic purposes of indirect compensation and benefits programs?

2. How and in what ways do legal considerations impinge on benefits programs in organizations?

3. What are the three basic mandated protection plans? Summarize each one.

4. What are the more common forms of optional protection plans? Summarize each one.

5. What are the basic forms of paid time off provided by some organizations?

6. What are some of the important issues associated with managing paid time off?

7. Identify and summarize four basic kinds of indirect or nonfinancial benefits.

8. What is an employee assistance program?

9. What is a cafeteria-style benefits plan? What are its strengths and weaknesses?

10. Why is it especially important to evaluate the effectiveness of an organization's indirect compensation and benefits plans?

Closing Case

Flexible Benefits Are All the Rage

Once most benefits packages all looked about the same, but in today's competitive business climate, flexible benefits programs are all the rage. By *flexible,* experts mean that companies are giving employees more choices about their benefits and/or providing benefits that add flexibility to the daily lives of employees.

For example, take the case of Katherine Lechler, a young graphics designer for a trade publication. Her employer provides high-quality on-site childcare for her two children. She pays about 20 percent less than she would for commercial childcare, has lunch with her children each day, and knows that she can be at their side at a moment's notice. For its part, the company gets a higher percentage of Lechler's work time, and she is less likely to look for a job with another company that might not provide the same benefits.

Another increasingly popular benefit is on-site counseling of various types. ATS, a large telecommunications firm, provides psychological counseling for its employees. People use the service to work through personal and/or family problems, career issues, or just about anything else where a trained psychologist can be of help. Again, the firm's program has advantages. The part-time psychologist costs about one-fifth of what ATS saves on hiring new people—its turnover is one-third of the industry average.

Similarly, Marriott International provides a twenty-four-hour toll-free hotline for its employees and it is staffed by social workers. Employees can call for advice on everything from setting up a family budget to dealing with a child's problems at school, to selecting the best automobile insurance policy. Marriott spends about $1 million annually to operate the service, but it estimates that it saves $4 million in reduced absenteeism and lower turnover.

Small businesses are also getting in on the act. Russell, Karsh, & Hagen, an eleven-person public relations firm in Denver, Colorado, allows its employees to donate public relations work—on company time—to their favorite charity. While this program might not be a benefit per se, it nevertheless helps employees see

that the firm is interested in supporting issues that they value.

Another small public relations firm in New Jersey, Daly Gray, allows staffers to add a couple of extra vacation days whenever they travel on company business. The president even donates some of his own frequent flyer miles to make it easier for his employees to travel. And again, both the firm and its employees benefit.

Indeed, these and other kinds of benefits continue to grow in popularity. One recent survey found, for example, that human resource managers expect part-time work options, telecommuting, and flexible work hours to grow significantly by the year 2004. In addition, the same survey found rapid and continuing growth in other benefits options, including long-term care insurance, group financial planning, prepaid legal services, group auto insurance, and group homeowners insurance.[21]

Case Questions

1. What do you see as the pluses and minuses for the growing array of benefits for employees? For employers?

2. What circumstances, if any, might prompt a reversal of this trend?

3. What benefits appeal most to you personally?

Building HR Management Skills

Purpose: The purpose of this exercise is help you assess the issues associated with cafeteria-style benefits programs.

Step 1: Assume that you are the human resource manager of a midsized manufacturing company. Your company currently offers a relatively traditional benefits program. The specifics are as follows:

1. Health insurance: the organization contributes $250 per employee per month, which covers the cost for the employee; the employee pays an additional $50 per month per covered dependent.

2. Dental insurance: the organization contributes $50 per month, which covers the cost for the employee; the employee pays an additional $10 per month per covered dependent.

3. Life insurance: the organization contributes $20 per month for $40,000 in term life insurance; the employee can buy additional units of coverage as a function of annual salary.

4. Vacation: everyone gets two weeks per year.

5. Holidays: everyone gets ten paid holidays per year.

6. Sick time: everyone gets ten sick days per year.

Step 2: Assume that your boss has indicated that the firm wants to adopt a cafeteria-style benefits plan, and that you are to devise such a plan.

Step 3: Outline as many options as you can think of for such a plan. Use the set of benefits listed above as a starting point.

Ethical Dilemmas in HR Management

 Assume that you are the human resource manager for a service organization. Your boss recently read that most employees underestimate the value of the benefits provided to them by their employer. He has instructed you to develop a plan for communicating the costs of benefits to your employees. You agree that communicating this information is a good idea; however, he has instructed that you should manipulate the information so that it looks better than the reality.

For example, your firm offers ten sick days per year. The average employee takes only eight days per year and forfeits the unused number of days. Your boss wants you to talk about this benefit as though everyone took their full allotment. Your firm offers two health insurance options: a basic or standard plan and a premium plan. Both the company and the individual pay more if the premium plan is chosen. He wants you to quote only the cost for the more expen-

sive plan, even though more than half of your workers have chosen the standard plan.

When you questioned his ideas, your boss simply said, "These are the potential costs that we could incur for everyone. Just because people don't take all their sick days or they select the basic insurance plan, that's their choice. The company is willing to pay for ten sick days and for the high-end insurance. So we should get credit for being generous."

Questions

1. What are the ethical issues in this situation?

2. What are the basic arguments for and against what your boss is instructing you to do?

3. What do you think most managers would do? What would you do?

HR Internet Exercise

 Many companies today post information about their benefits on their websites. Select any five companies in which you have a personal interest. Visit their websites and learn about their benefits. If any of them don't list benefits on their websites, continue exploring until you obtain information on five different companies.

Questions

1. Compare and contrast the different benefits packages offered among the set of firms.

2. What are the advantages and disadvantages of posting information about benefits on a website?

3. How effective do you think each site is in terms of communicating information about company benefits?

14

Managing Labor Relations

CHAPTER OBJECTIVES

After studying this chapter you should be able to:

■ Describe the role of labor unions in organizations.

■ Identify and summarize trends in unionization.

■ Discuss the unionization process.

■ Describe the collective-bargaining process.

■ Discuss how labor agreements are negotiated.

■ Summarize how labor agreements are administered.

■ Discuss labor unions and social issues.

Sometimes it takes three, not two, to tango. In late 2002 a labor union and management needed federal intervention to force them to reach a labor agreement. The dispute started when the International Longshore and Warehouse Union could not reach a new labor agreement with the Pacific Maritime Association representing twenty-nine West Coast ports.

According to the port association, the union instructed its workers to begin a systematic work slowdown to improve its bargaining position. The union meanwhile argued that it simply told its members to work in strict accordance with all safety and health rules because the employers were bargaining in bad faith. In response, the port association imposed a lockout, which prevented all port workers from getting to their job sites.

The resulting chaos was disastrous for the limping U.S. economy. Foreign automobile parts sat on ships, forcing several assembly plants to be idle. Toys and other holiday merchandise bound for retailers across the country sat in cargo hulls. And fruits, vegetables, and other perishables began to rot. Finally, after ten days, President Bush invoked federal legislation to force the ports to reopen, and a federal mediator stepped in to help the two sides reach an agreement.

Finally, as 2002 drew to a close, the two sides began to compromise with the help of the federal mediator. The resulting agreement increased worker pension benefits and required employers to pay all insurance costs for the workers. But the ports also received union authorization to develop new productivity-enhancing technologies and to cut 400 marine clerk jobs. In February 2003, the union members voted overwhelmingly to accept the new contract, which runs through 2008.[1] ■

"It's a disaster. Our Christmas merchandise . . . is sitting in boats or over in Asia."

(Robin Lanier, spokesperson for Target*)

The Pacific Maritime Association and its managers had to contend with one of the most significant challenges facing many businesses today—dealing with organized labor in ways that optimize the needs and priorities of both the business and its employees. When this challenge is handled effectively and constructively, both sides benefit. But when relationships between an organization and its unions turn sour, both sides can suffer great costs. In the chapter-opening vignette, workers lost ten days of income. The ports also lost millions of dollars in revenues, and the shock waves spread across several different industries.

In this part of the book, we focus on the fundamental issues and challenges associated with managing a workforce. The preceding parts dealt with entry-level processes based on the mechanisms of staffing and the strategies and techniques used to enhance motivation and performance among workers. By definition, then, these subjects have focused on dynamic, changing, and evolutionary processes. But organizations must also attend to the management of an existing and ongoing workforce, which is the focus of this part.

This chapter focuses on the management of labor relations. We start by assessing the role of labor unions in organizations. We examine trends in unionization and describe the unionization process itself. Collective bargaining is discussed, followed by a description of the issues involved in negotiating labor agreements. A discussion of the administration of labor agreements concludes Chapter 14. In Chapter 15 we examine the management of different aspects of the work environment. Managing a diverse workforce is the subject of Chapter 16. Chapter 17 concludes this part with a discussion about managing new employment relationships.

THE ROLE OF LABOR UNIONS IN ORGANIZATIONS

Labor relations can be defined as the process of dealing with employees who are represented by a union. A **labor union**, in turn, is a legally constituted group of individuals working together to achieve shared job-related goals. As we will see later, these goals often include issues such as higher wages, enhanced benefits, and/or better working conditions. **Collective bargaining**, a specific aspect of labor relations discussed more fully later in this chapter, is the process by which managers and union leaders negotiate acceptable terms and conditions of employment for those workers represented by the unions.[2] Although *collective bargaining* is a term that technically and properly is applied only in settings where employees are unionized, similar processes, of course, often exist in nonunionized settings as well. In these cases, however, they are likely to be labeled *employee relations* rather than labor relations.

Historical Development of Unions

Figure 14.1 shows the major historical events in the emergence and growth of labor unions in the United States. Indeed, the historical formation of labor unions closely parallels the history of the country itself. For example, the earliest unions in the United States emerged during the Revolutionary War. These unions were called craft unions. By "craft unions" we mean that each such union limited itself

■ **Labor relations** is the process of dealing with employees who are represented by a union.

■ A **labor union** is a legally constituted group of individuals working together to achieve shared, job-related goals, including higher pay and shorter working hours.

■ **Collective bargaining** is the process by which managers and union leaders negotiate acceptable terms and conditions of employment for those workers represented by the unions.

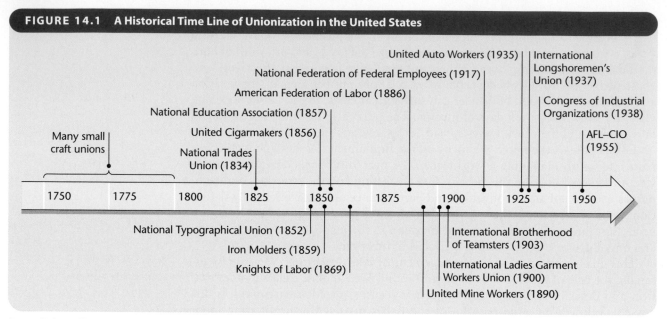

FIGURE 14.1   A Historical Time Line of Unionization in the United States

United Auto Workers (1935)

International Longshoremen's Union (1937)

National Federation of Federal Employees (1917)

American Federation of Labor (1886)

Congress of Industrial Organizations (1938)

National Education Association (1857)

United Cigarmakers (1856)

AFL–CIO (1955)

Many small craft unions

National Trades Union (1834)

1750   1775   1800   1825   1850   1875   1900   1925   1950

National Typographical Union (1852)

Iron Molders (1859)

Knights of Labor (1869)

International Brotherhood of Teamsters (1903)

International Ladies Garment Workers Union (1900)

United Mine Workers (1890)

Source: Ricky Griffin and Ronald Ebert, *Business*, 3rd ed., © 2000. Reprinted by permission of Prentice-Hall, Inc., Upper Saddle River, N.J.

to representing groups of workers who performed common and specific skilled jobs. For example, one of the first unions—the Journeyman Cordwainers Society of Philadelphia—was formed by shoemakers in Philadelphia in 1794. The union's goal was to enhance the pay and working conditions of all shoemakers.

Many of the earliest unions were localized in nature and often confined their activities to a single setting. But in 1834 the first national unions in the United States began to emerge. Throughout the remainder of the nineteenth century, one major union after another began to appear. Among the most significant were the National Typographical Union in 1852, the United Cigar Makers in 1856, and the National Iron Molders in 1859. The nineteenth century ended with thirty national unions, with a combined membership of around 300,000 individuals.

The first major union to have a significant impact in the United States, however, was the **Knights of Labor**, which was founded in 1869. Like most other unions, the Knights originally represented crafts and sought to improve the lot of its members. But unlike most other national unions that restricted their organizing activities to a single craft or job, the Knights of Labor expanded its goals and its membership to include workers in numerous fields. Their objective was quite simple—the leaders of the Knights of Labor believed that if they could control (or represent) the entire supply of skilled labor in the United States, their ability to negotiate favorable wages would be significantly enhanced. Members joined the Knights directly, as opposed to a later model where members joined a separate union that was affiliated with other more specific unions loosely coordinated under an umbrella organization.

The Noble and Holy Order of the Knights of Labor (the union's full name) admitted anyone to membership, regardless of race or creed (which typically *were* important considerations for membership in unions at the time), except for those they considered to be "social parasites" (such as bankers). In addition to

■ The **Knights of Labor** was an important early union that expanded its goals and its membership to include workers in numerous fields rather than a single industry.

improving wages, the Knights of Labor sought to replace capitalism with worker cooperatives. The union enjoyed incredible growth for several years, growing from 52,000 members in 1883 to 700,000 members in 1886. But internal strife about goals and disagreement over what should replace the capitalist model all led to the eventual demise of the Knights of Labor. The single event that contributed most to its demise, however, was a mass meeting in Chicago's Haymarket Square on May 4, 1886. The meeting was held to protest some earlier violence stemming from an attempt to establish an eight-hour workday. When the May 4 meeting was over, further violence left 200 wounded and resulted in the hanging of several leaders of the Knights. By the end of the century, the Knights of Labor had all but disappeared from the labor scene.

Even as the Knights of Labor union was dying, however, its replacement was already beginning to gather strength. The **American Federation of Labor (AF of L)** was founded in 1886 by Samuel Gompers. Like the Knights of Labor, the American Federation of Labor was comprised of various craft unions. Unlike the Knights of Labor, the AF of L sought not to get involved in legislative and political activities, but instead focused its efforts on improved working conditions and better employment contracts. Also unlike the Knights of Labor, the AF of L served as an umbrella organization, with members joining individual unions affiliated with the AF of L, as opposed to joining the AF of L itself.

■ The **American Federation of Labor (AF of L)** was another early union; it focused its efforts on improved working conditions and better employment contracts rather than getting involved in legislative and political activities.

While the AF of L focused exclusively on the "business" of unions, several more radical and violent union movements developed after the demise of the Knights of Labor. For example, under the leadership of Eugene V. Debs, the American Railway Union (ARU) battled the railroads (especially the Pullman Company—of Pullman car fame) mostly over wages, and many people were killed during strike violence. Debs also became a leader of the Socialist Party and actually ran for president of the United States on the Socialist ticket in 1920. The Industrial Workers of the World consisted mostly of unskilled workers and advocated extreme violence as a means of settling labor disputes. The mining companies and textile mill owners with which they battled also believed in violence as a means of settling labor disputes, and many people were killed during strikes organized by the "Wobblies," as they were called. The union's opposition to U.S. involvement in World War I led to its being prosecuted for treason and most of the leaders being jailed.

For the more mainstream organized labor movement, many of these fringe groups were too radical, and workers preferred the businesslike approach of the AF of L. As a result, the AF of L grew rapidly throughout the early decades of the twentieth century. Indeed, by the end of World War I, it had a total membership of more than 5 million individuals. Over the next several years, however, membership in the AF of L began to decline, and by the mid-1930s its membership stood at approximately 2.9 million members.

One of the weaknesses of the AF of L was its continued focus on crafts. That is, only skilled craftspersons performing specifically defined jobs were allowed to join. During the 1930s, however, a new kind of unionization began to emerge that focused on industrial unionization. Rather than organizing workers across companies or across industries based on their craft, this new type of union activity focused on organizing employees by industry, regardless of their craft, skills, or occupation.

In the late 1930s, John L. Lewis of the United Mine Workers lead a dissenting faction of the AF of L to form a new labor organization called the **Congress of Industrial Organizations (CIO)**. The CIO was the first major representative of

■ Another important early union was the **Congress of Industrial Organizations (CIO),** which focused on organizing employees by industry, regardless of their craft, skills, or occupation.

the new approach to unionization noted above. The CIO quickly began to organize the automobile, steel, mining, meat-packing, paper, textile, and electrical industries. By the early 1940s, CIO unions had almost 5 million members.

In the years following World War II, union memberships in the AF of L and the CIO, as well as other unions, gradually increased. However, a series of bitter strikes during that same era also led to public resentment and calls for union reform. And Congress did indeed intervene to curtail the power of unions. The AF of L and the CIO then began to contemplate a merger as a way of consolidating their strength. Eventually, in 1955, the AFL-CIO was formed, with a total membership of around 15 million employees. Union membership since 1955 has been quite erratic, however, and we will discuss that fact more fully in the next section. The Point/Counterpoint feature for this chapter highlights some of the basic arguments for and against the viability of unions today and sheds some light on the question of whether or not unions still have a role in contemporary society. Next, we will examine the legal context of unions and common union structures.

Legal Context of Unions

Partly because of the tumultuous history of labor unions in the United States, various laws and other regulations have been passed. Some are intended to promote unionization and union activities, while others are intended to limit or curtail union activities. As early as 1806, the local courts in Philadelphia declared

The legal context of labor unions is an important backdrop for all labor relations. Moreover, this context is strongly rooted in the historical evolution of labor relations. For example, the Taft-Hartley Act (more formally known as the Labor Management Relations Act) was passed in 1947 to curtail and limit certain union practices. These protesters are members of the International Ladies' Garment Workers Union. They are picketing nonunion garment shops in downtown Los Angeles in 1948 as a demonstration of their strength. Some of their signs are clearly directed at the Taft-Hartley Act and Taft himself. But the law remains intact and still plays an important role in labor relations today.

POINT | COUNTERPOINT

Are Labor Unions Still Necessary?

Labor unions were initially formed to try to equalize the power between labor and management. Because management controlled more resources, labor had power only if individual workers united in a concerted effort. This approach allowed workers to enjoy the rights they deserved and to deal with management as equals. Some people claim that unions have become too powerful and too interested in political agendas that are not always in the country's best interests. Others simply argue that labor is now the equal of management, and because effective management requires granting workers power and discretion, unions are simply no longer needed.

POINT... **Labor unions are no longer needed in the United States because...**	COUNTERPOINT... **But labor unions still serve an important function and so are needed because...**
Employees already have clear rights, and nonunion companies often offer better pay and conditions than do unionized companies.	Employees without unions have only the rights management chooses to grant, rather than the rights the workers might actually deserve. Would nonunion companies offer those levels of pay and benefits without the continued threat of unionization?
Unions raise pay without regarding costs and so hurt U.S. competitiveness.	What is the good of improving competitive position if it comes at the cost of jobs and fair pay for U.S. employees?
Unions are largely corrupt.	Many unions do have a history of corruption, but extensive efforts have been aimed at cleaning up this problem.
Union leaders pursue political agendas that are at odds with the interests of their members.	Individual workers often see only their own interests and don't understand how some policies can hurt other workers; thus, in the long run, they hurt themselves as well.
Unions interfere with more progressive management efforts aimed at improving competitiveness In international markets.	Union-management cooperation has led to situations where competitive advantage has been gained. The auto company Saturn claims that cooperation with the UAW has led to lower production costs and better quality—sources of competitive advantage. The key is to get unions involved in decision making.

So... It is reasonable to suggest that unions still have a function, and the threat of unionization probably continues to play a role in management decisions to implement more enlightened policies. But the role of unions will probably need to change (and already is changing). Unions need to become strategic partners with management to help ensure that U.S. companies survive and prosper—which is in everyone's best interest. But unions must also continue to fight for employee rights and to serve as the voice of employees who believe they have been wronged by management. It will be interesting to see how unions change, or whether they even manage to do so. If they do not adapt, they may well become obsolete.

the Cordwainers to be, by its very existence, in restraint of trade and thus illegal. This Cordwainer Doctrine, as it became known, dominated the law's view of unions until 1843, when the Massachusetts Supreme Court, in *Commonwealth* v. *Hunt,* ruled that unions were not by their very nature in restraint of trade but that this issue had to be proven in each individual case. This court decision led to increased union activity, but organizations responded by simply firing union organizers. After the Sherman Antitrust Act was passed in 1890, businesses once again sought (successfully) court injunctions against unions for restraint of trade. By the 1920s organizations also sought to identify union leaders as communists to reduce public sympathy toward them and to give the government an excuse to control the unions.

By the end of the 1920s, the country was in the grip of the Great Depression and the government soon intervened in an attempt to end work stoppages and start the economy on the road to recovery. The first significant piece of legislation was the **National Labor Relations Act,** which was passed in 1935. This act is more commonly referred to as the **Wagner Act** and still forms the cornerstone of contemporary labor relations law. The basic purpose of the Wagner Act was to grant power to labor unions and to put unions on a more equal footing with managers in terms of the rights of employees. It gives workers the legal right to form unions, to bargain collectively with management, and to engage in group activities such as strikes to accomplish their goals. This act also forces employers to bargain with properly elected union leaders and prohibits employers from engaging in certain unfair labor practices, including discriminating against union members in hiring, firing, and promotion.

The Wagner Act also established the **National Labor Relations Board** (**NLRB**) to administer its provisions. Today the NLRB still administers most labor law in the United States. For example, it defines the units with which managers must collectively bargain and it oversees most elections held by employees that will determine whether or not they will be represented by a union.

In the previous section, we noted congressional activity in the years following World War II that curtailed the power of the unions. The most important piece of legislation in this era was the **Labor Management Relations Act,** also known as the **Taft-Hartley Act,** which was passed in 1947. This act was a response to public outcries against a wide variety of strikes in the years following World War II. The basic purpose of the Taft-Hartley Act was to curtail and limit union practices. For example, the Taft-Hartley Act specifically prohibits practices such as requiring extra workers solely as a means to provide more jobs and refusing to bargain with management in good faith. It also outlawed an arrangement called the **closed shop,** which refers to a workplace in which only workers who are already union members may be hired by the employer.

Section 7 of the Taft-Hartley Act also allowed states, if they wished, to restrict union security clauses such as closed-shop agreements. Roughly twenty states took advantage of this opportunity and passed laws that also outlawed **union shop agreements** (where a nonunion member can be hired but must join the union within a specified time to keep his or her job) and various other types of union security agreements. These laws are known as right-to-work laws, and the states that have adopted them (located predominantly in the Southeast) are known as Right-to-Work States.[3]

The Taft-Hartley Act also established procedures for resolving strikes deemed threatening to the national interest. For example, the president of the United States has the authority under the Taft-Hartley Act to request an injunction to prohibit workers from striking for sixty days. The idea is that, during this so-called cooling-off period, labor and management stand a greater chance of

■ The **National Labor Relations Act,** passed in 1935 and more commonly referred to as the **Wagner Act,** granted power to labor unions and put unions on a more equal footing with managers in terms of the rights of employees.

■ The **National Labor Relations Board (NLRB)** administers most labor law in the United States.

■ The **Labor Management Relations Act,** also known as the **Taft-Hartley Act,** was passed in 1947 in response to public outcries against a wide variety of strikes in the years following World War II; it curtailed and limited union powers.

■ A **closed shop** refers to a workplace in which only workers who are already union members may be hired by the employer.

■ A **union shop agreement** includes various types of union security agreements in addition to a requirement that a nonunion member can be hired, but he or she must join the union within a specified time to keep his or her job.

resolving their differences. For example, in February 1997 the union representing the pilots at American Airlines announced that its members had voted to strike. Within minutes of this announcement, President Clinton invoked the Taft-Hartley Act and ordered the union to cancel its strike. His argument was that American Airlines is the nation's largest air carrier and a shutdown would be extremely detrimental to national interests. In addition, the Taft-Hartley Act extended the powers of the NLRB. For example, following passage of the act, the NLRB was also given the power to regulate unfair union practices.

A final significant piece of legislation affecting labor relations is the **Landrum-Griffin Act,** which was passed in 1959. Officially called the **Labor Management Reporting and Disclosure Act,** this law focused on eliminating various unethical, illegal, and undemocratic union practices. For instance, the Landrum-Griffin Act requires that national labor unions elect new leaders at least once every five years, and that convicted felons cannot hold national union office (which is why Jimmy Hoffa was removed as president of the teamsters union). It also requires unions to file annual financial statements with the Department of Labor. And finally, the Landrum-Griffin Act stipulates that unions provide certain information regarding their internal management and finances to all members.

- The **Landrum-Griffin Act** (officially called the **Labor Management Reporting and Disclosure Act**) was passed in 1959 and focused on eliminating various unethical, illegal, and undemocratic union practices.

Union Structures

All organizations have their own unique structure, and so do large labor unions. But most unions have some basic structural characteristics in common. Figure 14.2 shows the basic structure of most unions. The cornerstone of most labor unions, regardless of their size, is the local union, more frequently referred to as a local. **Locals** are unions organized at the level of a single company, plant, or small geographic region. Each local has an important elected position called the **shop steward.** The shop steward is a regular employee who functions as a liaison between union members and supervisors.

- **Locals** are unions organized at the level of a single company, plant, or small geographic region.

- The **shop steward,** an elected position in a local union, is a regular employee who functions as a liaison between union members and supervisors.

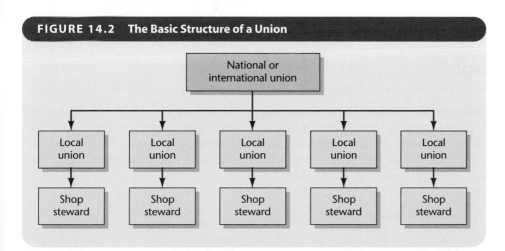

FIGURE 14.2   The Basic Structure of a Union

Source: Ricky Griffin and Ronald Ebert, *Business*, 3rd ed., © 2000. Reprinted by permission of Prentice-Hall, Inc., Upper Saddle River, N.J.

Unions are organized at both a local level and a national level and, in some cases, at an international level as well. But because most activity begins at the local level, local union officials, such as Bruce Hummel of the Chocolate Workers Local 464, are key players in labor-management relations at the plant level. Hummel's position is especially unique because his local operates in Hershey, Pennsylvania, headquarters of Hershey Foods. Hershey is probably as close an example as one can find today of a company town, where most of the people in the town depend on Hershey Foods for their living. In fact, the local union is so strong that it successfully fought the company's recent attempt to increase workers' portion of health care expenses.

Local unions are usually clustered by geographic region and coordinated by a regional officer. These regional officers in turn report to and are part of a national governing board of the labor union. The national affairs of a large union are generally governed by an executive board and a president. These individuals are usually elected by members of the union themselves. This election takes place at an annual national convention that all union members are invited to and are encouraged to attend.

The president is almost always a full-time union employee and may earn as much money as the senior manager of a business. The executive board functions much more like a board of directors and is generally comprised of individuals who serve on the board in addition to their normal duties as employees of an organization. Just as a large business has various auxiliary departments (such as a public relations and a legal department), so too do large national unions have auxiliary departments. These auxiliary departments may handle issues such as the legal affairs of the union. They may oversee collective bargaining issues and may provide assistance and services to the local unions as requested and needed.

TRENDS IN UNIONIZATION

While understanding the historical, legal, and structural context of labor unions is important, so too is an appreciation of other trends regarding union membership, union-management relations, and bargaining perspectives. These topics are each discussed in the sections that follow. HR in the 21st Century also describes some interesting trends in unionization.

Trends in Union Membership

Since the mid-1950s, labor unions in the United States have experienced increasing difficulty in attracting new members. While millions of U.S. workers still belong to labor unions, union membership as a percentage of the total workforce

Emerging Trends in Unionization

As noted in the text, unionization among U.S. workers has been on the decline for some time and will probably continue in that direction for the foreseeable future. Although unionization in the service sector of the economy has increased, this trend has been more than offset in the rest of the economy. Will unions disappear? Probably not, but they may look different in the next century than they have looked in the past. For example, some experts suggest that a basic transformation in unionism and the relationship between unions and management is already taking place. A key component of this transformation is an end to the adversarial relationship between labor and management.

The Saturn plant in Tennessee is often cited as an example of how such a system can work. Saturn was created several years ago by GM as a new kind of U.S. car maker modeled on the Japanese system of cooperation between management and workers. To understand how this model works, consider an event at the Saturn plant a few years ago: GM instructed Saturn management to increase its production quotas, and the UAW registered its strong opposition to the proposed change. Since workers in general have long resisted management's efforts to boost productivity, this stance may not sound so unusual on the surface. But the basis for the union's opposition was unusual in this instance—employees were concerned that increased production would come at the price of decreased quality, and they believed that producing high-quality automobiles was the more important goal. Eventually, GM management agreed and dropped its insistence on higher production. And while labor relations at Saturn aren't perfect, they are generally far better than throughout the rest of GM.

A related trend in unionization is an increase in concessionary bargaining. This type of bargaining, which gained popularity in the 1980s, involves unions making concessions in areas such as wages and work rules to help firms survive. In return, they obtained greater job security for union members. Recent debate has centered on

"[R]esearch has found ... that strikes may become less common, but that concessions involving benefits (rather than wages or work rules) are becoming more common."*

whether this new trend represents a real shift in the way unions and management work or is simply a blip due to hard economic times. But it has been widely argued that the only real future for unions in the United States lies with their working together with management to improve competitive position and to increase productivity.

Finally, some recent research sheds additional light on unionization trends. For example, research has found that bargaining relationships may be either more cooperative or more contentious than they have been in the past, that strikes may become less common, but that concessions involving benefits (rather than wages or work rules) are becoming more common. Thus, there is some reason to believe that the basic nature of the relationship between unions and management has already begun changing and will likely continue to change in the same direction.

But notice that the results of this study also point out that bargaining relationships that are not becoming more cooperative are becoming more contentious. That is, the disparity between contentious and cooperative relationships between unions and management may be growing. As a result, the future may find many instances where the new industrial relations model is firmly in place, but many others where hostilities are as strong as (or stronger than) they were in the past. Perhaps those firms that cannot establish more cooperative relationships will be less likely to prosper in the future, but that remains to be seen. In any case, the same company that has entered into a new type of agreement with its major unions—General Motors—was also described in the closing case as engaging in less than cooperative behavior.

Sources: "She's Jump-Starting Saturn," *USA Today,* February 19, 1999, p. 3B (*quote on p. 3B); "Union Battles," *Wall Street Journal,* January 11, 1999, p. R27; C. C. Heckscher, *The New Unionism: Employee Involvement in the Changing Corporation* (New York: Basic Books, 1988); J. Cutcher-Gershenfeld, P. McHugh, and D. Power, "Collective Bargaining in Small Firms: Preliminary Evidence of Fundamental Change," *Industrial and Labor Relations Review,* 1996, Vol. 49, pp. 195–212; "Cooperation Keeps Saturn Plant Working," *USA Today,* June 24, 1998, p. 1B.

has continued to decline at a steady rate. For example, in 1977, over 26 percent of U.S. wage and salary employees belonged to labor unions. But today, that figure is about 14 percent of those workers. If government employees are excluded from consideration, then only about 11 percent of all wage and salary employees in private industry currently belong to labor unions. These union membership trends are shown in Figure 14.3.

FIGURE 14.3 Trends in Union Membership

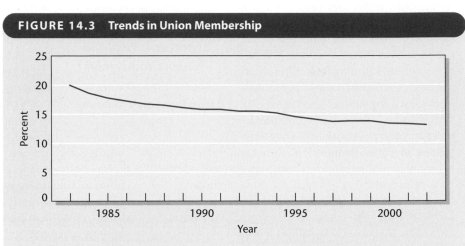

Year	Union or Employee Association Members (thousands)	Union or Association Members as Percent of Wage and Salary Employment (percent)
1983	17,717	20.1
1984	17,340	18.8
1985	16,996	18.0
1986	16,975	17.5
1987	16,913	17.0
1988	17,002	16.8
1989	16,960	16.4
1990	16,740	16.1
1991	16,568	16.1
1992	16,390	15.8
1993	16,598	15.8
1994	16,748	15.5
1995	16,360	14.9
1996	16,269	14.5
1997	16,110	14.1
1998	16,211	13.9
1999	16,477	13.9
2000	16,258	13.5
2001	16,387	13.4
2002	16,107	13.2

Sources: Wall Street Journal Almanac 1999, p. 248. U.S. Department of Labor, Bureau of Labor Statistics.

Just as union membership has continued to decline, so has the percentage of successful union organizing campaigns. In the years immediately following World War II and continuing through the mid-1960s, for instance, most unions routinely won certification elections. In recent years, however, labor unions are winning certification fewer than 50 percent of the times when workers are called on to vote. From most indications then, the power and significance of labor unions in the United States, while still quite formidable, is significantly lower than it was just a few decades ago. Several factors explain the declining membership in labor unions today.

One common reason is the changing composition of the workforce itself. Traditionally, union members have been predominantly white males in blue-collar jobs. But as most people are aware, today's workforce is increasingly composed of women and ethnic minorities. These groups have a much weaker tradition of union affiliation, so their members are less likely to join unions when they enter the workforce. A corollary to these trends has to do with the fact that much of the workforce has shifted toward geographic areas in the South and toward occupations in the service sector that have also been less heavily unionized.

A second reason for the decline in union membership in the United States is more aggressive anti-unionization strategies undertaken by businesses.[4] The National Labor Relations Act and other forms of legislation specify strict management practices vis-à-vis labor unions; nevertheless companies are still free to pursue certain strategies intended to eliminate or minimize unionization. For example, both Motorola and Procter & Gamble now offer no-layoff guarantees for their employees and have created a formal grievance system for all workers. These arrangements were once available only through unions. But because these firms offer them without any union contract, employees are likely to see less benefit from joining a union.

Some companies have also tried to create a much more employee-friendly work environment and strived to treat all employees with respect and dignity. One goal of this approach has been to minimize the attractiveness of labor unions for employees. Many Japanese manufacturers that have set up shop in the United States have successfully avoided unionization efforts by the United Auto Workers by providing job security, better wages, and a work environment in which employees are allowed to participate in the management of the facilities.

Trends in Union-Management Relations

The gradual decline in unionization in the United States has been accompanied by some significant trends in union-management relations. In some sectors of the U.S. economy, perhaps most notably the automobile and steel industries, labor unions still remain strong. In these areas, unions have a large membership and considerable power vis-à-vis the organizations in which their members work. The United Auto Workers, for example, is still one of the strongest unions in the United States today.

But in most sectors of the economy, labor unions are clearly in a weakened position; as a result many have had to take a much more conciliatory stance in their relations with managers and organizations.[5] This situation contrasts sharply with the more adversarial relationship that once dominated labor relations in this country. For instance, unions recognize that they don't have as much power as they once held and that it is in their best interests, as well as the best interests of the

This was the scene on September 18, 2003, as the United Auto Workers signed contracts with General Motors and Delphi, the world's largest auto parts company. The leaders of GM (Rick Wagoner, chairman, far left), Delphi (J. T. Battenberg, CEO, far right), and the UAW (Richard Shoemaker, vice president, left and Ron Gettelfinger, president, right) chat after agreeing on a contract only four days after the old contract covering 700,000 auto workers and retirees expired. The agreement included plant closings and scaled back demands for wages, but it also included guaranteed health benefits. Both sides attributed the quick settlement to the professionalism of the other side, but also to the reality that they must work together to protect the U.S. automobile industry from foreign competition.

workers they represent, to work with management as opposed to working against management. Hence, union-management relations are in many ways better today than they have been in years. Although this improvment is attributable in large part to the weakened power of unions, most experts would agree that union-management relations have still improved.

But this does not mean that unions are dead, or that unions and management do not still struggle with more basic issues as well as newer issues. In August of 2003, Verizon Communications faced a strike by the Communication Workers of America (CWA) and several other unions representing 85,000 employees. The issues were an interesting mix of traditional union concerns and some of the more recent concerns discussed above. For example, telephone operators and customer-service representatives complained that they were forced to work overtime and that the lack of sufficient break time had led to undue stress on the job. This "stress in the workplace" issue is surely typical of the more recent union issues. But there were also problems with pay raises, and the fact that the company was shifting jobs to lower-paying regions of the country.

There was one additional issue at stake that never made it to the bargaining table. The CWA, which represents about 75,000 Verizon employees, has been trying to unionize Verizon Wireless as well. The wireless communications sector has thus far resisted unionization, and since that sector is extremely competitive, Verizon has been fighting hard to keep it that way.

The strike lasted fifteen days. Verizon found that, in the high-tech sector of the economy, it was difficult to replace the striking workers, and that they needed to get their workers back on the job. As a result, the union won on most issues, including a 12 percent wage increase and a 14 percent pension increase over the three-year contract. The company also granted stock options to every union employee for the first time in the company's history. The company won some freedom to move around employees, in return for some job security promises, and service reps were guaranteed "close time" when they could shut down their station to relieve stress. But the unspoken issue remains unresolved as the CWA continues to try to unionize the Wireless employees. The strike, and the way it was settled, illustrates that, while basic issues can still lead to labor problems, the world of labor-management relations is indeed changing. It also illustrates that there may be cases where union power is not as low as had been reported. Specifically, in a competitive industry where there is a strong demand for well-trained, well-educated workers, the American union movement may find it has more leverage than has been the case for many years.

Trends in Bargaining Perspectives

Building on the trends identified in the two previous sections, bargaining perspectives have also altered in recent years. For example, in the past most union-management bargaining situations were characterized by union demands for dramatic increases in wages and salaries. A secondary issue was usually increased benefits for union members. But now unions often bargain for different goals, such as job security. Of special interest in this area is the trend toward moving jobs to other countries to take advantage of lower labor costs. Thus, unions might want to restrict job movement, whereas companies might want to maximize their flexibility vis-à-vis moving jobs to other countries.[6]

As a result of organization downsizing and several years of relatively low inflation in this country, many unions today opt to fight against wage cuts rather than strive for wage increases. Similarly, organizations might be prone to argue for less health care and other benefits for workers, and a common union strategy today is simply to attempt to preserve what workers currently have. Unions also place greater emphasis on improved job security for their members. An issue that has become especially important in recent years has been to focus on improved pension programs for employees.

THE UNIONIZATION PROCESS

The laws discussed earlier, as well as various associated regulations, prescribe a specific set of steps that employees must follow if they want to establish a union. These laws and regulations also dictate what management can and cannot do during an effort by employees to form a union.

Why Employees Unionize

Why do employees choose to join labor unions? In the simplest of terms, the answer is really straightforward: they believe that they are somehow better off as a result of joining a union.[7] More precisely, employees are more likely to unionize when they are dissatisfied with some aspect of their job, they believe that a union can help make this aspect of the job better, and they are not philosophically opposed to unions or to collective action.[8]

But the real answer is much more complex. In the early days of labor unions, people chose to join them because their working conditions were so unpleasant in many cases. In the eighteenth and nineteenth centuries, in their quest to earn ever-greater profits, some business owners treated their workers with no respect. They often forced their employees to work long hours, and minimum-wage laws and safety standards did not exist. As a result, many employees worked twelve, fifteen, or eighteen hours a day and sometimes were forced to work seven days a week. The pay was sometimes just pennies a day and employees received no vacation time or other benefits. They worked totally at the whim of their employer; if they complained about working conditions, they were dismissed. Thus, people initially chose to join labor unions because of the strength that lay in the numbers associated with the large-scale labor unions.

In many parts of the United States and in many industries, these early pressures for unionization became an ingrained part of life. Union values and union membership expectations were passed down from generation to generation. This trend typified many industrialized northern cities such as Pittsburgh, Cleveland,

and Detroit. In general, parents' attitudes toward unions are still an important determinant for whether or not an employee elects to join a union.[9] As noted earlier, strong unionization pressures still exist in some industries today, such as the automobile industry, the steel industry, and other economic sectors relying on heavy manufacturing.

Steps in Unionization

Several prescribed steps must be followed if employees are to form and join a labor union. These general steps are shown in Figure 14.4 and are described in more detail below.

First, employees must exhibit some interest in joining a union. In some cases, this interest may arise from among current employees who are dissatisfied with

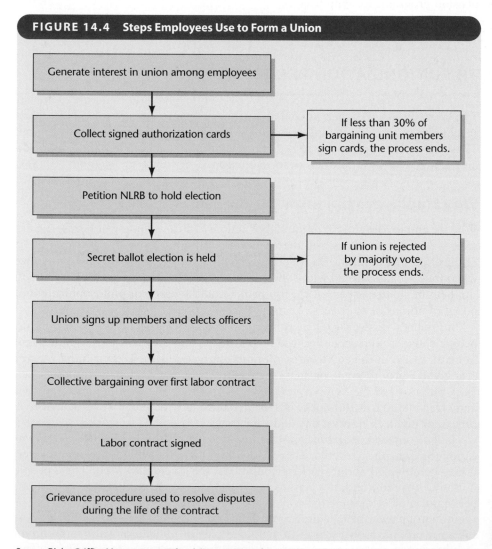

FIGURE 14.4   Steps Employees Use to Form a Union

Generate interest in union among employees

Collect signed authorization cards → If less than 30% of bargaining unit members sign cards, the process ends.

Petition NLRB to hold election

Secret ballot election is held → If union is rejected by majority vote, the process ends.

Union signs up members and elects officers

Collective bargaining over first labor contract

Labor contract signed

Grievance procedure used to resolve disputes during the life of the contract

Source: Ricky Griffin, *Management*, 7th ed. (Boston: Houghton Mifflin, 2002), p. 441. Copyright © 2002 by Houghton Mifflin Company. Reprinted with permission.

some aspects of the employment relationship. In other instances, existing labor unions may send professional union organizers to nonunionized plants or facilities to create interest in unionization.[10]

If interest in forming a union exists, the National Labor Relations Board is asked to define the bargaining unit. The **bargaining unit** refers to the specifically defined group of employees who will be eligible for representation by the union. For example, a bargaining unit might be all nonmanagement employees in an organization or perhaps all clerical workers at a specific site within the organization.

Once the bargaining unit has been defined, organizers must then strive to get 30 percent of the eligible workers within the bargaining unit to sign authorization cards requesting a certification election. Signing an authorization card does not necessarily imply that the individual signing the card wants to join a union. Rather, the authorization card simply indicates the individual's belief that a union election should be held. If organizers cannot get 30 percent of the workers to sign authorization cards, then the process ends.

But if the required number of signatures is obtained, the next step in forming a union is for organizers to petition the NLRB to conduct an election. The NLRB sends one or more representatives, depending on the size of the bargaining unit, to the facility and conducts an election. The election is always conducted via secret ballot. If a simple majority of those voting approve union certification, then the union becomes the official bargaining agent of the eligible employees. But if a majority fails to approve certification, the process ends. In this instance, organizers cannot attempt to hold another election for at least one year.[11]

If the union becomes certified, then its organizers create a set of rules and regulations that govern the conduct of the union. They also elect officers, establish a meeting site, and begin to recruit members from the labor force in the bargaining unit to join the union. Thus, the union comes into existence as a representative of the organization's employees who fall within the boundaries of the bargaining unit.

> ■ The **bargaining unit** refers to the specifically defined group of employees who are eligible for representation by the union.

Decertification of Unions

Just because a union becomes certified, however, does not necessarily mean that it will exist in perpetuity. Under certain conditions an existing labor union may be decertified. A company's workers, for example, might become disillusioned with the union and may even come to feel that they are being hurt by the presence of the union in their organization. They may believe that the management of the organization is trying to be cooperative and to bargain in good faith but that the union itself is refusing to cooperate.

For decertification to occur, two conditions must be met. First, no labor contract can currently be in force (that is, the previous agreement must have expired and a new one not yet been approved). Second, the union must have served as the official bargaining agent for the employees for at least one year. If both these conditions are met, employees or their representatives can again solicit signatures on decertification cards. As with the certification process, if 30 percent of the eligible employees in the bargaining unit sign the decertification cards, then the NLRB conducts a decertification election. Again, a majority decision determines the outcome. Thus, if a majority of those voting favor decertification, the union is then removed as the official bargaining agent for the unit. Once a union has been decertified, a new election cannot be requested for certification for at least one year.

THE COLLECTIVE-BARGAINING PROCESS

When a union has been legally certified, it becomes the official bargaining agent for the workers it represents. Collective bargaining can be thought of as an ongoing process that includes both the drafting and the administration of a labor agreement.

Preparing for Collective Bargaining

By definition, collective bargaining involves two sides: management representing the employing organization and the labor union representing its employees. The collective-bargaining process is aimed at agreement on a binding labor contract that will define various dimensions of the employment relationship for a specified period of time. Thus, it is incumbent on both management and union leaders to be adequately prepared for a bargaining and negotiation period because the outcome of a labor negotiation will have long-term effects on both parties.

Management can take several actions to prepare for collective bargaining. For example, the firm can look closely at its own financial health to work out a realistic picture of what it can and cannot offer in terms of wages and salaries for its employees. Management can also conduct a comparative analysis to see what kinds of labor contracts and agreements exist in similar companies and research what this particular labor union has been requesting—and settling for—in the past.

The union can and should undertake several actions to be effectively prepared for collective bargaining. It too should examine the financial health of the company through sources such as public financial records. Like management, the union can also determine what kinds of labor agreements have been reached in other parts of the country and can determine what kinds of contracts other divisions of the company or other businesses owned by the same corporation have negotiated recently.

Setting Parameters for Collective Bargaining

Another part of preparing for collective bargaining is prior agreement about the parameters of the bargaining session. In general, two categories of items may be dealt with during labor contract negotiations. One set of items, as defined by law, are **mandatory items**. Mandatory items include wages, working hours, and benefits. If either party expresses a desire to negotiate over one or more of these items, the other party has to agree.

Almost any other aspect of the employment relationship is also subject to negotiation, provided both sides agree. These items are called **permissive items**. For example, if the union expresses an interest in having veto power over the promotion of certain managers to higher level positions and if, for some reason, the company were willing to agree to this demand as a point of negotiation, then it would be permissible to enter this point into the negotiations.

But some items are not permissible for negotiation under any circumstances. For example, in a perfect world management might want to include a clause in the labor contract specifying that the union promises not to strike. However, legal barriers prohibit such clauses from being written into labor contracts, and therefore this item would not be permissible.

■ **Mandatory items,** including wages, working hours, and benefits, must be included as part of collective bargaining if either party expresses a desire to negotiate one or more of them.

■ **Permissive items** may be included in collective bargaining if both parties agree.

NEGOTIATING LABOR AGREEMENTS

After appropriate preparation by both parties, the negotiation process itself begins. Of course, barriers may also arise during this phase, and bargaining impasses may result in strikes or other actions.

The Negotiation Process

Generally speaking, the negotiation process involves representatives from management and the labor union meeting at agreed-on times and at agreed-on locations, and working together to attempt to reach a mutually acceptable labor agreement. In some instances, the negotiation process itself might be relatively brief and cordial. But in other instances it might be lengthy, spanning weeks or perhaps even months, and it might also be quite acrimonious. For example, the labor agreement reached between the team owners and the union representing baseball players that was settled in late 1996 took several years to negotiate and was interrupted by a strike by the baseball players.

A useful framework for understanding the negotiation process refers to the bargaining zone, which is illustrated in Figure 14.5.[12] During preparations for negotiation, both sides are likely to attempt to define three critical points. For the organization, the bargaining zone and its three intermediate points include the employer's maximum limit, the employer's expectation, and the employer's desired result on items being negotiated. For example, the organization might have a zero increase in wages and benefits as a desired result (also known as management's "target point"). But it also recognizes that this desired result is unlikely and so what it expects is to have to provide a modest increase in wages and benefits totaling perhaps 4 to 5 percent. But if preparations are done thoroughly, managers also know the maximum amount they are willing to pay, which might be as high as 7 or 8 percent (management's "resistance point"). Note that, in this example, management would rather suffer through a strike than pay more than an 8 percent pay increase.

On the other side of the table, the labor union also defines a bargaining zone for itself that includes three points. These three points include the union's minimum acceptable limit on what it will take from management (the union resistance point: the settlement level below which the union will strike), its own expectations about what management is likely to agree to, and the most it can reasonably expect to get from management (the union target point). For instance, the labor union might feel that it has to provide a minimum increase of 2 to 3 percent in wages

Of course, negotiations between labor and management are not always cordial and cooperative. As this GE worker's shirt suggests, the company's unionized workers have not reacted well to GE's attempts to raise worker co-payments for health benefits. In fact, in January of 2003, GE's 24,000 unionized workers went on strike for two days over the changes. GE's new CEO Jeffrey Immelt reacted to this strike by trying to impose even greater increases in worker co-pays, and the company's thirteen unions have reacted with accusations and threats. When former CEO Jack Welch entered into his first contract negotiations in 1982, he wanted to start off on the right foot and granted one of the largest settlements in the company's history. Present workers are looking for a similar sign of good faith from Welch's successor.

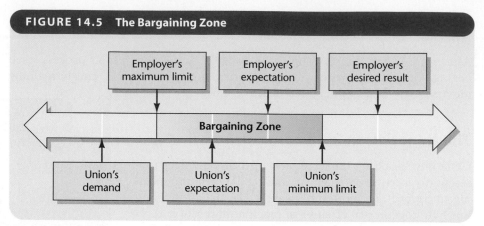

FIGURE 14.5   The Bargaining Zone

Source: Ricky Griffin and Ronald Ebert, *Business,* 6th ed. Reprinted by permission of Prentice-Hall, Inc., Upper Saddle River, N.J.

and benefits to its members. They expect a settlement of around 5 percent but would like to get 9 or 10 percent. In the spirit of bargaining, they may make an opening demand to management as high as 12 percent.

Hence, during the opening negotiation session, labor might inform management that it demands a 12 percent wage and benefit increase. And the employer might begin by stating emphatically that no increases should be expected. Assuming, however, that some overlap exists between the organization's and the union's demands and expectations in the bargaining zone (a positive settlement zone), and assuming that both sides are willing to compromise and work hard at reaching an agreement, it is likely that an agreement will in fact be attained. Where exactly within that range the final agreement falls depends on the relative bargaining power of the two parties. This power is a function of many factors, such as negotiating skills, data on other settlements, and the financial resources needed either to call for (for the union) or to survive (for management) a strike.

Much of the actual negotiations revolve around each party trying to discover the other's resistance point without revealing its own. Because this point represents the least favorable settlement the party is willing to accept, the opponent who discovers that point then makes a "final" offer exactly at the resistance point. For example, if the union discovers that management is willing to go as high as 8 percent before breaking off negotiations and facing a strike, the union would then make an offer at 8 percent and indicate that this was its final offer. Management would rather pay 8 percent than have a strike, so they should settle at 8 percent, which is actually the most favorable contract the union could have possibly won. Incidentally, once a party makes a true final offer, they cannot back away from that position without losing face in the negotiations. Parties usually leave themselves some room for further negotiations and use statements such as the following: "I cannot imagine our members accepting anything less than an 8 percent raise, and I'm sure they would walk out on strike if we came back with less."

The resulting agreement is not necessarily the end of the bargaining process. First, the new contract agreement must be ratified by the union membership. If the union membership votes to reject the contract (which typically reflects internal union politics more than anything else), the parties must return to the bargaining table. But even before the union membership votes, a final step in the bargaining process must be followed. As soon as an agreement is reached, both parties begin to make public statements about how tough a negotiator the other party was. Both acknowledge that they really wanted a lot more and that they hope they can live with this agreement, but that the other party was such a good negotiator that this agreement was the best they could come up with. This posturing helps both parties "sell" the agreement to their constituencies and also allows both parties to maintain their image as a strong negotiator no matter how one-sided the final agreement might be. Once ratified, this agreement then forms the basis for a new labor contract.

Barriers to Effective Negotiation

The foremost barrier to effective negotiation between management and labor is the lack of an overlap for the bargaining zones of the respective sides (i.e., there is a negative settlement zone). That is, if management's upper limit for a wage increase is 3.5 percent and if the union's minimum limit for what it is willing to accept is 5 percent, then no overlap exists in the bargaining zones and the two sides will almost certainly be unable to reach an agreement. Beyond such differences in bargaining zones, however, other barriers to effective negotiation can also come into play.

For example, sometimes a long history of acrimonious relationships between management and labor make it difficult for the two sides to negotiate in good faith. If, for example, the labor union believes that the management of the firm has a history of withholding or distorting information and that management approaches negotiations from the standpoint of distrust and manipulation, then the union will be suspicious of any proposal made by management and may in fact be unwilling to accept almost any suggestion made by management. Of course, the same pattern can occur for the other side, with management exhibiting extreme distrust of the labor union.

Negotiations can also be complicated by inept negotiators and poor communication between negotiators. Effective negotiation is a critical skill and one that not everyone possesses. Thus, if managers select as a representative someone who doesn't understand the negotiation process, then difficulties are likely to arise.

As a result of diligent negotiation, however, management and labor should be able to agree on a mutually acceptable labor contract. On the other hand, if management and labor cannot agree on a new contract or one to replace an existing contract after a series of bargaining sessions, then either or both sides might declare that they have reached an impasse. An **impasse** is simply a situation in which one or both parties believe that reaching an agreement is not imminent.

> ■ An **impasse** is a situation in which one or both parties believe that reaching an agreement is not imminent.

Resolving Impasses

If labor and management have reached an impasse, several actions can be taken by either or both sides in an attempt to break the impasse. The basic objective of most of these tactics is to force the other side to alter or redefine its bargaining zone so that an accord can be reached.

The most potent weapon that the union holds is the potential for a strike. A **strike** occurs when employees walk off their jobs and refuse to work. In the United States, most strikes are called economic strikes because they are triggered

> ■ A **strike** occurs when employees walk off their jobs and refuse to work.

by impasses over mandatory bargaining items such as salaries and wages. During a strike, workers represented by the union frequently march at the entrance to the employer's facility with signs explaining their reasons for striking. This action is called **picketing** and is intended to elicit sympathy for the union and to intimidate management.

Two less extreme tactics that unions sometimes use are boycotts and slowdowns. A **boycott** occurs when union members agree not to buy the products of a targeted employer. A **slowdown** occurs when workers perform their jobs at a much slower pace than normal. A variation on the slowdown occurs when union members agree, sometimes informally, to call in sick in large numbers on certain days, an action called a sickout. Pilots at American Airlines engaged in a massive sickout in early 1999, causing the airline to cancel thousands of flights before a judge ordered the pilots back to work.

Some kinds of strikes and labor actions are illegal. Foremost among these illegal actions is the so-called **wildcat strike**. A wildcat strike occurs during the course of a labor contract and is usually undertaken in response to a perceived injustice on the part of management. Because strikes are not legal during the course of a binding labor agreement, a wildcat strike is also unauthorized, at least theoretically, by the strikers' union.

Management also has certain tactics that it may employ in its efforts to break an impasse. One possibility is called a lockout. A **lockout** occurs when the employer denies employees access to the workplace. Managers must be careful when they use lockouts, however, because the practice is closely regulated by the government. A firm cannot lock out its employees simply to deprive them of wages or to gain power during the labor negotiations. Suppose, however, that the employer can meet a legitimate business need by locking out its employees. If this business need can be carefully documented, then a lockout might be legal. For example, in 1998 ABC locked out its off-camera employees because they staged an unannounced one-day strike during a critical broadcasting period.[13] Almost half of the 1998–1999 NBA season was lost when team owners locked out their players over contract issues.[14] Management occasionally uses temporary workers or replacements for strikers. These individuals are called strikebreakers. Conflict sometimes erupts between strikebreakers attempting to enter an employer's workplace and picketers representing the interests of the union at the employer's gates.

Sometimes the various tactics described above are successful in resolving the impasse. For instance, after workers have gone out on strike, the organization may change its position and indeed modify its bargaining zone to accommodate potentially larger increases in pay. After management experiences a strike, it sometimes realizes that the costs of failing to settle are greater than previously believed, and so managers are willing to give more to avoid a longer strike (i.e., their resistance point has shifted). But in many situations other alternatives for resolving an impasse are also available. Common alternatives include the use of mediation and arbitration.

In **mediation** a neutral third party, called the mediator, listens to and reviews the information presented by both sides. The mediator then makes an informed recommendation and provides advice to both parties about what she or he believes should be done. For example, suppose the impasse centers around wage increases, with the union demanding 8 percent and the company willing to pay only 5 percent. The mediator listens to both sides and reviews all the evidence,

■ **Picketing** occurs when workers representing the union march at the entrance to the employer's facility with signs explaining their reasons for striking.

■ A **boycott** occurs when union members agree not to buy the products of a targeted employer.

■ A **slowdown** occurs when workers perform their jobs at a much slower pace than normal.

■ A **wildcat strike** occurs during the course of a labor contract and is usually undertaken in response to a perceived injustice on the part of management.

■ A **lockout** occurs when an employer denies employees access to the workplace.

■ In **mediation** a neutral third party, called the mediator, listens to and reviews the information presented by both sides and then makes an informed recommendation and provides advice to both parties about what she or he believes should be done.

and may subsequently conclude that because of the financial profile of the company and because of other labor negotiations in other industries, 5 percent is both fair and all the organization can afford to pay. This advice is then provided to both sides. The union doesn't have to accept this information, however, and can continue its efforts to exact a higher wage increase from the employer.

Another alternative to resolving impasses is arbitration. In **arbitration** both sides agree in advance that they will accept the recommendations made by an independent third-party arbitrator. Like a mediator, the arbitrator listens to both sides of the picture and presents and reviews all the evidence. But in arbitration, the information that results is placed in the form of a proposed settlement agreement that the parties have agreed in advance to accept. Thus, a settlement is imposed on the parties and the impasse is ended. But some believe that arbitrators tend to impose settlements that "split the difference." If both parties believe that the arbitrator has proposed such a settlement, they have an incentive to stick to their original positions and not move toward a settlement because such a move shifts the middle further away from their target point.[15] As such, the threat of arbitration may "chill" the negotiation process and actually make a negotiated settlement *less* likely.

> ■ In **arbitration** both sides agree in advance that they will accept the recommendations made by an independent third-party arbitrator.

An alternative form of arbitration has therefore been proposed that should induce the parties, it is argued, to negotiate a settlement by potentially imposing strikelike costs on both parties.[16] Under **final-offer arbitration**, the parties bargain until impasse. At that point, the two parties' final offers are submitted to the arbitrator. Under traditional arbitration, the arbitrator is then free to impose a settlement at any point he or she wishes. But under final-offer arbitration, the arbitrator has only two choices for the imposed settlement—the two parties' final offers. That is, the arbitrator must select either one or the other party's final offer *as the imposed settlement*. Thus, the party that does not bargain in good faith may get everything he or she wants in the arbitrator's decision but may just as easily lose everything. Under such a system, the parties are more willing to try to reach a settlement on their own rather than go to the arbitrator. Professional baseball uses final-offer arbitration to resolve contract disputes between individual players and owners.

> ■ Under **final-offer arbitration,** the parties bargain until impasse and then the two parties' final offers are submitted to the arbitrator.

ADMINISTERING LABOR AGREEMENTS

Another key clause in the labor contracts negotiated between management and labor defines how the labor agreement will be enforced. In some cases, enforcement is clear. If the two sides agree that the company will increase the wages it pays to its employees by 2 percent a year over the next three years according to a prescribed increase schedule, then there is little opportunity for disagreement. Wage increases can be calculated mathematically and union members will see the effects in their paychecks. But other provisions of many labor contracts are much more subjective in nature and thus are more prone to misinterpretation and different perceptions.

For example, suppose a labor contract specifies how overtime assignments are to be allocated in the organization. Such allocation strategies are often relatively complex and suggest that the company may have to take into account various factors, such as seniority, previous overtime allocations, the hours or days in which the overtime work is needed, and so forth. Now suppose that a supervisor in the factory is attempting to follow the labor contract and offers overtime to a certain employee. This employee, however, indicates that before he or she can accept, he or she must check with a spouse or partner to learn more about previous obligations and commitments. The supervisor may feel a time crunch and be unable to wait as long as the employee would like. As a result, the supervisor gives the overtime opportunity to a second employee. The first employee may feel aggrieved by this course of action and elect to protest.

When such differences of opinion occur, the individual labor union member takes the complaint to her or his shop steward, a union officer described earlier in this chapter. The shop steward listens to the complaint and forms an initial impression. The shop steward has the option of advising the employee that the supervisor handled the matter appropriately. But other appeal mechanisms are also available so that the employee, even if refuted by the shop steward, still has channels for appeal.

Of course, if the shop steward agrees with the employee, she or he may also follow prescribed methods for dealing with the situation. The prescribed methods might include starting with the supervisor to listen to his or her side of the story and then continuing along the lines of appeal up the hierarchy of both the labor union and the company. In some cases, mediation and arbitration may be instigated in an effort to resolve the disagreement. For example, some of the potential resolutions to the grievance described above would be to reassign the overtime opportunity to the employee who was asked first. Or the overtime opportunity may stay with the second employee but the first employee would also receive overtime pay.

LABOR UNIONS AND SOCIAL ISSUES

Earlier in this chapter we discussed the historical roots of the U.S. labor movement. We noted that the labor movement in this country focused on bread-and-butter issues such as wages and hours of work, unlike the labor movement in many European countries. Early American unionists were less concerned with social issues and, partially as a result, a labor party in the United States never drew much interest. Unions and union members supported political candidates who favored their goals, and unions have spoken out on any number of political issues. But for the most part the issues in which U.S. labor unions became involved were pretty close to the basic issues facing U.S. labor. This situation is clearly changing, however.

U.S. labor unions have become quite vocal in several areas where they have traditionally been silent. For example, union leaders in this country have spoken out against child labor in Third World countries and the general exportation of jobs to lower-paying countries. Union positions on these issues (and some of the issues discussed below) represent union self-interests to some extent. For example, moving manufacturing jobs to Mexico also means that U.S. unions will lose members. But there is more to this issue than obvious self-interest. These public positions have changed the way many people think about unions.

Although union membership has declined over the past several decades,
these changes can enhance the power
of labor unions and thus affect the relationship between unions and management. A wide array of issues has
attracted the involvement of the U.S.
labor movement, but we will focus on
only a few. Note, however, that these
issues are simply meant to be illustra-
tive of the new scope of union interests
in this country.

Prison Labor

Most of us do not spend a lot of time
thinking about what prison inmates do
with their time, but in most cases they

work at jobs inside the prisons. Traditionally, these jobs included manufacturing
automobile license plates, repairing roads, or doing the laundry for other state
institutions, but that situation has been changing.

First, the number of prisoners involved has been changing. In 1990, there were
approximately 66,000 federal prisoners and 708,000 state and local prisoners. By
2000, those numbers had risen to 145,000 federal inmates and 1.8 million state
and local inmates. Many of these inmates work at paid jobs, but they earn somewhat less than workers on the outside. In fact, in 1991, prison wages ranged from
$0.23 to $1.15 per hour on a federal pay scale, although more than half these
workers earned $0.40 per hour or less.[17] Second, the laws regulating where and
how the goods produced by inmate labor can be sold have been changing, thus
making it easier to sell products produced by inmates on the open market.

The fact that goods produced at such a low cost can compete openly with
goods produced by workers who are paid a minimum wage is potentially a serious threat to the jobs of low-paid, unskilled workers in the general population.[18]
In fact, some argue that prison labor contributes little to the gross domestic product (GDP) but has a substantial effect on the employment opportunities and
wages of high school dropouts in this country.[19] These same critics also argue
that these jobs do not prepare prison inmates for outside jobs once they are released and so do not lessen the rate of subsequent arrest and incarceration. Thus,
the U.S. labor movement and its advocates argue that this system needs to be re-
formed to provide more rights to prison laborers and to ensure that prison labor
does not take away civilian population jobs, which in the long run can lead to
increased crime.

Contingent Workers

We discussed some issues surrounding the topic of contingent workers in Chapter 6. Perhaps it is not surprising that U.S. unions have taken a stand on the topic
of contingent workers. Under U.S. labor laws, contingent workers are considered
independent contractors or self-employed laborers, and in 1998 these self-
employed workers numbered about 10.3 million—or approximately 8 percent of

Unions have become much more involved in social issues over the past few years. One of the issues that unions have spoken out against is the use of prison labor. Here, a group of inmates at the Central California Women's Facil-ity, near Fresno, work on circuit boards for Joint Venture Electron-ics, which employs fifty-five in-mates. The inmates at the facility are excited about working on this job because it actually pays mini-mum wage. The other job avail-able to inmates in this facility is working in the state-sponsored denture lab for $.33 an hour. Of course, assemblers of circuit boards on the outside would earn several times the minimum wage, so relying on convict labor re-duces company costs. But it also reduces the number of jobs avail-able to non-inmates—which could lead to more crime.

the workforce.[20] As independent contractors, these workers are not covered by most employment and labor laws. In fact, to be covered by almost any legislation related to employment, a person must have some type of employment relationship with an entity, which is not the case for most contingent workers. This problem will become more serious as more organizations turn to contingent workers as a way of managing the demand for labor.

A Living Wage

In Chapters 3 and 11, we discussed the minimum wage and also noted the controversy over whether the minimum wage should be raised. This controversy continues, and a separate movement that is strongly supported by the U.S. labor movement advocates that all employees be paid a living wage.[21] This movement advocates that employers should pay all employees a wage that is at or above the government-defined poverty level for a family of specified size (e.g., four members). Such ordinances have been passed in several localities in the United States, and in these localities, minimum wages range from about $7 to $11 per hour.

The labor movement has been active in building coalitions with local communities to try to pass living-wage ordinances, and some scholars see this issue as a testing ground for the future. Specifically, they see these efforts as a test of whether the U.S. labor movement can build coalitions to help move a social agenda.[22] It is quite likely that the U.S. labor movement, while not abandoning bread-and-butter issues, will develop a much broader social agenda in the twenty-first century. If labor unions are losing some strength in more traditional areas, they may be able to compensate by becoming a serious social force. If they can win some power in less traditional areas, it will be interesting to see if they can leverage that social power back into the workplace and regain some of the power lost over the past few decades.

Unions and the Electronic Age

The Internet presents many interesting challenges for U.S. labor unions. The most obvious challenge stems from the fact that computers and new technology often mean that work can be done by fewer employees. We noted earlier that companies have been trying to move more production sites to foreign countries where labor costs are lower and where U.S. unions have no input. Thus, unions would lose members. At the same time, the introduction of technology is also reducing the number of workers and the number of union members. Although unions must oppose some of these technological advances for the sake of their members' jobs if nothing else, they cannot simply reject these advances wholesale. It is clear in many cases that the firms involved will lose business and perhaps even be forced out of business if they cannot keep pace with the technology (and cost control) of their competitors. Such outcomes are not desirable from the unions' perspective either, and so the U.S. labor movement is in a difficult position.

But changes in technology have also posed a much different set of challenges for unions and for the management of firms with unionized employees. For example, many firms who fear unionization efforts have no-solicitation rules at work. These rules simply mean that no employee can solicit other employees on company time for any cause except United Way campaigns. That is, under such rules, employees cannot sell candy for the high school band, raffle tickets for a new car, or even tickets for a church dinner. An important aspect of these rules is that they also outlaw any attempts by union organizers to solicit employees to sign cards appointing the union as sole bargaining agent. Organizations are usually vigilant about no-solicitation rules because they stop union-organizing efforts at work.

But the Internet presents a challenge to these no-solicitation rules. It is much more difficult to monitor solicitation on the Internet, and some of this solicitation may even come from outside the firm. If the company fails to stop these forms of solicitation, can they still legally stop union solicitation at work? Can unions use the Internet to solicit union membership if they do so from outside the company? Recent NLRB rulings and opinions have not clarified the answers to these questions. For example, if the organization allows employees to use the Internet (even if the computers are company owned) to post thank-you notes, it may be forced to allow union solicitation as well. The NLRB will have to deal with these issues in the coming years, but the key seems to be nondiscrimination. That is, companies cannot (apparently) forbid employees from using the Internet for union solicitation if companies allow employees to use the Internet for other non-business-related purposes.[23] In any case, the Internet has complicated the problem of solicitation—by any party—on the job.

It seems, however, that unions have generally seen Internet solicitation as a useful tool in a different setting. In many high-tech firms, it is common to outsource work and for people to work at home. In these situations, employees rarely meet face to face. How can a union hope to organize these workers? A recent article has pointed out that unions in the Silicon Valley area have been successful in using the Internet for union-organizing campaigns.[24] They have been active in trying to organize a wide variety of contingent workers in the area, and they successfully organized janitorial workers across firms in the Silicon Valley through Internet solicitation. This approach has enabled union organizers to reach workers they couldn't meet personally, and it plays on the fact that many workers at all levels in this area have easy access to computers. Unions in the Silicon Valley area have also used Internet-based campaigns to mount successful boycotts against some firms.

Finally, unions have found that the Internet has had a significant impact on the way they conduct their own internal business. It is now possible for unions in this country to communicate immediately with union leaders and members from around the world. This development has made unions more democratic in their internal policies. It has also enabled unions to mobilize international resources to deal with issues that all union members face wherever they work, such as the lower wages and looser labor regulations associated with agreements under the World Trade Organization.

It remains to be seen how unions will be able to use and be challenged by computers and the electronic age in the coming years. It is already clear, however, that new electronic technology has been a mixed blessing for the U.S. labor movement. While technology continues to threaten jobs, it also allows unions to reach workers in ways that were never possible before. It is not yet clear that computers will be able to revitalize the union movement in the United States, but they certainly seem capable of breathing new life into that movement.

Chapter Summary

Labor relations is the process of dealing with employees who are represented by a union. A labor union is a legally constituted group of individuals working together to achieve shared job-related goals. Collective bargaining is the process by which managers and union leaders negotiate acceptable terms and conditions of employment for those workers represented by the unions. The historical formation of U.S. labor unions closely parallels the history of the United States itself. Many laws and other regulations have been passed, some of which are intended to promote unionization and union activities; others are intended to limit or curtail union activities. Like any large organization, labor unions also have structures that facilitate their work.

Since the mid-1950s, labor unions in the United States have experienced increasing difficulty in attracting new members. Indeed, while millions of U.S. workers still belong to labor unions, union membership as a percentage of the total workforce has continued to decline at a steady rate. Unions recognize that they don't have as much power as they once held and that it is in their best interests, as well as the best interests of the workers they represent, to work with management as opposed to working against management. Bargaining perspectives have also altered in recent years.

Employees must follow a specific set of steps if they want to establish a union. First, employees must express some interest in joining a union. If interest exists in forming a union, the National Labor Relations Board (NLRB) is asked to define the bargaining unit. Once the bargaining unit has been defined, organizers must then strive to get 30 percent of the eligible workers within the bargaining unit to sign authorization

cards requesting a certification election. If organizers cannot get 30 percent of the workers to sign authorization cards, then the unionization process ends. But if the required number of signatures is obtained, the next step in forming a union is for organizers to petition the NLRB to conduct an election. If the union becomes certified, then its organizers create a set of rules and regulations that will govern the conduct of the union. Under certain conditions, an existing labor union may be decertified.

Collective bargaining involves management representing the employing organization and the labor union representing its employees. The collective-bargaining process is aimed at agreement on a binding labor contract that will define various dimensions of the employment relationship for a specified period of time. One important part of preparing for collective bargaining is prior agreement on the parameters of the bargaining session.

Generally speaking, the negotiation process involves representatives from management and the labor union meeting at agreed-on times and at agreed-on locations, and working together to attempt to reach a mutually acceptable labor agreement. A useful framework for understanding the negotiation process is the bargaining zone. Of course, numerous barriers to effective negotiation exist, and several methods are available for both management and labor to use in their attempts to overcome an impasse.

A key clause in the labor contracts negotiated between management and labor defines how the labor agreement will be enforced. While some enforcement issues are relatively straightforward, others may rely heavily on a formal grievance procedure.

Key Points for Future HR Managers

▶ Despite declines in union membership, unionization of employees remains a reality for many large firms in the United States and even more so internationally.

▶ The relationship between unions and management is strictly regulated by law, and these regulations are much more comprehensive in Europe and other parts of the world.

▶ Although some evidence suggests that union-management relations are improving in the United States, other evidence suggests that, in some cases, these relations are getting worse.

▶ Most employees join unions because they are dissatisfied with the way they are treated and they feel that management is not responsive to their concerns. Some employees join unions, though, because of social norms and the fact that unions helped their parents.

▶ Effective human resource practices can reduce the desire of employees to unionize, but organizations are limited in what they can do to prevent unionization. Also, while unions can be decertified, management cannot advocate decertification.

▶ Collective bargaining is a reality in unionized firms, and many critical issues must be part of the bargaining process with the union.

▶ When bargaining fails, slowdowns, strikes, and lockouts are possible alternatives.

▶ Third-party intervention, in the form of mediation and arbitration, is becoming common in labor-management disputes.

▶ Although U.S. labor unions continue to be concerned with basic issues of wages and work conditions, the labor movement has become much more involved in social issues in recent years and has become a vocal advocate for social change.

▶ The Internet may change the way unions do business and the way management must relate to unions.

▶ Unions have traditionally played an important role in improving working conditions for U.S. workers, and many workers still view unions in this light. Therefore, if a firm has a union, it may be difficult to vote it out; if a firm does not have a union, it may be more difficult than some managers believe to keep a union out.

▶ Some firms have found unions to be helpful partners as they explore new ways to organize work, while others have found unions to be tenacious opponents to any change. It is important to think

Key Points for Future General Managers

seriously about the kind of relationship management wants to have with unions.

▶ A well-developed legal framework is in place to guide management in dealing with unions, and enforcement of these laws has been fairly consistent over the years.

▶ Unions have become effective at calling for social reform, and such actions have increased their popularity in the media.

Review and Discussion Questions

1. Discuss the historical evolution of labor unions in the United States.

2. Identify and briefly explain each of the major laws affecting unionization in the United States.

3. What is a shop steward?

4. Is your state a right-to-work state? What are your personal opinions about this issue?

5. Discuss trends in unionization.

6. What steps would you take to increase union membership?

7. Summarize the basic steps employees must follow to create a union.

8. What is the bargaining zone?

9. Identify and describe the three general areas that relate to collective bargaining.

10. Identify and discuss the methods for resolving impasses.

Closing Case

Winning the Battle but Losing the War?

It's Sunday of Memorial Day weekend in Flint, Michigan. A line of big flatbed trucks pulls up to the delivery doors of the General Motors (GM) Flint Metal Center. Drivers and crew members get out and look around nervously. A few minutes later the big doors are open and more than a dozen two-ton metal dies, valued at over $300,000 each, are loaded on the trucks. When they are all loaded and tied down, the drivers and crew members again look around nervously, then get back into the trucks and drive off.

Was this incident a serious case of industrial espionage? After all, these dies are used to turn sheets of steel into the hoods and fenders of the new GMC Sierra pickup trucks and are extremely valuable. Or perhaps it was the work of the United Auto Workers (UAW). After all, the union had been feuding with GM over the new trucks, with GM trying to cut labor costs by reducing the workforce and the union fighting to save jobs and keep them from moving to Mexico. In truth, the real culprits were neither the competition nor the union. GM itself "stole" the dies from one of its own plants that was being threatened with a strike.

In June 1998 the UAW had threatened to shut down the metal-stamping plant. The threat of a shutdown represented a major concern for GM because this particular plant was being set up to make fenders and bumpers for a new truck model that had the potential to be the best-selling and highest profit margin vehicle in GM's 1999 lineup. As a result, GM couldn't risk losing production time because of a strike and was simply taking extreme measures to protect itself.

The dies and other key components for the new trucks were secretly stored in old factories—and even a few bowling alleys—in the area and were then shipped to another stamping plant in Mansfield, Ohio. The Ohio plant had a contract with GM that would not allow a strike at that critical time, and so GM could produce the needed parts if the Flint plant were closed. GM later justified its actions on the grounds that the truck was its most promising new product in a long time and it was crucial that it be available at the start of the new model year. The UAW, on the other hand, felt that it was fighting for jobs for its workers and against trends by GM to move auto jobs outside the United States.

GM did get the trucks out on time, but it also endured one of the costliest strikes in its history. The dispute was so bitter, the loss of jobs so substantial, and the concessions made by GM so sweeping that it is not clear who ultimately "won." As explained more fully below, the heart of the issue involved the loss of jobs by U.S. workers. So, on June 5, 1998, 25,000 workers from the firm's Flint, Michigan, plants went on strike. The strike spread quickly and lasted until July 28. By the time the strike was settled, GM estimated that it lost $2.2 billion in sales and even more in terms of lost market share, making it the costliest labor battle GM had fought in decades.

GM had argued earlier that the project would result in 20,000 new jobs across five plants. But UAW officials countered that the accompanying efficiencies and automation could also result in the long-term reduction of 50,000 jobs, and even more jobs would be moved to Mexico and Asia. The UAW also alleged that GM had not followed through on promises to spend millions on modernizing U.S plants because, it claimed, the company was planning to shift more production to other countries. Therefore, the UAW was opposing GM at every step of the way. In fact, there had been strikes the previous year that were also called in reaction to this plan.

During one of these earlier strikes at a Pontiac, Michigan, plant, a union official commented that, to settle the strike, the union made several concessions, including agreeing to have repairpersons fix problems with the trucks while they were still on the assembly line instead of at the end of the line. This "concession" sounds more like the enlightened employee involvement systems described in this chapter: it would give the workers more say on when and what type of repairs were needed. But the union claimed that these systems have not worked at GM due to a lack of trust. As the union official put it, stopping the line by pulling the "stop-line chord" to make repairs often got workers in trouble with management.

GM was trying to circumvent these labor problems by shifting production to sites that were less likely to be disrupted by work stoppages. The dies that had been spirited away on the Sunday of Labor Day weekend, were finally returned to the plant on July 26, but by that point, the strike had been going on for some time and had become ugly. In fact, during the course of the strike, GM had attempted to have the strike declared illegal and then, failing in that, threatened to stop medical benefits for striking workers—an unheard-of move!

When the fifty-four-day strike finally ended, it was difficult to see what GM had won. The union did agree to new work rules that would increase productivity at the Flint stamping plant, and it also agreed to settle several other disputes that would ensure labor peace until the national contract expired. But in return, GM had to agree to invest about $180 million in plant modernization and to hold onto several plants that were planned for divestiture. Perhaps more critically, the relationship between the UAW and GM had been damaged. It is not clear if it can be improved, although UAW Vice President William Shoemaker urged cooperation in a speech he made before 2,000 GM managers. On the other hand, employees at the Lordstown, Ohio, GM plant have complained that they are being pressured to increase productivity or GM will move most of the jobs from that plant to Mexico.

The real issue, then, is whether the relationship between unions and management is really changing.

Cases of increased cooperation and partnering have occurred. But unions see membership dwindling and jobs being shifted to other countries, so they are unlikely to view the situation as one where "everyone wins." In the coming years, GM will have to reduce its workforce and cut labor costs if it is to retain its leadership in the auto industry. Both Ford and Daimler-Chrysler are already way ahead in modernization. If GM can accomplish this modernization with the cooperation of the UAW, it will truly signal the beginning of a new era in union-management relations, but for now it may just be business as usual.[25]

Case Questions

1. Which side do you think had a better argument for its position, General Motors or the United Auto Workers?

2. Which side do you think won? Why?

3. What general insights can be gleaned from this case regarding labor-management relations?

Building HR Management Skills

Purpose: The purpose of this exercise is to help you understand the bargaining process and how the bargaining-zone model can help facilitate negotiation and bargaining.

Step 1: Your instructor will divide the class into an even number of small groups. Half the groups will be designated as management and the other half as labor. Assume that you are about to negotiate and bargain over a potential wage increase.

Step 2: Your instructor will provide each group with information corresponding to the three parts of the bargaining-zone model as it applies to your role.

Step 3: Your group should spend a few minutes discussing the best way to handle negotiations so you can meet or exceed your expectations.

Step 4: Your instructor will pair teams of labor negotiators with teams of management negotiators. Within a time limit specified by your instructor, engage in bargaining until you reach an agreement (if possible).

Step 5: Each group should share its negotiated agreement on the wage increase with the rest of the class.

Step 6: Respond to the following questions:

1. Explain differences and/or similarities in negotiated agreements.

2. How useful did you find the bargaining-zone model? Without using this model, would your bargaining have been more or less difficult?

3. Can you see other areas of applicability besides collective bargaining for the bargaining-zone model?

Ethical Dilemmas in HR Management

Assume that you work for a midsized nonunion company. The firm is facing its most serious union-organizing campaign in years, and your boss is determined to keep the union out. He has just given you a list of tasks that should thwart the efforts of the organizers. For example, he has suggested the following:

▶ Whenever you learn about a scheduled union information meeting, you should schedule a worker appreciation event at that same time. He wants you to offer free pizza and barbecue and to give cash prizes. The winners have to be present to receive their prizes.

▶ He wants you to look at the most recent performance evaluations of the key union organizers and to terminate the one with the lowest overall evaluation.

▶ He wants you to make an announcement that the firm is seriously considering new benefits such as on-site childcare, flexible work schedules, telecommuting options, and exercise facilities. While you know the firm is indeed looking into these benefits

and several others, you also know that ultimately what is provided will be far less lavish than your boss wants you to intimate.

When you questioned the ethics and legality of these practices, he responded by saying, "Look, all's fair in love and war, and this is war." He went on to explain that if the union wins, the company might actually shut down its domestic operations altogether and move all its production capacities to lower-cost foreign plants. He concluded by saying that he was really looking out for the benefit of the employees, even if he had to play hardball to help them. And indeed, while you can see through his hypocrisy, you also recognize that there is some potential truth in his warning—if the union wins, jobs may actually be lost.

Questions

1. What are the ethical issues in this situation?

2. What are the basic arguments for and against taking extreme measures to fight unionization efforts?

3. What do you think most managers would do in this situation? What would you do?

HR Internet Exercise

Both the AFL-CIO and the NLRB maintain websites to help explain what they do and why. Visit each of their websites at these addresses:

http://www.aflcio.org/
http://www.nlrb.gov/

Questions

1. What specific information can you find on each site that might be of benefit to you as a manager?

2. What specific information can you find on each site that might be of benefit to you as an individual worker interested in forming a union?

3. What improvements might you suggest to make each website more effective for its intended audience?

15

Managing Careers and Work Environments

CHAPTER OBJECTIVES

After studying this chapter you should be able to:

■ Describe the nature of careers.

■ Relate human resource management to career development.

■ Discuss career planning and career management for new entrants, mid-career employees, and late-career employees.

■ Identify and describe related contemporary career development issues and challenges.

■ Discuss the importance to an organization of evaluating its career management activities.

■ Discuss the physical environment at work.

■ Discuss employee safety and health.

■ Describe health- and stress-management programs in organizations.

Around the middle of the twentieth century, experts forecasted a utopian society in which leisure time was abundant and people had little hard work to do. When was this prediction supposed to come true? Just about now. But in reality, of course, almost the opposite has happened. Many people report that they work longer hours than ever before, worry about job security, and feel an array of workplace pressures ranging from stress to tension, to anxiety.

These circumstances have been brought about by several factors. In this age of doing more with less, managers are sometimes simply pressuring their employees to work harder and/or longer hours. Similarly, because people can no longer expect to work for one employer over their entire careers, they may focus more attention on the possibilities of layoffs and/or outright job loss. And the proliferation of dual-career couples, single parents, and other demographic changes make it harder for people to find time to attend to normal activities like banking, exercise, and so forth. In 1973, the median number of work hours per week in the United States was 40.6, and the median number of leisure hours was 26.2. By 2000, however, the median number of work hours per week had increased to 51.2, and the median

> *"You could feel the tension. It wasn't anything to see somebody cry over stress. When a job gets you to that point, it's not worth it."*
>
> (Teresa Williford, former customer-service representative at BellSouth)*

number of leisure hours per week had declined to 18.5.

So what are the effects of these trends? Employers may be getting more work out of their employees, but some experts suggest that stress and stress-related problems cost U.S. companies over $200 billion annually. These costs include higher health-care costs, turnover, unscheduled absenteeism, and declining morale. In particular, more workers are filing stress-related claims under worker's compensation programs. These claims have increased from 911 in 1981 to 4,997 in 1996, to 6,875 in 2001.

How are companies responding? More and more companies and their managers are recognizing both the organizational and the human costs of excess stress. As a result, many are now actively seeking ways to lower stress by reducing job demands and/or offering stress-reduction benefits. For example, Public Service Electric & Gas, a New Jersey firm, offers yoga and stress-management classes to its employees. Rourke, MS&L, a Boston-based public relations firm, gives its employees $75 a quarter to spend on exercise classes, massages, and similar stress-reduction activities. These kinds of programs are proliferating rapidly. At the same time, though, stress is still a major problem in many companies and for many workers.[1] ■

Many different aspects of the work environment are of concern to the human resource manager. When we think of work environments, we think most typically about the physical environment. Specifically, we think about noise, lighting, and stress and how these factors influence an employee's behavior at work. While all are important (and will be discussed in this chapter), for many individuals, the more immediate work environment also involves their jobs and their careers. We discussed the nature of work and work design in Chapter 5. We now turn to a broader view of the individual work environment to discuss some issues associated with careers and career management. Thus, this chapter begins with the concepts of career planning and development. We first establish the nature of careers and then relate human resource management and career management more explicitly. We also discuss how organizations can evaluate career management activities. The chapter then focuses on the more traditional aspects of the physical environment at work.

THE NATURE OF CAREERS

Most people have a general idea of the meaning of *career*. For instance, people generally agree that careers have something to do with the work a person does in an organization, but they also recognize that a career is a broader and more general concept than a single job or task in an organization.

The Meaning of *Career*

We define a **career** as the set of experiences and activities that people engage in related to their job and livelihood over the course of their working life. This definition, then, suggests that a career includes the various specific jobs that a person performs, the kinds of responsibilities and activities that comprise those jobs, movements and transitions between jobs, and an individual's overall assessment of and feelings of satisfaction with these various components of her or his career.

■ A **career** is the set of experiences and activities that people engage in related to their job and livelihood over the course of their working life.

Most people have historically thought of the various components comprising a person's career as having some degree of interrelation. This perspective stems from the fact that, in the past at least, people generally wanted to work for a single organization and spent most of their work life within that single organization. Presumably, if they performed effectively and were successful at their work, they advanced up the organizational hierarchy. Even when people changed jobs, they tended to work for other organizations in the same industry. For example, while Lee Iacocca is perhaps best remembered for saving Chrysler several years ago, at earlier times in his career he worked for both General Motors and Ford.

But in recent times, conceptualizations of careers have become considerably more general. Because of organizational downsizing efforts and innovations in strategies such as outsourcing and shared services, considerably more change has occurred in the work patterns of individuals than in the past.[2] For instance, people are likely to leave an organization in one industry and go to work for an organization in a totally different industry, and they may also spend some time between jobs and organizations consulting or working in otherwise independent contractor-type positions.

Carol Thompson spent years working in her practice as a licensed clinical social worker. She saw private patients and worked for the courts in San Francisco, and she found her work very rewarding if rather draining. When she finally decided to retire from her practice after closing it down gradually over several years, she was not ready to totally "retire." She responded to a call for volunteers at the Botanical Gardens at the University of California at Berkeley, and eventually began taking classes in horticulture. She is now a full-time volunteer, working with professional botanists on plant propagation at the Botanical Gardens. She says that this new work has reinvigorated her, and is quite rewarding. In this decision to find something to do after retirement, Thompson is not alone. It is estimated that in 2000, 37 percent of men and 31 percent of women aged fifty-five to sixty-four were employed full- or part-time while receiving pensions.

More and more frequently, people are taking breaks from their work. These breaks include sabbaticals, discretionary periods of unemployment, and similar activities that may make a positive contribution to a person's overall work life but do not involve formal employment by an organization. People who return to school to enhance their education now more than ever before are likely to consider that period of their lives as part of their career.

Traditional Career Stages

A long-time, generally accepted view of a career included stages that a typical individual progresses through. As shown in Figure 15.1, the first stage is called **exploration**. During this period of a person's life, he tries to identify the kind of work that he is interested in doing. This period of a typical person's career starts in his mid- to late teens and lasts through his mid- to late twenties. It generally encompasses the time when he tries to assess his own interests, values, preferences, and career opportunities and to relate them to what he thinks represents a feasible career option for himself. His coursework in school and his first jobs play an important role in the exploration stage of career development.

For example, it is not uncommon for someone who anticipates majoring in a certain field of study to change his

■ **Exploration** is the first traditional career stage and involves identifying interests and opportunities.

■ The **establishment** stage of the traditional career model involves creating a meaningful and relevant role in the organization.

major once he begins taking courses in that area. Sometimes people take their first job in a particular field only to discover it's not what they expected it to be and then begin to look for alternative options. Of course, sometimes people are perfectly happy with the outcome of the exploration stage. They find that the coursework of their field is indeed of interest to them and their first job assignment is exciting, challenging, and just what they expected it to be.

The second stage of a typical career is called the **establishment** stage. During this period, the individual begins to create a meaningful and relevant role for herself and the organization. She may, for example, become a valuable member of a work team, achieve success and recognition by her superior, and be acknowledged by the organization as someone that the company values and wants to retain. While considerable range in terms of age and time exists in this stage, it

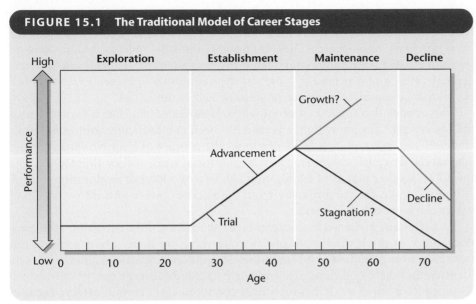

FIGURE 15.1 The Traditional Model of Career Stages

Source: Adapted from *Careers in Organizations*, by Douglas T. Hall. Copyright © 1976 by Scott, Foresman, and Co. Reprinted by permission of Douglas T. Hall and Lyman Porter.

generally encompasses the period of time when an individual is in her late twenties through her mid- to late thirties.

The **maintenance** stage is the next stage in a typical career. During this period, the individual begins to reach a level in the organization that optimizes his talents or capabilities. Not everyone can become a CEO, however, and only a small percentage of the total workforce in any organization attains the rank of top executive. Thus, for many employees, this stage also marks a **midcareer plateau.** Many successful managers, especially in larger companies, may never progress beyond the rank of middle manager, and so end their careers on this plateau, but nevertheless enjoy careers considered to be highly productive and worthwhile. Individuals in the maintenance stage of their career must often devote extra effort to learning new job skills and remaining current in their professional skills and abilities. They are also frequently called on to fill mentoring roles in which they help newcomers to the organization to get their feet on the ground and to launch their own careers.[3]

> ■ The **maintenance** stage involves optimizing talents or capabilities.

Finally, the fourth stage of a typical career is the **disengagement** stage. During this period, the individual gradually begins to pull away from her work in the organization, her priorities change, and work may become less important to her. Consequently, she begins thinking more and more about leaving the organization and finding other sources for fulfilling her personal needs and goals. Some may evolve toward part-time work status, some retire from the organization, some simply cut back on their activities and responsibilities.

> ■ The fourth traditional career stage, **disengagement,** involves the individual gradually beginning to pull away from work in the organization. Priorities change and work may become less important.

New Views of Career Stages

Of course, in the contemporary era of downsizing and layoffs, sometimes people go through these four stages of career development in a relatively short period of time. People may find themselves disengaging from the organization at a relatively young age, and they may also anticipate beginning the entire process again by seeking new opportunities, new challenges, and new interests.[4] Many experts agree that while the traditional model of careers summarized above still has conceptual value, a new perspective such as the one shown in Figure 15.2 is a more accurate representation of career stages now and in the future.

This model also suggests a progression of career stages, but it focuses more on "career age" (i.e., how long a person has been in a particular job) rather than chronological age and directly incorporates the premise of multiple career stages. The model describes career stages of exploration, trial, and establishment, followed by another period of exploration. This second level of exploration in turn is likely to take the person away from the current career and into a new one where the process begins again.

At each stage in the person's career he or she faces a different set of issues and decisions.[5] At the beginning of one's career there are issues about making the transition from a student to an employee. This involves questions about one's self identity, and these questions also influence decisions about exactly what career someone plans to enter. Individuals may choose to enter certain careers because they are considered "hot," or because of general economic trends. They also choose careers because they are more consistent with their own interests, education, and values.

Once a career has been chosen and the person begins to build on that career, a different set of issues emerges. Most of these issues relate to trying to establish the proper balance between work and family life. It is at this point in one's career where these issues become more salient and the individual must deal with the potential tradeoff between working hard to build and advance a career, and establishing lasting relationships with others, including building a strong family

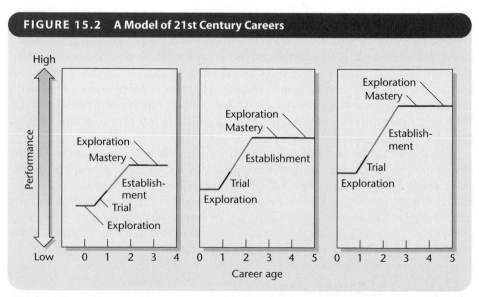

FIGURE 15.2   A Model of 21st Century Careers

Source: Douglas T. Hall, "Protean Careers in the 21st Century," *Academy of Management Executive,* Vol. 10, No. 4, 1996, p. 9. Copyright © 1996 by Academy of Management. Reprinted by permission of the Academy of Management via Copyright Clearance Center.

life. Also, at this stage, decisions are more frequent regarding whether or not the person should remain with a given firm or move to a different organization. The decision as to how best to advance one's career in terms of moving is, of course, also tied to the growing importance of balancing work and family. By the time a person reaches some sort of mid-career point, there are often questions about the worth of continuing to work on one's career, and new questions about self-identity emerge (sometimes leading to a "mid-life crisis").

Issues Facing Older Workers and the Decision to Retire

As the workers continues to age there are new issues to deal with, and some of them relate to potential age discrimination. As noted in Chapter 3, person over forty years of age are protected by the Age Discrimination in Employment Act, but the fact remains that many people assume that abilities and job performance decline with age. In fact, the evidence regarding such declines is rather mixed and generally weak. For example, although there is evidence of declines in abilities such as motor coordination and dexterity, the relationship between age and the levels of these abilities almost completely disappears when we control for education and job type. Furthermore, there is no evidence of any meaningful relationship between age and such abilities as intelligence, verbal ability or numerical ability.[6] Perhaps more critically, there is almost no relationship between age and job performance—in fact, some studies have found a curvilinear relationship between age and performance where performance is highest when a worker is youngest *and* when a worker gets older.[7]

In any event, eventually older workers must confront the decision to retire. In truth, however, the decision to retire is not as simple as it once was. Today, there is really a whole continuum of choices available to a person contemplating retirement. The person can actually retire, take a pension and begin some other nonwork activities (the traditional view of retirement), but this is becoming less common. More commonly, individuals retire and then take on full-time work at another organization, or retire and then take on part-time work, or work as a consultant, either at their former employer or somewhere. Over time, they may reduce the amount of time they spend at work until they gradually move into full retirement, but retirement has become much more of a process than an event.[8]

Nonetheless, there are a number of factors that appear related to the decision to retire (or to begin the retirement process). For example, individuals are more likely to retire when they have the financial resources needed to maintain their preretirement lifestyles, and they are more likely to retire when their health makes continuing to work excessively burdensome. Individuals are also more likely to retire when their spouses have retired. In addition, there are a number of factors that are related to adjustment after retirement. Of course, as noted above, many people tend to continue with some type of "bridge work," and these people generally adjust well to retirement. Also individuals who have structured leisure activities and those who do volunteer work tend to adjust better to retirement. But one of the most important factors related to adjustment is one's health. Individuals who avoid serious health problems adjust better, in part, because they can engage in the kinds of activities outlined above.

In conclusion, a person's career can be viewed as extending past the time of full-time work, as it becomes more difficult to tell who is really retired and who is simply doing some type of bridge work in preparation for full retirement.

Although issues relating to retirement have always been important, they will become even more so in the future. The aging workforce, combined with longer life spans and longer productive work careers, means that the issues will become much more important for the HR manager in the future.

HUMAN RESOURCE MANAGEMENT AND CAREER MANAGEMENT

Most successful organizations and managers today recognize that careers aren't something that simply happen, that they must be planned and managed. Part of the responsibility for this career planning resides with the organization, but the individual her- or himself must also play an important role.[9] This section examines the organizational and individual perspectives on careers shown in Figure 15.3.

Organizational Perspectives on Careers

Organizations are generally responsible for determining the jobs that people will perform for the organization, the pattern of interrelationships between jobs in an organization, the kinds of people that will be hired for those jobs, the development of those individuals to prepare them for more meaningful jobs, and decisions regarding the movement of people from one job to another. Clearly, it is in the organization's best interest to take an active role in career management for people in the firm.[10]

The organization can take steps from the outset to facilitate career management. For example, in Chapter 7 we discussed the idea of selecting individuals not because of their match with the requirements of a specific job but because of their fit with the organization. Despite any other problems associated with this selection strategy, it seems helpful for career management because the organization presumably hires individuals who fit different jobs. In fact, even when organizations select individuals for a specific job, it is still possible to do so with subsequent career moves in mind. That is, if an entry-level position is not particularly demanding, it is possible for an organization to hire people whose skills and abilities

FIGURE 15.3 Individual and Organizational Perspectives on Career Planning

match a higher-level job that they might be expected to move into later. This practice can be defended as long as the employee will likely move up to the higher-level job eventually.

If an organization does indeed help its employees plan and manage their careers more effectively, it can expect to achieve several benefits. It will find itself with a larger pool of talented individuals. In addition, this workforce will generally be more satisfied and motivated because they will have recognized the opportunities that the organization has provided for them and the care with which their job assignments are managed. When an organization finds that it must reduce the size of its workforce, it will have a better understanding of which individuals are more likely to contribute to the success and effectiveness of the organization itself.

On the other hand, if the organization does a poor job with managing the careers of people in the organization, it will face several difficulties. The quality of its talent pool might vary in inefficient and erratic ways. That is, it might have an abundance or surplus of highly talented and qualified employees in some areas and at some levels of the firm but have a shortage of talented and capable people at other levels or areas of the organization. In addition, the workforce of such an organization might be more dissatisfied and unmotivated because people are not given appropriate promotion opportunities and/or are not placed in appropriate positions. When the organization needs to transfer people or lay people off, it may be unsure about who can handle the new assignments.

Individual Perspectives on Careers

Individuals obviously have an important stake in their own careers. They experience most directly the benefits and rewards of successful careers and incur the costs and frustrations of unsuccessful careers. A person's perceived and experienced career success or failure is also likely to have a major impact on his or her self-esteem and similar indications of self-worth.

A person who understands and carefully monitors his or her career is likely to understand the reasons behind his or her successes and failures. That is, this individual will know why she or he has been promoted or not and will have an accurate assessment of future promotion prospects and possibilities. In addition, an individual who accepts responsibility for managing her or his career will also be better prepared to deal with an unanticipated career setback such as job loss or demotion.

But many people are surprisingly uninformed and uninvolved in their own careers. They accept jobs and go to work but pay relatively little attention to their roles in the organization beyond the scope of a specific job. Thus, they may have little understanding about how they landed in a particular position and may have little understanding about what their next position is likely to be and how they might prepare themselves for that position when they are placed in it.

CAREER PLANNING AND CAREER MANAGEMENT

Career planning is clearly important to both organizations and employees. Most organizations that are genuinely interested in the careers of their employees develop sophisticated career management systems. These systems are based in turn on career planning.

The Importance of Career Planning

Career planning requires careful coordination between individual employees and the organization itself. Usually human resource managers represent the organization in the career planning process. General Electric and Shell Oil are known to be especially effective in the area of career planning and development for their managers. In general, most career planning systems involve the steps shown in Figure 15.4.

The first step is generally called the **individual assessment phase**. As the term suggests, individual assessment requires that individuals analyze carefully what they perceive to be their own abilities, competencies, skills, and goals. Many organizations provide employees with forms or questionnaires to help them develop this information. These forms may be tests or personality inventories, or they may simply be open-ended questions for the individual to answer.

The organization also plays an important role in career planning. From the organization's standpoint, human resource managers should develop specifications about where individuals in each position might be most likely to advance. That is, a determination might be made about where a person in a particular job category is likely to be promoted in one of two or three other job categories. Thus, the organization is specifying potential career paths that an individual might take up the organizational hierarchy.[11] Shell's career-path model, for example, is available to managers on the firm's corporate intranet. HR Around the Globe highlights the growing importance of international assignments as part of career management.

The organization must also integrate its performance management system with its career management system. That is, a person should not expect to progress automatically from one job to another along a certain path but instead recognize that this movement will be determined in part by his or her performance effectiveness. That is, occupying a certain job for a few years may potentially lead to a promotion into a particular area, but that potential doesn't make such a progression automatic. If an individual does poor work in the first job, for example, the individual may be demoted, terminated, or transferred laterally into another job without a promotion.

Communication is also an important part of this process. For example, the organization may know the paths that are most likely to be followed from one position to another and may be able to gauge the probability or likelihood that a specific individual will follow this path or a prescribed path for a promotion to

■ The **individual assessment phase** of career planning requires that individuals analyze carefully what they perceive to be their own abilities, competencies, skills, and goals.

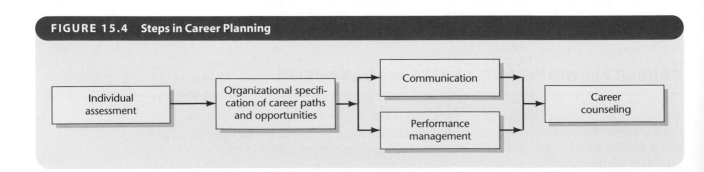

FIGURE 15.4   Steps in Career Planning

International Assignments and Career Development

The importance of global thinking in business is becoming more obvious with each passing day. If firms are to be truly competitive in the future, they need to think strategically on a global level. Many leading firms today believe that international assignments are the single best means to help managers to start thinking globally. As a result, it may become increasingly important that anyone who hopes to rise through the levels of management in the future to have had as many international assignments as possible.

But before you volunteer for the next international assignment that becomes available, you must be sure that you work for an organization that has a strategic view of international assignments and globalization. If you don't, you might want to think twice about that six-month assignment in Europe, or think about finding a job with a company that does understand the broader role of international assignments.

Many managers were traditionally somewhat reluctant to accept international assignments because these assignments were viewed as a hindrance to an employee's future career potential, and they were in fact often seen as risky from a career management perspective. Many managers were especially concerned about what they would face when they returned from the international assignment. Many feared that they would not be able to return to their old job (or a similar job), and that they would actually be demoted when they returned. In addition, they may have missed out on different performance incentives while they were away, and they would clearly be out of the sight (and out of mind?) of senior management. And the shocks associated with repatriation, including the loss of status, and the higher cost of living when perks such as rent subsidies, domestic help, chauffeur services, or club memberships disappeared, were also considered disadvantages.

It is also typical for companies to lose about 20 percent of their returning expatriate managers within a year of repatriation, and many more returning managers re-

> *"The next head of General Electric will be someone who spent time in Bombay, in Hong Kong.... We have to send our best and brightest overseas and make sure they have the training that will allow them to be the global leaders who will make GE flourish in the future."*
>
> (Jack Welch, legendary former CEO of General Electric)*

port that they have seriously thought about leaving their organization. Much of this turnover is due to failure on the part of the organization to manage the repatriation process effectively and also due to the problems outlined above, but some of it is due to a simple failure to communicate effectively about the importance placed on international experience. The overall problem is quite serious in any case. Unless the organization can do something to reduce this turnover, it will not reap the benefits of an international assignment (in terms of increasing global thinking), and it will also pay for its competitors to gain such an advantage.

But many of these problems stem from a narrow view, on the company's part, of the role of international assignments. Many companies offer such assignments only when a person with a specific set of skills is needed and this need cannot be filled by a host-country national. The realization that organizations must compete globally in the future, however, has also begun to change organizations' thinking about international assignments. More organizations are beginning to see these assignments as a developmental activity rather than a response to a specific need. It is becoming clearer that successful leaders in the future will be those who can understand and appreciate cultural differences and understand how to integrate needed company practices with these cultural differences and the expectations associated with those cultural differences. In an attempt to ensure that future managers have this understanding, multinational organizations are increasingly viewing an international assignment as a prerequisite to upper management assignments.

This recognition also makes it more important that the organization manage the international assignment properly and thus avoid losing its repatriated managers. It is clearly important, then, to select the right people for international assignments, provide them with the training they need, support them (financially and psychologically) while they are abroad, and successfully repatriate them when they return.

Organizations are also becoming more creative and thoughtful about the exact nature of international assignments. For example, an organization such as Exxon would traditionally send domestic managers to Venezuala or would have Venezuelan managers come to the United States. But more strategic thinking about international assignments might well have Exxon sending Venezuelan managers to eastern Europe to familiarize them with the eastern European culture. Once international assignments are viewed in this new way, the key is to expose the manager to a range of cultures and countries to prepare him or her for the future.

The implications of this new thinking for career management should be obvious. Surely some risks are still as-sociated with an international assignment, especially if the organization is not sensitive to the problems of repatriation. But in the global firm of the future, it will be impossible to advance up the management career ladder without some international experience. Thus the successful career of the future will be sure to include one or more such international assignments.

Sources: J. S. Black, H. B. Gregersen, M. E. Mendenhall, and L. K. Stroh, *Globalizing People Through International Assignments* (Reading, Mass.: Addison-Wesley, 1999) (*quote on p. 1); "An American Expatriate Finds Hong Kong Post a Fast Boat to Nowhere," *Wall Street Journal*, January 21, 1999, pp. A1, A8.

■ **Career counseling** involves interaction between an individual employee or manager in the organization and either a line manager or a human resource manager.

another position. But if this information isn't communicated to the individual employee, then it is of little or no value to anyone.

The final step in effective career planning is career counseling. As the term suggests, **career counseling** involves interaction between an individual employee or manager in the organization and either a line manager or a human resource manager. This counseling session typically involves frank and open dialogue, with the goal of making sure that the individual's assessment and the organization's assessment of the individual's role and prospects in the organization are congruent. We will discuss career counseling programs in more detail later in this chapter.

The Consequences of Career Planning

When an organization does an effective job of career planning, both it and its employees can expect to achieve numerous benefits. As noted earlier, for example, effective career development and management can result in a more effective workforce and employees who are more motivated and satisfied with their organization. But the organization that engages in effective career management should also expect to achieve cost savings. A higher level of person-job fit should be achieved, with the resulting benefits of lower absenteeism, lower turnover, and a more satisfied and productive workforce. The organization's costs of identifying managers for promotion should be lowered because that identification is part of its regular and ongoing career development processes.

Individuals in organizations that handle career planning effectively should also achieve numerous benefits. They should have a better understanding of their place in the organization, and they should avoid the feelings of resentment or betrayal that occur when people expect to succeed and find out in fact that their organization sees them in a different light. In addition, they can make more informed decisions about alternative career options, educational opportunities, and so forth.

Limitations and Pitfalls in Career Planning

Even though career planning is important to both organizations and individuals, and effective career planning benefits both, everyone should also recognize that career planning has limitations and potential pitfalls. For example, no amount of sophisticated forecasting can predict with absolute certainty the level of talent, expertise, motivation, or interest a given individual will have in the future. People experience changes in interests, for example, and they may redefine their priorities. Even though the organization and the individual may expect that the individual will be capable of performing a certain job in the future, it may turn out that both parties are wrong.

The organization's future human resource needs can also change. For example, it may become more successful or less successful than it originally envisioned, or it may decide on new strategies to pursue. Or new managers may come in and want work done differently than in the past. And new opportunities may present themselves to both the individual and the organization. For instance, an organization may have a certain current member of its workforce who has been tapped to assume an important position in a couple of years. But a substantially stronger individual for that same position may unexpectedly emerge. In this case, the organization may have to alter its original strategy, even at the risk of alienating the individual originally tapped for the job.

Similarly, individuals sometimes find new opportunities at unexpected times. Both an individual and the organization, for instance, may expect that individual to take a certain job in the future. But another organization may appear on the scene to lure the individual away, perhaps at a substantially higher salary. In this instance, the individual is likely to be happy with this turn of events because he or she will have a new position and a higher salary. The organization, on the other hand, may face disruption and may have to alter its existing plans.

Unanticipated mergers and acquisitions can also result in changes in career opportunities. For example, when Amoco was acquired by British Petroleum (BP) a few years ago, the new organization found itself with a surplus of qualified managers and had to offer early retirement incentives to some of them. Others were presented with unanticipated opportunities for new assignments that were substantially different from what they expected. For example, a senior Amoco manager based in Houston, Texas, had been on a career path that did not include the possibility of an international assignment. But shortly after the integration of the firms, this manager was offered a promotion to a new job in London.

CAREER DEVELOPMENT ISSUES AND CHALLENGES

Regardless of the career stages for individual employees, many organizations who are sincerely interested in more effective career management for their employees deal with and address various issues and challenges. In this section we introduce and describe some of these issues and challenges in more detail.

Career Counseling Programs

As already noted, career counseling programs are important to an organization interested in career development for its employees. Such programs usually address a wide variety of career-related issues and are readily accessible to people in the organization. Some programs are formal while others are considerably informal.

Formal career counseling programs usually take the form of workshops, conferences, and career development centers. In some cases, the organization establishes general-purpose career counseling programs that are available to all employees. They may also create special programs targeted for certain categories of employees. Among the more popular special programs are counseling programs for fast-track managers, women managers, and minority managers. These special programs serve various purposes in addition to addressing the specific needs of certain categories of employees. They also help to integrate those employees into the mainstream of the overall organization, and they create important networking opportunities for these individuals.

Organizations also have informal counseling programs. Much of this counseling takes the form of one-on-one interactions between an employee and the employee's supervisor and typically occurs during the performance appraisal period. For example, when supervisors appraise and evaluate the performance of a subordinate and then provide performance feedback to that individual, part of the conversation also deals with issues such as promotion prospects, skill development, and so forth. Sometimes employees may simply drop by the human resource department for advice on career-related questions and issues. When drop-ins are common, it is important for the human resource department to fulfill its center of expertise role to be able to provide useful and accurate information.

When a person reaches the midcareer stage, he or she is often faced with dual career challenges as well as work-family conflicts. Women especially are forced to deal with the conflicts between raising a family and managing a career. Liz Ryan, shown here with her five children, founded World Women in Technology (World-WIT; www.worldWIT.org) to help them. The organization, which she runs from her home, has 20,000 members and forty discussion groups designed to help women deal with the conflicts between career and family. Ryan manages to juggle both WorldWIT and her own consulting business, which requires her to travel. Ryan says she hates the phrase "work-life balance" because it implies a stable state of equilibrium that no one ever really achieves.

Dual-Career and Work-Family Issues

Back in the 1950s and into the 1960s, most married couples in the United States were characterized by roles that gave the male partner's career precedence over the female partner's career. That is, the family tended to live where the husband needed to live. When the husband was given a job transfer, his decision to take it wasn't usually questioned. And if the wife happened to be employed outside the home, it was assumed that she would resign from her job and that the family would move.

But as more and more women entered the workforce, primarily beginning in the mid- to late 1960s, this pattern changed substantially. For many married couples now the wife's career is on an equal footing with the husband's or perhaps may be given precedence over that of the husband. Thus, when organizations offer a transfer to an employee, they must be prepared to deal with the complexities associated with another career. The entire process of career planning must take into consideration the fact that another career must often be managed simultaneously.

Perhaps related to this trend is the growing concern over balancing family needs with the demands of work. As noted above, as dual-career and single-parent employment increases, these concerns pose yet another challenge to career management, especially in the midcareer stages.[12] First, concerns over family-friendly work practices (such as childcare, eldercare, and flexible work schedules) have an influence over the choices that employees make concerning where to work. In fact, many organizations are now advertising their family-friendly practices as a means of competing for employees.[13] Also, it is increasingly clear that concerns at home and with the family affect an employee's behavior at work. Stress over how to arrange for childcare or who will care for an ailing parent can cause the employee problems at work. Relieving these pressures allows the employee to concentrate more on the job and so more fully realize his or her career potential.[14]

Finally, evidence shows that work stressors influence family stress, which in turn is related to long-term health.[15] Thus, as the workforce becomes more diverse, organizations have to recognize that both dual-career issues and concerns over work-family balance will become increasingly important factors for determining career success and must be considered as part of career management. Some of these issues will be taken up in more detail later in this chapter.

EVALUATING CAREER MANAGEMENT ACTIVITIES

The ultimate goals of career management are to have employees reach their full potential at work, enjoy productive and satisfying work careers, and then make a successful transition to retirement. Full appreciation of career management activities on the part of the employee may not come until after retirement. But as employees are increasingly unlikely to spend their entire careers in a single organization, success in retirement is much more likely to be a function of the individual's own career management efforts (as well as the good fortune to remain healthy through the retirement years). For a large number of employees, especially those in higher-status jobs or those for whom work is an important part of self-image, leaving one's career does not mean the end of work. For these employees, managing the transition to what have been called "bridge" jobs (and eventually to full retirement) is most important for their continued satisfaction.[16]

Therefore, career management activities can be judged only by their success at any one point in time. If an employee is satisfied with his or her career at this point, then career management must be judged successful *up to that point*. We have focused primarily on actions the organization can take to manage this process, but clearly a great deal also depends on the employee's efforts at managing his or her career. Employees who go into careers for which they are not well suited (either in terms of abilities or temperament) will obviously be more likely to suffer dissatisfaction with their careers. Although organizational career management efforts are important, the successful management of one's career depends heavily on the employee's efforts to assess his or her own abilities and interests accurately and to formulate a plan for what a successful career should look like.

THE PHYSICAL ENVIRONMENT

The actual physical environment in which an employee works is also extremely important. It can have an effect on safety and health, and later in the chapter we will discuss these issues. Now we concentrate on how the physical environment affects the pleasantness (or unpleasantness) of the work setting. Many aspects of the physical environment may affect an employee's attitudes and behavior on the job, but we will discuss just a few.

Hours of Work

In Chapter 17 we will discuss new trends toward nontraditional workweeks, such as the compressed workweek. Although working four days for three days off a week may be attractive to some people, this approach can create problems too. Also, it may not be equally attractive to all employees. For example, one study found that young males were much more receptive to compressed workweeks than were any other group.[17] Preferences aside, studies of compressed work schedules have found that construction accidents are more likely to occur later in the day (which would be ten hours long) due to fatigue on construction jobs, and generally mixed results were found for productivity in jobs with compressed work schedules.[18]

The design of offices has always been a significant part of the work environment for many workers. But Cisco Systems in the Silicon Valley is about to embark upon a new age of office design. Cisco VP Dave Rossetti heads a 100-person team (some of whom are pictured here) that is charged with completely redesigning Cisco's work environment. They realize that work is increasingly done in groups that form and disband as needs arise. Therefore they envision a workplace where free-floating employees can find a generic empty office nearest to their current group of collaborators and set up operations. The office will feature blank white boards when unoccupied, but when someone enters the space, the room will sense the employee's presence and, by scanning the person's ID badge, the room will automatically configures itself to suit the needs of the individual. The room will even automatically update the computer system with the proper e-mail address and the phone with the employee's extension. Cisco is still developing some of the software that will make this possible, but it is clear that the company sees the workplace of the future as one that will require a work space for the future.

In many industries, the problems of shiftwork present another challenge to managing the work environment effectively. All human beings are subject to **circadian rhythms**, which tell our bodies when to eat and sleep. When employees work a night shift, their bodies must adapt to sleeping during the day and staying awake at night. Although this change is disruptive, the body adapts and learns to switch day and night. But employees who must work on rotating shifts are never quite able to establish a new rhythm. As a result, employees working rotating shifts are more likely to have ulcers than are other employees because their bodies struggle to find an equilibrium.[19] Nonetheless, other research has indicated that some workers, especially older, more experienced employees, may actually like the variety and can cope with the changes in biological rhythms.[20]

■ **Circadian rhythms** are natural cycles that indicate when a body needs to eat or sleep.

Illumination, Temperature, and Office and Work-Space Design

One phase of the Hawthorne studies, which were conducted in 1924 in a Western Electric plant outside Chicago, was concerned with the effects of illumination on productivity. The results indicated that changes in the level of illumination were *not* responsible for the changes in productivity observed. This failure discouraged scholars from examining the effects of illumination on workplace behavior for quite some time. Considerable evidence shows that extremes of temperature (in either direction) can affect both attitudes and decision making on the job.[21] It has even been suggested that ambient temperature helps explain national differences in stress on the job.[22] Research has also shown that different tasks require different levels of optimal lighting, and that employees who perceive their work environments as dark are generally less satisfied with their jobs.[23]

Other aspects of the physical work environment that have received attention over the years include the use of music in the workplace. These studies, many of them going back over fifty years, have indicated that almost any type of background music can improve employee attitudes and performance on the job.[24] A recent study found that the use of personal stereos on the job improved both attitudes and performance, especially on relatively simple jobs.[25] Also, the physical layout of office space and the use of dividers and cubicles have been found to influence attitudes and behavior at work.[26] HR in the 21st Century explores some modern twists on workplace design.

Although many of these studies found that changes in the physical environment affect performance, the physical environment seems to have the strongest affect on attitudes. That is, even when light, temperature, or office layout didn't influence performance, these factors were associated with differences in how employees felt about their jobs and where they worked. It is clear, however, that some aspects of the environment can influence employee safety and health, a topic we will turn to now.

EMPLOYEE SAFETY AND HEALTH

Another important part of managing the work environment deals with employee safety and health. As we will see, employee safety and health in general and the Occupational Safety and Health Act of 1970 (described in Chapter 3) in particular have a significant impact on human resource management. Basic issues

Building the Perfect Work Environment

One of the more interesting changes sweeping corporate America today involves architecture. Specifically, many companies are seeking new and innovative designs for the workplace to make it more interesting and appealing and to promote interaction and spontaneity. Traditionally, offices were arrayed down long corridors; the further a manager moved up the hierarchy, the bigger the office until the ultimate prize was obtained—the corner office.

The next major trend was the installation of cubicles. These modular constructions afforded only a modicum of privacy but still defined specific work space for each employee. Workplace arrangements could be dismantled and/or rearranged with minimal difficulty. But cubicles also reduce individuality and interaction, partially explaining why they became the object of derision in *Dilbert* and other cartoons. So today, many firms are moving in new and nontraditional ways as they seek to redefine their physical environment.

Several characteristics generally are reflected in how companies structure their space today. A movement toward large, well-lit, open spaces where people can gather,

"Before, we were in a typical office. Nothing stood out about the space. We wanted atmosphere that was comfortable, untraditional and more open."

(Debbie Shecterle, director of human resources, Doane Pet Care Company)*

talk, and interact is becoming popular. Designers often hope that such features promote greater interaction among employees. Whereas workplaces used to be developed around straight lines, squares, and rectangles, today they are more likely to feature curves, circles, and other oblique lines and spaces. Right angles are avoided whenever possible, ceilings rise and fall, and bright colors intermix with more somber wood tones.

Of course, such designs have problems as well. Furniture may not fit into a round office as well as in a square one. And if a design is too idiosyncratic, landlords may worry that if the current tenant leaves, it may be difficult to find a new one. But still, many companies are attracted to the benefits of this new model. Doane Pet Care, for example, eliminated all of its cubicles and redesigned its workspace with curved walls; few interior walls; and gold, brown, and green colors. First Bank Systems in Minneapolis; Sears, Roebuck & Co.; and The Gap, Inc. are also adopting this new approach.

Sources: "Pride of Place," *Business Week*, November 2, 1998, pp. 61–81; Dominic Bencivenga, "A Humanistic Approach to Space," *HRMagazine*, March 1998, pp. 68–74; "Curves Ahead," *Wall Street Journal*, March 10, 1999, pp. B1, B10 (*quote on p. B1).

■ **Safety hazards** refer to those conditions in the work environment that have the potential to cause harm to an employee.

■ **Health hazards** are characteristics of the work environment that more slowly and systematically, and perhaps cumulatively, result in damage to an employee's health.

involve actions that the organization can and should take to control or eliminate safety hazards and health hazards.

Safety hazards refer to those conditions in the work environment that have the potential to cause harm to an employee. **Health hazards,** on the other hand, are characteristics of the work environment that more slowly and systematically, and perhaps cumulatively, result in damage to an employee's health. Thus, a poorly connected string of wiring that might result in electrical shock to an employee poses a safety hazard, whereas continuous and ongoing exposure to chemicals that may increase the risk of cancer represents a health hazard.

Table 15.1 lists several of the most injury-prone businesses and occupations in the United States. For example, eating and drinking establishments reported 289,100 nonfatal injuries in 2001, representing about five injuries for every 100 employees. Similarly, among the most dangerous occupations was construction. In 2001, 349 construction workers lost their lives, 42 percent of them from falling.

TABLE 15.1   Injury-Prone Businesses and Dangerous Occupations

Selected Injury-Prone Businesses
Nonfatal Occupational Injuries: Number of Cases and Incidence Rates per 100
Full-Time Workers, 2001

Industry	Total Cases (thousands)	Incidence Rate
Health services	594.6	7.2
Construction, special trade contractors	320.6	8.2
Eating and drinking establishments	289.1	5.3
Grocery stores	190.5	7.5
General merchandise stores	166.2	7.8
Trucking and warehousing transportation	156.6	8.4
Social services	138.3	5.9
Air transportation	135.5	13.3
Automotive dealers and services	122.8	5.5
Hotels and lodging	102.8	7.2

Dangerous Occupations
Index of Relative Risk and Number of Occupational Fatalities Resulting from
Injuries in 2001 (Average Fatality Rate for All Occupations = 4.3)

Occupation	Index of Relative Risk	Number of Fatalities	Major Deadly Event
Construction	33.5	349	Fall (42%)
Farming	27.9	499	Struck by object (17%)
Truck driver	25.3	799	Highway accident (68%)
Groundskeeper	13.7	120	Fall (23%)
Police and detective	13.5	159	Homicide (39%)
Manual labor, excluding construction	13.2	167	Highway accident (14%), struck by object (14%), fall (14%)
Electrician	12.5	109	Fall (16%)
Military	9.3	110	Highway accident (15%)
Carpenter	7.5	112	Fall (62%)

Source: U.S. Department of Labor, Bureau of Labor Statistics, http://www.bls.gov.

Common Workplace Hazards and Threats

First, we address some of the more frequent causes of accidents and then describe some of the more pervasive health hazards. One major category of factors that can cause accidents in the workplace is the characteristics of the physical environment. At a general level, of course, accidents can happen anywhere. People can slip on wet flooring or a loose piece of carpeting or can drop something heavy on a foot in almost any setting. But in manufacturing settings, several specific conditions of the work environment might prove to be potentially dangerous. Among the more common are unguarded or improperly guarded machines. In this instance, "guarding" refers to a shield or other piece of equipment to keep body parts from coming in contact with moving machine parts, such as gears or conveyor belts.

Defective equipment and tools can also cause accidents. Poor lighting and poor or improper ventilation can also be dangerous. Improper dress poses a hazard. For example, if a person wears loose clothing, she or he runs the risk that the clothing might get caught in the moving part of a machine. Sharp edges around machinery can be a hazard. And finally, poor housekeeping resulting in dirty or wet floors, improperly stacked materials, and congested storage areas can result in accidents. Of course, hazards are not restricted to manufacturing settings; they can occur in almost any work setting. As we noted in Chapter 3, for example, home-office safety is becoming a concern for businesses that allow telecommuting.[27]

Personal actions of individual employees can also represent a common workplace hazard. Among the more frequently described and identified personal actions that result in accidents include taking unnecessary risks, failing to wear protective equipment such as goggles or gloves, using improper tools and equipment for specific jobs, taking unsafe shortcuts, and simply engaging in foolish horseplay. Any of these actions has the potential to bring harm or injury to people in the workplace quickly and without warning. These kinds of actions caused an excessive number of injuries for years at Georgia-Pacific, as detailed later in this chapter's closing case.

A separate set of workplace factors may produce negative health effects that appear much more gradually. Chemicals, toxic fumes, and similar workplace factors may fall into this category. Secondary smoke may also be a factor. And some buildings themselves have relatively unsafe characteristics, including asbestos insulation and carpeting that has been treated with improper combinations of chemicals and dyes.

In many cases, these sorts of health hazards are occupational. For example, people who work in coal mines and pesticide plants may be especially prone to come into contact with potential health hazards. The U.S. Department of Labor has identified seven major categories of occupational illnesses:

1. Occupational skin diseases or disorders
2. Dust diseases of the lungs
3. Respiratory conditions due to toxic agents
4. Poisoning
5. Disorders due to physical agents
6. Disorders associated with repeated trauma
7. Other categories of occupational illness

Organizations and OSHA

Widespread concern about employee safety and health led to the passage in 1970 of the most comprehensive law regarding worker safety. This act is technically known as the Occupational Safety and Health Act of 1970 but is most frequently referred to simply by its initials: OSHA. At the time OSHA was passed, approximately 15,000 work-related deaths occurred in the United States every year.

OSHA authorized the U.S. government to create and enforce various standards regarding occupational safety and health. The responsibility for enforcing the provisions of OSHA was assigned to the Department of Labor. In concert with the Department of Labor, the Department of Health was also given the task of sponsoring research to establish the criteria for various tasks and occupations and for training employees to comply with the act. Most of this work is conducted by an agency called the National Institute for Occupational Safety and Health. A sample of the guidelines developed from this work is shown in Table 15.2.

■ **OSHA** authorized the U.S. government to create and enforce various standards regarding occupational safety and health.

TABLE 15.2   Some Sample General Industry Safety and Health Regulations from OSHA

For drinking water . . .

■ Potable water shall be provided in all places of employment.

■ The nozzle of a drinking fountain shall be set at such an angle that the jet of water will not splash back down the nozzle; and the end of the nozzle shall be protected by a guard to prevent a person's mouth or nose from coming in contact with the nozzle.

■ Portable drinking water dispensers shall be designed and serviced to ensure sanitary conditions, shall be capable of being closed, and shall have a tap. Unused disposable cups shall be kept in a sanitary container, and a receptacle shall be provided for used cups. The "common drinking cup" is prohibited.

For fire protection . . .

■ Portable fire extinguishers, suitable to the conditions and hazards involved, shall be provided and maintained in effective operating condition.

■ Portable fire extinguishers shall be given maintenance service at least once a year. A durable tag must be securely attached to show the maintenance or recharge date.

■ In storage areas, clearance between sprinkler systems deflectors and the top of storage varies with the type of storage. For combustible material, stored over 15 feet, but not more than 21 feet high, in solid piles, or over 12 feet, but not more than 21 feet, in piles that contain horizontal channels, the minimum clearance shall be 36 inches. The minimum clearance for smaller piles, or for noncombustible materials, shall be 18 inches.

And for portable ladders . . .

■ The maximum length for portable wooden ladders shall be as follows: step, 20 feet; single straight ladders, 30 feet; sectional ladders, 60 feet; trestle ladders, 20 feet; platform stepladders, 20 feet; painter's stepladders, 12 feet; mason's ladders, 40 feet.

■ Non-self-supporting ladders shall be erected on a sound base at a 4 to 1 pitch, and placed to prevent slippage.

■ The top of a ladder used to gain access to a roof should extend at least 3 feet above the point of contact.

Source: General Industry Standards and Interpretations, U.S. Department of Labor, OSHA (Vol. 1, Revised 1989, Part 1910).

Through research and analysis of workplace statistics, OSHA has created various safety standards. These standards are defined as "practices, means, operations, or processes, reasonably necessary to provide safe . . . employment." The various standards that OSHA creates are regularly published and disseminated to employers across the country. Organizations are responsible for keeping up to date on all current OSHA standards, which can be difficult because of the length and volume of the various sets of regulations and standards. Each year new standards, revisions of old standards, or extensions or reinterpretations of various existing standards are updated by OSHA in volumes that total hundreds of pages in length. Thus, managers frequently feel that OSHA represents unnecessary regulation of their activities.

To ensure compliance with OSHA, inspectors from the U.S. Department of Labor visit places of employment, either on a random basis or by the invitation of an employer, an employee, or a union. If an employee requests an OSHA inspection, her or his identity is kept confidential. If the OSHA inspector determines that the employer is guilty of major violations, significant penalties can result. For example, an employer can be fined $10,000 per violation for willful or repeated major violations. In addition, company officials may be personally fined for failure to comply with OSHA regulations and can conceivably be sentenced to jail time.

OSHA also requires that employers keep highly specific and standardized records of illnesses and injuries that occur in the workplace. These records must be produced and shown to any OSHA compliance officer who requests them. In addition to routine record keeping, employers must also report directly to OSHA and immediately all accidents and illnesses that result in deaths in the workplace or that pose a serious health hazard to all employees in the organization. Of course, employers have avenues for appeal. For example, if they disagree with the recommendations of an OSHA compliance officer, they can turn to the Occupational Safety and Health Review Commission. They can also pursue their claim through the federal courts.

Most people believe that OSHA has not been terribly effective. They argue, for example, that the standards are too comprehensive, too technical, and often too arbitrary. Critics also point out that enforcement of OSHA standards is still relatively uneven. And even in terms of actual measurable effects, OSHA has been less than successful. While awareness of safety issues has undoubtedly increased, the number of occupational accidents and occupational illnesses has not been significantly diminished.[28]

Controlling Accidents at Work

Regardless of whether OSHA is involved or not, an organization can take several precautions in its effort to create a safer work environment, especially regarding accidents at work. One important approach is to design more safety into the workplace through a process called safety engineering. **Safety engineers** are experts who carefully study the workplace, try to identify and isolate particularly dangerous situations, and recommend solutions for dealing with those situations.

In addition, organizations can sometimes help control accidents at work by providing protective clothing and related devices to employees. Among the more common kinds of protective clothing and devices are various types of head protection, eye goggles and face shields, hearing protection for loud noise environments,

■ **Safety engineers** are experts who carefully study the workplace, try to identify and isolate particularly dangerous situations, and recommend solutions for dealing with those situations.

gloves for hand protection, safety shoes for foot protection, waist support belts for people lifting heavy objects, and belts and lifelines for employees who work in high places. And in today's technology-driven workplaces, safety equipment also includes wrist and elbow supports and screen filters for people who keyboard several hours a day, and properly designed chairs and desk surfaces for people who sit for most of their workday.

In addition, employee training is an important ingredient in attempts to control accidents at work. Employees should be taught the safest work procedures that the organization can identify, and they should be taught to follow safe work procedures and to report unsafe conditions to managers. Finally, providing safety incentives and behavior modification training to employees has also been found effective in reducing the number of accidents on the job.[29]

An organization can try to make the workplace safer in either one of two ways. One is to emphasize a reduction in the number of accidents or in the number of workdays lost to accidents. You have probably walked by a construction site or been inside a facility that has a sign indicating how long it has been since someone missed work because of an accident. Accidents and lost workdays can be counted and so can easily be used to justify whatever measures the organization takes. But it is also possible to focus on safe behaviors (the second approach to making the workplace safer) rather than on accidents themselves. An example of an emphasis on safe behavior would be training and rewards for people who engage in safe behaviors (e.g., wearing their hard hats), with the assumption that this behavior will lead to a decrease in the number of accidents. Although safe behavior is a step removed from reduced numbers of accidents, increasing safe behaviors is clearly a necessary step in reducing accidents. Both approaches can work, but they operate in much different ways.

Controlling Occupational Diseases

Controlling occupational diseases is a bit more complex. The effects of occupational diseases are often observable only after extended periods of time, so it may be difficult for the organization to know if its precautions are effective against occupational diseases. For example, several years ago it was determined that a disproportionate number of workers at an Amoco research facility had contracted brain cancer. Experts have been studying the problem for over ten years. While some observers theorize that chemicals at the work site are responsible, neither the independent researchers nor the company itself have been able to pinpoint the problem or to establish conclusively that the work site is to blame.[30]

However, certain precautions can still be taken. For example, the organization should be thoroughly familiar with all hazardous circumstances in the work environment that might cause occupational diseases. If these hazards can be eliminated or minimized, then the organization should attempt to do so. If the hazardous environment is unavoidable, the organization can still take precautions.

For example, all employees should be clearly informed of the various risks and hazards associated with their jobs. This information should enable the employees themselves to take a larger role in maintaining their own health. Again in many cases, proper equipment might be helpful. Respiratory shields for breathing, pressurized or rubberized body suits, and appropriate safety materials and equipment such as gloves and masks might also be helpful.

HEALTH- AND STRESS-MANAGEMENT PROGRAMS

Organizations today are increasingly becoming involved in health- and stress-management programs for their employees.[31] For such programs to be effective, it is first necessary to understand the causes and consequences of stress at work. Figure 15.5 notes the major causes and consequences.

Causes of Stress at Work

■ **Stress** is a person's adaptive response to a stimulus that places excessive psychological or physical demands on him or her.

Stress is a person's adaptive response to a stimulus that places excessive psychological or physical demands on him or her. The stimuli that cause stress are called *stressors*. Organizational stressors are various factors in the workplace that can cause stress. We mentioned this topic briefly in Chapter 8, when we discussed the importance of job satisfaction at work. Four general sets of organizational stressors are task demands, physical demands, role demands, and interpersonal demands.

Task demands are stressors associated with the specific job a person performs. Some occupations are by nature more stressful than others. The jobs of surgeon, air traffic controller, and professional football coach obviously are more stressful

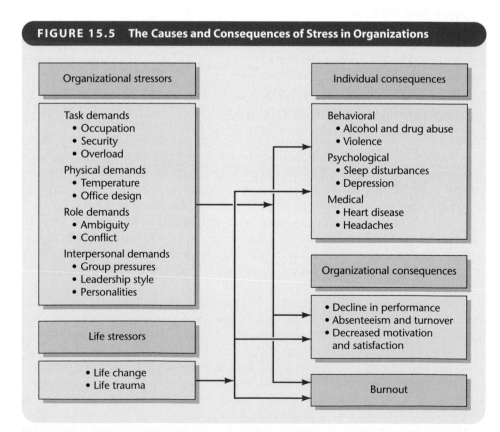

FIGURE 15.5   The Causes and Consequences of Stress in Organizations

Source: Reprinted from James C. Quick and Jonathan D. Quick, *Organizational Stress and Preventive Management*, McGraw-Hill, 1984, pp. 19, 44, and 76. Copyright © 1984 by The McGraw-Hill Companies. Reprinted with the permission of James C. Quick.

than those of a general practitioner, airplane baggage loader, and football team equipment manager, respectively. Beyond specific task-related pressures, other task demands may pose physical threats to a person's health. Such conditions exist in occupations like coal mining, toxic-waste handling, and so forth. Security is another task demand that can cause stress. Someone in a relatively secure job is not likely to worry too much about losing that position. On the other hand, if job security is threatened, stress can increase dramatically. For example, stress generally increases throughout an organization during a period of layoffs or immediately following a merger with another firm. Such a phenomenon has been observed at several organizations, including AT&T, Safeway, and Digital Equipment.

Another task demand stressor is overload. Overload occurs when a person simply has more work to do than he or she can handle. The overload can be either quantitative (the individual has too many tasks to perform or too little time in which to perform them) or qualitative (the person may believe she or he lacks the ability to do the job). More managers report going to their office on weekends to get their jobs done, a direct result of overload.[32] We should also note that the opposite of overload may also be undesirable—low task demands can result in boredom and apathy just as overload can cause tension and anxiety. Thus, a moderate degree of workload-related stress is optimal because it leads to high levels of energy and motivation. HR Tech Talk discusses how electronic communication may result in information overload and cause heightened stress for managers.

Physical demands relate to the job setting. Many of the physical aspects of the work environment that we discussed earlier, such as working in extreme temperatures, have been associated with stress on the job. Also, office design can be related to stress if its end result is isolation or boredom or too much interaction with coworkers. Strenuous labor such as loading heavy cargo or lifting packages can also lead to stress, as can poor lighting or inadequate work surfaces.

Role demands can cause stress too. A role is a set of expected behaviors associated with a position in a group or organization. Stress can result from either role ambiguity or role conflict that people experience in groups. For example, an employee who is feeling pressure from her boss to work longer hours and from her family for more time at home will almost certainly experience stress. A new employee experiencing role ambiguity because of poor orientation and training practices by the organization will also suffer from stress.

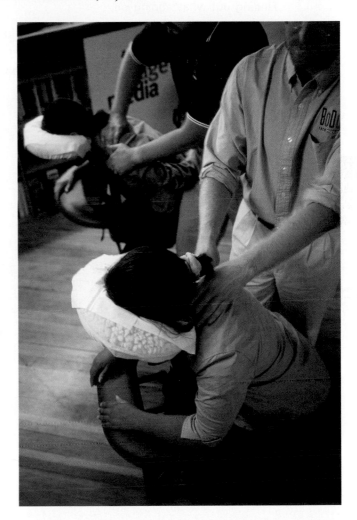

Wellness programs at work are becoming much more common as employers recognize the importance of keeping employees healthy and relatively stress free. Third Age Media, a media consulting firm in San Francisco, has taken this approach very seriously. Here, two employees receive massages offered by the company throughout the day for employees who need a bit of relaxation. On-site gyms, workout facilities, and aerobics classes are all becoming quite commonplace in corporate America. These facilities tend to increase employee satisfaction and can reduce stress at work, but they can also pay for themselves by improving the general health of employees, which decreases their need for medical attention and increases productivity.

HR Tech Talk

Too Much Technology?

Information and communication lie at the heart of what most human resource managers do. Finding out what's going on, thinking about what it means and what else is going on, and then telling others what's going on are constant rituals that define much of the work of many managers. Today's cutting-edge information technology makes it possible for these managers to keep in constant touch with all their information contacts regardless of time or location. Need to get a quick message to someone? Send them an e-mail. Need an important document from the office? Have it faxed. Need to talk to someone right away? Use the cell phone.

Are these developments positive? Certainly, new information technology has enabled many human resource managers to make decisions better and faster than ever before. And this technology also promotes more frequent communication among people, resulting in improved coordination and enhanced organizational flexibility and response times. Managers can keep in constant touch with others, and a manager's boss, colleagues, and subordinates can get in touch anytime.

But some trouble spots also crop up. For example, information technology makes it easier than ever before for human resource managers to suffer from information overload. One recent survey, for example, found that managers in typical large corporations send or receive an astonishing 177 messages each day. The forms of these messages run the gamut from e-mail to Post-it Notes. And many human

"Critical thinking and analysis get lost in an interrupt-driven workplace."

(Nancy Ozawa, consultant)*

resource managers fall into the trap of thinking that because they *can* always be in touch, they *must* always be in touch. Thus, they check their e-mail constantly, carry their cell phones on vacation or to the golf course, and keep a pager strapped around their waist at all times.

If these behaviors are left unchecked, managers risk various problems. From an organizational perspective, for example, people may begin to spend so much time communicating that other parts of their work suffer. And instant access to information and the pressure that accompanies modern technology may lead managers to make decisions too rapidly, without taking proper time to reflect and consider all alternatives. From an information-processing perspective alone, a single daily issue of the *New York Times* today contains more information than an average person in the seventeenth century would have encountered in a lifetime!

And the pressure itself can carry with it dire consequences for the individuals themselves. They risk losing balance in their lives, for example, and may be so "connected" that they are never away from their work. As a result, they become prime candidates for burnout and end up falling behind others who take a more ordered and balanced approach not only in their work but also in their lives.

Sources: Gina Imperato, "The E-Mail Prescription," *Fast Company*, May 1999, pp. 90–92; "Drowning in Data," *Newsweek*, April 28, 1997, p. 85; "Memo 4/8/97, FYI: Messages Inundate Offices," *Wall Street Journal*, April 8, 1997, pp. B1, B10 (*quote on p. B1).

Another set of organizational stressors consists of three *interpersonal demands*. Group pressures include pressure to restrict output, pressure to conform to the group's norms, and so forth. For instance, it is quite common for a work group to arrive at an informal agreement about how much each member will produce. Individuals who produce much more or much less than this level may be pressured by the group to get back in line. An individual who feels a strong need to vary from the group's expectations (perhaps to get a pay raise or promotion) will experience a great deal of stress, especially if acceptance by the group is also important to him or her.

Leadership style can cause stress. Suppose an employee needs a great deal of social support from his leader. The leader, however, is quite brusque and shows no concern or compassion for the employee. This employee will likely feel stressed. Similarly, assume that an employee feels a strong need to participate in decision making and to be active in all aspects of management. Her boss is autocratic and refuses to consult subordinates about anything. Once again, stress is likely to result.

Conflicting personalities and behaviors may cause stress. Conflict can occur when two or more people must work together even though their personalities, attitudes, and behaviors differ. For example, a person with an internal locus of control—that is, who always wants to control events—might get frustrated working with an external person who likes to wait and see what happens. A smoker and a nonsmoker who are assigned adjacent offices obviously will experience stress. Table 15.3 provides a subjective list of the most and least stressful jobs. The list is based on factors such as quotas and deadlines, long workweeks, and various other factors. Finally, it is important that all of the stressors noted above exist against a background of general life events that can also cause stress.

Consequences of Stress at Work

Stress can lead to several positive and negative consequences. If the stress is positive, the result may be more energy, enthusiasm, and motivation. Of more concern, of course, are the negative consequences of stress. Three sets of consequences that can result from stress are individual consequences, organizational consequences, and burnout.[33]

Behavioral consequences of stress are responses that may harm the person under stress or others. One such behavior is smoking. Research has clearly documented that people who smoke tend to smoke more when they experience stress. Other possible behavioral consequences are accident tendencies, violence, and appetite disorders. Psychological consequences of stress relate to an individual's mental health and well-being. When people experience too much stress at work, they may become depressed or may find themselves sleeping too much or not enough. Stress may also lead to family problems and sexual difficulties. The medical consequences of stress affect a person's physical well-being. Heart disease and stroke, among other illnesses, have been linked to stress. Other common medical problems resulting from too much stress include headaches, backaches, ulcers and related stomach and intestinal disorders, and skin conditions like acne and hives. The Lighter Side of HR on page 497 illustrates how these consequences can occur and provides a humorous solution.

Clearly, any of the individual consequences just discussed can also affect the organization, but other consequences of stress have even more direct consequences for organizations. One clear organizational consequence of too much stress is a decline in performance. For operating workers, such a decline can translate into poor-quality work or a drop in productivity. For managers, it can mean faulty decision making or disruptions in working relationships as people become irritable and hard to get along with. As discussed in Chapter 8, withdrawal behaviors such as absenteeism and turnover can result from stress on the job.

Another direct organizational consequence of employee stress relates to attitudes. As we just noted, job satisfaction, morale, and organizational commitment can all suffer, along with motivation to perform at high levels. As a result, people may be more prone to complain about trivialities, do only enough work to get by, and so forth. Burnout, another consequence of stress, has clear implications

TABLE 15.3   Most and Least Stressful Jobs

The most and least stressful jobs, based on factors such as quotas and deadlines, long workweeks, the hazards involved, level of competitiveness, physical demands, environmental conditions, contact with the public, need for precision, and amount of stamina required.

Most Stressful Jobs	Least Stressful Jobs
1. U.S. president	1. Medical records technician
2. Firefighter	2. Janitor
3. Senior corporate executive	3. Forklift operator
4. Race car driver (Indy class)	4. Musical instrument repairperson
5. Taxi driver	5. Florist
6. Surgeon	6. Actuary
7. Astronaut	7. Appliance repairperson
8. Police officer	8. Medical secretary
9. Football player (NFL)	9. Librarian
10. Air traffic controller	10. Bookkeeper
11. Highway patrol officer	11. File clerk
12. Public relations executive	12. Piano tuner
13. Mayor	13. Photographic process worker
14. Jockey	14. Dietitian
15. Basketball coach (NCAA)	15. Paralegal assistant
16. Advertising account executive	16. Vending machine repairperson
17. Real estate agent	17. Bookbinder
18. Photojournalist	18. Barber
19. Member of Congress	19. Medical laboratory technician
20. Stockbroker	20. Electrical technician
21. Fisherman	21. Typist/word-processor
22. Airplane pilot	22. Broadcast technician
23. Lumberjack	23. Mathematician
24. Emergency medical technician	24. Dental hygienist
25. Architect	25. Jeweler

Source: The Wall Street Journal Almanac 1999, p. 232. Copyright © 1999 Dow Jones and Company. Republished by permission of Dow Jones, Inc. via Copyright Clearance Center, Inc.

■ **Burnout** is a general feeling of exhaustion that develops when an individual simultaneously experiences too much pressure and too few sources of satisfaction.

for both employees and organizations. **Burnout** is a general feeling of exhaustion that develops when an individual simultaneously experiences too much pressure and too few sources of satisfaction.

Other consequences of stress include various dysfunctional behaviors that detract from, rather than contribute to, organizational performance. Two of the

The Lighter Side of HR

Stress is a major problem in many organizational settings. As illustrated in this cartoon, people often bring their work-related problems home with them. While a small amount of this kind of behavior is generally unavoidable, it can result in sleep disturbances, depression, and similar problems if it is carried to excess. One method for helping counter stress, however, is a good support network. A partner and friends, for example, can help people cope better with stress, keep things in perspective, and take their minds off work, as also shown in this cartoon.

more common are absenteeism and turnover. Some absenteeism, of course, has a legitimate cause, such as illness, jury duty, or death or illness in the family. At other times, the employee may feign a legitimate cause as an excuse to stay home. When an employee is absent, legitimately or not, her or his work does not get done at all or a substitute must be hired to do it. In either case, the quantity or quality of actual output is likely to suffer. Obviously, some absenteeism is expected, but organizations strive to eliminate feigned absenteeism and reduce legitimate absences as much as possible.

Turnover occurs when people quit their jobs. An organization usually incurs costs when replacing workers who have quit; if turnover involves especially productive people, it is even more costly. Turnover seems to result from several factors, including aspects of the job, the organization, the individual, and the labor market and family influences. In general, a poor person-job fit is also a likely cause of turnover. People may also be prone to leave an organization if its inflexibility makes it difficult to manage family and other personal matters; they may be more likely to stay if an organization provides sufficient flexibility to make it easier to balance work and nonwork considerations.

Other forms of dysfunctional behavior may be even more costly for an organization. Theft and sabotage, for example, result in direct financial costs for an organization. Sexual and racial harassment are also costly to an organization, both indirectly (by lowering morale, producing fear, and driving off valuable employees) and directly (through financial liability if the organization responds inappropriately).

Workplace violence and aggression are also growing concerns in many organizations. People who are having problems coping with stress may vent their difficulties by yelling at or harassing their colleagues. They may also engage in other destructive behaviors such as damaging company property or physically assaulting their boss or a coworker. Violence by disgruntled workers or former workers results in dozens of deaths and injuries each year.[34]

But it is also possible that stress has some positive effects on behavior at work. Several studies[35] have suggested that not all stress is the same and that some sources of stress can actually lead to positive outcomes at work.[36] Also, it has been argued that without stress, there is little stimulation and employees can become bored. This perspective leads to the question, Is it possible to have too little stress on the job? The Point/Counterpoint feature for this chapter presents some different views on this question.

Wellness Programs in Organizations

Two basic organizational strategies for helping employees manage stress are institutional programs and collateral stress programs. **Institutional programs** for managing stress are undertaken through established organizational mechanisms. For example, properly designed jobs and work schedules, as discussed earlier, can help ease stress. Shiftwork, in particular, can cause major problems for employees because they have to adjust their sleep and relaxation patterns constantly. Thus, the design of work and work schedules should be a focus of organizational efforts to reduce stress.

■ **Institutional programs** for managing stress are undertaken through established organizational mechanisms.

The organization's culture can also be used to help manage stress. Some organizational cultures, for example, have a strong norm against taking time off or going on vacation. In the long run, such norms can cause major stress. Thus, the organization should strive to foster a culture that reinforces a healthy mix of work and nonwork activities. Supervision can play an important institutional role in managing stress. A supervisor is a potential major source of overload. If made aware of their potential for assigning stressful amounts of work, supervisors can do a better job of keeping workloads reasonable.

In addition to their institutional efforts aimed at reducing stress, many organizations are turning to collateral stress programs. A **collateral stress program** is an organizational program created specifically to help employees deal with stress. Organizations have adopted stress-management programs, health-promotion programs, and other kinds of programs for this purpose. More and more companies are developing their own programs or adopting existing programs of this type. For example, Lockheed Martin offers screening programs for its employees to detect signs of hypertension, and Hospital Corporation of America offers its employees four cents a mile for cycling, sixteen cents a mile for walking or jogging, and sixty-four cents a mile for swimming.

■ **Collateral stress programs** are organizational programs created specifically to help employees deal with stress.

Many firms today also have employee fitness programs. These kinds of programs attack stress indirectly by encouraging employees to exercise, which in turn is presumed to reduce stress. On the negative side, this kind of effort costs considerably more than stress-management programs because the firm must invest in exercise facilities. Still, more and more companies are exploring this option. Both Tenneco and L.L.Bean, for example, have state-of-the-art fitness centers available for their employees' use.

Organizations try to help employees cope with stress through other kinds of programs. For example, existing career development programs like that at General Electric are used for this purpose. Other companies use programs promoting everything from humor to massage as antidotes for stress. Of course, little or no research supports some of the claims made by advocates of these programs. Thus, managers must take steps to ensure that any organizational effort to help employees cope with stress is at least reasonably effective.

Not Enough Stress?

Is stress always a bad thing? Considerable evidence suggests that more stress is not always related to decreased job satisfaction and physical problems. In fact, in some cases, stress can be seen as representing a challenge to the employee and can be quite stimulating. Given this finding, it is not clear whether we should be advocating more or less stress on the job, and some suggest that stress should be increased in some cases.

POINT... We should always seek to reduce the levels of stress on the job because ...	COUNTERPOINT... Sometimes we can have too little stress and should increase the stress on the job because ...
High levels of stress have been related to burnout and physical problems.	Overcoming some stress results in feelings of mastery.
High levels of stress are related to dissatisfaction and turnover.	Dealing effectively with stress is important for the development of managers.
High levels of stress lead to declines in performance on the job.	Jobs with no stress also present no challenge, which leads to boredom.

So... We can have too much stress on the job, but we should also consider the possibility of too little stress and stimulation. The key is to identify the levels of stress that lead to challenge and stimulation but do not reach the levels of producing burnout and dissatisfaction.

AIDS in the Workplace

Acquired immune deficiency syndrome (AIDS) has become a major problem in the world today. AIDS is relevant to employers for several reasons. An employee with AIDS must cope with a life-threatening medical issue, but it is also important to that individual's coworkers. Unfortunately, there is no clear-cut solution for dealing with this issue. Individuals who publicly disclose their condition increase the potential for retaliation from coworkers—many people fear the disease and may shun those who have it. And the organization faces various privacy-related issues.

In general, an organization that wants to deal with this issue must start by developing and implementing a comprehensive AIDS policy. As a premise for developing a policy, however, all employers must keep in mind certain points. First, it is illegal to ask an applicant if she or he has AIDS. Some states allow organizations to require applicants to take an AIDS test, whereas other states do not. Regardless of the outcome, an employee can be denied employment on the basis of AIDS only if it is determined that the applicant cannot perform the job. As long as the individual who is already hired is capable of performing the job, he or she cannot be terminated or placed on leave. All medical information regarding the individual and her or his condition must be kept absolutely confidential.

In general, organizations can adopt three strategies in trying to deal with AIDS from a management perspective. One strategy is to categorize AIDS under a comprehensive life-threatening illness policy. In this instance, AIDS is treated like terminal cancer or any other life-threatening illness. The organization can then apply the same sorts of insurance coverage provisions, early-retirement and leave provisions, and so forth.

Another strategy is to form an AIDS-specific policy. This action is completely legal for an organization to contemplate as long as neither the intent nor the implementation of the policy results in discrimination against people on the basis of an AIDS condition. In general, most companies that form an AIDS-specific policy do so in an affirmative way. That is, the essence of the policy is to affirm the organization's stance that employees with AIDS are still entitled to work, receive benefits, and be treated comparably to all other employees.

The third approach that some companies take is to have no policy at all, an approach taken by far too many companies. The organization either doesn't want to confront the necessity for having an AIDS policy, is afraid to confront the need for such a policy, or doesn't know how to approach such a policy. In any of these events, managerial ignorance can potentially result in serious problems for both the employer and the employees.

Chapter Summary

A career is the set of experiences and activities that people engage in related to their job and livelihood over the course of their working life. Historically most people have thought of the various components comprising a person's career as having some degree of interrelation. A long-time, generally accepted view of the career stages a typical individual progresses through consists of exploration, establishment, maintenance, and disengagement. A more recent perspective refocuses career stages on career age and acknowledges the likelihood of multiple careers, and this more recent perspective also recognizes that retirement is a part of the career progression.

Most successful organizations and managers today recognize that careers don't just happen. Indeed, successful careers must be planned and managed. Part of the responsibility for this career management resides with the organization, but the individual her- or himself must also play an important role.

Career planning is important to both organizations and individuals. Most organizations that are genuinely interested in the careers of their employees develop sophisticated career management systems. These systems are based in turn on career planning. Career planning requires careful coordination between individual employees and the organization itself. Even though career planning is important and beneficial to both organizations and individuals, everyone should also recognize that career planning has limitations and potential pitfalls.

In many ways, the early career stages faced by an individual are the most tumultuous. Regardless of whether they are taking their first jobs or whether they are moving into one job after a long period of employment elsewhere, new entrants into an organization always feel a certain degree of uncertainty and apprehension about their new employer. Thus, an important starting point for human resource managers interested in managing the careers of their employees more effectively is understanding some of the early career problems that such employees often encounter.

After an individual completes the first few years of a job successfully, many of the early career problems may have been addressed. But some problems still loom on the horizon for these individuals once they reach the midcareer stage. The most common midcareer problem faced by most individuals in corporations today is what is generally referred to as the midcareer plateau.

In the latter stages of a person's career, it is perhaps even more important for the organization to provide career management services. Many of these services try to solve the problems faced by people in the later stages of their careers. Many of these problems revolve around issues associated with retirement.

Regardless of the career stage of each employee, many organizations that are sincerely interested in more effective career management for their employees deal with and address various issues and challenges. Career counseling programs are important to an organization interested in career development for its employees. Such programs usually address a wide variety of career-related issues and are readily accessible to people in the organization. Dual-career and work-family issues are also an important part of today's career management activities and concerns.

The success of career management activities can only be judged according to their success at any one point in time. If an employee is satisfied with his or her career at one point, then career management must be judged successful up to that point.

The actual physical environment in which an employee works is also extremely important. Many aspects of the physical environment may affect an employee's attitudes and behavior on the job. Work hours reflect one such aspect. Illumination, temperature, and office and work-space design are also important.

Another important part of managing a work environment deals with employee safety and health. Basic issues involve actions that the organization can and should take to control or eliminate safety hazards and health hazards. Safety hazards refer to those conditions in the work environment that have the potential to cause harm to an employee. Health hazards are those characteristics of the work environment that more slowly and systematically, and perhaps cumulatively, result in damage to an employee's health. OSHA authorized the U.S. government to create and enforce various standards regarding occupational safety and health.

Stress is a person's adaptive response to a stimulus that places excessive psychological or physical demands on him or her. The stimuli that cause stress are called stressors. Organizational stressors are various factors in the workplace that can cause stress. Four general sets of organizational stressors are task demands, physical demands, role demands, and interpersonal demands. If the stress is positive, the result may be more energy, enthusiasm, and motivation. Three other sets of consequences that can result from stress are individual consequences, organizational consequences, and burnout. Two basic organizational strategies for helping employees manage stress are institutional programs and collateral stress programs. AIDS is also relevant to employers for various reasons.

▶ The nature of careers is changing, but it is still important to recognize that effective human resource management requires career planning, not just filling jobs.

▶ Dual-career and work-family issues will remain the most challenging aspects of career planning in the new century.

▶ Managing the physical work environment is another critical aspect of the human resource function.

▶ Decisions about shiftwork, illumination, temperature, and workplace design can have a significant

Key Points for Future HR Managers

impact on employee productivity, employee health, employee safety, and employee attitudes toward their jobs.

▶ Occupational safety and health is important because of legal requirements and also because of its impact on productivity and employee attitudes.

▶ Stress at work plays a major role in employee health, attitudes, and productivity, and much of this stress comes from the way work is designed.

▶ AIDS in the workplace will continue to be an important health issue in the new century.

Key Points for Future General Managers

▶ Although the traditional career may be dead, it is still critical to think through and plan an employee's entire career.

▶ The physical work environment is critical for productivity, health, safety, and employee attitudes.

▶ Employee safety is not only a matter of the law, it is good business because it reduces costs and increases productivity.

▶ Careers and work environment issues are rarely areas for increasing competitive advantage. Instead, if these areas are not properly managed, a firm can incur crippling costs.

Review and Discussion Questions

1. What is a career?

2. Compare and contrast the traditional and emerging career models. Which model are you most comfortable with? Why?

3. If you are soon becoming a new career entrant, what issues are you most concerned about? How might an employer help you deal with these issues?

4. From the standpoint of an individual employee, under what circumstances might a career plateau be a positive challenge?

5. Would you like to have an international assignment as part of your career? What issues and concerns might you have about such a possibility?

6. Describe the kind of physical environment in which you would most like to work.

7. What are the differences between safety hazards and health hazards?

8. Review the list of injury-prone jobs and dangerous occupations in Table 15.2. Identify five other jobs that you think might also belong on each list.

9. Research the OSHA guidelines and regulations that relate most directly to your current or anticipated job.

10. What are the primary causes and consequences of stress in organizations?

Closing Case

Safety Comes to Georgia-Pacific

Georgia-Pacific Corporation is the world's largest distributor of building products (such as wood panels, lumber, and gypsum products) and among the five largest manufacturers of packaging materials, correspondence paper (such as office printing products and stationery), wood pulp, and tissue paper. The firm is based in Atlanta, Georgia, and has more than 100 distribution centers scattered across North America. It controls more than 6 million acres of timberland in the United States and Canada. Its annual revenues generally run about $15 billion.

Forest-products businesses have never been known for their safe, pleasant, and comfortable work environments. Paper mills, sawmills, and plywood factories, for example, are generally characterized by constant, deafening noise; huge, razor-toothed blades, shredders, and grinders; long chutes loaded with rumbling tons of lumber; and giant vats full of boiling water and caustic chemicals. The products they make are awkward in size, heavy, and often full of painful splinters, and the machinery used to make them requires frequent maintenance and close contact with sharp edges and dangerous moving parts.

Throughout much of its history, Georgia-Pacific had an unenviable accident record, even for what experts see as a highly dangerous and hazardous industry. For example, between 1986 and 1990 the firm averaged nine serious injuries per year per 100 employees, and twenty-six workers lost their lives on the job. Two factors contributing to these statistics were unrelenting pressure to keep productivity high and a macho organization culture that promoted risk-taking and bravado.

For example, top management continually reinforced the importance of keeping production lines moving, no matter what. As a result, workers would often attempt to perform routine maintenance or repair broken equipment parts without shutting down the line. And if they didn't have a pair of safety gloves handy, they would carry around heavy—and sharp—saw blades with their bare hands rather than "waste" an extra few minutes to take appropriate safety precautions. Indeed, one observer noted that you weren't considered a real Georgia-Pacific "mill guy" unless you were missing a finger or two!

But this situation started to change about ten years ago when a new top management team came in. The new managers were appalled by the firm's poor safety record and vowed to make it a source of pride rather than a source of embarrassment. The starting point was creating a task force charged with learning more about operating practices that contributed to accidents and then figure out how to change those practices. The next step was altering the firm's basic culture so that it reinforced safe rather than risky practices and behaviors. And finally, Georgia-Pacific implemented an array of new rules and regulations that explicitly promoted safe work and punished those responsible for unnecessarily hazardous or dangerous actions.

So far, the results have been impressive. Accident rates dropped consistently every year in the 1990s, and few workers lose their lives anymore. At one of the firm's most hazardous plants, injuries run about 0.7 per 100 workers annually. OSHA indicates that this ratio is about one-third the injury rate at the average bank! And the company has realized that being more cautious and following safer work procedures has boosted its productivity rather than lowering it. Stopping a production line to correct a problem usually takes only a few minutes, whereas stopping it because of an accident or injury might shut down production for hours—or even days.

Injury rates now play a major role in the performance evaluation and compensation for all supervisors and managers at Georgia-Pacific. Safety equipment is an absolute requirement. One top manager, for example, happily tells the story of how he was recently chewed out by an hourly worker while visiting a sawmill because he carelessly stepped too close to a dangerous piece of equipment. All employees in the mills have to wear earplugs, hardhats, goggles, gloves, and steel-toed shoes at all times. Failure to follow these regulations can result in immediate dismissal. And indeed, Georgia-Pacific is so proud of its achievements in safety that it's working to extend the same principles used to make these changes to other areas of its business, including quality and customer service.[37]

Case Questions

1. Why do you think Georgia-Pacific has been so successful in reducing its accident and injury rates?

2. What other industries and businesses might benefit from the same kind of approach?

3. Research Georgia-Pacific's most recent safety statistics and see if the firm is still doing as well.

Building HR Management Skills

Purpose: The purpose of this exercise is to help you appreciate the similarities and differences in career management from the standpoint of individuals and of organizations.

Step 1: Outline an ideal career management plan from your own standpoint. Start by selecting an entry-level job in an organization for which you might have an interest in working. Then outline the various jobs you would be interested in moving into, the time you would like to spend in each, the salary you might expect to receive, and similar considerations, up to the position of CEO. Be realistic, but also design the plan with your personal interests in mind.

Step 2: Now assume that you are the senior human resources executive in the firm you selected in step 1. Look at the same entry-level position you used as a starting point there. Outline a career development plan for someone else starting in that position. As in step 1, outline the jobs and expectations for a person progressing all the way through the hierarchy to the very top, noting time and salary at each job along the way. Be fair to the individual, but keep the best interests of the organization first and foremost in your mind at all times.

Step 3: Compare and contrast the two different career management plans you developed. Identify the particular areas where the plans are similar and where they are different. Note the reasons for these similarities and differences.

Questions

1. Is it possible for a career management plan to be perfectly fair and equitable for both the individual and the organization? Why or why not?

2. Do you think it would be a good idea for an organization to have its employees develop their own career management plans, as you did in step 1, and then compare them with organizational plans? Why or why not?

3. Which type of plan—the individual or the organization plan—is likely to be the most flexible? Why?

Ethical Dilemmas in HR Management

 You are the owner/manager of a small software enterprise. You employ a total of 150 people, all of whom have stock options in the business. Working in consultation with several of your designers, you are closing in on a major breakthrough with a software product that can dramatically reduce manufacturing costs for firms in several different industries. You are also aware, however, that several larger competitors are working hard to develop the same basic technology. If your firm is to achieve the breakthrough first, a major push is needed.

You are sitting in your office weighing the following basic facts:

1. All of your employees are on the verge of exhaustion; each one has been putting in sixty to eighty hours per week for the last four months, and no one ever takes a day off. You know that a couple of employees are drinking more than normal, and at least three are reportedly having marital difficulties.

2. You estimate that another six to eight weeks of intense work and long hours will likely allow your firm to get the new product up and running first.

3. If your firm is the first to get the new software finished, everyone in the firm will reap a huge financial reward. The most senior employees (and you, of course) will likely become millionaires; even the newest employees should see their stock options increase in value to near $100,000 more than their current value.

4. It will take an all-or-nothing effort if you are to succeed. That is, you cannot cut back on work schedules or give people time off, or else you will fall behind your competitors. Every single worker will need to work hard until the project is finished, or else you might as well give up now.

You see yourself as having two options. On the one hand, you can cut back on the workload and reduce the stress and pressure on your employees. While your firm would almost certainly lose the race for the software breakthrough, the company is nevertheless quite profitable and your employees earn an above-market income. Other opportunities for major breakthroughs may occur in the future. On the other hand, you can keep the work pace as it is; after all, it's only for a few more weeks and then everyone will share in what will likely be a major reward.

Questions

1. What are the ethical issues in this situation?

2. What are the basic arguments for and against continuing an all-out push to achieve the breakthrough?

3. What do you think most owners/managers would do? What would you do?

HR Internet Exercise

 The Occupational Safety and Health Administration (OSHA), part of the U.S. Department of Labor, maintains an extensive website. Start by visiting the site at http://www.osha.gov/.

Now, assume that you have just been placed in charge of workplace safety for a midsized manufacturing firm plagued by a high rate of injuries and accidents. Based on your review of the OSHA website, respond to the following questions:

Questions

1. How helpful do you think the OSHA website might be to you in lowering your plant's accident and injury rate?

2. What parts of the site do you think are most and least helpful?

3. Do you think a manager in your position can rely solely on the OSHA website to deal with problems, or will other information be required?

16

Managing the Diverse Workforce

Diversity is a fact of life in organizations today. And while diversity has many benefits, the potential for conflict increases significantly. Different backgrounds, perspectives, customs, and values combine to make it ever more likely that people will disagree and see situations differently.

For example, take the Marriott Marquis Hotel in New York City's Time Square. The hotel employs 1,700 people from seventy countries and who speak forty-seven languages. One major reason for the hotel's diversity is its labor pool—the area is populated by a diverse set of immigrants and these residents often apply for these kinds of jobs. But the hotel managers also strongly believe that the diverse workforce is an asset in part because it fits the multicultural clientele who frequent the hotel.

But managing the diversity at Marriott can be a challenge. For example, consider the case of Jessica Brown, an African-American quality-assurance manager

"[A]ll you can really do is hope [the resentment] goes away eventually. And it usually does."

(Cynthia Keating, Marriott manager)*

responsible for housekeeping. Brown says that when she rewards other African-Americans, some of her Hispanic employees criticize her for playing favorites. But when she rewards the Hispanic employees, some African-Americans accuse her of ignoring them.

Balancing religious preferences is also complicated. One manager, Victor Aragona, recently sought out a room attendant to fix an overflowing bathtub. The attendant was found prostrate on a towel in the housekeeper's closet bowing to Mecca and saying his daily Islamic prayers. Rather than disturb him, Aragona fixed the bathtub himself.

To help cope with these challenges, Marriott offers frequent training programs in multiculturalism and conflict management. These courses are required for all managers and are open to most nonmanagers as well. Even so, the hotel still finds it necessary to offer periodic and regular refresher courses to help people work together with a minimum of conflict.[1] ■

anagers at the Marriott Marquis Hotel face a complex set of challenges and opportunities. On the one hand, the diverse workforce they oversee poses far more complications and complexities than would a more homogenous one. On the other hand, the diverse workforce employed at the hotel also provides competitive advantages and opportunities to cater more effectively to the multinational clientele who frequent the area. Balancing the complications and the benefits of diversity is among the most important workplace issues facing most managers and their organizations today.

This chapter is about workforce diversity in organizations. We begin by exploring the meaning and nature of diversity. We distinguish between diversity management and equal employment opportunity. Next we identify and discuss several common dimensions of diversity. The impact of diversity on the organization is explored. We address how diversity can be managed for the betterment of both individuals and organizations. Finally, we characterize and describe the fully multicultural organization.

THE NATURE OF WORKFORCE DIVERSITY

Workforce diversity has become an important issue in many organizations, both in the United States and abroad. A logical starting point in understanding this phenomenon better is to establish the meaning of the word *diversity* and then to examine why such diversity is increasing today.

The Meaning of Workforce Diversity

Diversity exists in a group or organization when its members differ from one another along one or more important dimensions.[2] If everyone in the group or organization is exactly like everyone else, no diversity exists. But if everyone is different along every imaginable dimension, total diversity exists. In reality, of course, these extremes are more hypothetical than real; most settings are characterized by a level of diversity somewhere between. Thus, diversity is not an absolute phenomenon wherein a group or organization is or is not diverse. Instead, diversity should be conceptualized as a continuum. Therefore, diversity should be thought of in terms of degree or level of diversity along relevant dimensions.[3]

These dimensions of diversity might include gender, age, and ethic origin, among many others. A group comprised of five middle-aged white male U.S. executives has relatively little diversity. If one member leaves and is replaced by a young white female executive, the group becomes a bit more diverse. If another member is replaced by an older African-American executive, diversity increases a bit more. And when a third member is replaced by a Japanese executive, the group becomes even more diverse.

■ **Diversity** exists in a group or organization when its members differ from one another along one or more important dimensions.

Trends in Workforce Diversity

As we noted earlier, organizations today are becoming increasingly diverse along many different dimensions. Several different factors have accounted for these trends and changes. One factor that has contributed to increased diversity is

Increasing workforce diversity is largely viewed as something a company should do because it is the right thing and also because it improves performance. Fannie Mae, the mortgage guarantor group, with a 2002 ranking of #1 and a 2003 ranking of #2 has topped the list of Fortune's best places for minorities to work. The company recognizes the importance of internal diversity because each person's unique attributes translate to key skills, talents, and potential within the company. In addition, Fannie Mae's Office of Diversity, Health, and Work Life Initiatives offers external diversity training to customers, partners, and other businesses. Fannie Mae's Chairman and Chief Executive Officer Franklin D. Raines is pictured here (third from right) along with key members of his management team.

changing demographics in the labor force. As more women and minorities have entered the labor force, for example, the available pool of talent from which organizations hire employees has changed in both size and composition. If talent within each segment of the labor pool is evenly distributed (for example, if the number of talented men in the workforce as a percentage of all men in the workforce is the same as the number of talented women in the labor force as a percentage of all women in the workforce), it follows logically that, over time, proportionately more women and proportionately fewer men will be hired by an organization compared to the employees who were hired in the past.

A related factor that has contributed to diversity has been the increased awareness by organizations that they can improve the overall quality of their workforce by hiring and promoting the most talented people available, regardless of gender, race, or any other characteristics. By casting a broader net in recruiting and looking beyond traditional sources for new employees, organizations are finding more broadly qualified and better qualified employees from many different segments of society. Thus, these organizations are finding that diversity can be a source of competitive advantage.

Another reason for the increase in diversity has been legislation and legal actions that have forced organizations to hire more broadly. Organizations in the United States were once free to discriminate against women, blacks, and other minorities. Thus, most organizations were dominated by white males. But over the last thirty years or so, various laws have outlawed discrimination against these and other groups. As we detailed in Chapter 3, organizations must hire and promote people today solely on the basis of their qualifications.

A final contributing factor to increased diversity in organizations has been the globalization movement. Organizations that have opened offices and related facilities in other countries have had to learn to deal with different customs, social norms, and mores. Strategic alliances and foreign ownership have also contributed because managers today are more likely to have job assignments in other countries and/or to work with foreign managers within their own countries. As employees and managers move from assignment to assignment across national boundaries, organizations and their subsidiaries within each country thus become more diverse. Closely related to this pattern is a recent increase in immigration into the United States. As illustrated in Figure 16.1, for example, immigration declined steadily from 1900 until around 1930 but has been increasing since that time, except for a slight dip in the last decade.

FIGURE 16.1   Immigration Trends into the United States

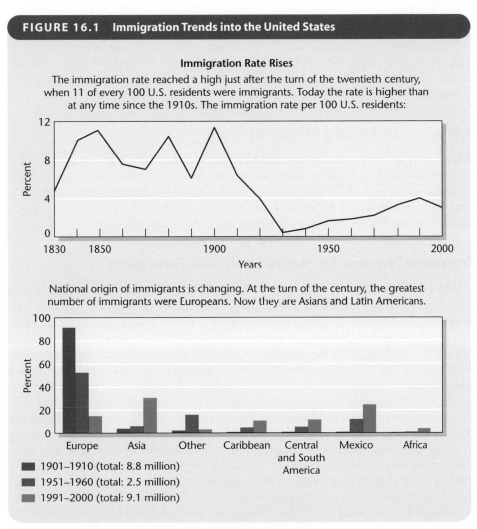

Immigration Rate Rises

The immigration rate reached a high just after the turn of the twentieth century, when 11 of every 100 U.S. residents were immigrants. Today the rate is higher than at any time since the 1910s. The immigration rate per 100 U.S. residents:

National origin of immigrants is changing. At the turn of the century, the greatest number of immigrants were Europeans. Now they are Asians and Latin Americans.

- 1901–1910 (total: 8.8 million)
- 1951–1960 (total: 2.5 million)
- 1991–2000 (total: 9.1 million)

Sources: USA Today, February 28, 1997, p. 7A; *2000 Statistical Yearbook of the Immigration and Naturalization Service* (Washington, D.C.: U.S. Government Printing Office, 2002).

DIVERSITY MANAGEMENT VERSUS EQUAL EMPLOYMENT OPPORTUNITY

■ **Equal employment oppor-tunity** means treating people fairly and equitably and taking actions that do not discriminate against people in protected classes on the basis of some illegal criterion.

■ **Diversity management** places a much heavier empha-sis on recognizing and appreci-ating differences among people at work and attempting to pro-vide accommodations for those differences to the extent that is feasible and possible.

Many managers assume that diversity and equal employment opportunity are the same. In fact, they have completely different meanings. **Equal employment oppor-tunity** means treating people fairly and equitably and taking actions that do not discriminate against people in protected classes on the basis of some illegal crite-rion. But **diversity management** places a much heavier emphasis on recognizing and appreciating differences among people at work and attempting to provide ac-commodations for those differences to the extent that is feasible and possible.

Similarities Among People at Work

Regardless of how different people appear to be, almost all employees share some fundamental similarities.[4] For example, most people work to satisfy some set of needs that are almost always based on financial criteria. Most people have a fundamental and basic desire to be treated with respect and dignity by their employer. And third, most people have a capacity for being reasonable and un-derstanding when confronted with reasonable behavior by others and when they recognize all the information relevant to a work setting.

Differences Among People at Work

Many people share some basic set of similar characteristics, but they also display various fundamental differences, a topic that will be discussed more fully in the next major section of the chapter. Common differences include gender, ethnicity, and age. But the list of differences among individuals is much longer and ranges from religious beliefs to dietary preferences, to political philosophies.

Identical Treatment Versus Equitable Treatment

In the years immediately following passage of Title VII of the 1964 Civil Rights Act, many human resource managers operated under the assumption that they were required by law to treat everyone equally. But in reality, that assumption is neither the intent of the law nor really even possible. The real essence not only of Title VII but of the more contemporary perspective on workforce diversity is that it is appropriate to acknowledge differences among people as long as people are treated fairly.

Consider religion, for example. A typical company in the United States rou-tinely gives days off to employees for basic Christian holidays such as Christmas. But people who have different religious beliefs may not acknowledge the sanctity of these religious holidays and instead have a different set of days that they asso-ciate with strong religious beliefs. Thus, an employer who provides Christian holidays off should also be sensitive to the need to provide important religious holidays off for various employees of different beliefs and faiths. The Whirlpool appliance factory near Nashville, Tennessee, for example, employs about 200 Muslims (about 10 percent of its workforce). The factory found it necessary to adjust its work schedules, cafeteria menus, and dress codes to accommodate workers who pray several times a day; don't eat pork; and wear loose-fitting clothing, head coverings, and sandals.[5]

Men and women are also fundamentally different in various ways that cannot be ignored. For example, on average, men have greater muscle mass than do women and can therefore lift heavier weight. And women have the biological capacity to bear children. Consequently, men and women may need fundamentally different treatment in work organizations. For example, women may need to be given longer periods of time off during the time immediately preceding and after the birth of a child. When a woman chooses to return to work after birth, the organization may need to provide a transitional period during which her work-related demands are lessened at first but then gradually increased over time.

The Americans with Disabilities Act (ADA) presents a serious challenge to managers who try to balance treating everyone the same with treating everyone equitably. The ADA specifically states that an organization cannot discriminate against a person with a disability as long as he or she can perform the essential functions of the job *with or without a reasonable accommodation.* Therefore, an employee who requests such an accommodation must be accommodated. At first glance, this situation may not appear problematic because the employee presumably needs this accommodation to perform his or her job. Many of the accommodations requested and granted, such as large-print computer screens, allowances for guide dogs, wheelchair ramps, or amplified phones, don't present a problem.

But what about an accommodation requested by a person with a disability that would be desirable and/or useful to other employees who do not have a disability? An interesting example of this dilemma occurred in early 1998 when the Professional Golf Association (PGA) ruled that Casey Martin, whose serious back problems made walking a golf course dangerous, would be allowed to use a golf cart in tournament play. Although there was disagreement over exactly how much of a difference this accommodation would make, many other golfers claimed that if they too were allowed to ride around the course, they would be less tired and so would play better. In this case, not only did other golfers want the same accommodation that had been granted to Martin, they also felt that it gave him an unfair competitive advantage.

Although Martin's case may be a particularly dramatic example of the problem, we can easily imagine other accommodations requested by a person with a disability would also be valued by other employees or that other employees might perceive the accommodation as an unfair advantage. Even in classroom settings, students often perceive it as unfair when a student with a disability is granted extra time for a test. Coworker resentment over the granting of accommodations can be a problem for all concerned. For the able-bodied employee, these accommodations may be perceived as unjust, leading to dissatisfaction on the job. For the disabled employee, the anticipated resentment may discourage him or her from asking for the accommodation needed to perform the job effectively. The manager's perspective, of course, focuses on the problem of balancing the concerns of the different parties.[6]

Again, the important message is for managers to recognize that differences among people exist. It is important first to acknowledge the differences and then to make reasonable accommodation to deal with these differences. The key issue, however, is to make sure that the acknowledgment and the accommodation are equitable—everyone needs to have an equal opportunity to contribute to and advance within the organization.

DIMENSIONS OF DIVERSITY

As indicated earlier, many different dimensions of diversity can be used to characterize an organization. In this section we discuss age, gender, ethnicity, disability, and other dimensions of diversity.

Age Distributions

One key dimension of diversity in any organization is the age distribution of its workers.[7] The average age of the U.S. workforce is gradually increasing and will continue to do so for the next several years. Several factors contribute to this pattern. The baby-boom generation (a term used to describe the unusually large number of people who were born in the twenty-year period following World War II) continues to age. Declining birth rates among the post-baby-boom generations simultaneously account for smaller percentages of new entrants into the labor force. Another factor that contributes to aging of the workforce is improved health and medical care. As a result of these improvements, people can remain productive and active for longer periods of time. Combined with higher legal limits for mandatory retirement, more and more people are working beyond the age at which they might have retired just a few years ago.

How does this trend affect human resource management? Older workers tend to have more experience, may be more stable, and can make greater contributions to productivity. On the other hand, despite the improvements in health and medical care, older workers are nevertheless likely to require higher levels of insurance coverage and medical benefits. As shown in Figure 16.2, accident rates increase substantially for older workers. After a person reaches the age of sixty-five, the likelihood of a fatal injury increases significantly. As discussed in HR in the 21st Century, the overall number of retirees combined with fewer younger members of the workforce may lead to future labor shortages, even though some workers are staying in the workforce longer.

In the U.S. there has been criticism of the "glass ceiling," which limits the ability of female managers to reach the top levels of management. While there is some evidence of cracks in this ceiling, female managers in some other countries face even more difficult barriers. For example, in Finland the sauna is as common a recreational activity for managers as golf is in the U.S. But as Finnish companies such as Nokia step onto the world stage, they are facing criticism for their sauna culture. The problem is rather simple. In Finland business is often conducted in saunas, most deals are made in saunas, and even visiting foreign business leaders are usually entertained in saunas. But the saunas are segregated by gender, so female managers (almost half the Finnish workforce is female) are excluded from the setting where much important business takes place. Although some multinationals have moved away from saunas as a place to do business, the sauna is very much part of the Finnish culture—and the sauna door is much harder to break through than the glass ceiling.

Gender

As more and more females have entered the workforce, organizations have subsequently experienced changes

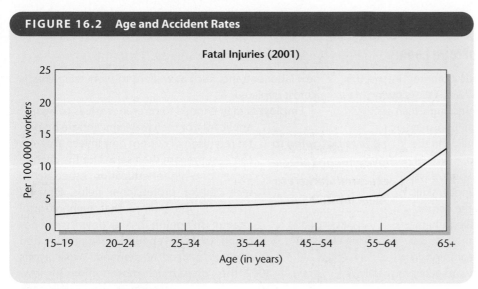

FIGURE 16.2 **Age and Accident Rates**

Fatal Injuries (2001)

*Excluding fatalities from September 11, 2001.

Source: Census of Fatal Occupational Injuries, Bureau of Labor Statistics, U.S. Department of Labor, 2001.

in the relative proportions of male and female employees. Figure 16.3 on page 517 highlights trends in gender composition (as well as ethnicity) in the workplace. As the figure shows clearly, the proportion of female employees to male employees has and will continue to increase gradually. For instance, projections show that by 2010 women will comprise 47.9 percent of the workforce, up from 45.2 percent in 1990 and 46.6 percent in 2000.

These trends aside, a significant gender-related problem that many organizations face today is the so-called glass ceiling, which was introduced in Chapter 2. The **glass ceiling** describes a barrier that keeps many females from advancing to top management positions in many organizations. This ceiling represents a real nonphysical barrier that is difficult to break but is also subtle. While women comprise almost 45 percent of all managers, only two female CEOs head two of the 1,000 largest businesses in the United States. Similarly, the average pay of females in organizations is lower than that of males. While the pay gap is gradually shrinking, inequalities are still present.

Why does the glass ceiling exist? One reason is that some male managers are still reluctant to promote female managers. Another is that many talented women choose to leave their jobs in larger organizations and start their own businesses. Still another factor is that some women choose to suspend or slow their career progression to have children.

■ The **glass ceiling** describes a barrier that keeps females from advancing to top management positions in many organizations.

Ethnicity

A third major dimension of cultural diversity in organizations is ethnicity. **Ethnicity** refers to the ethnic composition of a group or organization. Within the United States, most organizations reflect varying degrees of ethnicity and are comprised of whites, African-Americans, Hispanics, and Asians. Figure 16.3 also shows trends in the ethnic composition of the U.S. workforce.

■ **Ethnicity** refers to the ethic composition of a group or organization.

HR in the 21st Century

On the Horizon, a Labor Shortage Looms

 Layoffs have become common in the U.S. economy as businesses face slowing demand and a slackening high-tech sector. In October 2002, 4.1 million persons, out of a workforce of 130 million in the United States, were unemployed. However, James E. Oesterreicher, labor expert, says, "The U.S. faces a worker gap and a skills gap—and both are right around the corner." Even as the economy remains stalled, unemployment has held steady, at a modest 5.6 percent. Labor shortages are beginning in health care and construction. Harvard economist Dale W. Jorgenson claims, "If employers thought the '90s were the decade of the worker, the next decade will be even more that way."

The retirement of aging baby boomers is just one reason for the shortage. Another factor is the lower numbers of twenty-somethings entering the workforce. No untapped pockets of labor supply, such as women or immigrants, can contribute workers, as they did during the 1990s. In addition, work attitudes have shifted, and workers are more willing to leave jobs to gain time for leisure or family. The productivity gains that occurred over the last decade may be at a limit. "It would be almost impossible to match the increases of the past 20 years," says David T. Ellwood, Harvard economist. Finally, the pool of

"[W]e're not going to have enough college-educated workers to meet the demand."

(Harvard economist
David T. Ellwood)*

new labor entrants, such as welfare-to-work recipients, is almost depleted.

Employers may choose to offer incentives to attract applicants, or they may concentrate on better retention of current employees. Workers can best prepare themselves for the change by seeking higher education, especially in technical or professional fields. Ellwood states, "If you believe that technological change isn't going to slow down, we're not going to have enough college-educated workers to meet the demand." While layoffs grew in 2002, they grew much more rapidly for low-skilled workers than for professionals. John Challenger, CEO of an outplacement firm, claims, "Even when the economy is fully recovered and companies are back in expansion mode, we may not see a revival in hiring of the rank-and-file worker." The proverb "A rising tide raises all boats" may be true, but it may not raise all boats equally.

Sources: Aaron Bernstein, "Too Many Workers? Not for Long," *Business Week,* May 20, 2002, pp. 45–48 (*quote on p. 45); "Lower Paid Workers Face Job Cuts," *CNN Money,* September 10, 2002, money.cnn.com, accessed November 23, 2002; "Statement of U.S. Secretary of Labor Elaine L. Chao on Unemployment Numbers for October 2002," U.S. Department of Labor, November 23, 2002, www.dol.gov, accessed November 23, 2002; "Table A-7. Reason for Unemployment," *U.S. Bureau of Labor Statistics,* November 1, 2002, www.bls.gov, accessed November 23, 2002.

The biggest projected changes involve whites and Hispanics. In particular, the percentage of whites in the workforce is expected to drop to 69.2 percent by 2010, down from 73.1 percent in 2000 and 77.7 percent in 1990. At the same time, the percentage of Hispanics is expected to climb to 13.3 percent by 2010, up from 10.9 percent in 2000 and 8.5 percent in 1990. The percentage of blacks is expected to remain relatively stable (10.9 percent in 1990, 11.8 percent in 2000, and 12.7 percent in 2010). Finally, Asians and others are expected to represent 6.1 percent of the U.S. workforce in 2010, up from 4.7 percent in 2000 and 3.7 percent in 1990.

As with women, members of the African-American, Hispanic, and Asian groups are generally underrepresented in the executive ranks of most organizations today, as well as in several different occupational groups. And their pay is similarly lower than might be expected. But as is the case for women, the differences are gradually disappearing as organizations fully embrace equal employment opportunity and recognize the higher overall level of talent available to them. Table 16.1 shows

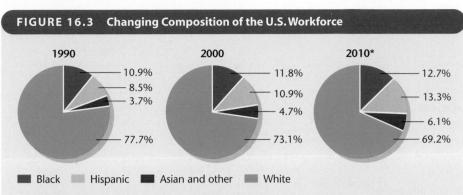

FIGURE 16.3   Changing Composition of the U.S. Workforce

The shifting racial and ethnic makeup of the U.S. work force: number of workers by race and ethnic origin and their share of the total civilian labor force.

Numbers (thousands)	1990	2000	2010*	Percent	1990	2000	2010*
Total	125,840	140,863	157,721	Total	100.0	100.0	100.0
Men	69,011	75,247	82,221	Men	54.8	53.4	52.1
Women	56,829	65,616	75,500	Women	45.2	46.6	47.9
White, non-Hispanic	97,818	102,963	109,118	White, non-Hispanic	77.7	73.1	69.2
Men	53,731	55,359	57,538	Men	42.7	39.3	36.5
Women	44,087	47,604	51,580	Women	35.0	33.8	32.7
Black, non-Hispanic	13,740	16,603	20,041	Black, non-Hispanic	10.9	11.8	12.7
Men	6,802	7,816	8,991	Men	5.4	5.5	5.7
Women	6,938	8,787	11,050	Women	5.5	6.2	7.0
Hispanic origin	10,720	15,368	20,947	Hispanic origin	8.5	10.9	13.3
Men	6,546	8,919	11,723	Men	5.2	6.3	7.4
Women	4,174	6,449	9,224	Women	3.3	4.6	5.8
Asian and other, non-Hispanic	4,653	6,687	9,636	Asian and other, non-Hispanic	3.7	4.7	6.1
Men	2,572	3,570	5,070	Men	2.0	2.5	3.2
Women	2,081	3,116	4,566	Women	1.7	2.2	2.9

Projection

Source: U.S. Department of Labor, Bureau of Labor Statistics, *Monthly Labor Review,* November 2001, http://www.bls.gov.

trends in different occupations for blacks and Hispanics (see the next page). For example, the percentage of blacks and Hispanics comprising several different kinds of business roles plus various professional specialties increased substantially from 1983 to 2002.

Disability

Disability is another significant dimension of diversity. Disabilities can range from hearing impairments to missing fingers or limbs, to blindness, to paralysis.

TABLE 16.1   Employment of Blacks and Hispanics in Selected Occupations, 1983 and 2002*

	Blacks		Hispanics	
	1983	2002	1983	2002
Total workforce, 16 years of age and over	9.3%	10.9%	5.3%	12.2%
Occupation				
Executive, administrative, and managerial	4.7	7.6	2.8	6.3
Officials and administrators in public administration	8.3	13.0	3.8	7.6
Financial managers	3.5	8.4	3.1	6.8
Personnel and labor relations managers	4.9	8.0	2.6	5.1
Purchasing managers	5.1	6.6	1.4	4.7
Managers in marketing, advertising, and public relations	2.7	3.7	1.7	4.9
Managers in medicine and health care	5.0	9.5	2.0	6.2
Accountants and auditors	5.5	9.0	3.3	6.0
Management analysts	5.3	6.2	1.7	2.5
Professional specialty	6.4	8.3	2.5	5.3
Architects	1.6	2.3	1.5	5.2
Engineers	2.7	4.5	2.2	4.0
Mathematical and computer scientists	5.4	7.3	2.6	5.1
Natural scientists	2.6	4.1	2.1	2.9
Physicians	3.2	5.0	4.5	5.8
Dentists	2.4	4.0	1.0	3.3
College and university teachers	4.4	5.4	1.8	5.4
Economists	6.3	6.2	2.7	4.6
Psychologists	8.6	9.5	1.1	3.8
Lawyers	2.6	4.6	0.9	3.1
Authors	2.1	2.3	0.9	3.8
Musicians and composers	7.9	12.9	4.4	5.8
Editors and reporters	2.9	4.7	2.1	3.3

*Data for 1983 and 2002 are not strictly comparable.
Minorities as a percentage of total employed.

Sources: Data for 1983: *The Wall Street Journal Almanac 1999,* p. 241. © 1999 Dow Jones and Company, Inc. All rights reserved. Data for 2002: U.S. Department of Labor, Bureau of Labor Statistics, http://www.bls.gov.

The presence of a disability represents another aspect of diversity in organizations, but among persons who have disabilities, some differences are important as well. That is, unlike other dimensions of diversity, reactions to persons with disabilities vary dramatically as a function of several dimensions of the disability. One of these dimensions is termed "origin." That is, if the disability is perceived as being avoidable (for example, someone who has been injured while driving drunk), coworkers are likely to react more negatively to the disability than when the problem was unavoidable (for example, a person who was born blind).

Another dimension is the aesthetic aspect of the disability, with disabilities that are more disfiguring being perceived more negatively. A third and critical dimension refers to the nature of the disability itself. For example, although mental disabilities might be easier to conceal, they are also more frightening to coworkers. Disabilities related to stress or to back injuries are not as physically obvious and so, when individuals with these disabilities request and are granted an accommodation, resentment by coworkers is more likely.[8]

Other Dimensions of Diversity

In addition to age, gender, ethnicity, and disability status, organizations are also confronting other dimensions of diversity. Country of national origin is a dimension of diversity that can be especially important for global organizations. This dimension can be particularly significant when different languages are involved. Single parents, dual-career couples, gays and lesbians, people with special dietary preferences (e.g., vegetarians), and people with different political ideologies and viewpoints also represent significant dimensions of diversity in today's organizations.

THE IMPACT OF DIVERSITY ON ORGANIZATIONS

No doubt organizations are becoming ever-more diverse. But what is the impact of this diversity on organizations? As we will see, diversity provides both opportunities and challenges for organizations. Diversity also plays several important roles in organizations today.

Diversity and Social Change

Diversity can have a significant impact on organizations as a force for social change. This change generally occurs as the composition of an organization's workforce gradually begins to mirror the composition of its surrounding labor market. For example, if a manager in an organization learns to interact effectively with a diverse set of people at work, it follows logically that she or he will be better equipped to deal with a diverse set of people in other settings. And conversely, an individual who is comfortable interacting in diverse settings should have little problem dealing with diversity at work. Thus, diversity in organizations both facilitates and is facilitated by social change in the environment.

Another way that organizations affect social change is through the images they use to promote themselves and their products. An organization that runs print ads showing nothing but white male executives in its workplace conveys a certain image of itself. In contrast, an organization that uses diverse groups as representatives conveys a different image.

Diversity and Competitiveness

Many organizations are also finding that diversity can be a source of competitive advantage in the marketplace. In general, six arguments have been proposed for how diversity contributes to competitiveness.[9] These six arguments are illustrated in Figure 16.4.

The *cost argument* suggests that organizations that learn to cope with diversity will generally have higher levels of productivity and lower levels of turnover and absenteeism. Organizations that do a poor job of managing diversity, on the other hand, will suffer from problems of lower productivity and higher levels of turnover and absenteeism. Because each of these factors has a direct impact on costs, the former organization will remain more competitive than will the latter. Ortho Pharmaceuticals estimates that it has saved $500,000 by lowering turnover among women and ethnic minorities.

The *resource acquisition argument* for diversity suggests that organizations that manage diversity effectively will become known among women and minorities as good places to work. These organizations will thus be in a better position to attract qualified employees from among these groups. Given the increased importance of these groups in the overall labor force, organizations that can attract talented employees from all segments of society are likely to be more competitive.

The *marketing argument* suggests that organizations with diverse workforces will be able to understand different market segments better than will less diverse organizations. For example, a cosmetics firm like Avon that wants to sell its products to women and blacks can better understand how to create such products and market them effectively if women and black managers are available to provide input into product development, design, packaging, advertising, and so forth.

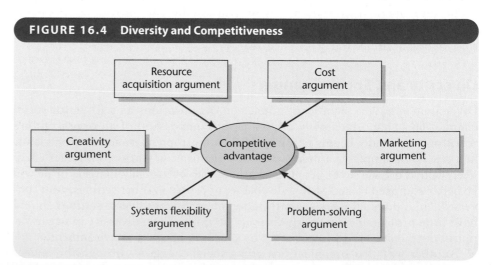

FIGURE 16.4   Diversity and Competitiveness

Source: Ricky W. Griffin, *Management*, 7th ed. (Boston: Houghton Mifflin, 2002), p. 175. Copyright © 2002 Houghton Mifflin Company. Reprinted by permission.

The *creativity argument* for diversity suggests that organizations with diverse workforces will generally be more creative and innovative than will less diverse organizations. If an organization is dominated by one population segment, its members will generally adhere to norms and ways of thinking that reflect that population segment. They will have little insight or few stimuli for new ideas that might be derived from different perspectives. HR Around the Globe explores this idea in more detail. The diverse organization, in contrast, will be characterized by multiple perspectives and ways of thinking and is therefore more likely to generate new ideas and ways of doing things.

Related to the creativity argument is the *problem-solving argument*. Diversity carries with it an increased pool of information. In almost any organization, there is some information that everyone has, and other information is unique to each individual. In an organization with little diversity, the larger pool of information is common and the smaller pool is unique. But in a more diverse organization, the unique information is larger. Thus, if more information can be brought to bear on a problem, the probability is higher that better solutions will be identified.[10]

Finally, the *systems flexibility argument* for diversity suggests that organizations must become more flexible as a way of managing a diverse workforce. As a direct consequence, the overall organizational system will also become more flexible. Organizational flexibility enables the organization to respond better to changes in its environment. Thus, by effectively managing diversity within its workforce, an organization simultaneously becomes better equipped to address its environment.[11]

Diversity and Conflict

Diversity in an organization can also become a major source of conflict.[12] This conflict can arise for different reasons. One potential avenue for conflict is when an individual thinks that someone has been hired, promoted, or fired because of her or his diversity status.[13] For example, suppose a male executive loses a promotion to a female executive. If he believes that she was promoted because the organization simply wanted to have more female managers rather than because she was the better candidate for the job, he will likely feel resentful toward both her and the organization itself.

Firms that have resisted efforts to diversify their workforce often argue that a diverse workforce can hurt a strong corporate culture. Critics of such firms have argued that maintaining a culture is merely an excuse to discriminate. The clash between diversity and culture has become quite clear at Wal-Mart. Wal-Mart, a company that likes to think of employees as family and vows to treat everyone with respect, is facing a huge discrimination suit on behalf of the firm's female employees. Stephanie Odle, a former assistant manager for Wal-Mart who discovered that she was being paid $10,000 less per year than a male assistant manager, was the catalyst for what will be the largest sex discrimination case (Dukes v. Wal-Mart) in history, covering some 1.5 million current and former Wal-Mart employees. Part of the problem is that the Wal-Mart culture is built upon the Wal-Mart way of doing things. For example, Wal-Mart does not post openings for management training positions because it believes that would be too bureaucratic; store managers are absolutely trusted to promote the most qualified people. Also, there are no companywide statistics on diversity because, again, managers are trusted to do what is right. However, it is alleged that these practices have been partly responsible for the fact that only 14.5 percent of Wal-Mart managers are women while 66 percent of the total workforce is female, and female managers earn an average of $89,000 annually versus almost $106,000 for male managers.

Too Little Diversity?

It's no secret, of course, that many businesses from Japan and South Korea have been highly successful in recent years. But some experts question whether or not the lack of diversity that exists in those firms will still be an advantage in the future. To see how little diversity exists, consider the case of Samsung Electronics, a huge Korean business. The firm's board of directors consists of nineteen members, all male. Fifteen of them have worked for the firm for at least twenty years, and eight even attended the same university. Japan's Honda Motor Co. is quite similar—its board is all Japanese, as is every president of each Honda foreign subsidiary.

Executives at these firms defend their hiring and promotion practices. They argue, for example, that their lack of diversity reduces management conflict, smoothes decision making, and ensures that top management is both

> *"Cohesiveness of corporation is more important to [the] Japanese. They are not well-trained in managing different nationalities. They are more comfortable in [their own] group."*
>
> (Kaoru Kobayashi, Japanese professor)*

loyal to and knowledgeable about the business. It also enhances cohesiveness among key leaders because they tend to see situations the same way and to have similar interests.

But critics point out that the lack of diversity also creates problems. For example, some experts contend that executives from Japan and Korea do not understand people from other cultures and thus treat them cavalierly and with disdain. By not relying more on foreigners, Japanese and Korean firms may also be less knowledgeable about international laws and regulations. And some critics even predict that the lack of executive diversity may dampen creativity and innovation, potentially causing Japanese and Korean firms to be less competitive in the future.

Sources: "Men's Club," *Wall Street Journal,* September 26, 1996, pp. A1, A8 (*quote on p. A1); "Tight Little Island," *Forbes,* January 12, 1998, pp. 52–53; "Seoul Is Still Teetering on the Edge," *Business Week,* January 5, 1998, pp. 56–57.

Continuing conflict apparently exists among whites and blacks within the ranks of the Federal Aviation Administration (FAA). Some blacks have charged that their white supervisors are prejudiced and that they are subject to various subtle forms of discrimination. Some whites, however, believe that the government agency has hired some blacks who really aren't qualified for the job of air traffic controller because it cannot attract a significant number of qualified employees.[14]

Another source of conflict stemming from diversity is through misunderstood, misinterpreted, or inappropriate interactions between people of different groups. For example, suppose a male executive tells a sexually explicit joke to a new female executive. He may intentionally be trying to embarrass her, he may be trying clumsily to show her that he treats everyone the same, or he may think he is making her feel like part of the team. Regardless of his intent, however, if she finds the joke offensive, she will justifiably feel anger and hostility. These feelings may be directed only at the offending individual or more generally toward the entire organization if she believes that its culture facilitates such behavior. Of course, sexual harassment itself is both unethical and illegal.

Some evidence suggests that conflict may be especially pronounced between older and younger women in the workplace. Older women may be more likely to have sacrificed family for career and to have overcome higher obstacles to get ahead—they were, in a sense, trailblazers. Younger women, on the other hand, may find that organizational accommodations make it relatively easy for them to balance multiple roles and may also have a less pronounced sense of having to fight to get ahead.[15]

Conflict can also result from other elements of diversity. For example, suppose a U.S. manager publicly praises the work of a Japanese employee for his outstanding work. The manager's action stems from the dominant cultural belief in the United States that such recognition is important and rewarding. But because the Japanese culture places a much higher premium on group loyalty and identity than on individual accomplishment, the employee will likely feel ashamed and embarrassed. Thus, a well-intentioned action may backfire and result in unhappiness.

Conflict can arise as a result of fear, distrust, or individual prejudice. Members of the dominant group in an organization may worry that newcomers from other groups pose a personal threat to their own position in the organization. For example, when U.S. firms have been taken over by Japanese firms, U.S. managers have sometimes been resentful or hostile to Japanese managers assigned to work with them. People may also be unwilling to accept people who are different from themselves. And personal bias and prejudices are still very real among some people today and can lead to potentially harmful conflict. The Lighter Side of HR cleverly illustrates this point.

The Lighter Side of HR

While any number of strong arguments—legal, moral, ethical, and economic—can be offered for increased diversity in organizations, costs and/or inconveniences must also be borne. Differences among people may increase conflict and make it more complicated for them to work together. As shown in this cartoon, individuals sometimes lament the "old days" when everyone they worked with was alike. Nevertheless, these arguments against diversity are extremely modest when compared to the myriad reasons for greater diversity in organizations. (The New Yorker Collection 1993 Mort Gerberg from cartoonbank.com. All Rights Reserved.)

"I think I preferred it *before* he became an equal-opportunity employer."

MANAGING DIVERSITY IN ORGANIZATIONS

Because of the tremendous potential that diversity holds for competitive advantage, as well as the possible consequences of diversity-related conflict, much attention has been focused in recent years on how individuals and organizations can manage diversity better. In the following sections we first discuss individual strategies for dealing with diversity and then summarize organizational approaches to managing diversity.

Individual Strategies for Dealing with Diversity

One key element of managing diversity in an organization consists of actions that individuals themselves can take. Individuals can strive for understanding, empathy, tolerance, and communication.

Understanding   The first element in the strategy is understanding the nature and meaning of diversity. Some managers have taken the basic concepts of equal employment opportunity to an unnecessary extreme. They know that, by law, they cannot discriminate against people on the basis of gender, race, and so forth. Thus, in following this mandate they come to believe that they must treat everyone the same.

But this belief can cause problems when it is translated into workplace behaviors among people after they have been hired. As noted earlier, people are not the same. While people need to be treated fairly and equitably, managers must understand that differences do exist among people. Thus, any effort to treat everyone the same, without regard to their fundamental human differences, only leads to problems. Therefore it is important for managers to understand that cultural factors cause people to behave in different ways and that these differences should be accepted.

Empathy   Related to understanding is empathy. People in an organization should try to understand the perspective of others. For example, suppose a group that has traditionally been comprised of white males is joined by a female member. Each male may be a little self-conscious about how to act toward its new member and may be interested in making her feel comfortable and welcome. But they may be able to do this even more effectively by empathizing with how she may feel. For example, she may feel disappointed or elated about her new assignment, she may be confident or nervous about her position in the group, and she may be experienced or inexperienced in working with male colleagues. By learning more about these and similar circumstances, the existing group members can facilitate their ability to work together effectively.

Tolerance   A third related individual approach to dealing with diversity is tolerance. Even though managers learn to understand diversity, and even though they may try to empathize with others, the fact remains that they may still not accept or enjoy some aspect or behavior on the part of others. For example, one organization recently reported that it was experiencing considerable conflict among its U.S. and Israeli employees. The Israeli employees always seemed to want to argue about every issue that arose. The U.S. managers preferred a more harmonious way of conducting business and became uncomfortable with the conflict. Finally, after considerable discussion, it was learned that many Israeli employees simply enjoy arguing and see it as part of getting work done. The firm's U.S. employees still do not enjoy the arguing but are more willing to tolerate it as a fundamental cultural difference between themselves and their Israeli colleagues.

Communication   A final individual approach to dealing with diversity is communication. Problems often become magnified over diversity issues because people are afraid or otherwise unwilling to discuss issues that relate to diversity. For example, suppose a younger employee has a habit of making jokes about the age of an elderly colleague. Perhaps the younger colleague means no harm and is just engaging in what she sees as good-natured kidding. But the older employee may find the jokes offensive. If the two do not communicate, the jokes will continue and the resentment will grow. Eventually, what started as a minor problem may erupt into a much bigger one.

For communication to work, it must be two-way. If a person wonders if a certain behavior on her or his part is offensive to someone else, the curious individual should probably just ask. Similarly, if someone is offended by the behavior of another person, he or she should explain to the offending individual how the behavior is perceived and request that it stop. As long as such exchanges are handled in a friendly, low-key, and nonthreatening fashion, they will generally have a positive outcome. Of course, if the same message is presented in an overly combative manner or if a person continues to engage in offensive behavior after having been asked to stop, the problem will escalate. At this point, third parties within the organization may have to intervene. And in fact, most organizations today have one or more systems in place to address questions and problems that arise as a result of diversity. We now turn our attention to the various ways that organizations can indeed manage diversity better.

Organizational Strategies for Dealing with Diversity

Individuals can play an important role in managing diversity, but the organization itself must also play a fundamental role. Through its various policies and practices, people in the organization come to understand which behaviors are appropriate and which are not. Diversity training is an even more direct method for managing diversity. The organization's culture is the ultimate context that diversity must address.

Organizational policies   Managing diversity starts with the policies that an organization adopts because they directly or indirectly affect how people are treated. Obviously, the extent to which an organization embraces the premise of equal employment opportunity determines to a large extent the potential diversity within an organization. But differences exist between the organization that follows the law to the letter and practices passive discrimination and the organization that actively seeks a diverse and varied workforce.

Another aspect of organizational policies that affects diversity is how the organization addresses and responds to problems that arise from diversity. Consider the example of a manager charged with sexual harassment. If the organization's policies put an excessive burden of proof on the individual being harassed and invoke only minor sanctions against the guilty party, it is sending a clear signal about the importance of such matters. But the organization that has a balanced set of policies for addressing questions like sexual harassment sends its employees a different message about the importance of diversity and individual rights and privileges.

Indeed, perhaps the major policy through which an organization can reflect its stance on diversity is its mission statement. If the organization's mission statement articulates a clear and direct commitment to diversity, everyone who reads that mission statement will grow to understand and accept the importance of diversity, at least to that particular organization.

As a result of some of the issues raised above, people have argued that increased diversity should not be a major goal of most organizations. These individuals are not necessarily arguing that diversity is not worth achieving but simply that so many problems are associated with increased diversity that it should not be a major focus of organizations. Our Point/Counterpoint feature for this chapter addresses some of these disagreements.

Organizational practices   Organizations can also help manage diversity through various ongoing practices and procedures. Avon's creation of networks for various groups represents one example of an organizational practice that fosters diversity. In general, the idea is that, because diversity is characterized by differences among people, organizations can manage that diversity more effectively by following practices and procedures based on flexibility rather than rigidity.

Benefits packages, for example, can be structured to accommodate individual situations. An employee who is part of a dual-career couple and has no children may require relatively little insurance (perhaps because his spouse's employer provides more complete coverage) and would like to be able to schedule vacations to coincide with those of his spouse. Another employee who is a single parent may need a wide variety of insurance coverage and prefer to schedule his vacation time to coincide with school holidays.

Flexible working hours can help an organization accommodate diversity. Differences in family arrangements, religious holidays, cultural events, and so forth, may each require that employees have some degree of flexibility in their work schedules. For example, a single parent may need to leave the office every day at 4:30 to pick up the children from their daycare center. An organization that truly values diversity will make every reasonable attempt to accommodate such a need.

Organizations can also facilitate diversity by making sure that diversity exists in its key committees and executive teams. Even if diversity exists within the broader organizational context, an organization that does not reflect diversity in groups like committees and teams implies that diversity is not a fully ingrained element of its culture. In contrast, if all major groups and related work assignments reflect diversity, the message is a quite different one.

Diversity training   Many organizations are finding that diversity training is an effective means for managing diversity and minimizing its associated conflict. **Diversity training** is specifically designed to enable members of an organization to function better in a diverse workplace. This training can take various forms.[16] As discussed in HR Legal Brief, diversity training has to be undertaken all too often to remedy specific problems or crises that have erupted. But many organizations find it useful to help people learn more about their similarities and differences for other reasons.

■ **Diversity training** is specifically designed to enable members of an organization to function better in a diverse workplace.

POINT | COUNTERPOINT

Should Organizations Strive to Increase Diversity?

We have discussed the various advantages associated with increased diversity. These advantages range from reduced legal problems to improving social welfare and increasing productivity. Yet increased diversity can also bring problems and so increase costs. Some of these potential costs are serious enough for some to argue that increased diversity should not be a major goal of organizations.

POINT... Organizations should strive to increase diversity because...	COUNTERPOINT... Organizations should *not* strive to increase diversity because...
It leads to a wider set of ideas and viewpoints to consider.	It results in more conflict.
It allows an organization to take full advantage of all available human resources.	Strong organizational cultures require more homogeneity.
It makes an organization more competitive.	Selection approaches that emphasize fit between employees and organizations suggest that diverse employees will not fit in as well.
It is the socially responsible thing to do.	It is important that an organization *not* violate the law; striving toward diversity is superfluous.

So... Increased diversity clearly has some advantages, but arguments against diversity as an important goal still exist. The organization must decide how important are the advantages and how critical are the potential costs. In most cases, though, increasing diversity seems to make sense as an important organizational goal.

Men and women can be taught to work together more effectively and can gain insights into how their own behaviors affect and are interpreted by others. In one organization, a diversity training program helped male managers gain insights into how various remarks they made to one another could be interpreted by others as being sexist. In the same organization, female managers learned how to point out their discomfort with those remarks without appearing overly hostile.

Similarly, white and black managers may need training to understand each other better. Managers at Mobil noticed that four black colleagues never seemed to eat lunch together. After a diversity training program, they realized that the black managers felt that if they ate together, their white colleagues would be overly curious about what they were talking about. Thus, they avoided close associations with one another because they feared calling attention to themselves.

Some organizations go so far as to provide language training for their employees as a vehicle for managing diversity. Motorola, for example, provides English language training for its foreign employees on assignment in the United States. At Pace Foods in San Antonio, Texas, staff meetings and employee handbooks are translated into Spanish for the benefit of the company's 100 Hispanic employees (out of a total payroll of 350 employees).

HR Legal Brief

The Merits of Diversity Training?

Texaco executives made headlines a few years ago when a tape-recorded conversation in which they made racially insulting remarks was made public. About the same time, AT&T came under fire when a company newsletter used images of monkeys to represent people in Africa. And Denny's, the popular restaurant chain, attracted national attention over charges that it discriminated against minority customers and employees.

In each case, company officials made public apologies and offered restitution to those who were most directly offended. Another response from each company was an announcement that key managers throughout the firm must participate in diversity training. Diversity training, as the term suggests, is designed to help individuals better understand people who are different from themselves.

"The objective is to help managers and supervisors to understand how unconscious behavior can impact employees, how differences can get in the way of productivity in the workplace and how to leverage diversity as a competitive advantage."

(Edward N. Gadsden, Jr., Texaco's diversity director)*

Such training is supposed to help people understand the beliefs, values, and life styles of others and to make them more tolerant and accepting of diverse points of view. Many experts believe that a well-planned and well-delivered diversity training program can indeed help people become more tolerant of others. On the other hand, some critics believe that such training addresses only surface-level issues. For example, some of the terms that the Texaco executives used disparagingly had been learned in a diversity program!

Sources: "A 3Com Factory Hires a Lot of Immigrants, Gets Mix of Languages," *Wall Street Journal,* March 30, 1998, pp. A1, A12; "Do Diversity Programs Make a Difference?" *Wall Street Journal,* December 4, 1996, p. B1 (*quote on p. B1).

Organizational culture   The ultimate test of an organization's commitment to managing diversity is its culture. Unless there is a basic and fundamental belief that diversity is valued, it cannot become a truly integral part of an organization, regardless of what managers say or put in writing. An organization that really wants to promote diversity must shape its culture so that it clearly underscores top management commitment to and support of diversity in all of its forms throughout every part of the organization. With top management support, and reinforced with a clear and consistent set of organizational policies and practices, diversity can become a basic and fundamental part of an organization.

THE MULTICULTURAL ORGANIZATION

■ The **multicultural organization** is one that has achieved high levels of diversity, one that can capitalize fully on the advantages of the diversity, and one that has few diversity-related problems.

Many organizations today are grappling with cultural diversity. While organizations are becoming more diverse, there are few truly multicultural organizations. The **multicultural organization** is one that has achieved high levels of diversity, one that can capitalize fully on the advantages of the diversity, and one that has few diversity-related problems.[17] One recent article described the six basic characteristics of such an organization.[18] These six basic characteristics are illustrated in Figure 16.5.

FIGURE 16.5 The Multicultural Organization

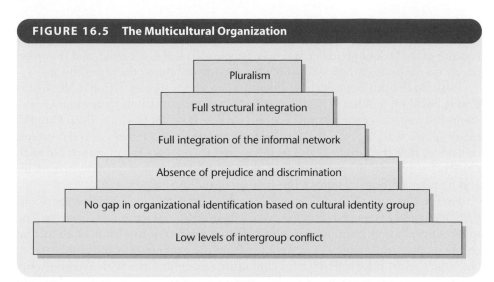

Pluralism

Full structural integration

Full integration of the informal network

Absence of prejudice and discrimination

No gap in organizational identification based on cultural identity group

Low levels of intergroup conflict

Source: Based on Taylor H. Cox, "The Multicultural Organization," *Academy of Management Executive*, May 1991, pp. 34–47. Copyright © 1991 by Academy of Management. Reprinted by permission of Academy of Management via Copyright Clearance Center.

A multicultural organization is one in which diversity and the appreciation of all cultures is simply the way business is done. Some people think of UPS as a somewhat old-fashioned company, and it certainly isn't as splashy as some of its competitors in the shipping industry. But that doesn't mean that UPS is behind the curve in multiculturalism. Jovita Carranza, the company's highest-ranking Hispanic female executive, began working at UPS twenty-seven years ago. She says she never asked for a promotion, but more responsibility came as a result of doing a good job. She now oversees the daily loading and unloading of 1.5 million packages and the 20,000 employees who handle them as they come through UPS Worldport, a four-million-square-foot facility, in Louisville. She notes that there is no diversity officer or diversity committee at UPS. Instead, she notes that diversity and multiculturalism are just part of the way UPS does business.

First, the multicultural organization is characterized by pluralism. Every group represented in an organization works to understand every other group better. Thus, black employees try to understand white employees, and white employees try just as hard to understand their black colleagues. In addition, every group represented within an organization has the potential to influence the organization's culture and its fundamental norms.

Second, the multicultural organization achieves full structural integration. Full structural integration suggests that the diversity within an organization is a complete and accurate reflection of the organization's external labor market. If about half of the labor market is female, then about half of the organization's employees are female. This same proportion is reflected at all levels of the organization. No glass ceilings or other subtle forms of discrimination exist in the organization.

Third, the multicultural organization achieves full integration of its informal networks. This characteristic suggests that no barriers to entry and participation in any organizational activity exist. For example, people enter and exit lunch groups, social networks, communication grapevines, and other informal aspects of organizational activity without regard to age, gender, ethnicity, or other dimension of diversity.

Fourth, the multicultural organization is characterized by an absence of prejudice and discrimination. No traces

of bias exist and prejudice is eliminated. Discrimination is not practiced in any shape, form, or fashion. Discrimination is nonexistent not because it is illegal but because of the lack of prejudice and bias. People are valued, accepted, and rewarded purely on the basis of their skills and what they contribute to the organization.

Fifth, in the multicultural organization, no gap in organizational identification is based on a cultural identity group. Many organizations tend to make presumptions about organizational roles based on group identity. For example, many people walking into an office and seeing a male and female conversing tend to assume that the female is the secretary and the male is the manager. No such tendencies exist in the multicultural organization. People recognize that males and females are equally likely to be managers and secretaries.

Finally, the multicultural organization experiences low levels of intergroup conflict. We noted earlier that conflict is a likely outcome of increased diversity. The multicultural organization has evolved beyond this point to a state of almost no conflict among different people. People within the organization fully understand, empathize with, have tolerance for, and openly communicate with everyone else. Values, premises, motives, attitudes, and perceptions are so well understood by everyone that any conflict that does arise involves meaningful and work-related issues as opposed to differences in age, gender, ethnicity, or other dimensions of diversity.

Chapter Summary

Diversity exists in a group or organization when its members differ from one another along one or more important dimensions. Diversity is increasing in organizations today because of changing demographics, the desire by organizations to improve their workforce, legal pressures, and increased globalization.

Diversity management and equal employment opportunity may appear to be the same, but they are in fact quite different. Equal employment opportunity is intended to eliminate discrimination in the workplace; management diversity focuses on recognizing and accommodating differences among people.

Diversity involves several key dimensions. Four of the more common are age, gender, ethnicity, and disability. The overall age of the workforce is increasing. More women are also entering the workplace, although a glass ceiling still exists in many settings. In the United States, more Hispanics are entering the workplace as the percentage of whites in the general population gradually declines.

Diversity affects organizations in many different ways. Diversity also serves as a force for social change. Many organizations are realizing that diversity can be a major force for competitive advantage. Finally, diversity can also be a significant source of conflict.

Managing diversity in organizations can be done by both individuals and the organization itself. Individual approaches to dealing with diversity include understanding, empathy, tolerance, and communication. Major organizational approaches are through policies, practices, diversity training, and culture.

Few, if any, organizations have become truly multicultural. The key dimensions that characterize organizations as they eventually achieve this state are pluralism, full structural integration, full integration of the informal network, an absence of prejudice and discrimination, no gap in organizational identification based on a cultural identity group, and low levels of intergroup conflict attributable to diversity.

Key Points for Future HR Managers

▶ While equal employment opportunity is the law, effective management of diversity in the workplace is critical for gaining and maintaining competitive advantage.

▶ Effective diversity management requires recognition of how people are similar to and how they are different from one another. It also requires respect for the differences that do exist.

▶ The workforce is becoming much more diverse. The workforce is aging, more women have entered the workforce, the workforce is becoming more ethnically diverse, and the number of persons with disabilities is rising. Each of these trends presents special challenges to human resource managers.

▶ Increased diversity has the potential to allow the firm to acquire more valued employees, to raise levels of productivity, to market its goods and services more effectively to a broader segment of the population, and to increase its levels of creativity. Conflict can also increase as diversity increases.

▶ Effective management of diversity and the development of multicultural organizations require a clear and strong commitment from the highest levels in the organization.

Key Points for Future General Managers

▶ Managing diversity is critical for the company that wants to remain competitive in the new century. Extremely effective diversity management can lead to a strong competitive advantage as a firm becomes more attractive to a broader set of applicants, has easier access to a broader set of markets, and increases creativity within the firm.

▶ Effective diversity management is a full-time job and requires strong and consistent support from top management.

Review and Discussion Questions

1. Define diversity.

2. What are the basic trends in diversity in the United States today? What accounts for these trends?

3. Distinguish between identical treatment and equitable treatment in an organizational setting.

4. What are the four most common bases of diversity that are relevant to managers and their organizations?

5. What trends are apparent regarding age, gender, and ethnicity in the workplace?

6. How does diversity contribute to competitiveness?

7. How does diversity contribute to conflict?

8. Identify and discuss various individual strategies for managing diversity.

9. Identify and discuss various organizational strategies for managing diversity.

10. What is a multicultural organization? Do you think such an organization exists?

Closing Case

The Avon Way

Women have always played an important role at Avon, the largest cosmetics firm in the United States. Starting with the first Avon Lady in 1886, women have long been the foundation of the firm's marketing and sales efforts. And Avon has always employed a lot of women throughout its organization. But control always remained in the hands of the small group of men who ran the company. A series of disastrous decisions and setbacks in the 1980s, however, caused the firm to rethink its philosophies and to promote its best middle managers, many of them women, into the executive ranks. And as a result, Avon has turned itself around. Today the firm is known for both its exemplary financial performance and its acceptance of all people, regardless of their gender, skin color, or age.

Avon's problems started in the 1970s, when its top management team tried to change the firm's strategy. This group of predominantly male managers first ignored their own marketing research about women consumers and shifting career patterns, which had indicated that more women were entering the workforce and seeking professional careers. In particular, they failed to recognize that the personal-care products preferred by women were also changing. Then, in the 1980s, they tried to buck emerging trends and to diversify with a number of ill-conceived acquisitions. Finally, as the firm was on the brink of bankruptcy, a new top management team was brought in. Led by chief executive officer (CEO) Jim Preston, Avon refocused itself on its roots and began to market cosmetics again to a largely female market, albeit a very different market.

But this time the firm adopted new approaches. It decided to recognize and reward managerial talent rather than the gender of the individual manager. As a result, more women were promoted into higher-level positions. In addition, Preston shifted the firm's organization culture to be more accommodating to all its employees—to value differences among people rather than attempting to impose a rigid and controlling model for accomplishing goals. For example, the firm dropped its season-ticket purchases to Knick and Yankee games and replaced them with season tickets for the New York City Ballet and the New York Philharmonic. And the company eliminated its annual hunting retreat, a male bastion of drinking and card playing.

Avon is also moving aggressively into foreign markets. For example, Avon products are now sold in mature markets like western Europe and Japan. In addition, the firm sells its products throughout China, Russia, and eastern Europe. All told, Avon manufactures its products in eighteen countries and sells them in 125. Preston credits several key female executives for championing the international push and for making sure that it was done right. And many new managers at the firm have come from international contacts, organizations, and networks that the firm did not previously see as a valuable source of executive talent.

But perhaps the biggest testament to the "new" Avon is its new top management team. In 1999, after Preston's departure, Andrea Jung was named chair and CEO; at the same time Susan Kropf was appointed president and chief operating officer (COO). All told, over half of the firm's top officers are women and more than 40 percent of its global managers are women. Almost half of the firm's board of directors is female. Clearly, Avon is a firm that has changed its own culture and appreciates the power of diversity and multiculturalism.[19]

Case Questions

1. What underlies Avon's commitment to diversity?

2. Why don't more companies follow Avon's lead?

3. Can any of the dimensions of diversity derail Avon's success?

Building HR Management Skills

Purpose: The purpose of this exercise is to help develop increasingly important human resource skills as they relate to multicultural issues and challenges.

Step 1: Read and reflect on the scenario that follows:

Your firm has recently undergone a significant increase in its workforce. Many of the new workers you have hired are immigrants from eastern Europe and Asia. Several do not speak English very well, but all are hard workers who appear to want to be successful and to fit in with their coworkers.

Recently, however, some problems have come to your attention. Several of your female workers have begun to complain about an increase in sexual harassment. Your supervisors have noticed an increase in tardiness and absenteeism among all your workers. You have decided that some action is needed. You are unsure, however, about how to proceed. Consequently, you have decided to spend a few days thinking about what to do.

Step 2: Respond to the questions that follow:

1. Think of as many causes as you can for each of the two problems you face.

2. Determine how you might address each problem, given the potential array of factors that might have contributed to each.

3. What role might the organization culture be playing in this situation, apart from issues of multiculturalism?

4. What role might multiculturalism be playing in this situation, apart from issues of organization culture?

Ethical Dilemmas in HR Management

Assume that you are the senior human resource executive in your company. For years your firm had relatively little diversity. The 1,000-member workforce was almost exclusively white and male. But in recent years you have succeeded in increasing diversity substantially. Almost one-third of your employees are now female, while over 40 percent are Hispanic or African-American.

Your firm has recently had some unfortunate financial setbacks. You feel that you have no choice but to lay off about 300 employees for a period of at least six months. If everything goes well, you also expect to be able to rehire them at the end of the six-month period.

You are currently puzzling over what criteria to use in selecting people for layoffs. If you use strict seniority, women and ethnic minorities will bear the brunt of the layoffs because they are almost all among the newest employees in the firm. If you use strict performance, however, your older and more senior (and predominately white male) workers will bear the brunt because your newer employees have the most current training and job skills. You also wonder what role loyalty should play because many of your older workers could have left for higher-paying jobs a few years ago but chose to stay.

Questions

1. What are the ethical issues in this situation?

2. What are the basic arguments for and against the different criteria in selecting employees to be laid off?

3. What do you think most managers would do? What would you do?

HR Internet Exercise

One of the most important multicultural challenges facing managers today involves language skills. Assume that you are the human resource manager for a large domestic company. Your firm has recently decided to enter into a joint venture with three foreign companies, one each from France, Germany, and Korea. The terms of this joint venture involve your three partners each sending a team of managers to your corporate headquarters for a period of two years.

You must make sure that your own top management team has the basic language skills in each of the three languages represented among your partners.

With the background information above as context, do the following:

1. Use the Internet to obtain information about language-training programs and methods.

2. Obtain information about one or more programs or methods and decide how you should proceed.

17

Managing Employment Relationships

CHAPTER OBJECTIVES

After studying this chapter you should be able to:

- Understand the nature of employee rights at work

- Discuss the nature of employment contracts between organizations and employees.

- Identify and describe the issues involved in managing knowledge workers

- Discuss the use of contingent and temporary workers.

- Describe new forms of work arrangements.

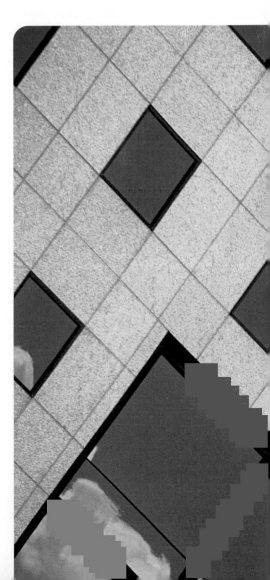

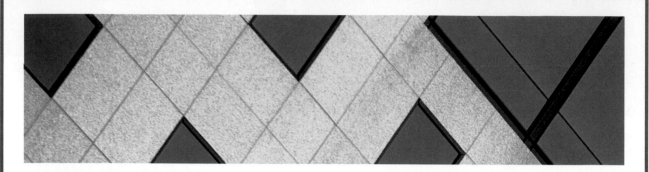

No one argues that the fundamental relationship between employers and employees has changed dramatically over the last several years. As one case in point, consider the recent series of events that took place at Merrill Lynch. The firm recruited Alexander Lambros, Jr., in 1989 to open a new office in Cape Coral, Florida, by giving him a $50,000 signing bonus, a 50 percent cut of the commissions, and a free rein to decorate and staff the office to his own tastes. He quickly became a company star, and his performance was never questioned.

Health problems subsequently forced him out of the branch manager position, but he stayed with the office and maintained a large and loyal client base, with a sales base of $88 million. But Lambros began to question the ethics of some of his predecessor's business practices. Later still, Lambros was asked to serve in the position of branch manager during the holiday period so the official manager could take a vacation. While acting in that capacity one day, he accepted an important document addressed to the branch manager. A sales assistant saw him take possession of the document and reported that to the real manager.

"The easiest way for managers of a firm to get new clients is to fire a broker and take his accounts. It's very common."

(Brad Hopper, brokerage executive)*

A few days later, the manager stormed into Lambros's office and fired him for "destroying company property." He claimed that the sales assistant supported his charges that Lambros had opened the envelope. A series of suits and countersuits have failed to uncover what really happened, however, and why. Lambros argues that the firm wanted him out, in part so that other managers could divide his customer base and in part because he had been so critical of certain business practices that he thought were unethical.

Merrill Lynch argues that neither issue played a role in his departure. Company officials instead point out concerns about Lambros funneling business to his wife, who worked for a different brokerage company. They also charged that he was undermining the authority of the official branch manager in ways that were damaging morale in the Cape Coral office. They also charged that he did, in fact, inappropriately "damage company property" by opening an envelope that was not really his, and that a witness observed his behavior. But in a bizarre turn, the sales assistant later claimed she had never said that she saw Lambros open the letter, merely that she saw it in his possession. She also charged that Merrill Lynch had tried to pressure her into lying to support its case. Ah, the tangled webs![1] ■

The case involving Lambros and Merrill Lynch underscores several important issues regarding businesses today. Most important, it reflects the fundamental change in relationships between employers and employees that has taken place during the last several years. In many firms, employees no longer trust their employer to treat them fairly and equitably. And employers often believe their employees act too much in their own self-interests. As a result, the fundamental nature of the employment relationship continues to change in various ways.

Many Americans grew up with clear expectations concerning the relationship they would have with the organization where they worked. Traditional models of this relationship suggested that an employee could expect to have a job as long as he or she worked hard and followed the rules. Employees understood that they were expected to exhibit loyalty and commitment to the organization. These contributions from the employee, along with inducements from the organization, formed the basis of the relationship between the employee and the organization. But the nature of this relationship has been changing and continues to change.

When we consider the relationship between the organization and the employee, we can talk about the basic legal employment contract, the psychological contract between employee and employer, or the social contract that involves both these parties plus the government. But in each case, the nature of these contracts is not what many people today grew up to expect. As a result, a much wider variety of relationships between organization and employee are possible in today's workplace, and the nature of these varied relationships poses a new set of challenges for the human resource manager.

EMPLOYEE RIGHTS IN THE WORKPLACE

The view that many people in the United States hold toward the concept of "individual rights" is derived from the U.S. Constitution, which guarantees certain fundamental rights to everyone—the rights to free speech and freedom of religion, for example. But some rights are unique to the workplace. This section introduces the concept of workplace rights, then discusses the preservation of employee rights at work.

The Meaning of Employee Rights

The foundation of workplace rights is the employment-at-will doctrine, which was discussed earlier in the book (Chapter 3). The concept of **employment-at-will** suggests that people work at the sole discretion of their employer and thus can be terminated at any time for any reason. This viewpoint, however, represents one extreme perspective on employee rights in the workplace. Essentially, the employment-at-will doctrine suggests that individuals have relatively few rights.

In fact, however, many of the laws and regulations governing human resource management that have been described earlier, most notably in Chapter 3, have been created to help define, maintain, and preserve various employee rights. For example, discrimination law essentially gives people the right to work without being evaluated on the basis of non-job-relevant factors such as gender or race.

■ **Employment-at-will** is a nineteenth-century common-law rule that allows an employer to terminate any employee at any time, for any reason (good or bad), or for no reason at all.

Similarly, minimum-wage legislation gives people the right to expect a certain base level of compensation for their work. And labor law gives employees the right to organize and join a labor union under certain prescribed circumstances.

More recently, various other issues concerning employment rights have arisen. One important rights issue today is the employee's right to privacy. This issue centers around points such as access to e-mail and voice mail in a job location. For instance, what rights does the employee have to maintain the privacy of his or her e-mail? Can the employer, who perhaps owns the computer and the computer system that the employee is using, have the right to enter the employee's computer without the employee's knowledge or consent and review the e-mails? This emerging legal issue, also discussed in Chapter 3, is one that will not likely be resolved for at least a few more years.

What about an employee's private life? Is an employee's private life truly private, or does the organization have a right to monitor and be concerned about how an employee spends his or her personal time? Some have argued that employees, especially higher-ranking and more visible employees, are *always* representatives of the company, and so the company always has a right to monitor and deal with their behavior. Obviously, others disagree with this point of view and argue that behavior that does not affect performance on the job is the employee's business. (We will revisit this issue later when we talk about substance abuse.) Wal-Mart once had a policy of not hiring divorced persons because they believed hiring such employees clashed with their family-oriented image. But a court in New York ruled that Wal-Mart could not discharge an employee who obtained a divorce. Clearly, the issue about an employee's right to privacy will continue to be debated.

In general, an employee's rights in any organizational setting are determined in part by the law and in part by the nature of the contract between the employee and the employer. In unionized settings, these contracts are quite formal and clear about the nature of the relationships. Formal, well-articulated contracts are common in other settings (e.g., professional sports). But in most employment settings, the rules governing the relationship are not so clear, nor are they as well specified. Nonetheless, we can discuss the notion of a psychological contract that governs all relationships at work.

THE NATURE OF EMPLOYMENT CONTRACTS

■ The **collective-bargaining agreement** between the organization and a labor union defines the nature of the employment relationship precisely.

When they begin a job today, many new employees sign a formal contract with the employing organization. These legal employment contracts usually set out each party's responsibilities and rights and specify the length of the contract terms. In some cases, the organization agrees to a legal contract called a **collective-bargaining agreement** between the organization and the employees as a group, although individuals do not sign the contract. As noted in Chapter 16, management and a labor union, which functions as the bargaining agent of the employees as a group, typically negotiate the specific terms of these contracts. These contracts are legal documents and are enforceable in a court of law. Therefore, if either party fails to live up to its responsibilities, the other party can sue for breach of contract. Although these issues are important, recent interest centers on the changing nature of a different kind of contract between employer and employee, and that is where we will focus most of our attention in this section.

The Nature of Psychological Contracts

A **psychological contract**, which is illustrated in Figure 17.1, can be defined as the set of expectations held by an employee concerning what he or she will contribute to the organization (referred to as **contributions**) and what the organization, in return, will provide to the employee (referred to as **inducements**). Thus, psychological contracts define the most basic relationship that employees expect to have with an organization.

These contracts are typically not written, so they are not formal contracts in any legal sense and are not enforceable in court. Nonetheless, an organization that believes an employee has violated his or her commitment and reduced contributions below an acceptable level often disciplines or terminates that employee. On the other hand, an employee who feels the organization has violated its commitment to provide inducements either reduces contributions to the company or leaves. Note that the employee's contributions include intangibles such as loyalty, and so a reduction in contributions might not be simply a reduction in effort or output but a basic change in attitude toward the organization.

Not all psychological contracts are the same, of course. Some experts have characterized these contracts as falling on a continuum from *transactional* to *relational*.[2] Contracts that are more transactional in nature typically involve a shorter time horizon, contain specific obligations, and stress financial inducements or inducements that can be converted into money (e.g., salary, benefits). Contracts that are more relational in nature involve longer and indeterminate time horizons and nonspecific and wide-ranging obligations, and stress nonfinancial (e.g., socioemotional) inducements as well as financial inducements. These latter contracts are much more fluid and so are more likely to change over time.

Traditionally, one of the inducements offered by an organization was employment security. The basic understanding was that, if an employee continued to contribute to the organization, he or she could expect to remain employed.

> ■ A **psychological contract** is the set of expectations held by an employee concerning what he or she will contribute to the organization (referred to as **contributions**) and what the organization will provide to the employee in return (referred to as **inducements**).

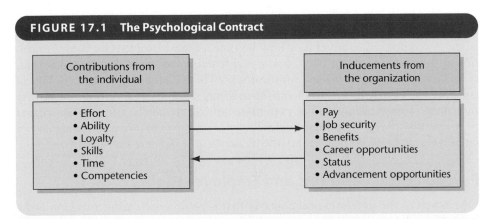

FIGURE 17.1   The Psychological Contract

Source: Adapted from Gregory Moorhead and Ricky W. Griffin, *Organizational Behavior*, 7th ed. (Boston: Houghton Mifflin, 2004), p. 87. Copyright © 2004 Houghton Mifflin Company. Reprinted with permission.

Although some have argued (probably correctly) that this kind of employment security was never really an inducement offered by U.S. corporations, the fact that many employees perceived it to be the case is enough for it to become part of their view of the contract.[3]

But as noted in earlier chapters, this inducement has not been available to employees over the last few years because downsizing and layoffs have become common. In many cases, organizations have tried to substitute training and development opportunities for job security. In other words, the organization was admitting that hard work no longer guaranteed a job, but if the organization was considering laying off a worker who was productive, they would at least provide that employee with some skills and competencies that would make him or her more employable elsewhere. Thus, even if the nature of the contract had not changed, the terms of the psychological contract often had.

But for many employees this shift represented a violation of the contract. As a result, employees felt they could reduce their contributions and their obligations to the organization.[4] As long as unemployment was rising, the employee could not afford to reduce effort on the job or to reduce output for fear of being fired. Instead, the employee reduced contributions in the areas of loyalty and commitment. To some extent this change made the terms of the contract less specific (and more transactional in nature), but again, the real change was in the terms of the psychological contract. HR in the 21st Century explores some of the more unpleasant results that might occur as a consequence of this trend.

At the end of the 1990s, however, unemployment in the United States was at an all-time low. Employees no longer needed to fear losing their jobs because other jobs were available. Therefore, it was possible to reduce effort and output on the job, but this possibility was not the worst of it for organizations. As unemployment shrunk, organizations found they again had to compete for employees. The reduced rate of population growth also began to play a role in reducing the supply of workers in the economy. (We will discuss special problems with certain types of employees below.) Instead of workforce reductions, organizations began to think about ways of retaining employees, and retention bonuses and sign-on bonuses have become more popular. But the beginning of the twenty-first century has brought a return to cutbacks and rising unemployment. As a result, employees are much more concerned with the rights they have.

As we noted above, the terms of the psychological contract have already changed. As a result, employees feel less loyalty and attachment to an organization and so are quite willing to be lured away by competing offers. The changing terms of the psychological contract may now become a bigger problem for the organization than it was for the employees who had felt violated when they lost their jobs, regardless of the levels of their contributions. These changes in the psychological contract will clearly be one of the major challenges facing organizations in the new millenium. This challenge will be even more difficult to meet as organizations come to realize that they can no longer offer lifetime employment as an inducement after employees experienced how empty the inducement was a few years earlier.

Psychological Contracts and Employee Rights

One aspect of the psychological contract that is getting increasing attention is the issue of employee rights. That is, in addition to inducements offered by the organization, employees have certain expectations about their rights while at work.

HR in the 21st Century

An Eye for an Eye

Going postal is a phrase that has become all too common today. Coined in response to several high-profile incidents in the U.S. Postal Service, the phrase is generally used when a worker or former employee takes violent action against a manager, coworker, or other employee in the organization. The highest-profile examples involve homicides in the workplace, something that happens today with alarming regularity.

While these homicides grab the headlines, some experts fear a growing epidemic of violence of a different sort—action taken for purposes of revenge, retribution, or retaliation, or to cause the company or its employees problems of various kinds. For example, among the more common acts of revenge reported in recent years are acts such as spitting in the boss's food, calling a co-worker's spouse and hinting at an extramarital affair, and tampering with computers. Other common "pranks" include duplicating someone's car keys and moving his or her car to a different area of the parking lot, spreading malicious rumors, and leaking important confidential information.

> *"For some people, sabotage can give a feeling of fairness and closure."*
>
> (Daniel Levine, editor of Internet e-zine *Disgruntled*)*

A former broker at Smith Barney was recently arrested after eighteen months of e-mail and Internet mischief aimed at company managers whom he believed had wronged him in some way. A former worker at Omega Engineering has been charged with planting a software "bomb" in the firm's computer system, causing critical software to be erased and costing the company about $10 million in sales. And a North Carolina theater worker has been charged with trying to blackmail his employer by threatening to tell people he had put the ashes of his recently cremated aunt into the popcorn!

Many experts believe that rather than companies being able to end them, these kinds of actions will continue to increase. The bond that once connected employers and their employees continues to weaken as a result of layoffs and other factors, and some people will continue to feel cheated, misled, and/or shortchanged by their employers. If these feelings become strong enough, some form of sabotage or revenge is increasingly likely.

Sources: "Employees, Ex-Workers Get Even," *USA Today*, August 20, 1998, pp. 1B, 2B (*quote on p. 2B); Paul Falcone, "Dealing With Employees in Crisis," *HR Magazine*, May 2003, pp. 117–126.

As we noted above, an employee's right to a job are rather limited in most cases because he or she can be terminated at will. But beyond the right to a job, other employee rights might be challenged at work. An important part of the psychological contract involves expectations about these rights.

Freedom of speech is guaranteed by the first amendment to the U.S. Constitution. Many of us know that this right does not extend to yelling "fire" in a crowded movie theater, but at work other limitations restrict rights. Private-sector employees who publicly disagree with management or who say something that damages the reputation of the company, for instance, can be disciplined for this behavior. The more visible the employee and the more the employee "represents" the organization (e.g., someone in top management), the more this type of freedom of speech is limited. Even in the public sector, employees cannot use their position to endorse political candidates (although they can do so as private citizens).

Another area of employee rights that is often disputed is the right to privacy. Privacy rights at work also vary considerably by state and even by economy sector. Public-sector employers cannot search employee desks unless they have probable cause (i.e., a real basis for suspecting wrongdoing), but private-sector employers typically can conduct a search with much less justification. Although most states outlaw an employer listening to private phone conversations (or reading e-mail) without probable cause, not all do. Also, in some states, random drug testing of employees (as opposed to job applicants) is outlawed but not in others.

New technology has also introduced new challenges to employee rights to privacy. Traditionally, employee personnel files contained paper records that were stored in one location and could be kept secure. Many organizations now keep employee records electronically, however, and it is more difficult to keep these electronic records secure and confidential. In fact, many organizations design human resource information systems that are meant to create easy access to information about employees. We discuss these systems and the problems they pose for privacy rights in more detail in Appendix 1.

In addition, as noted in Chapter 8, employees in many organizations are under electronic surveillance to prevent theft—and many of these employees are not even aware of the surveillance. In fact, a report by the Office of Technology Assessment (conducted several years ago) reported that about 10 million workers in the United States are secretly monitored at work.[5] The purpose of this surveillance ranges from checking on unauthorized breaks to attempts to increase quality control. Whatever the purpose, the threat of invasion of privacy from these programs is considerable.

One interesting application of electronic monitoring at work has been in the area of performance appraisal. These systems are usually widely publicized, so the issue is not clearly one of privacy rights. It is now possible for organizations to monitor the number of keystrokes entered by a data-entry clerk or to monitor the number of calls handled by a reservations clerk. Many employees have complained about this situation. They feel that it *is* an invasion of privacy and that this monitoring results in increased stress and more work time lost due to stress-related pressure and illness.[6] Yet evidence also suggests that computer-monitored performance can lead to more fair appraisals and can actually increase productivity. The success or failure of these systems seems to depend on the nature of the job and the way the monitoring is introduced, as well as whether individuals or groups are monitored.[7] Thus, more must be learned about computer-monitored appraisal systems, but they are likely to grow in popularity in the future—and to grow in controversy as well.

The Nature of Social Contracts

■ A **social contract** expands the relationship between employer and employee to include the government.

A **social contract** simply refers to expanding the relationship between employer and employee to include a third party—the government. This view recognizes that public policies such as minimum-wage levels, taxes, union-management relations, and health-care provisions are an important part of the relationship between employer and employee. For example, we discussed in Chapter 13 how many of the benefits given by organizations are mandated by law. These mandated benefits are an important part of a total benefits package. (And, in fact, we noted that mandated benefits in the United States are relatively low compared to benefits in most European countries.) Therefore, an employee should expect that, in exchange for his or her efforts and loyalty, the organization would provide, at a minimum, those benefits mandated by law.

But the terms of the social contract are changing. Some of the nontraditional work relationships discussed below have resulted in more employees not having even basic benefits usually mandated by law. Years of organizational downsizing have led to many workers not having any type of health insurance (even employees who have started their own businesses are less likely to be covered by health-insurance plans). As a result, the government may need to do more to ensure a minimum safety net for all employees. President Clinton's attempt to provide minimum mandated health-care benefits was a concrete manifestation of this growing concern. The Dunlop Commission report, released in 1995, noted that workplace productivity and a hard-working labor force are important assets for any nation and that the government should move to protect these assets, suggesting increased government involvement.[8]

Increased government involvement in providing benefits and guaranteeing worker rights will surely have implications for human resource managers. At the very least it will require increased paperwork and record keeping, but it will also likely involve newer restrictions on how employees can be treated at work. In fact, some have argued that the "new" social contract should have organizations no longer competing on the basis of costs but instead pursuing a high-productivity, high-wage strategy that allows a voice for all employees.[9] Such a strategy would surely change the nature of the human resource function in organizations.

MANAGING KNOWLEDGE WORKERS

Traditionally, employees added value to organizations because of what they did or because of their experience. As we enter the information age in the workplace, however, many employees add value simply because of what they know.[10] This new reality creates new problems and challenges for managing work relationships.

The Nature of Knowledge Work

Employees who add value simply because of what they know are usually referred to as **knowledge workers,** and how well these employees are managed is seen as a major factor in determining which firms will be successful in the future.[11] Knowledge workers include computer scientists, engineers, and physical scientists, and they provide special challenges for the human resource manager. They tend to work in high-technology firms and are usually experts in some abstract knowledge base. They often believe they have the right to work autonomously and they identify more strongly with their profession than they do with any organization—even to the extent of defining performance in terms recognized by other members of their profession.[12]

As the importance of information-driven jobs grows, the need for knowledge workers will also grow. But these employees require extensive and specialized training, and not everyone is willing to make the human capital investments necessary to move into these jobs. In fact, even after knowledge workers are on the job, retraining and training updates are critical so that their skills do not become obsolete. It has been suggested, for example, that the "half-life" for a technical education in engineering is about three years. Failure to update the required skills by the end of that time not only results in the organization losing competitive advantage but also increases the likelihood that the knowledge worker will go to another firm that is more committed to updating these skills.[13]

■ **Knowledge workers** add value simply because of what they know.

Sun Yunbo and Fang Zhen are auto designers in Shanghai working on the Buick Excelle, a new car that GM will build and sell in China beginning in 2004. They represent a new breed of knowledge worker that is becoming critical to China's future. Many people have seen products that are made in China, but the goal in China is to have more products that are designed in China. This goal requires training and retaining knowledge workers capable of generating designs that will sell. Some argue that traditional Chinese education encourages rote memorization and discourages creative thinking, which is not conducive to the kind of creativity needed for innovative product design. But a growing number of design schools in China and a new generation of young designers seem to be making a difference. Chinese designed mobile phones account for over 30 percent of that market in China, and companies such as Black & Decker and Philips feature products designed in China. The problem, however, may come as Chinese designers become more popular and successful— the competition for successful knowledge workers worldwide is becoming fiercer by the day, and China may have trouble keeping these young designers from moving to other countries.

Compensation and career development policies for knowledge workers must also be specially tailored. For example, in many high-tech organizations, engineers and scientists have the option of entering a technical career path that parallels a management career path. This option allows the knowledge worker to continue to carry out specialized work without taking on management responsibilities; at the same time the organization offers the knowledge worker compensation that is equivalent to the compensation available to management. Also, in many high-tech organizations, salary adjustments within various classifications for management workers are most frequently based on maturity curves rather than on performance. That is, because performance is difficult to quantify for these employees, and because a great deal of research and development (R&D) activity may not have an immediate payoff, salary is based on the employee's years of work experience. The assumption is that, in a technical area, more experience makes the employee more valuable to the organization.[14]

But in other high-tech firms, the emphasis is on pay for performance, with profit sharing based on projects or products developed by the knowledge workers. In addition, the tendency in most firms employing these workers is to reduce the number of levels of the organization to allow the knowledge workers to react more quickly to the external environment and to reduce the need for bureaucratic approval.[15]

An Expanded View of Knowledge Work

Our discussion thus far has concentrated on employees who have knowledge-related jobs, known as knowledge workers. But organizations are increasingly coming to view "knowledge" more broadly: as the ultimate source of competitive advantage. That is, according to a popular view of strategic management known as the resource-based view of the firm, firms gain competitive advantage by developing resources that are rare, valuable, and difficult to copy or substitute.[16]

Traditionally, these resources were considered to be technology or specialized suppliers, for example, but more recent thinking suggests that intangible resources based on knowledge and the capabilities of workers is a more sustainable source of competitive advantage. Thus, any employee who can bring some unique insights to the job is potentially seen as a source of competitive advantage. As a result, most employees are viewed as knowledge workers and should be rewarded and valued because of the knowledge they possess.

Knowledge Worker Management and Labor Relations

In any event, the demand for knowledge workers has been growing dramatically in recent years. As a result, organizations that hire these workers need to introduce regular market adjustments (upward) to employee pay if they want to retain them. This approach is especially critical in an area where demand is growing because entry-level wages for these employees are skyrocketing. Once an employee accepts a job with a firm, he or she is more subject to the internal labor market, which is not likely to grow as quickly as the external market for the knowledge workers. As a result, the longer an employee remains with a firm, the further behind the market rate his or her pay falls—unless it is regularly adjusted.

Of course, the growing demand for these workers also results in organizations going to rather extreme measures to attract them in the first place.[17] High starting salaries and sign-on bonuses are common. British Petroleum Exploration was recently paying starting petroleum engineers with undersea platform drilling knowledge (not experience, just knowledge) salaries in the six-figure range, with sign-on bonuses of over $50,000 and immediate profit sharing. Even with these incentives, human resource managers from the organization complained that in the Gulf Coast region, they could not retain these specialists because the young engineers would leave to accept a sign-on bonus with a competitor after just a few months.

But these phenomena occur in times when unemployment is relatively low, and the demand for certain types of knowledge workers is relatively recent. As time goes on and college students learn about the salaries paid to these specialists, more of them will gravitate to programs in areas such as undersea drilling. More universities will respond with larger and larger programs in these and other areas to accommodate the new demand. As a result, enough of these specialists will be available in a few years to meet the demand, and the frenzy over hiring and retaining these employees will subside.

This information takes time to filter down to new students, and some students are already on the academic track in these areas. Therefore, the future will likely see a surplus of ocean-drilling engineers, for example. This situation will drive salaries down, which in the long run will discourage new students from making the human capital investments needed to perform these jobs. Then another shortage of these knowledge workers will trigger a new round of efforts to attract and retain those employees who are available. While these patterns greatly complicate the lives of human resource professionals, organizations will have to do better long-term planning so they can manage the supply and demand of knowledge workers rather than react to the labor market conditions. The knowledge base about the issues related to managing knowledge workers is growing, and organizations can build competitive advantage by better utilizing the knowledge resources they have.[18] These skills will be critical to human resource managers in the new century.

CONTINGENT AND TEMPORARY WORKERS

As we noted in Chapter 6, alternatives to recruiting full-time permanent employees exist, and in fact the use of contingent and temporary workers by organizations has exploded.[19] We turn now to some of the issues associated with managing relationships with those workers.

Trends in Contingent and Temporary Workers

■ A **contingent worker** is a person who works for an organization on something other than a permanent or full-time basis.

In recent years the number of contingent workers in the workforce has increased dramatically. Table 17.1 summarizes recent statistics. We define a **contingent worker** as a person who works for an organization on something other than a permanent or full-time basis. Categories of contingent workers include independent contractors, on-call workers, temporary employees (usually hired through an outside agency), and contract and leased employees. Another category is part-time workers. For example, Citigroup makes extensive use of part-time sales agents to pursue new clients.[20] About 10 percent of the U.S. workforce currently works in one of these alternative forms of employment relationships. Experts suggest, though, that this percentage is increasing at a consistent pace.

For some jobs temporary workers simply make the most sense. The Lear Corporation in Southfield, Michigan, makes automobile seats. In fact, J. D. Power has deemed it the best in the auto industry, and with nearly $14 billion in annual sales it is the world's largest manufacturer of auto seats. At the Lear plant giant robotic arms with plastic attachments swivel in and out of car seats as they move across the factory. But the company credits its success to the human touch. Four-day-a-week students, housewives, and retirees, such as the gentleman pictured here, report to the plant to test car seats. They rest their rears on sensors that record pressure and stress, and they are asked to report how good the seat feels. They are paid $25 per car, and their opinions are the final test for car seat designs. Company spokespersons note that even though a computer says a new design is better, the company won't adopt a new design unless the human testers can tell the difference and like it.

Advantages and Disadvantages of Using Contingent and Temporary Workers

Companies that use contingent and temporary workers face several advantages and disadvantages. The primary advantage that most companies seek to achieve with the use of contingent workers is cost savings. For the most part an organization that uses contingent workers does not have to pay for their benefits, such as health insurance, vacation time, and sick days. Usually the agency that provides the contingent workers absorbs these costs. In some arrangements, tax burdens can also be shifted to either the employee him- or herself or to the provider of the contingent worker.

Another major advantage that companies derive from the use of contingent workers is increased flexibility. Recruiting and hiring permanent workers is a

TABLE 17.1 Employed Workers with Alternative Work Arrangements by Occupation and Industry (Percentage Distribution*)

Characteristic	Workers with Alternative Arrangements			
	Independent Contractors[†]	On-Call Workers	Temporary Agency Workers	Workers Provided by Contract Firms
Total, 16 years of age and over (in thousands)	8,585	2,089	1,169	633
Occupation				
Executive, administrative, and managerial personnel	19.4%	5.5%	6.7%	13.1%
Professional specialty personnel	16.8	25.9	10.4	25.4
Technicians and related support personnel	1.2	4.2	6.5	9.1
Sales professionals	15.6	6.6	7.7	3.1
Administrative support, including clerical personnel	3.9	8.7	29.5	4.4
Service workers	10.7	18.8	7.6	18.6
Precision production, craft, and repair personnel	19.5	13.0	7.5	19.3
Operators, fabricators, and laborers	7.3	15.0	23.2	6.3
Farming, forestry, and fishing personnel	5.6	2.2	0.9	0.7
Industry				
Agriculture	5.7	2.1	0.5	0.5
Mining	0.3	0.4	0.9	1.1
Construction	19.6	10.1	2.9	5.8
Manufacturing	3.7	5.3	21.1	20.8
Transportation and public utilities	5.6	9.7	7.3	6.4
Wholesale trade	2.7	2.3	2.8	3.6
Retail trade	8.8	11.8	3.7	2.6
Finance, insurance, and real estate	9.2	2.4	6.6	4.1
Services	44.4	50.5	45.5	36.8
Public administration	0.1	5.3	0.0	11.9

*Data for February 2001.
†About 10 percent of the U.S. workforce is employed under an alternative arrangement, particularly as independent contractors.
Source: U.S. Department of Labor, Bureau of Labor Statistics, http://www.bls.gov.

costly proposition. If the organization miscalculates its workforce needs and hires more employees than it can adequately support, it may then face expensive and painful layoffs and downsizing efforts. But using contingent workers helps an organization address this predicament more effectively. That is, the organization can maintain a permanent and full-time workforce of somewhat less than it really needs to conduct its business and then make up the difference with contingent workers. Then, as its demand for human resources increases or decreases, it can bring in more or fewer contingent workers.

But the use of contingent workers also has some significant disadvantages. One major disadvantage is productivity. While few studies have been conducted to document this belief scientifically, it seems reasonable to believe that the average contingent worker is not as well-versed in the organization and how it conducts its business as is a permanent and full-time employee. That is, the individual contingent worker may possess adequate generalized skills but may lack firm-specific skills. Consequently, the contingent worker may not understand enough about specific organizational procedures and operations to be able to function efficiently, at least during the early period of work.

Another disadvantage that firms confront when using contingent workers is decreased organizational commitment and loyalty. The Lighter Side of HR illustrates this disadvantage. When an employee is a permanent and full-time member of a firm's staff and has spent years working for the organization, it follows that she or he will develop a reasonably strong loyalty and commitment to the organization. This loyalty and commitment is a function of well-established working relationships, common and shared experiences, and the security of employment. But none of these characteristics are likely to exist in the work relationship an organization has with contingent workers. Thus, contingent workers will almost surely be less committed and less loyal to the organization.

Another disadvantage is that an organization may fail to develop a strong human resource base of its own if it relies too heavily on contingent workers. In today's environment, an organization can staff almost all skilled positions with contingent workers. But if it takes this course of action, it may end up with few or even no employees of its own who possess some of these fundamental skills. In the short run, this situation might not be a particularly big problem. But in the long term, the organization may face at least some problems of decreased effectiveness as a result of a weaker human resource foundation of its own. The HR Legal Brief summarizes another disadvantage, namely, the potential for legal complications if it mismanages its contingent workers.

The Lighter Side of HR

Companies everywhere seem to be making greater use of contingent and part-time workers. But as illustrated in this cartoon, trying to change the employment status of people from contingent to permanent, or vice versa, must be handled carefully. If workers see the costs of changing as outweighing the benefits, they are likely to resist the change. Thus, managers need to have a full and complete understanding of all the issues before proceeding to attempt to impose changes. (The New Yorker Collection 1987 Mischa Richter from cartoonbank.com. All Rights Reserved.)

"We're just like one big happy family here."

When Is Temporary Permanent?

For the last several years more and more big companies have hired a growing number of temporary workers. Some companies have come to rely so heavily on temporary workers that these individuals almost become a permanent part of the organization. One of the primary reasons that employers use temporary workers is because they are generally not covered under various benefits plans, especially pensions.

But what happens when a firm hires temporary workers and then keeps them on for an extended period of time? For example, over 29 percent of the workers employed by temp agencies remain on their assignments for a year or longer. The question becomes, Who is the primary employer: the temp agency who first hired the individual and then gave him or her an assignment, or the firm that contracted for the individual's services with the temp agency but then kept the employee for an extended period of time?

This kind of situation has prompted a close look by the courts. For example, the Labor Department recently filed a lawsuit against Time Warner. The suit charges that some of Time Warner's temp workers actually qualify now as permanent employees and thus should be covered by the

> *"Any company with any sense is going to be aware of these [new legal questions] and is talking to counsel about the potential liabilities."*
>
> (Ed Lenz, general counsel for the National Association of Temporary & Staffing Services)*

same benefits agreements that apply to other workers. An even more significant case, however, has been filed by a group of Microsoft workers. A group of 6,000 such workers claim that they are essentially common-law Microsoft employees now and should have the same pension coverage as the firm's permanent employees. Other recent cases have involved Allstate and Pacific Gas & Electric.

The critical factor in determining which side is "right," so far at least, is the nature of the employment relationship. If the firm itself decides who it will employ, provides the same supervision for temporary workers as for permanent workers, and uses its own payroll system to compensate them, the courts are generally finding that the workers qualify for all other benefits afforded regular employees. Only when the temp agency itself makes the assignment decision, provides at least part of the supervision, and handles compensation do the individuals remain temporary workers. A pattern seems to be emerging, but more court decisions are no doubt on the horizon before these issues are settled once and for all.

Sources: "When Is a Temp Not a Temp?" *Business Week*, December 7, 1998, pp. 90–92 (*quote on p. 90); "Programmers of the World ...," *Business Week*, December 7, 1998, pp. 92–94.

Managing Contingent and Temporary Workers

Given the widespread use of contingent and temporary workers today, it follows logically that managers should understand how to utilize these kinds of employees more effectively. That is, they need to understand how to manage contingent and temporary workers.

One key to the effective management of contingent and temporary workers is careful planning. Even though one of the presumed benefits of using contingent workers is flexibility, it is still important for managers to try to use such workers in a relatively smooth and coordinated fashion. Rather than having to call in contingent workers sporadically and with no prior notice, it is beneficial for the organization to be able to bring in specified numbers of contingent workers for well-defined periods of time. And this approach calls for careful planning.

A second important part of managing contingent and temporary workers more effectively is to understand and acknowledge the advantages and disadvantages described in the preceding section. That is, the organization needs to recognize what

Managing work relationships is becoming more difficult with such a great reliance on outsourcing. When work is outsourced the people performing the job are not employees of the company, but work for the contractor who provides the service. Yet these workers provide services that customers see as coming from the parent company. So the parent company must manage these people, even though they work for someone else and may be located far away from the parent company. Organizations such as Convergys specialize in providing outsourced services. Their main call center located in Cincinnati, Ohio, handles billing for many firms in the customer care industry, and the company has recently won a $280 million contract to perform many human resource management functions for the State of Florida. The services, of course, will be provided from the headquarters in Ohio.

it can and can't achieve from the use of contingent and temporary workers. Expecting too much from such workers, for example, is a mistake that the manager should avoid.

Third, it is important that managers carefully assess the real cost of using contingent workers. For example, we noted above that many firms adopt this course of action as a way of saving labor costs. And the organization should be able to document precisely its labor costs savings. It can document this information by looking at how much it would be paying people in wages and benefits if they were on permanent staff, comparing this figure with how much they are paying the agency providing the contingent workers, and assessing the difference. But this difference might be misleading. For instance, we also noted above that contingent workers might not be as effective performers as permanent and full-time employees. So comparing employees on a direct cost basis is not necessarily valid. Instead, the organization has to adjust the direct differences in labor costs with the differences in productivity and performance.

Managers also need to articulate and understand fully their own strategies and decide in advance how they intend to manage their temporary workers, specifically focusing on how to integrate these workers into the organization. At a simplistic level, for example, an organization with a large contingent workforce needs to make some decisions about the treatment of contingent workers relative to the treatment of permanent, full-time workers. For example, should contingent workers be invited to the company holiday party? Should contingent workers have the same access to employee auxiliary benefits, such as counseling services or childcare facilities, as do permanent and full-time employees? These questions don't have clear, right or wrong answers. The point simply is that managers must understand that they need to develop a strategy for integrating contingent workers according to some sound logic and rationale and then follow that strategy consistently over time.

Human Resource Architecture

Earlier, in both Chapters 2 and 6, we referred to a strategic model for deciding what types of employees a firm should hire. We now need to spend more time discussing this model, which has been termed human resource architecture.[21] This approach is based on the calculation of two critical terms: the value of human capital (i.e., employees) and the uniqueness of human capital. In this view, value is determined by the extent to which an employee helps an organization to accomplish its major strategic objectives. Core assets are those assets that are vital for the organization's strategic position (and are thus more valuable), while peripheral assets are those employees who do not serve those strategic goals directly (and are thus less valuable). Uniqueness refers to the ease with which the organization can find another employee with the same skills—the more difficult it is to replace the skills, the more unique the human capital.

The human resource architecture consists of four quadrants, which are formed by crossing two levels of value (high and low) with two levels of uniqueness (high and low) for human capital (see Figure 17.2). In quadrant I, human capital is *both* valuable and unique. In this quadrant we rely on permanent, full-time employees and work to develop those employees to their full potential. Thus, the organization should hire employees at the entry level (for the most part) and should provide all necessary training and developmental experience. The nature of the psychological contract in this quadrant should focus on the organization and should encourage mutual investment on the part of the employees and the organization.

Quadrant II is where human capital is valuable but not unique. Here the organization should hire employees who have already developed the necessary skills at another organization. Although these employees should also be full-time and permanent, the nature of the psychological contract should be much different. Here, the focus should be on a symbiotic relationship where both parties benefit, but the organization should appreciate that these employees are less likely to be fully committed to the organization, and vice versa.

In quadrant III both value and uniqueness are low. Needed skills are not strategic and many workers possess them, and so the firm would be wise to contract for the services externally. This approach translates into a strong reliance on contract labor, or even temporary and part-time labor, and the psychological contract is transactional. That is, the employees are hired to do a job only and are not expected to have much commitment to (or involvement in) the overall

FIGURE 17.2   Human Resource Architecture

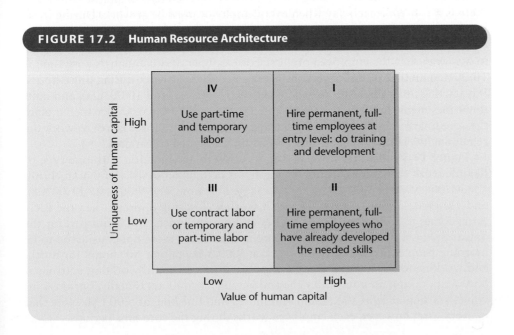

organization. Finally, in quadrant IV human capital is unique but not valuable. Thus, the skills are not critical for achieving strategic objectives, but they are important and not easy to find. In this quadrant the nature of the psychological contract is one where both parties enter a partnership, and part-time and temporary work relationships are likely to be widely used.

To date, little empirical research supports (or refutes) this model, but it does provide a potentially useful framework for organizations deciding where and when nontraditional employment relationships are more likely to be successful.

MANAGING NEW FORMS OF WORK ARRANGEMENTS

Even when organizations continue to employ people on a permanent, full-time basis, the work schedules and arrangements for these employees are changing rapidly. Traditionally, if employees worked forty hours a week, they were expected to be physically present at work five days a week, eight hours a day, unless the nature of the job was such that the employee was required to spend time on the road. In modern organizations, however, it is becoming increasingly common for people to work on a schedule other than five days/forty hours and/or to work at a place other than the office or place of business.

Managing Alternative Work Schedules

■ **Flexible work hours** programs involve employees working forty hours per week and five days a week, but with the potential for flexible starting and ending times.

The two most common alternatives to the traditional workweek are programs known as flexible work hours and compressed workweeks. Employees working under **flexible work hour** plans usually must still work a full forty hours per week and, typically, they must work five days a week. The employees have control, however, over the starting and ending times for work on each day. In almost every case, there is a *core time* each day when every employee must be at work. During these hours the organization can schedule meetings or any other activities that require coordination among employees. The remaining hours (*flex time*) can be made up in any way that the employee prefers. For example, if a company's core time is 10:00 A.M. until 2:00 P.M., everyone is expected to be at work during those hours. But starting times might be anywhere between 7:00 A.M. and 10:00 A.M., and quitting times might be anywhere between 2:00 P.M. and 7:00 P.M. Under such a plan, the core time represents twenty hours a week, and the employee is free to work the remaining twenty hours in any fashion within the stated constraints.

Figure 17.3 illustrates how an organization might function with one type of flexible work schedule. This organization has defined 6:00 A.M.–9:00 A.M., 11:00 A.M.–1:00 P.M., and 3:00 P.M.–7:00 P.M. as flexible time, and 9:00 A.M.–11:00 A.M. and 1:00 P.M.–3:00 P.M. as core time. A worker choosing option 1 (i.e., the early riser) comes to work at 6:00 A.M., takes an hour for lunch, and is finished for the day at 3:00 P.M. Option 2, perhaps more attractive for those not considered to be morning people, involves starting work at 9:00 A.M., taking two hours for lunch, and working until 7:00 P.M. Option 3 is closest to a standard workday, starting at 8:00 A.M., taking an hour at lunch, and leaving at 5:00 P.M. Finally, option 4 involves starting at 9:00 A.M., taking no lunch, and finishing at 5:00 P.M. Note that in every case, however, each employee works during the core time periods.

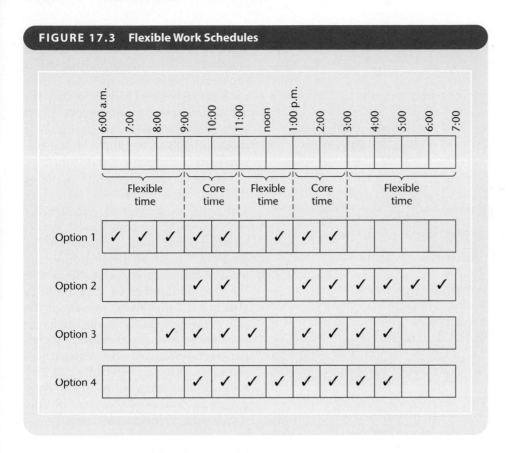

FIGURE 17.3   Flexible Work Schedules

These plans are believed to reduce stress because the employee does not have to travel during peak commuting times and can have more control over the commute.[22] They are also believed to increase job satisfaction because the employee is given more control over the work environment and a stronger feeling that he or she is trusted by the organization.[23] They are not as feasible in organizations that place a strong emphasis on teams; otherwise, no serious problems associated with their use are reported.

Compressed workweeks are arrangements in which the employee works the required number of hours (typically forty) but does so in less than five days. For example, a four-day, ten-hour-a-day work schedule is fairly common, and schedules that involve four days with twelve hours a day, followed by four days off, are also fairly common. The employee gains the flexibility of three days off a week, presumably making it less likely that he or she will lose work time to deal with personal business. These schedules are also well suited for employees who work at sites that are difficult to get to, such as offshore drilling rigs. These schedules are not for everyone, however, and longer workdays are related to increased accidents in some settings.[24] Nonetheless, compressed workweeks are extremely popular with some employees.

Both of these alternative schedule plans are growing in popularity, and few problems seem to be associated with them (except as noted). These alternative schedules present some unique challenges to the human resource manager, however. As noted above, flexible schedules are often not feasible in organizations that rely heavily on

■ **Compressed workweeks** are arrangements where the employee works the required number of hours (typically forty) but does so in less than five days.

In the age of the Internet working from home has become more feasible and more common. Jill Smith lives in Utah and works as a reservations clerk for JetBlue Airlines, which is based at New York's Kennedy International Airport. The fact that she works at home is probably not that unique, but the fact that every one of JetBlue's 550 reservations clerks works at home is rather unique. Smith and each of her 549 colleagues are required to pay $45 a month for extra phone lines that allow them to take calls and dial into the booking system. In return, they can work on a very flexible schedule. Smith works about twenty-five hours a week—in her slippers. This arrangement helps JetBlue keep down its costs (i.e., no office and no furniture) and helps improve employee satisfaction, which reduces turnover. The arrangement is also helpful to Smith who can stay at home, care for her four children, and still earn a reasonable salary.

teams. In fact, whenever one employee's work depends on input from another employee, these schedules may be a problem. Even when they are not a problem, flexible schedules reduce the amount of time that employees interact with their coworkers, which makes it more difficult to develop a strong culture or even a strong esprit de corps.

Although employees are at work the same number of hours as before and have the opportunity to interact with coworkers, compressed work-weeks present similar challenges because the stress of longer hours may make social interaction less likely, and the greater number of days off may also affect some social aspects of the job. The human resource manager must try to find ways to replace socializing activities with other experiences so that employees, especially new employees, can learn more about their coworkers and can become more fully socialized into the organization.

Managing Alternative Work Sites

In addition to employees working on alternative schedules, employees performing their work at a location other than the place of business, most likely at home, is a growing trend. Home work and telecommuting are two popular variations on this theme. Table 17.2 shows the number and characteristics of people currently working under one or the other of these options. **Home work programs** include arrangements that are often referred to as cottage industries. In the earliest days of the industrial revolution, before many factories were built, employees would take parts back home to their cottages and manufacture them, then return them to a central point where they could be assembled. Similar types of cottage industries still exist for the manufacturing of small and not very complex items.

It is more common, however, to operate in what can be called an electronic cottage. Employees take office work home with them and complete it on home computers. They can then return to the office to collect more work. They are connected to that office via a modem, fax machine, and e-mail. These arrangements can even result in a virtual office and are becoming especially popular with people who want (or need) to work but do not wish to work full-time or who have other responsibilities such as child- or eldercare.[25]

■ **Home work programs** include arrangements that are often referred to as cottage industries.

TABLE 17.2   Number of People Doing Job-Related Work at Home, 2001

Characteristic	Number (thousands)	Wage and Salary			Self-Employed
		Rate*	Paid	Unpaid	
Total, 16 years of age and over	19,759	15.0%	17.4%	52.0%	29.7%
Without children under age 18	11,121	13.7	15.7	52.3	31.0
With children under age 18	8,638	17.0	19.6	51.6	27.9
With children under age 6	3,580	16.6	21.8	49.9	27.2
Men, 16 years of age and over	10,291	14.8	16.0	50.5	32.6
Without children under age 18	5,763	13.2	14.6	48.5	35.8
With children under age 18	4,527	17.4	17.7	53.1	28.4
With children under age 6	1,875	15.9	19.1	56.1	23.9
Women, 16 years of age and over	9,468	15.2	18.9	53.7	26.5
Without children under age 18	5,357	14.3	16.9	56.5	25.8
With children under age 18	4,111	16.6	21.6	50.0	27.4
With children under age 6	1,705	17.6	24.8	43.1	30.7

*Refers to the number of persons working at home as a percentage of the total at work.

Source: U.S. Department of Labor, Bureau of Labor Statistics, http://www.bls.gov.

Telecommuting is simply the logical extension of the electronic cottage. Under this arrangement, employees may do almost all of their work at home and may even receive assignments electronically. This arrangement provides employees with the ultimate in flexibility because they can choose the hours they work and even the location. A growing body of evidence suggests that this arrangement increases job satisfaction and even productivity, and it also allows organizations to use the services of individuals who may not be able to work at a given site.[26] For example, an employee can live many hours from his or her office if he or she performed most of the work via telecommuting. Finally, larger organizations can save considerable amounts of money if they do not need large (or any) real office space. Cisco Systems, a pioneer in telecommuting, estimates that, by allowing employees to work at home, it has boosted productivity by 25 percent, lowered its own overhead by $1 million, and retained key knowledge workers who might have left for other jobs without the flexibility provided by the firm's telecommuting options.[27]

Alternative work sites present a more serious challenge to the human resource manager. In the past, the AFL-CIO has complained that home work arrangements allow management to impose unfair working conditions on employees, and it also makes it more difficult for unions to organize workers. So unions continue to oppose these arrangements. As with alternative work schedules, communication among employees is difficult under these arrangements, and it is extremely difficult for a new employee to become socialized. But in fact little socialization may

■ **Telecommuting** involves employees doing almost all of their work at home, perhaps even receiving assignments electronically.

Should You Work at Home?

Most organizations evaluate telecommuting relationships from their own perspective, that is, whether it works for the organization. Many employees who feel the need to work from home or who would prefer to do so usually fail to consider the disadvantages to such arrangements. These potential problems affect the individual rather than the organization and should be considered before any individual employee chooses to accept a telecommuting relationship.

POINT... Employees should work at home when they can because ...	COUNTERPOINT... Employees should not work at home, even when they can, because ...
It makes the balance between work and family easier to manage.	It blurs the separation between work life and family life.
It affords the employee maximum control and flexibility over his or her work schedule.	It makes it more difficult for the employee to impress managers with work behavior.
It avoids the stress of commuting.	Employees who are out of sight may also be out of mind for promotions and other opportunities.
It allows the employee to work in a more pleasant work environment.	It makes it more difficult for the employee to network with coworkers.

So... Although employees often see a telecommuting relationship as a positive option, it clearly has some disadvantages. As in most cases, the employee should weigh the benefits against these potential costs before deciding to accept the telecommuting option. It is critical to appreciate that costs *can* be incurred.

be possible if many of the employees are working under nontraditional work arrangements and many are working at home.

In addition, some individuals may simply lack the self-discipline to get the work done in a completely unconstrained environment, although the available evidence suggests that this outcome is not much of a problem. What does seem to be a problem is that these alternative work sites are likely to increase employees' sense of alienation at work.[28] They have no social connections and no support from coworkers, and so loyalty or commitment to the organization is unlikely to develop. Companies are trying, however, to overcome these problems. For example, Merrill Lynch allows potential telecommuters a two-week dry run to see how they like it. Aetna assigns each of its telecommuters an office buddy to help those working at home to stay in touch with what's going on at the office. And America West even arranges monthly potluck dinners to maintain social interaction among employees who work at home.[29]

Some disagree about whether telecommuting can aid the employee in the long run. Even if the employee has some need or desire to work from home, is it always in his or her best interests to do so? Our Point/Counterpoint feature for this chapter examines some of the issues involved.

Chapter Summary

One important part of a legal employment contract covers the conditions and terms under which an employee can be terminated. Employment-at-will asserts that an employer can terminate any employee at any time, for any reason or for no reason at all. A psychological contract is the set of expectations held by an employee concerning what he or she will contribute to the organization and what the organization, in return, will provide to the employee. Because job security is less prevalent now, many companies find that they must redefine the psychological contracts they have with their employees. One aspect of the psychological contract that is getting increased attention is the issue of employee rights. The notion of a social contract simply refers to expanding the relationship between employer and employee to include the government.

As we enter the information age in the workplace, many employees add value simply because of what they know. These employees are usually referred to as knowledge workers, and how well these employees are managed is seen as a major factor in determining which firms will be successful in the future. Compensation and career development policies for knowledge workers must also be specially tailored.

Over the past several years, the greatest growth in jobs and employment has been in the service sector of the economy. Service jobs include accounting, real estate, and other professional service functions. But many service jobs tend to lack glamour, be low paying, and require little skill. What is most challenging about this trend is the shortage of employees for these jobs.

A great deal of interest has focused on outsourcing certain functions in organizations today. The major issue for managers interested in this tactic is to decide what kinds of functions or activities are suitable for outsourcing. While lower-level jobs are often outsourced first, in some organizations higher-level functions are also being outsourced.

An explosion has occurred in the use of contingent and temporary workers by organizations. Contingent workers work for an organization on something other than a permanent or full-time basis. Categories of contingent workers include independent contractors, on-call workers, temporary employees, contract and leased employees, and part-time workers. Companies that choose to use contingent and temporary workers face several advantages and disadvantages.

Even when organizations continue to employ people on a permanent, full-time basis, the work schedules and arrangements for these employees are changing rapidly. In modern organizations, however, it is becoming increasingly common for people to work on a schedule other than five days/forty hours per week and/or to work at a place other than the office or place of business.

Key Points for Future HR Managers

- Employee rights in the workplace are becoming more important in human resource decisions.

- Employment contracts are important, but psychological contracts—which specify the expectations of the two parties and which are often not written down—may be even more important for managing human resources.

- The nature of the psychological contract has changed at many organizations. The firm typically views employees in more transactional terms, and the firm should therefore expect lower levels of commitment from its employees.

- Social contracts involve relationships among organizations, employees, and the government.

- Knowledge workers are seen by many as the new source of competitive advantage, but these workers often require special sets of human resource practices.

- The use of contingent workers is on the rise, and these employees pose special problems for human resource managers. They typically have lower levels of involvement in and commitment to the organization.

- Organizations should be careful in deciding how and when to employ contingent workers, and a model known as human resource architecture can provide some guidelines for these decisions.

- Alternative work schedules and work sites are also becoming more popular, and each of these alternatives also brings additional problems requiring planning.

Key Points for Future General Managers

▶ Traditional work relationships are becoming much less common than they were ten or twenty years ago.

▶ New employment relationships afford the organization much more flexibility and they can be quite cost effective, but employees hired under these new arrangements are often less committed and less involved than are those hired under more traditional arrangements.

▶ The human resource architecture model may offer guidance about when to employ contingent workers (i.e., workers with nontraditional employment relationships).

▶ The psychological contract between employer and employee is usually not written. It specifies the nature of expectations for each party in the employment relationship. These contracts change, but a violation of the psychological contract by either party, can create many problems.

▶ Additional flexibility can come through the use of alternative work schedules (such as compressed workweeks) or even alternative work sites (such as the use of telecommuting), but these relationships come with costs that must be considered.

Review and Discussion Questions

1. What is employment-at-will? Do you agree or disagree with its basic premise?

2. Distinguish between a psychological contract and a social contract.

3. What contributions and inducements typify a psychological contract in a class such as this one?

4. What are knowledge workers? What are the special challenges involved in managing knowledge workers?

5. What are the special challenges involved in managing low-skill workers?

6. What are the various kinds of contingent workers that organizations use?

7. What are the primary advantages and disadvantages in using contingent and temporary workers?

8. What are the differences between flexible work schedules and compressed workweeks?

9. Which would you personally prefer, a flexible work schedule or a compressed workweek?

10. Identify and discuss some of the major issues involved in allowing people to work at alternative work sites, such as their home office.

Closing Case

Temps, Temps, Everywhere!

Charleston Naval Shipyard, Charleston, SC: Like other pieces of complicated equipment, navy ships at the Charleston Naval Shipyard, Charleston, South Carolina, must have regular maintenance and service work, as well as major overhauls and upgrades, which are done less frequently. This work is usually done by one of several naval shipyards around the country. Whenever a ship is scheduled for service, each shipyard (including the Charleston Naval Shipyard) can bid for that work. Over the years it has specialized in working on nuclear missile submarines, although it

also works on every type of ship. The civilian employees in Charleston, like those at other shipyards, work for the Department of Defense. But they are limited to one year of continuous employment. If they work for more than one year, they attain a certain status and privileges as government workers that the government does not wish to bestow.

Whenever the shipyard wins a bid, therefore, an interesting employment process begins. The shipyard immediately begins advertising for temporary (one-year) employees who have the exact skills needed to perform the required maintenance work on the project. These skills obviously vary from project to project. The shipyard can usually hire many of the workers it needs, but it may have to train others. In either case, on the day the ship arrives for its maintenance work, the shipyard must have in place all the systems and the employees needed to carry out the work.

The fact that these temporary employees can work only for one year presents a dilemma for the shipyard. What if the work takes longer than is anticipated? What if employees are needed for more than one year? The regulations say that employees cannot work for more than one year continuously. If they are needed longer, they are terminated. Then, after one week of not being employed, they can be rehired by the shipyard for another year. Of course, skilled workers are always needed by the shipyard, and so some people attain almost permanent employee status as they move from one project to another. Nonetheless, all the employees are officially classified as temporary, and all hiring is done on an as-needed basis.

Macy's, Herald Square, New York City, NY:

There are few more enduring symbols of the onset of the traditional Christmas season than the Macy's Thanksgiving Day parade in New York City. But before the parade is over and the official shopping season begins, one of the largest programs of temporary hiring in the United States has already taken place. Indeed, the process is repeated all over the country as department and specialty stores get ready for the Christmas rush.

Every year in stores such as Macy's, hundreds of temporary employees are hired to supplement the regular staff. Although the demands of the season are substantial, the Christmas season does not last long enough to justify hiring more full-time people. On the other hand, the amount of time required makes it unreasonable to try to meet this demand by extending overtime to existing employees. Instead, notices go out in early November and the hiring process begins. Few applicants have had meaningful retail selling experience, although a large cadre of people return every year to Macy's to work during the holiday season.

What kind of person applies for and gets these temporary jobs? The most typical applicants are retired persons, students, and housewives. These are people unwilling or unable to work full-time, yet it is easy to find among them several hard-working and loyal employees. The employees typically receive employee discounts (10–15 percent, even off sale prices), as well as extra money for the holiday season.

Macy's and similar stores can meet the demands of the holiday shopping period without increasing the basic payroll. And for all, another holiday tradition is continued.

Collin Street Bakery, Corsicana, TX:

While many people associate the holiday rush with retailers like Macy's, many other kinds of employers also find it necessary to make seasonal adjustments in their workforce. Consider the Collin Street Bakery, a 100-year-old firm in Corsicana, Texas. For much of the year the bakery is a small, family-operated enterprise selling cookies, pies, cakes, and bread and employing fewer than fifty people. Although fruitcakes are often the brunt of jokes, they are serious business to the folks at the Collin Street Bakery.

As it turns out, the Collin Street Bakery sells more fruitcakes during the holiday season than any other producer in the world. The firm sells about 1.5 million fruitcakes a year, with about one-fourth of them being shipped to foreign countries. During the period starting in September each year, the bakery expands its workforce, first for the preparation of fruitcakes and later for their mailing and shipping. By Thanksgiving, more than 500 temporary workers are employed at the bakery.

But unlike Macy's in New York City, the Collin Street Bakery has a much smaller labor pool to draw from—the local community has only about 23,000 residents! Therefore, rather than market its jobs to seasonal workers, the bakery instead promotes opportunities to employees with full-time jobs elsewhere who might want to supplement their income during the holiday season. The shipping jobs, for instance, can be performed anytime, and most workers come in after their day jobs are finished, perhaps working from 7:00 P.M. (after dinner) or so until 11:00 P.M. two or three nights a week. This approach gives the bakery an ample supply of talent while also benefiting local residents who want to supplement their pay.[30]

Case Questions

1. What are the similarities and differences among the temporary staffing situations faced by the shipyard, the department store, and the bakery?

2. Which of the three challenges is the biggest? Which is the smallest?

3. What changes might force each of the three employers to adjust its temporary staffing strategy?

Building HR Management Skills

Purpose: The purpose of this exercise is to help you better understand the implicit and explicit elements of psychological contracts in an organization.

Step 1: Assume that you are the senior human resource executive of a large service company. Your firm has undergone three different layoffs during the last five years, and your employees feel that they have little job security. While your pay and training opportunities are among the best in your industry, you can also foresee the possibility of additional workforce reductions.

Step 2: Your boss, the chief executive officer, has suggested that you develop what she calls a new covenant for your organization, something you see as really an explicit psychological contract. This document, to be committed to writing and shared throughout the organization, will outline exactly what the firm will offer to its employees and what it expects in return.

Step 3: Draft the new covenant for your organization.

Step 4: Repeat this process assuming each of the following different circumstances:

■ Your firm is a midsized distribution company; the pay is slightly below industry averages, but you have never laid anyone off.

■ You are the company owner; you pay above-average wages and provide superior benefits. You also expect your employees to work long and hard and to exhibit unerring loyalty to you and to your firm.

■ You manage a large domestic subsidiary of a foreign corporation. Your parent company wants to instill its own values and corporate culture in your firm. These changes will include a more paternalistic approach and more job security, but lower pay and less lavish benefits.

Step 5: Form groups with your classmates and compare your responses, then respond to the following questions:

1. What are the major similarities and differences in your new covenants for the four different situations?

2. How similar or different were the various covenants developed by your group members?

3. What are the advantages and disadvantages of formal and written psychological contracts compared to informal and unwritten ones?

Ethical Dilemmas in HR Management

Your firm has a major telecommuting program. Under the terms of the program, employees are allowed to work at home two days a week. Because you prefer the structure and routine of a regular work schedule and workplace, you have elected not to participate. One of your best friends, however, was an early participant and is today one of its most outspoken advocates.

You know from casual comments, however, that your friend recently spent part of a work-at-home day on the golf course. You also know that your friend occasionally buys the family groceries and/or runs other family errands during work-at-home time. You have asked your friend about these comments. Your friend

was clearly uncomfortable and embarrassed by your question, mumbled that it was just comp time to offset some work in the evening and on the weekend, and then quickly changed the subject.

Questions

1. What are the ethical issues in this situation?

2. What are the basic arguments for and against your friend's behavior?

3. What would you do in this situation? What do you think most people would do?

HR Internet Exercise

Assume that you are the human resource manager for a midsized manufacturing company. Your firm has just gotten a big contract that will boost your human resource requirements for the next eighteen months or so. You will need new production workers, office/administrative workers, truck drivers and warehouse personnel, and sales support personnel. You are uncertain about what might happen after the contract is over, so you do not want to add permanent employees, although your permanent workforce might also grow.

Search the Internet for temporary employment agencies that might be of value. Review each site carefully and prepare a memo to your boss outlining both how you should proceed and your degree of comfort/discomfort with this approach. Respond to the following questions:

1. Do you feel more comfortable working with a large national firm or a smaller local one? Why?

2. Do you feel more comfortable working with one agency for all your needs, or do you prefer to work with different agencies for each type of worker you need? Why?

3. What information was easiest to learn from the websites you visited? What information was the most difficult?

Human Resource Information Systems

The human resource manager's job requires a large number of decisions. These decisions, in turn, require access to a large amount of information. In simple cases, we can imagine an HR manager reading and analyzing the files for the ten applicants for a recent job opening and deciding who should receive an offer. Perhaps the position for which these applicants are applying is a new one within the organization, and so at some point the HR manager must determine the appropriate compensation for this position relative to other jobs within the firm. Furthermore, this new position may be the result of a new strategic initiative that requires information about the kinds of skills and abilities available inside the organization.

Clearly, these decisions require that various kinds of information be available for the HR manager. As we will see, there is also a fair amount of information that might be useful to new employees once they join the organization and to other individuals who may have to make very different kinds of decisions but might still need to know something about the current human resources in the organization. The need for this kind of information, in an easily accessible and ready to use form, is at the heart of human resource information systems.

WHAT ARE HUMAN RESOURCE INFORMATION SYSTEMS (HRISs)?

A human resource information system is a special form of a more general kind of information system. Thus we begin by briefly examining the nature of information technology in general, and then we focus more specifically on human resource information systems and their role in organizations.

The Nature of Information Technology

Information technology refers to the resources used by an organization to manage information that it needs to carry out its mission. Information technology is generally of two types—manual or computer based. All information technology, and the systems that it defines, has five basic parts. One part is the *input medium,* the device that is used to add data and information into the system. For example, an optical scanner at Kroger enters point-of-sale information. Likewise, someone can also enter data through a keyboard. And when people apply for jobs in an organization, their resumes and/or job applications might be scanned into the firm's information system.

The data that are entered into the system typically flow first to a processor. The *processor* is the part of the system that is capable of organizing, manipulating, sorting, or performing calculations or other transformations with the data. Most systems also have one or more *storage devices*—a place where data can be stored for later use. Floppy disks, hard drives, and CD-ROMs are common forms of storage devices. As data are transformed into usable information, the resulting information must be communicated to the appropriate person by means of an output medium. Common ways to display output are video displays, printers, other computers, and fax machines.

Finally, the entire information technology system is operated by a *control system*—most often software of one form or another. Simple systems in smaller organizations can use off-the-shelf software. Microsoft Windows, DOS, and Mac OS are general operating systems that control more specialized types of software. Microsoft Word and WordPerfect are popular systems for word processing. Microsoft Excel and Lotus 1-2-3 are popular spreadsheet programs, and Microsoft Access is frequently used for database management. Of course, elaborate systems of the type used by large businesses require a special customized operating system. Some firms create their own information system for human resources, whereas others buy existing software commercial products.[1] And when organizations start to link computers together into a network, the operating system must be even more complex.

Human Resource Information Systems

A human resource information system, as noted above, is a special form of information system oriented directly at an organization's HR management needs. That is, a **human resource information system** (or **HRIS**) is the entire set of people, procedures, forms, and data used to acquire, store, analyze, retrieve, distribute, and use information about an organization's human resources. The system is, therefore, much more than just computer hardware and software (although these components are critical to an effective HRIS). Finally, the major goal of the system is to provide needed information that is timely and accurate and to provide it in a way that it is useful to persons making HR-related decisions.

■ A **human resource information system (HRIS)** is the entire set of people, procedures, forms, and data used to acquire, store, analyze, retrieve, distribute, and use information about an organization's human resources.

In essence, the information contained in an HRIS is information that has always been available in books, reports, records, or forms. The key difference, though, is that the information is now computerized. There is no longer any need for paper forms or reports, for instance, and decision makers should be able to locate and access easily and exactly the information they need. For example, if there is a need to know exactly how many people are working in an area (the "head count"), when they began working with the company (perhaps to determine potential wage costs), or even the average number of dependents employees have (perhaps to project benefit costs), the person charged with obtaining the information should be able to access a computer database and retrieve the desired information.

Thus the specific nature of any HRIS will depend upon the needs of the organization. Organizations will differ, for example, in terms of what information they actually need to retrieve, and therefore need to store, as part of the HRIS. Some organizations may focus on race and gender characteristics of the workforce, while others might be concerned about accidents and work days lost. Furthermore, organizations will differ in terms of how they need the information to be presented. Some may need information at the aggregate level, about the organization as a whole (numbers of employees, average wages, average hours, and so on), while others might need more information about individuals (a person's work history, skills profile, and so on). The remainder of this appendix discusses some specific uses of HRISs in organizations, as well as some specific ideas about the kinds of information that might be needed. Finally, we will discuss some of the moral, ethical, and legal issues that are involved with setting up and using an HRIS.

POTENTIAL USES OF HRISs

Of course, the potential types of output from an HRIS depend on the nature of the input. But the decision concerning what information to input depends on how the system will be used. Ultimately, the HRIS should help the organization in its strategic planning process, but there are a number of other more focused applications.

HR Functions

At a very basic level, the HRIS can be used by the organization and its members to help them more effectively manage the employment relationship. For example, from the standpoint of the organization, the HRIS can be used in HR planning. Job openings can be posted as part of its recruiting efforts. Applications can be scanned (as already noted) and stored. Performance appraisal information can also be stored, as can the employee's history of training and development activities. Career path, compensation, and benefit information can also be an integral part of the HRIS. Individual employees should be able to scan the HRIS for new job possibilities within the organization and be better informed about training opportunities and benefit options.

Record Keeping and Report Generation

Perhaps the most common application of an HRIS, however, involves the generation of reports, especially reports that must be prepared on a regular basis. A good example of this would be the EEO-1 report on current employees that many organizations are required to file with the government. Data must be presented for all jobs using the following categories: officials and managers, professionals, technicians, sales workers, office and clerical, (skilled) craft workers, (semiskilled) operatives, (unskilled) laborers, and service workers. For each job category the organization is required to report how many incumbents can be classified as white (not of Hispanic origin), black (not of Hispanic origin), Hispanic, Asian or Pacific Islander, and Native American or Native Alaskan. Furthermore, the organization must report numbers within these groups for male and female employees separately.

Also, many organizations are required to regularly submit "eight factor" reports, which indicate both the availability and utilization of employees within the same categories (for both jobs and employees) as in the EEO-1 report. These reports depend on the same types of information as the EEO-1 reports, and an HRIS is extremely useful in supplying that information. Other reports requiring HRIS input involve the evaluation of training programs. Computation of cost-benefit ratios for these programs requires information about which training programs an employee has gone through, and some evaluation of past and current levels of job performance, turnover, or absenteeism. In fact, virtually any evaluation that deals with absenteeism and turnover data, or with any type of productivity data, requires input from an HRIS.

But perhaps the area where the most report generation activity requiring an HRIS takes place is the compensation and benefits area. For example, to "price" jobs, an organization needs data on how the jobs score on various compensable factors, as well as data on what other organizations are paying. The results of the wage surveys for comparison data and the results of the job evaluation are likely to be kept in an HRIS and thus made available to compensation analysts. Also, once jobs are priced, an HRIS can provide the data needed to compare current compensation rates with those generated through the pricing process and to indicate which jobs should have their compensation adjusted. HRIS data are also used to determine withholdings and generate rates of take-home pay for employees. In such cases the system must be flexible enough to deal with changes in the tax codes or in the number of dependents.

Similarly, recall that in Chapter 13 we discussed the idea of a cafeteria benefits program. These systems provide an allowance for benefits that employees can "spend" on any mix of benefits they want. It is virtually impossible to implement such a system and keep track of choices and changes in choices and allocations without an HRIS, and data from these systems are needed to provide reports to employees. Even without a cafeteria system, HRIS data are needed to generate annual reports informing employees of their present benefits and the value of those benefits. Here again, flexibility is vital, as choices and options are likely to change.

One final example of an area where an HRIS is critical is in the area of planning. Specifically, as an organization plans for its human resource needs for the following year, it needs information about planned changes in operations and the implications of those changes for human resources. But the organization also needs to know about its available human resources and what types of skills and experiences the present workforce possesses. Inventories of skills and experience provide a challenge not only because of the amount of information required but also because of the way the information is encoded and used.

In most of the other examples we have discussed, the kind of data required for the system is pretty clear. That is, if managers need to know the number of women in a certain job, encoding this information is straightforward. However, to prepare an inventory of skills and experiences, managers need to first decide which skills and experiences are relevant for the decisions to be made. Then they must decide exactly what information about those skills and experiences to include. For example, a manager might simply want to note whether an employee has had a certain job assignment or not. Or the manager might want to know how long the assignment lasted and how successful the employee was on the job. In the area of skills, an organization might simply rely upon self-reports that an employee can speak French, for example. But more complex systems might include information about scores on a French test or might indicate the level of speaking ability. Thus HRISs used for planning require the organization to make many more decisions than do systems used for other types of decisions.

These examples provide some idea of the range of information that might be included in an HRIS and what kinds of decisions this information might be used for. Nonetheless, the actual range of possibilities is almost endless, as organizations determine what kinds of information they need to have access to in order to make the decisions that need to be made. But regardless of the kinds of information included, a number of other issues must be considered as an organization designs and implements an HRIS.

ISSUES AND CONCERNS IN THE USE OF HRISs

Regardless of the exact information an organization retains in its HRIS and regardless of how that information is used, the fact that the organization collects and stores a large amount of information about its employees, and that this information can be easily retrieved, raises a number of other issues and concerns. Some of these are related to legal questions concerning privacy and the invasion of privacy, whereas others are related to the ethics of storing and retrieving personal information about employees.

Legal Issues

Most of the legal issues concerning HRISs are related to privacy. The Fourth Amendment to the U.S. Constitution guarantees protection from unreasonable search and seizure. The ability of an organization (or its representatives) to search an employee's files without his or her permission might well violate that protection. In addition, the Fifth Amendment provides protection against self-incrimination, and if an organization searches through an employee's personnel files and finds incriminating information, this action could be viewed as a violation of that protection.

As noted in Chapter 3, most of the legislation in the privacy area has been enacted by states, but the Privacy Act of 1974 requires federal agencies to open their personnel files for employee inspection. Furthermore, the law enables the employee to correct any incorrect or misleading information in those files, *and* allows the employee to prevent the use of the information in those files for anything other than its original intent. Several lawmakers have suggested that this protection be extended to employees in private industry, but such legislation has not yet been formally proposed. It seems clear, however, that in the future organizations might have more difficulty in deciding what kinds of information to keep about employees and how to use that information, which will have a substantial impact on the design of HRISs.

The Privacy Protection Study Commission was established in 1977 to determine which safeguards needed to be put in place to protect employee rights in this area. The commission has suggested a number of steps to help organizations protect employee rights as they set up HRISs. These include:

1. Organizations should collect and store only job-relevant information in their information systems.

2. Organizations should limit or completely avoid storing subjective information about employees (such as appraisal information) in their information systems.

3. Organizations should provide employees with information about exactly how their records will be used.

4. Organizations should allow employees to access their records and files and to correct any incorrect information.

5. Organizations should strictly limit internal access to employee information.

6. Organizations should strictly limit and always document the release of information to anyone outside the organization without employee approval.[2]

Clearly, these suggestions would significantly limit the organization's ability to rely on information systems for decision making, and the potential conflicts between an employee's rights to privacy and an organization's need to have information will continue to be an important issue.

Ethical Issues

Some legal restrictions already in place potentially limit the information an organization can store about employees and how that information is used. And these restrictions are likely to increase over time. But in addition to legal restrictions, a number of ethical considerations should guide the design and use of an HRIS.

For example, organizations are restricted in the information they can collect about an employee's health at the time of hiring. However, once a person is an employee, an organization might routinely collect and store information about insurance claims that possibly contain information about health issues. Likewise, organizations should not ask applicants (or even current employees) about any disabilities they might have. On the other hand, employees who have disabilities may be able to request certain accommodations in order to carry out their jobs. Furthermore, the organization would be likely to store information about these accommodations, especially if they dealt with hours or conditions of employment. But retaining such information in an employee's file could jeopardize opportunities in the future if some decision maker discovers the employee's "hidden" disability (for example, a learning disability).

Even if there were no tangible results of this information becoming known, coworkers might begin treating the employee differently. Therefore, the question arises of whether or not the organization should keep this kind of information. Clearly, there might be good reasons to keep such information, and doing so is probably legal, but the information could cause embarrassment or discomfort to the employee if it were known. Again, the solution to such dilemmas probably lies with tighter restrictions on who can access an employee's file. But of course, as these restrictions grow, the chances increase that someone who might need to have access to some information will be denied access because he or she would then also have access to more-sensitive information.

CONCLUSIONS

As organizations become more complex and as the amount of information they need increases, the need for automated information systems increases dramatically. The organization must determine what kinds of information it will need by deciding what kinds of decisions it will make based on the HRIS information and who will actually make the decisions. Because these needs are likely to change over time, it is also necessary to build in a certain amount of flexibility.

But the ultimate flexibility would involve having a maximum amount of information available for every employee and then making this information accessible by every employee. Such a system would almost certainly violate an employee's rights to privacy and might well cause the employee embarrassment. Weighing the present and future organizational needs for information against the employee's rights and well-being will remain a major challenge for designers of HRISs.

Data and Research in Human Resource Management

Many aspects of the HR manager's job require decisions to be made. Throughout this text we have tried to provide information about the nature of these decisions, as well as insights into potential solutions. But even after a decision is made, the job is not complete—it is still necessary to evaluate the decision. That is, the HR manager (or perhaps someone else in the organization) needs to determine whether the implemented decision or program worked as intended. To be able to evaluate the decision effectively, the HR manager needs some appreciation and understanding of research, data, and data analysis. Note that in this day of computerization, HR managers do not usually need to actually perform specific statistical tests, but they must be able to decide which data to collect and determine which tests to run; then they must be able to interpret the results.

This appendix provides an overview of some of these issues. Although the principles discussed here apply to a wide variety of settings, we place them in the context of HR decisions and HR programs. In addition, we discuss in some detail two HR issues of a fairly technical nature that are also mentioned in the body of the text—validity generalization and utility analysis. First, though, we discuss a general issue that underlies all research in the social sciences, including HR research: causality.

DETERMINING CAUSAL RELATIONSHIPS

When an HR manager implements a new pay plan as a means of reducing turnover and then observes that turnover has, in fact, been reduced, the manager would probably like to believe that the new pay plan *caused* the reduction in turnover. This desire to believe the new pay plan was responsible for the change in turnover is especially true if the new pay plan was implemented in one division, perhaps as a pilot project, and the organization must now decide whether to implement the plan throughout the organization. At first glance the issue may seem to be quite simple. Turnover was high (say, 15 percent), a new pay plan was implemented, and turnover subsequently went down (perhaps to 8 percent). What else could have caused the drop in turnover?

This is exactly the right question to be asking, but the answer is not obvious. Any number of factors other than the new pay system could conceivably influence turnover in the organization. For example, when unemployment rates are high, turnover generally drops in all organizations as employees see few alternatives to their present jobs. When unemployment rates are lower, alternatives are available, and so an unhappy employee might feel more secure in acting on the basis of his or her dissatisfaction. Therefore, if the local unemployment rate increased around the time the new pay plan was implemented, reduced employment alternatives, rather than the new pay plan, may have caused the turnover rate to change. In fact, in this case, if the organization had done nothing, the turnover rate would still have gone down as a result of the rise in unemployment.

Another possibility is that disgruntled employees have been leaving the organization at a fairly constant rate. However, at some point all the disgruntled employees have already quit, and all that are left are the satisfied employees who are not likely to quit. Perhaps this point occurred at about the same time the new pay plan was implemented. Here again, the turnover rate would have dropped even if the organization did nothing.

In yet one more scenario, perhaps the employees believed that the management didn't really care much about them, and so their leaving was in response to a perceived neglect. When the organization introduced a new pay system, the management signaled to the employees that it did care about them. But the important thing was the fact that the management did *something* for the employees, rather than the specific nature of the new pay plan. Here, turnover would not have gone down if the organization did nothing, but a much less expensive intervention that communicated concern on the part of the management might have been equally effective.

To establish that a causal relationship exists, we must be able to effectively rule out all other rival plausible explanations for the changes we have observed. If any or all of the explanations discussed above (or some other explanation) are possible, we cannot say with certainty that the new pay plan caused the reduction in turnover. In fact, under such a set of circumstances we cannot say exactly what caused the reduction in turnover.

Many times, when we want to examine the impact of some program on an outcome of interest, we simply examine the relationship between a variable corresponding to the program and a variable corresponding to the outcome of interest. For example, if an organization is interested in training employees as a means of increasing satisfaction (since the employees would have more skills and be able to do a wider variety of jobs), an HR manager might decide to correlate the amount of training employees have with their levels of satisfaction. This task would involve determining whether employees with more training were also more satisfied with their jobs. Assuming that the HR manager would find such a relationship, she or he might conclude that training causes higher levels of satisfaction and so recommend companywide training programs. (We discuss correlations in more detail a bit later.)

But again, there would be problems with such a statement. Because the HR manager did not provide the training (and so had no control over who was trained or how much training a person received), many other factors could explain the relationship observed. Perhaps being more satisfied on the job leads an employee to make more investments for the sake of the company, including seeking training. Thus increased satisfaction caused increased training, rather than vice versa. Alternatively, perhaps more highly motivated employees were more likely to seek training and more likely to be happy on the job. In this case, training would not have caused satisfaction, and satisfaction would not have caused employees to seek training. Instead, a third variable (the level of employee motivation) caused both, the seeking of training and the increase in satisfaction.

Therefore, we state again that we can make causal statements (changes in *a* caused changes in *b*) only when we have ruled out all plausible alternative explanations. Furthermore, we can never make causal statements when our conclusions are based on a correlation between two variables. Instead, if we wish to make causal statements, we need to be able to control for these alternative explanations. How do we do that? The simple answer is that we need to conduct an experiment in which two groups are equivalent on everything that might possibly be relevant, especially on levels of overall satisfaction. Then we introduce a treatment (for example, a new pay plan) to one group (at random), but not the other. After a suitable period of time, we measure the levels of satisfaction in the two groups. If the level of satisfaction (following the intervention) is higher in the group that received the new pay plan, we can be relatively sure that the new pay plan caused satisfaction to increase.

We have just described a true experiment that allowed us to make a causal statement. It is often difficult to conduct true experiments in organizational settings, but some variations are easier to carry out. The discussion of these different designs is beyond the scope of the present discussion. Nevertheless, without some type of experiment, we cannot make statements of the type that "*a* causes *b*."

COMMON HR RESEARCH ISSUES

Whether or not some type of experiment will be conducted, a number of issues must be considered whenever an organization does HR research. We will discuss sampling, measurement, and statistical issues in the context of various types of HR research issues. Again, these subjects are complex, and we can provide only an introduction to them here. The interested reader is encouraged to look for additional material.[1]

Samples and Sampling

In Chapter 7 we introduced the idea of validation as it relates to selection—demonstrating that persons who scored higher on some test (or other selection device) also performed better on the job. To demonstrate such a relationship (and so validate the test), we typically collect information on test scores and subsequent (or current) performance and then calculate a correlation to determine the extent of any relationship. Presumably, an organization could give this test to every employee and obtain performance information for every employee, but this would be extremely time consuming. The organization would be more likely to collect these data from some subset of employees, which we call a "sample." The organization would then determine the extent of the relationship in the sample data and infer that the same relationship holds true for the rest of the population.

Before discussing any details about samples, we must point out that even if the organization decided to test and collect performance data from every employee, sampling would still be involved. That is, managers are not really interested in the relationship between test scores and job performance for current employees—the organization already knows how well they are performing. Instead, managers want to use any information about test scores and performance with future applicants. If a relationship exists between the two, managers would use the test scores of applicants to predict their later performance on the job and hire only those expected to perform well. Therefore, managers would be using the relationship between scores and performance in current employees and assume that the same relationship would hold for new applicants.

For this logic to work, the sample must be representative of the population of interest. If we use current employees to compute a relationship that we hope will apply to later applicants, our current employees must be representative of future applicants. If, for example, our present employees are mostly white males and we expect many future applicants to be nonwhite and/or females, we can be pretty certain that our sample is not a good one for predicting performance of later applicants.

Effective sampling procedures allow television networks to predict the outcome of elections so early in the evening. When network executives tell us that 75 million families watched the last Super Bowl, they base this statement on the viewing patterns of a small sample of "typical" families—referred to as "Nielsen families" because of the name of the firm that compiles the ratings.

One of the most famous blunders based on poor sampling occurred during the presidential election of 1948. Harry Truman was running against a Republican named Thomas Dewey. Pollsters conducted an opinion poll to try to predict the outcome of the election. They sought a "representative" sample of all Americans they could poll and decided to draw the sample from local phone directories. The polls indicated that Dewey would be the easy winner, and everyone was surprised when Truman won handily. The problem was with the sample used in the polls. In 1948 many Americans did not own a phone because they could not afford one. Therefore, the phone directory only provided information about phone owners—not the general population. People with more money were more likely to own phones, and traditionally people with more money are more likely to vote Republican. The sample was therefore biased in that it overrepresented Republicans. Had the sample been more representative, the outcome would have been different. Modern pollsters have become much more sophisticated about drawing samples, and in fact, the phone directory might provide a much more representative sample of Americans today than it did in 1948.

Measurement Issues

If we were interested in measuring someone's height, we could do so with a yardstick and be pretty sure that we got it right. We can measure time and distance with amazing precision as well. But when we try to measure someone's level of ability, or personality or intelligence, we begin to have difficulties. In addition to measuring the level of someone's conscientiousness (for example), we are also measuring a lot of other things we don't really want to measure. This is the problem of unreliability we discussed in Chapter 7. Eventually, we could be measuring so many of these unwanted things that we are not measuring conscientiousness at all. We also discussed the validity problem in Chapter 7.

If we are interested in seeing whether a test for conscientiousness is related to performance on the job, we have to be sure that we can measure both conscientiousness and performance in a meaningful way. If our test is somehow biased, or requires a high level of reading ability, for example, we will have problems, since the test is supposed to measure conscientiousness not reading ability. As a result, we might conclude that conscientiousness does predict job performance when we have really only found that reading ability predicts job performance. Likewise, if we do not have a good measure of job performance (see Chapter 9), we may conclude that our test predicts performance on the job when it really only predicts a person's gender, since men consistently are rated higher on our (flawed) performance measure even when they do not perform better than women. Using the test in this case would then result in selecting only men, which, in this case, would almost certainly be illegal.

Statistical Issues

Despite our discussion of causality, the single most common statistical test used in HR is the correlation coefficient. A correlation coefficient indicates the degree of linear relationship between two sets of scores. When scores on, say, a test and job performance are correlated, we know that changes in test scores are associated with changes in job performance. If the correlation is positive, we further know that higher test scores are associated with higher levels of performance. The stronger the relationship, the higher the correlation, and the closer changes in one are associated with changes in the other. Notice that we are not saying that the test scores cause the changes in performance. Instead, we simply note that those who score higher also tend to perform better. In fact, correlations are used in settings where we do not have experimental designs and so we cannot assess causality.

Correlations can also be negative. The sign (positive or negative) indicates nothing about the strength of the relationship, only the nature of the relationship. When a correlation is negative it means that higher scores on one variable are associated with lower scores on the other. For example, we know that employees who are more satisfied on their jobs should be absent less frequently. Therefore, if we took a sample of employees, measured their job satisfaction, and noted how many days they missed work in the past year, we should find that those with higher satisfaction scores were absent fewer days—a negative correlation.

The strength of the correlation coefficient indicates the strength of the relationship between the two sets of scores. Correlations can range from -1.00 through 0 to $+1.00$. Since the sign of the correlation only tells us the direction of the relationship, we can see that a correlation of 0 indicates no relationship between the variables, whereas a correlation of 1 indicates the strongest relationship possible. In fact, a correlation of 1.00 is also referred to as a perfect correlation. It means that for every unit of change in one variable, there is exactly one unit of change in the other. Because the relationship is perfect, we can also perfectly predict the scores on one variable from the scores on the other variable. To help illustrate this principle and to help make the concept of correlations clearer, we have presented some correlation coefficients in Figure A2.1.

FIGURE A2.1   Diagrams Illustrating the Scatter Plots for Five Correlation Coefficients

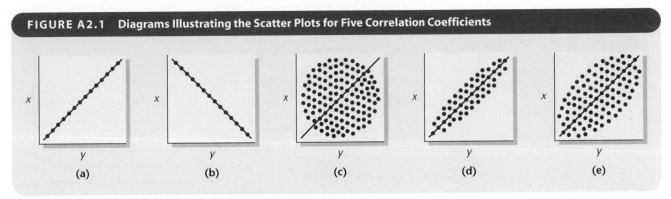

(a)　　　　(b)　　　　(c)　　　　(d)　　　　(e)

These diagrams illustrate correlations of 1.00 (a), −1.00 (b), zero (c), .80 (d), and .10 (e).

The first three diagrams illustrate correlations that are either perfect or 0. Specifically, these are the scatter plots that would correspond to each correlation. A scatter plot is obtained by simply graphing each person's scores on the two variables x and y (where x might be scores on a test and y might be job performance). For example, we have indicated the point corresponding to a person who scored 80 on x and 90 on y. Every other point in the scatterplot was determined in exactly the same way. You may wonder why if the correlation between the two variables is perfect, the person whose scores we have illustrated does not have exactly the same score on both variables. In order to explain that, we need one more piece of information that is presented in the figure.

Notice that in each case we draw a line, called the regression line, through the scatter plot. This represents the best straight-line fit to the information in the graph. The linear equations represented by those lines are always of the form $y = bx + c$ where y is the score on variable y; x is the score on variable x; c is a constant; and b is the regression coefficient, or the *slope* of the line. The constant term simply allows the scores on the two variables to differ by some constant and is also referred to as the *y intercept*, since it marks the point at which the line crosses the vertical axis. The slope of the line is a ratio of the number of units of change in one variable to the number of units of change in the other. In all the examples provided here, the slope is equal to 1.0. This slope is simply the easiest to illustrate and indicates that in the best-fitting line one unit of change in x is associated with one unit of change in y. The y intercept, or constant, in each case is 10, indicating that the two variables change on different scales, but that these scales differ by exactly 10 units. Thus for each case except for the negative correlation, the equation for the best-fitting regression line would be equal to

$$y = 1.0(x) + 10$$

In the first example, where there is a perfect and positive correlation, the best-fitting line fits the data perfectly—all the points on the scatter plot line up exactly on the regression line. Our equation would lead us to predict that for any value of x, if we simply add 10, we will get a corresponding value for y. In the first case, our predictions are exactly right each time, since every point is on the line. So if we knew someone had a score on x of 30, we would predict a score on y of 40, and in the first case we would be exactly right. The nature of the equation and prediction are the same for the negative correlation, except that the equation would have a negative slope, but prediction would still be perfect.

The regression line for the third correlation is the same as for the first but here the correlation is 0. Thus knowing a score on x provides absolutely no help in predicting a score on y. In fact, we can see that someone scoring 50 on x could score anywhere from 0 to 100 on y. This same range of predicted values will be obtained for every value of x. Notice here that the points in the scatter plot form more of a circle and, in any case, deviate far from the straight line. The only predictions we can make in all cases are those based on the simple linear regression equation, and the further the points deviate from the straight line, the less accurate our predictions until we reach this case, where the correlation is 0, and our predictions are no better than we could obtain if we just chose random numbers.

The remaining two graphs illustrate correlations greater than 0, but less than 1.00. In both cases the points in the scatter plot deviate from our best-line regression line, but the degree of deviation is quite different. In the fourth illustration, the correlation is computed to be $=.80$. Although prediction is not perfect here, notice the points do not deviate much from the regression line. As in the other cases, if a person had a score of 50 on x, we would predict that he or she should score 60 on y. Because prediction cannot be perfect here, we are not always right. But notice that a person scoring 50 on y will score somewhere between 55 and 65 on y. We predicted a score of 60, and we were off, but not by much. Thus, knowing someone's score on x does not perfectly predict the score on y, but it narrows things down considerably.

The final illustration involves a correlation of $+.10$. Here the points of the scatter plot deviate quite a bit from the regression line, and so we would expect predictions to be less accurate. The person scoring 50 on x would still be predicted to score 60 on y, but in fact, persons scoring 50 on x score anywhere from 10 to 90 on y. This is still better than the accuracy of prediction when the correlation is 0, but not by much, and we can predict very little about scores on y from scores on x.

Another statistical test that is encountered in HR is known as a t-test. This test, which compares two groups in terms of their mean scores, may well be used in experimental designs as a means of determining causality. For example, if we were interested in whether a group that had received a training program produced more "units" than one that wasn't trained (but was otherwise comparable to aid in determining causality), we would use a t-test to compare the mean levels of output in the two groups. If the trained group produced more units and the difference were greater than we would expect by chance alone (determined by comparing our obtained t-value with some critical value from a table), we would conclude that the training did cause an increase in output.

If, instead, there were three groups, we would need to employ a related but slightly different statistical test. So if we wanted to compare the output of a group receiving traditional training, a group receiving computer-aided training, and a group receiving no training, we could compare the mean levels of output for the three groups simultaneously, using a statistical test called analysis of variance (ANOVA). This technique would be preferable to conducting a series of *t*-tests among all the possible pairs of groups for a number of reasons that are beyond the scope of this discussion. Suffice it to say, however, that in this case ANOVA would be the best test to use. If we determined that the means differed at a level beyond what we would expect by chance, we would still need to conduct some follow-up (post hoc) tests to determine exactly which means differed from which other means.

These, then, are the statistical tests basic to HR operations. Using the right test, along with proper sampling techniques and sound measurement, allows HR managers to answer the questions needed to carry out their job effectively. Many of these questions deal with the evaluation of programs or interventions. That is, if an organization introduces a new appraisal or compensation program, the firm wants to be sure that the new program is accomplishing what was intended. An HR manager often deals with questions of this type, and the tools and techniques discussed here make it more likely that the manager can provide the organization with the answers it needs.

OTHER TECHNICAL ISSUES IN HR RESEARCH

In addition to using statistics and research techniques to answer specific questions, there are also at least two areas in which an HR manager needs some specialized technical expertise related to the treatment of data. We focus on the issues of validity generalization and utility analysis. In both cases the HR manager needs to understand something about data and analysis in order to provide the best services possible to the organization.

Validity Generalization

When we discussed test validation in Chapter 7, we discussed it in terms of separate validation efforts for each test on each job. In fact, organizations and courts have traditionally viewed the validation process this way. Each test must be validated for each job. Yet, at some level we recognize that this approach may be unnecessary. For example, let us say that State Farm Insurance Company develops a test to select insurance agents and goes through the process of validating the test. Let us say further that State Farm relies on a test of clerical abilities that is generally available to any interested organization. Now if Allstate decides to use the same abilities test to select its insurance agents, does it need to conduct a separate validity study? It would seem reasonable to assume that if scores on the test were related to performance at State Farm, they should be related to performance at Allstate as well.

In fact, Allstate would be able to "borrow" State Farm's validity data, and even rely on it in court if necessary, as long as Allstate could demonstrate through job analysis that the job requirements and the settings in the two firms were the same. In fact, in the simplest and least controversial form of validity generalization, one firm uses the validity study results of another firm, but both firms are interested in using the same test to select persons for the same job.

An extension of this type of validity generalization involves the use of the Position Analysis Questionnaire (or PAQ), which was designed to describe a wide variety of jobs using a common set of job dimensions (see Chapter 5). The developers of the PAQ extended some earlier work on synthetic validity[2] and argued that it was possible to show relationships between tests and job dimensions, just as one usually demonstrated relationships between tests and the entire job. If one could establish such relationships (that is, performance on a test was related to performance on some aspect of a job) and if a general set of job dimensions could be used that was believed to underlie all jobs, it would be possible to "construct" validity data for any job. That is, it would be possible to determine which job dimensions were important for a given job and then put together a selection battery by combining those tests that were related to performance on each dimension.

In fact, such a system has been developed for use with the PAQ and was introduced in Chapter 5. This system (which is referred to as job component validity) allows an organization to conduct a job analysis of a job, using the PAQ, and then rely on the already established relationships to construct a recommended test battery for use in selecting persons for the job in question. Although limited, the available information suggests that these recommendations, in fact, prove to be valid for the job in question when this is tested empirically.[3] Thus this approach would allow an organization to piece together validity information for a variety of jobs and tests and would require job analysis, rather than a formal validation study, to support the use of a test or tests in a selection setting. Whether the courts will accept this broader application is not clear.

The most far-reaching proposal for validity generalization, however, has been proposed by Frank Schmidt and John Hunter.[4] These authors and their associates have compiled an enormous amount of data clearly indicating that many of the differences we observe in the validity of a given test, across different jobs, can be attributed to problems of unreliability and measurement, rather than to true differences in the predictability of performance. In fact, these arguments even suggest that certain types of cognitive ability tests (such as intelligence tests), and certain other types of tests, are related to performance on *virtually all* jobs. Furthermore, these tests predict performance better than alternatives do, and so there is no need to conduct any validity studies. An organization can simply use these tests for selection and know it is selecting the best people.[5]

These arguments, although supported by a great deal of data, have not been completely accepted by the courts and are quite controversial. The controversy has been generated not only because these arguments obviate the need for separate validity studies but also because they propose tests such as intelligence tests, which tend to have adverse impact, as the best predictors of performance across a wide variety of jobs.

Utility Analysis

Test validation is concerned with demonstrating that persons who score higher on some test also perform better on some job. Once this relationship has been established, an organization can use the test to select applicants by hiring only those who score above a certain cutoff on the test. This approach will result in the organization hiring more people who are ultimately successful and fewer persons who would ultimately fail on the job. Therefore, the organization can be said to be improving its selection system and selecting better people. But how much better is the selection system, and how much better are the people selected? Utility analysis attempts to answer these critical questions.

For example, we do not need very sophisticated models to conclude that if 95 percent of the persons hired without the use of a test are successful, then even if the test is valid, if it improves the success rate to 96 percent, but costs the firm hundreds of thousands of dollars to administer, it probably is not worth the additional cost. Over the years a number of approaches to assessing utility have been proposed. An early approach used a series of charts (the Taylor Russell tables) that indicate the improvement in the selection of successful applicants by using a test with specified validity, given the percentage of successful employees selected without using the test and the selection ratio (explained below).[6] But this approach failed to consider the costs associated with selection. Therefore, more complete utility models have been proposed that do consider the costs associated with selection, training, or whatever the intervention is being evaluated.

An early utility model that considered costs, was proposed by Hubert Brogden[7] and is presented below. The original model had a problem calculating one critical component, but subsequent versions, as well as other models that further refined the basic relationships,[8] could be used to express exactly how much (in dollars) a new selection system or training program was worth to an organization. Conceptually, the model is as follows (mathematically, the model must be expressed differently):

$$\text{Savings per person selected} = z_y SD_y - \text{Cost of selecting the person}$$

The cost of selecting a person is the product of the cost of testing each applicant (which includes both actual testing costs and recruiting costs) and the selection ratio, or the ratio of applicants per job opening. If there were ten applicants for each job opening, the selection ratio would be 1/10 or .10. The greater the selection ratio, the more applicants per job, which allows the organization to be more selective, but also increases the cost of testing. So, if the cost to test each applicant is $10, and the selection ratio is .10, the cost to select an individual is $100 (plus recruiting costs). If the selection ratio goes to $i/100$, the cost to select an individual becomes $1,000 (plus recruiting costs).

The remaining terms in the expression require some explanation as well. The term z_y refers to the mean criterion score (in standard score units) of those selected. Basically, this value indicates how successful those selected with the test in question might be. The SD_y term refers to the variance in performance on the job, expressed in dollar terms. If this term is high, the performance, or output, of a high-performing individual is worth a lot more to the organization than the performance of a low-performing individual. In such a case the value to the company of selecting high-performing individuals would go up. But in other cases the difference between the value of a high- and low-performing employee might not be so great. The value of the SD_y term would be reduced, and the utility of the test would be less. That is, in such a case, high-performing employees would be worth less to the organization relative to low-performing employees as compared to a case where the utility of the test was high. More complete illustrations of the use of utility analyses can be found elsewhere,[9] but these analyses are an important weapon for HR managers who wish to demonstrate that their efforts yield financial returns to the organization.

Endnotes

Chapter 1

1. Matthew Boyle, "The Right Stuff," *Fortune*, March 4, 2002, pp. 85–86 (*quote on p. 86); Matthew Boyle, "The Shiniest Reputations in Tarnished Times," *Fortune*, March 4, 2002, pp. 70–72; Wendy Zellner, "Southwest: After Kelleher, More Blue Skies," *Business Week*, April 2, 2001, p. 45; "America's Top 500 Companies," *Forbes*, April 14, 2003, pp. 144–172.

2. Robert M. Grant, "Toward a Knowledge-Based View of the Firm," *Strategic Management Journal*, 1996, Vol. 17, pp. 109–122.

3. Jeffrey Pfeffer, "Producing Sustainable Competitive Advantage Through the Effective Management of People," *The Academy of Management Executive*, February 1995, pp. 55–69; Peter Cappelli and Anne Crocker-Hefter, "Distinctive Human Resources Are Firms' Core Competencies," *Organizational Dynamics*, Winter 1996, pp. 7–22.

4. See Charles R. Greer, *Strategy and Human Resources* (Englewood Cliffs, N.J.: Prentice-Hall, 1995), for an overview of the strategic importance of human resources.

5. Robert R. Blake, "Memories of HRD," *Training & Development*, March 1995, pp. 22–28.

6. Randall S. Schuler, "Repositioning the Human Resource Function: Transformation or Demise?" *The Academy of Management Executive*, August 1990, pp. 49–60.

7. For an excellent review of some of the problems involved in selecting employees in the context of high security settings, see Paul R. Sackett, Neal Schmitt, Jill E. Ellingson, and Melissa Kabin, "High-Stakes Testing in Employment, Credentialing, and Higher Education," *The American Psychologist*, April 2001, pp. 302–418.

8. "Life Goes On," *HR Magazine*, September 2002, pp. 42–49.

9. Daniel Wren, *The Evolution of Management Thought*, 4th ed. (New York: Wiley, 1994).

10. Thomas A. Mahoney, "Evolution of Concept and Practice in Personnel Administration/Human Resource Management (PA/HRM)," *Journal of Management*, 1986, Vol. 12, No. 2, pp. 223–241.

11. Frederick W. Taylor, *Principles of Scientific Management* (New York: Harper, 1911).

12. Oliver E. Allen, "'This Great Mental Revolution,'" *Audacity*, Summer 1996, pp. 52–61.

13. J. M. Fenster, "How General Motors Beat Ford," *Audacity*, Fall 1992, pp. 50–62.

14. Wren, *The Evolution of Management Thought*.

15. Elton Mayo, *The Human Problems of an Industrial Civilization* (New York: Macmillan, 1933).

16. Abraham Maslow, "A Theory of Human Motivation," *Psychological Review*, July 1943, pp. 370–396.

17. Douglas McGregor, *The Human Side of Enterprise* (New York: McGraw-Hill, 1960).

18. James H. Dulebohn, Gerald R. Ferris, and James T. Stodd, "The History and Evolution of Human Resource Management," in Gerald R. Ferris, Sherman D. Rosen, and Harold T. Barnum (eds.), *Handbook of Human Resource Management* (Cambridge, Mass.: Blackwell, 1995), pp. 18–41.

19. For example, see John E. Delery and D. Harold Doty, "Modes of Theorizing in Strategic Human Resource Management: Tests of Universalistic, Contingency, and Configurational Performance Predictions," *Academy of Management Journal*, August 1996, pp. 802–835.

20. Dave Ulrich, "A New Mandate for Human Resources," *Harvard Business Review*, January–February 1998, pp. 124–133.

21. Brian Becker and Barry Gerhart, "The Impact of Human Resource Management on Organizational Performance: Progress and Prospects," *Academy of Management Journal*, August 1996, pp. 779–801; Russell A. Eisenstat, "What Corporate Human Resources Brings to the Picnic: Four Models for Functional Management," *Organizational Dynamics*, Autumn 1996, pp. 7–22.

22. John W. Kendrick, *Understanding Productivity: An Introduction to the Dynamics of Productivity Change* (Baltimore, Md.: Johns Hopkins, 1977).

23. Ross Johnson and William O. Winchell, *Management and Quality* (Milwaukee, Wis.: American Society for Quality Control, 1989).

24. Rudy M. Yandrick, "Help Employees Reach for the Stars," *HRMagazine*, January 1997, pp. 96–100

25. Michelle Martinez, "Prepared for the Future," *HRMagazine*, April 1997, pp. 80–87.

26. Susan Brooks, "Managing a Horizontal Revolution," *HRMagazine*, June 1995, pp. 52–58.

27. See, for example, Brian E. Becker, and Mark A. Huselid, "High Performance Work Systems and Firm Performance: A Synthesis of Research and Managerial Implications," *Research in Personnel and Human Resource Management*, 1998, Vol. 16, pp. 53–101; John W. Boudreau and Peter R. Ramsted, "Human Resource Metrics: Can Measures Be Strategic?" in Patrick Wright, Lee Dyer, John Boudreau, and George Milkovich (eds.), *Strategic Human Resources Management in the Twenty-First Century*, (Stamford, Conn.: JAI Press, 1999, pp. 75–98).

28. Stephenie Overman, "A Day in the Life of a HR Generalist," *HRMagazine*, March 1993, pp. 78–85.

29. For an excellent review, see John W. Boudreau, "Utility Analysis for Decisions in Human Resource Management," in Marvin D. Dunnette and Leatta M. Hough (eds.), *Handbook of Industrial and Organizational Psychology,* Vol. 2, 2nd ed. (Palo Alto, Calif.: Consulting Psychologists Press, 1991), pp. 621–745.

30. See, for example, Mark A. Huselid, "The Impact of Human Resource Management Practices on Turnover, Productivity, and Corporate Financial Reporting," *Academy of Management Journal,* 1996, Vol. 39, pp. 779–801.

31. See Martha I. Finney, "The Catbert Dilemma," *HRMagazine,* February 1997, pp. 70–76, for an interesting discussion of the relationship between human resource managers and other managers in organizations.

32. For an interesting contrast between large and small firms and human resource management activities, see Allison E. Barber, Michael J. Wesson, Quinetta M. Roberson, and M. Susan Taylor, "A Tale of Two Job Markets: Comparing the Hiring Practices of Large and Small Organizations," *Personnel Psychology,* 1999, Vol. 52, pp. 841–861.

33. Lotte Bailyn, "Patterned Chaos in Human Resource Management," *Sloan Management Review,* Winter 1993, pp. 77–89.

34. Martha Finney, "Degrees That Make a Difference," *HRMagazine,* November 1996, pp. 74–82; Bruce Kaufman, "What Companies Want from HR Graduates," *HRMagazine,* September 1994, pp. 84–90.

35. Steve Bates, "Facing the Future," *HRMagazine,* July 2002, pp. 26–32.

36. Brian D. Steffy and Steven D. Maurer, "Conceptualizing and Measuring the Economic Effectiveness of Human Resource Activities," *Academy of Management Review,* 1988, Vol. 13, No. 2, pp. 271–286.

37. Sources: *Hoover's Handbook of Private Companies 2003* (Austin, Tex.: Hoover's Business Press, 2003), pp. 148–159; Brian O'Reilly, "The Rent-a-Car Jocks Who Made Enterprise #1," *Fortune,* October 28, 1996, pp. 125–128; "Enterprise Takes Idea of Dressed for Success to a New Extreme," *Wall Street Journal,* November 20, 2002, p. B1.

Chapter 2

1. "The Starbucks Strategy," *Washington Post,* September 1, 2002, pp. E1, E6; "Brewing a British Coup," *USA Today,* September 16, 1998, pp. 1D, 2D; Jennifer Reese, "Starbucks—Inside the Coffee Cult," *Fortune,* December 9, 1996, pp. 190–200 (*quote on p. 196).

2. Charles R. Greer, *Strategy and Human Resources* (Englewood Cliffs, N.J.: Prentice-Hall, 1995).

3. The points in the debate are best explained in Brian Becker and Barry Gerhart, "The Impact of Human Resource Management on Organizational Performance: Progress and Prospects," *Academy of Management Journal,* August 1996, pp. 779–801. The different sides are represented in Mark A. Huselid, "The Impact of Human Resource Management Practices on Turnover, Productivity, and Corporate Financial Reporting," *Academy of Management Journal,* 1995, Vol. 38, pp. 635–672; John Delery and D. Harold Doty, "Modes of Theorizing in Strategic Human Resource Management: Tests of Universalistic, Contin-

gency, and Configurational Performance Predictions," *Academy of Management Journal,* 1995, Vol. 38, pp. 802–835; and Patrick Wright, Dennis Smart, and Gary McMahan, "Matches Between Human Resources and Strategy Among NCAA Basketball Teams," *Academy of Management Journal,* Vol. 38, No. 5, pp. 1052–1074.

4. See Charles W. L. Hill and Gareth R. Jones, *Strategic Management: An Analytical Approach,* 6th ed. (Boston, Mass.: Houghton Mifflin, 2004).

5. Janine Nahapiet and Sumantra Ghoshal, "Social Capital, Intellectual Capital, and the Organizational Advantage," *Academy of Management Review,* 1998, Vol. 23, pp. 242–266.

6. Catherine M. Daily and Charles Schwenk, "Chief Operating Officers, Top Management Teams, and Boards of Directors: Congruent or Countervailing Forces?" *Journal of Management,* 1996, Vol. 22, No. 2, pp. 185–208.

7. S. A. Kirkpatrick and Edwin A. Locke, "Direct and Indirect Effects of Three Core Charismatic Leadership Components on Performance and Attitudes," *Journal of Applied Psychology,* 1996, Vol. 81, pp. 36–51; see also Harry G. Barkema and Luis R. Gomez-Mejia, "Managerial Compensation and Firm Performance: A General Research Framework," *Academy of Management Journal,* 1998, Vol. 41, pp. 135–145.

8. See, for example, Donald C. Hambrick and Sidney Finkelstein, "Managerial Discretion: A Bridge Between Polar Views on Organizations," in L.L. Cummings and B. Staw (eds.) *Research in Organizational Behavior,* Vol. 9 (Greenwich, Conn.: Jai Press, 1987, pp. 369–406); or Sidney Finkelstein and Donald Hambrick, "Top Management Team Tenure and Organizational Outcomes: The Moderating Role of Managerial Discretion," *Administration Science Quarterly,* Vol. 35, 1990, pp. 484–503.

9. Hill and Jones, *Strategic Management: An Analytical Approach.*

10. Brian Becker and Barry Gerhart, "The Impact of Human Resource Management on Organizational Performance: Progress and Prospects," *Academy of Management Journal,* August 1996, Volume 39, No. 4, pp. 779–801.

11. Kenneth Andrews, *The Concept of Corporate Strategy,* rev. ed. (Homewood, Ill.: Dow Jones–Irwin, 1980).

12. David M. Schweiger and James P. Walsh, "Mergers and Acquisitions: An Interdisciplinary View," in Kenneth Rowland and Gerald Ferris (eds.), *Research in Personnel and Human Resource Management,* Vol. 8 (Greenwich, Conn.: JAI Press, 1990), pp. 41–107.

13. David M. Schweiger and Angelo DeNisi, "Communications with Employees Following a Merger: A Longitudinal Field Study," *Academy of Management Journal,* 1991, Vol. 34, pp. 110–135.

14. Hill and Jones, *Strategic Management: An Analytical Approach.*

15. Jay Barney and Ricky W. Griffin, *The Management of Organizations* (Boston, Mass.: Houghton Mifflin, 1992).

16. Russell A. Eisenstat, "What Corporate Human Resources Brings to the Picnic: Four Models for Functional Management," *Organizational Dynamics,* Autumn 1996, pp. 7–21.

17. John O. Whitney, "Strategic Renewal for Business Units," *Harvard Business Review,* July–August 1996, pp. 84–98.

18. Raymond E. Miles and Charles C. Snow, *Organizational Strategy, Structure, and Process* (New York: McGraw-Hill, 1978).

19. Michael Porter, *Competitive Strategy* (New York: Free Press, 1980).

20. Robert L. Cardy and Gregory H. Dobbins, "Human Resource Management in a Total Quality Organizational Environment: Shifting from a Traditional to a TQHRM Approach," *Journal of Quality Management,* 1996, Vol. 1, No. 1, pp. 5–20.

21. Henry Mintzberg, "Patterns in Strategy Formulation," *Management Science,* October 1978, pp. 934–948.

22. David Fiedler, "Know When to Hold 'Em," *HR Magazine,* August 2002, pp. 89–94.

23. Edilberto F. Montemayor, "Congruence Between Pay Policy and Competitive Strategy in High-Performing Firms," *Journal of Management,* 1996, Vol. 22, No. 6, pp. 889–912.

24. David Lepak and Scott Snell, "The Human Resource Architecture: Toward a Theory of Human Capital Allocation and Development," *Academy of Management Journal,* Vol. 24, No. 1, pp. 31–48; David Lepak and Scott Snell, "Examining the Human Resource Architecture: The Relationships Among Human Capital, Employment, and Human Resource Configuration," *Journal of Management,* 2002, Vol. 28, No. 4, pp. 517–544; David Lepak and Scott Snell, "Managing the Human Resource Architecture for Knowledge-Based Competition," in Susan Jackson, Michael Hitt, and Angelo DeNisi (eds.), *Managing Knowledge for Sustained Competitive Advantage: Designing Strategies for Effective Human Resource Management* (San Francisco, Calif: Jossey-Bass, 2003).

25. Peter Bamberger and Avi Fiegenbaum, "The Role of Strategic Reference Points in Explaining the Nature and Consequences of Human Resource Strategy," *Academy of Management Review,* October 1996, pp. 926–958.

26. Richard L. Daft, *Organization Theory and Design* (St. Paul, Minn.: West, 2003).

27. John Purcell and Bruce Ahlstrand, *Human Resource Management in the Multi-Divisional Company* (Oxford: Oxford University Press, 1994).

28. Terrence E. Deal and Allan A. Kennedy, *Corporate Cultures: The Rights and Rituals of Corporate Life* (Reading, Mass.: Addison-Wesley, 1982).

29. Jay Barney, "Organizational Culture: Can It Be a Source of Sustained Competitive Advantage?" *Academy of Management Review,* July 1986, pp. 656–665.

30. See, for example, David Jemison and Sim Sitkin, "Corporate Acquisitions: A Process Perspective," *Academy of Management Review,* 1986, Vol. 11, No.1, pp. 145–163; or Nancy Napier, "Mergers and Acquisitions, Human Resource Issues and Outcomes: A Review and Suggested Typology," *Journal of Management Studies,* 1989, Vol. 26, No. 3, pp. 271–289.

31. See discussion of this strategy in Bruce Nissen, "The 'Social Movement' Dynamics of Living Wage Campaigns," in Paula Voos (ed.), *Proceedings of the 53rd Annual Meeting of the Industrial Relations Research Association,* Industrial Relations Research Association, Washington D.C., January 2001, pp. 232–240.

32. Lee Dyer, "Human Resource Planning," in K. Rowland and G. Ferris (eds.), *Personnel Management* (Boston, Mass.: Allyn & Bacon, 1982), pp. 52–77.

33. R. G. Murdick and F. Schuster, "Computerized Information Support for the Human Resource Function," *Human Resource Planning,* 1983, Vol. 6, No. 1, pp. 25–35.

34. Taylor H. Cox and Stacy Blake, "Managing Cultural Diversity: Implications for Organizational Competitiveness," *The Academy of Management Executive,* August 1991, pp. 45–56.

35. "The Geography of Work," *Time,* June 22, 1998, pp. 98–102

36. Carla Johnson, "Developing a Strong Bench," *HRMagazine,* January 1998, pp. 92–97.

37. "P&G Will Make Jager CEO Ahead of Schedule," *Wall Street Journal,* September 10, 1998, pp. B1, B8.

38. "Firms Plan to Keep Hiring, Spending," *USA Today,* January 26, 1995, p. B1.

39. "Firms Find Ways to Grow Without Expanding Staffs," *Wall Street Journal,* March 18, 1993, pp. B1, B2.

40. "When UPS Demanded Workers, Louisville Did the Delivering," *Wall Street Journal,* April 24, 1998, pp. A1, A10.

41. "Layoffs on Wall Street Will Bruise Big Apple," *USA Today,* October 15, 1998, p. 1B; "Its Share Shrinking, Levi Strauss Lays Off 6,395," *Wall Street Journal,* November 4, 1997, pp. B1, B8.

42. Denise Rousseau, "Changing the Deal While Keeping the People," *The Academy of Management Executive,* February 1996, pp. 50–61.

43. Elizabeth Wolfe Morrison and Sandra L. Robinson, "When Employees Feel Betrayed: A Model of How Psychological Contract Violation Develops," *Academy of Management Review,* January 1997, pp. 226–256; Sandra Robinson, Matthew Kraatz, and Denise Rousseau, "Changing Obligations and the Psychological Contract," *Academy of Management Journal,* 1994, Vol. 37, No. 1, pp. 137–152.

44. Murray Barrick and Michael Mount, "The Big Five Personality Dimensions and Job Performance: A Meta-Analysis," *Personnel Psychology,* 1991, Vol. 44, No. 1, pp. 1–26.

45. Several critical measurement issues are raised in Barry Gerhart, Patrick Wright, Gary McMahan, and Scott Snell, "Measurement Error in Research on Human Resources and Firm Performance: How Much Error Is There and How Does It Influence Size Estimates?" *Personnel Psychology,* 2000, Vol. 53, No. 4, pp. 803–834.

46. See, for example, Mark A. Huselid, "The Impact of Human Resource Management Practices on Turnover, Productivity, and Corporate Financial Reporting," *Academy of Management Journal,* 1995, Vol. 38, pp. 635–672; or Rajiv Banker, Joy Field, Roger Schroeder, and Kingshuk Sinha, "Impact of Work Teams on Manufacturing Performance: A Longitudinal Study," *Academy of Management Journal,* 1996, Vol. 39, No. 4, pp. 867–890.

47. Source: "While Hiring at Most Firms Chills, Wal-Mart's Heats Up," from *USA Today,* August 26, 2002, p. 3B. Copyright ©2002 USA Today. Reprinted with permission.

Chapter 3

1. "Workers File Suit Over Long Hours," Associated Press news story published in the *Bryan-College Station Eagle,* August 3, 2002, pp. B1, B7.

2. David Israel, "Learn to Manage the Legal Process," *HRMagazine,* July 1993, pp. 83–87.

3. "HR and the Government," *HRMagazine,* May 1994, pp. 43–48. See also J. Ledvinka, *Federal Regulation of Personnel and Human Resource Management* (Boston, Mass.: Kent, 1982).

4. Jon M. Werner and Mark C. Bolino, "Explaining U.S. Court of Appeals Decisions Involving Performance Appraisal: Accuracy, Fairness, and Validation," *Personnel Psychology,* Spring 1997, pp. 1–24.

5. See Philip E. Varca and Patricia Pattison, "Evidentiary Standards in Employment Discrimination: A View Toward the Future," *Personnel Psychology,* Summer 1993, pp. 239–250.

6. *Diaz* v. *Pan American World Airways, Inc.,* 442 F. 2d 385 (5th Cir. 1971).

7. James E. Jones, William P. Murphy, and Robert Belton, *Discrimination in Employment,* 5th ed., American Casebook Series (St. Paul, Minn.: West Publishing Co., 1987, p. 381).

8. *Griggs* v. *Duke Power Company,* 401 U.S. 424 (1971).

9. Technically, neither guilt nor innocence is determined in civil cases. The defendant either is liable for discrimination or is not liable for discrimination. We will use the terms *guilty* and *innocent* occasionally, however, because readers are more comfortable with these terms.

10. *Wards Cove Packing Co., Inc.* v. *Antonio,* U.S. Sup. Ct. 1387 (June 5, 1989).

11. *McDonnell-Douglas Corporation* v. *Green,* 411 U.S. 792 (1973).

12. "Culture of Racial Bias at Shoney's Underlines Chairman's Departure," *Wall Street Journal,* December 21, 1992, p. A1.

13. "When Quotas Replace Merit, Everybody Suffers," *Forbes,* February 15, 1993, pp. 80–102.

14. *Bakke* v. *The Regents of the University of California at Davis,* 438 U.S. 265 (1978).

15. *United Steelworkers of America, AFL-CIO* v. *Weber,* Sup. Ct. (1979); 443 U.S. 193; 99 S. Ct. 2721; 61 L. Ed. 2d 480.

16. *Wygant* v. *Jackson Board of Education,* Sup. Ct. (1986); 106 S. Ct. 1842; 90 L. Ed. 2d 260.

17. *Local 93 of the International Association of Firefighters, AFL-CIO, C.L.C.* v. *City of Cleveland,* Sup. Ct. (1986); 106 S. Ct. 3063, 92 L. Ed. 2d 405.

18. *U.S.* v. *Paradise,* Sup. Ct.; 478 US 1019; 106 S. Ct. 3331, 92 L. Ed. 2d 737 (1986).

19. *Einsley Branch, NAACP* v. *Seibels,* 60 F. 3d 717 (11th Cir. 1994).

20. *Hopwood* v. *State of Texas,* 78 F. 3d 932 (5th Cir. 1996).

21. Jonathan A. Segal, "Sexual Harassment: Where Are We Now?" *HRMagazine,* October 1996, pp. 68–73; Gerald D. Bloch, "Avoiding Liability for Sexual Harassment," *HRMagazine,* April 1995, pp. 91–94.

22. *Meritor Savings Bank, FSB* v. *Vinson et al.,* Sup. Ct.; 477 U.S. 57 (1986).

23. *Harris* v. *Forklift Systems* 510 U.S. 17 (1993).

24. Jonathan A. Segal, "Proceed Carefully, Objectively to Investigate Sexual Harassment Claims," *HRMagazine,* October 1993, pp. 91–95.

25. *Scott* v. *Sears Roebuck,* 798 F. 2d 210 (7th Cir. 1986).

26. *Oncale* v. *Sundowner Offshore Servs.,* 96 Sup. Ct. 568, 523 U.S. 75; S. Ct. 998; 140 L. Ed. 2d 201 (1998).

27. "Justices' Ruling Further Defines Sexual Harassment," *Wall Street Journal,* March 5, 1998, p. B1.

28. "How to Shrink the Pay Gap," *Business Week,* June 24, 2002, p. 151.

29. *Johnson* v. *Mayor and City Council of Baltimore,* Sup. Ct. 105; S. Ct. 2717; 86 L. Ed. 2d 286 (1985).

30. "As Workers Grow Older, Age-Bias Lawsuits Decline," *USA Today,* June 26, 1998, p. B1.

31. "Recent Suits Make Pregnancy Issues Workplace Priorities," *Wall Street Journal,* January 14, 1998, p. B1.

32. The most noteworthy of these are the *Wards Cove* (1989) case discussed earlier, *Patterson* v. *McLean Credit Union* [109 S. Ct. 2363 (1989)], and *Price Waterhouse* v. *Hopkins* [109 S. Ct. 1775 (1989)].

33. Most of these issues were decided in *EEOC* v. *Arabian American Oil Co.,* 89 Sup. Ct. 1838, 1845; 498 U.S. 808; 111 S. Ct. 40; 112 L. Ed. 2d 17 (1990).

34. Francine S. Hall and Elizabeth L. Hall, "The ADA: Going Beyond the Law," *The Academy of Management Executive,* February 1994, pp. 17–26.

35. Albert S. King, "Doing the Right Thing for Employees with Disabilities," *Training & Development,* September 1993, pp. 44–46.

36. "Disabilities Act Abused?" *USA Today,* September 25, 1998, pp. 1B, 2B.

37. Michael Barrier, "A Line in the Sand," *HRMagazine,* July 2002, pp. 35–43.

38. "Court Narrows Disability Act," *USA Today,* June 23, 1999, p. 1A.

39. For a review and a discussion of the determinants of this problem, see Adrienne Colella, "Coworker Distributive Fairness Judgments of the Workplace Accommodation of Employees with Disabilities," *Academy of Management Review,* Vol. 26, No. 1, pp. 100–116.

40. David Stamps, "Just How Scary Is the ADA?" *Training,* 1995, Vol. 32, pp. 93–101.

41. Michelle Neely Martinez, "FMLA––Headache or Opportunity?" *HRMagazine,* February 1994, pp. 42–45.

42. Jonathan A. Segal, "Traps to Avoid in FMLA Compliance," *HRMagazine,* February 1994, pp. 97–100. See also Timothy Bland, "The Supreme Court Reins in the FMLA (Slightly)," *HRMagazine,* July 2002, pp. 44–48.

43. John Montoya, "New Priorities for the '90s," *HRMagazine,* April 1997, pp. 118–122.

44. David Israel, "Check EEOC Position Statements for Accuracy," *HRMagazine,* September 1993, pp. 106–109.

45. William R. Tracey, "Auditing ADA Compliance," *HRMagazine,* October 1994, pp. 88–93.

46. David C. Ankeny and David Israel, "Completing an On-Site OFCCP Audit," *HRMagazine,* March 1993, pp. 89–94.

47. *Electromation* v. *NLRB,* US Court of Appeals for the 35 F. 3d 1148 (7th Cir. 1994).

48. *E. I. Du Pont de Nemours and Company* v. *NLRB,* 12 F. 3d 209 (5th Cir. 1993).

49. "Fewer Employers Are Currently Conducting Psych and Drug Tests," *HR Focus,* October 2000, p. 78.

50. Stephanie Overman, "Splitting Hairs," *HRMagazine,* August 1999, pp. 42–48.

51. "Laws, Juries Shift Protection to Terminated Employees," *USA Today,* April 2, 1998, pp. 1B, 2B.

52. For more information about the requirements of the act and the exceptions, see Joshua Ditelberg, "A Practical Guide to Workforce Reductions," *SHRM Legal Report,* March–April 2002, pp. 1–5.

53. "What to Do with Bad News," *HRMagazine,* July 2002, pp. 58–63.

54. Sources: "The *Seinfeld* Firing," *Wall Street Journal,* May 11, 1998, p, A20; "Ex-Miller Executive Wins Award in 'Seinfeld' Case," *Wall Street Journal,* July 16, 1997, p. B13.

Chapter 4

1. *Hoover's Handbook of World Business 2002* (Austin, Tex.: Hoover's Business Press, 2002); "In Mexico, a GM Worker Springs into the Middle Class," *Wall Street Journal,* July 29, 1998, pp. B1, B4; Ricky W. Griffin and Michael W. Pustay, *International Business—A Managerial Perspective Forecast 2003* (Upper Saddle River, N.J.: Prentice-Hall, 2003).

2. Martha I. Finney, "Global Success Rides on Keeping Top Talent," *HRMagazine,* April 1996, pp. 68–74.

3. Gregory D. Chowanec and Charles N. Newstrom, "The Strategic Management of International Human Resources," *Business Quarterly,* Autumn 1991, pp. 65–70.

4. Griffin and Pustay, *International Business.*

5. Richard M. Steers, "The Cultural Imperative in HRM Research," in Albert Nedd (guest ed.), Gerald R. Ferris, and Kendrith M. Rowland (eds.), *Research in Personnel and Human Resources Management* (Supplement 1: International Human Resources Management) (Greenwich, Conn.: 1989), pp. 23–32.

6. Geert Hofstede, *Culture's Consequences: International Differences in Work-Related Values,* (Beverly Hills, Calif.: Sage Publishers, 1980).

7. Nakiye Boyacigiller, "The Role of Expatriates in the Management of Interdependence, Complexity, and Risk in Multinational Corporations," *Journal of International Business Studies,* Vol. 21, No. 3, pp. 357–382.

8. Sakhawat Hossain and Herbert J. Davis, "Some Thoughts on International Personnel Management as an Emerging Field," in Albert Nedd (guest ed.), Gerald R. Ferris, and Kendrith M. Rowland (eds.), *Research in Personnel and Human Resources Management* (Supplement 1: International Human Resources Management) (Greenwich, Conn.: 1989, pp. 121–136).

9. Griffin and Pustay, *International Business.*

10. Ibid.

11. "The High Cost of Expatriation," *Management Review,* July 1990, pp. 40–41.

12. Cynthia Fetterolf, "Hiring Local Managers and Employees Overseas," *The International Executive,* May–June 1990, pp. 22–26.

13. "Bringing Back the Beetle," *Forbes,* April 7, 1997, pp. 42–44.

14. Carla Johnson, "Save Thousands per Expatriate," *HRMagazine,* July 2002, pp. 73–77.

15. Winfred Arthur, Jr., and Winston Bennett, Jr., "The International Assignee: The Relative Importance of Factors Perceived to Contribute to Success," *Personnel Psychology,* Fall 1995, pp. 99–113.

16. J. Steward Black, Hal B. Gregersen, and Mark E. Mendenhall, *Global Assignments* (San Francisco, Calif.: Jossey-Bass, 1992).

17. See, for example, Ian Torbion, "Operative and Strategic Use of Expatriates in New Organizations and Market Structures," *International Studies of Management and Organization,* 1994, Vol. 24, pp. 5–17.

18. "Global Managers Need Boundless Sensitivity, Rugged Constitutions," *Wall Street Journal,* October 13, 1998, p. B1.

19. "Firms in Europe Try to Find Executives Who Can Cross Borders in a Single Bound," *Wall Street Journal,* January 25, 1991, p. B1.

20. "Younger Managers Learn Global Skills," *Wall Street Journal,* March 31, 1992, p. B1.

21. "As Costs of Overseas Assignments Climb, Firms Select Expatriates More Carefully," *Wall Street Journal,* January 9, 1992, pp. B1, B6.

22. J. Stewart Black and Hal B. Gregersen, "The Right Way to Manage Expats," *Harvard Business Review,* March–April 1999, pp. 52–62; see also Carla Johnson, "Save Thousands per Expatriate," *HRMagazine,* July 2002, pp. 73–77.

23. For example, see Paula Caligiuiri, MaryAnne Hyland, Aparna Joshi, and Allon Bross, "Testing a Theoretical Model for Examining the Relationship Between Family Adjustment and Expatriate Work Adjustment," *Journal of Applied Psychology,* 1998, Vol. 83, pp. 598–614.

24. Margaret Shaffer and David Harrison, "Expatriates' Psychological Withdrawal from International Assignments: Work, Nonwork, and Family Influences," *Personnel Psychology,* 1998, Vol. 51, pp. 87–96

25. See review by Denis Ones and Chockalingam Viswesvaran, "Personality Determinants in the Prediction of Expatriate Job Success," in D. Saunders and Z. Aycan (eds.), *New Approaches to Employee Management,* 1994, Vol. 4, pp. 63–92; and the study by Paula Caligiuiri, "The Big Five Personality Characteristics as Predictors of Expatriate's Desire to Terminate the Assignment and Supervisor-Rated Performance," *Personnel Psychology,* 2000, Vol. 53, pp. 67–88.

26. See G. W. Florkowski and D. S. Fogel, "Expatriate Adjustment and Commitment: The Role of Host-Unit Treatment," *International Journal of Human Resource Management,* 1999, Vol. 10, pp. 783–807.

27. For a more complete discussion of this potential problem, see Soo Min Toh and Angelo DeNisi, "Host Country National Reactions to Expatriate Pay Policies: A Proposed Model and Some Implications," *Academy of Management Review,* 2003, Vol. 28, pp. 606–621.

28. "Companies Use Cross-Cultural Training to Help Their Employees Adjust Abroad," *Wall Street Journal,* August 9, 1992, pp. B1, B6.

29. Paul Vanderbroeck, "Long-Term Human Resource Development in Multinational Organizations," *Sloan Management Review,* Fall 1992, pp. 95–99.

30. Kathryn Tyler, "Targeted Language Training is Best Bargain," *HRMagazine,* January 1998, pp. 61–68.

31. Frank Jossi, "Successful Handoff," *HRMagazine,* October 2002, pp. 48–52.

32. K. Cushner and Richard Brislin, *International Interactions: A Practical Guide* (Thousand Oaks, Calif.: Sage Publishing, 2000).

33. Simca Ronen, "Training the International Assignee," in I. L. Goldstein and Associates, *Training and Development in Organizations* (New York: Jossey-Bass, 1989), p. 418.

34. Richard M. Hodgetts and Fred Luthans, "U.S. Multinationals' Compensation Strategies," *Compensation & Benefits Review,* January–February 1993, pp. 57–62.

35. Michael J. Bishko, "Compensating Your Overseas Executives, Part 1: Strategies for the 1990s," *Compensation & Benefits Review,* May–June 1990, pp. 33–43.

36. "For Executives Around the Globe, Pay Packages Aren't Worlds Apart," *Wall Street Journal,* October 12, 1992, pp. B1, B5.

37. Stephanie Overman, "In Sync," *HRMagazine,* March 2000, pp. 86–92.

38. See Carla Johnson, "Save Thousands per Expatriate," *HRMagazine,* July 2002, pp. 73–77.

39. Robert O'Connor, "Plug the Expat Knowledge Drain," *HRMagazine,* October 2002, pp. 101–107.

40. Andrea Poe, "Welcome Back," *HRMagazine,* March 2000, pp. 94–105.

41. National Foreign Trade Council report, cited in Carla Johnson, "Save Thousands per Expatriate," *HRMagazine,* July 2002, pp. 73–77.

42. Sources: "Gentlemen, Start Your Engines," *Fortune,* June 8, 1998, pp. 138–146; James Aley and Matt Siegel, "The Fallout from Merger Mania," *Fortune,* March 2, 1998, pp. 26–56; "Labor Holds a Key to Fate of Daimler-Chrysler Merger," *Wall Street Journal,* May 7, 1998, pp. B1, B18; "Oil Companies Pump Out $50 Billion Merger Deal," *USA Today,* August 12, 1998, pp. 1B, 2B.

Chapter 5

1. Clare Ansberry, "In the New Workplace, Jobs Morph to Suit Rapid Pace of Change," *Wall Street Journal,* March 22, 2002, pp. A1–A7 (*quote on p. A7); E. Jeffrey Hill, "Flexible Schedules Help Employees Work More Without Complaint," Brigham Young University, May 19, 2001, accessed at www.newswise.com on May 5, 2002; Peter Cappelli and David Neumark, "External Job Churning and Internal Job Flexibility," National Bureau of Economic Research, Working Paper No. 8111, February 2001, accessed at papers.nber.org on May 2, 2002.

2. E. J. McCormick, *Job Analysis: Methods and Applications* (New York: American Management Association, 1979).

3. Greer, *Strategy and Human Resources.*

4. A. S. DeNisi, "The Implications of Job Clustering for Training Programmes," *Journal of Occupational Psychology,* Vol. 49, pp. 105–113.

5. K. Pearlman, "Job Families: A Review and Discussion of Their Implications for Personnel Selection," *Psychological Bulletin,* Vol. 87, pp. 1–27.

6. McCormick, *Job Analysis: Methods and Applications.*

7. U.S. Department of Labor, Employment, and Training Administration, *The Revised Handbook for Analyzing Jobs* (Washington, D.C.: U.S. Government Printing Office, 1991).

8. Frank Landy and Joseph Vasey, "Job Analysis: The Composition of SME Samples," *Personnel Psychology,* Vol. 44, No. 1, 1991, pp. 27–50.

9. Ibid.

10. U.S. Department of Labor, Employment, and Training Administration, *The Revised Handbook for Analyzing Jobs.*

11. E. A. Fleishman, *Manual for the Ability Requirements Scale* (MARS, revised) (Palo Alto, Calif.: Consulting Psychologists Press, 1991).

12. For example, see J. E. Morsh, *Job Types Identified with an Inventory Constructed by Electronics Engineers* (Lackland Air Force Base, San Antonio, Tex. U.S. Air Force Personnel Research Laboratory, 1966).

13. S. A. Fine and W. W. Wiley, *An Introduction to Functional Job Analysis* (Kalamazoo, Mich.: W. E. Upjohn Institute for Employment Research, 1971).

14. E. J. McCormick, P. R. Jeanneret, and R. C. Mecham, "A Study of Job Characteristics and Job Dimensions as Based on the Position Analysis Questionnaire (PAQ), *Journal of Applied Psychology,* 1972, Vol. 56, pp. 347–368.

15. McCormick, *Job Analysis: Methods and Applications.*

16. See, for example, E. J. McCormick, P. R. Jeanneret, and R. C. Mecham, "A Study of Job Characteristics and Job Dimensions as Based on the Position Analysis Questionnaire (PAQ), *Journal of Applied Psychology,* 1972, Vol. 56, pp. 347–368; or E. J. McCormick, A. S. DeNisi, and J. B. Shaw "The Use of the Position Analysis Questionnaire (PAQ) for Establishing the Job Component Validity of Tests," *Journal of Applied Psychology,* 1978, Vol. 64, pp. 51–56.

17. A. S. DeNisi, E. T. Cornelius, and A. G. Blencoe, "A Further Investigation of Common Knowledge Effects on Job Analysis Ratings: On the Applicability of the PAQ for All Jobs," *Journal of Applied Psychology,* 1987, Vol. 72, pp. 262–268.

18. J. C. Flanagan, "The Critical Incident Technique," *Psychological Bulletin,* Vol. 51, 327–358.

19. Milan Moravec and Robert Tucker, "Job Descriptions for the 21st Century," *Personnel Journal,* June 1992, pp. 37–40.

20. Ricky W. Griffin, *Task Design* (Glenview, Ill.: Scott, Foresman, 1982).

21. Michael Campion, "Interdisciplinary Approaches to Job Design: A Constructive Replication with Extension," *Journal of Applied Psychology,* 1988, Vol. 73, pp. 467–481.

22. Frederick Herzberg, *Work and the Nature of Man* (Cleveland, Ohio: World Press, 1966).

23. Robert Ford, "Job Enrichment Lessons from AT&T," *Harvard Business Review,* January–February 1973, pp. 96–106.

24. J. Richard Hackman and Greg R. Oldham, *Work Redesign* (Reading, Mass.: Addison-Wesley, 1980).

25. Eric Trist and Kenneth Bamforth, "Some Social and Psychological Consequences of the Longwall Method of Coal-Getting," *Human Relations,* 1965, Vol. 4, pp. 3–38.

26. *Albermarle Paper Co.* v. *Moody,* Sup. Ct. of the U.S., 1975, 422 U.S. 405, 95 S. Ct. 2362, L. Ed. 2d. 280.

27. For a complete discussion of these sources of inaccuracy, see Frederick Morgeson and Michael Campion, "Social and Cognitive Sources of Potential Inaccuracy in Job Analysis," *Journal of Applied Psychology,* 1998, Vol. 82, pp. 627–655.

28. Richard Arvey, "Sex Bias in Job Evaluation Procedures," *Personnel Psychology,* 1986, Vol. 39, pp. 315–335.

29. *Electromation Inc. v. National Labor Relations Board,* 1992.
30. Sources: "These Six Growth Jobs Are Dull, Dead-End, Sometimes Dangerous," *Wall Street Journal,* December 1, 1994, pp. A1, A8; *Hoover's Handbook of American Business 2003* (Austin, Tex.: Hoover's Business Press, 2003).

Chapter 6

1. "9.11.02," *Business Week,* September 16, 2002, pp. 34–38; "Airport Screening Hits Barrier: No Staff," Associated Press wire story as published in the *Bryan-College-Station Eagle,* July 29, 2002, p. A3 (*quote on p. A3); "Feds Take Over Airport Screening," *USA Today,* November 18, 2002, pp. 1A, 2A.
2. James A. Breaugh. *Recruitment: Science and Practice* (Boston, Mass.: PWS-Kent, 1992).
3. Robert Bretz, Jr., and Timothy Judge, "The Role of Human Resource Systems in Job Applicant Decision Processes," *Journal of Management,* 1994, Vol. 20, No. 3, pp. 531–551.
4. Allison Barber, Christina Daly, Cristina Giannatonio, and Jean Phillips, "Job Search Activities: An Examination of Changes Over Time," *Personnel Psychology,* 1994, Vol. 47, pp. 739–750.
5. Timothy Judge and Robert Bretz, "Effects of Work Values on Job Choice Decisions," *Journal of Applied Psychology,* Vol. 77, No. 3, pp. 261–271.
6. "Right Here in Dubuque," *Forbes,* March 29, 1993, pp. 86–88.
7. Charles Williams, Chalmer Labig, Jr., and Thomas Stone, "Recruitment Sources and Posthire Outcomes for Job Applicants and New Hires: A Test of Two Hypotheses," *Journal of Applied Psychology,* Vol. 78, No. 2, pp. 163–172.
8. Andy Bargerstock and Hank Engel, "Six Ways to Boost Employee Referral Programs," *HRMagazine,* December 1994, pp. 72–77.
9. "Your Buddy May Be Worth 30 Grand," *Business Week,* October 12, 1998, p. 8.
10. "Executive Recruiter Scored Major Coup by Enticing Motorola's Fisher to Kodak," *Wall Street Journal,* November 1, 1993, p. B8.
11. "Software Firm Tests College Job Hopefuls," *USA Today,* April 8, 1993, pp. B1, B2.
12. Beth McConnell, "Companies Lure Job Seekers in New Ways," *HRNews,* April 2002, pp. 1–5.
13. Peter Cappelli, "Making the Most of Online Recruiting," *Harvard Business Review,* March 2001, pp. 139–146.
14. Bill Leonard, "Online and Overwhelmed," *HRMagazine,* August 2000, pp. 37–42.
15. Candee Wilde, "Recruiters Discover Diverse Value in Websites," *Informationweek,* February 7, 2000, p. 144.
16. Kuhn and Mikal Skuiterud, "Job Search Methods: Internet Versus Traditional," *Monthly Labor Review,* October 2000, pp. 3–11.
17. Cappelli, "Making the Most of Online Recruiting."
18. J. P. Wanous and A. Colella, "Organizational Entry Research: Current Status and Future Directions, in K. Rowland and G. Ferris (eds.), *Research in Personnel and Human Resource Management* (Greenwich, Conn.: JAI Press, 1989).
19. "It's Not Easy Making Pixie Dust," *Business Week,* September 18, 1995, p. 134.
20. B. M. Meglino and A. S. DeNisi, "Realistic Job Previews: Some Thoughts on Their More Effective Use in Managing the Flow of Human Resources," *Human Resource Planning,* 1987, Vol. 10, pp. 157–167.
21. Jean Phillips, "Effects of Realistic Job Previews on Multiple Organizational Outcomes: A Meta-Analysis," *Academy of Management Journal,* 1998, Vol. 41, pp. 673–690.
22. R. A. Dean and J. P. Wanous, "Effects of Realistic Job Previews on Hiring Bank Tellers," *Journal of Applied Psychology,* 1984, Vol. 69, pp. 61–68.
23. B. M. Meglino, A. S. DeNisi, S. A. Youngblood, and K. J. Williams, "Effects of Realistic Job Previews: A Comparison Using Enhancement and Reduction Previews," *Journal of Applied Psychology,* 1988, Vol. 73, pp. 259–266.
24. B. M. Meglino, A. S. DeNisi, and E. C. Ravlin, "The Effects of Previous Job Exposure and Subsequent Job Status on the Functioning of Realistic Job Previews," *Personnel Psychology,* 1993, Vol. 46, pp. 803–822.
25. "Living Overtime: A Factory Workaholic," *Wall Street Journal,* October 13, 1998, p. B1.
26. Gilbert Nicholson, "Get Your Benefit Ducks in a Row," *Workforce,* September 2000, pp. 78–84.
27. Lee Phillion and John Brugger, "Encore! Retirees Give Top Performance as Temporaries," *HRMagazine,* October 1994, pp. 74–78.
28. See especially David Lepak and Scott Snell, "The Human Resource Architecture: Toward a Theory of Human Capital Allocation and Development," *Academy of Management Review,* 1999, Vol. 24, pp. 31–48.
29. S. L. Rynes, R. D. Bretz, and B. Gerhart, "The Importance of Recruitment in Job Choice: A Different Way of Looking," *Personnel Psychology,* 1991, Vol. 44, pp. 487–521.
30. See the review in Allison Barber, *Recruiting Employees: Individual and Organizational Perspectives* (Thousand Oaks, Calif.: Sage Publishing, 1998).
31. Barbara Rau and Maryanne Hyland, "Roe Conflict and Flexible Work Arrangements: The Effects on Applicant Attraction," *Personnel Psychology,* 2002, Vol. 55, pp. 111–136.
32. A. Saks, "A Psychological Process Investigation for the Effects of Recruitment Source and Organizational Information on Job Survival," *Journal of Organizational Behavior,* 1994, Vol. 15, pp. 225–244.
33. C. R. Williams, C. E. Labig, and T. Stone, "Recruitment Sources and Posthire Outcomes for Job Applications and New Hires," *Journal of Applied Psychology,* 1993, Vol. 78, pp. 163–172.
34. Sources: David Leonhardt, "Did Pay Incentives Cut Both Ways?" *New York Times,* April 7, 2002, pp. BU1–BU3; "A Smarter Squeeze?" *Business Week,* December 31, 2001, pp. 42–44; "Agency Workers Mull Pay Cut for Time Off," *The Indianapolis Star,* March 11, 2002; Rick Perera, "Siemens Offers Workers 'Time-Outs' to Save Cash," *The Industry Standard,* August 31, 2001, pp. 32–33.

Chapter 7

1. "Personnel File," *Fast Company,* January 2001, pp. 118–122 (*quote on p. 118); *Hoover's Handbook of American Business 2003* (Austin, Tex.: Hoover's Business Press, 2003), pp. 615–616.

2. See Neal Schmitt and Ivan Robertson, "Personnel Selection," *Annual Review of Psychology,* 1990, Vol. 41, pp. 289–319.

3. "Auto Plants, Hiring Again, Are Demanding Higher-Skilled Labor," *Wall Street Journal,* March 11, 1994, pp. A1, A4.

4. Wendy Dunn, Michael Mount, Murray Barrick, and Deniz Ones, "Relative Importance of Personality and General Mental Ability in Managers' Judgments of Applicant Qualifications," *Journal of Applied Psychology,* 1995, Vol. 80, No. 4, pp. 500–509.

5. Michael Stevens and Michael Campion, "The Knowledge, Skill, and Ability Requirements for Teamwork: Implications for Human Resource Management," *Journal of Management,* 1994, Vol. 20, No. 2, pp. 503–530.

6. M. R. Barrick and M. K. Mount, "The Big Five Personality Dimensions and Job Performance: A Meta-Analysis," *Personnel Psychology,* 1991, Vol. 44, pp. 1–26.

7. It is not always clear that recruiters and interviewers can effectively distinguish between the two types of fit. See, for example, Amy Kristof-Brown, "Perceived Applicant Fit: Distinguishing Between Recruiters' Perceptions of Person-Job and Person-Organization Fit," *Personnel Psychology,* 2000, Vol. 53, pp. 643–672.

8. Orlando Behling, "Employee Selection: Will Intelligence and Conscientiousness Do the Job?" *Academy of Management Executive,* February 1998, pp. 77–86.

9. J. E. Hunter and R. F. Hunter, "Validity and Utility of Alternative Predictors of Job Performance," *Psychological Bulletin,* Spring 1984, pp. 72–98.

10. C. J. Russell, J., Mattdson, S. E. Devlin, and D. Atwater, "Predictive Validity of Biodata Items Generated from Retrospective Life Experience Essays," *Journal of Applied Psychology,* 1990, Vol. 75, pp. 569–580.

11. See "Can You Tell Applesauce from Pickles?" *Forbes,* October 9, 1995, pp. 106–108 for several examples.

12. J. E. Hunter, "Cognitive Ability, Cognitive Aptitudes, Job Knowledge, and Job Performance," *Journal of Vocational Behavior,* 1986, Vol. 29, pp. 340–362.

13. A. R. Jensen, *Bias in Mental Testing* (New York: Free Press, 1980).

14. M. K. Mount and M. R. Barrick, *Manual for the Personal Characteristics Inventory* (Iowa City, Iowa: 1995).

15. Daniel P. O'Meara, "Personality Tests Raise Questions of Legality and Effectiveness," *HRMagazine,* January 1994, pp. 97–104.

16. See L. M. Hough, "The Big Five Personality Variables—Construct Confusion: Description Versus Prediction," *Human Performance,* 1992, Vol. 5, pp. 139–155; for an opposing view, see J. E. Hunter and R. F. Hunter, "Validity and Utility of Alternative Predictors of Job Performance," *Psychological Bulletin,* 1984, Vol. 96, pp. 72–98.

17. "Employers Score New Hires," *USA Today,* July 9, 1997, pp. 1B, 2B.

18. P. R. Sackett, "Integrity Testing for Personnel Selection," *Current Directions in Psychological Science,* 1994, Vol. 3, pp. 73–76.

19. R. C. Hollinger and J. P. Clark, *Theft by Employees* (Lexington, Mass.: Lexington Books, 1983).

20. U.S. Congress, Office of Technology Assessment, *The Use of Integrity Tests for Pre-Employment Screening* (Washington, D.C.: U.S. Government Printing Office, 1990); S. W. Gilliland, "Fairness from the Applicant's Perspective: Reactions to Employee Selection Procedures," *International Journal of Selection and Assessment,* 1995, Vol. 3, pp. 11–19.

21. Michael McDaniel, Deborah Whetzel, Frank Schmidt, and Steven Maurer, "The Validity of Employment Interviews: A Comprehensive Review and Meta-Analysis," *Journal of Applied Psychology,* 1994, Vol. 79, No. 4, pp. 599–616.

22. "Think Fast!" *Forbes,* March 24, 1997, pp. 146–151.

23. Elaine Pulakos and Neal Schmitt, "Experience-Based and Situational Interview Questions: Studies of Validity," *Personnel Psychology,* 1995, Vol. 48, pp. 289–308.

24. M. A. McDaniel, D. L. Whetzel, F. L. Schmidt, and S. D. Maurer, "The Validity of Employment Interviews: A Comprehensive Review and Meta-Analysis," *Journal of Applied Psychology,* 1994, Vol. 79, pp. 599–616.

25. *Watson v. Fort Worth Bank and Trust,* 108 Sup. Ct. 2791 (1988.)

26. See Thomas Dougherty, Daniel Turban, and John Callender, "Confirming First Impressions in the Employment Interview: A Field Study of Interviewer Behavior," *Journal of Applied Psychology,* 1994, Vol. 79, No. 5, pp. 659–665.

27. Paul Falcone, "Getting Employers to Open Up on a Reference Check," *HRMagazine,* July 1995, pp. 58–63.

28. "Think Fast!" *Forbes,* March 24, 1997, pp. 146–151.

29. Richard Campbell and Douglas Bray, "Use of an Assessment Center as an Aid in Management Selection," *Personnel Psychology,* Autumn 1993, pp. 691–698.

30. Annette C. Spychalski, Miguel A. Quinones, Barbara B. Gaugler, and Katja Pohley, "A Survey of Assessment Center Practices in Organizations in the United States," *Personnel Psychology,* Spring 1997, pp. 71–82.

31. Justin Martin, "So, You Want to Work for the Best . . . ," *Fortune,* January 12, 1998, pp. 77–85.

32. See especially *Washington v. Davis,* Sup. Ct; 426 U.S. 229; S. Ct. 2040, L. Ed. 2d 597 (1976).

33. See, for example, *Albermarle Paper Company v. Moody,* Sup. Ct.; 422 U.S. 405; 95 S. Ct. 2362, 45 L.Ed. 2d 280 (1975); *Connecticut v. Teal,* Sup. Ct; 457 U.S. 440; 102 S. Ct. 2525; L. Ed. 2d 190 (1982); and *Watson v. Fort Worth Bank and Trust,* Sup. Ct.; 487 U.S. 977; 108 S. Ct. 2777; L. Ed. 2d 827 (1988).

34. Sources: "Worker Shortage Forces Small Businesses into Creative Hiring," *USA Today,* October 30, 1998, pp. 1B, 2B; "Making Risky Hires into Valued Workers," *Wall Street Journal,* June 19, 1997, pp. B1, B2.

Chapter 8

1. Lisa Takeguchi Cullen, "Where Did Everyone Go?" *Time,* November 18, 2002, pp. 64–66 (*quote on p. 65); "Lower Paid Workers Face Job Cuts," CNN Money website, cnnmoney.com, accessed on November 23, 2002; "Pink Slip Blizzard," CBS News website, www.cbsnews.com, accessed on November 23, 2002; Yahoo! News website, story. news.yahoo.com, accessed on November 23, 2002.

2. J. Stacy Adams, "Inequity in Social Exchange" in L. Berkowitz (ed.), *Advances in Experimental Social Psychology,* Vol. 2 (New York: Academic Press, 1965), pp. 267–299.

3. Gerald Leventhal, "The Distribution of Rewards and Resources in Groups and Organizations," in L. Berkowitz and W. Walster (eds.), *Advances in Experimental Social*

Psychology, (Vol. 9) (New York: Academic Press, 1976), pp. 91–131.

4. Joel Brockner and Batia Wiesenfeld, "An Integrative Framework for Explaining Reactions to Decisions: Integrative Effects of Outcomes and Procedures," *Psychological Bulletin*, 1996, Vol. 120, pp. 189–298.

5. Robert Bies and Joseph Moag, "Interactional Justice: Communication Criteria of Fairness," in R. Lewicki, B. Sheppard, and M. Bazerman (eds.), *Research on Negotiations in Organizations*, Vol. 1 (Greenwich, Conn.: JAI Press, 1986), pp. 43–55.

6. Jerald Greenberg, "The Social Side of Fairness: Interpersonal and Informational Classes of Organizational Justice," in R. Cropanzano (ed.), *Justice in the Workplace: Approaching Fairness in Human Resource Management* (Hillsdale, N.J.: Erlbaum, 1993), pp. 79–103.

7. Wayne Cascio, Clifford Young, and James Morris, "Financial Consequences of Employment Change Decisions in Major U.S. Corporations," *Academy of Management Journal*, 1997, Vol. 40, pp. 1175–1189.

8. For example, see Dan Worrell, Wallace Davidson, and Varinder Sharma, "Layoff Announcements and Stockholder Wealth," *Academy of Management Journal*, 1991, Vol. 34, pp. 662–678.

9. Joel Brockner, "The Effects of Work Layoffs on Survivors: Research, Theory and Practice," in B. Staw and L. Cummings (eds.), *Research in Organizational Behavior*, Vol. 10. (Greenwich, Conn.: JAI Press, 1988), pp. 213–215.

10. American Management Association, *Corporate Job Creation, Job Elimination, and Downsizing: Summary of Key Findings* (New York: American Management Association, 1997).

11. Fay Hansen, "Employee Assistance Programs (EAPs) Grow and Expand Their Reach," *Compensation and Benefits Review*, March–April 2000, p. 13.

12. See, for example, Meg Bryant, "Testing EAPs for Coordination," *Business and Health*, August 1991, pp. 20–24; or Barbara Pflaum, "Seeking Sane Solutions: Managing Mental Health and Chemical Dependency Costs," *Employee Benefits Journal*, 1992, Vol. 16, pp. 31–35.

13. James Smith, "EAPs Evolve to Health Plan Gatekeepers," *Employee Benefit Plan Review*, 1992, Vol. 46, pp. 18–19.

14. M. R. Buckley and W. Weitzel, "Employment at Will," *Personnel Administrator*, 1988, Vol. 33, pp. 78–80.

15. *Toussaint v. Blue Cross and Blue Shield of Michigan*, 408 Michigan, 529, 292 N.W. 2d 880 (1980).

16. *Fortune v. National Cash Register*, 364 Massachusetts 91, 36 N.E. 2d 1251 (1977).

17. This approach was pioneered by Union Carbide; see A. B. Chimezie, Osigweh Yg, and William Hutchinson, "To Punish or Not to Punish: Managing Human Resources Through Positive Discipline," *Employee Relations*, March 1990, pp. 27–32. For a more complete picture, see Dick Grove, *Discipline Without Punishment* (New York: American Management Association, 1996).

18. See, for example, Michael Abelson and Barry Baysinger, "Optimal and Dysfunctional Turnover: Toward an Organizational Level Model," *Academy of Management Review*, 1984, Vol. 9, pp. 331–341.

19. On the positive side, job satisfaction has been defined as the positive feeling that "results from the perception that one's job fulfills . . . one's important job values." See, Edwin Locke, "The Nature and Causes of Job Dissatisfaction," in M. Dunnette (ed.), *Handbook of Industrial and Organizational Psychology* (Chicago, Ill.: Rand McNally, 1976), pp. 901–969.

20. For an excellent review of this literature, see Charles Hulin, Mary Roznowski, and Dan Hachiya, "Alternative Opportunities and Withdrawal Decisions," *Psychological Bulletin*, 1985, Vol. 97, pp. 233–250.

21. The original model was presented in William Mobley, "Intermediate Linkages in the Relationship Between Job Satisfaction and Employee Turnover," *Journal of Applied Psychology*, 1977, Vol. 62, pp. 237–240. A refined model was later presented in Peter Hom and Roger Griffeth, "A Structural Equations Modeling Test of a Turnover Theory: Cross Sectional and Longitudinal Analysis," *Journal of Applied Psychology*, 1991, Vol. 76, pp. 350–366.

22. John Sheridan and Michael Abelson, "Cusp-Catastrophe Model of Employee Turnover," *Academy of Management Journal*, 1983, Vol. 26, pp. 418–436.

23. Thomas Lee and Terrence Mitchell, "An Alternative Approach: The Unfolding Model of Voluntary Employee Turnover," *Academy of Management Review*, 1994, Vol. 19, pp. 51–89.

24. Terrence Mitchell, Brooks Holtom, Thomas Lee, Christopher Sablynski, and Miriam Erez, "Why People Stay: Using Job Embeddedness to Predict Voluntary Turnover," *Academy of Management Journal*, 2001, Vol. 44, pp. 1102–1121.

25. Richard Arvey, Thomas Bouchard, Neal Segal, and Len Abraham, "Job Satisfaction: Genetic and Environmental Components," *Journal of Applied Psychology*, 1989, Vol. 74, pp. 187–193.

26. See, for example, Barry Staw, Nancy Bell, and J. Clausen, "The Dispositional Approach to Job Attitudes: A Lifetime Attitudinal Test," *Administrative Science Quarterly*, 1986, Vol. 31, pp. 56–78; and Timothy Judge, "Does Affective Disposition Moderate the Relationship Between Job Satisfaction and Affective Turnover?" *Journal of Applied Psychology*, 1993, Vol. 78, pp. 395–401.

27. Barry Gerhart, "How Important Are Dispositional Factors as Determinants of Job Satisfaction? Implications for Job Design and Other Personnel Programs," *Journal of Applied Psychology*, 1987, Vol. 72, pp. 493–502.

28. See Locke, "The Nature and Causes of Job Dissatisfaction," for a review of the literature on these determinants of job satisfaction.

29. Bruce Meglino, Elizabeth Ravlin, and Cheryl Adkins, "A Work Values Approach to Corporate Culture: A Field Test of the Value Congruence Process and Its Relationship to Individual Outcomes," *Journal of Applied Psychology*, 1989, Vol. 74, pp. 424–433.

30. For an excellent review of the relationship between leader behavior and employees' reactions, such as satisfaction, see Victor Vroom, "Leadership," in M. Dunnette (ed.), *Handbook of Industrial and Organizational Psychology* (Chicago, Ill.: Rand McNally, 1986), pp. 560–663.

31. Rick Hackett and Robert Guion, "A Re-evaluation of the Job Satisfaction-Absenteeism Relation," *Organizational*

Behavior and Human Decision Processes, 1985, Vol. 35, pp. 340–381.

32. Richard Mowday, Richard Steers, and Lyman Porter, "The Measurement of Organizational Commitment," *Journal of Vocational Behavior,* 1979, Vol. 14, pp. 224–247.

33. See, for example, Chester Schriesheim, "Job Satisfaction, Attitudes Towards Unions, and Voting in a Union Representation Election," *Journal of Applied Psychology,* 1978, Vol. 63, pp. 548–553; for a somewhat more complex model that still focuses on job dissatisfaction, see Stuart Youngblood, Angelo DeNisi, Julie Molleston, and William Mobley, "The Impact of Worker Attachment, Instrumentality Beliefs, Perceived Labor Union Image, and Subjective Norms on Voting Intentions and Union Membership," *Academy of Management Journal,* 1994, Vol. 15, pp. 576–590.

34. The original research is summarized in Dennis Organ, *Organizational Citizenship Behavior: The Good Soldier Syndrome* (Lexington, Mass.: Heath, 1988).

35. See Walter Borman, "Job Behavior, Performance and Effectiveness," in M. Dunnette and L. Hough (eds.), *Handbook of Industrial and Organizational Psychology,* Vol. 1, 2nd ed. (Palo Alto, Calif.: Consulting Psychologists Press, 1991), pp. 271–326.

36. See the discussion in Susan Jackson, Donald Schwab, and Randall Schuler, "Toward an Understanding of the Burnout Phenomenon," *Journal of Applied Psychology,* 1986, Vol. 71, pp. 630–640. For an update and a more complex model, see Evangelia Demerouti, Arnold Bakker, Friedhelm Nachreiner, and Wilmar Schaufei, "The Job Demands-Resources Model of Burnout," *Journal of Applied Psychology,* 2001, Vol. 86, pp. 499–512.

37. See Locke, "The Nature and Causes of Job Dissatisfacton," for a review.

38. Patricia Smith, Lorne Kendall, and Charles Hulin, *The Measurement of Satisfaction in Work and Retirement.* (Chicago, Ill.: Rand McNally, 1969).

39. Theodore Kunin, "The Construction of a New Type of Attitude Measure," *Personnel Psychology,* 1955, Vol. 8, pp. 65–78.

40. Sources: Andrea Poe, "Keeping Hotel Workers," *HRMagazine,* February 2003, pp. 91–93; "America's Top 500 Companies," *Forbes,* April 14, 2003, pp. 144–172.

Chapter 9

1. Leanne Atwater and David Waldman, "Accountability in 360 Degree Feedback," *HRMagazine,* May 1998, pp. 96–104; David Waldman, Leanne Atwater, and David Antonioni, "Has 360 Degree Feedback Gone Amok?" *Academy of Management Executive,* 1998, Vol. 12, No. 2, pp. 86–94; Bruce Pfau and Ira Kay, "Does 360-Degree Feedback Negatively Affect Company Performance?" *HR Magazine,* June 2002, pp. 54–59 (*quote on p. 57)

2. See Chapter 8 in Charles R. Greer, *Strategy and Human Resources* (Englewood Cliffs, N.J.: Prentice-Hall, 1995), for a review of the strategic importance of performance management in organizations.

3. W. Timothy Weaver, "Linking Performance Reviews to Productivity and Quality," *HRMagazine,* November 1996, pp. 93–98.

4. A. S. DeNisi, *Cognitive Approach to Performance Appraisal: A Program of Research.* (London: Routledge, 1996).

5. For several excellent reviews of these "cognitive" decision-making processes on the part of the rater, see A. S. DeNisi, T. P. Cafferty, and B. Meglino, "A Cognitive Model of the Performance Appraisal Process," *Organizational Behavior and Human Decision Processes,* 1984, Vol. 33, pp. 360–396; and D. R. Ilgen and J. M. Feldman, "Performance Appraisal: A Process Focus," in B. Staw and L. Cummings (eds.), *Research in Organizational Behavior* Vol. 5 (Greenwich, Conn.: JAI Press, 1983).

6. Arup Varma, Angelo S. DeNisi, and Lawrence H. Peters, "Interpersonal Affect and Performance Appraisal: A Field Study," *Personnel Psychology,* Summer 1996, pp. 341–360.

7. K. Kraiger and K. Ford, "A Meta-Analysis of Ratee Race Effects in Performance Rating," *Journal of Applied Psychology,* 1985, Vol. 70, pp. 56–65.

8. See, for example, J. N. Cleveland, R. M. Festa, and L. Montgomery, "Applicant Pool Composition and Job Perceptions: Impact on Decisions Regarding an Older Applicant," *Journal of Vocational Behavior,* 1988, Vol. 32, pp. 112–125.

9. For example, see the review by V. F. Nieva and B. Gutek, "Sex Effects in Evaluations," *Academy of Management Review,* 1980, Vol. 5, pp. 267–276.

10. A. Colella, A. S. DeNisi, and A. Varma, "A Model of the Impact of Disability on Performance Evaluations," *Human Resource Management Review,* 1997, Vol. 7, pp. 27–53.

11. Kevin R. Murphy and Jeanette N. Cleveland, *Understanding Performance Appraisal: Social, Organizational, and Goal-Based Perspectives* (Thousand Oaks, Calif.: Sage Publications, 1995).

12. Forest J. Jourden and Chip Heath, "The Evaluation Gap in Performance Perceptions: Illusory Perceptions of Groups and Individuals," *Journal of Applied Psychology,* 1996, Vol. 81, No. 4, pp. 369–379.

13. Angelo S. DeNisi, W. Alan Randolph, and Allyn G. Blencoe, "Potential Problems with Peer Ratings," *Academy of Management Journal,* 1983, Vol. 26, pp. 457–467.

14. Leanne Atwater, Paul Roush, and Allison Fischtal, "The Influence of Upward Feedback on Self- and Follower Ratings of Leadership," *Personnel Psychology,* Spring 1995, pp. 35–59.

15. See, for example, Alan Walker and James Smither, "A Five-Year Study of Upward Feedback: What Managers Do with Their Results Matters," *Personnel Psychology,* 1999, Vol. 52, pp. 393–423.

16. For a good review of the work in this area, see David Waldman and Leanne Atwater, *The Power of 360-Degree Feedback: How to Leverage Performance Evaluations for Top Productivity* (Houston, Tex.: Gulf Publishing, 2000).

17. James M. Conway, "Analysis and Design of Multitrait-Multirater Performance Appraisal Studies," *Journal of Management,* Vol. 22, No. 1, pp. 139–162.

18. For an in-depth discussion of these problems, see Susan Haworth, "The Dark Side of Multi-Rater Assessments," *HRMagazine,* May 1998, pp. 106–112; or Angelo DeNisi and Avraham Kluger, "Feedback Effectiveness: Can 360-Degree Appraisals Be Improved?" *Academy of Management Executive,* Vol. 14, pp. 129–139.

19. See discussions of these processes in Walter Borman, "Exploring the Upper Limits of Reliability and Validity in Job Performance Ratings," *Journal of Applied Psychology,* 1978, Vol. 63, pp. 135–144; and Angelo DeNisi, Thomas Cafferty, and Bruce Meglino, "A Cognitive Model of the Performance Appraisal Process," *Organizational Behavior and Human Decision Processes,* 1984, Vol. 33, pp. 360–396.

20. See, for example, H. John Bernardin and C. S. Walter, "Effects of Rater Training and Diary Keeping on Psychometric Errors in Ratings," *Journal of Applied Psychology,* 1977, Vol. 62, pp. 64–69; or Angelo DeNisi, Tina Robbins, and Thomas Cafferty, "The Organization of Information Used for Performance Appraisals: The Role of Diary Keeping," *Journal of Applied Psychology,* 1989, Vol. 74, pp. 124–129.

21. For an excellent review of some relevant court cases, see Jon Werner and Mark Bolino, "Explaining U.S. Courts of Appeals Decisions Involving Performance Appraisal: Accuracy, Fairness, and Validation," *Personnel Psychology,* 1997, Vol. 50, pp. 1–24.

22. For a more complete discussion of the proper focus for appraisals in different settings, see Angelo DeNisi, "Performance Appraisal and Control Systems: A Multilevel Approach," in K. Klein and S. Kozlowski (eds.), *Multilevel Theory, Research, and Methods in Organizations,* SIOP Frontiers Series (San Francisco, Calif.: Jossey-Bass, 2000), pp. 121–156.

23. E. D. Sisson, "Forced Choice: The New Army Rating," *Personnel Psychology,* 1948, Vol. 1, pp. 365–381.

24. J. C. Flanagan, "The Critical Incident Technique," *Psychological Bulletin,* 1954, Vol. 51, pp. 327–358.

25. J. C. Flanagan and R. K. Burns, "The Employee Performance Record: A New Appraisal and Development Tool," *Harvard Business Review,* September–October 1955, pp. 95–102.

26. H. J. Bernardin and C. S. Walter, "The Effects of Rater Training and Diary Keeping on Psychometric Errors in Ratings," *Journal of Applied Psychology,* 1977, Vol. 62, pp. 64–69; A. S. DeNisi, T. Robbins, and T. P. Cafferty, "The Organization of Information Used for Performance Appraisals: The Role of Diary Keeping," *Journal of Applied Psychology,* 1989, Vol. 74, pp. 124–129.

27. P. C. Smith and L. M. Kendall, "Retranslation of Expectations: An Approach to the Construction of Unambiguous Anchors for Rating Scales," *Journal of Applied Psychology,* 1963, Vol. 47, pp. 149–155.

28. H. J. Bernardin, M. B. LaShells, P. C. Smith, and K. M. Alvares, "Behavioral Expectation Scales: Effects of Development Procedures and Formats," *Journal of Applied Psychology,* 1976, Vol. 61, pp. 75–79.

29. G. P. Latham, C. H. Fay, and L. M. Saari, "The Development of Behavioral Observation Scales for Appraising the Performance of Foremen," *Personnel Psychology,* 1979, Vol. 33, pp. 815–821.

30. For an excellent review of the variations on these methods, see Chapter 4 in H. J. Bernardin and R. W. Beatty, *Performance Appraisal: Assessing Human Behavior at Work* (Boston, Mass.: PWS-Kent, 1984).

31. See, for example, Joseph Mishra and Susan Crampton, "Employee Monitoring: Privacy in the Workplace?" *SAM Advanced Management Journal,* 1998, Vol. 53, p. 4.

32. See Elizabeth Douthitt and John R. Aiello, "The Role of Participation and Control in the Effects of Computer Monitoring on Fairness Perceptions, Task Satisfaction, and Performance," *Journal of Applied Psychology,* 2001, Vol. 86, pp. 867–874.

33. American Management Association, *Workplace Monitoring and Surveillance: A 1999 AMA Survey* (New York: American Management Association, 2000).

34. See, for example, reviews by Frank Landy and James Farr, "Performance Rating," *Psychological Bulletin,* 1980, Vol. 87, pp. 72–102; or Angelo DeNisi, *A Cognitive Approach to Performance Appraisal* (London: Routledge, 1996), pp. 1–20.

35. W. C. Borman, "Job Behavior, Performance, and Effectiveness," in M. D. Dunnette and L. Hough (eds.), *Handbook of Industrial and Organizational Psychology,* Vol. 2, 2nd ed. (Palo Alto, Calif.: Consulting Psychologists Press, 1991); W. C. Borman and S. J. Motowidlo, "Expanding the Criterion Domain to Include Elements of Contextual Performance," in N. Schmitt and W. Borman (eds.), *Personnel Selection in Organizations* (San Francisco, Calif.: Jossey-Bass, 1993).

36. D. W. Organ and K. Ryan, "A Meta-Analytic Review of Attitudinal and Dispositional Predictors of Organizational Citizenship Behavior," *Personnel Psychology,* 1995, Vol. 48, pp. 775–802.

37. J. M. Werner, "Dimensions That Make a Difference: Examining the Impact of In-Role and Extrarole Behaviors on Supervisory Ratings," *Journal of Applied Psychology,* 1994, Vol. 79, pp. 98–107.

38. Maria Rotundo and Paul Sackett, "The Relative Importance of Task, Citizenship, and Counterproductive Performance to Global Ratings of Job Performance: A Policy-Capturing Study," *Journal of Applied Psychology,* 2002, Vol. 87, pp. 66–80.

39. Neal P. Mero and Stephan J. Motowidlo, "Effects of Rater Accountability on the Accuracy and the Favorability of Performance Ratings," *Journal of Applied Psychology,* 1995, Vol. 80, No. 4, pp. 517–524.

40. Jeffrey S. Kane, H. John Bernardin, Peter Villanova, and Joseph Peyrefitte, "Stability of Rater Leniency: Three Studies," *Academy of Management Journal,* 1995, Vol. 38, No. 4, pp. 1036–1051.

41. Walter C. Borman, Leonard A. White, and David W. Dorsey, "Effects of Ratee Task Performance and Interpersonal Factors on Supervisor and Peer Performance Ratings," *Journal of Applied Psychology,* 1995, Vol. 80, No. 1, pp. 168–177.

42. Juan I. Sanchez and Phillip De La Torre, "A Second Look at the Relationship Between Rating and Behavioral Accuracy in Performance Appraisal," *Journal of Applied Psychology,* 1996, Vol. 81, No. 1, pp. 3–10.

43. Kate Ludeman, "To Fill the Feedback Void," *Training & Development,* August 1995, pp. 38–43.

44. Allan H. Church, "First-Rate Multirater Feedback," *Training & Development,* August 1995, pp. 42+.

45. Avraham Kluger and Angelo DeNisi, "Feedback Interventions: An Historical Review, and Meta-Analysis and a Proposed New Model," *Psychological Bulletin,* 1996, Vol. 119, pp. 254–284.

46. For a full description of the model and its effectiveness, see Robert Pritchard, Steven Jones, Phillip Roth, Karla Stuebing, and Steven Ekeberg, "Effects of Group Feedback, Goal-Setting, and Incentives on Organizational Productivity," *Journal of Applied Psychology* (Monograph), 1988, Vol. 73, pp. 337–358; and Robert Pritchard, Steven Jones, Phillip Roth, Karla Steubing and Steven Ekeberg, "The Evaluation of an Integrated Approach to Measuring Organizational Productivity," *Personnel Psychology,* 1989, Vol. 42, pp. 69–115.

47. *Brito v. Zia Company,* 478 F. 2d 1200 (10th Cir. 1973).

48. Sources: "New Hires Win Fast Raises in Accelerated Job Reviews," *Wall Street Journal,* October 6, 1998, pp. B1, B16; "Your Year-End Review Doesn't Have to Be Quite That Horrible," *Wall Street Journal,* December 23, 1997, p. B1.

Chapter 10

1. Frank Jossi, "Lesson Plans," *HRMagazine,* February 2003, pp. 72–76 (*quote on p. 74); *Hoover's Handbook of American Business 2003* (Austin, Tex.: Hoover's Business Press, 2003), pp. 148–149.

2. See Chapter 1 in Charles R. Greer, *Strategy and Human Resources* (Englewood Cliffs, N.J.: Prentice-Hall, 1995), for an overview of the importance of training and development.

3. Paul Chaddock, "Building Value with Training," *Training & Development,* July 1995, pp. 22–25.

4. Marcia Atkinson, "Build Learning into Work," *HRMagazine,* September 1994, pp. 60–66.

5. J. Bruce Tracey, Scott I. Tannenbaum, and Michael J. Kavanagh, "Applying Trained Skills on the Job: The Importance of the Work Environment," *Journal of Applied Psychology,* 1995, Vol. 80, No. 2, pp. 239–252.

6. Kathryn Tyler, "Take New Employee Orientation Off the Back Burner," *HRMagazine,* May 1998, pp. 49–51.

7. "Corporate America Goes to School," *Business Week,* October 20, 1997, pp. 66–72.

8. Teresa L. Smith, "The Basics of Basic Skills Training," *Training & Development,* April 1995, pp. 4447.

9. R. M. Gagne, "Learning Outcomes and Their Effects: Useful Categories of Human Performance," *American Psychologist,* 1984, Vol. 39, pp. 377–385.

10. Jack Stack, "The Training Myth," *Inc.,* August 1998, pp. 41–42.

11. Kathryn Tyler, *HRMagazine,* February 2003, pp. 78–84.

12. "Training Takes Front Seat at Offices," *USA Today,* January 19, 1999, p. 6B.

13. "U.S. Airlines They Should Offer Peanut-Free Rows," *The Wall Street Journal,* September 2, 1998, pp. A1, A8.

14. Jane Webster and Joseph J. Martocchio, "The Differential Effects of Software Training Previews on Training Outcomes," *Journal of Management,* 1995, Vol. 21, No. 4, pp. 757–787.

15. Elizabeth Goodridge, "Slowing Economy Sparks Boom in e-learning," *Information Week,* November 12, 2001, pp. 100–104.

16. Kathryn Tyler, "Take E-Learning to the Next Step," *HRMagazine,* February 2002, pp. 56–61.

17. "Leader of the Pack in Wilderness Training Is Pushed to the Wall," *Wall Street Journal,* July 24, 1997, pp. A1, A6.

18. "Work Week," *Wall Street Journal,* November 24, 1998, p. A1.

19. Christine Clements, Richard J. Wagner, and Christopher C. Roland, "The Ins and Outs of Experiential Training," *Training & Development,* February 1995, pp. 52–59.

20. Kathryn Tyler, "Simon Says, 'Make Learning Fun'," *HRMagazine,* June 1996, pp. 162–165.

21. M. D. Dunnette and J. P. Campbell, "Laboratory Education: Impact on People and Organizations," *Industrial Relations,* 1968, Vol. 8, pp. 1–27, 41–44.

22. The relationship between individual and organizational learning is discussed in much more detail in Lois Tetrick and Nancy Da Silva, "Assessing the Culture and Climate for Organizational Learning," in Susan Jackson, Michael Hitt and Angelo DeNisi (eds.), *Managing Knowledge for Sustained Competitive Advantage.* (San Francisco, Calif.: Jossey-Bass, 2003), pp. 333–360.

23. See, for example, Michael Hitt, Barbara Keats, and Sam DeMarie, "Navigating in the New Competitive Landscape: Building Strategic Flexibility and Competitive Advantage in the 21st Century," *Academy of Management Executive,* 1998, Vol. 12, pp. 22–42; and Angelo DeNisi, Michael Hitt and Susan Jackson, "The Knowledge-Based Approach to Sustainable Competitive Advantage," in Susan Jackson, Michael Hitt and Angelo DeNisi (eds.), *Managing Knowledge for Sustained Competitive Advantage* (San Francisco, Calif.: Jossey-Bass, 2003), pp. 3–36.

24. Hyuckseung Yang, Paul R. Sackett, and Richard D. Arvey, "Statistical Power and Cost in Training Evaluation: Some New Considerations," *Personnel Psychology,* Autumn 1996, pp. 651–668.

25. Sources: *Hoover's Handbook of American Business 2003* (Austin, Tex.: Hoover's Reference Press, 2003), pp. 256–257; "'Boeing U': Flying by the Book," *USA Today,* October 6, 1997, pp. 1B, 2B; "Is Your Airline Pilot Ready for Surprises?" *Time,* October 14, 2002, p. 72.

Chapter 11

1. "A Little Less in the Envelope This Week," *Business Week,* February 18, 2002, pp. 64–66; "Pay? How About a Pizza?" *Newsweek,* April 20, 1998, pp. 42–43 (*quote on p. 43); "'Off-the-Clock' Time: More Work for No Pay," *USA Today,* April 24, 1997, p. 1B.

2. Kathryn Tyler, "Compensation Strategies Can Foster Lateral Moves and Growing in Place," *HRMagazine,* April 1998, pp. 64–69.

3. J. Stacey Adams, "Inequity in Social Exchange," in L. Berkowitz (ed.), *Advances in Experimental Social Psychology* (New York: Academic Press, 1965), pp. 267–299.

4. Jeffrey Pfeiffer, "Six Dangerous Myths About Pay," *Harvard Business Review,* May–June 1998, pp. 109–119.

5. See "Is Minimum Wage Minimum Life?" Associated Press news story, January 23, 1995, as published in the *Bryan-College Station Eagle,* p. B1.

6. Brian S. Klaas and John A. McClendon, "To Lead, Lag, or Match: Estimating the Financial Impact of Pay Level Policies," *Personnel Psychology,* 1996, Vol. 49, No. 1, pp. 88–98.

7. Edward E. Lawler III, "The New Pay: A Strategic Approach," *Compensation & Benefits Review,* July–August 1995, pp. 145–154.

8. Sandra O'Neil, "Aligning Pay with Business Strategy," *HRMagazine,* August 1993, pp. 76–80.

9. Charles Greer, *Strategy and Human Resources* (Englewood Cliffs, N.J.: Prentice-Hall, 1995).

10. "Many Companies Lower Pay Raises," *USA Today,* April 4, 2002, p. 1B.

11. Emily Pavlovic, "Choosing the Best Salary Surveys," *HRMagazine,* April 1994, pp. 44–48.

12. Judith Collins and Paul Muchinsky, "An Assessment of the Construct Validity of Three Job Evaluation Methods: A Field Experiment," *Academy of Management Journal,* 1993, Vol. 36, No. 4, pp. 895–904.

13. George Milkovich and Jerry Newman, *Compensation* (Homewood, Ill.: Irwin/BPI, 1990).

14. Milkovich and Newman, *Compensation.*

15. Ibid.

16. G. D. Jenkins and N. Gupta, "The Payoffs of Paying for Knowledge," *National Productivity Review,* 1985, Vol. 4, pp. 121–130.

17. Sources: *Hoover's Handbook of American Business 2003* (Austin, Tex.: Hoover's Business Press, 2003); " 'I'm Proud of What I've Made Myself Into—What I've Created,'" *Wall Street Journal,* August 28, 1997, pp. B1, B5; " 'That's Why I Like My Job . . . I Have an Impact on Quality,'" *Wall Street Journal,* August 28, 1997, pp. B1, B8.

Chapter 12

1. "Going Sideways on the Corporate Ladder," *Business Week,* September 30, 2002, p. 39 (*quote on p. 39); "A Little Less in the Envelope This Week," *Business Week,* February 18, 2002, pp. 64–66.

2. For a review, see G. Moorhead and R. W. Griffin, *Organizational Behavior,* 7th ed. (Boston, Mass.: Houghton Mifflin, 2004).

3. Matt Bloom and George Milkovich, "Relationships Among Risk, Incentive Pay, and Organizational Performance," *Academy of Management Journal,* 1998, Vol. 41, No. 3, pp. 283–297.

4. Matt Bloom, "The Performance Effects of Pay Dispersion on Individuals and Organizations," *Academy of Management Journal,* 1999, Vol. 42, No. 1, pp. 25–40.

5. Edward E. Lawler, *Strategic Pay: Aligning Organizational Strategies and Pay Systems* (San Francisco, Calif.: Jossey-Bass, 1990).

6. G. D. Jenkins, G. E. Ledford, N. Gupta, and D. H. Doty, *Skill-Based Pay* (Scottsdale, Ariz.: American Compensation Association, 1992).

7. John L. Morris, "Lessons Learned in Skill-Based Pay," *HRMagazine,* June 1996, pp. 136–142.

8. Daniel Wren, *The Evolution of Management Theory,* 4th ed. (New York: Wiley, 1994).

9. C. Wiley, "Incentive Plan Pushes Production," *Personnel Journal,* August 1993, p. 91.

10. "When Money Isn't Enough," *Forbes,* November 18, 1996, pp. 164–169.

11. Jacquelyn DeMatteo, Lillian Eby, and Eric Sundstrom, "Team-Based Rewards: Current Empirical Evidence and Directions for Future Research," in L. L. Cummings and Barry Staw (eds.), *Research in Organizational Behavior,* Vol. 20 (Greenwich, Conn.: JAI Press, 1998), pp. 141–183.

12. Theresa M. Welbourne and Luis R. Gomez-Mejia, "Gainsharing: A Critical Review and a Future Research Agenda," *Journal of Management,* 1995, Vol. 21, No. 3, pp. 559–609.

13. "Executive Pay," *Business Week,* April 15, 2002, pp. 80–100.

14. T. A. Steward, "The Trouble with Stock Options," *Fortune,* January 1, 1990, pp. 93–95.

15. "Sign of Times: GE Chief Immelt to Get Stock—Not Options," *Wall Street Journal,* September 18, 2003, pp. B1, B4.

16. Harry Barkema and Luis Gomez-Mejia, "Managerial Compensation and Firm Performance: A General Research Framework," *Academy of Management Journal,* 1998, Vol. 41, No. 2, pp. 135–145.

17. Rajiv D. Banker, Seok-Young Lee, Gordon Potter, and Dhinu Srinivasan, "Contextual Analysis of Performance Impacts of Outcome-Based Incentive Compensation," *Academy of Management Journal,* 1996, Vol. 39, No. 4, pp. 920–948.

18. M. Blair, "CEO Pay: Why Such a Contentious Issue?" *The Brookings Review,* Winter 1994, pp. 23–27.

19. J. Pfeffer and N. Langton, "The Effects of Wage Dispersion on Satisfaction, Productivity and Working Collaboratively: Evidence from College and University Faculty," *Administrative Science Quarterly,* 1993, Vol. 38, pp. 382–407.

20. R. G. Ehrenberg and M. L. Bognanno, "The Incentive Effects of Tournaments Revisited: Evidence from the European PGA Tour," *Industrial and Labor Relations Review,* 1990, Vol. 43, pp. 74–88.

21. Sources: "Continental Is Winning the Battle for Share in New York Market," *Wall Street Journal,* January 9, 1999, pp. A1, A11; *Hoover's Handbook of American Business 2003* (Austin, Tex.: Hoover's Business, 2003); "Explorer Possibilities," *Continental Magazine,* October 1997, p. 19.

Chapter 13

1. "Now It's Getting Personal," *Business Week,* December 16, 2002, pp. 90–92 (*quote on p. 90); "Firms Brace for a Worker Shortage," *Time,* May 6, 2002, p. 44.

2. Bureau of National Affairs, U.S. Chamber of Commerce data, January 5, 1995.

3. "Detroit Meets a 'Worker Paradise,'" *Wall Street Journal,* March 3, 1999, pp. B1, B4.

4. Randall S. Schuler and Susan E. Jackson. *Human Resource Management: Positioning for the 21st Century,* 6th ed. (Minneapolis, Minn: West Publishing Company, 1996), p. 309.

5. Fran Lipson, "How to Cut the Waste from Workers' Compensation," *HRMagazine,* June 1993, pp. 83–87.

6. Richard Wolfe and Donald Parker, "Employee Health Management: Challenges and Opportunities," *The Academy of Management Executive,* 1994, Vol. 8, No. 2, pp. 22–31.

7. For a recent discussion of these issues, see Maureen Minehan, "Islam's Growth Affects Workplace Policies," *HRMagazine,* November 1998, p. 216.

8. Mina Westman and Dov Eden, "Effects of Respite from Work on Burnout: Vacation Relief and Fade-Out," *Journal of Applied Psychology,* August 1997, pp. 516–527.

9. "Employer Benefit Surveys Target Unhealthy Habits," *USA Today,* May 28, 1998, p. 1B.

10. S. Caudron, "The Wellness Pay Off," *Personnel Journal,* July 1990, pp. 55–60.

11. Shirley Hand and Robert Zawacki, "Family-Friendly Benefits: More Than a Frill," *HRMagazine,* October 1994, pp. 79–74.

12. E. E. Kossek and V. Nichol, "The Effects of On-Site Child Care on Employee Attitudes and Performance," *Personnel Psychology,* 1992, Vol. 45, pp. 485–509.

13. "Gay Employees Win Benefits for Partners at More Corporations," *Wall Street Journal,* March 18, 1994, p. A1.

14. Rudy Yandrick, "The EAP Struggle: Counselors or Referrers?" *HRMagazine,* August 1998, pp. 90–91.

15. W. J. Sonnenstuhl and H. M. Trice, *Strategies for Employee Assistance Programs: The Crucial Balance* (Ithaca, N.Y.: Cornell University ILR Press, 1990).

16. Melissa Barringer and George Milkovich, "A Theoretical Exploration of the Adoption and Design of Flexible Benefit Plans: A Case of Human Resource Innovation," *Academy of Management Review,* April 1998, pp. 305–324.

17. A. E. Barber, R. B. Dunham, and R. A. Formisano, "The Impact of Flexible Benefits on Employee Satisfaction: A Field Study," *Personnel Psychology,* 1992, Vol. 45, pp. 55–57.

18. For a more in-depth discussion of the requirements and advantages of qualification, see Michael Sarli, "Nondiscrimination Rules for Qualified Plans: The General Test," *Compensation and Benefits Review,* September 1991, pp. 56–67.

19. H. W. Hennessey, P. L. Perrewe, and W. A. Hochwarter, "Impact of Benefit Awareness on Employee and Organizational Outcomes: A Longitudinal Field Experiment," *Benefits Quarterly,* 1992, Vol. 8, No. 2, pp. 90–96.

20. M. Wilson, G. B. Northcraft, and M. A. Neale, "The Perceived Value of Fringe Benefits," *Personnel Psychology,* 1985, Vol. 38, pp. 309–320.

21. Sources: "Perks That Work," *Time,* November 9, 1998, pp. 126–130; "An Apple a Day—On the Boss," *Business Week,* October 4, 2002, pp. 122–124.

Chapter 14

1. "29 Ports All Stopped Up," *USA Today,* October 1, 2002, p. 3B (*quote on p. 3B); "West Coast Ports Still Closed as Talks Break Down," *USA Today,* October 2, 2002, p. 1B; "West Coast Port Labor Contract Ratified," *The Journal of Commerce,* January 24, 2003, p. 1.

2. David Lipsky and Clifford Donn, *Collective Bargaining in American Industry* (Lexington, Mass.: Lexington Books, 1981).

3. Alabama, Arkansas, Florida, Georgia, Iowa, Kansas, Kentucky, Louisiana, Mississippi, Nebraska, Nevada, North Carolina, North Dakota, South Carolina, South Dakota, Tennessee, Texas, Utah, Virginia, and Wyoming are right-to-work states, although a state can change its status on this issue at any time.

4. "Companies Counter Unions," *USA Today,* September 1997, pp. 1B, 2B.

5. Edward E. Lawler III and Susan A. Mohrman, "Unions and the New Management," *The Academy of Management Executive,* 1987, Vol. 1, No. 3, pp 65–75.

6. "Why Mexico Scares the UAW," *Business Week,* August 3, 1998, pp. 37–38.

7. Clive Fullagar, Paul Clark, Daniel Gallagher, and Michael E. Gordon, "A Model of the Antecedents of Early Union Commitment: The Role of Socialization Experiences and Steward Characteristics," *Journal of Organizational Behavior,* 1994, Vol. 15, pp. 517–533.

8. Stuart Youngblood, Angelo DeNisi, Julie Molleston, and William Mobley, "The Impact of Worker Attachment, Instrumentality Beliefs, Perceived Labor Union Image, and Subjective Norms on Voting Intentions and Union Membership," *Academy of Management Journal,* 1984, Vol. 27, pp. 576–590.

9. J. Barling, E. K. Kelloway, and E. H. Bremermann, "Pre-employment Predictors of Union Attitudes: The Role of Family Socialization and Work Beliefs," *Journal of Applied Psychology,* 1991, Vol. 75, pp. 725–731.

10. "Some Unions Step Up Organizing Campaigns and Get New Members," *Wall Street Journal,* September 1, 1995, pp. A1, A2.

11. See Jeanette A. Davy and Frank Shipper, "Voter Behavior in Union Certification Elections: A Longitudianl Study," *Academy of Management Journal,* 1993, Vol. 36, No. 1, pp. 187–199, for a discussion of some of the determinants of individual voting behavior in union elections.

12. Adapted from R. E. Walton and R. B. McKersie, *A Behavioral Theory of Labor Negotiations* (New York: McGraw-Hill, 1965). Note that we have used the terminology used by those authors, which is adapted from game theory. The reader might encounter different terms in other treatments of bargaining, but the concepts are the same as those described here.

13. "ABC Locks Out Striking Employees," *USA Today,* November 3, 1998, p. B1.

14. Phil Taylor, "To the Victor Belong the Spoils," *Sports Illustrated,* January 18, 1999, pp. 48–52.

15. H. S. Farber and H. C. Katz, " Interest Arbitration, Outomes, and the Incentive to Bargain," *Industrial and Labor Relations Review,* 1979, Vol. 33, pp. 55–63.

16. P. Feuille, "Final Offer Arbitration and the Chilling Effect," *Industrial Relations,* 1975, 14, pp. 302–310.

17. Lynn Gibson, "Implications of the FLSA for Inmates, Correctional Institutions, Private Industry and Labor," statement before the U.S. Senate Hearings of the Committee on Labor and Human Resources, October 18, 1993.

18. For a more in-depth discussion of these issues, see Ray Marshall, "Industrial Relations and Inmate Labor," *Proceedings of the 53rd Annual Meeting of the Industrial Relations Research Association,* New Orleans, 2001, pp. 339–348.

19. Jeffrey Kling and Alan Krueger, "Costs, Benefits, and Distributional Consequences of Inmate Labor," *Proceedings of the 53rd Annual Meeting of the Industrial Relations Research Association,* New Orleans, 2001, pp. 349–358.

20. See Kevin Banks, "Contingent and Informal Workers in North America: Workplace Human Rights," *Proceedings of the 53rd Annual Meeting of the Industrial Relations Research Association,* New Orleans, 2001, pp. 90–98.

21. See, for example, Janice Fine, "Community Unionism: The Key to the New Labor Movement," *Perspectives on Work,* 1997, Vol. 1, pp. 32–35; or Bruce Nissen, "Living Wage Campaigns from a 'Social Movement' Perspective," *Labor Studies Journal,* 2000, Vol. 25, pp. 29–50.

22. For example, see Greg Muntsios, *A New Labor Movement for the New Century* (New York: Garland, 1998).

23. For a complete discussion of the issues and the rulings in this area, see Camille Olson and Michael Rybick, "Spotlight on Union Organizing: 'No Solicitation No Distribution' and Related Rules in the Age of E-mail and the Internet," *Legal Report* (published by Society of Human Resource Managers), May–June 2002, pp. 5–7.

24. Nathan Newman, "Union and Community Mobilization in the Information Age," *Perspectives on Work,* 2002, Vol. 6, No. 2, pp. 9–11.

25. Sources: "What's Really Behind GM's Strike? A Battle Over a Hot New Truck," *Wall Street Journal,* July 28, 1998, pp. A1, A5; "What Price Peace?" *Business Week,* August 10, 1998, pp. 24–25; "GM Might Stop Benefits for Workers," *USA Today,* June 26, 1998, p. B1; "Rivals Make Strides After Nasty Strike," *USA Today,* December 16, 1998, pp. B1, B2.

Chapter 15

1. "Workplace Hazard Gets Attention," *USA Today,* May 5, 1998, pp. 1B, 2B ("quote on p. 1B); *The Wall Street Journal Almanac 1999* (New York: Ballantine Books, 1999), p. 231; "The New Paternalism," *Forbes,* November 2, 1998, pp. 68–70; "More Work, Less Play," *New York Times,* December 15, 2002, p. 15A.

2. Manuel London, "Redeployment and Continuous Learning in the 21st Century: Hard Lessons and Positive Examples from the Downsizing Era," *The Academy of Management Executive,* November 1996, pp. 67–79.

3. Adrianne H. Geiger-DuMond and Susan K. Boyle, "Mentoring: A Practitioner's Guide," *Training & Develoment,* March 1995, pp. 51–55.

4. Douglas T. Hall, "Protean Careers of the 21st Century," *The Academy of Management Executive,* November 1996, pp. 8–16.

5. For a discussion of a wide variety of issues at every stage in one's career, see Daniel Feldman (ed.), *Work Careers: A Developmental Perspective* (San Francisco: Jossey-Bass, 2002).

6. Bruce Avolio and David Waldman, "Variations in Cognitive, Perceptual, and Psychomotor Abilities Across the Working Life Span: Examining the Effects of Race, Sex, Experience, Education, and Occupational Type," *Psychology and Aging,* 1994, Vol. 9, pp. 430–442.

7. See for example, reviews by Glen McEvoy and Wayne Cascio, "Cummulative Evidence of the Relationship Between Employee Age and Job Performance," *Journal of Applied Psychology,* 1989, Vol. 74, No. 1, pp. 11–17; and Susan Rhoades, "Age-related Differences in Work Attitudes and Behavior: A Review and Conceptual Analysis," *Psychological Bulletin,* Vol. 93, pp. 328–367.

8. Terry Beehr, "The Process of Retirement: A Review and Recommendations," *Personnel Psychology,* 1986, Vol. 39, No. 1, pp. 31–55.

9. Gregory K. Stephens, "Crossing Internal Career Boundaries: The State of Research on Subjective Career Transitions," *Journal of Management,* 1994, Vol. 20, No. 2, pp. 479–501.

10. Suzyn Ornstein and Lynn A. Isabella, "Making Sense of Careers: A Review 1989–1992," *Journal of Management,* 1993, Vol. 19, No. 2, pp. 243–267.

11. Kenneth R. Brousseau, Michael J. Driver, Kristina Eneroth, and Rikard Larsson, "Career Pandemonium: Realigning Organizations and Individuals," *The Academy of Management Executive,* November 1996, pp. 52–66.

12. M. Ferber, B. O'Farrell, and L. Allen, *Work and Family: Policies for a Changing Workforce* (Washington, D.C.: National Academy Press, 1994).

13. H. Morgan and K. Tucker, *Companies That Care: The Most Family-Friendly Companies in America, What They Offer, and How They Got That Way* (New York: Simon & Schuster, 1991).

14. S. Zedeck and K. L. Mosier, "Work in Family and Employing Organizations," *American Psychologist,* 1990, Vol. 45, pp. 240–251.

15. V. J. Doby and R. D. Caplan, "Organizational Stress as Threat to Reputation: Effects on Anxiety at Work and at Home," *Academy of Management Journal,* 1995, Vol. 38, pp. 1105–1123.

16. P. B. Doeringer, "Economic Security, Labor Market Flexibility, and Bridges to Retirement," in P. B. Doeringer (ed.), *Bridges to Retirement* (Ithaca, N.Y.: Cornell University ILR Press, 1990), pp. 3–22.

17. Myron D. Fottler, "Employee Acceptance of a Four Day Work Week," *Academy of Management Journal,* 1977, Vol. 20, pp. 656–668.

18. S. Ronen and S. B. Primpts, "The Compressed Work Week as Organizational Change: Behavioral and Attitudinal Outcomes," *Academy of Management Review,* 1981, Vol. 6, pp. 61–74.

19. A. Purach, "Biological Rhythm Effects of Night Work and Shift Changes on the Health of Workers," *Acta Medica Scandinavia,* 1973, Vol. 152, pp. 302–307.

20. S. Zedeck, S. E. Jackson, and E. S. Marca, "Shift Work Schedules and Their Relationship to Health, Adaptation, Satisfaction, and Turnover Intentions," *Academy of Management Journal,* 1983, Vol. 26, pp. 297–310.

21. G. B. Meese, M. I. Lewis, D. P. Wyon, and R. Kok, "A Laboratory Study of the Effects of Thermal Stress on the Performance of Factory Workers," *Ergonomics,* 1982, Vol. 27, pp. 19–43.

22. E. VanDeVliert and N. W. Van Yperen, "Why Cross National Differences in Role Overload? Don't Overlook Ambient Temperature," *Academy of Management Journal,* 1996, Vol. 39, pp. 986–1004.

23. D. G. Hayward, "Psychological Factors in the Use of Light and Lighting in Buildings," in J. Lang, C. Burnette, W. Moleski, and D. Vachon (eds.), *Designing for Human Behavior: Architecture and the Behavioral Sciences* (Stroudsburg, Penn.: Dowden, Hutchinson, & Ross, 1974), pp. 120–129.

24. R. I. Newman, D. L. Hunt, and F. Rhodes, "Effects of Music on Employee Attitude and Productivity in a Skateboard Factory," *Journal of Applied Psychology,* 1956, Vol. 50, pp. 493–496.

25. G. R. Oldham, A. Cummings, L. J. Mischel, J. M. Scmidtke, and J. Zhou, "Listen While You Work? Quasi-Experimental Relations Between Personal Stereo Headset Use and Employee Work Responses," *Journal of Applied Psychology,* 1995, Vol. 80, pp. 547–564.

26. G. R. Oldham, "Effects of Changes in Workspace Partitions and Spatial Density on Employee Reactions: A Quasi-Experiment," *Journal of Applied Psychology,* 1988, Vol. 73, pp. 253–258.

27. "Working at Home Raises Job Site Safety Issues," *USA Today,* January 29, 1998, p. 1A.

28. "Labor Secretary's Bid to Push Plant Safety Runs into Skepticism," *Wall Street Journal,* August 19, 1994, pp. A1, A5.

29. R. S. Haynes, R. C. Pine, and H. G. Fitch, "Reducing Accident Rates with Organizational Behavior Modification," *Academy of Management Journal,* 1988, Vol. 25, pp. 407–416.

30. "In an Amoco Lab, Researchers Hunt for Colleagues' Killer," *USA Today,* April 13, 1999, p. 8D.

31. Karen Danna and Ricky W. Griffin, "Health and Well-Being in the Workplace," *Journal of Management,* 1999, Vol. 19, pp. 125–146.

32. "Workplace Demands Taking up More Weekends," *USA Today,* April 24, 1998, p. 1B.

33. Richard S. DeFrank and John M. Ivancevich, "Stress on the Job: An Executive Update," *The Academy of Management Executive,* 1998, Vol. 12, No. 3, pp. 55–67.

34. See Anne O'Leary-Kelly, Ricky W. Griffin, and David J. Glew, "Organization-Motivated Aggression: A Research Framework," *The Academy of Management Review,* January 1996, pp. 225–253.

35. See, for example, Wendy Boswell, Julie Olson-Buchanan, and Marcie Cavanaugh, "Investigation of the Relationship Between Work-Related Stress and Work Outcomes: The Role of Felt Challenge, Psychological Strain, and Job Control," paper presented at the Academy of Management meetings, Toronto, Ontario, 2000; and Marcie Cavanaugh, Wendy Boswell, Mark Roehling, and John Boudreau, "An Empirical Examination of Self-Reported Work Stress Among U.S. Managers," *Journal of Applied Psychology,* 2000, Vol. 85, pp. 65–74.

36. See, for example, Cynthia McCauley, Marian Ruderman, Patricia Ohlott, and Jane Morrow, "Assessing the Developmental Components of Managerial Jobs," *Journal of Applied Psychology,* 1994, Vol. 79, pp. 544–560.

37. Sources: Anne Fisher, "Danger Zone," *Fortune,* September 8, 1997, pp. 165–167; *Hoover's Handbook of American Business 2003* (Austin, Tex.: Hoover's Business Press, 2003).

Chapter 16

1. "How One Hotel Manages Staff Diversity," *Wall Street Journal,* November 20, 1996, pp. B1, B11 (*quote on p. B11); *Hoover's Handbook of American Business 2003* (Austin, Tex.: Hoover's Business Press, 2003), pp. 904–905; "In a Factory Schedule, Where Does Religion Fit In?" *Wall Street Journal,* March 4, 1999, pp. B1, B12; Roy Johnson, "The 50 Best Companies for Blacks & Hispanics," *Fortune,* August 3, 1998, pp. 94–106.

2. David A. Thomas and Robin J. Ely, "Making Differences Matter: A New Paradigm for Managing Diversity," *Harvard Business Review,* September–October 1996, pp. 79–90.

3. Dora C. Lau and J. Keith Murnighan, "Demographic Diversity and Faultlines: The Compositional Dynamics of Organizational Groups," *Academy of Management Review,* 1998, Vol. 23, No. 2, pp. 325–340.

4. Frances J. Milliken and Luis L. Martins, "Searching for Common Threads: Understanding the Multiple Effects of Diversity in Organizational Groups," *Academy of Management Review,* 1996, Vol. 21, No. 2, pp. 402–433.

5. "In a Factory Schedule, Where Does Religion Fit In?" *Wall Street Journal,* March 4, 1999, pp. B1, B12.

6. Adrienne Colella, "The Work Group Perspective: Co-Worker Responses to Group Member Accommodations," in D. Harrison (chair), "Implementing What Matters Most: Multiple Stakeholders in Accommodating People with Disabilities at Work. All- Academy Symposium," presented at annual meeting of the Academy of Management, San Diego, Calif., August 1998.

7. Barbara L. Hassell and Pamela L. Perrewe, "An Examination of Beliefs About Older Workers: Do Stereotypes Still Exist?" *Journal of Organizational Behavior,* 1995, Vol. 16, pp. 457–468.

8. For a more complete discussion of these dimensions, see Diane L. Stone and Adrienne Colella, "A Model of Factors Affecting the Treatment of Disabled Individuals in Organizations," *Academy of Management Review,* 1996, Vol. 21, pp. 352–401.

9. Based on Taylor H. Cox and Stacy Blake, "Managing Cultural Diversity: Implications for Organizational Competitiveness," *The Academy of Management Executive,* August 1991, pp. 45–56; see also Gail Robinson and Kathleen Dechant, "Building a Business Case for Diversity," *The Academy of Management Executive,* August 1997, pp. 21–30.

10. C. Marlene Fiol, "Consensus, Diversity, and Learning in Organizations," *Organization Science,* August 1994, pp. 403–415.

11. Douglas Hall and Victoria Parker, "The Role of Workplace Flexibility in Managing Diversity," *Organizational Dynamics,* Summer 1993, pp. 5–14.

12. Janice R. W. Joplin and Catherine S. Daus, "Challenges of Leading a Diverse Workforce," *The Academy of Management Executive,* August 1997, pp. 32–44.

13. "As Population Ages, Older Workers Clash with Younger Bosses," *Wall Street Journal,* June 13, 1994, pp. A1, A8.

14. "Pursuit of Diversity Stirs Racial Tension at an FAA Center," *Wall Street Journal,* December 3, 1998, pp. A1, A8.

15. "Generational Warfare," *Forbes,* March 22, 1999, pp. 62–66.

16. Karen Hildebrand, "Use Leadership Training to Increase Diversity," *HRMagazine,* August 1996, pp. 53–57.

17. Patricia L. Nemetz and Sandra L. Christensen, "The Challenge of Cultural Diversity: Harnessing a Diversity of Views to Understand Multiculturalism," *Academy of Management Review,* 1996, Vol. 21, No. 2, pp. 434–462.

18. This discussion derives heavily from Taylor H. Cox, "The Multicultural Organization," *The Academy of Management Executive,* May 1991, pp. 34–47.

19. Sources: Betsy Morris, Patricia Sellers, "The 50 Most Powerful Women in American Business," *Fortune,* October 12, 1998, pp. 76–89; "If Women Ran the World, It Would Look a Lot Like Avon," *Fortune,* July 21, 1997, pp. 74–79; *Hoover's Handbook of American Business 2003* (Austin, Tex.: Hoover's Business Press, 2003), pp. 216–217.

Chapter 17

1. "Merrill Broker Protests Policies, Is Fired, Finds His Clients Divvied Up," *Wall Street Journal,* February 27, 1998, pp. A1, A8 (*quote on p. A1); *Hoover's Handbook of American Business 2003* (Austin, Tex.: Hoover's Business Press, 2003).

2. D. M. Rousseau and J. McLean Parks, "The Contracts of Individuals and Organizations," in L. L. Cummings and B. M. Staw (eds.), *Research in Organizational Behavior,* Vol. 15 (Greenwich, Conn.: JAI Press, 1993), pp. 1–43.

3. D. T. Hall and J. E. Moss, "The New Protean Career Contract: Helping Organizations and Employees Adapt," *Organizational Dynamics,* Winter 1998, pp. 22–37.

4. S. L. Robinson, M. S. Kraatz, and D. M. Rousseau, "Changing Obligations and the Psychological Contract: A Longitudinal Study," *Academy of Management Journal,* 1994, Vol. 37, pp. 137–152.

5. J. J. Laabs, "Surveillance: Tool or Trap?" *Personnel Journal,* 1992, Vol. 71, pp. 96–104.

6. B. Garson, *The Electronic Sweatshop: How Computers Are Transforming the Office of the Future into the Factory of the Past* (New York: Simon & Schuster, 1988).

7. J. R. Aiello, "Computer-Based Work Monitoring: Electronic Surveillance and Its Effects," *Journal of Applied Social Psychology,* 1993, Vol. 23, pp. 499–507.

8. Commission on the Future of Worker-Management Relations, *Final Report* (Washington, D.C.: Department of Labor–Department of Commerce, 1995; Also known as the Dunlop Report).

9. R. Marshall, "A New Social Contract," in J. Auerbach and J. Welsh (eds.), *Aging and Competition: Rebuilding the U.S. Workforce* (Washington, D.C.: The National Planning Association, 1994), pp. 207–224.

10. Max Boisot, *Knowledge Assets* (Oxford, England: Oxford University Press, 1998).

11. M. L. Tushman and C. A. O'Reilly, *Winning Through Innovation* (Cambridge, Mass.: Harvard Business School Press, 1996).

12. M. A. Von Glinow, *The New Professionals* (Cambridge, Mass.: Ballinger, 1988).

13. T. W. Lee and S. D. Maurer, "The Retention of Knowledge Workers with the Unfolding Model of Voluntary Turnover," *Human Resource Management Review,* 1997, Vol. 7, pp. 247–276.

14. J. C. Kail, "Compensating Scientists and Engineers," in D. B. Balkin and L. R. Gomez-Mejia (eds.), *New Perspectives on Compensation* (Englewood Cliffs, N.J.: Prentice-Hall, 1987), pp. 278–281.

15. G. T. Milkovich, "Compensation Systems in High-Technology Companies," in A. Klingartner and C. Anderson (eds.), *High Technology Management* (Lexington, Mass.: Lexington Books, 1987).

16. Jay Barney, "Firm Resources and Sustained Competitive Advantage," *Journal of Management,* 1991, Vol. 17, pp. 99–129.

17. Thomas Stewart, "In Search of Elusive Tech Workers," *Fortune,* February 16, 1998, pp. 171–172.

18. See, for example, the various discussions in the edited volume by Susan Jackson, Michael Hitt, and Angelo DeNisi, *Managing Knowledge for Sustained Competitive Advantage: Designing Strategies for Effective Human Resource Management* (San Francisco, Calif.: Jossey-Bass, SIOP Frontiers Series, 2002).

19. Daniel C. Feldman, Helen I. Doerpinghaus, and William H. Turnley, "Managing Temporary Workers: A Permanent HRM Challenge," *Organizational Dynamics,* Autumn 1994, pp. 49–63.

20. "Citibank Hitches Itself to Primerica's Team to Peddle Accounts," *Wall Street Journal,* April 19, 1999, pp. A1, A6.

21. The term was introduced by the authors who originally presented the model. See David P. Lepak and Scott A. Snell, "The Human Resource Architecture: Toward a Theory of Human Capital Allocation and Development," *Academy of Management Review,* 1999, Vol. 24, pp. 31–48.

22. A. N. Kluger, "Commute Variability and Strain," *Journal of Organizational Behavior,* 1998, Vol. 19, pp. 147–166.

23. D. Denton, "Using Flextime to Create a Competitive Workforce," *Industrial Management,* January–February 1993, pp. 29–31.

24. J. Pearce and R. Dunham, "The 12-Hour Work Day: A Forty-Eight-Hour, Eight-Day Week," *Academy of Management Journal,* 1992, Vol. 35, pp. 1086–1098.

25. S. Greengard, "Making the Virtual Office a Reality," *Personnel Journal,* September 1994, pp. 66–79.

26. S. Cauderon, "Working at Home Pays Off," *Personnel Journal,* November 1992, pp. 40–49.

27. "Making Stay-at-Homes Feel Welcome," *Business Week,* October 12, 1998, pp. 155–156.

28. S. D. Atchison, "The Care and Feeding of 'Lone Eagles'," *Business Week,* November 15, 1993, p. 58.

29. "Saying Adios to the Office," *Business Week,* October 12, 1998, pp. 152–153.

30. Sources: "Seasonal Businesses Bustle to Find Teen Workers," *USA Today,* May 15, 1997, p. B1; "Industries Crying Out for Help Wanted," *USA Today,* May 5, 1997, p. B1; "Worker Shortage Forces Small Business into Creative Hiring," *USA Today,* October 30, 1998, pp. B1, B2.

Appendix 1

1. Bill Roberts, "Software Selection Made Easier," *HRMagazine,* June 1998, pp. 44–49.
2. Privacy Protection Study Commission, *Personal Privacy in an Information Society* (Washington, D.C.: Government Printing Office, 1977).

Appendix 2

1. For excellent overviews see Floyd J. Fowler Jr., *Survey Research Methods* (Beverly Hills, Calif.: Sage Publications, 1984); and Randall B. Dunham and Frank J. Smith, *Organizational Surveys* (Glenview, Ill.: Scott, Foresman, 1979).
2. M. J. Balma, "The Concept of Synthetic Validity," *Personnel Psychology,* 1959, Vol. 12, pp. 395–396; C. H. Lawshe, and M. D. Steinberg, "Studies in Synthetic Validity I: An Exploratory Investigation of Clerical Jobs," *Personnel Psychology,* 1955, Vol. 8, pp. 291–301.
3. Ernest J. McCormick, Angelo S. DeNisi, and James B. Shaw, "The Use of the Position Analysis Questionnaire (PAQ) for Establishing the Job Component Validity of Tests," *Journal of Applied Psychology,* 1979, Vol. 64, pp. 51-56; John R. Hollenbeck and Ellen M. Whitener, "Criterion-Related Validity for Small Sample Context: An Integrated Approach to Synthetic Validity," *Journal of Applied Psychology,* 1988, Vol. 73, pp. 536–544.
4. Frank L. Schmidt and John E. Hunter, "Development of a General Solution to the Problem of Validity Generalization," *Journal of Applied Psychology,* 1977, Vol. 62, pp. 529–540.
5. Frank L. Schmidt, Deniz S. Ones, and John E. Hunter, "Personnel Selection," *Annual Review of Psychology,* 1992, Vol. 43, pp. 627–670.
6. H. C. Taylor and J. T. Russell, "The Relationship of Validity Coefficients to the Practical Effectiveness of Tests in Selection. *Journal of Applied Psychology,* 1939, Vol. 23, pp. 565–578.
7. Hubert E. Brogden, "When Testing Pays Off," *Personnel Psychology,* 1949, Vol. 2, pp. 171–185.
8. For example, see proposals by Wayne F. Cascio and Robert A. Ramos, "Development and Application of a New Method for Assessing Job Performance in Behavioral/Economic Terms," *Journal of Applied Psychology,* 1986, Vol. 71, pp. 20–28; or John W. Boudreau, "Utility Analysis for Decision Making in Human Resource Management," in Marvin D. Dunnette and Leaetta M. Hough (eds.), *Handbook of Industrial and Organizational Psychology,* Vol. 2 (Palo Alto, Calif.: Consulting Psychologists Press, 1991), pp. 621–745.
9. Wayne F. Cascio, *Costing Human Resources: The Financial Impact of Behavior in Organizations,* 2nd ed. (Boston, Mass: PWS-Kent, 1987).

ADA *See* Americans with Disabilities Act.

adaptation model A popular approach to business strategy. It describes different ways businesses can seek to adapt to their environment. (2)

ADEA *See* Age Discrimination in Employment Act.

AF of L *See* American Federation of Labor.

affirmative action A set of steps taken by an organization to seek qualified applicants from groups underrepresented in the workforce. (3)

Age Discrimination and Employment Act (ADEA) Legislation that prohibits discrimination against employees over the age of forty. (3)

agency theory Theory concerned with the diverse interests and goals held by the organization's stakeholders, including its employees and managers, and the methods through which the organization's reward system can be used to align these diverse interests and goals. (12)

American Federation of Labor (AF of L) An early union that focused its efforts on improved working conditions and better employment contracts rather than getting involved in legislative and political activities. (14)

Americans with Disabilities Act of 1990 (ADA) Legislation that prohibits discrimination based on disability and applies to all aspects of the employment relationship such as job application procedures, hiring, firing, promotion, compensation, and training, as well as other employment activities such as advertising, recruiting, tenure, layoffs, leave, and fringe benefits. (3)

apprenticeship Training method involving a combination of on-the-job and classroom instruction. (10)

arbitration Conflict resolution process in which both sides agree in advance that they will accept the recommendations made by an independent third-party arbitrator. (14)

assessment center An approach to selecting managers based on measuring and evaluating their ability to perform critical work behaviors. (7)

banding Approach that creates clusters of job applicants who do not differ substantially from one another, thus allowing an organization to select an applicant from an underrepresented group in the organization while still ensuring high performance standards. (7)

bargaining unit The specifically defined group of employees who are eligible for representation by the union. (14)

BARS *See* Behaviorally Anchored Rating Scales.

base salary A guaranteed amount of money that the individual will be paid. (12)

Behaviorally Anchored Rating Scales (BARS) A performance appraisal method representing a combination of the graphic rating scale and the critical incident method. (9)

Behavioral Observation Scales (BOS) A performance appraisal method developed from critical incidents like BARS but uses substantially more critical incidents to define specifically all the measures necessary for effective performance. (9)

benefits Various rewards, incentives, and other items of value that an organization provides to its employees beyond their wages, salaries, and other forms of direct financial compensation. (13)

BFOQ *See* bona fide occupational qualification.

big five personality traits These traits tend to be more behavioral than cognitive or emotional, and they are likely to be more important for job performance than are more traditional personality traits. They include *neuroticism, extraversion, openness to experience, agreeableness*, and *conscientiousness*. (7)

biodata applications These applications focus on the same type of information found in a regular application but they go into more complex and detailed assessments about that background. (7)

bona fide occupational qualification (BFOQ) Legal requirement for performing a particular job such that race, gender, or other personal characteristic legitimately affects a person's ability to perform the job. (3)

BOS *See* Behavioral Observation Scales.

boycott Action in which union members agree not to buy the products of a targeted employer. (14)

burnout A general feeling of exhaustion that develops when an individual simultaneously experiences too much pressure and too few sources of satisfaction. (15)

business necessity A practice that is important for the safe and efficient operation of the business. It is a permissible BFOQ exception. (3)

business strategy Strategy explaining how the firm will compete in each market where it conducts business. (2)

cafeteria-style benefits plans Plans that allow the employee to choose those benefits he or she really wants. (13)

career The set of experiences and activities that people engage in related to their job and livelihood over the course of their working life. (15)

career counseling Discussion that involves interaction between an individual employee or manager in the organization and either a line manager or a human resource manager. (15)

CIO *See* Congress of Industrial Organizations.

circadian rhythms Natural cycles that indicate when a body needs to eat or sleep. (15)

Civil Rights Act of 1991 Legislation that makes it easier for individuals who feel they have been discriminated against to take legal action against organizations and provides for the payment of compensatory and punitive damages in cases of discrimination under Title VII. (3)

classification system A job evaluation method attempting to group sets of jobs together into clusters, often called grades. (11)

closed shop A workplace in which only workers who are already union members may be hired by the employer. (14)

cognitive ability test A measure of mental skills. (7)

collateral stress programs Organizational programs created specifically to help employees deal with stress. (15)

collective bargaining The process by which managers and union leaders negotiate acceptable terms and conditions of employment for those workers represented by the unions. (14)

collective-bargaining agreement A formal and written agreement between the organization and a labor union defining the precise nature of the employment relationship. (17)

compensable factors In job evaluation, any aspects of a job for which an organization is willing to provide compensation. (11)

compensation The set of rewards that organizations provide to individuals in return for their willingness to perform various jobs and tasks within the organization. (11)

competencies Relatively broad capabilities necessary for effective job performance. They vary from organization to organization. (5)

competitive strategies A framework suggesting that three basic strategies are appropriate for a wide variety of organizations in diverse industries. (2)

compressed workweeks Arrangements where the employee works the required number of hours (typically forty) but does so in less than five days each week. (17)

computer-assisted instruction Instruction that involves a trainee sitting at a personal computer and operating software that has been developed specifically to impart certain information to the individual. (10)

Congress of Industrial Organizations (CIO) An early union that focused on organizing employees by industry, regardless of their craft, skills, or occupation. (14)

contextual performance Tasks an employee does on the job that are not required as part of the job but that still benefit the organization in some way. (9)

contingent worker A person who works for an organization on something other than a permanent or full-time basis. (17)

contingent workforce All temporary, part-time, or leased employees who are employed by organizations to fill in for permanent employees during times of peak demand. (6)

contrast error Comparing people against one another instead of against an objective standard. (9)

corporate strategy A strategy that deals with determining what businesses the corporation will operate. (2)

cost leadership strategy A strategy that focuses on minimizing costs as much as possible. (2)

country's culture The set of values, symbols, beliefs, and languages that guide the behavior of people within that culture. (4)

critical incidents approach Job analysis method focusing on the critical behaviors that distinguish between effective and ineffective performers. (5)

critical incident method Performance appraisal method that relies on instances of especially good or poor performance on the part of the employee. (9)

culture The set of values that helps an organization's members understand what the organization stands for, how it does things, and what it considers important. (2)

defined benefit plan A private pension plan in which the size of the benefit is precisely known and is usually based on a simple formula using input such as years of service. (13)

defined contribution plan A private pension plan in which the size of the benefit depends on how much money is contributed to the plan. (13)

development Teaching managers and professionals the skills needed for both present and future jobs. (10)

differentiation strategy A strategy that attempts to develop an image or reputation for products or services that sets them apart from competitors. (2)

direct applicants Individuals who apply for a position with the organization without any action on the part of the organization. (6)

direct foreign investment Occurs when a firm headquartered in one country builds or purchases operating facilities or subsidiaries in a foreign country. (4)

discipline A formal organizational action taken against an employee as a result of a rules violation, below-par performance, or other dysfunctional behavior. (8)

disengagement The fourth stage of the traditional career model in which the individual gradually begins to pull away from work in the organization. Priorities change and work may become less important. (15)

disparate impact discrimination Occurs when an apparently neutral employment practice disproportionately excludes a protected group from employment opportunities. (3)

disparate treatment discrimination When individuals in similar situations are treated differently and when the differential treatment is based on the individuals' race, color, religion, gender, national origin, age, or disability status. (3)

distributional error When a rater tends to use only one part of the rating scale. (9)

distributive justice Perception that the outcomes a person faces are fair when compared to the outcomes faced by others. (8)

diversification strategy A strategy used by companies in which they add new products, product lines, or businesses to their existing core products, product lines, or businesses. (2)

diversity Exists in a group or organization when its members differ from one another along one or more important dimensions. (16)

diversity management Places a much heavier emphasis on recognizing and appreciating differences among people at work and attempts to provide accommodations for those differences to the extent that is feasible and possible. (16)

diversity training Training designed specifically to enable members of an organization to function better in a diverse workplace. (16)

Drug-Free Workplace Act of 1988 A law aimed at reducing the use of illegal drugs at work, primarily aimed at federal contractors. The law provides for regular drug testing for certain jobs such as long-haul truck drivers. (3)

EAP *See* employee assistance plan.

economic communities Sets of countries that agree to reduce or eliminate trade barriers among their member nations. (4)

education Formal classroom training that an individual has received in public or private schools and college, university, and/or technical school. (7)

employee assistance plan (EAP) Plan designed to assist employees who have chronic problems with alcohol or drugs or who have serious domestic or personal problems. (13)

employee leasing An alternative to recruiting in which the organization pays a fee to a leasing company that provides a pool of employees to the organization. (6)

Employee Retirement Income Security Act (ERISA) of 1974 Legislation that guarantees a basic minimum benefit that employees can expect to be paid at retirement. (3)

employee stock ownership plan (ESOP) A group-level reward system in which employees are gradually given a major stake in the ownership of a corporation. (12)

employee training A planned attempt by an organization to facilitate employee learning of job-related knowledge, skills, and behaviors. (10)

employment application A form that asks individuals for various bits of information pertaining to their personal background. (7)

employment-at-will A nineteenth-century common-law rule that allows an employer to terminate any employee, at any time, for any reason (good or bad) or for no reason at all. A traditional view of the employment relationship that both employer and employee have the mutual right to terminate an employment relationship at any time, for any reason, and with or without advance notice to the other. (3; 8; 17)

employment test A device for measuring the characteristics of an individual, such as personality, intelligence, or aptitude. (7)

equal employment opportunity Treating people fairly and equitably and taking actions that do not discriminate against people in protected classes on the basis of some illegal criterion. (16)

Equal Pay Act of 1963 Law requiring organizations to pay the same wage or salary to men and women doing equal work. (3)

ergonomics The study of the interface between an individual's physical characteristics and the environmental requirements of the job. (5)

ERISA *See* Employee Retirement Income Security Act of 1974.

ESOP *See* employee stock ownership plan.

establishment The second stage of the traditional career model in which a meaningful and relevant role in the organization is created by the employee for him- or herself. (15)

ethics An individual's beliefs about what is right and wrong and what is good and bad. (3)

ethnicity The ethic composition of a group or organization. (16)

ethnocentric staffing model An approach in which an organization uses primarily parent-country nationals to staff higher-level foreign positions. (4)

Executive Order 11246 Law that prohibits discrimination based on race, color, religion, gender, or national origin for organizations that are federal contractors and/or subcontractors. (3)

Executive Order 11478 Law that requires the federal government to base all its employment policies on merit and fitness and specifies that race, color, gender, religion, and national origin should not be considered. (3)

executive succession Systematically planning for future promotions into top management positions. (2)

expatriates Employees who are sent by a firm to work in another country. They may be either parent-country nationals or third-country nationals. (4)

experience The amount of time the individual may have spent working, either in a general capacity or in a particular field of study. (7)

exploration The first traditional career stage in which interests and opportunities are identified. (15)

exporting The process of making a product in the firm's domestic marketplace and then selling it in another country. (4)

external equity In compensation, refers to comparisons made by employees to others employed by different organizations and performing similar jobs. (11)

external recruiting The process of looking to sources outside the organization for prospective employees. (6)

factor comparison method Method of job evaluation assessing jobs, on a factor-by-factor basis, using a factor comparison scale as a benchmark. (11)

Fair Labor Standards Act (FLSA) Legislation passed in 1938 that established a minimum hourly wage for jobs. (3)

false negatives Applicants who are predicted to fail and who are not hired, but if they had been hired, they would have been successful. (7)

false positives Applicants who are predicted to be successful and who are hired, but who ultimately fail. (7)

Family and Medical Leave Act of 1993 Legislation that requires employers having more than fifty employees to provide up to twelve weeks of unpaid leave for employees after the birth or adoption of a child; to care for a seriously ill child, spouse, or parent; or in the case of an employee's own serious illness. (3)

final-offer arbitration A conflict resolution process in which the parties bargain until impasse, at which point the two parties' final offers are submitted to the arbitrator. (14)

Fleishman job analysis system A job analysis procedure that defines abilities as enduring attributes of individuals that account for differences in performance. It relies on the taxonomy of abilities that presumably represents all the dimensions relevant to work. (5)

flexible work hours Programs in which employees work forty hours per week and five days a week, but with the potential for flexible starting and ending times. (17)

focus strategy Strategy in which an organization tries to target a specific segment of the marketplace for its products or services. (2)

forced distribution method A performance appraisal method in which employees are grouped into predefined frequencies of performance ratings. (9)

foreign-service premium *See* hardship premium.

four-fifths rule Guideline for determining if disparate impact exists. If a selection criterion (such as a test score) results in a selection rate for a protected class that is less than four-fifths (80 percent) of that for the majority group, then disparate impact exists. (3)

functional strategy Strategy describing how the firm will manage each of its major functions, such as marketing, finance, and human resources. (2)

gainsharing   A team- and group-based incentive system designed to share the cost savings from productivity improvements with employees. (12)

general labor pool   The local labor market from which a firm hires its employees. (6)

general training   Providing trainees with skills and abilities that can be applied in any organization. (10)

geocentric staffing model   Approach that puts parent-country nationals, host-country nationals, and third-country nationals in the same category, with the firm attempting always to hire the best person available for a position. (4)

geographical comparisons   A method for establishing disparate impact that compares the potential pool of qualified applicants from a protected class with the number of present employees from that class. (3)

glass ceiling   The barrier that keeps females from advancing to top management positions in many organizations. (16)

goal-based system   Also known as the *management-by-objectives (MBO) system*. A performance appraisal method based largely on the extent to which individuals meet their personal performance objectives. (9)

grand strategy   A single overall framework for action developed by the top management team at the corporate level. (2)

graphic rating scale   A performance appraisal method consisting of a statement or question about some aspect of an individual's job performance. The rater provides an evaluation on a numerical scale corresponding to his or her response to the statement or question about the employee. (9)

halo error   When one positive performance characteristic causes the manager to rate all other aspects of an employee's performance positively. (9)

hardship premium   Also known as *foreign-service premium*. An additional financial incentive offered to individuals to entice them to accept a less-than-attractive international assignment. (4)

Hawthorne studies   Series of research studies that led to the human relations era. (1)

headhunter   An individual working for an executive search firm that seeks out qualified individuals for higher-level positions. (6)

health hazards   Characteristics of the work environment that more slowly and systematically, and perhaps cumulatively, result in damage to an employee's health. (15)

health maintenance organization (HMO)   Medical organization that provides medical and health services to employees on a prepaid basis. (13)

hierarchy of human needs   Theory of motivation based on differentially important needs. It was developed during the human relations era by Abraham Maslow. (1)

high-performance work systems   Approaches that rely on a set of best practices for using human resources to gain a meaningful competitive advantage. (2)

HMO   *See* health maintenance organization.

home work programs   Programs that include arrangements often referred to as cottage industries. (17)

horns error   When a manager downgrades other aspects of an employee's performance because of a single performance dimension. (9)

hostile work environment   Sexual harassment resulting from a climate or culture that is punitive toward people of the opposite gender. (3)

human relations era   School of thought that supplanted scientific management as the dominant approach to management during the 1930s. (1)

human resource information system   An integrated and increasingly automated system for maintaining a database regarding the employees in an organization. (2; App 1)

human resource management   The comprehensive set of managerial activities and tasks concerned with developing and maintaining a qualified workforce—human resources—in ways that contribute to organizational effectiveness. (1)

human resource management system   An integrated and interrelated approach to managing human resources that fully recognizes the interdependence among the various tasks and functions that must be performed. (1)

human resource planning   The process of forecasting the supply and demand for human resources within an organization and developing action plans for aligning the two. (2)

human resources   The people an organization employs to carry out various jobs, tasks, and functions in exchange for wages, salaries, and other rewards. (1)

illegal discrimination   Discrimination resulting from behaviors or actions by an organization or managers within an organization that cause members of a protected class to be unfairly differentiated from others. (3)

impasse   A situation in which one or both parties believe that reaching an agreement is not imminent. (14)

in-baskets   Special forms of work simulation for prospective managers. They consist of collections of hypothetical memos, letters, and notes that require responses. (7)

individual assessment phase   Part of career planning that requires individuals to analyze carefully what they perceive to be their own abilities, competencies, skills, and goals. (15)

individual incentive plans   Incentives that reward individual performance on a real-time basis. (12)

in-house training   Also known as a *development program*. Training that is conducted on the organization's premises, primarily by the organization's employees. (10)

instructional-based programs   Programs that approach training and development from a teaching and learning perspective. (10)

institutional programs   Programs for managing stress that are undertaken through established organizational mechanisms. (15)

integrity tests   Tests that attempt to assess an applicant's moral character and honesty. (7)

interactional justice   The quality of the interpersonal treatment people receive when a decision is implemented. (8)

internal equity   In compensation, refers to comparisons made by employees to other employees within the same organization. (11)

internal recruiting   The process of looking inside the organization for existing, qualified employees who might be promoted to higher-level positions. (6)

interviews   Face-to-face conversations between prospective job applicants and representatives of the organization. (7)

job analysis The process of gathering and organizing detailed information about various jobs within the organization so that managers can better understand the processes through which they are performed most effectively. (5)

job analysts Individuals who perform job analysis in an organization. (5)

job characteristics approach An alternative to job specialization that takes into account the work system and employee preferences. It suggests that jobs should be diagnosed and improved along five core dimensions. (5)

job description Written document that lists the tasks, duties, and responsibilities for a particular job; specifies the major job elements; provides examples of job tasks; and provides some indication of the relative importance in the effective conduct of the job. (5)

job design The determination of an individual's work-related responsibilities. (5)

job dissatisfaction The feeling of being unhappy with one's job. It is a major cause of voluntary turnover. (8)

job embeddedness The fact that some people stay on their jobs, even when they decide they are unhappy and should leave. Other ties in the community or obligations keep the employee on the job. (8)

job enlargement Approach developed to increase the total number of tasks workers perform. It is based on the assumption that doing the same basic task over and over is the primary cause of worker dissatisfaction. (5)

job enrichment Attempts to increase both the number of tasks a worker does and the control the worker has over his or her job. (5)

job evaluation A method for determining the relative value or worth of a job to the organization so that individuals who perform that job can be compensated adequately and appropriately. (11)

job families Groups of jobs with similar task and KSA requirements. (5)

job posting A mechanism for internal recruiting in which vacancies in the organization are publicized through various media such as company newsletters, bulletin boards, internal memos, and the firm's intranet. (6)

job ranking A job evaluation method requiring the manager to rank-order jobs, based on their relative importance to the organization, from most important to least important. (11)

job rotation Moving employees systematically from one job to another. (5)

job specialization The degree to which the overall task of the organization is broken down and divided into smaller component parts. (5)

job specification Document that focuses on the individual who will perform the job and indicates the knowledge, abilities, skills, and other characteristics that an individual must have to be able to perform the job. (5)

joint venture Also known as a *strategic alliance*. An arrangement in which two or more firms cooperate in the ownership and/or management of an operation on an equity basis. (4)

Knights of Labor An important early union that expanded its goals and its membership to include workers in numerous fields rather than a single industry. (14)

knowledge workers Employees who add value simply because of what they know. (1; 17)

knowledge, skills, and abilities (KSAs) The fundamental requirements necessary to be able to perform a job. (5)

KSAs *See* knowledge, skills, and abilities.

Labor Management Relations Act Also known as the *Taft-Hartley Act*. Legislation passed in 1947 in response to public outcries against a wide variety of strikes in the years following World War II. It curtails and limits union powers, and it regulates union actions and their internal affairs in a way that puts them on an equal footing with management and organizations. (3; 14)

Labor Management Reporting and Disclosure Act Also known as the *Landrum-Griffin Act*. Legislation passed in 1959. It focuses on eliminating various unethical, illegal, and undemocratic union practices. It regulates union actions and their internal affairs in a way that puts them on an equal footing with management and organizations. (14)

labor relations The process of dealing with employees who are represented by a union. (14)

labor union A legally constituted group of individuals working together to achieve shared job-related goals, including higher pay and shorter working hours. (14)

Landrum-Griffin Act *See* Labor Management Reporting and Disclosure Act.

learning A relatively permanent change in behavior or behavioral potential that results from direct or indirect experience. (10)

learning organization An organization whose employees continuously attempt to learn new information and to use what they have learned to improve product or service quality. (10)

lecture or discussion approach Approach that involves a trainer presenting the material in a descriptive fashion to those attending the program. (10)

licensing Arrangement in which one company grants its permission to another company in a foreign country to manufacture and/or market the first company's products in the second company's local market. (4)

life-cycle benefits Benefits that are based on a person's relative life cycle. The most common examples include childcare and eldercare. (13)

line managers Managers directly responsible for creating goods and services. (1)

locals Unions organized at the level of a single company, plant, or small geographic region. (14)

lockout When an employer denies employees access to the workplace. (14)

maintenance The third stage of the traditional career model in which an employee optimizes talents or capabilities. (15)

management-by-objectives (MBO) system *See* goal-based system.

mandatory items Items that must be included as part of collective bargaining if either party expresses a desire to negotiate one or more of them. Common examples are wages, working hours, and benefits. (14)

maturity curve A schedule specifying the amount of annual increase a person will receive. (11)

McDonnell-Douglass test A method for establishing dispartate impact. It requires that a qualified member of a protected class applies for a job, is rejected for that job, but the company continues to search for someone with the same qualifications. (3)

mediation A conflict resolution process in which a neutral third party, called the mediator, listens to and reviews the information presented by both sides, makes an informed recommendation, and provides advice to both parties about what she or he believes should be done. (14)

merit-pay plans Compensation plans that formally base at least some meaningful portion of compensation on merit. (12)

merit pay Pay awarded to employees on the basis of the relative value of their contributions to the organization. (12)

midcareer plateau A point that many people reach in their careers at which they do not receive additional promotions or advancement opportunities in the organization. (15)

mission A statement of how an organization intends to fulfill its purpose. (2)

multicultural organization An organization that has achieved high levels of diversity, can capitalize fully on the advantages of the diversity, and has few diversity-related problems. (16)

National Labor Relations Act Also known as the *Wagner Act*. It was passed in 1935 in an effort to control and legislate collective bargaining between organizations and labor unions. It granted power to labor unions and put unions on a more equal footing with managers in terms of the rights of employees. (3; 14)

National Labor Relations Board (NLRB) Legal body that administers most labor law in the United States. (14)

needs analysis The assessment of an organization's job-related needs and the capabilities of its current workforce. (10)

NLRB *See* National Labor Relations Board.

Occupational Safety and Health Act (OSHA) of 1970 Legislation that grants the federal government the power to establish and enforce occupational safety and health standards for all places of employment dealing directly with interstate commerce. (3; 15)

Old Age Survivors and Disability Insurance Program *See* social security.

on-the-job training The most common method of work-based training. It involves having employees learn their job while they are performing it. (10)

operating managers An increasingly popular term for managers previously called line managers. (1)

organizational citizenship behaviors Employee behaviors that are beneficial to the organization but are not formally required as part of an employee's job. (8)

organizational commitment The degree to which an employee identifies with an organization and is willing to exert effort on its behalf. (8)

organization design The framework of jobs, positions, clusters of positions, and reporting relationships among positions that is used to construct an organization. (2)

organization development An effort that is planned systemwide and managed from the top of the organization to increase the organization's overall performance through planned interventions. The technique relies heavily on behavioral science technology. (10)

orientation The process of introducing new employees to the organization so that they can become effective contributors more quickly. (10)

OSHA *See* Occupational Safety and Health Act of 1970.

outsourced training Also known as a *development program*. Program that involves having people from outside the organization perform the training. (10)

outsourcing When an organization brings in help from outside instead of hiring or buying it. The practice of hiring external vendors to provide basic human resource management services for an organization based on their ability to perform them more efficiently than the organization itself can. (1)

overtime An alternative to recruiting in which current employees are asked to work extra hours. (6)

paired comparison method A performance appraisal method that compares each individual employee with every other individual employee, one at a time. (9)

PAQ *See* position analysis questionnaire.

part-time workers Individuals who routinely expect to work less than forty hours a week. (6)

pattern or practice discrimination Discrimination that is similar to disparate treatment but occurs on a classwide basis. (3)

pay compression When individuals with substantially different levels of experience and/or performance abilities are paid wages or salaries that are relatively equal. (11)

pay-for-knowledge Compensating employees for learning specific information. (11)

pay secrecy The extent to which the compensation of any individual in an organization is secret or the extent to which it is formally made available to other individuals. (11)

pay surveys Surveys of compensation paid to employees by other employers in a particular geographic area, industry, or occupational group. (11)

performance appraisal The specific and formal evaluation of an employee conducted to determine the degree to which the employee is performing his or her job effectively. (9)

performance management The general set of activities carried out by the organization to change (improve) employee performance. (9)

perk *See* perquisite.

permissive items Items that may be included in collective bargaining if both parties agree. (14)

perquisite Also known as *perk*. An extra benefit that may or may not have any direct financial value but is considered to be an important reward by employees. (13)

personality tests Tests that measure traits, or tendencies to act, that are relatively unchanging in a person. (7)

personnel departments The original name for specialized organizational units for hiring and administering human resources. The term became popular during the 1930s and 1940s. (1)

personnel management The original name for human resource management. It grew from the recognition that human resources needed to be managed. (1)

picketing The action taken by workers representing a striking union in which they march at the entrance to the employer's facility with signs explaining their reasons for striking. (14)

Glossary

piece-rate incentive plan Compensation plan in which the organization pays an employee a certain amount of money for every unit she or he produces. (12)

point manual A technique used to implement the point system of job evaluation. It defines carefully and specifically the degrees of points from first to fifth. (11)

point system A job evaluation method requiring managers to quantify, in objective terms, the value of the various elements of specific jobs. (11)

polycentric staffing model An approach that calls for heavy use of host-country nationals throughout the organization. (4)

Position Analysis Questionnaire (PAQ) A standardized job analysis instrument consisting of 194 items that reflect work behavior, working conditions, or job characteristics and are assumed to be generalizable across a wide variety of jobs. (5)

Pregnancy Discrimination Act of 1979 Legislation that protects pregnant women from discrimination in the workplace. (3)

Privacy Act of 1974 Applies directly to federal employees, but has influenced other legislation. It allows employees to periodically review and contest information in their personnel files. (3)

private pension plan A prearranged plan administered by the organization that provides income to the employee at her or his retirement. (13)

procedural justice The perception that the process used to determine the outcomes was fair. (8)

productivity An economic measure of efficiency that summarizes and reflects the value of the outputs created by an individual, organization, industry, or economic system relative to the value of the inputs used to create the outputs. (1)

profit sharing An incentive system in which, at the end of the year, some portion of the company's profits is paid into a profit-sharing pool that is distributed to all employees. (12)

programmed instruction A training method wherein the material to be learned is prepared in a manual or training booklet, and the individual takes the manual or booklet and studies at his or her own pace. (10)

progressive discipline plans Systems in which the organization defines a sequence of penalties, each somewhat more severe than the previous one, and a time frame across which an individual's continued rules violations will escalate to higher levels of discipline. (8)

projection When we tend to see in others characteristics that we ourselves have and that we think contribute to effectiveness. (9)

projective technique A technique in which an individual is shown an ambiguous stimulus, such as an ink blot or a fuzzy picture, and then asked what he or she sees. (7)

protected class A group that consists of all individuals who share one or more common characteristic as indicated by law. (3)

protection plans Benefits designed to provide protection to employees when their income is threatened or reduced by illness, disability, death, unemployment, or retirement. (13)

psychological contract The set of expectations held by an employee concerning what he or she will contribute to the organization (referred to as *contributions*) and what the organization will provide to the employee in return (referred to as *inducements*). (2; 17)

psychomotor ability tests Tests that measure physical abilities such as strength, eye-hand coordination, and manual dexterity. (7)

punishment Any behavior or action, formal or informal, that results in unpleasant effects or consequences for someone else. (8)

purpose An organization's basic reason for existence. (2)

quality The total set of features and characteristics of a product or service that bears on its ability to satisfy stated or implied needs. (1)

quid pro quo harassment Sexual harassment in which the harasser offers to exchange something of value for sexual favors. (3)

quota A limit on the number or value of goods that can be traded. (4)

realistic job preview Steps undertaken to ensure that job seekers understand the actual nature of the jobs available to them. (6; 8)

recruiting The process of developing a pool of qualified applicants who are interested in working for the organization and from which the organization might reasonably select the best individual or individuals to hire for employment. (6)

referral An individual who is prompted to apply for a position by someone within the organization. (6)

regression-based system A method of job evaluation utilizing a statistical technique called multiple regression to develop an equation that establishes the relationship between different dimensions of the job and compensation. (11)

reliability The consistency of a particular selection (measurement) device. (7)

reverse discrimination Any practice that has disparate impact on members of nonprotected classes. (3)

rightsizing The process of monitoring and adjusting the composition of the organization's workforce to it optimal size. (8)

safety engineers Experts who carefully study the workplace, try to identify and isolate particularly dangerous situations, and recommend solutions for dealing with those situations. (15)

safety hazards Conditions in the work environment that have the potential to cause harm to an employee. (15)

salary Income paid to an individual on the basis of performance, not on the basis of time. (11)

sales commission An incentive paid to salespeople. (12)

Scanlon plan A type of gainsharing plan in which the distribution of gains is tilted much more heavily toward employees and across the entire organization. (12)

scientific management One of the earliest approaches to management. It was concerned with structuring individual jobs to maximize efficiency and productivity. (1)

screening process A series of decisions, each resulting in some candidates being eliminated and others being kept for continued consideration. (7)

selection process   The process of identifying the best candidate or candidates for jobs from among the pool of qualified applicants developed during the recruiting process. (7)

self-report inventory   A paper-and-pencil measure in which an applicant responds to a series of statements that might or might not apply to the applicant. (7)

shop steward   An elected position in a local union. The shop steward is a regular employee who functions as a liaison between union members and supervisors. (14)

simple ranking method   A performance appraisal method in which the manager simply rank-orders, from top to bottom or from best to worst, each member of a particular work group or department. (9)

skill-based pay   Pay that rewards employees for acquiring new skills. (11)

skills and abilities   The specific qualifications and capabilities of an individual to perform a specific job. (7)

slowdown   When workers perform their jobs at a much slower pace than normal. (14)

SMEs   *See* subject matter experts.

social contract model   A model that expands the relationship between employer and employee to include the government. (17)

social security   Officially known as the *Old Age Survivors and Disability Insurance Program*. A mandated program originally designed to provide limited income to retired individuals to supplement their personal savings, private pensions, part-time work, and so forth. (13)

specific training   Training that provides the trainee with skills or information that are of use only to his or her current organization. (10)

staffing   The process of determining the organization's current and future human resource needs and then taking steps to ensure that those needs are met effectively. (5)

staff managers   Managers who are responsible for an indirect or support function that has costs but whose bottom-line contributions are less direct. (1)

stock-option plan   An incentive plan established to give managers the option to buy the company stock in the future at a predetermined fixed price. The plan was once reserved for senior managers only, but it is increasingly offered now to other managers too. (12)

strategic alliance   Also known as a *joint venture*. An arrangement in which two or more firms cooperate in the ownership and/or management of an operation. (4)

stress   A person's adaptive response to a stimulus that places excessive psychological or physical demands on him or her. (15)

strike   An action in which employees walk off their jobs and refuse to work. (14)

subject matter experts (SMEs)   Individuals presumed to be highly knowledgeable about jobs and who provide data for job analysis. They may be existing job incumbents, supervisors, or other knowledgeable employees. (5)

suspension   A temporary layoff. It is usually a second step in progressive disciplinary plans. (8)

SWOT analysis   A conceptual framework useful in formulating strategies. SWOT is an acronym for "strengths, weaknesses, opportunities, and threats." (2)

systematic job rotation and transfer   An approach in which the employee is rotated or transferred systematically from one job to another. (10)

Taft-Hartley Act   *See* Labor Management Relations Act.

tariff   A tax collected on goods that are shipped across national boundaries. (4)

task analysis inventory   A family of job analysis methods, each with unique characteristics. Each method focuses on analyzing all the tasks performed in the focal job. (5)

telecommuting   An arrangement in which employees do almost all their work at home, perhaps even receiving assignments electronically. (17)

temporary employees   Employees who join the organization to work a specific period of time, rather than with the expectation of permanent or continued employment. Temporary employees are hired as an alternative to recruiting. (6)

termination   The final step in progressive disciplinary plans in which the employee is fired. (8)

Theory X and Theory Y   An important framework reflecting the different ways that managers can view employees. It was developed by Douglas McGregor during the human relations movement. (1)

360-degree feedback   An approach to performance appraisal that involves gathering performance information from people on all sides of the manager—above, beside, below, and so forth. (9)

Title VII of the Civil Rights Act   Legislation that makes it illegal for an employer to fail or refuse to hire or to discharge any individual or to in any other way discriminate against any individual with respect to any aspect of the employment relationship on the basis of that individual's race, color, religious beliefs, gender, or national origin. (3)

top management team   The group of senior executives responsible for the overall strategic operation of the firm. (2)

unemployment insurance   A mandated protection plan intended to provide a basic subsistence payment to employees who are between jobs. (13)

union shop agreement   Various types of union security agreements that include a requirement that a nonunion member can be hired but must join the union within a specified time to keep his or her job. (14)

utility analysis   An attempt to measure, in a more objective way, the impact and effectiveness of human resource management practices in terms of metrics such as firm financial performance. An attempt to determine the extent to which a selection system provides real benefit to the organization. (1; 7)

utilization analysis   A comparison of the racial, gender, and ethnic composition of the employer's workforce compared to that of the available labor supply. (3)

validity   The extent to which a measure or indicator measures what it is assumed to measure. (7)

verbal warnings   The first step in most progressive disciplinary programs in which cautions are conveyed orally to the employee. (8)

vestibule training   A work simulation situation in which the job is performed under a condition that closely simulates the real work environment. (10)

vesting rights   Guarantees that pension benefits will be provided. (13)

Vietnam Era Veterans' Readjustment Act of 1974 Legislation that requires federal contractors and subcontractors to take affirmative action toward employing Vietnam veterans. (3)

Vocational Rehabilitation Act of 1973 Legislation that requires executive agencies and subcontractors and contractors of the federal government receiving more than $2,500 a year from the government to engage in affirmative action for disabled individuals. (3)

wage and salary administration The ongoing process of managing a wage and salary structure. (11)

wages Generally, the hourly compensation paid to operating employees. The basis for wages is time. (11)

Wagner Act *See* National Labor Relations Act.

weighted application blank An application that relies on the determination of numerical indices to indicate the relative importance of various personal factors for predicting a person's ability to perform a job effectively. (7)

wellness programs Special benefit programs that concentrate on keeping employees from becoming sick rather than simply paying expenses when they do become sick. (13)

wildcat strike A strike that occurs during the course of a labor contract (and is therefore generally illegal) and is usually undertaken in response to a perceived injustice on the part of management. (14)

word-of-mouth recruiting Recruitment technique in which the organization simply informs present employees that positions are available and encourages them to refer friends, family members, or neighbors for those jobs (6)

work-based programs Programs that tie training and development activities directly to the performance of the task. (10)

Worker Adjustment and Retraining Notification (WARN) Act of 1988 Stipulates that an organization employing at least 100 persons must provide at least 60 days notice in advance of plans to close a facilty or lay off 50 workers or more. (3, 8)

workers' compensation A mandated protection program that provides insurance for individuals who suffer a job-related illness or accident. (13)

work simulation Also known as *work samples*. An approach that asks the prospective employee to perform tasks or job-related activities that simulate or represent the work for which the person is being considered. (7)

work team An arrangement in which a group is given responsibility for designing the work system to be used in performing an interrelated set of jobs. (5)

written warnings The second step in most progressive disciplinary programs in which cautions to the employee are given in writing and become part of the employee's permanent record. (8)

Photo and Cartoon Credits

Organization and Product Index